Greek Cypriots worldwide

~

A directory of who's who

compiled and produced by

Michael Yiakoumi

First published in Great Britain by Pen Press

All paper used in the printing of this book has been made from wood grown in managed, sustainable forests.

ISBN13: 978-1-907172-33-5

Printed and bound in the UK
Pen Press is an imprint of Indepenpress Publishing Limited
25 Eastern Place, Brighton, BN2 1GJ

A catalogue record of this book is available from
the British Library

Cover design by Matthew Ward Design
matthew.ward10@btinternet.com

Greek Cypriots in the UK, 111 St Thomas's road, London, N42QJ
Tel: 020 7503 3498 Email: cypriotwhoswho@aol.com

To all those people and to the memory of those who are not any more with us but helped in creating a second Cyprus abroad, this book is dedicated.

Kyriacos Tsioupras
Editor

CREDITS AND ACKNOWLEGEMENTS

Edited by Kyriakos Tsioupras

Compiled by Michael Yiakoumi

Researchers
Koulla Anastasi
Bernadette Dunphy
Gabriel Gabrilatsou
Nick Lazari
Vasilia Michael
Chris Neophytou
Jon Pishiri
George Ttofi
Savvas Savva
Beccy Sheriteh
Wendy Stanbridge
Dimitri Yiakoumi
Maria Yiakoumi
Joanna Zampas

Photography
Peter Pentayiotis

Creative Designers
Panicos Michael
Savvas Pavlou
Matthew Ward

Web Site
Dino Hadjinicola
Web Theoria

Copy Editor
Idelia Roark

Production
Kathryn Harrison

Acknowledgements
Ministry of Foreign Affairs Cyprus
Cyprus High Commissions and
Embassies
Greek Orthodox Church
Parikiaki Newspaper
Eleftheria Newspaper
Neos Kosmos Newspaper
Cyprus Mail Newspaper
Cyprus Weekly Newspaper
Politis Newspaper
London Greek Radio
Rik Tv
Sophie Toumazis
Dinos Nicolas
Harry Shiamaris
Louis Kyriacou
Louis Loizou
Kyriacos Elles
Dino Sophocleous
Tony Vourou
Metropolis of Cape Of Good Hope
Metropolis of Johanesburg
Cypriot Communities all over the world.

by **Kyriacos Tsioupras**
Editor

$\mathcal{S}$ome of the most moving scenes I experienced in life were the ones related to the departure of people from their villages in Cyprus to emigrate abroad. It was an atmosphere of near mourning, with relatives, friends and neighbours, sometimes all the inhabitants, accompanying the ones to leave to the village bus to say their goodbyes. Even heavier was the atmosphere at the quays of Famagusta and Limassol ports with parents and other close relatives and friends in tears waving their handkerchiefs to their loved ones on the boat slowly moving away. In those difficult years of the thirties and forties parents were wondering whether they would be able to see their sons or daughters again.

The first big wave of Cypriot immigrants to Britain was after the Second World War which continued well into the fifties. In employment they followed the pattern of those few thousands who had arrived before the war and, as a rule, they went into catering apart from a few who had found work as barbers and carpenters and in some other trades. It was much easier to get into the catering industry for two main reasons: There was no need for much training which would entail some knowledge of the language and a number of restaurants were already in the hands of Cypriots, in many cases relatives to the new arrivals. Their whole world for a number of years was within the square mile between Mornington Crescent in the north and Soho in the south settling mostly around Goodge Street, Charlotte Street, Rathbone Street and Windmill Street. That was also the area where the first Cypriot Brotherhood, established in 1935, was located.

Before the war the overwhelming majority of Cypriot immigrants were single or married men who had left their wives and children behind so that they could see how the situation was and decide whether their family could follow them or whether they themselves would go back. Cypriot women started emigrating in small numbers around 1935 when marriages became part of community life. Many single men would go back to the island to get married. That was the time when some people used the bizarre method of marriage by photograph by which the candidate girl would send a photo of herself to the one seeking a bride and wait for a positive answer. This method was used more widely in cases where the candidate groom was further away like Australia, South Africa and the United States.

The second big wave of migration to England as well as to Australia and South Africa was just before and immediately after the declaration of independence of Cyprus in 1960. The only explanation that can be given to that is the widely held anxiety at that time on the island about what independence would actually mean in economic terms. That was the time when Turkish Cypriots also emigrated in considerable numbers to England and Australia.

The third wave of immigration was after the coup and the Turkish invasion in 1974 mainly to Greece but in smaller numbers also to England, Australia, South Africa and Canada. Most of those who had arrived in England at that time, returned to Cyprus as soon as the situation on the island normalised.

The overwhelming majority of people who had left Cyprus in those three waves of immigration were economic immigrants. Certainly not in the sense of being faced with hunger. Even those who had left Cyprus in the thirties, at the time of high depression, did not do so as a result of not being able to make a living on the island. The real reason for so many people taking the decision to leave their country was the hope for a better future for themselves and, more so, for their children. If all those people were asked the question *"why?"* the answer would be, as a rule, *"for my children"* by which they actually meant the opportunity for better education for them. That was the time when there was no University on the island and in most cases the parents could not afford secondary education for their children anyway.

From the fifties onwards the scope of employment for the Cypriots in Britain widened. While catering remained the main area of engagement extending into ownership of restaurant and fish and chips shops, many of them would find work in factories, in building, hairdressing, carpentry and several other sectors. The new area of employment where more and more Cypriots got into from the middle fifties was that of clothing. They had the advantage of many of them, especially women, having had some kind of training in sewing in Cyprus. That meant a ready workforce extending to many thousands of women employed through the home work system which allowed them to work while attending to their children at home and taking them to school. Clothing became increasingly the main sector of what we can call the community economy. The period between 1955 and 1985 clothing gave the Cypriot community its golden years. At a point it was reliably estimated that 90% of the London area clothing industry was under the control of Cypriots. A big achievement by any standard!

In the meantime Cypriots moved from the West end to Camden Town and from there to Finsbury Park, Haringey, Wood Green and Palmers Green. Those who lived on the other side of the Thames moved further south. As a result of their tendency for self-employment in clothing and the catering industry, Cypriots worked and lived in their own semi-native environment. With two Cypriot banks operating from various branches, groceries and other shops supplying products from Cyprus, coffee-shops and places of entertainment copying the ones on the island, day-to-day life was as near as possible to life back home.

There are dozens of community Associations related in name and other forms of ties with villages and towns in Cyprus. Especially strong and influential are those relating to villages under the Turkish occupation with the best example that of Risokarpasso Association. Various other organisations – professional, cultural, educational, scientific and others – enrich community life. The religious needs of the community are most generously tended to by the Thyateira and Great Britain Archdiocese, established by the Oecumenical Patriarchate in 1922, now under Archbishop Gregorios. More than 120 churches – 25 of them in the Greater London area – serve the Greek community all over the United Kingdom. In the majority of cases the churches are freehold properties of the parishes which are of satisfactory economic standing.

A rather strong network of community schools set up by the church and various organisations , aided financially by the governments of Greece and Cyprus , provide Saturday and evening classes for the Greek language as well as Greek music and traditional dancing to relate the younger generations as closely as possible to their national and cultural roots.

The Greek Cypriot community is served by two weekly and one bimonthly newspapers as well as by the 24hour service London Greek Radio and the Hellenic TV. It also has its own Sunday football league run by the community organisation KOPA.

Out of this picture of a strong community entity one could get the impression of a ghetto image. That would be certainly a wrong impression. While trying to preserve their national and cultural identity, Greek Cypriots are outward looking people with active interest in improving the wider environment they live in – be that of the neighbourhood or of the local school, of professional or other organisations they belong to, or local government. They will take part in whatever is needed to be done to improve things and they will make their presence and their interest felt. It is true that first generation Cypriots would tend to take a back seat in relation to main stream activities because of language and other difficulties . Nevertheless, most of the Greek Cypriot Councillors elected in the last 30 years in Haringey, Barnet and Enfield have been first generation people who have been active in political parties. Indeed, their work and their overall contribution has been appreciated greatly by their colleagues, so much so that in all three Councils Greek Cypriots Councillors have been awarded with the honorary post of the Mayor.

Cypriots with a numerical strength of around 300,000 boast of a political weight higher than its numbers would imply. As a result of such a big number of Cypriots residing in North London the cypriot vote plays an important role in the outcome of elections in at least six constituencies in that area. Less important but nevertheless an influential role is attributed to the cypriot vote in a number of other constituencies in other parts of London and in other areas of the country. The National Federation of Cypriots, part of the worldwide movement of overseas Cypriots, as well as the London sections of political parties on the island and other community organisations are very active in lobbying and in other forms of political mobilisation . Therefore the cypriot vote is used as a means of pressure on candidates to take a position in support of Cyprus.

On one particular issue, that of Cyprus' entry to the European Union, the cypriot vote was a contributory factor in changing the position of the conservative government under John Major. Its original stand had been that Cyprus could not accede to the European Union while its political problem remained unresolved. Then it changed to there were many difficulties in acceding while the problem was not solved. And then, on the eve of the 1990 local elections, the government stated that there were difficulties in the way of Cyprus' entry but those difficulties were not insurmountable.

What is not widely realised is that with so many votes given to overseas Cypriots their vote is very important, possibly decisive, in the outcome of the presidential elections and certainly influential in parliamentary elections in Cyprus.

All we have said with regard to the ties with Cyprus refer mainly to the first generation Cypriots and, partly, to the second. Now we are going through the stage of the third generation and the beginning of the fourth. It is a completely different world The bulk of the community is made up of professions – lawyers, doctors, accountants, business executives, architects, teachers, actors, journalists. We are really proud of people like Andrew Adonis, who served as a member and head of 10, Downing Street Policy Unit and then as member of the House of Lords and Minister at the Department of Education, responsible for Schools. He is now Minister at the Department of Transport, responsible for Trains. As we are proud of Jane Paraskeva who had served as Chief Executive of the Law Society and now is Civil Service Commissioner. She holds also the position of the Head of the New Olympic Lottery Distributor as well as that of Chairman of the Child Maintenance and Enforcement Commission.

We are proud of Tony Clements, Minister for Health in Canada, of Charlie Crist, elected Governor of Florida in the United States where Gene Rossides had served, years ago, as Assistant Secretary at the Treasury. And people like Senator Nick Xenophontos in Australia. We also have the singers George Michael, Peter Andre and Diam in business Stelios Haji-Ioannou and Theo Paphitis. The list goes on and on as you will read on in the book.

We are also proud of thousands of people who have served in the United Kingdom, in Australia, the United States, Canada, South Africa and in other countries as local councillors, as Mayors and have stood and are standing as candidates for Parliament and the Euro-Parliament. As we are proud of so many achievers in many walks of life.

For the real heroes of this marvellous and at the same time noble story, though, we must go back to the beginning of the adventure. To those moving scenes at the ports of Famagusta and Limassol in the thirties, the forties and the fifties. To those people who were leaving beloved homes, people and places, going to the unknown, in most cases without any knowledge of another language and in some cases without any money in their pockets. They were determined to succeed, though, and, mostly, they succeeded. Through many years of hard work which would mean many kinds of suffering, physical and psychological, in an environment so different from what they had known back home, they prevailed over hardships and other difficulties, to prosper and see their dreams for a better life for themselves and, more so, for their children, largely realised.

To all those people and to the memory of those who are not any more with us but helped in creating a second Cyprus abroad, this book is dedicated.

by **Michael Yiakoumi**
Compiler

Greek Cypriots in the UK – A directory of who's who was a phenomenal success. What Greek Cypriot could flick through its pages and not marvel with pride at the fascinating achievements of so many of our people in Britain?

So it was the obvious next step to expand this listing to include the accomplishments of Greek Cypriots worldwide. After all, people from our small island have settled, prospered and distinguished themselves in all parts of the globe.

What a wonderful, inspiring task it was! It meant embarking on a fascinating, year-long odyssey that took me to Europe, Africa, Asia and America. The company that provided me with invaluable help and support is aptly named – *Travelmania*.

I attended Cyprus festivals in cities as different and far-flung as Melbourne and Toronto. I travelled to Moscow, Los Angeles, Cape Town and Sydney.

Names and profiles for this ambitious new work came flooding in from community events and the print and broadcast media. Regretfully, I could not include them all. But we still have around 2000 people who will be included in our new worldwide edition.

They include Greek Cypriots who have contributed socially or professionally to their communities. There are individuals involved in politics, media, business, sports, theatre, music and the arts. We also included those who have carried out invaluable social and charitable work.

By visiting all these countries I was able to see how our Greek Cypriot communities have prospered in their adopted countries and how they compared to and differed from each other. I found that the Greek Cypriot community in the United States was dispersed throughout that vast country, although the majority were located in the New Jersey area. The more recent immigrants, I discovered, went to study there and decided to stay after graduation. I also found that the sizeable mainland Greek communities in the US and indeed Canada influenced smaller Greek Cypriot communities providing them with a distinct Hellenic outlook.

In Australia and South Africa, however, the Greek Cypriot communities have been large enough to sustain the Greek Cypriot identity without significant influence from the large mainland Hellenic communities. The spirit is kept alive through Greek Cypriot festivals, community centres and churches that have large Greek Cypriot congregations.

Britain, of course, is home to the largest concentration of Greek Cypriots outside Cyprus. Many among this flourishing community of 350,000 visit the island regularly: the flight takes a mere four-and-a-half hours. Most Greek Cypriots in the UK started life in the clothing and catering trades in the 1950s. Their children and grandchildren are educated and are now flourishing in many professions.

It has taken me three years to compile this book, and I've enjoyed every minute. I was privileged to meet many notable, charismatic and engaging Greek Cypriots and travelled to many countries.

The book is a snapshot of our worldwide community today, a celebration of what we Greek Cypriots have achieved outside of our homeland and the greater potential that awaits us in the future.

I hope you find this book a useful, informative and entertaining resource.

Michael Yiakoumi

Washington, USA

Niagra Falls, Canada

Malibu, California

Cape Town, South Africa

Sydney, Australia

Soweto, South Africa

Cannes, South of France

by **Chris Neophytou**
a second generation
Cypriot living in
Melbourne

Greek Cypriots first arrived in Australia in the 1850's, as gold prospectors. The majority settled in Victoria and established small businesses.

More Cypriots arrived after the British take-over of Cyprus in 1878, many working their way to Australia as crewmen on board British ships.

Many Cypriots began to arrive in Australia after World War II, due to the violence and political instability facing Cypriots. The population of Cypriots living in Victoria increased from 169 in 1947 to 2,396 in 1954.

After the Turkish invasion of Cyprus in 1974, many Cypriots migrated to Australia. The population of Cypriots living in Victoria almost doubled in size between 1971 and 1981.

In more recent years Victoria is the most popular destination for Cyprus-born migrants to Australia, with 8,839 recorded in 2001.

In Melbourne, Greek Cypriot migrants have mainly settled in the outer suburbs of Sunshine, Broadmeadows, Keilor and Whittlesea, largely working as tradespeople, labourers and professionals. Organisations such as the Cypriot Community of Melbourne and Victoria provide support to the community. They are now spread all over Australia we have large Cypriot communities in Sydney, Perth, Adelaide and Brisbane again with their own community centres and organisations. There are the annual Cyprus wine festivals which take place in Melbourne and Sydney who receive thousands of visitors. The weather and culture is similar to their homeland but so far away it will take us a whole day to travel to Cyprus but still most of us still make the trip back to see our families and friends.

The Greek Cypriots are now making paths and integrating into the Australian community we now have Cypriots in Government we have Senator Nick Xenophon, Minister Theo Theophanous. MP Michael Costa. We have the Chief Executive of Aussie Rules Football Andrew Demetriou you will also watch TV and see Cypriot names coming up on the credits.

It is estimated there is 80,000 Cypriots born in Cyprus or of origin living there.

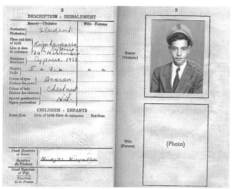

This was the passport issued to Nicholas Neophytou in 1955, to come to Australia

Kyrikou & Nichola Pallikarou arriving in Australia in 1955 from Cyprus

Cypriot Centre in Melbourne

Cypriot Centre in Sydney

Cyprus Festival in Melbourne

CANADA

by **Kyriakos Elles**
The President of the
Federation of Cypriots
in Canada.

The first Cypriots arrived in Canada between 1950 and 1953 then again after the Independence of Cyprus 1961 to 1968 and the invasion from 1974 to 1995.

There is estimated to be 35,000 Cypriots living in Canada. They are mainly concentrated in Toronto and surrounding areas such as Mississauga, Kitchener, Winnipeg and Ottowa. You will also find them in Vancouver and Montreal.

Most of the Cypriots originally worked in factories and catering now the next generation are mainly educated and have entered into professions such as Lawyers, Accountants and Doctors.

They try to keep their identity through having Cypriot Community Centres in Toronto and Kitchener which also include schools.They also hold events like Cypriot festivals, it's difficult for them because there is a large Greek community and they follow their traditions too as the Church congregations will be mainly Hellenic.

In Canada they have several organisations under the umbrella of their Federation of Cypriots in Canada and PSEKA Canada and many Greek Cypriots are involved in the lobbying of the Cyprus problem.

Cypriot Community Centre in Toronto

Photos of Cypriot Festivals in Toronto

The Population of Greek Cypriots in Greece is estimated to be around 60,000 mainly situated in the capital of Athens and the Cities of Thessaloniki and Pireaus.

The short distance and the understanding of the language was the founding reason they immigrated there. The first known Greek Cypriots were from Petulas and they came and settled in Peloponissos where they also built a church.

The Greek Cypriots here are professionals for example, doctors, accountants and lawyers they are involved in the shipping industry and lecturers both in schools and Universities. There are also a lot of students and actors, actresses and musicians who have gone to Greece to progress their careers. There are Cypriot community Centres, Schools and Cypriot themed events to help keep our identity.

Information given by the Republic of Cyprus Embassy in Greece.

by **Demetrios
Constantinides**
The Honorary Consul of
the Republic of Cyprus
Cape Town,
South Africa

The first Greek Cypriots arrived in South Africa in the 1930's and then after the independence of Cyprus at one time there was estimated to be 25,000 and they were situated mainly in Johannesburg and Cape Town but also in Durban and Port Elizabeth many from the Paphos and Karpassia areas.

The first immigrants were involved in farming, factories and the catering industry now they have their own property businesses also involved in mining and are educated so they are in professions like Doctors, Dentists, Lawyers and Accountants.

In recent years this population due to the political problems in South Africa has decreased to 10,000 with several going back to Cyprus, Australia, USA and even the United Kingdom.

The Greek Cypriots have tried to keep their Cypriot identity they have a community Centre in Johannesburg with a School they have churches that has a mainly Cypriot congregation and Cypriot Community organisations. South Africa has a large Greek community so you will find the Cypriots integrating into their community so you will find there is a Hellenic outlook.

Greek Cypriot Community Centre in Johannesburg

UK

by **Maria Yiakoumi**
Third Generation
Cypriot

Prior to the First World War, very few Cypriots migrated to the UK and the British Cypriot population at this time was around 150, according to historian Stavros Panteli. Only a handful of marriages involving Cypriots are recorded at London's Greek Orthodox Cathedral of Saint Sophia in the years before 1918. During the First World War many Cypriots joined the allied forces. When the British annexed Cyprus in 1914, Cypriots' political status changed and they found it easier to travel.

The 1931 British Census recorded more than 1,000 Cypriot-born people, but many of these were the children of British military personnel serving in the Mediterranean. However, some Greek Cypriots did migrate to the UK in the 1920s and 1930s, often finding jobs in the catering industry in Soho. By the start of the Second World War, there were around 8,000 Cypriots in London. More Cypriot immigrants arrived in the UK from 1955 onwards to 1960 approximately 20,000,. Migration peaked following independence in 1960, with around 25,000 Cypriots migrating in the year that followed. Many migrants joined family already living in Britain. Further migration accompanied the Turkish invasion of the island in 1974 Home Office figures show that roughly 10,000 Cypriots fled to the UK, the majority of them refugees, but many of them subsequently returned to the island.

The increase in post-war rents in central London had forced many Cypriot immigrants to move north within the city. With them settling mainly in Camden and then to Haringey. Robert Winder reported that "Haringey became the second biggest Cypriot town in the world". Many Cypriots set up restaurants, filling a gap left by Italians, many of whom had been interned during the Second World War. Greek Cypriots are found in large numbers in the London boroughs of Enfield, Haringey, Barnet and Hackney and outside of London in Manchester, Birmingham and Bristol. It is estimated there may be 300,000 Greek Cypriot's born in Cyprus or of Cypriot Ancestry living in the UK.

The first generation of Cypriots were involved in the catering trade as kitchen staff and waiters in the hotels and restaurants by the late 60's some realised their dreams and owned restaurants and cafés. Some were tailors who then became involved in the ladies garment industry who were followed by their mothers, wives and sister's who became machinists. Most of the dress factories in the 60's and 70's were owned by the Greek Cypriots.

Today the second generation through the hard work of their parents and grandparents have had the chance to have a further education and have gone into professions, medical, teaching, law, accountancy and media to name a few. We have Greek Cypriots who have advanced into politics, a minister, councillor's. Some who have made it into the world of music, sport media and the arts you will read about these people in this book. We have in the UK three newspapers a radio station, a cable TV Station, churches in every major town, a Cypriot football league consisting of about thirty teams and now several school age football teams that play in English leagues.

It's a future to look forward to.

Cypriot Centre Wood Green

Greek Cypriot Brotherhood Centre

Scene from Cyprus Wine Festival

Cypriots in the early 60's

Cypriots in the early 70's

by **Joanna Zampas**
Second generation
Cypriot

The story of Greek-Cypriot immigrants to the USA is the story of nearly all immigrants coming to the country – the story of generations of people who sacrificed themselves through hard work, often manual labor, so their children and future generations could have a life of the mind.

As a second generation Greek-Cypriot American, I pay homage to all those hardworking people, foremost my father. He uprooted himself from his home and family and supplanted himself into the US without having many friends or knowing the language well. My father, as most Greek-Cypriot immigrants, managed to achieve a certain level of prosperity in his new country and passed on to his children a driven work ethic and importance of education, so they could excel.

Community Organizations
The initial hardship of their new country was offset by close community ties. Community organizations, such as Lampousa, served as a link between new arrivals and ones already settled. These organizations played a pivotal role in maintaining and preserving traditional values and consolidating the Greek-Cypriot community during the early years of settlement.

1930s
The first wave of Greek-Cypriot immigrants was in 1930. My uncle, Costas Zampas, was included in this group. He came to the US through Ellis Island and served in the Navy which turned out to be his career. He passed away a decade ago at the age of 86. We are blessed to still have with us Mr. Aristedes (Aris) Demetriou born in Karavas in 1910. He, too, came to New York through Ellis Island on February 18, 1930 and set up a beauty parlor in Manhattan and he continued to work until 2006! He founded Lampousa in 1937.

1950s and beyond
The periods of greatest emigration were 1955-65 and after the Turkish invasion, 1974-79. In the early years, the Greek-Cypriot immigrants generally settled in the areas of the US where their compatriots from Greece were already settled decades before, primarily New York and Chicago. Employment opportunities were in the area of cooks, tailors, shoe repairers, hair dressers – trades learned from their homeland.

During the post-invasion years, the progressive Greek-Cypriot community moved away from traditional work to occupations that require a high level of education.

A common sentiment among them is their feeling of good fortune in being able to live and thrive in the US, while still maintaining their roots in Cyprus.

Many Greek-Cypriot Americans remain involved in political and lobby issues of importance to Cyprus. A solution to the present situation of the country continues to remain on the edge of a dream for all justice seekers in the world.

Aris Demetriou's Hair Parlor, Manhattan, 1933

Leaving for USA Dec 1960 – Stavros & Maro Zampas

Stavros Zampas in Chicago, Summer 1961

Cyprus Embassy, Washington

Winter 1962

Wedding Day, Oct. 16 1960

Greek Orthodox Church in Los Angeles

Australia

Australia

PETER ABRAAM
Chief Executive Officer of a Major Events Company. Previously Event Planning Manager, Formula One Grand Prix

DATE OF BIRTH: 04-Jul-1961
PLACE OF BIRTH: Melbourne, Australia, Grandparents from Aradippou, Cyprus.
MARITAL STATUS: Married to Penelope Abraam, Melbourne-Greek Parents.
SCHOOLS/COLLEGE: RMIT, Royal Melbourne University.
QUALIFICATIONS: Bachelor of Applied Science.
MEMBERSHIPS: South Melbourne Football Club, National Union of Greek Australian Students.
HONOURS/AWARDS: Numerous Community Awards.
HOBBIES AND INTERESTS: Football, History.
PERSONAL PROFILE: Chief Executive Officer of a Major Events Company. Previously Event Planning Manager, Formula One Grand Prix.

PANICOS ACHILLEOUS
President of Cyprus Hellenic Club in Sydney

DATE OF BIRTH: 02-Feb-1945
PLACE OF BIRTH: Pedhoulas.
MARITAL STATUS: Married to Thalia, Pedhoulas.
CHILDREN: Stelios, National Manager RESI. Nasia, Finance Dept. Quantas Holidays.
SCHOOLS/COLLEGE: Pedhoulas Gymnasium. Thessaloniki University, Military Academy, Police Academy.
HOBBIES AND INTERESTS: Community Work.
PERSONAL PROFILE: President of Cyprus Hellenic Club in Sydney. President of Pedhoulas Association, Australia. Member of SEKA.

MIRANDA ADAMOU
President of Justice for Cyprus Committee Australia. Vice President of Pseka, on the board of Trustees of the Radio Marathon Committee

DATE OF BIRTH: 25-Mar-1960
PLACE OF BIRTH: Kythrea.
MARITAL STATUS: Single.
CHILDREN: Michael, Student. Stelios, Student. Elli, Student.
SCHOOLS/COLLEGE: Pancyprian Gymnasium, Glades Ville High. Sydney University.
QUALIFICATIONS: BDS- Dentistry.
HOBBIES AND INTERESTS: Charity work, Women's Issues.
PERSONAL PROFILE: Dentist. Member of the Sydney Uni Greek Society. Committee member of Greek Australian Professional Association. President of Justice for Cyprus Committee Australia. Vice President of Pseka, on the board of Trustees of the Radio Marathon Committee, Secretary OEGGA, Australia.

MELISSA ANASTASI
Sydney based Film-maker

DATE OF BIRTH: 30-Sep-1978
PLACE OF BIRTH: Sydney, Australia, Father from Famagusta. Mother from Ayios Amvrosios.
MARITAL STATUS: Single.
SCHOOLS/COLLEGE: Macquarie University, Sydney University.
QUALIFICATIONS: Bachelor of Media, Certificate IV in Film & Video.
HOBBIES AND INTERESTS: Reading, film watching, walking, working, traveling, photography.
PERSONAL PROFILE: She is a Sydney based Film-maker, who has recently secured funding for a medium length film about a Cypriot family in Australia. She has made two other short films, and worked on both feature films and short films as an Assistant Director.

Entrants in Greek Cypriots Worldwide have been nominated for their achievements and contributions.
It is free to nominate someone, or yourself, who deserves to be in the book, just send in the name, contact address, telephone number and email to:
Greek Cypriots Worldwide
111 St Thomas's Road London N4 2QJ
Telephone 0044 207503 3498
cypriotwhoswho@aol.com
www.greekcypriotsworldwide.com

Australia

MARIA ANASTOPOULOS
Education

DATE OF BIRTH: 24-Aug-1973
PLACE OF BIRTH: Sydney, father and mother from Famagusta.
MARITAL STATUS: Married to John Anastopoulos, Greek.
CHILDREN: Sophia, School. Andreanna, School.
SCHOOLS/COLLEGE: Loxton high School. Sydney University.
QUALIFICATIONS: B. Ed mathematics & Computing.
HOBBIES AND INTERESTS: Keep-fit, Socialising.
PERSONAL PROFILE: Teaches Maths and Computing at a High School. Active in the Cypriot Community of Sydney.

ANDREA (GEORGIOU) ANDRONICOU
Electrochemist

DATE OF BIRTH: 26-Nov-1964
PLACE OF BIRTH: Limassol, Cyprus.
MARITAL STATUS: Married to Con, Civil Engineer-runs family business, Fast Fuel chain of Petrol Stations.
CHILDREN: Angelica, School. Andreas, School. Felicia, School.
SCHOOLS/COLLEGE: Brighton Secondary College, RMIT, Monash University.
QUALIFICATIONS: B. App. Science (Chemistry), Postgraduate. Business (Marketing).
HOBBIES AND INTERESTS: Reading, Movies, Running, Friends, Travel.
PERSONAL PROFILE: Prior to having children she was a Product Manager she specialised in Electrochemistry. Since having children she and her husband started to import car-wash consumables and started the Company Carwash Supply Industries. Active member of the Cypriot Community in Australia.

CON ANDRONICOU
Director of Fast Fuel' which is an independantly branded Petrol Station

DATE OF BIRTH: 02-Jun-1963.
PLACE OF BIRTH: Australia, Father - Cyprus, Mother - Greece.
MARITAL STATUS: Married to Andrea Georgiou, Greek Cypriot.
CHILDREN: Angelica, Andreas, Felicia.
SCHOOLS/COLLEGE: Monash University.

QUALIFICATIONS: B. Engineering - Civil.
HOBBIES AND INTERESTS: Stock Market, Cycling, friends.
PERSONAL PROFILE: Runs a successful business with two brothers. 'Fast Fuel' which is an independantly branded Petrol Station. Con also started up his own business supplying carwash consumables 'Carwash Supply Industries'.

STELIOS ANGELODEMOU
President of the Cyprus Community of Melbourne

DATE OF BIRTH: 14-Nov-1951
PLACE OF BIRTH: Varishia.
MARITAL STATUS: Married.
CHILDREN: Three Children.
PERSONAL PROFILE: Stelios Angelodemou is the President of the Cyprus Community of Melbourne.

ANDREANA ANGELOS
Lawyer/Vice President of Innerwest Law Society

DATE OF BIRTH: 28-Apr-1974
PLACE OF BIRTH: Sydney, Father from Ayios Amvrosios, Mother from Khirokitia.
MARITAL STATUS: Single.
SCHOOLS/COLLEGE: St. Catherines School. University of NSW.
QUALIFICATIONS: BA in Psychology, LLB.
HOBBIES AND INTERESTS: Travel, sports.
PERSONAL PROFILE: Lawyer in Family Law Firm. She was involved in Hellenic Society in University. Involved in S. A. E. and is Vice President of Innerwest Law Society.

DIONE ANGELOS
Voted No 1 Financial Planner in Westpac in Australia in 2007

DATE OF BIRTH: 31-Aug-1975.
PLACE OF BIRTH: Sydney, Father from Ayios Amvrosios, Mother from Khirokitia.
MARITAL STATUS: Single.
SCHOOLS/COLLEGE: St. Catherines School. University of New South Wales.

QUALIFICATIONS: BSC in Economics, M. Com Banking and Finance, CFP, SIA (AFF).
HONOURS/AWARDS: Voted No 1 Financial Planner in Westpac in Australia in 2007.
HOBBIES AND INTERESTS: Music, Share market, travel, jewellery.
PERSONAL PROFILE: Senior Financial Planner with Westpac Banking Corporation. Appeared on Ready, Steady, Cook as a guest cook.

NICOLAS PANAYI ANGELOS
Lawyer/Former President of Cyprus Community of New South Wales

DATE OF BIRTH: 10-Feb-1945
PLACE OF BIRTH: Ayios Amvrosios.
MARITAL STATUS: Married to Sophia, Khirokitia.
CHILDREN: Andrianna, Lawyer. Antigoni, Financial Planner. Yiota, Lawyer. Christopher, 3rd Year Commerce, Law Sydney University.
SCHOOLS/COLLEGE: Pancyprian Gymnasium. Sydney University, Law School LLB.
QUALIFICATIONS: Solicitor.
HOBBIES AND INTERESTS: Reading, Politics.
PERSONAL PROFILE: Has had his own Law office for 30 years. Secretary of SEKA. Former President of Cyprus Community of New South Wales. PASEKA (Justice committee for Cyprus Australia committee).

PANAYIOTA ANGELOS
Lawyer in family law business. During University was a finalist in The Mooting Competition and appeared in the Supreme Court

DATE OF BIRTH: 18-Feb-1983
PLACE OF BIRTH: Sydney, father from Ayios Amvrosios, Mother from Khirokitia.
MARITAL STATUS: Single.
SCHOOLS/COLLEGE: Ascham School. University of NSW, McGill Montreal.
QUALIFICATIONS: Lawyer.
HOBBIES AND INTERESTS: Music, singing, travel.
PERSONAL PROFILE: Lawyer in family law business. During University was a finalist in The Mooting Competition and appeared in the Supreme Court, was selected for Prestigious Exchange to McGill University. Appeared on TV ' Ready, Steady, Cook, as a guest cook.

ACHILLEAS ANTONIADES
High Commissioner to the High Commission of the Republic of Cyprus in Australia

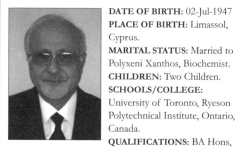

DATE OF BIRTH: 02-Jul-1947
PLACE OF BIRTH: Limassol, Cyprus.
MARITAL STATUS: Married to Polyxeni Xanthos, Biochemist.
CHILDREN: Two Children.
SCHOOLS/COLLEGE: University of Toronto, Ryeson Polytechnical Institute, Ontario, Canada.
QUALIFICATIONS: BA Hons, Sociology, Political Economy, MSW, Policy Planning, Administration, Certificate, Business Administration.
HOBBIES AND INTERESTS: Tennis, golf, gardening.
PERSONAL PROFILE: Achilleas has held many important Political posts over his career. He holds the post of High Commissioner to the High Commission of the Republic of Cyprus in Australia from February 2004 -date.

CHARALAMBOUS ANTONIOU
Treasurer of the Cyprus Community of New South Wales

DATE OF BIRTH: 07-Dec-1941
PLACE OF BIRTH: Athienou.
CHILDREN: Eleana, BA in Accounting now Housewife. Antonis, Sales, specialising in Books.
SCHOOLS/COLLEGE: Athienou Elementary School, Samuell Gymnasium, Nicosia.
HOBBIES AND INTERESTS: Community Work.
PERSONAL PROFILE: Treasurer of the Cyprus Community of New South Wales.

Greek Cypriot Walter Ionas was born in Cyprus in 1857, arrived in Adelaide in 1883 and worked as a tailor in the early 1890's.

Australia

SAVVAS ANTONIOU
Elderly Group Committee Treasurer,
Cyprus Community of Melbourne, Victoria

PLACE OF BIRTH: Karpassia
MARITAL STATUS: Married to Niki, Greek.
CHILDREN: Tony, IT Specialist. Andrew, Road Traffic. Marie, Housewife.
SCHOOLS/COLLEGE: Elementary School.
HOBBIES AND INTERESTS: Soccer, tennis.
PERSONAL PROFILE: Elderly Group Committee Treasurer, Cyprus Community of Melbourne, Victoria.

TONY ANTONIOU
Secretary of the Cypriot Community of Melbourne

DATE OF BIRTH: 16-Mar-1956
PLACE OF BIRTH: London, parents from Morphou.
MARITAL STATUS: Married to Sophie, Greek Cypriot.
CHILDREN: Tiffany, Human Resources. Luke, University, studying IT.
SCHOOLS/COLLEGE: Morphou Gymnasium. UCL.
QUALIFICATIONS: BSc in Civil Engineering.
HOBBIES AND INTERESTS: Soccer one of the founders of Bentley Green Football Club.
PERSONAL PROFILE: Secretary of the Cypriot Community Melbourne Victoria. General manager of Operations Melbourne Water.

STELIOS ARCADIOU
Artist

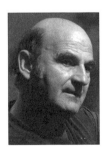

DATE OF BIRTH: 19-Jun-1946
PLACE OF BIRTH: Australia Parents from Cyprus.
PERSONAL PROFILE: Stelios Arcadiou is an Australian performance artist whose works focus heavily on futurism and extending the capabilities of the human body.

DR JOHN ARGYRIDES
Doctor in the Gastroenterology and Hepatology Unit at the Royal Adelaide Hospital

DATE OF BIRTH: 24-Dec-1957
PLACE OF BIRTH: Nicosia, Cyprus.
MARITAL STATUS: Married to Margo, Australian, Doctor.
CHILDREN: Michael, Nick, Tom.
SCHOOLS/COLLEGE: Proton Gymnasium, Ammochostos Lanition. Flinders University of South Australia.
QUALIFICATIONS: MBBS, FRACP.
HOBBIES AND INTERESTS: Cyprus politics and history, travelling, sports.
PERSONAL PROFILE: Doctor in the Gastroenterology and Hepatology Unit at the Royal Adelaide Hospital.

ANNA ATHANASIOU
OHS Practitioner

PLACE OF BIRTH: Cyprus.
PERSONAL PROFILE: Anna Athanasiou is an OHS Practitioner to the Office of Consumer and Business Affairs and to the field of Occupational Health and Safety in South Australia.

MICHALIS ATHANASIOU
General Manager of Laiki Bank, Austrailia

DATE OF BIRTH: 09-Jan-1974
PLACE OF BIRTH: Larnaca, Cyprus.
MARITAL STATUS: Married.
CHILDREN: Thanasis, St. Spyridon College, Sydney. Petros, Kindergarden.
SCHOOLS/COLLEGE: American Academy, Larnaca.
QUALIFICATIONS: BA Hons, Accounting Finance, MSC (Distinction) Securities & Investment Banking.
HOBBIES AND INTERESTS: Football, Scuba Diving, Politics.
PERSONAL PROFILE: General Manager of Laiki Bank, Australia. Formerly Group Treasurer of Laiki Group. He is heavily involved with Radiomarathon Australia (Chairman). Elected and served in Oroklini Council from 2001-2006 until he moved to Australia.

AVGOUSTINOS AVGOUSTOU
Head Teacher

DATE OF BIRTH: 11-Aug-1966
PLACE OF BIRTH: Nicosia, Cyprus.
MARITAL STATUS: Married to Anna, Greek/Australian, Banking.
CHILDREN: Chloe, Stephanie.
SCHOOLS/COLLEGE: Newtown high School. University of Sydney.
QUALIFICATIONS: Bachelor of Education.
MEMBERSHIPS: NSW Teachers Federation.
HOBBIES AND INTERESTS: Reading, bike riding, Greek music, travelling.
PERSONAL PROFILE: Secondary teacher of Modern Greek & English- Head Teacher Administration. Served as Committee Member of the Cyprus Community Centre of NSW in Sydney.

KYRIAKOS BARACKAS
Active Member of the Cypriot Community of Melbourne, Victoria

DATE OF BIRTH: 24-Mar-1946
PLACE OF BIRTH: Kalavasos.
MARITAL STATUS: Married to Maria, Menoico.
CHILDREN: Chris, Irine, Vasiliki.
SCHOOLS/COLLEGE: Elementary School Kalavasso.
HOBBIES AND INTERESTS: Soccer.
PERSONAL PROFILE: Former President and treasurer of the dancing group Cypriot Community of Melbourne, Victoria.

VASILIKI VICKI BARACKAS
Active member of the Cypriot Youth Community of Melbourne

DATE OF BIRTH: 09-Apr-1986
PLACE OF BIRTH: Australia, Mother from Menoiko Father from Kalavasos.
MARITAL STATUS: Single.
SCHOOLS/COLLEGE: Pascoe Vale Girls College. University of Melbourne.
HOBBIES AND INTERESTS: Travelling and Jewellery making.

PERSONAL PROFILE: Vicky is an active member of the Cypriot Youth Community of Melbourne and a volunteer for Starlight Foundation 2007.

ELENA CARAPETIS
Actress appears in Heartbreak TV Soap in Australia High

PLACE OF BIRTH: Australia her mother is from Cyprus
SCHOOLS/COLLEGE: National Institute of Dramatic Art.
QUALIFICATIONS: Degree in Performing Arts.
PERSONAL PROFILE: Elena Carapetis is known for her role as Jackie Kassis in Heartbreak High.

COSTA CHARALAMBOUS
Principal of Laing&Simmons Coogee/ Clovelly/Marouba Property company

PLACE OF BIRTH: Born in Australia Parents from Paphos
QUALIFICATIONS: Bachelor of Land Economics(Honours).
PERSONAL PROFILE: Principal –licencee in charge of Laing&Simmons Coogee/ Clovelly/Marouba Property company.

JOHN CHARALAMBOUS
shortlisted for the Commonwealth Writers Prize Best First Book in the South East Asia and Pacific region

DATE OF BIRTH: 24-Oct-1956
PLACE OF BIRTH: Melbourne, Australia, Parents from Cyprus.
MARITAL STATUS: Married to Evelyn, Australian, Teacher.
SCHOOLS/COLLEGE: Hampton High School. Melbourne State College.
QUALIFICATIONS: Bachelor of Education, Arts and Crafts.
PERSONAL PROFILE: He writes literary fiction and has had two novels published by University of Queensland Press: 'Furies' in 2004 and 'Silent Parts' in 2006. 'Furies' was shortlisted for the Commonwealth Writers Prize Best First Book in the South East Asia and Pacific region.

Australia

LISA MARIE CHARALAMBOUS
Actress appeared in the Theatrical Productions We will rock you and West Side Story

PLACE OF BIRTH: Parents from Cyprus
SCHOOLS/COLLEGE: Penleigh & Essendon Grammar School. Victorian College of Arts.
QUALIFICATIONS: Bachelor of Music Performance.
PERSONAL PROFILE: Lisa Marie Charalambous is an Actress has appeared in the Theatrical Productions We will Rock You, West Side Story and Les Miserables and several others.

CHARALAMBOS CHRISTODOULIDES
Web Services Manager, Macquarie University, Sydney, Australia

DATE OF BIRTH: 22-Jan-1974
PLACE OF BIRTH: London. Mother from Kyrenia. Father from Morphou.
MARITAL STATUS: Single.
SCHOOLS/COLLEGE: College of North East London. Kingsway College London. University of Portsmouth.
QUALIFICATIONS: BA Hons Design and Media.
PERSONAL PROFILE: Background: Senior Web Designer/Developer for a London based Interactive Web Agency. Currently: Web Services Manager, Macquarie University, Sydney, Australia.

ROULA CHRISTODOULIDES
Education, Cyprus Community School in Sydney

DATE OF BIRTH: 14-Dec-1958
PLACE OF BIRTH: Sydney, Australia, Father from Limassol Mother from Leonarisso.
MARITAL STATUS: Married to Michael Christodoulides.
CHILDREN: Georgia, Sales Support. Sam, University. Demetra, School.
SCHOOLS/COLLEGE: Strathfield Girls High School. University of NSW, Southern Cross University.
QUALIFICATIONS: Graduate Certificate in Management.

PERSONAL PROFILE: Business manager, Cyprus Community Greek School, Auburn.

CHRIS CHRISTODOULOU
Chairperson Wollongong sportsground trust

DATE OF BIRTH: 01-Feb-1960
PLACE OF BIRTH: Sydney, Parents from Nicosia.
MARITAL STATUS: Married to Gelsomina, Italian descent, Fitness Instructor-Respite Care.
CHILDREN: Elizabeth, High School. Isaac, High School.
SCHOOLS/COLLEGE: Wollongong Primary, Figtree High. Wollongong University.
QUALIFICATIONS: Bachelor of Arts- Industrial Relations.
MEMBERSHIPS: Life Member of the Liquor, Hospitality Miscellaneous Union, Member of the United Services Union.
HOBBIES AND INTERESTS: Bicycle riding.
PERSONAL PROFILE: 2000-present- Deputy Assistant Secretary, Unions NSW. Chairperson Wollongong sports ground trust.

CHRISTODOULOS CHRISTODOULOU
Associate Professor Australian Graduate School of Entrepreneurship

DATE OF BIRTH: 25-Apr-1955
PLACE OF BIRTH: Melbourne, Father: Acheritou, Mother: Ayia Triada, Yialousa.
MARITAL STATUS: Married to Despina, Limnia, Housewife.
SCHOOLS/COLLEGE: Melbourne High School. University of Melbourne, Monash University.
QUALIFICATIONS: B. Agric Science, Master of Science, MBA. Ph. D.
MEMBERSHIPS: Strategic Management Society, Australian. and New Zealand Academy of Management.
HOBBIES AND INTERESTS: Travel, Handyman.
PERSONAL PROFILE: Christodoulos Christodoulou is an Associate Professor Australian Graduate School of Entrepreneurship.

JOHN CHRISTODOULOU
Clinical Geneticist

DATE OF BIRTH: 15-Jan-1958
PLACE OF BIRTH: Sydney Australia Parents from Cyprus.
MARITAL STATUS: Married to Catherine, Australian, occupational Therapist.
CHILDREN: Thomas John, College. Callum Peter, High School.
SCHOOLS/COLLEGE: East Hills Boys High. University of Sydney.
QUALIFICATIONS: MB BS (Hons), PhD, FRACP, FRCPA, FHGSA (Clinical Genetics).
MEMBERSHIPS: American Society of Human Genetics, Australian Society for Biochemistry and Molecular Biology.
HOBBIES AND INTERESTS: Fencing.
PERSONAL PROFILE: John is a clinical geneticist, specialising in the field of inborn errors of metabolism, and his research interests in Rett Syndrome, mitochondrial respiratory disorders and Rett Syndrome. In 2006 he was invited to join the scientific advisory board of the Cyprus Institute for Neurology and Genetics.

MICHAEL CHRISTODOULOU
President of the Federation of Cypriot Communities in Australia and New Zealand

DATE OF BIRTH: 08-Aug-1955
PLACE OF BIRTH: Oroklini.
MARITAL STATUS: Married.
SCHOOLS/COLLEGE: Oroklini. Sydney University.
QUALIFICATIONS: Dr in Osteopathy and Chiropractice.
HONOURS/AWARDS: Recipient of the 2006 Government of NSW Community Service Award.
Recipient of the 2005 Community service Award from the Federation of Ethnic Communities Councils of Australia.
Recipient of the 2003 Centenary from the Australian Government.
PERSONAL PROFILE: Michael Christodoulou is the President of the Federation of Cypriot Communities in Australia and New Zealand. National President justice for Cyprus Coordinating Committee. Chairperson Maymurray neighbourhood Centre. Co, ordinator United Nations Human Rights Day Committee. Chiropractor by occupation in private practice since 1977.

ERIC CHRISTOFI
Telecommunications, General manager of M8 Telecom

DATE OF BIRTH: 08-Sep-1976.
PLACE OF BIRTH: Sydney Australia, Parents from Limassol.
MARITAL STATUS: Married to Stella.
SCHOOLS/COLLEGE: St. George College, Sydney.
QUALIFICATIONS: Computer Programming.
HOBBIES AND INTERESTS: Yachting.
PERSONAL PROFILE: General manager of M8 Telecom.

PETER CHRISTOFI
Secretary of the Federation of the Cyprus Community of Australia and New Zealand

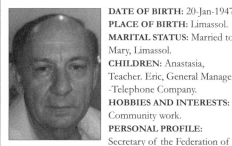

DATE OF BIRTH: 20-Jan-1947
PLACE OF BIRTH: Limassol.
MARITAL STATUS: Married to Mary, Limassol.
CHILDREN: Anastasia, Teacher. Eric, General Manager -Telephone Company.
HOBBIES AND INTERESTS: Community work.
PERSONAL PROFILE: Secretary of the Federation of the Cyprus Community of Australia and New Zealand. Former Secretary of Cyprus Committee of Sydney, New South Wales.

EMILY CHRISTOFIDES
National Marketing Manager for Wollongong University College

PLACE OF BIRTH: Australia Parents from Cyprus
SCHOOLS/COLLEGE: University of Wollongong.
QUALIFICATIONS: Bachelor of creative arts and master of marketing.
PERSONAL PROFILE: Emily Christofides is the National Marketing Manager for Wollongong University College.

Australia

LEE CHRISTOFIS (CHRISTOPHIDES)
Curator of Dance at the National Library of Australia

DATE OF BIRTH: 08-Feb-1948
PLACE OF BIRTH: Brisbane, Australia, Father from Odou.
MARITAL STATUS: Single.
SCHOOLS/COLLEGE: Brisbane State High. Brisbane Kindergarden Teachers College.
QUALIFICATIONS: Diploma in Early Childhood Teaching.
MEMBERSHIPS: Australian Dance Council-Ausdance (1990), Australian Early Childhood Association (1981-1999).
HONOURS/AWARDS: Honorary Life Member of Ausdance, Inaugural Victorian Government Award for Service to Multicultural Communities in the Arts.
HOBBIES AND INTERESTS: Ballet, contemporary dance, classical music, visual arts, literature, history, travel, culture, food, gardening, conversation, politics, debate.
PERSONAL PROFILE: After a brief career as a Ballet dancer, he became the first male kindergarden teacher to graduate in Queensland. His other life has been as a dance critic since 1981, in national print and broadcast media. His current position is Curator of Dance at the National Library of Australia.

STRATIS CHRISTOFIS
President Cypriot Brotherhood Queensland Australia (Deceased)

PLACE OF BIRTH: Odou, Cyprus in 1896
MARITAL STATUS: Married to Evangila Mousouris, Greek-British, Wife.
CHILDREN: Julie, Fund-raiser. Chris, Dental Surgeon. Helen, Pedagogue and Family Therapist. Lee child 5. John, Dancer, Critic child 5. Sculptor-Stone Mason.
SCHOOLS/COLLEGE: Village School.
HONOURS/AWARDS: Invested as Archon of the Greek Orthodox by His Grace Ezekiel Kefalas, Archbishop of Australia and New Zealand c. 1970.
HOBBIES AND INTERESTS: opera, singing, music, entertaining, politics, cricket, history, religion.
PERSONAL PROFILE: Cypriot Brotherhood of Queensland (President and executive for several years), 1930s-1960s Greek Orthodox Community of St George (president for more than 20 years).

ANASTASIA CHRYSOSTOMOU
Consultant at the Royal Melbourne Hospital

PLACE OF BIRTH: Parents from Larnaca.
QUALIFICATIONS: MBBS. FRACP.
PERSONAL PROFILE: DR Anna Chrysostomou is a consultant at the Royal Melbourne Hospital and also sees private patients at Emerald Hill Clinic. She has a particular interest in diseases of Kidneys(nephrology).

CON CONSTANTINE
Owner of the Australian Football Club Newcastle Jets

PLACE OF BIRTH: Cyprus
PERSONAL PROFILE: Con Constantine is the owner and Chairman of Newcastle Jets who play in the A division of the Australian League. He is the owner of Parklea Markets one of the premier retail destinations in Western sydney. He has recently purchased two Newcastle Community Newspapers The Newcastle & Lake Macquarie Post and the Hunter Post.

JOHN CONSTANTINE
Chairman of the Australian Soccer Federation

PLACE OF BIRTH: Parents from Cyprus.
QUALIFICATIONS: BA LLB.
PERSONAL PROFILE: John Constantine was the Chairman of the Australian Soccer Federation and President of Sydney Olympic FC he also served as a member of FIFA's Committee for Youth Competitions. John works as a Solicitor/Barrister.

Sir GEORGE CONSTANTINOU
Deceased
Cyprus HonoraryConsul at Papua New Guinea

DATE OF BIRTH: 11-May-1930.
HONOURS/AWARDS: Awarded knighthood by the Queen for his charitable work.
PERSONAL PROFILE: Sir George Constantinou was Cyprus Honorary Consul at Papua New Guinea. He established one of the most successful business and construction empires in the country Papuan welders and Papuan Transport Contractors Roadmakers.

Australia

MARIA CONSTANTINOU
Awarded the Australian Physiotherapy Association sport therapist title in 2001

PLACE OF BIRTH: Australia parents from Cyprus
SCHOOLS/COLLEGE: University of Queensland.
QUALIFICATIONS: MPhtySt(sports), BPhty. GradCertEd and MPhil.
HONOURS/AWARDS: Awarded the Australian Physiotherapy Association sport therapist title in 2001.
PERSONAL PROFILE: Maria teaches at the school of physiotherapy and exercise science at Griffin University on the Gold Coast, her primary teaching responsibilities are in the area of musculoskeletal, orthopaedic and sports physiotherapy. She has also worked as a sports physiotherapist at the Sydney 2000 and Athens 2004 Olympic games and at the Melbourne 2006 Commonwealth games.

STELLA COSMOS
Marketing Manager of Carrick Institute of education

DATE OF BIRTH: 01-Apr-1976
PLACE OF BIRTH: Melbourne, Parents from Anoyira.
SCHOOLS/COLLEGE: Swinburne University.
QUALIFICATIONS: Bachelor of Business (Marketing).
MEMBERSHIPS: Australian Institute Management.
HOBBIES AND INTERESTS: Music, travel.
PERSONAL PROFILE: Marketing Manager of Carrick Institute of Education.

Con Constantine is the owner and chairman of Newcastle Jets who play in the A division of the Australian league.

DIMITRIS COSTA
President of the Elderly Group of Cyprus Community, Melbourne, Victoria

DATE OF BIRTH: 06-May-1928
PLACE OF BIRTH: Karmi, kyrenia.
MARITAL STATUS: Married to Emilia.
CHILDREN: James, Store Manager. Helen, Supervisor-Remand Centre. Mary, Bachelor of Science-Theraputic Medicine.
SCHOOLS/COLLEGE: Kyrenia Gymnasium.
HOBBIES AND INTERESTS: Soccer, Community work.
PERSONAL PROFILE: President of the Elderly Group of Cyprus Community, Melbourne, Victoria.

MICHAEL COSTA
Treasurer and Minister of infrastructure New South Wales

DATE OF BIRTH: 15-Jul-1956
PLACE OF BIRTH: Newcastle Australia Parents from Cyprus.
PERSONAL PROFILE: Australian Politician, Currently Treasurer and Minister of Infrastructure New South Wales. Served as Police Minister from 2001 to 2003, Transport services Minister from 2003 to 2005. also served as Roads Minister in year 2005.

THOMAS COSTA
Former Secretary and Member of Cyprus Community of NSW. Justice of the Peace

DATE OF BIRTH: 10-Feb-1927
PLACE OF BIRTH: Akaki, Cyprus.
MARITAL STATUS: Married to Froso, Greek Cypriot.
CHILDREN: Mary, Travel Agent. Costas, G. P. Dorothy, Social Worker. Andrew, High School.
SCHOOLS/COLLEGE: Akaki Elementary.
QUALIFICATIONS: Self-educated.
HOBBIES AND INTERESTS: Souvla, gardening.
PERSONAL PROFILE: Justice of the Peace, NSW, 1950-date. Former Secretary and Member of Cyprus Community of NSW. Cyprus Self Determination Committee (General Secretary).

Australia

ANGELA COSTI
Lawyer/Writer

DATE OF BIRTH: 14-Jan-1968
PLACE OF BIRTH: Australia
Father from Kyrenia, Mother from Vasa.
MARITAL STATUS: Married to Joshua Koch, American, Promotions Officer.
CHILDREN: Elias, Theodore.
SCHOOLS/COLLEGE: Lalor Secondary. Melbourne University.
QUALIFICATIONS: LLB BA.
MEMBERSHIPS: Victorian Writers Centre.
HONOURS/AWARDS: Travel award from the Australian National Languages and Literacy Board in 1993.
HOBBIES AND INTERESTS: Reading, Literature, Music and History.
PERSONAL PROFILE: Angela Costi is a Lawyer she currently has a freelance writing business, her poems, dramatic narratives, stories and essays have been published. She has also produced plays.

GEORGE COSTI
Founder of De Costi Foods Australia's leading name in seafood retail

PLACE OF BIRTH: Cyprus
HONOURS/AWARDS: Awarded "Ambassador of Seafood" in 2003 in recognition of his enormous contribution to the seafood industry, spanning more than 30 years.
PERSONAL PROFILE: De Costi Seafoods was established at the Sydney Fish Markets, Pyrmont in 1981. Recognised as the most popular fresh seafood brand name in Australia, De Costi Seafoods operates in retail and wholesale seafood markets. Sourcing the finest quality seafood from all over Australia, New Zealand and the Asia Pacific Region, wherever the catch is being landed. They now have seventeen stores.

JOHN COSTI
Director, Orthopaedic Biomechanics Laboratory

DATE OF BIRTH: 11-Oct-1969
PLACE OF BIRTH: Adelaide, South Australia Parents from Cyprus.
MARITAL STATUS: Married to Kerry, Australian, Research Officer.
CHILDREN: Jake, Georgian.
SCHOOLS/COLLEGE: Seaton High School. The University of Adelaide, Flinders University.
QUALIFICATIONS: B. E. Mechanical (Hons). Ph. D. Biomechanics.
MEMBERSHIPS: Orthopaedic Research Society, Spine Society of Australia.
HONOURS/AWARDS: Finalist-International Society of Biomechanics (ISB)- Clinical Biomechanics Award 2007.
HOBBIES AND INTERESTS: Martial Arts, reading, computers, self development, continual pursuit of knowledge.
PERSONAL PROFILE: Director, Orthopaedic Biomechanics Laboratory, Repatriation General Hospital and Senior Lecturer, the University of Adelaide and Flinders University.

CHRISTOPHER COUDOUNARIS
Former Chairman of Stratfield Group over 80 Retail Outlets in Australia

PLACE OF BIRTH: Cyprus.
PERSONAL PROFILE: Christopher Coudounaris was the Chairman of Strathfield Group involved in retailing car audio products, home entertainment, home office and mobile telephone products, with over 80 shops in Australia.

COSTAS DEMETRIADES
President of the Cypriot Association of Western Australia

DATE OF BIRTH: 21-Aug-1948
PLACE OF BIRTH: Nicosia, Cyprus.
MARITAL STATUS: Married to Athena, Australian, Housewife.
CHILDREN: Alexandra, BA Fine Arts. Toula, BA English. Eleni, BA Environment & Planning. Andrea, BA (National Institute of Dramatic Art).
SCHOOLS/COLLEGE: Pancyprian Gymnasium, Nicosia, Cyprus. TAFE WA. RMIT University Melbourne Australia.

QUALIFICATIONS: Graduate Diploma in Educational Studies, Diploma in Accounting.
MEMBERSHIPS: NAATI (National Accreditation Authority of Translators and Interpreters), Curriculum Council of Western Australia.
HOBBIES AND INTERESTS: Radio (SBS Journalist), writing, music, dancing, Cyprus.
PERSONAL PROFILE: President of the Cypriot Association of WA. Teacher-Headmaster Greek Community Schools in WA, Journalist with SBS Radio (Australia).

ANDREA DEMETRIOU
Teacher/Writer

PLACE OF BIRTH: Morphou, Cyprus
MARITAL STATUS: Single.
SCHOOLS/COLLEGE: Albert Park and Princess Hill High School, Melbourne, Australia. Athens University.
QUALIFICATIONS: Degree in English and Greek Literature, Postgraduate in History of Philosophy.
HOBBIES AND INTERESTS: Singing, dancing, swimming.
PERSONAL PROFILE: Has written a Poetry Book called 'The mountains couldnt walk away', which refers to nostalgia and its consequences for a world which was lost after the Turkish invasion in 1974.

ANDREAS DEMETRIOU
Vice President of the Cyprus Community of Melbourne and Victoria, Australia

DATE OF BIRTH: 25-Aug-1959
PLACE OF BIRTH: Nicosia, Cyprus.
MARITAL STATUS: Married to Chrysoulla, Greek.
CHILDREN: Elizabeth, Eva, Christina.
SCHOOLS/COLLEGE: Famagusta Gymnasium, Pancyprian Gymnasium.
HOBBIES AND INTERESTS: Community work.
PERSONAL PROFILE: Company Director- manufacture Clothing. Vice President of the Cyprus Community of Melbourne and Victoria, Australia.

ANDREW DEMETRIOU
Chief executive Officer of the Australian Football League

DATE OF BIRTH: 14-Apr-1961
PLACE OF BIRTH: Australia Parents from Cyprus.
SCHOOLS/COLLEGE: La Trobe University.
QUALIFICATIONS: BA and a Diploma of Education.
PERSONAL PROFILE: Andrew Demetriou was an Australian Aussie rules Footballer playing for the North Melbourne Football club and later Hawthorn. At the end of the 2003 season Demetriou was elected Chief executive Officer of the Australian Football League. Andrew is also a qualified Teacher having taught Business, Law and Politics at both Trinity Grammar School and RMIT University.

ANTHONY DEMETRIOU
Lecturer at Macquarie University

DATE OF BIRTH: 07-Oct-1980.
PLACE OF BIRTH: Australia.
MARITAL STATUS: Single.
SCHOOLS/COLLEGE: Sydney Grammar. Macquarie University.
QUALIFICATIONS: BSc Computing and Information Systems.
PERSONAL PROFILE: Web Co-ordinator & Adjunct Lecturer at Macquarie University.

HARRY DEMETRIOU
Winner of the Best Fish and Chips Award in Queensland, Australia 2001

PLACE OF BIRTH: Parents from Cyprus.
MARITAL STATUS: Married to Helen.
CHILDREN: Maria, Business. Lisa, Business.
HONOURS/AWARDS: Winner of the Best Fish and Chips Award in Queensland Australia 2001.
PERSONAL PROFILE: Harry Demetriou is the co owner of one of the Gold Coasts largest Seafood Outlets at Harley Park.

Australia

Australia

JAMES DEMETRIOU
Lawyer/Chairman of Sports without Borders

DATE OF BIRTH: 07-Jun-1955
PLACE OF BIRTH: Melbourne, Australia, Mother - Kathikas, Father Kili.
MARITAL STATUS: Married to Toni Demetriou, Australian, Nurse.
CHILDREN: Thomas, Journalist. Lauren, Engineer. Tim, Student.
SCHOOLS/COLLEGE: North Coburg Primary School, Newlands High School. University of Melbourne, Anderson Business School, U.C.L.A.
QUALIFICATIONS: Bachelor of Laws, Masters of International Business.
MEMBERSHIPS: Law Institute of Victoria.
HOBBIES AND INTERESTS: Australian Rules Football, Soccer, Reading, the Classics-Ancient History.
PERSONAL PROFILE: Barrister, Solicitor and Company Director-Managing Director of The Acquis Group Pty Ltd. A Corporate advisory firm that provides strategic, transactional and compliance services to large SME's/midcap companies. James is well known for his involvement in the recent high profile sale of Taverner Hotel Group Pty Ltd to ALH Ltd. He is also Chairman of Sports without Borders.

JASON DEMETRIOU
Professional Rugby Player Club Captain of Wakefield Trinity Wild Cats

DATE OF BIRTH: 13-Jan-1976
PLACE OF BIRTH: Sydney Grandparents from Cyprus.
MARITAL STATUS: Married to Natalie.
CHILDREN: Isabella, Maddison.
SCHOOLS/COLLEGE: Kingsgrove High.
HONOURS/AWARDS: He was Wakefield's player of the season in 2006 and 2007 and was named in the Super League Dream Team in 2007 as well as being nominated for the Man of Steel award.
HOBBIES AND INTERESTS: Golf and Tennis.
PERSONAL PROFILE: Jason Demetriou is a Professional Rugby Player Club Captain of Wakefield Trinity Wild Cats who play in the Rugby Super League.

TONY DEMETRIOU
Former Editor of the English Section of the Parikiaki Newspaper

DATE OF BIRTH: 10-Jul-1978
PLACE OF BIRTH: London. Father from Nicosia; Mother, from Ayios Sergios.
MARITAL STATUS: Married to Josiane.
SCHOOLS/COLLEGE: Hadley Wood Primary School, Chancellors Secondary School, Oaklands College, London. Guildhall University, London.
QUALIFICATIONS: 9 GCSEs BTEC Higher Diploma in Media, BA Honours Media Communications. Qualified Journalist, Sports Reporter.
HOBBIES AND INTERESTS: Football (Arsenal Fan) music, travelling, going out, clubs, restaurants.
PERSONAL PROFILE: Tony Demetriou is the Former Editor of the English Section of the Parikiaki Newspaper. Now working in media in Australia.

ANDREW DEMOSTHENOUS
Active Member of Cypriot Community of Melbourne Victoria

DATE OF BIRTH: 13-Sep-1958
PLACE OF BIRTH: Cyprus.
MARITAL STATUS: Married to Emma, Australian.
CHILDREN: Helen, Chrissy.
SCHOOLS/COLLEGE: Technical School, Limassol.
HOBBIES AND INTERESTS: Soccer, fishing.
PERSONAL PROFILE: Works in the Transport Industry. Active member of Cypriot Community of Melbourne Victoria.

ZOE DEMOSTHENOUS
Dentist

DATE OF BIRTH: 15-Apr-1980.
PLACE OF BIRTH: Australia.
MARITAL STATUS: Single.
SCHOOLS/COLLEGE: Newtown High School of the Performing Arts. Sydney University.
QUALIFICATIONS: Bachelor of Medical Science, Bachelor of Dentistry.
HOBBIES AND INTERESTS: Beach, shopping, reading, pilates.
PERSONAL PROFILE: Dentist.

Australia

ELIAS ERACLEOUS
Structural Engineer 2006 ACSEV Award- Residential Design winner

DATE OF BIRTH: 05-Jun-1982
PLACE OF BIRTH: Limassol, Cyprus.
MARITAL STATUS: Single.
SCHOOLS/COLLEGE: University of Melbourne.
QUALIFICATIONS: Bachelor of Engineering, B. E (Civil) (Hons).
MEMBERSHIPS: Institution of Engineers Australia. (ACSEV) Association of Consulting Structural Engineers Victoria.
HONOURS/AWARDS: 2006 ACSEV Award - Residential Design.
HOBBIES AND INTERESTS: Backgammon, Judo, camping, chess, reading, problem solving, politics.
PERSONAL PROFILE: Involved with the Cypriot Youth Committee and Justice for Cyprus (PSEKA Vic). He has also represented the community at the World Council of Hellenes Abroad (SAE) in Thessaloniki on two occassions.

RITA GARRAD (KYPRIANOU)
Travel Agent and active member of Melbourne Community

DATE OF BIRTH: 19-Jan-1975
PLACE OF BIRTH: Melbourne, Australia, Father from Nicosia, Cyprus.
MARITAL STATUS: Married to Brad Garrad, Anglo-Indian-Australian.
SCHOOLS/COLLEGE: Lyndale Secondary College, Tafe.
QUALIFICATIONS: Associate Diploma.
HOBBIES AND INTERESTS: Travelling.
PERSONAL PROFILE: Owns a Travel Agency, specialist in tours to Cyprus, active member of Melbourne Community.

Andrew Demetriou is Chief Executive Officer of the Australian football league. his parents are from Cyprus.

GEORGE GEORGIADES
Former Vice President of the Cypriot community of Melbourne Victoria

DATE OF BIRTH: 21-Dec-1945
PLACE OF BIRTH: Nicosia, Cyprus.
MARITAL STATUS: Married to Della.
CHILDREN: Christina, Teacher. Michael, Businessman. Nicholas, Businessman.
SCHOOLS/COLLEGE: Kings Way College, London.
HOBBIES AND INTERESTS: Backgammon, football, tennis.
PERSONAL PROFILE: Ex Committee Member and ex vice president of Cyprus Community of Melbourne & Victoria. Company Director.

MICHAEL GEORGIADES
Business/Philanthropist

DATE OF BIRTH: 28-Feb-1962
PLACE OF BIRTH: South Africa both parents from Ktima.
MARITAL STATUS: Married to Philio, Cyprus, Real Estate Marketing.
CHILDREN: Alexandros, Student. Christopher, School.
SCHOOLS/COLLEGE: Spring boys High. Witwatersrand University.
QUALIFICATIONS: Accounting Degree.
MEMBERSHIPS: CPA AUSTRALIA.
HOBBIES AND INTERESTS: Sports, Golf, Cycling, Soccer, Tennis and Squash.
PERSONAL PROFILE: Michaels business helps support the Cyprus Club and the Greek Community of Australia, they are the sole agents for Pittas Halloumi and importers of many Greek products.

ANASTASIA GEORGIOU
Medical

PLACE OF BIRTH: Egypt grand Parents from Cyprus.
QUALIFICATIONS: BDS MDSC FRACDS.
PERSONAL PROFILE: Anastasia Georgiou is based at the university of Sydney, Institute of Clinical and Pathological Medical Research, Westmead Centre for Oral Health at Westmead Hospital.

Australia

ANDREW GEORGIOU
Senior Research Fellow at the University of New South Wales

DATE OF BIRTH: 28-Feb-1956
PLACE OF BIRTH: Australia Father from Kalavasos Mother from Gaidoura.
MARITAL STATUS: Married to Kathleen, Australian, Legal Secretary.
SCHOOLS/COLLEGE: La Trobe University, University of Sydney and the University of Southampton.
QUALIFICATIONS: BA MSc.
MEMBERSHIPS: Fellow of the Australian College of Health InformaticsAssociate fellow of the Australian College of Health Service Executives.
HOBBIES AND INTERESTS: History, ornithology, reading, art and literature.
PERSONAL PROFILE: Andrew Georgiou is a senior research fellow at the centre for Health Informatics at the University of New South Wales. He has worked as a senior researcher in a number of areas including public health, primary care, health informatics and outcomes measurement.

ANDREW CONSTANTINE GEORGIOU
magazine section Editor with 'Time Out', Sydney magazine

DATE OF BIRTH: 10-Feb-1972
PLACE OF BIRTH: Sydney Australia parents from Paphos.
SCHOOLS/COLLEGE: Marcellin College and University of NSW, Australia.
QUALIFICATIONS: Bachelor of Fine Arts and Masters in the Fine Arts.
HOBBIES AND INTERESTS: Interviews with people of artistic backgrounds, satirical cartooning, animal liberation, independent cinema.
PERSONAL PROFILE: magazine section Editor with 'Time Out', Sydney magazine. His work as a journalist and editor has meant he has interviewed such celebrities as Cyndi Lauper, Olivia Newton John, Duran Duran, Margaret Cho, Kathy Griffin and many other people from creative backgrounds.

BASIL GEORGIOU
Barrister/Solicitor/also on the Board at St Andrews Greek Orthodox Grammar School in Perth, Western Australia

DATE OF BIRTH: 06-Dec-1956
PLACE OF BIRTH: South Africa Parents from Cyprus.
MARITAL STATUS: Married to Athena, South African Parents from Cyprus, Company Director.
CHILDREN: Marina, Student. Phivo, Architect. Philip, Student.
SCHOOLS/COLLEGE: University of Witwatersrand, Johanesburg.
QUALIFICATIONS: B. Comm, LLb.
PERSONAL PROFILE: Basil Georgiou is a Barrister/Solicitor and Partner in Jackson Mcdonald Lawyers. He is also on the Board at St Andrews Greek Orthodox Grammar School in Perth, western Australia.

GEORGE GEORGIOU
Australian Commonwealth Award for Services to Sport

DATE OF BIRTH: 30-Nov-1959
PLACE OF BIRTH: Melbourne, Australia, Parents from Cyprus.
MARITAL STATUS: Married to Vita, Australian, Housewife.
CHILDREN: Alexander, Stefan.
SCHOOLS/COLLEGE: Moreland High School.
HONOURS/AWARDS: Australian Commonwealth Award for Services to the Community, Australian Commonwealth Award for Services to Sport, Victorian State Government Award for Promoting Multi-Cultural Affairs.
HOBBIES AND INTERESTS: Cricket, reading, music.
PERSONAL PROFILE: President of East Coburg Cricket Club.

It is free to nominate someone, or yourself, who deserves to be in the book, just send in the name, contact address, telephone number and email to:
Greek Cypriots Worldwide
111 St Thomas's Road London N4 2QJ
Telephone 0044 207503 3498
cypriotwhoswho@aol.com
www.greekcypriotsworldwide.com

KAITH GEORGIOU
Active Member of Cultural League of the Cyprus Community of Victoria

DATE OF BIRTH: 18-Nov-1949
PLACE OF BIRTH: Limassol, Cyprus.
MARITAL STATUS: Single.
SCHOOLS/COLLEGE: 2nd Gymnasium, Limassol, Santa Maria Terra Santa, Limassol.
HOBBIES AND INTERESTS: Community work.
PERSONAL PROFILE: Member of Cultural League of the Cyprus Community of Victoria. Teaching children the History of Cyprus and Greek language and Drama. Choreographer of the plays of Greek School.

SOZOS GEORGIOU
Assistant Treasurer of Cyprus Community of New South Wales

DATE OF BIRTH: 01-Sep-1935.
PLACE OF BIRTH: Drynia.
MARITAL STATUS: Married to Christalla, Athienou.
CHILDREN: Antonia, Assistant Manager Wetspak. Christakis, Computer Company.
SCHOOLS/COLLEGE: Drynia Elementary School.
HOBBIES AND INTERESTS: Shooting, soccer.
PERSONAL PROFILE: Assistant Treasurer of Cyprus Community of New South Wales. Previously owner of a supermarket.

STAVROS GEORGIOU
Economist and Research Scientist

DATE OF BIRTH: 08-Sep-1966
PLACE OF BIRTH: Birkenhead, UK, Father from Larnaca, Cyprus.
MARITAL STATUS: Single.
SCHOOLS/COLLEGE: Henry Meoles Comprehensive, Wirral, UK. University College, London, University of East Anglia.
QUALIFICATIONS: BSc MSc, PhD.
MEMBERSHIPS: European Association of Environment and Resource Economics.
PERSONAL PROFILE: Based in Sydney Australia Stavros is an Economist and research Scientist in the field of environmental decision-making and resource management. Has been a consultant and/or advisor to a number of UK Government Departments, the OECD, the European Commission, the World Bank and UNEP. Has published a number of co-authored books and many scientific papers in international journals, book chapters and other reports.

LINDA ANDREA GREGORIOU
Award Winning Property Developer

DATE OF BIRTH: 19-Nov-1964
PLACE OF BIRTH: Melbourne Australia, father from Limassol, Cyprus.
SCHOOLS/COLLEGE: Monash University, Melbourne, Australia.
QUALIFICATIONS: Bachelor of Arts, Graduate Diploma Urban Planning, Masters Urban Planning.
HONOURS/AWARDS: Chosen for design magazine 'Indesign' for their International Design Luminary for 2004; Sinclair Knight Merz, Best Development 2004; ARUP Award for Most Innovative Development 2004; Lend Lease Development Award for best overall development, 2002;.
HOBBIES AND INTERESTS: Cities, Architecture, Urban Design, Contemporary Art, Australian Idigenous Art, Gardens.
PERSONAL PROFILE: Managing Director of FTB Group, Property Development Company. Takes a multidisciplinary approach as a property developer, academic, commentator, interior designer, urban planner and publisher.

SOTERIS HADJIKYRIAKOU
Head of Branch Network, Laiki Bank, Australia. Radiomarathon Australia-Trust Member

DATE OF BIRTH: 27-Oct-1960
PLACE OF BIRTH: Nicosia, Cyprus.
MARITAL STATUS: Married to Anastasia, Greek Cypriot.
CHILDREN: Maria, Teacher. Helen, University (teacher).
SCHOOLS/COLLEGE: Nicosia Economic Lyceum.
QUALIFICATIONS: London Chamber of Commerce-Accounting, Certificate in Business Studies.
HOBBIES AND INTERESTS: Sports, music.
PERSONAL PROFILE: Head of Branch Network, Laiki Bank, Australia. Radiomarathon Australia-Trust Member.

Australia

ELEFTHERIA HADJISTEPHANOU (LAOUTA)
Teacher/Active member of the Melbourne Cypriot community

DATE OF BIRTH: 08-May-1952
PLACE OF BIRTH: Karavas, Cyprus.
CHILDREN: Natasha, Beauty Therapist (Australia). Andrew, (Chef) NMIT, Australia.
SCHOOLS/COLLEGE: LaTrobe University, Australia, Athens University.
QUALIFICATIONS: Maths/ Science, Greek Teacher.
HOBBIES AND INTERESTS: Travelling.
PERSONAL PROFILE: High School Teacher, Marian College, Catholic School. Greek Orthodox Community of Melbourne and Victoria.

DR JOHN ANDREW HAGILIASSIS
Dentist/Vice president of Cypriot Youth Club of Melb. 1993-1995

DATE OF BIRTH: 08-Jul-1975
PLACE OF BIRTH: Melbourne, Australia, Father from Rizokarpasso, Mother from Paphos.
MARITAL STATUS: Married to Joanne Flessas, Australian (parents from Kalamata, Greece), Speech Pathologist.
CHILDREN: Andy.
SCHOOLS/COLLEGE: Strathmore High School. University of Queensland, University of Melbourne.
QUALIFICATIONS: BDSC.
MEMBERSHIPS: ADA.
HONOURS/AWARDS: Golden Key Honour Society.
HOBBIES AND INTERESTS: AFL Football and poker.
PERSONAL PROFILE: Dentist, Private Practice. Clinical demonstrator for dentist students at Uni of Melbourne. Volunteer at Cypriot community of Melb. Vice president of Cypriot Youth Club of Melb. 1993-1995.

GEORGE HARRISON
Mayor of Wollongong on the coast of New South Wales in Australia

PLACE OF BIRTH: Cyprus
PERSONAL PROFILE: George Harrison was the Mayor of Wollongong on the coast of New South Wales in Australia.

MARIA HERODOTOU
University lecturer and Coordinator of the Greek studies Programs at La Trobe and Melbourne Universities

DATE OF BIRTH: 12-Feb-1951
PLACE OF BIRTH: Cyprus.
MARITAL STATUS: Married to Stephanos, Australian Greek Cypriot, Doctor of Medicine.
CHILDREN: Angie, Psychologist. Nicholas, Student.
SCHOOLS/COLLEGE: Pancyprian Gymnasium, Nicosia. University of Athens, La Trobe and Melbourne University.
QUALIFICATIONS: BA, Litt B, Dip Ed, MA, PhD.
MEMBERSHIPS: Greek Teachers Assoociation of Victoria and also Modern Greek Studies Association of Australia and New Zealand(she is vice president elected).
HOBBIES AND INTERESTS: Reading, music and travelling.
PERSONAL PROFILE: Maria Herodotou is a University lecturer and Coordinator of the Greek studies Programs at La Trobe and Melbourne Universities, she is a specialist vetter for the Greek exam for the Victorian Certificate of Education.

Entrants in Greek Cypriots Worldwide have been nominated for their achievements and contributions.
It is free to nominate someone, or yourself, who deserves to be in the book, just send in the name, contact address, telephone number and email to:
Greek Cypriots Worldwide
111 St Thomas's Road London N4 2QJ
Telephone 0044 207503 3498
cypriotwhoswho@aol.com
www.greekcypriotsworldwide.com

Australia

DR STEPHANOS HERODOTOU
Senior Consultant in Emergency Medicine, Emergency Department of the Northern Hospital

DATE OF BIRTH: 09-Sep-1948
PLACE OF BIRTH: Yeroskipou.
MARITAL STATUS: Married to Maria Herodotou- from Nicosia, Cyprus- University Lecturer).
CHILDREN: Angie, Clinical Psychologist. Nicholas, Student.
SCHOOLS/COLLEGE: School of Medicine, University of Athens.
QUALIFICATIONS: Bachelor of Medicine. Dr of Medicine.
MEMBERSHIPS: Member of the Medical Board of Victoria, member of the Association of General Practitioners.
HOBBIES AND INTERESTS: Tennis, Golf, reading, music, politics.
PERSONAL PROFILE: Senior Consultant in Emergency Medicine, Emergency Department of the Northern Hospital. Honorary Associate, School of Medicine of the University of Melbourne. Clinical Teacher in charge of the training/ clinical program for the medical students. Honorary member of the Greek Cyprian Community of Melbourne. He served as an elected vice-president for many years and as a committee member.

DR GEORGE IOANNOU
Radiologist

DATE OF BIRTH: 06-Mar-1958.
PLACE OF BIRTH: Cyprus.
SCHOOLS/COLLEGE: University of Queensland.
QUALIFICATIONS: MBBS.
HOBBIES AND INTERESTS: Golf and Soccer.
PERSONAL PROFILE: Dr George Ioannou is a Radiologist based at South Coast Radiology previous to that he was staff Radiologist at Queensland X-ray.

NORIS IOANNOU
Executive Director of Nexus Multicultural Arts Center

DATE OF BIRTH: 22-Feb-1947
PLACE OF BIRTH: Larnaca, Cyprus.
MARITAL STATUS: Single.
SCHOOLS/COLLEGE: Adelaide High School. University of Adelaide & Flinders University of SA.
QUALIFICATIONS: Bachelor of Science (Hons), Diploma of Education, Doctor of Philosophy.
MEMBERSHIPS: Independant Scholars Association of Australia, Australian Society of Authors.
HONOURS/AWARDS: Peer Advisor, Australia Council (1997), Honorary Fellow, History, Flinders University, Winner of Australian Heritage Award (1987) and various others.
HOBBIES AND INTERESTS: Keen painter has had some landscape paintings exhibited. Involved in conservational work and has planted over 40, 000 Australian forest trees.
PERSONAL PROFILE: Dr Noris Ioannou decided to switch careers after 11 years of teaching science and biology in Australia and London, he is now a cultural historian and writer. After publishing his first major book in 1986, sixteen additional books written or edited by him to date. Norris is the Executive Director of Nexus Multicultural Arts Center.

SIMON IOANNOU
Managing Director of Mcintyre Steel Industries

PLACE OF BIRTH: Australia. Parents from Paphos.
PERSONAL PROFILE: Simon Ioannou is the Managing Director of Mcintyre Steel Industries a Melbourne based company that supplies structural steel products and services to the building industry.

SIMON IOANNOU
Co Founder of Australia's first multi cultural network SBS-TV

PERSONAL PROFILE: Simon Ioannou is the Co Founder of Australia's first multi cultural network SBS-TV. Was appointed on the Commonwealth Film Censorship Board 1980.

There is an estimated 80,000 Cypriots living in Australia.

STEVEN JACOVOU
Specialist for a pharmaceutical company that specialises in Human Blood Products

DATE OF BIRTH: 07-Oct-1977
PLACE OF BIRTH: Melbourne, Australia, Mother from Larnaca, Father from Nicosia.
MARITAL STATUS: Married to Andrea Karas, Personal Assistant.
SCHOOLS/COLLEGE: Penola Catholic College, RMIT-Royal Melbourne Institute of Technology, Swinburn University of Technology.
QUALIFICATIONS: Bachelor of Applied Science (Human Biology), Diploma in business (Frontline Management).
HOBBIES AND INTERESTS: Bonsai, Automotive enthusiast.
PERSONAL PROFILE: Technical Improvement Specialist for a pharmaceutical company that specialises in Human Blood Products.

ELENI (ELLI) (MORNEHIS) KAMBOS
Vice President of the Cyprus Community of New South Wales

DATE OF BIRTH: 31-Jan-1932
PLACE OF BIRTH: Athienou, Cyprus.
MARITAL STATUS: Married to Yiannis, Gos.
CHILDREN: Katerina, Housewife. Vasilia, Business. Andreas, Optalmetrist.
SCHOOLS/COLLEGE: Athienou Elementary.
HOBBIES AND INTERESTS: Community Work.
PERSONAL PROFILE: Eleni is Vice President of the Cyprus Community of New South Wales. Co-ordinator for a Home for the Aged. She is also a Radio Broadcaster twice a week for 1683AM, Radio Club.

ANNA KANNAVA
Her film The Butler was a Finalist New York Short Film expo

PLACE OF BIRTH: Cyprus
SCHOOLS/COLLEGE: Deakin University.
QUALIFICATIONS: Bachelor of Education in Drama and Media.
HONOURS/AWARDS: Her film The Butler Finalist New York Short Film expo.
PERSONAL PROFILE: Anna Kannava has worked as an actor and directed several plays and short films.

NICKI KARAKATSANIS
Journalist and Radio Presenter on Australian Government Radio SBS. (Special Broadcasting Services)

DATE OF BIRTH: 16-Dec-1945
PLACE OF BIRTH: Paphos, Cyprus.
MARITAL STATUS: Married to Nick Karakatsanis, Mydelini.
CHILDREN: Christos, Safety manager. Michael, Solicitor (specialises in industrial relations).
SCHOOLS/COLLEGE: Pancyprian Gymnasium. University of New South Wales.
QUALIFICATIONS: BA in Languages.
HONOURS/AWARDS: Honoured by the Greek Cypriot Womens Organisation of Australia for services to the community.
HOBBIES AND INTERESTS: Cooking, music.
PERSONAL PROFILE: Senior Manager, Business Development and Marketing Co-ordination Bank of Cyprus. Journalist and Radio Presenter on Australian Government Radio SBS. (Special Broadcasting Services).

In 1914 Australia's second Greek language newspaper Oceanis was published in Adelaide by George Nicolaides. He was a Greek Cypriot from the village of Livadia near Larnaca. He published the book international directory of 1927,which aimed to be a guide for Greeks in Australia. The book was written in English, Greek and French.

NELLIE GEORGIOU KARISTIANIS
Associate Professor in Psychology at Monash University

DATE OF BIRTH: 15-Nov-1970
PLACE OF BIRTH: Australia. Father from Innia and mother from Lefkoniko, Cyprus.
MARITAL STATUS: Married to Steve, Australia Parents from Greece, Computers.
SCHOOLS/COLLEGE: Secondary John Paul College, Melbourne. Tertiary Monash University, Melbourne, Bachelor of Science, Honours (1989-1992). Monash University, PhD (1993-1997), Melbourne. John Paul College, Monash University.
QUALIFICATIONS: BSc(Hons) PhD.
MEMBERSHIPS: Victorian Psychologists Registration Board.
HONOURS/AWARDS: Australian of the Year, Science and Technology Category (1995).
HOBBIES AND INTERESTS: Walking, bike riding, painting, playing piano, singing.
PERSONAL PROFILE: Associate Professor in the School of Psychology, Psychiatry and Psychological Medicine, Monash University. Heads the Experimental Neuropsychology Research Unit.

JOAN KAVALLARIS
Medical Practitioner

PLACE OF BIRTH: Australia Parents from Cyprus.
PERSONAL PROFILE: Medical Practitioner in Burwood, was an educator Sydney Institute of General Practice Education and Training.

MARIA KAVALLARIS
Associate Professor President of the Australian Society for Medical Research

PLACE OF BIRTH: Australia Parents from Cyprus
QUALIFICATIONS: In 1996 she received one of only 12 worldwide cancer research fellowships to the Albert Einstein College of Medicine, New York.
PERSONAL PROFILE: Maria Kavallaris is an Associate Professor holds co joint appointments with the faculty of Medicine and Faculty of Sciences, University of New South Wales. She leads a group of Researchers focused on identifying the mechanisms of action and resistance to anti cancer drugs.

Maria is also the President of the Australian Society for Medical Research.

STAVROS KAZANTZIDIS
Films scooped the 1992 Channel Four Young Film maker of the Year Award at the Edinburgh Film festival

PLACE OF BIRTH: Famagusta
SCHOOLS/COLLEGE: University of Sydney and Australian Film Television & Radio School.
HONOURS/AWARDS: His film Road to Alice was the winner of the 1992 Australian Film Institute Best Short Film Award. It also scooped the 1992 Channel Four Young Film maker of the Year Award at the Edinburgh Film festival.
PERSONAL PROFILE: Stavros Kazantzidis is an Australian based Film Writer, Director, Producer and Actor.

EMILY KILIAS (MELETIOU)
Culinary consultant/Restaurant Owner

DATE OF BIRTH: 09-Nov-1961
PLACE OF BIRTH: Melbourne, Australia, Parents from Larnaca and Famagusta.
MARITAL STATUS: Married.
CHILDREN: Twin Boys, Melbourne University.
SCHOOLS/COLLEGE: Methodist Ladies College. MEWB University, Deacon University.
QUALIFICATIONS: Science, Nutrition and Dietetics.
PERSONAL PROFILE: Was a Fashion Buyer for Coles/Myer Group. She now is a Culinary consultant/Restaurant Owner.

Australia

DIMITRIOS KOMODROMOS
Active Member of the Cypriot Community Melbourne Victoria

DATE OF BIRTH: 18-Aug-1937
PLACE OF BIRTH: Paralamni.
MARITAL STATUS: Married to Paduru, Greek Cypriot.
CHILDREN: Maria, Teacher. Costas, Business. Theodoros, Chemical Engineer.
SCHOOLS/COLLEGE: Kenton Antoros Spoudon, Famagusta, Cyprus.
HOBBIES AND INTERESTS: Community work.
PERSONAL PROFILE: Member of the Cypriot Community Melbourne Victoria. He helped economically to establish in 1963 the Scouts 10th Group in Melbourne.

JOHN KOULLAS
Software Developer who is a Microsoft Certified Professional

DATE OF BIRTH: 22-Dec-1975
PLACE OF BIRTH: Geelong, Australia, Father born in Rizokarpaso, Mother born in Louvara.
MARITAL STATUS: Married to Katie Koullas, Australian, parents from Kalamta, Greece, Marketing Manager.
CHILDREN: Kikki.
SCHOOLS/COLLEGE: Oberon High School (Geelong). Deakin University (Geelong).
QUALIFICATIONS: Bachelor of Computing.
HOBBIES AND INTERESTS: Texas Hold'em Poker, football, watching TV.
PERSONAL PROFILE: Software Developer who is a Microsoft Certified Professional.

ALEX KOUNTOURI
Australian National Cricket Team Physiotherapist

PLACE OF BIRTH: Cyprus
PERSONAL PROFILE: Alex Kountouri was the former Sri Lanka National Cricket Side Physiotherapist now the Australian National Cricket Team Physiotherapist.

MYRA KOUREAS
Education

PLACE OF BIRTH: Australia Father from Athienou Mother from Arakaba.
PERSONAL PROFILE: Myra Koureas is the Marketing and Scholarship Officer, Faculty of Engineering, The University of Sydney.

DR KYPROS KOUTSOULLIS
General Practitioner

PLACE OF BIRTH: Athienou.
SCHOOLS/COLLEGE: University of Sydney.
QUALIFICATIONS: MBBS.
MEMBERSHIPS: Cypriot Australian Professional Association.
PERSONAL PROFILE: Dr Kypros Koutsoullis is a General Practitioner in Riverwood New South Wales. He is also the Secretary of the St Georges Division of General Practice.

GEORGE KOUVAROS
University Lecturer University of New South Wales

PLACE OF BIRTH: Australia parents from Cyprus
SCHOOLS/COLLEGE: University of Sydney.
QUALIFICATIONS: PhD.
PERSONAL PROFILE: Dr George Kouvaros is an Acting Associate Dean(Research) and Director of Post Graduate Research at the School of English Media, Film and The Performing Arts at the University of New South Wales.

THEOPHANIS KRAMBIAS
Member of the committe of Cyprus Community of Melbourne Victoria

DATE OF BIRTH: 12-Mar-1965
PLACE OF BIRTH: Morphou.
MARITAL STATUS: Married.
CHILDREN: Chris, Elly.
QUALIFICATIONS: BA, BSc MBA.
PERSONAL PROFILE: Theophanis Krambias Member of the committee of Cyprus Community of Melbourne Victoria. Board member of Ozchilds.

KYPROS KYPRI PHD

Senior Lecturer at the University of Newcastle in Australia

DATE OF BIRTH: 24-Feb-1971
PLACE OF BIRTH: Sydney, Australia, Father born in Geri.
MARITAL STATUS: Married to Johanna Ilona Dean, New Zealand, Clinical Psychologist.
CHILDREN: Stassi, Luke, Bonita.
SCHOOLS/COLLEGE: University of NSW, Sydney, University of Otago, New Zealand, University of California San Diego, USA.
QUALIFICATIONS: BA (Hons I) in Psychology, PhD in Public Health.
MEMBERSHIPS: Research Society on Alcoholism, Australian Professional Society on Alcohol and Drugs.
HONOURS/AWARDS: Gladys Brawn Postdoctoral Fellowship, University of Newcastle, Australia, Giordis Postdoctoral Research Award.
HOBBIES AND INTERESTS: Soccer, cycling.
PERSONAL PROFILE: He is a behavioural scientist interested in the social and environmental determinants of hazordous alcohol consumption, and in the prevention of alcohol related harm. He is also senior lecturer in population health at the University of Newcastle (Australia), and he is involved in a number of international collaborative research projects.

MELANI KYPRI

lawyer she runs a sponsorship programme for children in 7 different orphanages around the world

DATE OF BIRTH: 08-Nov-1960
PLACE OF BIRTH: Australia, Father from Geri.
MARITAL STATUS: Married to David Bradley, Australian, Lawyer.
CHILDREN: Stacy Kypri, Owns a clothes shop called Zivania. Sebastian, School. Valentina.
SCHOOLS/COLLEGE: North Sydney Girls' High.
QUALIFICATIONS: Higher School Certificate.
MEMBERSHIPS: Australian Caring for Children Inc. Australian Families for Children.

HOBBIES AND INTERESTS: Music, dance.
PERSONAL PROFILE: Melani is a lawyer she runs a sponsorship programme for children in 7 different orphanages around the world. It is a voluntary role which means all funds raised go to the children that need them. Her husband and herself have also adopted 2 children from Colombia.

REBECCA KYPRI

Singer

DATE OF BIRTH: 10-Oct-1972
PLACE OF BIRTH: Australia, Father from Geri.
MARITAL STATUS: Married to Nelson Inacio, Portuguese, Electrician.
SCHOOLS/COLLEGE: Killara High School. UNSW & Ensemble Acting Studios.
QUALIFICATIONS: Bachelor of Music, Diploma of Acting.
HOBBIES AND INTERESTS: Theatre, music, sports.
PERSONAL PROFILE: Has been a stage performer for 15 years. Has also worked in theatres all over Sydney and currently has her own Music Store and shop in the Newtown area where she teaches and sells music related products.

Dr KYPROS M. KYPRIANOU

Young Australian of the year (Victoria semi Finalist 2000)

DATE OF BIRTH: 1978
PLACE OF BIRTH: Melbourne, Australia, Mother from Paphos, Father from Nicosia
MARITAL STATUS: Single.
SCHOOLS/COLLEGE: Lyndale Secondary College. Monash University.
QUALIFICATIONS: Bachelor of Medicine and Bachelor of Surgery (Hons) Victorian Certificate of Education.
HONOURS/AWARDS: Young Australian of the year (Victoria semi Finalist 2000).
HOBBIES AND INTERESTS: Photography, music.
PERSONAL PROFILE: Currently working as Rural Paediatric Registrar in Mckay, Queensland, Australia, working at the Royal childrens Hospital, Melbourne.

"Their homeland is so far away the weather in Australia is similar to their homeland but so far away it takes them a whole day to travel back to Cyprus but still most of them do to see their family and friends."

Australia

ELIZABETH KYRIACOU
Science

PLACE OF BIRTH: Parents from Cyprus
SCHOOLS/COLLEGE: University of Sydney.
QUALIFICATIONS: B. E.
PERSONAL PROFILE: Elizabeth Kyriakou after working as an engineer both locally and internationally, she returned to academia to undertake her Phd in biomedical engineering. Her focus is the fluid structure interaction of the spinal cord under both normal conditions and in the presence of post-traumatic syringomyelia.

LOUIS KYRIACOU
Federal Secretary for the Federated Furnishing Trades Society(FFTS)

DATE OF BIRTH: 02-Jan-1933
PLACE OF BIRTH: Komi Kebir.
MARITAL STATUS: Married to Eleni, Pano Lefkara.
CHILDREN: Julie, George.
PERSONAL PROFILE: Louis Kyriacou was a union Activist and became a shop steward at his job at Gainsborough for the Federated Furnishing Trades Society(FFTS) initiating and leading a number of successful campaigns including equal pay for women and redundancy packages for the staff who worked at his factory. In the 70's Louis was invited to become an Industrial Organiser with the Victorian Branch of the FFTS eventually Louis was elected by the membership to become the Federal Secretary of the FFTS he is now retired.

MICHAEL KYRIACOU
Awarded place in Australia's 30 most inspiring young engineers

PLACE OF BIRTH: Australia parents from Cyprus
SCHOOLS/COLLEGE: University of New South Wales.
QUALIFICATIONS: BEng MBT MIE.
HONOURS/AWARDS: Awarded place in Australia's 30 most inspiring young engineers.
PERSONAL PROFILE: Michael Kyriacou is the Founder of the investment and consultancy firm Strattica Group.

TONY KYRIACOU
Executive officer Cypriot Community Melbourne Victoria

DATE OF BIRTH: 21-Mar-1966
PLACE OF BIRTH: Kambos.
MARITAL STATUS: Married to Mary, Greek/Australian.
CHILDREN: Philippe, School. Marcus, School.
SCHOOLS/COLLEGE: Preston College.
QUALIFICATIONS: Management Diploma.
HOBBIES AND INTERESTS: Soccer, Community work, outdoor activities.
PERSONAL PROFILE: Executive officer Cypriot Community Melbourne Victoria. Relationship Manager of Brotherhood of Cyprus, Australia.

CHRIS LAMBROU
Architecture

DATE OF BIRTH: 01-Feb-1960
PLACE OF BIRTH: Tavros.
MARITAL STATUS: Married to Kim, British.
CHILDREN: Alexander, Student. Anna Sophia, Student.
SCHOOLS/COLLEGE: Islington Green. Tottenham Technical College and Chelsea School of Art.
QUALIFICATIONS: BTEC, Chartered Architectural Technologist.
MEMBERSHIPS: Member of the Chartered Institute of Architectural Technologist.
HOBBIES AND INTERESTS: DIY, Greek Music and Travel.
PERSONAL PROFILE: Chris Lambrou was raised in London and is now living in Sydney Australia provides Architectural Design Services- residential renovations and refurbishments.

GEORGE LAZARIS
Former President of Cyprus Community of new South Wales

DATE OF BIRTH: 20-Nov-1930
PLACE OF BIRTH: Oroklini.
MARITAL STATUS: Married to Athanasia, Australian (Parents from Larnaca).
CHILDREN: Fiona, Travel Agent. Helen, School Teacher. William, Real Estate.
SCHOOLS/COLLEGE: Lykeion, Larnaca. American Academy, Larnaca.
HOBBIES AND INTERESTS: Community Work.
PERSONAL PROFILE: President of the Cyprus Hellene Club for 12 years. Two terms as president of Cyprus Community of New South Wales.

ANDREAS LAZAROU
Management-Hotels

DATE OF BIRTH: 26-May-1958
PLACE OF BIRTH: Morphou.
MARITAL STATUS: Married to Mary, Australian.
CHILDREN: Chloe, Adam, Matthew.
SCHOOLS/COLLEGE: RMIT.
QUALIFICATIONS: Bachelor of Engineering, MBA.
HOBBIES AND INTERESTS: Tennis, dancing.
PERSONAL PROFILE: Manages a chain of Reception Centres and Hotels in Australia.

PETER LAZAROU
Former President of the Cyprus Community, New South Wales

DATE OF BIRTH: 29-Aug-1931
PLACE OF BIRTH: Vatili.
MARITAL STATUS: Married to Terry, Vatili.
CHILDREN: Helen, PA. Mary, Housewife.
SCHOOLS/COLLEGE: Vatili Elementary School.
HOBBIES AND INTERESTS: Gardening.
PERSONAL PROFILE: Former President of the Cyprus Community, New South Wales. Involved with the Community for 13 years. Occupation was a Fish Wholesaler.

SAVVAS LIMNATITIS
Journalist for Kosmos and Epsilon in Sydney

DATE OF BIRTH: 23-Sep-1967
PLACE OF BIRTH: Limassol, Cyprus.
MARITAL STATUS: Married to Sophia, Greek Cypriot.
CHILDREN: Eleni, School. Nicki, School.
SCHOOLS/COLLEGE: 3rd Lyceum Limassol, Cyprus. Aristoteleion University, Tessaloniki.
HOBBIES AND INTERESTS: Art, literature, sport.
PERSONAL PROFILE: Journalist for Kosmos and Epsilon in Sydney.

ATHENA LIMNIOS
Senior Hospital Scientist

DATE OF BIRTH: 25-Nov-1952
PLACE OF BIRTH: Australia, Parents from Limassol, Cyprus.
MARITAL STATUS: Married to John Limnios, Greek (Australian Born), Professional Mechanical Engineer.
CHILDREN: George, Peter, Anna Eleni, All three at High School.
SCHOOLS/COLLEGE: Petersham Girls' High. University of Technology, Sydney.
QUALIFICATIONS: BSc MSc.
MEMBERSHIPS: Member of the Australian Society for Microbiology MASM, Member of the National Neissara Network, Australia.
HOBBIES AND INTERESTS: Greek Orthodox Fellowship, St Spyridon Parish, Kingsford, Sydney. Cooking and entertaining. Family outings and swimming.
PERSONAL PROFILE: Athena is a senior hospital scientist. Fund raises to assist nuns to build Monastory of Panagia Gorgoipikoos in Geelong, Victoria, and most recently assisted with fundraising to provide adequate schooling for orphans by Archibishop Makarios Monastery in Nairobi, Kenya.

Australia

LOIZOS ANDREAS LOIZOU
Councillor Burdekin, Queensland

DATE OF BIRTH: 17-Jun-1937
PLACE OF BIRTH: Queensland, Australia Parents from Cyprus.
MARITAL STATUS: Married to Kalotina Ginis, Island of Kalymnos, Housewife.
CHILDREN: Isodia, Housewife. Xanthipi, Housewife. Andreas, Marine and Engine Technician. Theofilos, Sugar Cane Grower.
SCHOOLS/COLLEGE: he only attended Primary School, due to a labour shortage during World War 2, his father needed his help on the Sugar Cane Farm.
HOBBIES AND INTERESTS: Fishing and being a Councillor.
PERSONAL PROFILE: Sugar Cane Farmer. Councillor, South Burdekin Water Board Director, Director on the Board of Bendigo Community Bank, Member of the Burdekin Shire Rivers Improvement Trust, Council member of Crime Stoppers Burdekin Branch, Council member of the Burdekin Counter Disaster Committee, also a member of St Stephanos Greek Orthodox, Home Hill for 45 years and Chairman of the Church Committee for 12 years, Also serves on various other committees.

LOUIS LOIZOU
Medical Practitioner

DATE OF BIRTH: 24-Aug-1955
PLACE OF BIRTH: Melbourne, Australia Parents from Cyprus.
MARITAL STATUS: Married to Andrea, Cypriot, Pharmacist.
CHILDREN: Anthony, Student at University. Alexia, High School.
SCHOOLS/COLLEGE: Maribyrnong High School. Monash University.
QUALIFICATIONS: MBBS (Hons) Fellow of the Australian College of Phlebiology.
HOBBIES AND INTERESTS: Golf.
PERSONAL PROFILE: Began General Practice in 1981 and looked after the Greek community in MT region for 20 years. He then up-skilled and became a Phlebiologist which manages any disorder pertaining to veins.

ANTHEA LOUCAS
Editor of the Gourmet Traveller Magazine

PLACE OF BIRTH: Australia Parents from Cyprus
PERSONAL PROFILE: Anthea Loucas is the Editor of the Gourmet Traveller a mainstream monthly magazine on food and travel.

PETER LOUKAS
In-house Tax Lawyer at Pitcher Partners active member of the youth cypriot Community of Melbourne

DATE OF BIRTH: 01-Oct-1977
PLACE OF BIRTH: Melbourne, Australia. Parents from Cyprus.
MARITAL STATUS: Single.
SCHOOLS/COLLEGE: Melbourne High. Monash University, Melbourne University.
HOBBIES AND INTERESTS: Guitar, Languages.
PERSONAL PROFILE: In-house Tax Lawyer at Pitcher Partners.

The first Cypriots arrived in Australia in the 1850's as gold prospectors

BETH MAGANN
Residential and Conference Services Manager, University College Melbourne

DATE OF BIRTH: 28-May-1965
PLACE OF BIRTH: Melbourne Australia, Mother from Athienou, Cyprus, Father from Yialoussa, Cyprus.
MARITAL STATUS: Married, Australian, Firefighter.
CHILDREN: Jarrod, Montgomery Secondary College. Jake, Montgomery Secondary College.
SCHOOLS/COLLEGE: Phillip Institute of Technology, RMIT.
QUALIFICATIONS: BA in Fine Arts, Graduate Diploma in Arts Education.
MEMBERSHIPS: ACHU HO.
HOBBIES AND INTERESTS: Arts, reading.
PERSONAL PROFILE: Residential and Conference Services Manager, University College Melbourne. Previously was Coordinator, Int. Program of Menzies College, La Trobe University.

DR MARIA MAKRIDES
Senior research fellow of the National Health and Medical Research Council of Australia

PLACE OF BIRTH: Cyprus
QUALIFICATIONS: Ph. D.
MEMBERSHIPS: Child health Research Institute.
PERSONAL PROFILE: Maria Makrides is a senior research fellow of the National Health and Medical Research Council of Australia and head of the Applied Nutrition Group at the Child Health Research Institute, Women's and Children's Hospital, Adelaide, Australia. Her work is focused on optimizing nutrition interventions at the perinatal stage to improve maternal and infant outcomes.

DESPINA (nee Vasili) MAVRIS
Pharmacist

PLACE OF BIRTH: Sydney Father from Troulli Mother from Arsos
MARITAL STATUS: Married to Jim Mavris, Company Director.
CHILDREN: Antoni, Nicola, Christothea.
SCHOOLS/COLLEGE: Kambala Church of England Girls School. University of Sydney.
QUALIFICATIONS: Bachelor of Pharmacy.
MEMBERSHIPS: Pharmaceutical Guild and Pharmaceutical Society.
PERSONAL PROFILE: Pharmacist.

ANDREAS MESSIOS
Member of the Community of Cyprus Communities of NSW, was previously Secretary (1952)

DATE OF BIRTH: 30-Nov-1925
PLACE OF BIRTH: Trikomo.
MARITAL STATUS: Married to June.
CHILDREN: Five Children.
SCHOOLS/COLLEGE: English School, Tricomo.
HOBBIES AND INTERESTS: Gardening.
PERSONAL PROFILE: Came to Australia in 1948. One of the first to venture to Australia, worked in restaurants and was a Taxi Driver, worked in Sydney for 11 years. Member of the Community of Cyprus Communities of NSW, was previously Secretary (1952).

ANASTASIA MICHAEL
Education

DATE OF BIRTH: 02-Aug-1972.
PLACE OF BIRTH: Australia, Parents from Ayios Athanasios.
MARITAL STATUS: Married to Michael, Australian.
CHILDREN: Charilao, Peter.
SCHOOLS/COLLEGE: Harrison School. University of New South Wales.
QUALIFICATIONS: Teaching Diploma.
PERSONAL PROFILE: Teacher in Primary School.

Australia

DESPINA MICHAEL
Lecturer at La Trobe University

DATE OF BIRTH: 17-Nov-1958
PLACE OF BIRTH: Melbourne, Australia. Father: Acheritou, Mother: Pyla.
MARITAL STATUS: Married to Christodoulos, Cyprus, Systems Analyst.
SCHOOLS/COLLEGE: Prahran Secondary College. University of Melbourne. Deakin University.
QUALIFICATIONS: Bachelor of Arts PhD Classical Studies.
MEMBERSHIPS: Modern Greek Studies Association of Australia and New Zealand.
HONOURS/AWARDS: Citation from Vice Chancellor, La Trobe University, for excellence in teaching, 2006.
HOBBIES AND INTERESTS: Visual arts and love to draw, music I also enjoy cooking and Cinema.
PERSONAL PROFILE: Dr Despina Michael teaches Greek History and popular culture. Ethnic and civil conflict in Southern europe at La Trobe University in Melbourne. Currently she is also assisting a theatrical group (sponsored by the Australia Council of the Arts) in their development of a play on Rebetika music called Café Rebetika.

LEFKIOS MICHAEL
Treasurer of the Cypriot Community Melbourne Victoria

DATE OF BIRTH: 08-Dec-1954
PLACE OF BIRTH: Paphos.
MARITAL STATUS: Married to Helen, Greek Cypriot.
CHILDREN: Danielle, Architect. Anthony, Imports Manager. Christina, Solicitor. Stephanie, Student.
SCHOOLS/COLLEGE: Technical School, Limassol, Cyprus. RMIT, Australia.
QUALIFICATIONS: Electrical Engineering.
HOBBIES AND INTERESTS: Soccer, movies, cars, travelling.
PERSONAL PROFILE: Electrical Engineer. Treasurer of the Cypriot Community Melbourne Victoria.

MICHALIS STAVROU MICHAEL
Research Fellow, Centre for Dialogue, La Trobe University

DATE OF BIRTH: 29-Jun-1960
PLACE OF BIRTH: Sydney, Australia (origin Ayios Epiktitos.
MARITAL STATUS: Married to Maria Vamvakinou, Australian, Member of Federal Parliament (Australia).
CHILDREN: Stavros Michael, Student. Stella Michael, Student.
SCHOOLS/COLLEGE: Ayios Epiktitos Primary, Famagusta Gymnasium. University of Sydney, La Trobe University.
QUALIFICATIONS: BA MA PhD.
HONOURS/AWARDS: Honorary Research Fellow, School of Sciences, La Trobe Uni.
HOBBIES AND INTERESTS: Football, reading, painting, conversation, cooking.
PERSONAL PROFILE: Co-ordinator of the newly established Institute of Cypriot Studies, whilst teaching at the schools of Historical and European Studies and Social Sciences at La Trobe University. Dr Michael has written and published extensively on Cyprus conflict he has also served on numerous Greek and Cypriot community organisations in Australia. Deputy Editor, Global Change, Peace & Security.

HARRY MICHAELS
From 1984 to present he has directed most of the coverage of Australia's International Soccer games

PLACE OF BIRTH: Cyprus
MARITAL STATUS: Married to Effie, TV Aerobic Demonstrator.
CHILDREN: Natalie, TV presenter.
SCHOOLS/COLLEGE: Independant Theatre School of Acting.
PERSONAL PROFILE: Harry Michaels started off as an Actor. He played the Delicatessen Staffer Giovanni Lenzi in the top rating series Number 96. Harry is now the owner and Managing Director of zer01zer0 major innovator of studio and digital outside broadcast facilities. From 1984 to present Harry Michaels directed most of the coverage of Australia's International Soccer games. He created and directed over 4000 episodes of the fitness show. Aerobics OZ Style seen today by an estimated 40 million viewers in 47 countries around the world.

NATALIE MICHAELS

Australian television presenter on the Sky News Showbiz programme on Foxtel

PLACE OF BIRTH: Australia Father From Cyprus **SCHOOLS/COLLEGE:** University of New South Wales. **QUALIFICATIONS:** Bachelor of Media Communications. **PERSONAL PROFILE:** Natalie Michaels is currently the entertainment reporter and producer for 'Showbiz' on Foxtel's popular Sky News Channel. Her credentials and interviewing skills have been honed by the hundreds of media assignments she has been involved with around Australia. These include interviews with celebrities such as Cameron Diaz, Lucy Lui, Keeanu Reeves, Renee Zellweger, Drew Barrymore, Linda Evangelista, Elle MacPherson, Jodi Kidd, Helena Christensen, Jade Jagger, Jane Brikin, Megan Gale, Beyonce Knowles, Cate Blanchett, Russell Crowe. Also the Author of the book When your Mr Right is Mr Wrong.

PANICOS MINA

President of the Community of Cypriots from N&S Melbourne

DATE OF BIRTH: 04-Jul-1952 **PLACE OF BIRTH:** Kontea. **MARITAL STATUS:** Married to Androulla, Lysi. **CHILDREN:** Maria, Paul, Dino. **SCHOOLS/COLLEGE:** Technical School Famagusta, Cyprus. **HOBBIES AND INTERESTS:** Soccer. **PERSONAL PROFILE:** Former President of the Federation of Cypriots in Australia and New Zealand and is President of the Community of Cypriots from N&S Melbourne.

JOHN MITAS

Chief Inspector of Mines and Quarries for Victoria, Australia

DATE OF BIRTH: 07-Oct-1951 **PLACE OF BIRTH:** Born Limassol parents from Rizokarpasso and Famagusta. **MARITAL STATUS:** Married to Mary, Born in Australia, Parents from Rizokarpaso and Famagusta. **CHILDREN:** Stephen, Data Engineer for BMW Formula One. Tina, Lawyer. Christopher, Technical Officer. **SCHOOLS/COLLEGE:** Swinburn Uni, RIMIT Melbourne, Ballarat University. **HOBBIES AND INTERESTS:** Golf, walking, gardening. **PERSONAL PROFILE:** Chief Inspector of Mines and Quarries for Victoria, Australia.

ANDREW NEOPHYTOU

Technical Consultant, Microsoft Certified Professional (MCP)

DATE OF BIRTH: 27-Feb-1972 **PLACE OF BIRTH:** Melbourne, Australia, Mother and Father from Cyprus. **MARITAL STATUS:** Single. **SCHOOLS/COLLEGE:** Essendon High School. Victoria University. **QUALIFICATIONS:** Bachelor of Business in Computing. **HOBBIES AND INTERESTS:** Building/Renovation, cars, computing. **PERSONAL PROFILE:** Technical Consultant, Microsoft Certified Professional (MCP).

Australia

Entrants in Greek Cypriots Worldwide have been nominated for their achievements and contributions.
It is free to nominate someone, or yourself, who deserves to be in the book, just send in the name, contact address, telephone number and email to:
Greek Cypriots Worldwide
111 St Thomas's Road London N4 2QJ
Telephone 0044 207503 3498
cypriotwhoswho@aol.com
www.greekcypriotsworldwide.com

Australia

CHRIS NEOPHYTOU
Co-author of IBM Redbook/President of Cypriot Youth Group (1997-2000) Contributor to the book Greek Cypriots Worldwide

DATE OF BIRTH: 24-Feb-1976
PLACE OF BIRTH: Australia, Father from Rizokarpasso, Mother from Paphos.
MARITAL STATUS: Single.
SCHOOLS/COLLEGE: Essendon High School. Royal Melbourne Institute of Technology.
QUALIFICATIONS: Bachelor of Engineering (Hons).
MEMBERSHIPS: Cyprus Community of Melbourne and Victoria.
HOBBIES AND INTERESTS: Swimming, walking.
PERSONAL PROFILE: Co-author of IBM Redbook, Tuning Netfinity Servers for Performance, 2000. IBM Maintenance Engineer (1997-present). president of Cypriot Youth Group (1997-2000). Active committee member of Cypriot Young Professionals. Chris is also a contributor to the book Greek Cypriots Worldwide.

KERRIE NEOPHYTOU
Head of preparatory school

DATE OF BIRTH: 04-Apr-1970
PLACE OF BIRTH: Melbourne, Australia, Father from Rizokarpasso, Mother from Paphos.
MARITAL STATUS: Single.
SCHOOLS/COLLEGE: Aberfeldie Primary School, Essendon High School. Philip Institute of Technology, RMIT, University of Melbourne.
QUALIFICATIONS: Diploma of Teaching (Primary), Bachelor of Education, Graduate Certificate in Early Childhood Teaching, Masters in Education.
MEMBERSHIPS: Greek Orthodox Archdiocese of Australia (Central Youth Committee of Victoria), Member of Australian College of Educator.
HOBBIES AND INTERESTS: Crafts/floristry, baking and reading.
PERSONAL PROFILE: Primary School Teacher and Special Education Teacher. Active member of a Greek Orthodox parish and fellowship group. Supports the inclusion of children with special needs into the community. Head of preparatory school.

ADA NICODEMOU
Australian actress, best known for her role as Leah Patterson-Baker in the soap opera Home and Away

DATE OF BIRTH: 14-May-1977
PLACE OF BIRTH: Larnaca.
MARITAL STATUS: Married to Chrys.
HONOURS/AWARDS: She has been nominated several times for the Gold Logie as Australia's Most Popular Television Performer at the Logie Awards. In 2005, she and professional dancer Aric Yegudkin won the final of Dancing with the Stars.
PERSONAL PROFILE: Australian actress, best known for her role as Leah Patterson-Baker in the soap opera Home and Away She made her TV debut in 1991, in an episode of Police Rescue. Nicodemou first auditioned for Home and Away at the age of 16, losing the role to Laura Vasquez, the audition led to some work as an extra on the show.
In 1994, at the age of 17, Nicodemou was cast as the rebellious Katarina on Heartbreak High. Although the role was initially to be a 12-week stint, she remained on the show for three years. After leaving Heartbreak High, Nicodemou studied Tourism at TAFE. She returned to television in 1998, playing Fiona Motson on the short-lived Breakers. In 1999, she played DuJour (the White Rabbit Girl) in The Matrix. Nicodemou made several other television appearances before joining the cast of Home and Away in 2000 as a regular cast member

ANASTASIOS NICOLAOU
Consultant Gastroenterologist

DATE OF BIRTH: 09-Apr-1961
PLACE OF BIRTH: Nicosia.
MARITAL STATUS: Married to Violet, Argentina.
CHILDREN: Stephanos, School.
SCHOOLS/COLLEGE: Kykkos Pancyprian Gymnasium, South Sydney Boys High School. University of Sydney.
QUALIFICATIONS: MBDS, FRACP.
MEMBERSHIPS: Fellow of the Royal Australian College of Physicians. Gastroenterology Society of Australia.
HOBBIES AND INTERESTS: Sport, soccer.
PERSONAL PROFILE: Consultant Gastroenterologist. Trustee of Pan Australian Radio Marathon.

Most popular destination for Cypriot born migrants is Victoria.

DESPOULLA NICOLAOU
Business

DATE OF BIRTH: 21-May-1976
PLACE OF BIRTH: Larnaca, Cyprus.
MARITAL STATUS: Married to Emmanuel Karantonis, Australian, Cabinet Maker (Own Business).
CHILDREN: Anthony.
SCHOOLS/COLLEGE: The Broadmedow Performing Arts School. Newcastle University.
QUALIFICATIONS: Bachelor of Social Science.
MEMBERSHIPS: South Junior Social Club, The Cypriot Club, Oz Poker Tour.
HONOURS/AWARDS: Circuit breaker. 1st in Ancient History, (Year 12), 1st in 3 Unit Modern Greek (Year 11 and 12).
HOBBIES AND INTERESTS: NRL Football, Soccer, reading.
PERSONAL PROFILE: Despoulla has own business with 20 employees. Volunteered for Salvation Army and also volunteered for Mission Australia door knock.

TONY NICOLAOU
Physiotherapist with Back in Motion Corporate Health

PLACE OF BIRTH: Cyprus.
SCHOOLS/COLLEGE: Monash University and Charles Sturt University.
QUALIFICATIONS: BSC and a Bachelor of Physiotherapy.
HOBBIES AND INTERESTS: Travel, soccer and keeping fit.
PERSONAL PROFILE: Tony Nicolaou is a Physiotherapist with Back in Motion Corporate Health and he has also worked out of the Wantirna South Practice in Australia.

CHRYSOULLA NICOTRA
Accountant/Active Member of the Sydney Cypriot Community

DATE OF BIRTH: 02-Jan-1968
PLACE OF BIRTH: Nicosia.
MARITAL STATUS: Married to Luciano.
CHILDREN: Francesco, School. George, School.
SCHOOLS/COLLEGE: Marrickville High School. University of Western Sydney.
QUALIFICATIONS: Bachelor of Business, Accounting and Law.
HOBBIES AND INTERESTS: Secretary of Parents and Friends Association, Tennis.

PERSONAL PROFILE: Accountant in Commerce, Active Member of the Sydney Cypriot Community.

NICHOLAS PAGONIS
Trade Unionist

DATE OF BIRTH: 24-Nov-1923
PLACE OF BIRTH: Aradippou.
MARITAL STATUS: Married to Helen.
CHILDREN: Con, Leigh, Catherine.
SCHOOLS/COLLEGE: Faraday Street Primary School. Collingwood Technical School and Royal Melbourne Institute of Technology.
QUALIFICATIONS: Computer Electronics.
HONOURS/AWARDS: As a result of his voluntary work with Fronditha Care the Greek Australian Nursing Home for the Elderly he was awarded a Life Governorship by the Board.
PERSONAL PROFILE: Nicholas Pagonis after serving in the Royal Australasian Air Force in the Second World War Nicholas worked in aviation electronics with the Commonwealth Aircraft Corporation(CAC) it was here he was elected the Electrical Trades Union shop Steward and later the Secretary of the Inter Union area Committee representing all the CAC workforce. Nicholas's father went to Australia in 1926.

PANAYIOTIS PANAYI
Barrister at Law served as Senior Political Advisor to a former Australian Foreign Minister

DATE OF BIRTH: 08-Mar-1973
PLACE OF BIRTH: Nicosia, Cyprus.
MARITAL STATUS: Single.
SCHOOLS/COLLEGE: James Cook University, Australia.
QUALIFICATIONS: BSc, LLB (Hons).
MEMBERSHIPS: Victorian Bar Association.
HONOURS/AWARDS: The Australian Defence Medal and the Australian Defence Force Commendation.
HOBBIES AND INTERESTS: travel, food and wine, sports and the arts.
PERSONAL PROFILE: Currently practices as a Barrister in Melbourne, Australia. He is also a Commissioned Officer of the Royal Australian Navy Reserve. Was previously an Australian Diplomat, and Senior Political Adviser to a former Australian Foreign Minister.

PETER PANAYI

Diving Coach coaches divers at the Melbourne Sports and Aquatic Centre most of them successful at major International Diving Exhibitions

PLACE OF BIRTH: London father from Tymbou
MARITAL STATUS: Married to Shirley, Diving Coach.
PERSONAL PROFILE: Peter Panayi has been a competitive, diver, coach and judge.
Peter is a level 3 coach and currently coaches divers at the Melbourne Sports and Aquatic Centre. Over the years Peter's divers have won in excess of 500 medals at State level and 400 medals at the National level. Peter's divers have also been successful at all major international diving competitions.

SHAUN PANAYI

Gold medal in 3 meters springboard diving in the Edinburgh Commonwealth Games in 1986

PLACE OF BIRTH: Australia Grandfather from Tymbou
HONOURS/AWARDS: Gold medal in 3 meters springboard diving in the Edinburgh Commonwealth Games in 1986.
PERSONAL PROFILE: Shaun Panayi Was one of the top Australian Divers.

SKEVI PANAYI (NEE PITTAS)

Director in the NSW Dept of Community Services

DATE OF BIRTH: 01-Apr-1964
PLACE OF BIRTH: Famagusta.
MARITAL STATUS: Married to George Panayi, Kiti, Self-employed.
CHILDREN: Jonathan, Ellen, Both at School.
SCHOOLS/COLLEGE: Enfield Public School, Burwood Girls' High School. Petersham College of Technical & Further Education, Macquarie University.

QUALIFICATIONS: Masters in Politics and Public Policy, Diploma in early Childhood.
MEMBERSHIPS: Member of the Institute of Public Policy Administration.
HOBBIES AND INTERESTS: Dancing, arts and politics.
PERSONAL PROFILE: At present she is a Director in the NSW Dept. of Community Services overseeing funding, monitoring and planning of community and regulating children's services. She has been influential in furthering multiculturalism and social Justice issues for disadvantaged communities. She has been Chair of a community based children's service and has served on a number of other community based organisations including the Cypriot Community Dance School.

LUCAS PANTELIS

Footballer in 1999 played for Australia in the under 17's World Championship and the final v Brazil

PLACE OF BIRTH: Adelaide Parents from Cyprus
HONOURS/AWARDS: Played for the Australian National under 17, 20 and 23 sides. In 1999 played for Australia in the under 17's World Championship and in the final v Brazil.
PERSONAL PROFILE: Luke is an Australian soccer player who plays as a central midfielder. He currently plays for Adelaide United in the Hyundai A League.

CHRISTODOULOS PAPAS

Director of Cyprus Community of New South Wales

DATE OF BIRTH: 29-Nov-1938
PLACE OF BIRTH: Mammari.
MARITAL STATUS: Married.
CHILDREN: Alexander, Electrical Engineer. Michael, Dentist.
SCHOOLS/COLLEGE: Samuel's Commercial Practical School.
QUALIFICATIONS: High School.
HOBBIES AND INTERESTS: Gardening and Fishing.
PERSONAL PROFILE: Printer. Sydney Olympics and Para-Olympics volunteer. Director of Cyprus Community of New South Wales.

MICHAEL PAPAS
Dentist

PLACE OF BIRTH: Australia Father from Mammari.
SCHOOLS/COLLEGE: Sydney University.
QUALIFICATIONS: BDS.
MEMBERSHIPS: Australian Dental Association.
PERSONAL PROFILE: Michael Papas is a Dentist based in Crows Nest in New South wales.

CHRIS PARASKEVA
Active Member of the Cypriot Community Melbourne Victoria

DATE OF BIRTH: 21-Dec-1959
PLACE OF BIRTH: Limassol.
MARITAL STATUS: Married to Christine.
CHILDREN: James, Estelle.
SCHOOLS/COLLEGE: Technical School, Limassol, Cyprus.
QUALIFICATIONS: Year 12.
HOBBIES AND INTERESTS: Fishing, hunting.
PERSONAL PROFILE: Furniture Maker, Tiler. Active Member of the Cypriot Community Melbourne Victoria.

PETER PARASKEVAS
Director of Vein Health Medical College

PLACE OF BIRTH: Cyprus
QUALIFICATIONS: MBBS FRACGP.
MEMBERSHIPS: member and registrar of the Australian College of Phlebology and a Fellow of the Royal Australian College of General Practitioners.
PERSONAL PROFILE: Peter Paraskevas is a is the director of Vein Health Medical Clinic which is solely dedicated to the treatment of Chronic Venous Disease and Varicose Veins.

GEORGIOU PATROKLOS
Former Manager of Laiki Bank, Melbourne and Commonwealth Bank. Greek teacher in community schools

DATE OF BIRTH: 01-Sep-1945
PLACE OF BIRTH: Limassol.
MARITAL STATUS: Married to Joanne, Cypriot.
CHILDREN: Despina, Student. Mary, Legal Executive. Androulla, Legal Executive.
SCHOOLS/COLLEGE: Ekonomiko Gymnasium, Limassol. RMIT.
QUALIFICATIONS: Education.
HOBBIES AND INTERESTS: Church activities.
PERSONAL PROFILE: Former Manager of Laiki Bank, Melbourne and Commonwealth Bank. Greek teacher in community schools. He is currently running a finance company called ELPIS.

GEORGE PATTALIS
Hydraulic Designer

PLACE OF BIRTH: Farmakas
PERSONAL PROFILE: George Pattalis is an Hydraulic Designer working for Hughes Trueman. He is in the design, documentation and site supervision of various hydraulic protection and medical gases services for projects ranging from schools, office and retail developments, hotels, technical colleges, hospitals, retirement villages, industrial development, landscape watering systems and sport and recreational facilities.

Entrants in Greek Cypriots Worldwide have been nominated for their achievements and contributions.
It is free to nominate someone, or yourself, who deserves to be in the book, just send in the name, contact address, telephone number and email to:
Greek Cypriots Worldwide
111 St Thomas's Road London N4 2QJ
Telephone 0044 207503 3498
cypriotwhoswho@aol.com
www.greekcypriotsworldwide.com

Australia

PAUL PAVLI
Senior Specialist Gastroenterologist

DATE OF BIRTH: 01-May-1954
PLACE OF BIRTH: Sydney, Australia, Father from Limassol and Mother from Paphos.
MARITAL STATUS: Married to Janelle Gai Hamilton, General Practioner.
CHILDREN: Alexandra, Mark, Lauren.
SCHOOLS/COLLEGE: North Sydney Boy's High School. Australian national University, University of Sydney.
QUALIFICATIONS: MB BS PhD.
MEMBERSHIPS: Australian Drug Evaluation Committee, Australian College of Physicians.
HOBBIES AND INTERESTS: Running (completed the Canberra marathon in 1986 and 1988), Gardening.
PERSONAL PROFILE: Senior specialist Gastroenterologist, The Canberra Hospital from February 1993. Associate Professor, Australian National University (ANU) Medical School from May 2004. Has had over 60 research publications and reviews.

ANGELO PAVLIDES
On the Motor Accidents Insurance Board

PLACE OF BIRTH: Limassol.
PERSONAL PROFILE: Angelo Pavlides is based at the Department of Treasury and Finance of Tasmania and is on the Motor Accidents Insurance Board.

JOHN PAVLOU
Airline Pilot for Quantas 747

DATE OF BIRTH: 01-Feb-1977
PLACE OF BIRTH: Australia Father from Farmakas Mother from Menikou.
MARITAL STATUS: Married to Margarita, London Parents from Cyprus, IT Business analyst.
CHILDREN: Ava.
SCHOOLS/COLLEGE: North Sydney Boys High School.
QUALIFICATIONS: Air Transport Pilots Licence.
MEMBERSHIPS: Australian & International Pilots Association.
HOBBIES AND INTERESTS: Travelling, Football keen Arsenal supporter.
PERSONAL PROFILE: John is a Airline pilot for the Australian Quantas group flying mainly 747 airplanes. He will probably be the first Cypriot to fly the A380 Airbus the World's largest airplane.

KAY PAVLOU
Directed the documentary called a Cyprus, A People Divided for Australian TV

DATE OF BIRTH: 25-Oct-1960
PLACE OF BIRTH: Australia Parents from Cyprus.
SCHOOLS/COLLEGE: Marion High School. Flinders University and AFTRS.
QUALIFICATIONS: BA.
MEMBERSHIPS: Australian Directors Guild.
HONOURS/AWARDS: For the Feature Film Mary Polish Film Festival 1995. The Short Film The Killing of Angelo Tsakos. Golden Gate Film Festival 1989.
HOBBIES AND INTERESTS: Photography, Yoga and Filming.
PERSONAL PROFILE: Kay Pavlou is a Film and Television Director in both documentary and drama. She directed the documentary called a Cyprus, A People Divided for Australian TV.

MARGARITA PAVLOU
IT Business Analyst specialising in working for the Australian Government

DATE OF BIRTH: 23-Jul-1978
PLACE OF BIRTH: London Father from Karavas, Maternal grandparents from Limassol.
MARITAL STATUS: Married to John, Australian Parents from Cyprus, Airline Pilot.
CHILDREN: Ava.
SCHOOLS/COLLEGE: Edith Cowan University, Perth, Australia.
QUALIFICATIONS: BA in Interactive multi media technology.
HOBBIES AND INTERESTS: Travelling and socialising.
PERSONAL PROFILE: Margarita Pavlou is an IT Business Analyst working for the Australian Government.

EFSTRATIOS PHANI
Justice of the Peace in New South Wales

DATE OF BIRTH: 25-Feb-1931
PLACE OF BIRTH: Peyia.
MARITAL STATUS: Married to Magdaline Kyriacou (Deceased), Greek Cypriot, Housewife.
CHILDREN: Androulla, School Teacher. Odyseas, Mechanical Engineer.
SCHOOLS/COLLEGE: Paphos High School (Gymnasio).
MEMBERSHIPS: In Sydney the Cyprus Community Club and Burwood RSL Club.
HOBBIES AND INTERESTS: Active participant on Talk Back radio on SBS, 2MM and 1683am Greek Radio.
PERSONAL PROFILE: After migrating worked in factories and had his own cafe. He helped establish the first Greek Orthodox Church in Dubbo which was named Myrtythiodyssa. Also holds Office as a Justice of the Peace in New South Wales.

ADAM PHILIPPOU
Finalist in X Factor Australia

PLACE OF BIRTH: born Adelaide Parents from Cyprus
PERSONAL PROFILE: Adam Philippou and his two brothers George and Michael, moved to London together in 1995 to pursue their music, signed to RCA and recording under the name of Universal. They released three singles and made numerous television appearances including Top of the Pops. They reformed in 2005 in their home town of Sydney under the name The Brothership and made it into the group's final of the X factor(Australia). He was the Lead Singer and Frontman.

GEORGE PHILIPPOU
Finalist in X Factor Australia

PLACE OF BIRTH: Adelaide parents from Cyprus
PERSONAL PROFILE: George Philippou and his two brothers Adam and Michael, moved to London together in 1995 to pursue their music, signed to RCA and recording under the name of Universal, they released three singles and made numerous television appearances including Top of the Pops. They reformed in 2005 in their home town of Sydney under the name The Brothership and made it into the groups final of the X factor(Australia). He played the guitar and vocalist.

MICHAEL PHILIPPOU
Finalist in X Factor Australia

PLACE OF BIRTH: Adelaide Parents from Cyprus
PERSONAL PROFILE: Michael Philippou and his two brothers George and Adam, moved to London together in 1995 to pursue their music, signed to RCA and recording under the name of Universal. They released three singles and made numerous television appearances including Top of the Pops. They reformed in 2005 in their home town of Sydney under the name The Brothership and made it into the groups final of the X factor(Australia). Michael now works as a Business Sales Consultant. He was a songwriter, guitar player and vocalist.

DEAN PIERIDES
University Lecturer

PLACE OF BIRTH: Father from Limassol.
SCHOOLS/COLLEGE: University of Pennsylvania and University of Melbourne.
QUALIFICATIONS: BA MEd.
PERSONAL PROFILE: Dean Pierides is Lecturer within the Faculty of Education at the University of Melbourne.

GEORGE PIERIDES
Dental Prosthetist

DATE OF BIRTH: 12-Jan-1945
PLACE OF BIRTH: Limassol.
MARITAL STATUS: Married to Helen, Cypriot, Accounting.
CHILDREN: Dean, Lecturer at Melbourne University.
SCHOOLS/COLLEGE: Lanition Gymnasium. RMIT Melbourne.
MEMBERSHIPS: Australian Dental Prosthetists Association.
HOBBIES AND INTERESTS: Painting and Poetry.
PERSONAL PROFILE: Chairman of Dental Technicians Association Cyprus and Chairman of the Dental Technicians Board.

Australia

LEWIS PIERIDES
Medical Practitioner

DATE OF BIRTH: 17-Feb-1954
PLACE OF BIRTH: Australia, Parents from Cyprus.
MARITAL STATUS: Single.
SCHOOLS/COLLEGE: University of Adelaide.
QUALIFICATIONS: MBBS, FAFOEM.
PERSONAL PROFILE: Medical Practitioner.

MARIA PIEROU
General Secretary of NEPOMAK

DATE OF BIRTH: 24-Mar-1983
PLACE OF BIRTH: Australia, Father from Akaki and Mother from Assia.
SCHOOLS/COLLEGE: University of Western Sydney, Macquarie University.
QUALIFICATIONS: Bachelor of Laws, Bachelor of Commerce, Diploma of European Languages.
PERSONAL PROFILE: General Secretary of NEPOMAK. President of SEKA, New South Wales. Vice President of NEPOMAK, Australia.

CHRISTINA POLYKARPOU
Active member of the Cypriot Community in Melbourne

DATE OF BIRTH: 29-Jan-1986
PLACE OF BIRTH: Victoria, Australia, Parents from Cyprus.
SCHOOLS/COLLEGE: Preston East Primary, Holy Name Primary, Northcote High School, St Mary's in Cyprus. Helped to organise Miss Cyprus 2003 and helps in the Annual Cyprus Festival in Melbourne.
QUALIFICATIONS: Completion on VCE.
MEMBERSHIPS: CYP Group.
HOBBIES AND INTERESTS: Friends, movies, reading.
PERSONAL PROFILE: Works for Aami Insurance car and home sales and customer relations, she is currently team leader and referral point. She also has a Salon that she runs on Saturdays She helps organise Miss Cyprus event and the Annual Cypriot Wine Festival.

MARY-ANNE PONTIKIS
Volunteer role as Assistant stage Manager at the Opening and Closing Ceremonies of the 2006 Melbourne Commonwealth Games

DATE OF BIRTH: 06-Apr-1957
PLACE OF BIRTH: Mother-Kyrenia, Father-Alona.
MARITAL STATUS: Single.
SCHOOLS/COLLEGE: Hadfield High School. State College of Victoria.
QUALIFICATIONS: Higher School Certificate, Diploma of Teaching (Primary), Bachelor of Education.
MEMBERSHIPS: Australian Education Union, Primary Councillor, Executive Branch Member for Victorian Branch (AEU), Victorian Trades Hall Council Delegate and various others.
HOBBIES AND INTERESTS: Dancing, fitness work, reading, calligraphy, shopping, travelling, meeting new people.
PERSONAL PROFILE: Volunteer role as Assistant Stage Manager at the Opening and Closing Ceremonies of the 2006 Melbourne Commomwealth Games. She is an active member for the Australian Education Union and a strong advocate for promoting Public Education.

PANAYIOTIS (PETER) PPIROS
Deputy Chairman of the South Australian Multicultural and Ethnic Affairs Commission

DATE OF BIRTH: 12-Feb-1961
PLACE OF BIRTH: Lapithos, Cyprus.
MARITAL STATUS: Married to Stavroulla, Greek Cypriot, Office Manager.
CHILDREN: Mihalis, Charalambous, Both students.
SCHOOLS/COLLEGE: Lapithos Greek High School, Renmark English High School. South Australia TAFE.
QUALIFICATIONS: Journalist, Legal Studies.
HONOURS/AWARDS: Australian Centenary of Federation Medal for service to community through the advancement of Multiculturalism. Federation of Ethnic Communities Council of Australia 25th Anniversary Medal for service to the ethnic communities.
HOBBIES AND INTERESTS: Theatre, music, dance, reading.

PERSONAL PROFILE: Peter Ppiros was appointed Deputy Chairman of the South Australian Multicultural and Ethnic Affairs Commission in 2006. He is the founder and editor of the Greek Community Tribune, a national Greek language newspaper. He is also the founder of the Riverland Greek Festival.

CONSTANTINOS PROCOPIOU
President, Justice for Cyprus PSEKA for Melbourne and PSEKA for Australia and New Zealand

DATE OF BIRTH: 30-Sep-1942
PLACE OF BIRTH: Trikomo.
MARITAL STATUS: Married to Andrianna Pipingas, Rizokarpasso, Stenographer.
CHILDREN: Nellie, Pharmacist. Sotera, Architect.
SCHOOLS/COLLEGE: Greek Gymnasium of Famagusta: Graduated 1960 under the name Andreou Constantinos, Maraslios Paedagogigal Academy. Monash University Melbourne, Australia, Athens University.
QUALIFICATIONS: BA.
MEMBERSHIPS: Victoria Secondary Teachers Association, Academic Staff Association.
HONOURS/AWARDS: Hellenic Distinction Award in Education for Contribution to Tertiary Education. Urban Design Award- finalist best Alteration and Addition to existing building.
HOBBIES AND INTERESTS: Football, tennis, Athletics, socialising, networking.
PERSONAL PROFILE: Head, Greek Studies in tertiary institutions for 20 years. Chairman, panel of examiners for higher school certificate. President, Malvern City Football Club. President, Justice for Cyprus PSEKA for Australia and New Zealand.

NELLIE PROCOPIOU
Pharmacist

PLACE OF BIRTH: Father from Trikomo, Mother from Rizokarpasso.
PERSONAL PROFILE: Nellie Procopiou was a pharmacist within the Poly Clinic of the Melbourne Commonwealth Games.

KALLI PULOS
Freelance facilitator and executive coach

PLACE OF BIRTH: Adelaide Mother from Cyprus
QUALIFICATIONS: Dip. Ed.
PERSONAL PROFILE: Kalli Pulos is an Associate with the Institute of Executive Coaching, Freelance Facilitator and Executive coach.

ANTHEA SAKKOU
Chiropractor

DATE OF BIRTH: 24-Feb-1974
PLACE OF BIRTH: Mother from Ayios Theodoros, Larnaca, Father from Nicosia.
MARITAL STATUS: Married to Con Sakkou, Cypriot from Nicosia.
CHILDREN: Yiana.
SCHOOLS/COLLEGE: Geohegan College and Royal Melbourne Institute of Technology.
QUALIFICATIONS: Batchelor of Applied Science and Batchelor of Chiropractic Science.
MEMBERSHIPS: Chiropractic Association of Australia.
HOBBIES AND INTERESTS: Stamp Collecting, Gardening and Socialising.
PERSONAL PROFILE: Anthea Sakkou is a Chiropractor.

CON SAKKOU
Business

DATE OF BIRTH: 22-Feb-1974
PLACE OF BIRTH: Nicosia – Cyprus. Mother – Pentayia. Father – Morphou.
MARITAL STATUS: Married to Anthea Sakkou maiden name Jacovou.
CHILDREN: Yiana.
SCHOOLS/COLLEGE: Evangelistria College. Victoria University.
QUALIFICATIONS: Associate Diploma of Business (Marketing).
MEMBERSHIPS: Chiropractic Association of Australia.
HOBBIES AND INTERESTS: Fishing.
PERSONAL PROFILE: Sales and Marketing Manager for Melbourne Marble and Granite and active member of the Australian Community.

Australia

CON SARROU
Accountant

DATE OF BIRTH: 07-Mar-1958
PLACE OF BIRTH: Victoria, Australia parents from Cyprus.
MARITAL STATUS: Married to Shelley, China.
SCHOOLS/COLLEGE: Mildura High School. Footscray Institute of Technology.
QUALIFICATIONS: Bachelor of Business.
HOBBIES AND INTERESTS: Golf, volleyball, gardening.
PERSONAL PROFILE: Accountant and P/Owner of Palace Complex in St. Kilda.

GEORGE SAVVA
Business

PLACE OF BIRTH: Cyprus.
PERSONAL PROFILE: George Savva is a Consultant with BDigital Ltd who together with its subsidiaries operates in the Telecommunications Industry in Australia.

NIKE SAVVAS
Artist with collections in Art Gallery of New South Wales, Sydney the British Library and the Tate Gallery Library as well as others

PLACE OF BIRTH: Sydney, Parents from Cyprus
SCHOOLS/COLLEGE: Sydney College of The Arts, University of New South Wales, University of Sydney and Goldsmiths College.
QUALIFICATIONS: BA MA.
HONOURS/AWARDS: 2006 New Work Grant, Australia Council 2005 Jury Prize 11th Triennale of India, Delhi 2003 Collex Primavera Acquisitive Art Award.
PERSONAL PROFILE: Nike Savvas is an Artist with collections in Art Gallery of New South Wales, Sydney the British Library and the Tate Gallery Library as well as others. She has had several solo exhibitions. Her last success was 2005 Atomic: Full of Love, Full of Wonder, Australian Centre for Contemporary Art, Melbourne, Australia.

GEORGE SAVVIDES
Managing Director- Medibank Private Ltd, (Private Health Insurer)

DATE OF BIRTH: 20-Oct-1956
PLACE OF BIRTH: Sydney, Australia, mother from Nicosia, father from Kyrenia.
MARITAL STATUS: Married to Vivian Symes, Australian.
CHILDREN: Peter Savvides, Luke Savvides, Both University Students.
SCHOOLS/COLLEGE: University of Technology, Sydney, University of New South Wales.
QUALIFICATIONS: BA MA MBA.
MEMBERSHIPS: Fellow, Australian Institute of Company Directors.
HOBBIES AND INTERESTS: Veterans hockey, boating.
PERSONAL PROFILE: Managing Director- Medibank Private Ltd, (Private Health Insurer). Board Member World Vision Australia. Board Member World Vision International.

IRINI SAVVIDES
Finalist in the 2002 Sydney Morning Herald Young Writer of The Year Award

PLACE OF BIRTH: Australia Parents from Cyprus
SCHOOLS/COLLEGE: Macquarie University and University of Sydney.
QUALIFICATIONS: BA Dp Ed M. ED MA.
HONOURS/AWARDS: Finalist in the 2002 Sydney Morning Herald Young Writer of The Year Award.
PERSONAL PROFILE: Irini Savvides is an Author her first Novel was called Willow Tree and Olive, Her second is Sky Legs.

HARRY SHIAMARIS
Journalist/Former Secretary of Cyprus Community of Melbourne, Victoria

DATE OF BIRTH: 21-Jan-1929
PLACE OF BIRTH: Lefkoniko.
MARITAL STATUS: Married to Popi, Limassol.
CHILDREN: Tasos, Businessman. Stella, Company Executive. Andre, Fashion Designer.
SCHOOLS/COLLEGE: Lefkoniko High School, Cyprus. Teacher Training College, Morphou.
QUALIFICATIONS: Teacher.
HOBBIES AND INTERESTS: Writing, journalism, TV, theatre.
PERSONAL PROFILE: Primary Teacher in Cyprus. Secondary Teacher in Australia. Author of two books. Former Secretary of Cyprus Community of Melbourne, Victoria.

CHRISTOS SHOLAKIS
Active member of Cypriot Community Melbourne Victoria

DATE OF BIRTH: 14-Sep-1932
PLACE OF BIRTH: Agros.
MARITAL STATUS: Married to Athena, Greek/Australian.
CHILDREN: Michalis, Computer Technician. Lazaros, Accountant. Andreas, Shops.
SCHOOLS/COLLEGE: Agros Gymnasium.
HOBBIES AND INTERESTS: Soccer Australian Rules.
PERSONAL PROFILE: Active member of the Cypriot Community Melbourne Victoria.

KYRIAKOS (KEN) SKOULLOS
Chief Executive Officer of Hudson Pacific Corporation

DATE OF BIRTH: 23-Nov-1953
PLACE OF BIRTH: Achna.
MARITAL STATUS: Married.
CHILDREN: Andreas, BA MBA Business Admin and logistics. Louis, BA business-commerce. Zoe, BA marketing /commerce. Stella, Primary School.
SCHOOLS/COLLEGE: American Academy.
MEMBERSHIPS: Lions, EKEME and Logistics Association of Australia.

HONOURS/AWARDS: Honorary recognition from La Trobe University for contribution and support to the Greek Centre(EKEME). Also Countrywide Chairman award 2005.
HOBBIES AND INTERESTS: Aussie Rules Football, Golf, Travel, Food and Wine.
PERSONAL PROFILE: Ken Skoullos is the Chief Executive Officer of Hudson Pacific. Established a number of businesses in Food service and manufacturing industries in the top 5 in its field in Australia. He has commercial interests in Virgin Airlines Lounges Australia wide, restaurants, commercial real estate, food manufacturing, importing and cheese trading.

COSTAS SOCRATOUS
Brimbank City Councillor

DATE OF BIRTH: 02-Jun-1952
PLACE OF BIRTH: Yeroskipou.
MARITAL STATUS: Married, Electoral Officer.
CHILDREN: Vera, Soulla, Melanie, Maria.
HONOURS/AWARDS: Volunteer Award, Multicultural and Centenary Awards.
HOBBIES AND INTERESTS: Soccer.
PERSONAL PROFILE: Brimbank City Councillor.

CHRISTOPHER SOZOU
Project Manager for Colonial First State

DATE OF BIRTH: 08-Apr-1977
PLACE OF BIRTH: Sydney Parents from Lefkara and Strovolos.
MARITAL STATUS: Married to Kathy Sozou.
SCHOOLS/COLLEGE: St Johns Lakemba. University of Sydney.
QUALIFICATIONS: BA Commerce (Accounting, Finance and Computer Science).
HOBBIES AND INTERESTS: Football and Formula One.
PERSONAL PROFILE: Project Manager for Colonial First State and three years as a project manager for Fidelity Investments UK(London).

Australia

KATHY SOZOU
Chartered Accountant

DATE OF BIRTH: 22-Nov-1980
PLACE OF BIRTH: Sydney
Parents from Troulli and
Aradippou.
MARITAL STATUS: Married
to Christopher Sozou, Sydney
Parents from Cyprus.
SCHOOLS/COLLEGE: Sydney
Civic High School. University
of New South Wales.
QUALIFICATIONS: BA
Commerce (Accounting and Finance).
MEMBERSHIPS: Institute of Chartered Accountants
Australia.
PERSONAL PROFILE: Kathy is a chartered accountant
working in insolvency/restructuring in Australia after a
3 year secondment working in KPMG London in the
same area.

SOPHIA SPYROU
Community Liason Officer, New South
Wales Police

DATE OF BIRTH: 25-Sep-1955
PLACE OF BIRTH: Famagusta,
Cyprus.
MARITAL STATUS: Married to
Andrea Vatili.
CHILDREN: Maria, High
School Teacher. Yiannis, Auto
Electrician. Pantellis, Apprentice
Electrician. Daniel, Apprentice
Mechanic.
SCHOOLS/COLLEGE:
Riverside Girls High School, Sydney.
QUALIFICATIONS: Diploma in Social Work.
HOBBIES AND INTERESTS: Music, dancing cooking,
travelling, socialising.
PERSONAL PROFILE: Community Liason Officer, New
South Wales Police. Previously worked with refugees
assisting with settlement issues.

ANDREAS STEPHANOU
Senior Research Fellow at the
Australian Council for Educational
Research

DATE OF BIRTH: 02-Dec-1946
PLACE OF BIRTH: Limassol,
Cyprus.
MARITAL STATUS: Single.
SCHOOLS/COLLEGE:
Universita' degli Studi di Roma.
University of Melbourne.
QUALIFICATIONS: PhD
(Melbourne), Laurea in Fisica
(Rome). Diploma of Education
(Melbourne).
MEMBERSHIPS: American Association
of Physics Teachers.
HOBBIES AND INTERESTS: Chess, football, gardening,
travelling, Computers, Photography. Main interest is in
Physics Education and Rasch measurement.
PERSONAL PROFILE: Senior Research Fellow at the
Australian Council for Educational Research. Taught
High school and University physics for 17 years.

FRIEDA STYLIANOU
Editor of the Local Government Reporter
published by Lexis Nexis

PLACE OF BIRTH: Parents from Cyprus.
PERSONAL PROFILE: Frieda Stylianou is a specialist
in personal injury law. Frieda is the Editor of the Local
Government Reporter published by Lexis Nexis.

STANLEY CHRIS STYLIS
ENT Surgeon

DATE OF BIRTH: 10-May-1932
PLACE OF BIRTH: Sydney,
Australia-Mother from Limassol.
MARITAL STATUS: Married to
Daphne.
CHILDREN: Andrew.
SCHOOLS/COLLEGE: Sydney
High School. Sydney University,
Royal College of Surgeons,
London.
QUALIFICATIONS: MB, BS
(hons) BSC (Med.) (Hons) FRCS, DLO.
PERSONAL PROFILE: Ex-Treasurer of Greek
Community-Wollongong, NSW. Member of committee
that built the first Greek Orthodox Church there in 1960.
Ex-Chairman of the ENT Dept. of Illawarra District
Area Hospital NSW. Director of the company which
owned and produced the Movie'Mad Max', directed and
written by George Miller (winner of the 2007 Hollywood
Logie Award), Founder of the Bondi Junction Private

Hospital in Sydney. Author of Medical Articles in Ear Nose and Throat Medical Journals. Presently involved with a patented and unique children's shoe for global distribution with partner John Karandonis to be globally launched 2008.

MARINA THEO
Commitee of the Ladies Cultural Group, Cypriot Community of Melbourne and Victoria

DATE OF BIRTH: 17-Mar-1959
PLACE OF BIRTH: Limassol.
MARITAL STATUS: Married to Theo Theophylactou.
CHILDREN: Andreas, Sales Manager. Panos, Student. Evangelia, School.
SCHOOLS/COLLEGE: St Mary's High School.
QUALIFICATIONS: Certified Travel Manager (CTM).
HOBBIES AND INTERESTS: Travel, Swimming.
PERSONAL PROFILE: Representative of Cyprus Airways in Australia, Commitee of the Ladies Cultural Group, Cypriot Community of Melbourne and Victoria.

CON THEOCHAROUS
Former Secretary of the International Academy of Pathology in Australia

PLACE OF BIRTH: Nicosia
PERSONAL PROFILE: Con Theocharous was the Secretary of the International Academy of Pathology in Australia.

ANDREW THEOPHANOUS
Parliamentary Secretary to Prime Minister Paul Keating

DATE OF BIRTH: 24-Mar-1946
PLACE OF BIRTH: Paphos.
MARITAL STATUS: Married to Dr Kathryn Eriksson, Archaeologist.
SCHOOLS/COLLEGE: Parliamentary Secretary to Prime Minister Paul Keating. Monash University, Oxford University and Melbourne University.
PERSONAL PROFILE: Andrew Theophanous lectured at Melbourne State College, Melbourne University, University of Nevada USA and Monash University. Andrew was elected as the Labour member for the Melbourne Electorate of Burke in 1980. From 1989 to 1993 he was Chairman of the joint Standing Committee on Migration. In 1993 Theofanous was appointed Parliamentary Secretary to the Minister of Housing and later Minister of Health and in 1994 he was appointed Parliamentary Secretary to Prime Minister Paul Keating. In April 2000 because of the allegations and evidence of fraud and corruption he retired from the Labor Party.

THEO CHARLES THEOPHANOUS
Victorian Minister for Industry & State Development, Major Projects and Small Business

DATE OF BIRTH: 16-Jun-1948
PLACE OF BIRTH: Polis, Cyprus.
MARITAL STATUS: Married to Margarita Toumbourou Theophanous, Cypriot, Pharmacist.
CHILDREN: Matthew, Personal Trainer. Harry, Solicitior. Kyriakos, University Student. Katerina, University Student.
SCHOOLS/COLLEGE: Glenroy High School. La Trobe University.
QUALIFICATIONS: Bachelor of Arts (HONS. FIRST CLASS) (LA TROBE).
MEMBERSHIPS: Australian Labour Party, Greek Community Melbourne Victoria, Cyprus Community Melbourne Victoria, Australian Workers Union, Fabian Society, Footscray Football Club.
HOBBIES AND INTERESTS: Multiculturalism, Economic and Social Justice Philosophy, Australian Rules Football, Fishing, Reading.
PERSONAL PROFILE: Victorian Minister for Industry and State Development Major Projects and Small Business. Previous work has been many political roles.

Australia

PETER (PANAYIOTIS) THEOPHILOU
Awarded Order of Australia Medal

DATE OF BIRTH: 15-May-1940
PLACE OF BIRTH: Monagrouli, Limassol, Cyprus.
MARITAL STATUS: Married to Christine, Cypriot, Accountant.
CHILDREN: Cynthia, Accountant.
SCHOOLS/COLLEGE: Sydney Technical College, Sydney University.
QUALIFICATIONS: Accountant Taxation Consultant.
MEMBERSHIPS: The Australian Association of Taxation.
HONOURS/AWARDS: 1996 - Citizen of the year, Banktown. 1997 - Order of Australia Medal (O. A. M) 2001 - Golden Cross of St Andrew's from the Greek Orthodox Church. Community service award from the government of New South Wales.
PERSONAL PROFILE: Accountant - Taxation Consultant. Instrumental in establishing St Euphemia Greek Orthodox College in Australia, established in 1989 with 24 students and now with 720 students.

ANDREW THOMAS
Former World Under 14 Tennis Champion

DATE OF BIRTH: 01-Mar-1990
PLACE OF BIRTH: Sydney Mother from Cyprus.
MARITAL STATUS: Single.
HONOURS/AWARDS: Former World Under 14 Tennis Champion.
PERSONAL PROFILE: Andrew Thomas is a Former World Under 14 Tennis Champion. He advanced to the final 16 in the junior boys single tournament at the US Open in 2007. He is ranked 27 in the World under 18 category. He is the only Australian tennis player to win the Les Petit in France, the most prestigious event for 14 year olds in the world. Past winners include Roger Federer, Juan Carlos Ferrero and Marat Safin. Andrew has also won the 12/U Orange Bowl in America, the most prestigious tennis event for 12 year olds in the world.

PATRICIA THOMPSON
Former General Secretary of POMAK

DATE OF BIRTH: 27-Dec-1956.
PLACE OF BIRTH: Paphos, Cyprus.

CHILDREN: Kosta, Bachelor in Tourism. Thomas, Certificate in Engineering.
SCHOOLS/COLLEGE: Kalogries, Cyprus. Didacta, Cyprus, Sydney University.
QUALIFICATIONS: Private Secretary, English and Greek Language.
MEMBERSHIPS: Cyprus Community, Sydney.
HOBBIES AND INTERESTS: Reading, swimming.
PERSONAL PROFILE: Has been in sub Committee for 10 years and 6 years as Director, Vice President of Cyprus Community Sydney and also 6 years as General Secretary of POMAK.

CHRISTIAN TOOULI
Business Development Manager Australian Technology Park, Sydney

PLACE OF BIRTH: Australia Father from Limassol
SCHOOLS/COLLEGE: Flinders University and University of Sydney.
QUALIFICATIONS: PhD.
PERSONAL PROFILE: Christian Toouli is the Business Development Manager Australian Technology Park, Sydney. Previous to this, he worked with Schering-Plough Biopharma as a Bio Chemist.

PROFESSOR JAMES TOOULI
Professor of Surgery at Flinders University

DATE OF BIRTH: 29-Nov-1945
PLACE OF BIRTH: Limassol, Cyprus.
MARITAL STATUS: Married to Helen, Australian, Administration.
CHILDREN: Christian, Molecular Biologist. Sarah, Primary School Teacher.
SCHOOLS/COLLEGE: Monash University, Melbourne.
QUALIFICATIONS: B (Med), SCi, MBBS, PhD, FRACS.
MEMBERSHIPS: International Surgical Group, World Gastroenterology Association.
HONOURS/AWARDS: Past President IHPBA, President Elect Asia Pacific HPBA, Past President GESA.
HOBBIES AND INTERESTS: Tennis, downhill skiing, cricket, Australian Rules Football, Building design and architecture.
PERSONAL PROFILE: Professor of Surgery at Flinders University.

Australia

ANTONI TOUMBOUROU
Co-founder and President of Cyprus Community of Melbourne Victoria for 30 years

DATE OF BIRTH: 14-Mar-1928
PLACE OF BIRTH: Assia, Cyprus.
MARITAL STATUS: Married to Evfrosini Agrata, Greek.
CHILDREN: John Rita, Noel Suzanna, Diasounas Panayiotis, Katerina.
SCHOOLS/COLLEGE: Assia Elementary School.
HOBBIES AND INTERESTS: Gardening, Backgammon, Social Work.
PERSONAL PROFILE: Co-founder and President of Cyprus Community of Melbourne Victoria for 30 years. Co-founder of ESEKA Worldwide. Previously had 42 shops in Australia selling menswear. initiated after the coup and invasion and started fund raising sent to Cyprus seven hundred thousand Australian dollars, over 2 years.

JASON TOUMBOUROU
Active member of the Cypriot Community of Melbourne, Youth President

DATE OF BIRTH: 29-Oct-1975
PLACE OF BIRTH: Melbourne, Father from Assia.
MARITAL STATUS: Married to Miranda, Australian originates from (Neo Chorio Polis).
CHILDREN: Elizabeth.
SCHOOLS/COLLEGE: Ivanhoe Grammar.
QUALIFICATIONS: Basic Accounting, Clothing Production Level 4.
MEMBERSHIPS: Cyprus Community, Melbourne & Victoria, Committee Member.
HOBBIES AND INTERESTS: History, Aviation, Sport, Soccer, Tennis, Golf, Fishing.
PERSONAL PROFILE: Ran a Factory for 10 years, production of mens suits. Youth Committee President. (Cub Rank, Cadet Corps), 1994-1996. Active member of the Cypriot Community of Melbourne.

JIMMY TSINDOS
Restauranter. TV Chef

DATE OF BIRTH: 08-Dec-1938
PLACE OF BIRTH: Vasa, Koilaniou.
MARITAL STATUS: Married to Christina, Alamynos, Skala.
CHILDREN: Charilaos, Businessman. Andreas, Surveyor/Computer Analyst.
SCHOOLS/COLLEGE: Paphos Gymnasium, Pancyprian, Nicosia.
HOBBIES AND INTERESTS: fishing, soccer.
PERSONAL PROFILE: Restauranter. TV Chef. Member of the Committee of Cyprus Community of Melbourne, Victoria.

PROCOPIS NICHOLAS VANEZIS
Cyprus High Commissioner in Australia 1982-88. Has written and published various books about Cyprus

DATE OF BIRTH: 01-Dec-1928
PLACE OF BIRTH: Rizokarpasso.
MARITAL STATUS: Married to Sotira (Lula), Cypriot, Teacher.
CHILDREN: Maria, Teacher, BSc, Dip Ed, TEFL. Nicholas, Chartered Accountant B Bus. M Ec. A. C. A. Andreas, Business Director B Ec.
SCHOOLS/COLLEGE: Paphos Greek Gymnasium. London University.
QUALIFICATIONS: BA Dip Ed EFL MA PhD.
HOBBIES AND INTERESTS: Politics, reading, writing, football, gardening.
PERSONAL PROFILE: Lectured in Cyprus at Pancyprian Gymnasium and the Technical Institute, Cyprus. Appointed Cultural Attache at Cyprus High Commission. London. 1963. Ministry of Foreign Affairs, Nicosia, served as Deputy Director. General and Chief Inspector of Embassies until 1982. transferred to Canberra, as Cyprus High Commissioner 1982-88. Has written and published various books about Cyprus.

Australia

CONSTANCE VASILI
Pharmacist

DATE OF BIRTH: 25-Aug-1982
PLACE OF BIRTH: Sydney parents from Troulli and Arsos.
MARITAL STATUS: Single.
SCHOOLS/COLLEGE: St Spyridon College. University of Sydney.
QUALIFICATIONS: BA in Pharmacy.
MEMBERSHIPS: Pharmaceutical Guild and Pharmaceutical Society.
HOBBIES AND INTERESTS: Sport and dancing.
PERSONAL PROFILE: Constance Vasili is a Pharmacist.

GEORGE VASILI
Director of Global/Galaxy Foods Property Ltd

DATE OF BIRTH: 06-Jun-1981
PLACE OF BIRTH: Sydney Father from Troulli and Arsos.
MARITAL STATUS: Single.
SCHOOLS/COLLEGE: St Spyridon College. University of New South Wales.
QUALIFICATIONS: Bachelor of Commerce -International Business.
HOBBIES AND INTERESTS: Soccer and Rugby.
PERSONAL PROFILE: Director of Global/Galaxy Foods Property Ltd a food supply and property company.

NICK VASILI
Retired Dentist/Businessman/Former President and member of the Cyprus Hellenic Club

DATE OF BIRTH: 28-Jan-1946
PLACE OF BIRTH: Troulli.
MARITAL STATUS: Married to Rea, Arsos.
CHILDREN: Despina, Pharmacist. George, Company Director. Constance, Pharmacist.
SCHOOLS/COLLEGE: Cleveland St Boys High. Sydney University.
QUALIFICATIONS: Dentist BDSc.
MEMBERSHIPS: Dental Association of New South Wales.
HOBBIES AND INTERESTS: Community Work.

PERSONAL PROFILE: Retired Dentist with own practice in Sydney. Director of family business involved in food distribution. Former president and member of the Cyprus Hellenic Club. Member of the Philoptocho of the Archdiosese and ESFKA.

GEORGE VASSILIOU
Managing Director HHO Multimedia in Australia

PLACE OF BIRTH: Parents from Cyprus
SCHOOLS/COLLEGE: University of East London.
PERSONAL PROFILE: George Vassiliou is the Managing Director HHO Multimedia in Australia based in Sydney it is a independant record company whose Head office is in the UK.

CHRISTOS VIOLARIS
Ex Treasurer of the Cyprus Community Group of Melbourne, Victoria

DATE OF BIRTH: 13-Oct-1941
PLACE OF BIRTH: Agros, Limassol, Cyprus.
SCHOOLS/COLLEGE: Agros High School.
HOBBIES AND INTERESTS: Politics, Community Work.
PERSONAL PROFILE: Treasurer of the Cyprus Community Group of Melbourne, Victoria for over 10 years. Co-ordinating Committee of Justice for Cyprus.

CHRISTOS VOYIAS
Banking

DATE OF BIRTH: 05-Feb-1970
PLACE OF BIRTH: Zambia, Africa, Parents from Pedhoulas, Cyprus.
MARITAL STATUS: Married to Derna, Home Duties.
CHILDREN: Andreas.
SCHOOLS/COLLEGE: English School, Nicosia, Cyprus. Salford University UK, Melbourne University.
QUALIFICATIONS: Bachelor Economics (Hons), MBA, Diploma in Financial Planning.
MEMBERSHIPS: Rotary.
HOBBIES AND INTERESTS: Soccer, Golf.

PERSONAL PROFILE: Bank of Cyprus, Senior Relationship Manager.

NICK XENOPHON
Elected to the Australian Senate

PLACE OF BIRTH: born 1959 Adelaide. Father from Cyprus **SCHOOLS/COLLEGE:** University of Adelaide. **QUALIFICATIONS:** Bachelor of Laws. **PERSONAL PROFILE:** Nick Xenophon was Elected to the Australian Senate in the 2007 federal election. He originally established and became principal of his own law firm Xenophon and Co.

HARRY XYDAS
Recipient Business Excellence Award in 2006

PLACE OF BIRTH: Cyprus.
QUALIFICATIONS: MSc FAIB.
MEMBERSHIPS: Fellow of the Australian Institute of Building for which he served as Councillor, Executive Board Member and President of WA Chapter.
HONOURS/AWARDS: His Company recipient Business Excellence Award in 2006.
PERSONAL PROFILE: Harry Xydas Founded Doric In 1989 they are a Construction and Engineering Group in Australia. Projects they have been involved in are Joondalup Shopping Centre, Edith Cowan University Library and Pearl room Entertainment Complex.

ROULLA YIACOUMI
One of the names behind Bran a weekly podcast company in Australia

PLACE OF BIRTH: Australia Father from Cyprus **PERSONAL PROFILE:** One of the names behind Bran a weekly podcast company in Australia that chat about the big news that have taken place in Australia and internationally each week. Roulla originally worked for Australia personal computer magazine.

MICHAEL YIALLOUROS
President of Cyprus Greek Orthodox Community, Apostolos Andreas Sunshine

DATE OF BIRTH: 01-Jul-1949 **PLACE OF BIRTH:** Geri, Nicosia. **MARITAL STATUS:** Married to Athena, Greek Cypriot. **CHILDREN:** Con, Engineering. Elpida, Advertising. **SCHOOLS/COLLEGE:** Pancyprian Gymnasium. **HOBBIES AND INTERESTS:** Gardening.
PERSONAL PROFILE: President of Cyprus Greek Orthodox Community, Apostolos Andreas Sunshine.

MILTIADES YIANGOU
Principal of St Euphemia College in Sydney, Australia

DATE OF BIRTH: 26-Feb-1943 **PLACE OF BIRTH:** Lemona. **MARITAL STATUS:** Married to Ioanna Charambous, Greek Cypriot, Teacher. **CHILDREN:** Con, Hairdresser. Helen, Fashion Designer. **SCHOOLS/COLLEGE:** Primary Education, Lemona Paphos, High School, Polemi Paphos. Armidale CAE, Sydney University.
QUALIFICATIONS: Graduate Diploma in Multicultural Education, BA.
MEMBERSHIPS: NSW Independent Education Union.
HOBBIES AND INTERESTS: Swimming, Bushwalking.
PERSONAL PROFILE: Teacher in Cyprus for 12 years and served in the National Guard. In 1989 he was interviewed and selected to become founding Principal of St Euphemia College in Sydney, which he still runs to date. St Euphemia College is under the auspices of the Greek Orthodox Archdiocese of Australia. He started the school with 29 students K-Y3 and now developed to a K_12 school with 700 students.

Australia

PANAYIOTIS YIANNOUDES
Entertainment/Business owner of 10 Cinemas in Australia

DATE OF BIRTH: 02-Feb-1935
PLACE OF BIRTH: Vouni.
MARITAL STATUS: Married to Katina Katopodis, Greek.
CHILDREN: Marilyn, Scientist in Immunology. Michael, Electronics/Cinema Manager. Irena, Teacher.
SCHOOLS/COLLEGE: Laniton Gymnasium, Limassol, Cyprus. Melbourne Taylors College.
HONOURS/AWARDS: Honoured in 1990, The Hellenic Award for Parikiaki Drastiriotita.
HOBBIES AND INTERESTS: Photography, travelling, gardening, camping.
PERSONAL PROFILE: From 1957 imported Greek Films in Australia, and after 1958 was a partner in Cosmopolitan Motion Pictures and then a partner in LYRA Films. During this time was owner of 10 cinemas around Australia. In 1985 created a Video Company with the name VideoStar releasing mostly Greek Films. Now his store has more than a 1000 Greek Films, and also has the biggest collection of advertising of Greek and American Films, historical archives for the Greek and Cypriot Communities in Australia.

ANGELICA YIANOULATOS
Active Member in the Cypriot Young Professionals

DATE OF BIRTH: 12-Jan-1987
PLACE OF BIRTH: Australia Grandparents born in Paphos.
MARITAL STATUS: Single.
SCHOOLS/COLLEGE: St John's Greek Orthodox College, Lowther Hall Anglican Grammar School. La Trobe University.
QUALIFICATIONS: Undergraduate of Bachelor Laws and Bachelor Arts. Double major in Greek language and History.
MEMBERSHIPS: Cyprus Community of Melbourne and Victoria, NUGAS.
HONOURS/AWARDS: Excellence in Philosophy Award.
HOBBIES AND INTERESTS: Greek history and Politics.
PERSONAL PROFILE: Active Member in the Cypriot Young Professionals.

DR MICHAEL ZACHARIA
Plastic Surgeon

DATE OF BIRTH: 05-Mar-1964
PLACE OF BIRTH: Adelaide parents from Aradippou.
SCHOOLS/COLLEGE: Pultney Grammar School. St Peters College, University of Adelaide and Adelaide Medical School.
QUALIFICATIONS: MBBS FRACS.
MEMBERSHIPS: Australasian Academy of Facial Plastic and Reconstructive Surgery and American Academy of Facial Plastic and Reconstructive Surgery.
HOBBIES AND INTERESTS: Golf, tennis, football, languages and wine.
PERSONAL PROFILE: Michael Zacharia is a Consultant ENT/Head & Neck/Facial Plastic Surgeon at Bondi Junction Private Hospital.

LAGIS ZAVROS
Chief Operating Officer/Director

DATE OF BIRTH: 15-Jun-1956
PLACE OF BIRTH: Nicosia, Cyprus.
MARITAL STATUS: Married to Theophano, Australian (Cypriot born), Teaches Greek.
CHILDREN: Alexios, Orios.
SCHOOLS/COLLEGE: Holloway School, Islington UK. Edith Cowan University (WA).
QUALIFICATIONS: Bachelor of Business (partial).
HONOURS/AWARDS: Worldwide Partner Advisory Council for Microsoft.
HOBBIES AND INTERESTS: Family, Property Investment, Current Affairs, Travel, Photography, Film-Making and Football.
PERSONAL PROFILE: Senior Executive involved in companies for the past 30 years. Involved in numerous community projects but in particular Produced and Directed a six part television series on Montessori Education. Sits on the Microsoft Worldwide ISV Advisory Council. The program is an exclusive invitation only membership to help Microsoft gather and disseminate Partner feedback on strategic Microsoft products, field engagement, programs and services. COO of WebSpy Ltd. and a Non-Executive Director of ICONIQ Pty Ltd.

MICHAEL ZAVROS

Artist 2004, 2005 and 2006 he was a finalist in Australia's most prestigious award for Portraiture Art

DATE OF BIRTH: 20-Aug-1974
PLACE OF BIRTH: Brisbane Australia, Grandparents lived in Agros, Cyprus.
MARITAL STATUS: Married to Alison Kubler, Australian, Visual Art Curator and Academic.
CHILDREN: Phoebe Zavros.
SCHOOLS/COLLEGE: Coombabh State High School. Queensland College of Art, Griffith university.
QUALIFICATIONS: Bachelor of Visual Art in Fine Art.
HONOURS/AWARDS: Primavera Collex Art Award 2004, through the Museum of Contemporary Art in Sydney. 2005 Robert jacks Drawing Prize through Bendigo Art Gallery, Victoria. In 2004, 2005 and 2006 he was a finalist in Australia's most prestigious award for portraiture The Art.
PERSONAL PROFILE: Michael Zavros' work has been included in numerous significant Australian and international exhibitions. Group exhibitions include Primavera 200 at the Museum of Contemporary Art, Sydney, and various others. Zavros' work is held in numerous international public and private collections. In 2001 he was awarded the Australia Council Visual Arts/Craft Fund, Milan Residency and more recently the VACF Barcelona Residency in 2005.

THEOPHANO ZAVROS

Co-Producer and Narrator of the six part television documentary 'Montessori an Inspiration

DATE OF BIRTH: 29-Jul-1955
PLACE OF BIRTH: Famagusta, Cyprus.
MARITAL STATUS: Married to Lagis Zavros, Australian (Cypriot born), Director, COO.
CHILDREN: Alexios, Marketing Manager. Orios, Auto Electrician.
SCHOOLS/COLLEGE: Bow Brook School. Hackney and Stoke Newington.
QUALIFICATIONS: Graduated from College.
HONOURS/AWARDS: Honorary Life Member of the Montessori School.
HOBBIES AND INTERESTS: Greek Music, Travel, Documentary Film-maker, Community work with elderly.
PERSONAL PROFILE: Cypriot Radio Producer 1985-2005, Teacher of the Greek Language to non-Greek students. Co-Producer and Narrator of the six part television documentary 'Montessori an Inspiration'. Co-Author of the poetry book 'Anemones', published in Australia.

Entrants in Greek Cypriots Worldwide have been nominated for their achievements and contributions to their community.

It is free to nominate someone, or yourself, who deserves to be in the book, just send in the name, contact address, telephone number and email to:

Greek Cypriots Worldwide
111 St Thomas's Road
London N4 2QJ
Telephone 0044 207503 3498
cypriotwhoswho@aol.com
www.greekcypriotsworldwide.com

PROFESSOR PANAYIOTIS AFXENTIOU
Professor of Economics University of Calgary

PLACE OF BIRTH: Cyprus.
PERSONAL PROFILE: Panayiotis Afxentiou is a Professor of Economics at the University of Calgary.

ANNA M. AGATHANGELOU
Associate Professor, York University, Toronto Ontario

PLACE OF BIRTH: Nicosia, Cyprus
MARITAL STATUS: Married to Dr. Kyle D. Killian, Professor and Family Therapist.
CHILDREN: Michael Lawrence, Aleksi Christos.
SCHOOLS/COLLEGE: Miami University, USA, Eastern Kentucky University, USA, Syracuse University, USA.
QUALIFICATIONS: PhD MA International Relations, MA Political Science, BS.
MEMBERSHIPS: American Political Science Association, National Women's Studies Association.
HONOURS/AWARDS: Who's Who Among America's Teachers, Tae Hwan Kwak Award in recognition for Outstanding Scholarship in International Relations.
HOBBIES AND INTERESTS: Studying Ancient Greek and Chinese philosophy, writing, poetry, and traveling.
PERSONAL PROFILE: Associate Professor, York University, Toronto Ontario, Author of the book 'The Global Political Economy of Sex: Desire, Violence and Insecurity in the Mediterranean National State's, and many articles.

CHRISTINE AMYGDALIDIS
Treasurer of The Cypriot Federation Canada/2002 Ontario Volunteer Service Award

DATE OF BIRTH: 26-Mar-1956
PLACE OF BIRTH: Nicosia.
MARITAL STATUS: Married to Stefano, Greece.
CHILDREN: Nicole, Stefani.
SCHOOLS/COLLEGE: Grammar School Nicosia.
QUALIFICATIONS: Graduation Diploma from Grammar School.
HONOURS/AWARDS: 2002 Ontario Volunteer Service Award.
HOBBIES AND INTERESTS: Reading, Dancing and Theatre.

PERSONAL PROFILE: Christine Amygdalides is the Treasurer of the Toronto Cypriot and of the Cypriot Federation of Canada.

EVE KOKKINOU ANDREOU
Nepomak Canada Secretary 03/05

DATE OF BIRTH: 31-Dec-1979
PLACE OF BIRTH: Canada.
MARITAL STATUS: Married to Nicholas, English, I. T. Professional.
SCHOOLS/COLLEGE: Centennial College.
QUALIFICATIONS: Diploma in Massage Therapy.
HOBBIES AND INTERESTS: Cypriot Dancing, Greek Dancing.
PERSONAL PROFILE: Eve was the Nepomak Canada Secretary 03/05 Massage Therapist by occupation.

DERMOT ANTONIADES
Scientist based at The University of Quebec specialising on Artic Research

PLACE OF BIRTH: Parents from Cyprus
SCHOOLS/COLLEGE: University of Toronto.
QUALIFICATIONS: PhD.
PERSONAL PROFILE: Dermot Antoniades is a Scientist based at The University of Quebec specialising on Artic Research.

MARGARITA LAM ANTONIADES
Family Physician at St Michaels Hospital in Toronto

DATE OF BIRTH: 02-Feb-1975
PLACE OF BIRTH: Toronto Father is from Potamos.
MARITAL STATUS: Married to Vincent Lam, Canadian of Chinese descent, Emergency Physician and Author.
CHILDREN: Theodore, Alexander.
SCHOOLS/COLLEGE: Acropolis Lyceum, Nicosia, Cyprus. University of Toronto.
QUALIFICATIONS: BSc. MD.
MEMBERSHIPS: Canadian College of Family Physicians. College of Physicians and Surgeons of Ontario.
HONOURS/AWARDS: Women's Health Scholarship

from the Ontario College of Family Physicians to pursue a fellowship in primary care for women with HIV.
HOBBIES AND INTERESTS: Healthcare for underprivileged populations, medical education and dance.
PERSONAL PROFILE: Margarita Antoniades works as a Family Physician at St Michaels Hospital in Toronto Canada. Her clinic serves an inner city population with a large proportion of new immigrants and persons with severe mental illness. They are part of a teaching hospital so she also enjoys teaching medical students and residents.

PROFESSOR ANDREAS ANTONIOU
Professor Emeritus at the University of Victoria

DATE OF BIRTH: 03-Mar-1938
PLACE OF BIRTH: Yerolakkos.
MARITAL STATUS: Married to Lynne Barrett, Canadian, Secretary.
CHILDREN: Tony, Engineer. Dave, Labour Relations Manager. Dino, Engineer. Helena, Interior Designer.
SCHOOLS/COLLEGE: Battersea College of Technology, University of London.
QUALIFICATIONS: BSc PhD.
MEMBERSHIPS: Fellow IEE.
HONOURS/AWARDS: Doctor Honoris Causa Metsovia, National Technical University of Athens, Greece 2002. IEEE Circuits and Systems Society Technical Achievement Award 2005.
HOBBIES AND INTERESTS: Classical Music, Cooking, Acoustic Guitar and Gardening.
PERSONAL PROFILE: Andreas Antoniou is a Professor Emeritus at the University of Victoria in the Department of Electrical and Computer Engineeringand is an Author of books and papers on associated subjects.

DR JOHN ANTONIOU
Gold Medal in Surgery for 2004 by the Royal College of Physicians and Surgeons of Canada

PLACE OF BIRTH: Parents from Cyprus
SCHOOLS/COLLEGE: Mcgill University.
QUALIFICATIONS: PhD.
HONOURS/AWARDS: Gold Medal in Surgery for 2004 by the Royal College of Physicians and Surgeons of Canada.
PERSONAL PROFILE: John Antoniou is an Assistant

Professor in the Division of Orthopaedic Surgery at Mcgill University and a Project Director in the Orthopaedic Research Lab at the Jewish General Hospital in Montreal.

MIKE ARGYRIDES
Organiser of the Cyprus Wine Festival in Toronto

DATE OF BIRTH: 02-Aug-1933
PLACE OF BIRTH: Prodromos.
MARITAL STATUS: Married to Androulla, Prodromos.
CHILDREN: Themis, Immigration. Julia, Law.
SCHOOLS/COLLEGE: Prodromos and Petula Elementary and Pedhoulas Gymnasium.
PERSONAL PROFILE: Mike Argyrides is a Restauranter and organiser of the Cyprus Wine Festival in Toronto and a member of the Cypriot community in Toronto.

STEPHANIE ATALIOTIS
Crowned Miss Vancouver 2008 in Canada

DATE OF BIRTH: 10-Jun-1987
PLACE OF BIRTH: Cyprus.
MARITAL STATUS: Single.
SCHOOLS/COLLEGE: Balmoral Hall School.
PERSONAL PROFILE: Stephanie is a Beauty Queen crowned Miss Vancouver 2008 in Canada.

KATHERINE AVRAAM
Chiropodist

PLACE OF BIRTH: Canada Parents from Cyprus.
PERSONAL PROFILE: Katherine Avraam is a Chiropodist in Toronto, Canada.

Canada

HELEN BUTTIGIEG
Television Host on HGTV in Canada

PLACE OF BIRTH: Limassol
MARITAL STATUS: Married.
CHILDREN: Two Daughters.
SCHOOLS/COLLEGE: Seneca College.
QUALIFICATIONS: Diploma in Radio and TV broadcasting.
PERSONAL PROFILE: Helen Buttiegieg is a Professional Organiser, Life Coach, Television Host and President of Weorganiseu, a company she founded. She hosted three seasons of the show 'Neat' on HGTV Canada and appeared as a guest on several Shows. Helen is a regular contributor to the magazines Home Digest and Home and Decor.

DR SAVVAS CHAMBERLAIN
Executive Chairman and Founder of Dalsa a world leader in Digital Imaging components and specialized semiconductor manufacturing

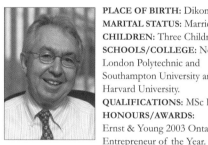

PLACE OF BIRTH: Dikomo
MARITAL STATUS: Married.
CHILDREN: Three Children.
SCHOOLS/COLLEGE: North London Polytechnic and Southampton University and Harvard University.
QUALIFICATIONS: MSc PhD.
HONOURS/AWARDS: Ernst & Young 2003 Ontario Entrepreneur of the Year.
Premiers Catalyst Award for Lifetime Achievement in innovation from Ontario Premier and Minister of Research and Innovation Dalton Mcguinty.
HOBBIES AND INTERESTS: Walking, hiking, tennis, music, books reading, live theatre and opera.
PERSONAL PROFILE: Dr Savvas Chamberlain is the Executive Chairman and Founder of Dalsa a world leader in Digital Imaging components and specialized semiconductor manufacturing. Dr Chamberlain was a Professor in the Electrical and Computer Engineering Department of the University of Waterloo. He continues his association with the University as a Distinguished Professor Emeritus.

ATHINA CHARALAMBIDES
Vice President of the Cypriot Federation Canada

PLACE OF BIRTH: Nicosia in 1971
MARITAL STATUS: Married to Andreas, Kathikas.
CHILDREN: Simon, Christina.
SCHOOLS/COLLEGE: American Academy Nicosia. School of Nursing, Nicosia, Humber College Toronto.
PERSONAL PROFILE: Athina Charalambides is Executive Vice President of the Cypriot Federation, Canada. Vice President of the World Federation of Overseas Cypriots.

CHARALAMBOS CHARALAMBOUS
Professor in the Department of Electrical and Computer Engineering at Mcgill University

PLACE OF BIRTH: Paphos
SCHOOLS/COLLEGE: Old Dominion University of Virginia.
QUALIFICATIONS: BS MS. PhD.
HONOURS/AWARDS: In 2001 Charalambos received the Premiers Research Excellence Award of the Ontario Province of Canada.
PERSONAL PROFILE: Charalambos Charalambous served as a Associate Professor at the University of Ottawa in the School of Information Technology and Engineering and as an Adjunct Professor in the Department of Electrical and Computer Engineering at Mcgill University Canada. He is now based in Cyprus.

DEMETRIOS CHIMONIDES
First team player with Pezoporikos Soccer Club in Cyprus now the coach of Cypriot Football team Kitchener in Canada

DATE OF BIRTH: 19-Jan-1938
PLACE OF BIRTH: Larnaca.
MARITAL STATUS: Married to Mary.
CHILDREN: Chris.
SCHOOLS/COLLEGE: Terra Santa High School.
HOBBIES AND INTERESTS: Soccer.
PERSONAL PROFILE: Demetrios Chimonides was a

Canada

first team player with Pezoporikos Soccer Club in Cyprus. He is also the coach of Cypriot football team Kitchener. Demetrios is the importer of Loel Wines and Spirits.

JOHN CHRISTODOULOU
Chairman and Chief Executive Officer of the Guardian Capital Group Ltd a Public listed Financial Services Company in Canada

DATE OF BIRTH: 19-Dec-1933.
PLACE OF BIRTH: Cyprus.
PERSONAL PROFILE: John Christodoulou is the Chairman and Chief Executive Officer of the Guardian Capital Group Ltd a public listed Financial Services Company employing 180 people based in Canada. John is also a Professor at the Graduate Schools of Business Administration Queens University and York University.

NICHOLAS CHRISTOU
Physician at the Royal Victoria Hospital in Montreal

PLACE OF BIRTH: Cyprus
PERSONAL PROFILE: Nicholas Christou is a Physician at the Royal Victoria Hospital in Montreal.

THE HONOURABLE TONY CLEMENT (BORN PANAYI)
Minister of Health Canada

DATE OF BIRTH: 27-Jan-1961
PLACE OF BIRTH: Manchester UK. Father from Liopetri Mother Canadian.
MARITAL STATUS: Married to Lynne Golding.
CHILDREN: Three Children.
SCHOOLS/COLLEGE: University of Toronto.
QUALIFICATIONS: BA.
PERSONAL PROFILE: Tony Clement is Canada's Minister of Health and Long Term Care. He initiated primary care reform, created the successful Telehealth system, oversaw the expansion of the hospital system and provided leadership for the country during SARS.

JOHN CLERIDES
Honoured in the Canadian Who's Who as the top buyer for private stores

PLACE OF BIRTH: Cyprus
PERSONAL PROFILE: John Clerides is a feature writer in the publication outstanding food and wine events calendar. He is also the owner of a Wine Cellar in Vancouver Canada.

STEPHANOS CONSTANTINIDES
Director of the Centre for Hellenic Studies and Research(Canada)

PLACE OF BIRTH: Cyprus.
SCHOOLS/COLLEGE: University of Athens and Paris University Sorbonne.
QUALIFICATIONS: BA. MA. and PhD.
PERSONAL PROFILE: Dr Stephanos Constantinides teaches Political Science at the University du Quebec a Montreal. He is the author of several books and articles on ethnic relations and also the director of the Centre for Hellenic Studies and Research (Canada).

ELEFTHERIOS DIAMANDIS
Professor and Head, Division of Clinical Biochemistry, Department of Laboratory Medicine and Pathobiology Faculty of Medicine, University of Toronto, Ontario.

DATE OF BIRTH: 08-Oct-1952
PLACE OF BIRTH: Limassol.
SCHOOLS/COLLEGE: Elementary and High School Limassol. University of Athens and University of Toronto.
QUALIFICATIONS: BSc PhD MD.
HONOURS/AWARDS: Miriam Reiner Award from the Capital Section of the American Association for Clinical Chemistry (December 2001).
PERSONAL PROFILE: Professor and Head, Division of Clinical Biochemistry, Department of Laboratory Medicine and Pathobiology Faculty of Medicine, University of Toronto, Ontario, Canada. Biochemist-in-Chief, Department of Clinical Biochemistry, University Health Network and Toronto Medical Laboratories, Toronto, Ontario, Canada. Head, Section of Clinical Biochemistry, Department of Pathology and Laboratory Medicine Mount Sinai Hospital, Toronto, Ontario, Canada

Canada

GEORGE ELEFTHERIADES
Professor in Electrical and Computer Engineering at the University of Toronto

PLACE OF BIRTH: Cyprus
SCHOOLS/COLLEGE: Swiss Federal Institute of Technology, University of Athens and University of Michigan.
QUALIFICATIONS: Phd and MSEE.
HONOURS/AWARDS: Ontario Premiers Research Excellence Award 2001.
PERSONAL PROFILE: George Eleftheriades is a Professor in the Department of Electrical and Computer Engineering at the University of Toronto.

NICHOLAS ANDREAS ELIADES
Businessman

DATE OF BIRTH: 29-Mar-1973
PLACE OF BIRTH: London. Parents from Pano Lefkara.
MARITAL STATUS: Single.
SCHOOLS/COLLEGE: Southgate School, Sussex University.
QUALIFICATIONS: BA Honours Economics with Economics, History, five years management.
HOBBIES AND INTERESTS: Football and table tennis.
PERSONAL PROFILE: Owner of ANC Worldwide Ltd "Advertising New Concepts" upmarketing in Canada.

CHARALAMBOS ELLES
Priest serving the Greek Community of Canada and has also formed a Byzantine School of Music

DATE OF BIRTH: 23-Aug-1936
PLACE OF BIRTH: Diorios.
MARITAL STATUS: Married to Kalliope, Avarita, Paphos.
CHILDREN: Kyriacos, Costa, Tryphon, Maria.
SCHOOLS/COLLEGE: Teacher's Training College Nicosia.
HOBBIES AND INTERESTS: Byzantine Music.
PERSONAL PROFILE: Charalambos Elles Teacher in Cyprus now a Priest serving the Greek Community of Canada and has also formed a Byzantine School of Music.

KYRIACOS ELLES
President of the Cypriot Federation of Canada

DATE OF BIRTH: 30-Aug-1960
PLACE OF BIRTH: Nicosia.
MARITAL STATUS: Married to Litsa, Cypriot.
CHILDREN: Marina, Kalia, Michael.
SCHOOLS/COLLEGE: University of Toronto and York University.
QUALIFICATIONS: BSc MSc MBA.
HOBBIES AND INTERESTS: Golf, Travel and Soccer.
PERSONAL PROFILE: Kyriacos Elles is the President of the Cypriot Federation of Canada and Chief Representative of the Bank of Cyprus in Canada and also former Chairman of the Cyprus Canada Chamber of Commerce.

PENELOPE EROTOKRITOU
Consul General of the Republic of Cyprus in Toronto

DATE OF BIRTH: 30-Oct-1974
PLACE OF BIRTH: Cyprus.
MARITAL STATUS: Married to Dr. Vaios Liapis, Professor of Classics.
SCHOOLS/COLLEGE: University of Cyprus, University of London.
QUALIFICATIONS: Holder of two graduate degrees from University of Cyprus one in Turkish Studies and one in Byzantine and modern Greek Literature.
PERSONAL PROFILE: Ms. Erotokritou joined the Diplomatic Service of the Ministry of Foreign Affairs of the Republic of Cyprus in August 1997. From 1997 to 2002 she served in the Cyprus Question Division and the Political Division of the Ministry of Foreign Affairs. In 2002 she was posted at the Permanent Mission of the Republic of Cyprus to the United Nations in New York, where she primarily focused on human rights issues. Since 2006 she is the Consul General of the Republic of Cyprus In Toronto.

STELIOS GEORGIADES
Academic Researcher in Child Psychiatry and Psychology

DATE OF BIRTH: 13-Nov-1975
PLACE OF BIRTH: Nicosia.
MARITAL STATUS: Married to Kathy Georgiades. Greek Canadian. Professor of Psychiatry.
SCHOOLS/COLLEGE: Palouriotissa Lyceum. Brock University (Canada) & University of Oregon (USA).
QUALIFICATIONS: BA MA in Psychology.
MEMBERSHIPS: Numerous psychological Associations, Numerous non-profit Organiziations.
HONOURS/AWARDS: Best Teenager Basketball Athlete in Cyprus. Awarded by the Cyprus Basketball Association in 1991.
HOBBIES AND INTERESTS: Poetry, Music, Non-Partisan Politics related to Cyprus.
PERSONAL PROFILE: Academic researcher with the Department of Psychiatry and Behavioural Neurosciences at McMaster University. He Serves as the Vice President of the Canadian Justice for Cyprus Committee and the Cypriot Community of Mississauga and District.

TASOS GEORGIADES
Assistant Professor in the Department of Mechanical Engineering, Dalhousie University, Halifax, Nova Scotia, Canada

PLACE OF BIRTH: Cyprus
SCHOOLS/COLLEGE: Technical University of Nova Scotia, Halifax and Dalhousie University Halifax Nova Scotia.
QUALIFICATIONS: BEng MSC and PhD.
PERSONAL PROFILE: Tasos served as an Assistant Professor (promoted to Associate Professor in year 2007 in the Department of Mechanical Engineering, Dalhousie University, Halifax, Nova Scotia, Canada. His research activities are primarily focused on fabrication, processing, testing, characterization, modeling and design of composite and smart composite materials and structures. He has over 40 publications in international peer-reviewed journals and conference proceedings.

COSTAS GEORGIADIS
Lecturer in Philosophy at Mcmaster University, Hamilton

PLACE OF BIRTH: Born 1929 Alexandria, Egypt. Father from Lapithos.
MARITAL STATUS: Married to Tania.
CHILDREN: Alex, Nina.
SCHOOLS/COLLEGE: Averofion Gymnasium in egypt. Athens, Warsaw and London Universities.
QUALIFICATIONS: MA PhD.
PERSONAL PROFILE: Costas Georgiadis taught Philosophy at Mcmaster University, Hamilton, Canada. Is also involved in the popularisation among Greek Canadians of Ancient and Modern Greek Culture especially Philosophy and Poetry.

LEN GEORGIOU
Board member of the Canadian Federal Liberal Political Party

DATE OF BIRTH: 25-May-1965
PLACE OF BIRTH: Nicosia Cyprus.
MARITAL STATUS: Married to Eleni Georgiou, Cypriot, Administers Housing Programs for The Region of Waterloo, Ontario, Canada.
CHILDREN: Maria Georgiou, Andreas Renee Georgiou.
SCHOOLS/COLLEGE: London Business School. University of Toronto Laurier University.
QUALIFICATIONS: BBA. Executive Leadership Management Program, Advanced Network Engineering Program, Professional Sales and Marketing.
MEMBERSHIPS: Federal Liberal Party--Board of Directors, Cypriot Community of Waterloo Region, Canada, Past President, PSEKA Canada.
HONOURS/AWARDS: CEO's Leadership Circle- Nortel Networks, Circle of Excellence - Nortel Networks. Frank Craft Citizenship Awards.
HOBBIES AND INTERESTS: Greek Music, Soccer, Golf, Travel.
PERSONAL PROFILE: 1st President PSEKA Canada, Master of Ceremonies, Dance Instructor of Cypriot Dance Group, Captain of Cyprus Brotherhood Soccer Team, Vice President, Global Sales at RL Solutions. Board member of the Canadian Federal Liberal Political Party.

Canada

PROFESSOR GEORGE HADJISOPHOCLEOUS
Professor and Vice President of the Cypriot Community of Ottawa

DATE OF BIRTH: 07-Feb-1956
PLACE OF BIRTH: Tsada.
MARITAL STATUS: Married to Sylvie Robidoux, Canadian, Computer Consultant.
CHILDREN: Christine, Alex, Mark, All Students.
SCHOOLS/COLLEGE: B Gymnasium Paphos. University of New Brunswick.
QUALIFICATIONS: BSc MSc PhD Mechanical Engineering.
MEMBERSHIPS: Vice President of the Cypriot Community of Ottawa, Vice President of the Parnassos Hellenic Cultural Society of Ottawa.
HOBBIES AND INTERESTS: Soccer, travel, reading, sailing.
PERSONAL PROFILE: Professor Hadjisophocleous leads a team of 20 students working in a number of areas including Fire Risk Analysis, Smoke Movement, Design Fires and Modelling. Prior to moving to Carleton University he was a Senior Research Officer at the Fire Risk Management Program of the National Research Council of Canada. He is the author of over 150 publications in the areas of fire research and fire risk assessment.

NICK HADJIYIANNIS
Assists Youth with disabilities achieve employment success and an active member of the Cypriot Community of Toronto

DATE OF BIRTH: 18-Mar-1966
PLACE OF BIRTH: Toronto Parents from Kathikas.
MARITAL STATUS: Married to Maria, Canadian Parents from Paphos.
CHILDREN: Georgina, Pavlina.
SCHOOLS/COLLEGE: Private Engineering College.
HOBBIES AND INTERESTS: Golf.
PERSONAL PROFILE: Nick Hadjiyiannis works for the Government with a non profit organisation assisting Youth with Disabilities achieve employment success. Nick is a committee member of the Cypriot Community of Toronto.

KYRIACOS HATZIPANAYIS
Vice President of the Cypriot Federation of Canada

DATE OF BIRTH: 24-Dec-1950
PLACE OF BIRTH: Mesoyi.
MARITAL STATUS: Married to Katherine, Canadian of Greek origin, Sales Rep.
CHILDREN: Constantine, Banking. Angelique, Health.
SCHOOLS/COLLEGE: 2nd High School of Paphos. University of Manitoba.
QUALIFICATIONS: BA MA.
MEMBERSHIPS: Manitoba Aerospace Association.
HONOURS/AWARDS: Deputy Ministers Award for Performance Measurement.
HOBBIES AND INTERESTS: Soccer, fishing.
PERSONAL PROFILE: Kyriacos Hatzipanayis is the Vice President of the Cypriot Federation of Canada. He is also the President of the Cypriot Association of Manitoba. Previously, Kyriacos was the trading commissioner with the Winnipeg Regional Office and is presently responsible for Aerospace & Defence, Building products and Construction, Enviromental industries and Service industries and Capital projects.

JANNETT IOANNIDES
Regional Director Helms Briscoe

PLACE OF BIRTH: Cyprus.
HOBBIES AND INTERESTS: Cooking and wine enthusiast.
PERSONAL PROFILE: Jannett Ioannides is a Regional Director in Helms Briscoe, a business advisory company.

CHRIS IOANNOU
Director of the Cypriot Community of Toronto and General Secretary and President of the Educational Committee

DATE OF BIRTH: 27-Aug-1953.
PLACE OF BIRTH: Nicosia.
MARITAL STATUS: Married to Angela, Nicosia.
CHILDREN: Leon, Constandia.
SCHOOLS/COLLEGE: Ryverson university.
QUALIFICATIONS: Business administration.
HOBBIES AND INTERESTS: Fishing.
PERSONAL PROFILE: Chris Ioannou is a Director of franchising Coffee time. He is the Director of the Cypriot Community of Toronto and General Secretary and President of the Educational Committee.

Canada

DEMOS IORDANOUS
President of Fredas Originals Inc

DATE OF BIRTH: 23-Sep-1951
PLACE OF BIRTH: Limassol, Cyprus.
MARITAL STATUS: Married to Freda Iordanous, Limassol, Cyrpus, Self-Employeed, Cypriot, Businesswoman.
CHILDREN: Paulina, Both University graduates now self employed. Elaine.
MEMBERSHIPS: Member of the Hellenic Business Association.
HOBBIES AND INTERESTS: Cars, Animals.
PERSONAL PROFILE: President of Freda's since 1971. Successfully manages and controls Freda's. Originals Inc.

FREDA IORDANOUS
Award winning Fashion Designer

DATE OF BIRTH: 04-Jun-1950
PLACE OF BIRTH: Limassol, Cyprus.
MARITAL STATUS: Married to Demos Iordanous, Cypriot, Businessman.
CHILDREN: Paulina, Business BA. Elaine, Business BA.
SCHOOLS/COLLEGE: Limassol, Cyprus – Fashion School.
MEMBERSHIPS: member of WPO (women presidents organization), WEC (Women Entrepreneurs of Canada).
HONOURS/AWARDS: In 1991 Freda's won the CABE AWARD (CANADA AWARD FOR BUSINESS EXCELLENCE) Canada's Best Employer for Women and was included in the Who's Who of Canadian Women.
HOBBIES AND INTERESTS: Gardening, Music.
PERSONAL PROFILE: Freda Iordanous Company is a fashion design leader who counts among her regular clients many media personalities. She is also a leading corporate apparel designer creating exclusive uniform packages for a number of companies Canada 3000, Air Transat, First Air Elizabeth Arden and many others.

IRENA JOANNIDES
Film maker has won 16 International Awards

PLACE OF BIRTH: Cyprus
SCHOOLS/COLLEGE: University of Toronto and Ryerson University.
QUALIFICATIONS: BA in Cinema studies.
HONOURS/AWARDS: Has won 16 International Awards grants awarded from Cyprus Ministry of Culture, Toronto Arts Council and Department of Canadian Heritage.
PERSONAL PROFILE: Irena Joannides is the Director of the films Her Violet Garden, Island and Frequency.

KYRIACOS KAKOULLIS
Real Estate Broker Musician Instrument Maker

DATE OF BIRTH: 12-Apr-1954
PLACE OF BIRTH: Larnaca.
MARITAL STATUS: Single.
CHILDREN: Savvas, Web Designer. Adrienne, Publicist for major Canadian TV Station.
SCHOOLS/COLLEGE: Canadian College.
MEMBERSHIPS: Toronto Real Estate Board, Ontario Real Estate Association, Canadian Mortgage Broker Association.
HOBBIES AND INTERESTS: Music plays the Bouzouki.
PERSONAL PROFILE: Licenced Real Estate Broker owner of Homelife/Vision Reality Inc. Musician Instrument Maker

NICHOLAS KARAISKOS
Orthodontic resident at the University of Manitoba

PLACE OF BIRTH: Canada Parents from Cyprus
QUALIFICATIONS: BSc(Hon) BSc(Dent), DMD.
PERSONAL PROFILE: Nicholas Karaiskos is an Orthodontic resident at the University of Manitoba, Winnipeg.

Canada

Dr STAVROS KARANICOLAS
Nephrologist

PLACE OF BIRTH: Cyprus.
PERSONAL PROFILE: Stavros Karanicolas is a Nephrologist based at St Johns Hospital, Toronto.

DR MARIO KASAPI
Education

PLACE OF BIRTH: Cyprus
SCHOOLS/COLLEGE: University of British Columbia.
QUALIFICATIONS: Ph. D.
PERSONAL PROFILE: Mario Kasapi is the Technology Transfer Manager at the University of British Columbia-industry liason Office.

NEOKLIS KOKKINOU
President of the Cypriot Community Mississauga and District

DATE OF BIRTH: 12-Jul-1952
PLACE OF BIRTH: Kaimakli.
MARITAL STATUS: Married to Vasso, Omorphita.
CHILDREN: Maria, Eve.
SCHOOLS/COLLEGE: Pancyprian Gymnasium, Nicosia.
HOBBIES AND INTERESTS: Music.
PERSONAL PROFILE: Neoklis Kokkinou is in the Construction Business, He is the President of the Cypriot Community Mississauga and District.

SONIA KYRIACOU
Sonias dancers have been representing Montreal at the annual Puerto Rico World Salsa Congress

PLACE OF BIRTH: Cyprus
PERSONAL PROFILE: Sonia Kyriacou is the Founder of Salsa Team Canada and coordinator for Montreal. Was also a Director and founder of the San Tropez dance School. For several years Sonia's dancers have been representing Montreal at the annual Puerto Rico World Salsa Congress.

TINA LOUCAIDES
Awarded the Osgoode Society for Canadian Legal History Prize in 2003

PLACE OF BIRTH: Parents from Cyprus.
SCHOOLS/COLLEGE: University of Toronto and Osgoode Hall Law School.
QUALIFICATIONS: BSc MSc LL. B.
MEMBERSHIPS: Canadian Bar Association.
HONOURS/AWARDS: Awarded the Osgoode Society for Canadian Legal History Prize in 2003.
PERSONAL PROFILE: Tina Loucaides is an Associate and a registered Canadian and United States patent agent with Bereskin & Parr.

GEORGE MAVROUDIS
Chief Executive Officer Guardian Capital Group Ltd

PLACE OF BIRTH: Cyprus
PERSONAL PROFILE: George Mavroudis is the Chief Executive Officer Guardian Capital Group Ltd. Prior to joining Guardian was a Managing Director with JP Morgan Asset Management and served for several years as a senior executive throughout their institutional investment management network in Toronto, New York, London and Moscow.

JOHN MICHAELIDES
Research Associate, Chemical Engineering Department University of Waterloo

DATE OF BIRTH: 11-Jun-1947
PLACE OF BIRTH: Milikouri Cyprus.
MARITAL STATUS: Married to Theodora Michaelides.
CHILDREN: Micheal, School Teacher. Maria, Registered Massage Therapist.
SCHOOLS/COLLEGE: Kykko Pancyprian Gymnasium. University of Waterloo Ontario Canada.
QUALIFICATIONS: BSc. MSc. PhD.
MEMBERSHIPS: Optimist Club Mannheim, Greek Cypriot Community of Kitchener Waterloo Ontario Canada.
HONOURS/AWARDS: International Multifoods Award on cost effectiveness.
HOBBIES AND INTERESTS: Photography, Hiking.

Canada

PERSONAL PROFILE: Research Associate, Chemical Engineering Department University of Waterloo. Director of research Robin Hood, International Multifoods. Current occupation Director Technical services Guelph Food Technology Centre.

FREDA MICHAELIDIS
Ex President of the Cypriot Community of Toronto

DATE OF BIRTH: 23-Aug-1954
PLACE OF BIRTH: Pelendri.
MARITAL STATUS: Married to George, Greek.
CHILDREN: Michael, Account Manager. Damian, General Contractor.
SCHOOLS/COLLEGE: Riverdale Collegiate, Ryerson University.
MEMBERSHIPS: Associate of the Institute of Canadian Bankers.
PERSONAL PROFILE: Freda Michaelidis is a Bank Branch Manager, She is the Ex President of the Cypriot Community of Toronto. Also involved with PSEKA and Hellenic Hope Centre for Children With Special Needs.

MICHAEL MIKELLIDES
Former President of the Cypriot Community of Toronto

DATE OF BIRTH: 21-Sep-1942
PLACE OF BIRTH: Limassol.
MARITAL STATUS: Married to Anastasia, Limassol.
CHILDREN: Helen, Professional organiser.
SCHOOLS/COLLEGE: Lanition High School Limassol. George Brown College.
MEMBERSHIPS: Cyprus Brotherhood Association and Cyprus Business Association.
HOBBIES AND INTERESTS: Travelling.
PERSONAL PROFILE: Michael Mikellides is the founder of Rotogran International designers of the Rotogran granulators a machine used for the plastics processing and recycling industries. He is a former President of the Cypriot Community of Toronto.

ANDREAS NICOLAIDES
Well known Restauranter in Calgary

PLACE OF BIRTH: Limassol.

PERSONAL PROFILE: Andreas Nicolaides is the owner of the well known Santorini Greek Restaurant in Calgary, Canada.

LENA NICOLAIDES
Vice President of Therma Wave

PLACE OF BIRTH: Canada Parents from Cyprus.
SCHOOLS/COLLEGE: Rutgers University and University of Toronto.
QUALIFICATIONS: BSc MSc and PhD.
PERSONAL PROFILE: Lena Nicolaides is theVice President of Therma Wave in marketing and applications she has authored more than 30 publications. She is also an inventor of issued and pending US patents.

COSTAS NICOLAOU
Represented Canada in Shooting at the World Championships in North America

DATE OF BIRTH: 04-Jun-1958
PLACE OF BIRTH: Pano Amiandos.
MARITAL STATUS: Married to Akrivi, Greece.
SCHOOLS/COLLEGE: George Brown College Toronto.
HOBBIES AND INTERESTS: Shooting.
PERSONAL PROFILE: Costas Nicolaou Represented Canada in shooting at the World Championships in North America. Costas is the President of the Canadian Cypriot Hunters and Trap Shooting Organisation. He is also on the Committee of the Cypriot Community of Toronto. Costas's occupation is civil engineering and technology.

Dr SAVVAS NICOLAOU
Assistant Professor in Radiology at the University of British Columbia

PLACE OF BIRTH: Cyprus
PERSONAL PROFILE: Dr Savvas Nicolaou is Assistant Professor in Radiology at the University of British Columbia and is based at the Vancouver General hospital.

MICHAEL PAIDOUSSIS
Honorary Consul General of the
Republic of Cyprus in Montreal

DATE OF BIRTH: 20-Aug-1935
PLACE OF BIRTH: Nicosia.
MARITAL STATUS: Married to
Vrisseis, Greece, Banker.
SCHOOLS/COLLEGE: Abet
Secondary School, Cairo. Mcgill
University and Cambridge
University.
QUALIFICATIONS: B. ENG
PhD.
MEMBERSHIPS: Canadian
Society for Mechanical Engineering. Institution of
Mechanical Engineers.
HONOURS/AWARDS: Awarded a Commemorative
Medal for the 125th Anniversary of the Confederation
of Canada.
PERSONAL PROFILE: Michael Paidoussis is the Thomas
Workman Professor Emeritus Department of Mechanical
Engineering of Mcgill University, Canada. Michael is the
Honorary Consul General of the Republic of Cyprus in
Montreal. Michael was also the President of the Hellenic
-Canadian Solidarity Committee for Cyprus and of the Pan
Canadian Solidarity Committee for Cyprus.

SAVVAS PALLARIS
Director at Alberta Treasury

PLACE OF BIRTH: Cyprus.
PERSONAL PROFILE: Savvas Pallaris is Director of
Structured Investments at Alberta Treasury.

MIKE PANAYI
Chartered Financial Analyst

DATE OF BIRTH: 30-Apr-1964
PLACE OF BIRTH: Milia.
MARITAL STATUS: Married to
Christina, Canadian, Accountant.
CHILDREN: Eleni Christina
Panayi, Jacqueline Mary Panayi.
SCHOOLS/COLLEGE: Wilfrid
Laurier University, Waterloo
Ontario, Canada.
QUALIFICATIONS: Holder
of Chartered Financial Analyst
designation and Chartered Business Valuator.
MEMBERSHIPS: Member of CFA Instiuteand Canadian
Institute of Chartered Business Valuators.
HOBBIES AND INTERESTS: Golf, Squash, Dining, Travel.
PERSONAL PROFILE: Incorporated Greek Cypriot
Community of Waterloo Region in 1990. Served on the
board of Directors of PSEKA Canada. Co-Founder of
Pinnacle Group of Companies.

Dr TED PANTELLI
Dentist

PLACE OF BIRTH: Cyprus.
PERSONAL PROFILE: Dr Ted Pantelli is a dentist with a
General Practice in Scarborough, Ontario.

MARIOS PAPAGAPIOU
Researcher in Chronic pain

DATE OF BIRTH: 22-Feb-1957
PLACE OF BIRTH: London
Parents from Alona and
Famagusta.
MARITAL STATUS: Married to
Panayiota, Pano Zodia.
CHILDREN: Andreas,
Christoforos, Alexandros.
SCHOOLS/COLLEGE: York
University, Calgary.
QUALIFICATIONS: BSc BEC MSc.
HOBBIES AND INTERESTS: Remote control
Aeroplanes and Aeronautics.
PERSONAL PROFILE: Marios Papagapiou is a
Researcher in chronic pain and teaching Science in a
High school.

MENELAOS PAVLIDES
Former Executive Vice President of the
Canadian Cypriot Federation

DATE OF BIRTH: 17-Mar-1924
PLACE OF BIRTH: Port Said
Egypt, Father from Cyprus.
MARITAL STATUS: Married to
Koulla.
CHILDREN: Angela, Anna.
SCHOOLS/COLLEGE: Abet
Greek High School in Cairo,
Egypt. St George Williams
College.
HONOURS/AWARDS: Long
Service Medal Scouts Canada, Queen Elizabeth 11
Jubilee Medal 2002.
PERSONAL PROFILE: Menelaos Pavlides was the
President of the Montreal Citizenship Council, Executive
Vice President of the Canadian Cypriot Federation as
well as many others. Served in the British Army in the
Second World War.

Canada

MICHAEL PETRIDES
Professor in Neurology

PLACE OF BIRTH: Famagusta
HONOURS/AWARDS: Elected to the American Academy of Arts and Sciences.
PERSONAL PROFILE: Michael Petrides is a Professor of the Psychology Dept/Neurology and Neurosurgery at Mcgill University in Canada. He is also the Director of the Neuropsychology/ Cognitive Neuroscience Unit, Montreal Neurological Institute and Hospital.

YIANNIS PSALIOS
Restaurant Owner whose Restaurants were featured on the Multi Show Series Food TV Canada

DATE OF BIRTH: 05-Nov-1950
PLACE OF BIRTH: Phini.
MARITAL STATUS: Married to Kally, Greek Canadian, restauranteur.
CHILDREN: Theo, Dina, Both Children Restauranteurs.
PERSONAL PROFILE: Yiannis Psalios restaurants were featured in a multi-show series on Food TV Network CANADA. The production company did another season culminating with the big family wedding back in Cyprus with "4, 000" guests.

SAM ROUSSOS
Business

PLACE OF BIRTH: Cyprus.
PERSONAL PROFILE: Sam is the Director of Operations for Toronto Parking Authority.

DR GEORGIA SAVVIDOU
Medical Practitioner in the Greek area of Toronto

DATE OF BIRTH: 02-Sep-1955
PLACE OF BIRTH: Tsada.
MARITAL STATUS: Married to George, Greek.
CHILDREN: Alexander, All Students. Nicholas, Constantine.
SCHOOLS/COLLEGE: University of Toronto.
QUALIFICATIONS: Bsc Msc MD.
MEMBERSHIPS: College of Physicians and Surgeons of Ontario.
HOBBIES AND INTERESTS: Travel.
PERSONAL PROFILE: Georgia Savvidou has a Medical Practice in the Greek area of Toronto.

GEORGE SERGIOU
Active member of the Cyprus Community Centre Toronto

DATE OF BIRTH: 19-Feb-1951
PLACE OF BIRTH: Nicosia.
MARITAL STATUS: Married to Anastasia.
CHILDREN: Chrysostomos, Mechanic. Iacovos, Electrician.
SCHOOLS/COLLEGE: Frederick Technical School.
HOBBIES AND INTERESTS: Music and Soccer.
PERSONAL PROFILE: George Sergiou is an Electrician also an active member of the Cyprus Community Centre Toronto.

GEORGE SOLEAS
Chair of the National Quality Assurance Committee of the Canadian Liquor Jurisdictions

PLACE OF BIRTH: Cyprus
SCHOOLS/COLLEGE: Mcmaster University and University of Toronto and University of California.
QUALIFICATIONS: MSC PhD.
MEMBERSHIPS: Chemical Institute of Canada and American Society for Enology and Viticulture.
PERSONAL PROFILE: George Soleas is the Vice President of the Liquor control Board of Ontario Quality Assurance. He is also the Chair of the National Quality Assurance Committee of the Canadian Liquor Jurisdictions and a Chartered Chemist.

Canada

57

GEORGE SOLOMOS
Founder and Former President of Neotel

PLACE OF BIRTH: Cyprus.
PERSONAL PROFILE: George Solomos is an experienced and seasoned executive in all facets of the high technology industry. He has been involved in the Securities and Exchanges Industry for the last ten years. He established his own communications Technology Corporation - Canada: President and CEO: Telion Technologies Inc. (public since 1993 as NEOTEL Inc.) Previously he worked with: AT&T/Rogers, Pitney Bowes, Bell Mobility, Clearnet, NEC, OKI, Motorola, NOKIA, Audiovox Corporation and other major Corporations in the Communications Industry; conceived and prepared several Business plans, (major ones of which have been very successfully implemented by NEC, Mitsubishi, Bell Mobility, etc); co invented and applied for patents on Biometric based technology; currently developing ideogram based biometric, high security devices.

DINO SOPHOCLEOUS
President of PSEKA Canada

DATE OF BIRTH: 20-May-1963
PLACE OF BIRTH: Nicosia.
MARITAL STATUS: Married to Melia, Nicosia.
CHILDREN: Alexander, Orestis.
SCHOOLS/COLLEGE: University of York, Toronto.
QUALIFICATIONS: BA Economics also holds the Qualification CFRE(Certified Fund Raising Executive). He raises funding for charities and specialises in multi million dollar capital campaigns.
PERSONAL PROFILE: Dinos Sophocleous is the President of the International Coordinating Committee for Justice for Cyprus in Canada (PSEKA). Member of the Board of the Canadian Ethno Cultural Council. Former President of the Cypriot Community of Toronto. Dinos is the Vice President, Resource development for the hearing Foundation of Canada.

JOHN SOPHOCLEOUS
Municipal Standards Officer in Toronto

DATE OF BIRTH: 03-May-1970
PLACE OF BIRTH: Toronto parents from Cyprus.
MARITAL STATUS: Married to Penny.
CHILDREN: Yianna, Kyra.
SCHOOLS/COLLEGE: Riverdale. Centenial College of Applied Arts and Technology.
QUALIFICATIONS: Diploma in Business Management.
HOBBIES AND INTERESTS: Keep Fit.
PERSONAL PROFILE: John Sophocleous is a Municipal Standards Officer in Toronto.

MARIA TASSOU
Civil Litigation Lawyer

PLACE OF BIRTH: Canada parents from Cyprus.
SCHOOLS/COLLEGE: University of Toronto.
MEMBERSHIPS: Maria is a member of the Criminal Injuries Compensation Board.
HONOURS/AWARDS: Recipient of the Brian David Radford Memorial Scholarship in Management.
PERSONAL PROFILE: Maria Tassou is a Civil Litigation Lawyer with Pallett Valo Lawyers Ontario, Canada.

THALIA TASSOU
Law

PLACE OF BIRTH: Cyprus.
SCHOOLS/COLLEGE: Paris University-Sorbonne and University du Quebec.
QUALIFICATIONS: MA. and LLB.
PERSONAL PROFILE: Thalia is a lawyer in Montreal, Quebec, Canada.

ACHILLEAS THOMA
Clinical Professor Department of Surgery Mcmaster University in Canada

PLACE OF BIRTH: Cyprus
SCHOOLS/COLLEGE: Mcmaster University.
QUALIFICATIONS: BSc MD FRCS FACS.
PERSONAL PROFILE: Achilleas Thoma is a Clinical Professor Department of Surgery and Associate member Dept of Clinical Epidemiology and Biostatistics at Mcmaster University in Canada.

Canada

ANDREAS TSANGARIS
Chief Scientist at Plasco Energy Group

PLACE OF BIRTH: Cyprus
PERSONAL PROFILE: Mr. Andreas Tsangaris is a Master of Mechanical Engineering and a Professional Engineer. He is the co-inventor of Plasco Energy Group's technology along with Mr. George Carter. He has led plasma research at Plasco Energy Group's facility since 1981. He is also responsible for the day to day engineering operations at the plant. He is well respected in the international plasma community and has appeared at many seminars where he has presented papers. He is now recognized as a leading authority in plasma processing.

DEMETRA VASSILIOU
Chief Physician at the Dermaworks Medical Aesthetics Clinic

PLACE OF BIRTH: Canada Father from Cyprus.
SCHOOLS/COLLEGE: Mcgill University.
QUALIFICATIONS: MD FRCSC.
PERSONAL PROFILE: Dr Demetra Vassiliou is Chief Physician at the Dermaworks Medical Aesthetics Clinic she has been a practising obstetrician and gynecologist at Ottowa Hospital for over 12 years.

DR ANDREAS VIKIS
Research Scientist Atomic energy of Canada

DATE OF BIRTH: 08-Jul-1942
PLACE OF BIRTH: Moni.
MARITAL STATUS: Married to Ava Vikis, Greek, General Surgeon.
CHILDREN: Haris, Assistant Professor Biochemistry. Elena, General Surgeon.
SCHOOLS/COLLEGE: Limassol Greek Gymnasium. College of Emporia. Kansas State University, University of Toronto.

QUALIFICATIONS: BSc PhD.
MEMBERSHIPS: American Chemical Society, Chemical Institute of Canada, Parnassos Hellenic Cultural Society (President).
HONOURS/AWARDS: Fellow Chemical Institute of Canada.
HOBBIES AND INTERESTS: Boating, Hiking, Public Speaking, Reading and Writing.
PERSONAL PROFILE: Dr. Vikis was a Lecturer/Assistant Professor at the University of Toronto and a Research Scientist Atomic energy of Canada, Currently a Science and Technology Consultant.

ELENA VIKIS
Physician

PLACE OF BIRTH: Parents from Moni and Limassol.
PERSONAL PROFILE: Dr Elena Vikis is a General Practitioner with her own practice in Vancouver Canada.

There is estimated to be 35,000 Cypriots living in Canada.

They are mainly concentrated in Toronto and surrounding areas such as Mississauga, Kitchener, Winnipeg and Ottawa.

They can also be found in Vancouver and Montréal.

Canada

NEKTARIOS ALEXANDROU
Footballer with Larissa

DATE OF BIRTH: 19-Dec-1983
PLACE OF BIRTH: Nicosia.
PERSONAL PROFILE: Started his career with Apoel in Cyprus as an attacker now plays for Larissa in Greece.

MARLAIN ANGELIDES
Singer Represented Cyprus in the Eurovision Song Contest in Jerusalem, 1999

PLACE OF BIRTH: born in 1969 in Athens, Greece. Father from Athens; Mother half-English, half-Cypriot from Paphos, Cyprus.
SCHOOLS/COLLEGE: Falcon School, Cyprus. Imperial College of Science, Technology and Medicine, London; Boston Conservatory, USA; Royal Academy of Music, London.
QUALIFICATIONS: Bsc in Biochemistry with Management; PGDip Musical Theatre.
HOBBIES AND INTERESTS: Dance, water-skiing, basketball, swimming, running, weight-training, theatre, cinema and socialising.
PERSONAL PROFILE: Represented Cyprus in the Eurovision Song Contest in Jerusalem, 1999 (with Thane Erotas). She has appeared in Saturday night Fever in Athens and is a member of the Band Dickens Zoo.

MARIA ANTONIOU
Assistant Prof of Parasitology at the Medical School, University of Crete

DATE OF BIRTH: 15-Aug-1952
PLACE OF BIRTH: Famagusta, Cyprus.
MARITAL STATUS: Married to Dr. Christos Kourouniotis, Greece, Professor of Mathematics.
CHILDREN: Antoniou, Melissa, Both Students.
SCHOOLS/COLLEGE: Famagusta Gymnasium. London University, Imperial College of Science.

QUALIFICATIONS: BSc. (Honours), ARCS Zoology(M. Sc.), DIC. Nematology (Parasitology PhD. Nematology (Parasitology).
MEMBERSHIPS: Zoological society. DIO organic agriculture association.
HOBBIES AND INTERESTS: Organic agriculture. Novel writting.
PERSONAL PROFILE: Maria is Assistant Professor at the University of Crete Medical School in the Laboratory of Clinical Bacteriology Parasitology Zoonoses and Geographical Medicine. Also in charge of the Diagnostic Serology Laboratory of the University Hospital in Heraklion.

MICHAEL CACOYANNIS
Filmaker produced and directed Zorba the Greek

DATE OF BIRTH: 11-Jun-1922
PLACE OF BIRTH: Limassol.
HONOURS/AWARDS: Cacoyannis has been nominated for an Academy Award 5 times. He Received Best Director, Best Adapted Screenplay and Best Film Nominations for Zorba the Greek and two nominations in the Foreign Language Category for Elektra and Iphigenia.
PERSONAL PROFILE: Michael Cacoyannis was sent to London by his family to become a Lawyer he ended up in the film industry and produced and directed Zorba The Greek, The Trojan Woman, Stella and many others.

CHARALAMBOS CHARALAMBIDES
Professor of Mathematics at the University of Athens

DATE OF BIRTH: 19-Dec-1945
PLACE OF BIRTH: Kilani.
MARITAL STATUS: Married to Lena Tsingaki, Greek.
CHILDREN: Angelos, University. Cassandra, University.
SCHOOLS/COLLEGE: Lanition Gymnasium Limassol.
QUALIFICATIONS: PhD.
MEMBERSHIPS: International Statistical Institute, Bernoulli Society, Greek Mathematical Society, Greek Statistical Institute.
HOBBIES AND INTERESTS: Reading and Travelling.
PERSONAL PROFILE: Lecturer, Professor in Mathematics at University of Athens, was assistant visiting professor, Mcgill University, Philadelphia, USA and visiting Professor, University of Cyprus.

Greece

CONSTANTINOS CHARALAMBIDES
Footballer with Panathinaikos in Greece

DATE OF BIRTH: 25-Jul-1981
PLACE OF BIRTH: Nicosia.
HONOURS/AWARDS: He has been capped over 20 times for the Cyprus national football team. He has scored 7 goals including two against Ireland coming on as a substitute.
PERSONAL PROFILE: He began his career with Cyprus club Apoel and then signed an 18th month contract with Panathinaikos FC in Greece, then was transferred to Paok then back to Panathinaikos. In August 2007 he signed a contract with the German club FC Carl Zeis Jena playing in the 2 Bundesliga.

ELIAS CHARALAMBOUS
South African born Cypriot Footballer playing for PAOK in Greece

DATE OF BIRTH: 25-Sep-1980
PLACE OF BIRTH: Johannesburg South Africa Parents from Cyprus.
PERSONAL PROFILE: Footballer midfielder but can also play as a defender played for Omonia from 1999 to 2005 he is currently playing for Paok FC of Greece. He is a regular in the Cyprus national team.

CONSTANTINOS CHRISTODOULOU
Registrar of the Department of Gynecology Laiko Hospital, Athens

DATE OF BIRTH: 01-Dec-1955.
PLACE OF BIRTH: Konia.
MARITAL STATUS: Single.
CHILDREN: Elektra, Student of Medicine. Alexandros, Student of Civil Engineering.
SCHOOLS/COLLEGE: First Gymnasium Paphos. Medical School Of Aristotelian University of Athens.
QUALIFICATIONS: MD PhD.
MEMBERSHIPS: Founding member of International Society of ultrasound in Obstetrics and Gynecology.
HONOURS/AWARDS: Awards from the Greek Society of Obstetrics and Gynecology.
HOBBIES AND INTERESTS: Tennis and Travelling.
PERSONAL PROFILE: Constantinos Christodoulou is a Registrar of the Department of Gynecology, Director of the Department of Ultrasound and pre natal diagnosis at Laiko Hospital Athens until 2001. Fetal Medicine in IASO Hospital Athens.

GEORGE CHRISTOFIDES
Professor School of Geology, Aristotle University of Thessaloniki

PLACE OF BIRTH: Limassol.
PERSONAL PROFILE: George Christofides is a Professor School of Geology, Aristotle University of Thessaloniki.

CONSTANTINOS CHRISTOFOROU
Musician, at the age of 17, he became the first Cypriot artist to achieve triple platinum sales

DATE OF BIRTH: 25-Apr-1977
PLACE OF BIRTH: Limassol.
PERSONAL PROFILE: At the age of 17 he became the first Cypriot artist to achieve triple platinum sales. In 1966 he represented Cyprus in the Eurovision song contest in Oslo, Norway with the song Only for us. In 1999 he was chosen by the successful Cypriot composer Georges Theofanous to be the lead singer in the first boy band of Greece One. The group One became very popular and commercially successful in Greece and Cyprus reaching Platinum sales. Then in 2002 Konstantinos participated again in the Eurovision song contest in Estonia this time as the lead singer of One representing Cyprus with the song "gimme" and finishing in sixth position. Konstantinos is now a solo singer and has produced the Albums "I love you" "private show"and "Giros tou kosmou".

CONSTANTINE CONSTANTINIDES
Specialist in Byzantine History and Literature teaches at the University of Ioannina

DATE OF BIRTH: 30-Dec-1949
PLACE OF BIRTH: Cyprus.
MARITAL STATUS: Married to Soteroula, Cypriot, Associate Professor.
SCHOOLS/COLLEGE: University of Athens, University of London.
QUALIFICATIONS: BA PhD Professor of Byzantine History.
MEMBERSHIPS: Scientific Association in Cyprus.
HONOURS/AWARDS: Fellow of Dumbarton Oaks, Fellow of Max-planck-Institut.
PERSONAL PROFILE: Professor Constantinides is a specialist in Byzantine History and Literature he teaches at the University of Ioannina.

Greece

STAVROS J. CONSTANTINIDES
President of Alpha Copy/Nokia

DATE OF BIRTH: 20-Jan-1956
PLACE OF BIRTH: Limassol.
MARITAL STATUS: Married to Constantina Calogeropoulou Athens Housewife.
CHILDREN: Eleni, School.
QUALIFICATIONS: BA in Economics MBA.
HONOURS/AWARDS: Several awards by Institutions: Infosystems, Leaders of the Year, Superbrands.
HOBBIES AND INTERESTS: Cars, Stamp collections, Antiques.
PERSONAL PROFILE: Businessman / President of Alpha Copy / Nokia.

SOTEROULLA DEMETRIADOU CONSTANTINIDOU
Associate Professor of Classics at the University of Ioannina

PLACE OF BIRTH: Nicosia.
MARITAL STATUS: Married to Constantine Constantinides, Cyprus, Professor of Byzantine History.
PERSONAL PROFILE: Soteroulla Demetriadou Constantinidou is an Associate Professor of Classics at the University of Ioannina, Greece.

DAMIANOS CONSTANTINOU
Founder of the Centre for Hellenism Damianos Foundation

PLACE OF BIRTH: Mitsero, Nicosia
CHILDREN: Constantino, Athena.
SCHOOLS/COLLEGE: Commercial Lyceum, Larnaca.
MEMBERSHIPS: Member and ex President of the Association of Certified Accountants and Auditors of Greece.
HONOURS/AWARDS: William Quitter Prize for Auditing and was sixth in the order of merit.
PERSONAL PROFILE: Moore Stephens the Accountancy Firm was established in Greece in 1963 by Mr. Damianos Constantinou and continues under his leadership for the past 45 years. Moore Stephens the first international accounting firm to set up an office in Greece, and the only one to continue in the same form for the last 40 years. Moore Stephens is the leading firm in the provision of services to the shipping sector. Damianos is also the Founder of the Centre for Hellenism Damianos Foundation. The Foundation carries out national activities in Greece and Cyprus and has been visited by his Holiness the Ecumenical Patriarch Bartholomew, the late Archbishop of Athens and Greece Christodoulos and other distinguished personalities. Within this centre there is a rose garden with over 600 different kinds of roses.

CONSTANTINOS N COUCCOULLIS
Lawyer, Founder and main partner of Constantinos N Couccoullis & Associates based in Athens

DATE OF BIRTH: 13-Nov-1945
PLACE OF BIRTH: Cyprus.
MARITAL STATUS: Married to Margarita, Administrative Executive of the legal firm.
CHILDREN: Alexia, Trainee lawyer.
SCHOOLS/COLLEGE: University of Athens. School of Law.
MEMBERSHIPS: Rotary HellasAthens Bar Association.
HONOURS/AWARDS: Benefactor of the Greek Orthodox Church.
PERSONAL PROFILE: Constantinos Couccoullis is a Lawyer. He is the founder and main partner of Constantinos N Couccoullis & Associates based in Athens.

PANOS DANOS
Member of the Board of Directors of RICS HELLAS

DATE OF BIRTH: 20-Apr-1968
PLACE OF BIRTH: Nicosia.
QUALIFICATIONS: BSc.
MEMBERSHIPS: Fellow of the Royal Institution of Chartered Surveyors. Member of the Board of Directors of RICS HELLAS. Board member of the Cyprus Valuers Association.
PERSONAL PROFILE: Panos Danos is the founder and managing director of Danos and Associates a property consulting company. Previously he was member of the Board of Directors at Lambert Smith Hampton Hellas Property Consultants and Valuers.

Greece

ARETI DEMOSTHENOUS

Director of the Institute of Historical Research for Peace She teaches Comparative Religious Law with emphasis on its Socio-Political Dimensions at the University of Athens

PLACE OF BIRTH: Cyprus
MEMBERSHIPS: She is Founding Member of the World Forum of Religions and Cultures (Nicosia-Athens) and of the International Association for the Promotion of Women of Europe (Branch: Cyprus). She is also member of the International Association of the Studies for Southeast Europe and the International Association for Intercultural Education.
PERSONAL PROFILE: Areti is a Director of the Institute of Historical Research for Peace She teaches Comparative Religious Law with emphasis on its Socio-Political Dimensions at the University of Athens. She has been visiting Lecturer at the Department of Sociology at Bogazici University, Turkey (2004-5) and visiting Scholar/Lecturer at the University of Cambridge, Faculty of Oriental Studies (2005-6). Since 2002 she is compiler and presenter of the weekly radio program "Culture and Peaceful Coexistence" in Cyprus Broadcasting Corporation (RIK 1).

KYRIACOS EFSTATHIOU

Associate Professor of the Mechanical Engineering Department, Polytechnical School of the Aristoteles University Thessaloniki

DATE OF BIRTH: 31-Aug-1952
PLACE OF BIRTH: Pretori.
MARITAL STATUS: Married to Maria.
CHILDREN: Two Daughters.
SCHOOLS/COLLEGE: University of Stuttgart and Aristotle University Greece.
QUALIFICATIONS: PhD.
PERSONAL PROFILE: Kyriacos Efstathiou is an Associate Professor of the Mechanical Engineering Department, Polytechnic School of the Aristoteles University Thessaloniki.

PROFESSOR KAKOUROS EFTHYMIOU

Professor of Child Psychopathology

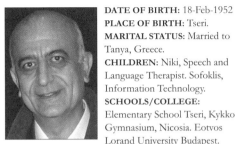

DATE OF BIRTH: 18-Feb-1952
PLACE OF BIRTH: Tseri.
MARITAL STATUS: Married to Tanya, Greece.
CHILDREN: Niki, Speech and Language Therapist. Sofoklis, Information Technology.
SCHOOLS/COLLEGE: Elementary School Tseri, Kykko Gymnasium, Nicosia. Eotvos Lorand University Budapest.
QUALIFICATIONS: MA PhD in Psychology.
HOBBIES AND INTERESTS: Current Affairs, technology and reading.
PERSONAL PROFILE: Kakouros Efthymios is a Professor of Child Psychopathology at TEI of Athens and head of the Department of Early Childhood Education. Founder and director of Psychological Centre for developmental and learning disabilities ARSI. Researcher and author of six books and 54 scientific articles in the field of child psychopathology.

PROFESSOR ELEFTHERIOU PANTELI ELEFTHERIOS

Professor of Botany University of Thessaloniki

DATE OF BIRTH: 10-Nov-1947
PLACE OF BIRTH: Derynia, Cyprus.
MARITAL STATUS: Married to Maria Christodoulou, Greek Cypriot, Teacher.
CHILDREN: Demetrios, Pantalis.
SCHOOLS/COLLEGE: 2nd Gymnasium Famagusta. Aristotle University of Thessaloniki, Faculty of Sciences, Department of Natural Sciences.
MEMBERSHIPS: Served as President of the Hellenic Botanical Society. Cyprus Academy of Sciences.
PERSONAL PROFILE: Professor of Botany, University of Thesalonniki.

ELEFTHERIOS EUGENIOU
Former Secretary of Greek Cypriot Brotherhood

DATE OF BIRTH: 02-Feb-1931
PLACE OF BIRTH: Pyrgos.
MARITAL STATUS: Married.
CHILDREN: Six.
HONOURS/AWARDS: Honoured by the Greek Orthodox Church in Great Britain for services to the Community.
PERSONAL PROFILE: Managing Director of group of companies. Was Secretary of Greek Cypriot Brotherhood and former Chairman of the Greek Cypriot Community Association in Hendon. Now living in Greece.

KYRIAKOS EVANGELOU
Head of Greek Branch of Eurohypo AG, a German bank specialising in real estate lending

DATE OF BIRTH: 03-Sep-1969
PLACE OF BIRTH: London. Parents from Akanthou.
MARITAL STATUS: Married to Elena, Athens, civil servant.
SCHOOLS/COLLEGE: Mill Hill High School. University of Westminster, City University Business School.
QUALIFICATIONS: BSc in Urban Estate Management, Msc in Property Investment. Chartered Surveyor.
MEMBERSHIPS: Member of the Royal Institution of Chartered Surveyors (RICS).
HONOURS/AWARDS: A. Johnson Award for graduating with highest marks in BSc Urban Estate Management from Westminster University (1991).
HOBBIES AND INTERESTS: Travel, current affairs, football.
PERSONAL PROFILE: Head of Greek Branch of Eurohypo AG, a German bank specialising in real estate lending. The branch won the Euromoney award in 2006 and 2007 for "Best Commercial Bank in Greece". Has over 17 years of experience in the property industry, and started his career with DTZ international property advisers in London in 1991. He has been involved in some of the largest property development projects in Greece, and is considered one of the countries leading property specialists, regularly making presentations at conferences. Between 2002-2005 he was Chairman of RICS Hellas.

MARIOS EVRYVIADES
Professor in International Relations at Athens University

PLACE OF BIRTH: Vasa.
SCHOOLS/COLLEGE: University of Tufts and University of New Hampshire.
QUALIFICATIONS: BA MA MALD and Ph. D.
PERSONAL PROFILE: Marios Evryviades is a Professor in International Relations at Athens University of Economics and Business. From 1989 to 1993 he was an adviser to and the speech writer for the President of Cyprus.

SAVVAS GEORGIADIS
BP Portrait Award 2004 National Portrait Gallery London

DATE OF BIRTH: 31-May-1975
PLACE OF BIRTH: Limassol.
MARITAL STATUS: Single.
SCHOOLS/COLLEGE: Athens School of Fine Arts.
HONOURS/AWARDS: BP Portrait Award 2004 National Portrait Gallery London.
HOBBIES AND INTERESTS: Music guitar.
PERSONAL PROFILE: Savvas Georgiadis is an artist exhibited in the UK, Greece and Cyprus.

ANDREAS GEORGIOU
Assistant Professor of Operations Research at the University of Macedonia, Thessaloniki, Greece

PLACE OF BIRTH: Cyprus.
SCHOOLS/COLLEGE: Aristotle University of Thessaloniki.
QUALIFICATIONS: PhD.
PERSONAL PROFILE: Andreas Georgiou is an Assistant Professor of Operations Research at the University of Macedonia, Thessaloniki, Greece. His research interests include mathematical human resource planning, locational analysis and applications of simulation.

PROFESSOR STELIOS GEORGIOU
University Professor at the Department of Mathematics at the University of Athens

DATE OF BIRTH: 24-Nov-1973
PLACE OF BIRTH: Limassol.
MARITAL STATUS: Married to Stella Stylianou, Cypriot, University Professor.
SCHOOLS/COLLEGE: University of Athens.
QUALIFICATIONS: BSc MSc Ph. D.
MEMBERSHIPS: Institute of Electrical and Electronic Engineers. The American Statistical Association. Greek Statistical Association.
HOBBIES AND INTERESTS: Tennis and Chess.
PERSONAL PROFILE: Stelios Georgiou is a University Professor at the Department of Mathematics at the University of Athens.

GIORGOS GEORGIS
Ambassador of Cyprus in Greece

PLACE OF BIRTH: Paralimni in 1948
MARITAL STATUS: Married.
CHILDREN: One Daughter.
SCHOOLS/COLLEGE: University of Athens.
QUALIFICATIONS: Ph. D.
HONOURS/AWARDS: For his contribution to the promotion of Cyprus studies and cultural relations with Greece he was awarded with the merit of the Commander of the Order of the Phoenix of the Hellenic Republic and with the merits of Honour by the University of Athens.
PERSONAL PROFILE: Giorgos Georgis is the Ambassador of Cyprus in Greece. From year 2000 he has been appointed as Professor of Contemporary History at the University of Cyprus and has since 2003 been a member of the Senate. He has been a teacher and lecturer in Cyprus and Greece. He has also published books on Sepheris and Greek Diplomatic History.

PROFESSOR IOANNIS HADJIAGAPIOU
Physics Professor at the University of Athens

DATE OF BIRTH: 15-Aug-1948
PLACE OF BIRTH: Ayios Dhometios.
MARITAL STATUS: Married to Louisa, Greek, Director at the ministry of development.
CHILDREN: Kyriaki, Doctor. Andreas, Physics student.
SCHOOLS/COLLEGE: Kykko Pancyprian Gymnnasium. Athens University.
QUALIFICATIONS: B. Sc, Ph. D.
MEMBERSHIPS: A. P. S.
PERSONAL PROFILE: Physics Professor at the University of Athens and Director at the Ministry of Development.

PROFESSOR IOANNIS HADJIMINAS
Professor Emeritus at the Medical and Dental School at the University of Athens

DATE OF BIRTH: 20-Dec-1920
PLACE OF BIRTH: Kyrenia.
CHILDREN: Stavro, Died in a car accident at the age of 18. Dimitri, Breast and Endocrine Surgeon.
SCHOOLS/COLLEGE: Kyrenia and Pancyprian University. Washington School of art and University of Athens.
QUALIFICATIONS: MD Ph. D.
MEMBERSHIPS: Member of the Physiological Society of GB.
HONOURS/AWARDS: Gold medal and Plaque from the City of Athens from the Union of Cypriots in Greece and the society of Cypriot Doctors.
HOBBIES AND INTERESTS: Art, Photography, Fishing, Swimming and skiing.
PERSONAL PROFILE: Ioannis Hadjiminas was a Lecturer at the Medical and Dental School at the University of Athens.

It is free to nominate someone, or yourself, who deserves to be in the book, just send in the name, contact address, telephone number and email to:
Greek Cypriots Worldwide
111 St Thomas's Road London N4 2QJ
Telephone 0044 207503 3498
cypriotwhoswho@aol.com
www.greekcypriotsworldwide.com

Greece

MICHALIS HADJIYIANNI

Musician Best pop artist, male singer, best selling albums and singles several times at both Greek and Cyprus music awards

DATE OF BIRTH: 05-Nov-1978
PLACE OF BIRTH: Nicosia parents from Kyrenia Cyprus.
MARITAL STATUS: Single.
SCHOOLS/COLLEGE: Cyprus Music academy.
QUALIFICATIONS: Degree in piano guitar and music.
HONOURS/AWARDS: Best pop artist, male singer, best selling albums and singles several times at both Greek and Cyprus music awards.
PERSONAL PROFILE: Started a music career in 1994 at the age of 16 when he won the first prize at a young talent show in Cyprus. in 1995 he gave his first concert and released his first cd single called Letter. In May 1998 he represented Cyprus in the Eurovision song contest singing his own composition Genesis. In march 2000 Hadjiyianni released his first solo album strange celebration which was to produce some of the biggest hits of that year. most of his albums have gone platinum. In the summer of 2004 he toured Greece and sang at the closing ceremony of the Olympic Games in Athens. In October 2005 he travelled to Australia for the first time and performed three concerts. Later in April 2006 he toured Canada and the USA with Giorgos Dalaras.

LOUCAS HAJI-IOANNOU

Shipping entrpreneur/Philanthropist (Deceased)

DATE OF BIRTH: 15-Sep-1927
PLACE OF BIRTH: Pedhoulas.
MARITAL STATUS: Married to Nedi, Limassol.
CHILDREN: Polys, Runs his own Shipping fleet. Stelios, Founder of Easy Jet. Clelia, President of the Haji-Ioannou Foundation.
SCHOOLS/COLLEGE: Pedhoulas Elementary.
PERSONAL PROFILE: Loucas Haji-ioannou first worked as a salesman in Nicosia then started a import export business in Saudi Arabia specialising on cement. In 1959 he bought his first dry cargo ship and in 1969 bought his first oil tanker. By 1990 he was the world's largest independant shipowner controlling a fleet of more than 50 vessels. He endowed the Haji-ioannou foundation with more than 10 million dollars. The Foundation built a school at his home village of Pedhoulas;It also supports drug rehabilitation programmes. marine

enviromental protection schemes and the Greek Institute of Cardiology.

PROFESSOR PANAYIOTIS IFESTOS

Lecturer and Professor in International Relations and Strategic Studies University of Piraeus

PLACE OF BIRTH: Cyprus
PERSONAL PROFILE: Panayiotis Ifestos is a Lecturer and Professor in International Relations and Strategic Studies University of Piraeus.

THOUKYDIDIS IOANNOU

Professor/Author. Visitor Professor at the University of Athens

DATE OF BIRTH: 14-Feb-1951
PLACE OF BIRTH: Kissousa Limassol.
MARITAL STATUS: Married to Cryssi, Greece, journalist.
CHILDREN: Petros, Postgraduate studies in Computing and Information Systems at the University of Piraeus.
SCHOOLS/COLLEGE: Pancyprian Gymnasium Nicosia. University of Athens and Piraeus.
QUALIFICATIONS: BA MA PhD.
MEMBERSHIPS: EUROCLIO (European Standing Conference of History Teacher's Association). Greek Pedagogigal Society. Union of Cypriots in Greece.
HOBBIES AND INTERESTS: Tennis, bowling, social actvities, writing.
PERSONAL PROFILE: Professor/Author. Visitor Professor at the University of Athens, National representative (of Greece) and Professor of Greek Language in Luxembourg (European Commission). Inspector of Secondary Education in Greece.

CONSTANTINOS JACOVIDES
Associate Professor of Physics at the University of Athens

DATE OF BIRTH: 18-Nov-1947
PLACE OF BIRTH: Kyrenia Cyprus.
MARITAL STATUS: Married.
SCHOOLS/COLLEGE: Gymnasium of Kyrenia Cyprus.
QUALIFICATIONS: Bsc in Physics, MSc in Meterorology, PhD, in Atmospheric Hydrodynamics.
MEMBERSHIPS: European Association for physics, Greek Physics Association, Cypriot Physics Association, Greek-Cypriot Union of Athens.
HOBBIES AND INTERESTS: Photo ad Informing Colleagues (Greek and Foreigner's) for my beloved country (Cyprus problem).
PERSONAL PROFILE: Associate Professor in Atmospheric Physics-University of Athens.

DAKIS JOANNOU
Appointed to the Chancellors Court of Benefactors at Oxford University

DATE OF BIRTH: 29-Dec-1939
PLACE OF BIRTH: Nicosia, Cyprus.
MARITAL STATUS: Married to Mrs Lietta Stavrakis, Nicosia.
CHILDREN: Maria, Christos, Ellie, Stelios.
SCHOOLS/COLLEGE: Athens College, Cornell University in 1962, his Master's from Columbia University, University of Rome, Italy.
QUALIFICATIONS: Bachelors and masters in Civil Engineering. PhD in Architecture.
MEMBERSHIPS: Founder of the DESTE Foundation for Contemporary Art, also serves on the councils of several museums worldwide. He is a member of the Board of Trustees of the New Museum of Contemporary Art in New York, while he is also a member of the Tate Modern International Council.
HONOURS/AWARDS: Dakis Joannou's family's recent support to the University of Oxford with the establishment of the Stelios Ioannou School for Research in Classical and Byzantine Studies, has honoured him with his appointment to the Chancellor's Court of Benefactors.
HOBBIES AND INTERESTS: Dakis Joannou is a major collector of contemporary art enjoying international recognition.

PERSONAL PROFILE: Dakis core business is Civil Engineering construction and energy with activities in the Middle East, North Africa and South Eastern Europe. He also has holdings in the Intercontinental Hotel and Yes Hotels a chain of Boutique Hotels. He is also involved in a wide range of other entrepreneurial activities holding Directorships in several companies.

MILTOS KAMBOURIDES
Bronze Medalist at the Balkan Math Olympiad and nomination by Property Week Magazine as Property Newcomer of the Year (2008)

PLACE OF BIRTH: Nicosia in 1972
MARITAL STATUS: Married to Maria Vernikou, Photographer.
CHILDREN: Two.
SCHOOLS/COLLEGE: Massachusetts Institute of Technology.
QUALIFICATIONS: BS MS.
HONOURS/AWARDS: Bronze Medalist at the Balkan Math Olympiad (Beijing 1990, Moscow 1992). Nomination by Property Week Magazine as Property Newcomer of the Year (2008) and Goldman Sachs Global Innovation Award 1998.
PERSONAL PROFILE: Milton Kambourides is the Founder and Managing Partner of Dolphin Capital Partners (DCP) and manages Dolphin Capital Investors one of the largest AIM listed real estate investment funds with an asset base of approximately 2. 5 billion. Euros. Miltos is a also a founding partner of Soros Real Estate Partners, a global real estate private equity business formed in 1999 by George Soros.

ANDREAS KATSOURIS
Professor, Ancient Greek Philology at the University of Ioannina

PLACE OF BIRTH: Cyprus.
PERSONAL PROFILE: Andreas Katsouris Professor, Ancient Greek Philology.

ANTONIS KATTAMIS
Professor of Pediatric Haematology and Oncology

PLACE OF BIRTH: Parents from Cyprus
SCHOOLS/COLLEGE: University of Athens.
MEMBERSHIPS: Hellenic Society of Pediatric Haematology and Oncology.
PERSONAL PROFILE: Antonis Kattamis is the Professor of Pediatric Haematology and Oncology at the University of Athens.

PROFESSOR CHRISTOS KATTAMIS
Professor of Pediatrics at the University of Athens

DATE OF BIRTH: 13-Sep-1930
PLACE OF BIRTH: Kythrea.
MARITAL STATUS: Married to Helen Taouki, Greek, Dentist.
CHILDREN: Chrystalena, Pyschologist PhD. Antonis, Pediatrician, Associate Professor. Eva, Biologist B. Sc.
SCHOOLS/COLLEGE: Secondary School: Pancyprian Gymnasium Nicosia. University : Medical School University of Athens.
QUALIFICATIONS: M. D. In Medicine. Doctor of Medicine Athens University, Thesis for Associate Professor, University of Athens.
MEMBERSHIPS: European Society Pediatric Research, European Pediatric Society Hematology-.
HONOURS/AWARDS: ARISTION Academy of Athens for outstanding research activities in Science.
HOBBIES AND INTERESTS: Music, Travelling.
PERSONAL PROFILE: Emeritus Professor Of Pediatrics At the University of Athens. Chairman of the Greek National Commitee for Poliomyelitis.

PASCHALIS KITROMILIDES
Professor, Dept. of Political Science, University of Athens

DATE OF BIRTH: 05-Nov-1949.
PLACE OF BIRTH: Nicosia.
SCHOOLS/COLLEGE: Harvard University and University of Athens.
PERSONAL PROFILE: Paschalis Kitromilides is a Professor, Dept. of Political Science, University of Athens.

MARCOS KOLOKOUDIAS
Assistant Professor University of Athens

PLACE OF BIRTH: Paralimni.
PERSONAL PROFILE: Markos Kolokoudias is an Assistant Professor University of Athens Department of Oral and Maxillofacial Surgery.

FROSOULLA KOLOSIATOU
Poet Awarded the First State Prize for Poetry in Cyprus in 2005 for the book

DATE OF BIRTH: 20-Mar-1954
PLACE OF BIRTH: Larnaca.
MARITAL STATUS: Married to Vasilis, Greek.
CHILDREN: Jason, Student.
SCHOOLS/COLLEGE: University of Athens.
MEMBERSHIPS: Cypriot Poetry Association.
HONOURS/AWARDS: Awarded the First State Prize for Poetry in Cyprus in 2005 for the book "When the Flamingos are leaving".
HOBBIES AND INTERESTS: Reading, writing and music.
PERSONAL PROFILE: Frosoulla Kolosiatou is a Poet she has written six books of poetry some have been translated into different languages. She is a Teacher in a Secondary School.

NICOLAOS KONOMIS
Professor of Greek Literature

PLACE OF BIRTH: Morphou
MARITAL STATUS: Married to Eleni.
CHILDREN: Maria, Christos.
SCHOOLS/COLLEGE: Pancyprian Gymnasium, University of Athens and University of Oxford.
QUALIFICATIONS: B. A. classics, Bachelor of Literature, D. Ph.
MEMBERSHIPS: Nicolaos Konomis is a Professor of Greek Literature and member of the Greek academy in Athens.
HONOURS/AWARDS: President of the Republic of Greece Kostis Stephanopoulos presented him a honorary distinction, award and medal, for his work and contribution to society.

STELIOS KONSTANTAS
Singer

PLACE OF BIRTH: Larnaca **MARITAL STATUS:** Married. **CHILDREN:** Three Children. **PERSONAL PROFILE:** He has participated in two national finals for the Eurovision song contest came second in 1997 and fourth in 1999. has since produced a single and an album.

MICHALIS KONSTANTINOU
all time leading goal scorer with 24 goals in 52 appearances for the Cyprus National Football Team

DATE OF BIRTH: 19-Feb-1978 **PLACE OF BIRTH:** Paralimni. **HONOURS/AWARDS:** In the National team he is the spearhead of the Cypriot national side and he is already the all time leading goal scorer with 24 goals in 52 appearances. **PERSONAL PROFILE:** Michalis Konstantinou a striker who started professional football for Cypriot side Enosis Neon Paralimni FC. For whom he scored 17 goals in 25 games in the 1996/97 season and was top goalscorer of the Cypriot Championship. Michalis then moved to Iraklis in Greece where in his four seasons produced a total of 60 goals in 119 appearances. In 2001 in a deal which took three Panathinaikos players to Iraklis Konstantinou was transferred to Panathinaikos for 11. 3 million euros the most ever paid for a Cypriot player. After a successful period at Panathinaikos he joined Olympiakos where he still plays here he helped his team win the double in 2005/6.

PHIDIAS KONTEMENIOTIS
Journalist/Lawyer

DATE OF BIRTH: 05-Sep-1947 **PLACE OF BIRTH:** Cyprus. **MARITAL STATUS:** Married to Fotini Mazonaki, Greek, Teacher. **CHILDREN:** Polixeni, Evangelia, Nicolas. **SCHOOLS/COLLEGE:** Greek Gymnasium, Morphou. Athens Law School, GW Uinversity. **QUALIFICATIONS:** Law Degree, Economics, Political, Science. **HOBBIES AND INTERESTS:** DIY, nature. **PERSONAL PROFILE:** Self made A to Z Professional journalist. 1965-1978 business executive, 1978-1984 Legal practice, 1984 - present.

PANTELIS KONTOPODIS
Lecturer School of Independent Faculties

PLACE OF BIRTH: Kyrenia.
PERSONAL PROFILE: Panteli Kontopodis is a Lecturer School of Independent Faculties of Physical education and Sport Science.

AGNI MYLONA KOSMA
Professor, Statistical Mechanics and Chemical System Dynamics

PLACE OF BIRTH: Cyprus.
PERSONAL PROFILE: Agni Mylona Kosma is a Professor, Statistical Mechanics and Chemical System Dynamics at the University of Ioannina.

ODYSSEAS KOUFOPAVLOU
Assistant Professor, University of Patras

PLACE OF BIRTH: Athienou **SCHOOLS/COLLEGE:** University of Patras. **QUALIFICATIONS:** PhD. **MEMBERSHIPS:** Institute of Electrical and Electronics Engineers (IEEE). Technical Chamber of Greece. **HONOURS/AWARDS:** IBM Research Division Award. **PERSONAL PROFILE:** Odysseas Koufopavlou is an Assistant Professor, University of Patras, Patras, Greece. Member of VLSI Design Laboratory.

Greece

GEORGE KOUMOULLIS
Professor of Mathematics University of Athens

DATE OF BIRTH: 03-Jul-1951.
PLACE OF BIRTH: Lefkara.
MARITAL STATUS: Married to Maria Bourika, Greek, High School teacher.
CHILDREN: Aglaia-Anna Kournoulli.
SCHOOLS/COLLEGE: Gymnasium of Lefkara. University of Athens.
QUALIFICATIONS: BSc in Mathematics, PhD in mathematics.
HOBBIES AND INTERESTS: Reading and traveling.
PERSONAL PROFILE: Professor of Mathematics, University of Athens.

MICHAEL KOUPPARIS
Professor of Analytical Chemistry University of Athens

PLACE OF BIRTH: Polis Chrysochous
PERSONAL PROFILE: Michael Koupparis is a Professor of Analytical Chemistry University of Athens.

ZAFIROULLA IAKOVIDOU KRITSI
Associate Professor in General Biology and Genetics, University of Thessaloniki

DATE OF BIRTH: 14-Nov-1948
PLACE OF BIRTH: Limassol.
MARITAL STATUS: Married to Evangelos, Chemist.
CHILDREN: Anna, Psychologist. Fotini, Teacher. Kosmas, Student.
SCHOOLS/COLLEGE: Greek High School of Soleas. Aristotle University of Thessaloniki, Yale University USA.
QUALIFICATIONS: BSc PhD.
MEMBERSHIPS: Hellenic Chemists Society.
EUROPEAN ENVIROMENTAL MUTAGEN SOCIETY.
PERSONAL PROFILE: Zafiroulla Kritsi is a Associate Professor in General Biology and Genetics, University of Thessaloniki.

GEORGE KYRIACOU
George Kyriacou is an Associate Professor, Democritus University of

PLACE OF BIRTH: Cyprus.
PERSONAL PROFILE: George Kyriacou is an Associate Professor, Democritus University of Thrace, Department of Electrical and Computer Engineering, Microwaves Lab.

KLEONIKI LAMNISOU
Lecturer at Department of Biology, School of Science, University of Athens

PLACE OF BIRTH: Dhali.
PERSONAL PROFILE: Kleoniki Lamnisou is a lecturer at Department of Biology, School of Science, University of Athens.

MARIOS LEONIDOU
Actor appeared in plays such as Romeo & Juliet(Shakespeare) and many more

DATE OF BIRTH: 15-Aug-1976
PLACE OF BIRTH: Nicosia.
MARITAL STATUS: Single.
SCHOOLS/COLLEGE: University of South Florida.
QUALIFICATIONS: Batchelor in Dramatic Arts/Performance.
HONOURS/AWARDS: Theatre, Snooker, Football, Tennis and Basketball.
PERSONAL PROFILE: Marios Leonidou is an Actor based in Athens. He has appeared in plays such as The Comedy of Error's, Romeo and Juliet (Shakespeare) and many more.

IOANNIS LOIZIDES
Lecturer at Department of International and European Economic Studies

PLACE OF BIRTH: Nicosia.
PERSONAL PROFILE: Ioannis Loizides is a Lecturer at Department of International and European Economic Studies Athens University of Economics and Business.

Greece

ARAVIS LOIZOU
General Secretary of PSEKA.
International Cordinating Committee
justice for Cyprus

DATE OF BIRTH: 16-Jul-1957
PLACE OF BIRTH: Piyi.
MARITAL STATUS: Married to
Helen Charalambous, Studied
Political Sciences and Public
Administration in Pantion
University of Athens.
CHILDREN: Mary, Greek
Philosophy Teacher. Kostas,
Hotel Receptionist. Christiana,
Fifth Class of Primary School.
SCHOOLS/COLLEGE: Hellenic Gymnasium of
Lefkonico. University of Athens.
HONOURS/AWARDS: Awards - Awarded by the
President of National Bank of Greece for his Study in
Non Performing Loans.
HOBBIES AND INTERESTS: Car Driving, Travel Greek
culture.
PERSONAL PROFILE: Director Manager of National
Bank of Greece S. A. Substitute of General Secretary
of OKOE, General Secretary of PSEKA. International
Cordinating Comittee justice for Cyprus.

KOSTAS MAVROS
Lecturer at The Universities of Athens
and Patras

DATE OF BIRTH: 13-Oct-1942
PLACE OF BIRTH: Nicosia.
MARITAL STATUS: Married to
Anthi, Greek.
CHILDREN: Michalis,
Cyprus Diplomat. Rea,
Teacher. Spyros, Tourist
Business.
SCHOOLS/COLLEGE:
Pancyprian Gymnasium.
University of Athens.
QUALIFICATIONS: Degree in Mathematics.
PERSONAL PROFILE: Kostas Mavros was a lecturer at
The Universities of Athens and Patras. Has also written
and published four books.

SARBEL MICHAEL
Singer has represented Greece in the
Eurovision Song Contest

DATE OF BIRTH: 14-May-1981
PLACE OF BIRTH: London
Parents from Cyprus and
Lebanon.
SCHOOLS/COLLEGE: English
National Opera.
PERSONAL PROFILE: Sarbel is
a singer and rising star in Greece
and Cyprus. He has represented
Greece in the Eurovision Song
Contest.

ADONIS MICHAELIDES
Lecturer in Chemistry at the University
of Ioannina

PLACE OF BIRTH: Limassol.
PERSONAL PROFILE: Adonis Michaelides is a Lecturer
in the Department of Chemistry at the University of
Ioannina.

GEORGE MICHAELIDES
Secretary of OKOE The Federation of
Cypriots in Greece

PLACE OF BIRTH: Cyprus.
PERSONAL PROFILE: George Michaelides is the
Secretary of OKOE The Federation of Cypriots in
Greece.

SPYROS MILTIADES
Consul for the Republic of Cyprus in
Greece

DATE OF BIRTH: 21-Aug-1977
PLACE OF BIRTH: Cyprus.
MARITAL STATUS: Married to
Maria, Famagusta.
SCHOOLS/COLLEGE:
University of Cyprus and L.
S. E.
QUALIFICATIONS: BA MA.
HOBBIES AND INTERESTS:
Theatre, sports and dancing.
PERSONAL PROFILE: Spyros
Miltiades is the Consul for the Republic of Cyprus in
Greece.

Greece

GEORGE MORARIS
Poet

PLACE OF BIRTH: Limassol in 1946
MARITAL STATUS: Single.
SCHOOLS/COLLEGE: University of Athens.
QUALIFICATIONS: Degree in Greek Philology.
MEMBERSHIPS: Association of Greek -Cypriot Scientists of Greece.
HONOURS/AWARDS: Awarded a first prize of poetry by the Minister of Education and Culture of the Republic of Cyprus.
HOBBIES AND INTERESTS: Archaeology, History of Fine Arts.
PERSONAL PROFILE: George Moraris is a Poet who has published two books of poetry one called "Association of Silence" and the other "Flowers of Rhamnous". He is a Teacher in Secondary Education in Athens.

GEORGE NICOLAIDES
Art

DATE OF BIRTH: 25-Jan-1948
PLACE OF BIRTH: Nicosia.
MARITAL STATUS: Married to Roulla, Greek, Dr of Maths, Philosophy and Psychology.
CHILDREN: Andrew, Computer Designing and Engineering. Theodoros, Logistics at the University of Piraeus.
SCHOOLS/COLLEGE: Pancyprian School. Athens School of Fine arts.
MEMBERSHIPS: Member of Greek Chamber of Arts.
HOBBIES AND INTERESTS: Classical Music and Reading.
PERSONAL PROFILE: George Nicolaides is a Painter and a Professor of Fine Arts 22 personal exhibitions and many group exhibitions too.

PROFESSOR CHRISTOS OLYMPIOS
Professor of vegetable production, Chairman of vegetable production department, Agricultural University of Athens

DATE OF BIRTH: 08-Dec-1942
PLACE OF BIRTH: Cyprus.
MARITAL STATUS: Married to Ero.
CHILDREN: Michalis, Kyriakos, Both University Students.
SCHOOLS/COLLEGE: Pancyprian Gymnasium. University of Thessaloniki, Agricultural University of Athens and University of London.
QUALIFICATIONS: BSc PhD.
MEMBERSHIPS: Member of the International Society for Horticultural Sciences. Member of the Greek Society for Horticultural Sciences.
HOBBIES AND INTERESTS: Music, Athletics, Traveling.
PERSONAL PROFILE: Christos is a Professor of vegetable production, Chairman of the vegetable production department and President of the Department of Horticulture, Agricultural University of Athens, Greece. In charge and co-ordinator of research projects financed by national funds and EU research projects, Establishment of a Seed-potato Center and a Farmers cooperative.

ALEXANDROS PANAYI
Musician involved with Cypriot entries in the Eurovsion song contest performing, backing vocal or composer

PLACE OF BIRTH: Nicosia, Cyprus
SCHOOLS/COLLEGE: Berklee College of Music Boston.
PERSONAL PROFILE: Alex Panayi grew up in a family of musicians and artists. His father was one of the founders of the first symphony orchestra in Cyprus and his mother Klairy acclaimed Cypriot pianist.
During his five year stay in the United States, he had the opportunity to perform with artists such as Gary Burton, Peter Erskine, Billy Joel and The Manhattan Transfer. Alex has been involved with Cypriot entries in the eurovision song contest performing, backing, vocal or composer.

Greece

TASOS PANAYIDES
Former High Commissioner of Cyprus in London

DATE OF BIRTH: 09-Apr-1934
PLACE OF BIRTH: Paphos.
MARITAL STATUS: Married to Pandora Constantinides.
CHILDREN: Two sons, one daughter.
SCHOOLS/COLLEGE: Paphos Gymnasium, University of London, University of Indiana.
QUALIFICATIONS: Diploma in Education, MA Political Science.
HOBBIES AND INTERESTS: Swimming, reading and books.
PERSONAL PROFILE: Teacher 1954-1959. 1st Secretary to President Makarios 60-63. Director Presidents Office 1963-1969. Ambassador of Cyprus to Federal Republic Germany, Switzerland & Austria 1969-1978. High Commissioner in UK and Ambassador to Sweden, Denmark, Norway and Iceland 1979-1990. Permanent Secretary, Ministry of Foreign Affairs Cyprus 1990-1994. Ambassador to Sweden, Finland, Norway, Denmark, Latvia, Lithuania & Estonia 1994-1996. Chairman Avra Ship Management SA June 1997.

KIKIS PANDEHIS
Founder of Kyprionics, a company in Cyprus in Radio Communications and Central Air Conditioning systems

DATE OF BIRTH: 20-Apr-1930.
PLACE OF BIRTH: Jaffa, Palestine Parents from Cyprus.
MARITAL STATUS: Married to Avgi, Larnaca.
CHILDREN: Mary, Economist.
SCHOOLS/COLLEGE: Freres College in Jerusalem and English School Nicosia.
QUALIFICATIONS: Electrical, Mechanical, Enviromental Engineer.
HOBBIES AND INTERESTS: Radio amateur and Astronomy.
PERSONAL PROFILE: Kikis Pandehis is the Founder of Kyprionics a company in Cyprus in Radio Communications and Central Air Conditioning systems. After 74 he moved to Greece and founded DCS Hellas an enviromental control, Building Management Systems and humidification with projects with Hospitals, Hotels Industries and many others.

DEMETRIOS PAPAGEORGIOU
Professor Laboratory of Milk Hygiene and Technology.

PLACE OF BIRTH: Kathikas
PERSONAL PROFILE: Demetrios Papageorgiou is a Professor Laboratory of Milk Hygiene and Technology at the University of Thessaloniki.

DR COSTAS PAPANICOLAS
Professor of Physics University of Athens

PLACE OF BIRTH: Paphos born 1950
SCHOOLS/COLLEGE: Famagusta High School. Massachusetts Institute of Technology.
QUALIFICATIONS: B. Sc. Ph. D.
MEMBERSHIPS: Member of the National Council of Research of Greece, Fellow of the American Physical society.
PERSONAL PROFILE: Costas Papanicolas is a Professor of Physics and Director of the Laboratory of Physics at the University of Athens. He is an adjunct Professor at the University of Illinois and visiting Professor at MIT, and a scientific collaborator at the Centre of Nuclear Research of France. He is also the Head of the Council for Educational Evaluation accreditation in Cyprus.

ANTONIA PAPASTYLIANOU
Lecturer in Psychology at the University of Thrace

PLACE OF BIRTH: Nicosia.
MEMBERSHIPS: Psychology Society of Northern Greece.
PERSONAL PROFILE: Antonia Papastylianou is a Lecturer in Psychology at the University of Thrace.

Greece

The population of Greek Cypriots in Greece is estimated to be around 60,000 mainly situated in the capital of Athens and the cities of Thessalonica and Piraeus.

CHRISTAKIS A. PARASKEVA
Assistant Professor in Chemical Engineering

DATE OF BIRTH: 07-Jun-1961
PLACE OF BIRTH: Famagusta, Cyprus.
MARITAL STATUS: Married to Penelope Moisiadou. Civil Engineer.
CHILDREN: Antonis, Student. Vaia, Student.
SCHOOLS/COLLEGE: Lanition Gymnasium Limassol. University of Patras Greece.
QUALIFICATIONS: Diploma in Chemical Engineering, Ph. D in Chemical Engineering.
MEMBERSHIPS: Technical Association of Greece (TEE) President of the Panhellenic Association of Chemical Engineers/Branch of Western Greece.
HOBBIES AND INTERESTS: Chess, Fishing, Greek Music.
PERSONAL PROFILE: Assistant Professor in Chemical Engineering at the University of Patras. Research Activities, Participation in Research Projects, Publications, Confrence Participation/Attendance, Teaching Activities.

PHILIPPOS PATSALIS
Professor at the University of Ioannina Medical School in Greece

PLACE OF BIRTH: Cyprus
PERSONAL PROFILE: Philippos Patsalis is a Professor at the University of Ioannina Medical School in Greece. He is also the Head of the Department of Cytogenetics at the University of Cyprus.

PROFESSOR ANDREAS PHILIPPOU
Professor of Statistics

DATE OF BIRTH: 15-Jul-1944
PLACE OF BIRTH: Nicosia.
MARITAL STATUS: Married to Athina, Journalist.
CHILDREN: Margarita, Medical Student. Melina, Architectural Student. Alexandra, Architectural Student.
SCHOOLS/COLLEGE: University of Athens and University of Wisconsin.
QUALIFICATIONS: BSc MSc PhD.

MEMBERSHIPS: Grande Ufficiale of Italy and Honorary Chairman of the Mathematical Association of Cyprus.
HOBBIES AND INTERESTS: Swimming and Sailing.
PERSONAL PROFILE: Andreas Philippou is a Professor of Probability and Statistics at the University of Patras. He was Minister of Education of the Republic of Cyprus 1988-90. Member of the House of Representatives of the Republic of Cyprus 2004-7.

STAVROS POLYVIOU
Vice-President of the Youth of The World Federation of Overseas Cypriots

DATE OF BIRTH: 25-Feb-1979
PLACE OF BIRTH: Athens.
MARITAL STATUS: Single.
SCHOOLS/COLLEGE: University of Greece, University of Patras, Greece, University of Kund Sweden.
QUALIFICATIONS: MD, MSc.
MEMBERSHIPS: President of the Youth of The Federation of Cypriot Organizations in Greece, Vice-President of the Youth of The World Federation of Overseas Cypriots.
HOBBIES AND INTERESTS: Sports, Literature, Piano, Foreign Languages and many others.
PERSONAL PROFILE: Pediatric Resident (Karamandaneion Childrens Hospital, Patra Greece), Speaks English, German, Italian, Swedish.

MEROPI (KYRIAKIDOU) POULAKI
Judge in the Court of Appeals, Greece

DATE OF BIRTH: 17-Apr-1952
PLACE OF BIRTH: Karavas.
MARITAL STATUS: Married to Nikolaos, Greece, Doctor.
CHILDREN: Christos, Graduated from Oslo University. Charitini, At Lancaster University doing a Masters.
SCHOOLS/COLLEGE: Greek Gymnasium Lapithos. Law School of Athens University.
MEMBERSHIPS: Greek Judges Society.
PERSONAL PROFILE: Meropi is a Judge in the Court of Appeals, Greece.

DR MARIA ROUSSOU
Senior Lecturer in Education at the
University of Aegean

DATE OF BIRTH: 15-Oct-1948
PLACE OF BIRTH: Nicosia.
MARITAL STATUS: Single.
CHILDREN: Constantinos,
Computer Programmer.
SCHOOLS/COLLEGE:
Pancyprian Gymnasium Nicosia.
Birkbeck College and University
of London.
QUALIFICATIONS: BEd, BA
PHD.
MEMBERSHIPS: Greek Diaspora Trust. Hellenic Centre.
PERSONAL PROFILE: Maria Roussou has written
several publications. Weekly contributions to the
Fileleftheros newspaper in Cyprus. 1974-1979 worked
with the Ministry of Education in Cyprus, Educator &
Counsellor for refugee children & displaced Cypriots.
Senior Lecturer in Education at the University of
Aegean.

CHRISTINE SKEMPA
Lawyer based in Athens

PLACE OF BIRTH: Athens Mother from Nicosia.
PERSONAL PROFILE: Christine Skempa is a Lawyer
based in Athens.

JOANNA SKEMPA
Arts

DATE OF BIRTH: 09-Nov-1934
PLACE OF BIRTH: Nicosia.
CHILDREN: Marinos, Geo
Technical Consultant. Christine,
Lawyer.
SCHOOLS/COLLEGE:
Pancyprian Gymnasium.
Neokleous Institute for
Advanced Secretarial Studies.
MEMBERSHIPS: Institute of
Inter Balkan relations.
HONOURS/AWARDS: From Antenna Channel for
Athletic records from 1952 to 1958 and from the Public
Power Corporation for services to the company.
HOBBIES AND INTERESTS: Sport and Painting.
PERSONAL PROFILE: Artist and Chief of the
personnel Department of supplies direction of Public
Power Corporation.

DR MARINOS SKEMPAS
Science

PLACE OF BIRTH: Athens Mother From Nicosia.
QUALIFICATIONS: MSc Ph. D. D. I. C.
PERSONAL PROFILE: Marinos Skempas is a Geo
Technical Consultant.

MICHAEL SKOULLOS
Associate Professor of Environmental
Chemistry, University of Athens,
Department of Chemistry

PLACE OF BIRTH: Athens family from Nicosia.
PERSONAL PROFILE: Michael Skoullos is an Associate
Professor of Environmental Chemistry, University of
Athens, Department of Chemistry. He is also director of
the Global Water Partnership-Mediterranean.

Dr COSTAS STAMATARIS
President of OKOE Organisation of
Cypriots in Greece

PLACE OF BIRTH: Cyprus.
PERSONAL PROFILE: Dr Costas Stamataris is President
of OKOE Organisation of Cypriots in Greece. He is
also Vice President of the World Federation of Overseas
Cypriots. He is a Researcher in the Department of
Animal Health and Husbandry, Faculty of Veterinary
Medicine Aristoleian University, Thessaloniki.

ANGELIKI STRINGOU
Artist

DATE OF BIRTH: 04-Feb-1937
PLACE OF BIRTH: Limassol,
Cyprus.
MARITAL STATUS: Single.
SCHOOLS/COLLEGE:
University College, Cardiff,
Wales. Art classes at the studio
of artist T. Stefopoulos, Athens,
Greece.
QUALIFICATIONS: Diploma in
Social Sciences. Artist.
MEMBERSHIPS: Greek Chamber of Arts, International
Feminine Cultural Association.
HOBBIES AND INTERESTS: Skiing, Swimming, Yoga.
PERSONAL PROFILE: Artist-14 one-woman exhibitions
in Greece and France and several group exhibitions. Her
paintings can be found in private collections in Greece,
Europe, Finland, USA. Canada, Australia, Cyprus, and in
the collection of Zampelas Art Limited, Nicosia, Cyprus.

Greece

Greece

PROFESSOR NICOS TEREZOPOULOS
Lecturer National Technical University of Athens, Laboratory of Metallurgy

DATE OF BIRTH: 25-Jul-1936
PLACE OF BIRTH: Kyrenia.
MARITAL STATUS: Married to Evangelia, Greek Diplomat.
CHILDREN: Zacharoulla, Maria and Georgia.
SCHOOLS/COLLEGE: Kyrenia Gymnasium, Imperial College, Trent Polytechnic, University of Nottingham.
QUALIFICATIONS: HND. Mining Engineering C. ENG (Chartered Engineer), MPhil (Master of Philosophy, Mining), PhD Mining.
HOBBIES AND INTERESTS: Travel.
PERSONAL PROFILE: Lecturer National Technical University of Athens, Laboratory of Metallurgy.

GIORGOS THEOFANOUS
A leading music producer and composer in Greece having sold more than one million CDs

PLACE OF BIRTH: Larnaca in 1968.
SCHOOLS/COLLEGE: Berklee college of music in Boston USA.
PERSONAL PROFILE: In 1990 he settled in Athens, Greece where he began his career in the music industry. At present he is considered one of the leading composers and music producers in Greece, having sold more than one million CDs and written more than 400 songs for some of the most successful singers in Greece. In 1999 Theofanous put together the first boy band in Greece ONE. ONE became very popular and commercially successful in Greece and Cyprus reaching Platinum sales. He also produced the song for them that got them to the 6th spot in the Eurovision song contest in 2002 in Estonia.

EVRIDIKI THEOKLEOUS
Represented Cyprus in two Eurovision song contests in 1992 and 1994

DATE OF BIRTH: 25-Feb-1968
PLACE OF BIRTH: Limassol.
CHILDREN: One son.
SCHOOLS/COLLEGE: National Conservatory of Cyprus, Le Studio des Varietes in Paris, Berklee college of music in Boston USA.
PERSONAL PROFILE: She moved to Athens in 1989 released her first album in 1991

gia proti fora has since produced several albums. One of the most popular Cypriot singers she has represented Cyprus in two Eurovision song contests in 1992 and 1994.

ANDREAS THEOPHILOU
Director of Research, Democritos National Center for Scientific Research in Athens

DATE OF BIRTH: 25-Mar-1940
PLACE OF BIRTH: Cyprus.
MARITAL STATUS: Married to Ntina Zioga, Greek, Economist, Banking.
CHILDREN: Theodoros, Iris.
SCHOOLS/COLLEGE: Paphos Gymnasium. University of Athens, Salford UK.
QUALIFICATIONS: Physics, Ph. D. Electrical Engineering, Professor, Postgraduate School.
HOBBIES AND INTERESTS: swimming, sailing, popularization of science.
PERSONAL PROFILE: Director of Research, Democritos National Center for Scientific Research in Athens, Research in Theoretical Physics: Development of new mathematical methods and applications in the theory of atoms, molecules, Solids, Surface phenomena.

PROFESSOR ANDREAS THRASYVOULOU
Professor of Apiculture, School of Agriculture, Aristotle University, Thessaloniki

DATE OF BIRTH: 03-Mar-1948
PLACE OF BIRTH: Nicosia Cyprus.
CHILDREN: Eleni Thrasyvoulou.
QUALIFICATIONS: BSc in Agriculture, MSc and PhD in Entomology.
HONOURS/AWARDS: President of the Hellenic Scientific Society of Apiculture-Sericulture, a member of the International Honey Commission and Honorary President of the Cyprian and Rhodes Beekeepers Association.
PERSONAL PROFILE: Professor Thrasyvoulou is the director of the laboratory of Apiculture-Sericulture, School of Agriculture of Aristotle University Thessaloniki he develops programs related with the Physicochemical Characteristics of honey. He has published more than 150 scientific papers in international and national magazines.

THEODORA TILEMAHOU

Doctor, Neurologist. Director of the Department of Neurology, Hippokration Hospital of Athens

DATE OF BIRTH: 16-Jun-1950
PLACE OF BIRTH: Paphos.
MARITAL STATUS: Married to Antonis Spanakos, Athens, Chemist.
CHILDREN: Peter, Student.
SCHOOLS/COLLEGE: Stroumpi Primary School. Medical School of University of Athens.
MEMBERSHIPS: Athens Medical Society and Greek Neurology Society.
HOBBIES AND INTERESTS: History and Astronomy.
PERSONAL PROFILE: Theodora Tilemahou is a Doctor, Neurologist. Director of the Department of Neurology, Hippokration Hospital of Athens.

PANAYIOTIS TSANGARIS

Assistant Professor of Mathematics

PLACE OF BIRTH: Lefkoniko.
PERSONAL PROFILE: Panayiotis Tsangaris is an Assistant Professor in the Department of Mathematics at the University of Athens.

SOTIRIS VARNAVAS

Professor of Geology

PLACE OF BIRTH: Cyprus.
PERSONAL PROFILE: Sotiris Varnavas is a Professor of Geology at the University of Patras he is also a poet. Member of the Committee of the The Poetry Symposium.

ALEXANDROS VASSILIADIS

Associated Professor, Technological Education Institute of Piraeus

DATE OF BIRTH: 22-Jul-1959
PLACE OF BIRTH: Athens Parents from Cyprus.
SCHOOLS/COLLEGE: High School Athens. University of Patras, University of Athens.
QUALIFICATIONS: BSc in Chemistry, PhD in Polymer Chemistry.
HOBBIES AND INTERESTS: Travelling, Sports.
PERSONAL PROFILE: Associated Professor, Technological Education Institute of Piraeus.

ALEXIA VASSILIOU

Musician represented Cyprus in the Eurovision song contest in 1987

DATE OF BIRTH: 05-Feb-1964
PLACE OF BIRTH: Famagusta.
SCHOOLS/COLLEGE: Berklee College of Music.
PERSONAL PROFILE: Prominent Cypriot singer represented Cyprus in the Eurovision song contest in 1987 the song she sung was "aspro mavro" and scored seventh in the competition. Has produced several albums since.

MICHALIS VIOLARIS

Musician written songs in Cypriot dialect that are immensely popular

DATE OF BIRTH: 09-Feb-1944
PLACE OF BIRTH: Ayia Varvara.
SCHOOLS/COLLEGE: Studied in Athens.
PERSONAL PROFILE: He is considered the musician who first made Cypriot music popular, throughout the Greek World, besides recording traditional Cypriot songs like Jasmin and Tyllirkotissa. He has also written songs in Cypriot dialect that are immensely popular.

ANNA VISSI

Singer Awarded 28 Platinum Discs

DATE OF BIRTH: 20-Dec-1957
PLACE OF BIRTH: Pyla.
CHILDREN: Sofia.
SCHOOLS/COLLEGE: National Conservatory and University of athens.
HONOURS/AWARDS: Awarded 28 Platinum Discs.
PERSONAL PROFILE: Anna Vissi is a singer who has represented both Cyprus and Greece in the Eurovision song contest. Anna has sold 9. 5 million Albums Worldwide. She has appeared in concerts in Cyprus, Greece, USA, Canada United Kingdom and Australia.

Greece

PROFESSOR ANDREAS VOSKOS
Professor of Classics at the University of Athens

DATE OF BIRTH: 08-Aug-1943
PLACE OF BIRTH: Pano Zodia.
MARITAL STATUS: Married to Aspasia, Greek, Lecturer.
CHILDREN: Ioanis, Lawyer. Christianna, Lawyer. Anastasi, School. Elysias, School.
SCHOOLS/COLLEGE: Greek Gymnasium Morphou. University of Athens.
QUALIFICATIONS: PhD.
PERSONAL PROFILE: Andreas Voskos is a Professor of Classics at the University of Athens. The Former Chairman of Federation of Cypriots in Greece and Vice Chairman of PSEKA.

IOANNIS VOSKOS
Law Lecturer, International Business Law, Business School of Athens (BCA),

DATE OF BIRTH: 12-Jun-1969
PLACE OF BIRTH: Famagusta.
MARITAL STATUS: Single.
SCHOOLS/COLLEGE: High School of Athens, Greece. University of Hull.
QUALIFICATIONS: L. L. M. Scholarship by the A. G. Leventis Foundation. Lawyer before the Supreme Courts of Greece.
MEMBERSHIPS: Member of the Athens Bar.
PERSONAL PROFILE: Internal Legal Counsel of SAP HELLAS S. A. - Systems, Applications & Products In Data Processing and Country Risk Manager (since Jan. 2000 onwards), where he has been managing cases ever since the establishment of the Company in Greece. Served as Associate Professor at the Athens Business School for the preparation of the Certificate of Qualified Accountant for the Institute of Chartered Accountant's of England and Wales. Also was Lecturer, International Business Law, Business School of Athens (BCA).

MARIOS VRYONIDES
Lecturer in Sociology of Education at the University of Aegean Greece

DATE OF BIRTH: 24-Apr-1972.
PLACE OF BIRTH: Cyprus.
SCHOOLS/COLLEGE: Panteion University Athens, University of Essex and University of London.
QUALIFICATIONS: BA MA PhD.

PERSONAL PROFILE: Marios Vryonidis is a Lecturer in Sociology of Education at the University of Aegean Greece.

HELEN GEORGE YIACOUMIS
Solicitor

DATE OF BIRTH: 06-Jun-1973
PLACE OF BIRTH: Birmingham. Father from Vatili; Mother from Kato Drys.
MARITAL STATUS: Single.
SCHOOLS/COLLEGE: Edgbaston High School for Girls, Birmingham. Kings College, London. College of Law, London.
QUALIFICATIONS: BA CPE Diploma in Law (Commendation).
HOBBIES AND INTERESTS: Fitness, an RSA, qualified instructor.
PERSONAL PROFILE: Helen trained and qualified as a solicitor with city shipping lawyers, Holman Fenwick & Willan, where she spent almost four years. She then gained a year's commercial dispute resolution experience at Hamonds, a top-ten commercial law firm. Helen joined North of England P&I Club, one of the world's leading marine insurance mutuals in 2002 and relocated to the Greek office in March 2003. Was Secretary of West Midlands British Cypriot Youth Committee and a representative of British Cypriot Youth at Biannual International Conference for overseas Cypriots.

CHRISTODOULOS YIALLOURIDES
International Professor in International Relations at Panteion University of Athens

PLACE OF BIRTH: Morphou 1949.
SCHOOLS/COLLEGE: University of Athens and University of Bochum Germany.
PERSONAL PROFILE: Christodoulos Yiallourides is a Professor in International Relations at Panteion University of Athens. He has written in several publications. He is also on the Board of Directors of Daedalos Institute of Geopolitics.

YIASOUMIS YIASOUMI

Footballer Cyprus International playing in Greece

DATE OF BIRTH: 31-May-1975
PLACE OF BIRTH: Larnaca.
PERSONAL PROFILE:
Yiasoumis Yiasoumi Is a Footballer playing for PAOK Fc in Greece he is a Cypriot International played previously for Paralimni and Apoel.

It is free to nominate someone, or yourself, who deserves to be in the book, just send in the name, contact address, telephone number and email to:

Greek Cypriots Worldwide
111 St Thomas's Road London N4 2QJ

Telephone 0044 207503 3498
cypriotwhoswho@aol.com
www.greekcypriotsworldwide.com

Greece

South Africa

ANTONIS ANTONIADES
Chairman of the West Rand Hellenic Community

DATE OF BIRTH: 02-Dec-1951
PLACE OF BIRTH: Strovolos.
MARITAL STATUS: Married to Annalie.
CHILDREN: Three children 2 daughters and one son.
SCHOOLS/COLLEGE: High School Kykkos.
HOBBIES AND INTERESTS: Motoring.
PERSONAL PROFILE: Antonis Antoniades is Chairman of the West Rand Hellenic Community and founder of Ace Packaging.

ARGYROS ANTONIOU
High Commissioner of Cyprus in South Africa

PLACE OF BIRTH: Kythrea 1950
MARITAL STATUS: Married.
CHILDREN: Three Children.
SCHOOLS/COLLEGE: University Nice and Panteion University Athens.
QUALIFICATIONS: BA.
PERSONAL PROFILE: Argyros Antoniou is the High Commissioner of Cyprus in South Africa. He was the Director of Bi Lateral Relations with European Countries Ministry of Foreign affairs in Cyprus.

ZENO APOSTOLIDES
Secretary of the Toxicology Society of Africa

PLACE OF BIRTH: Cyprus.
SCHOOLS/COLLEGE: University of Pretoria.
QUALIFICATIONS: MSc DSc.
MEMBERSHIPS: Secretary of the Toxicology Society of Africa.
PERSONAL PROFILE: Zeno Apostolides is a Senior Lecturer in the Faculty of Natural and Agricultural Sciences School of Biological Sciences, Department of Chemistry at the University of Pretoria.

JIMMY AUGOUSTI
Chairman and managing Director of Blomfontein Celtic

PLACE OF BIRTH: South Africa Parents from Cyprus.
PERSONAL PROFILE: Jimmy Augousti is the Chairman and Managing Director of Blomfontein Celtic Football Club.

ADONIS AVRAMIDES
Managing Director of the Food Emporium chain of Delis The Bread Basket in South Africa

DATE OF BIRTH: 27-Apr-1939
PLACE OF BIRTH: Rizokarpasso.
MARITAL STATUS: Married to Chryso, Cyprus.
CHILDREN: Maria, Katerina, Panos.
PERSONAL PROFILE: Adonis Avramides is the Managing Director of the Food Emporium chain of Delis called The Bread Basket in South Africa. He started the company with his wife in 1982.

KIMON BOYIATSIS
Founder and Director of Trident Capital

DATE OF BIRTH: 29-Aug-1961
PLACE OF BIRTH: Johannesburg Father from Paphos Mother from Morphou.
MARITAL STATUS: Single.
SCHOOLS/COLLEGE: St Johns College.
QUALIFICATIONS: Fellow Institute of Finance.
PERSONAL PROFILE: Kimon Boyiatsis is the Founder and Director of Trident Capital. He is also a Director of South African Institute Finance and a Director of Investment Managers Association of South Africa.

ARISTARGOS (HARRY) CHRISTODOULOU
Lawyer and Director of the Law firm Cliffe Dekker in South Africa

DATE OF BIRTH: 12-Mar-1976
PLACE OF BIRTH: Johannesburg, Grand parents from Paphos and Eurichou.
MARITAL STATUS: Married to Tania, Johannesburg, Attorney.
SCHOOLS/COLLEGE: University of Witwatersrand.
QUALIFICATIONS: BCOM, LLB.
HOBBIES AND INTERESTS: Wildlife Photography, Fly Fishing and Lawn Bowls.
PERSONAL PROFILE: Lawyer and Director of the the Law firm Cliffe Dekker in South Africa.

CHRISTOS CHRISTODOULOU
Lawyer

PLACE OF BIRTH: Paphos.
PERSONAL PROFILE: Christos Christodoulou is a lawyer and a partner in the law firm Christodoulos and Mavrakis based in Johannesburg.

CONSTANTINOS CHRISTODOULOU
President of the Greek Community in North Natal

PLACE OF BIRTH: Cyprus.
PERSONAL PROFILE: President of the Greek Community in North Natal. He is also the owner of a supermarket business.

STELLIANOS (STANLEY) CHRISTODOULOU
World Title Boxing Referee

DATE OF BIRTH: 31-Jan-1946
PLACE OF BIRTH: Johannesburg, Father from Eurichou, Mother from Paphos.
MARITAL STATUS: Married to Mary, South Africa, Housewife.
CHILDREN: Agathodoros, Chartered Accountant. Evgenia, Marketing. Aristargos, Lawyer. Antonios, Project Manager.
SCHOOLS/COLLEGE: Roosevelt.
MEMBERSHIPS: Johannesburg Country Club.
HONOURS/AWARDS: South Africa Presidential Sports Award 1995/1996. Appointed Official of the year 1999 by the World Boxing Association. Inducted into the International Boxing Hall of Fame 2004 in Canasota, New York. Inducted into the South African Sports Hall of Fame 2007, Johannesburg.
HOBBIES AND INTERESTS: Boxing, Golf Soccer, Bowls, Cycling and Squash.
PERSONAL PROFILE: Stanley Christodoulou has been a International Boxing Referee for 44 years including refereeing 115 World Title fights and judging 38 World Title fights. Two Fights that he did that stand out are Pedroza v Mcguigan and Marvin Hagler v Roberto Duran.

AMALIA CHRISTOFOROU
Investigative Journalist

PLACE OF BIRTH: South Africa parents from Cyprus.
SCHOOLS/COLLEGE: University of Witwatersrand in Johannesburg.
QUALIFICATIONS: Honours Degree in Zoology.
PERSONAL PROFILE: Amalia Christoforou began her career as a journalist for the Caxton community newspapers in Johannesburg in 2003. After two and a half years as a reporter and photojournalist she left Caxton to accompany a group of mountaineers to the summit of Kilimanjaro as a freelance journalist. Upon her return she joined the TV programme Carte Blanche team as a research journalist.

DEMETRIOS CONSTANTINIDES
Honorary Consul Of the Republic of Cyprus Cape Town

DATE OF BIRTH: 29-Sep-1966
PLACE OF BIRTH: Nicosia.
MARITAL STATUS: Married to Maria, Parents from Paphos, Lawyer.
CHILDREN: Marian.
SCHOOLS/COLLEGE: University of South africa.
QUALIFICATIONS: Degree in Marketing.
PERSONAL PROFILE: Dr Demetrios Constantinides is the Honorary Consul Of the Republic of Cyprus Cape Town. Also has a property development and retail Business.

> **Stanley Christodoulou has refereed 115 world title fights including the Marvin Hagler v Robert Duran fight.**

South Africa

GEORGE CONSTANTINIDES
Specialist in Water Supply Strategies

PLACE OF BIRTH: Nicosia
MARITAL STATUS: Single.
SCHOOLS/COLLEGE: Witwatersrand University.
QUALIFICATIONS: BSc In Civil Engineering.
PERSONAL PROFILE: George Constantinides is a specialist in Water Supply Strategies, water demand management, water conservation, distribution management, reticulation design and project management.

MARIA CONSTANTINIDES
Lawyer and active in community affairs in Cape Town

DATE OF BIRTH: 17-May-1966
PLACE OF BIRTH: South Africa Parents from Paphos.
MARITAL STATUS: Married to Demetrios Constantinides, Nicosia, Honorary Consul of the Republic of Cyprus Cape Town.
CHILDREN: Marian.
SCHOOLS/COLLEGE: University of Witwatersrand.
QUALIFICATIONS: BA LLB.
HOBBIES AND INTERESTS: Socialising.
PERSONAL PROFILE: Maria Constantinides is a qualified Lawyer and active in community affairs in Cape Town she is involved in the family business.

DEMITRI CONSTANTINOU
Director of the University of the Witwatersrand Centre for Exercise Science and Sports Medicine

DATE OF BIRTH: 20-Jan-1964
PLACE OF BIRTH: Johannesburg, South Africa Parents from Cyprus.
MARITAL STATUS: Married to Barbara, South African, Midwife.
CHILDREN: Jason, Stacey.
SCHOOLS/COLLEGE: The Hill High School, Johannesburg. University of the Witwatersrand, Johannesburg. The University of Cape Town, Cape Town.

QUALIFICATIONS: MBBCh (MD), BSc Med (Hons) Sport Science. : Medical doctor, Advanced Team and sports physician.
MEMBERSHIPS: South African Sports Medicine Association, American College of Sports Medicine, fellow of International Sports Medicine Federation.
HOBBIES AND INTERESTS: Sport, art.
PERSONAL PROFILE: Past President of South African Sports Medicine Association. Team physician to numerous international sporting events, current Director of the University of the Witwatersrand Centre for Exercise Science and Sports Medicine.

PANAYIOTIS DANIEL
Chief Representative at Bank Of Cyprus South Africa

DATE OF BIRTH: 30-Jul-1967
PLACE OF BIRTH: Nicosia.
MARITAL STATUS: Single.
SCHOOLS/COLLEGE: Grammar School Nicosia. University of Pretoria.
QUALIFICATIONS: BA Honours Economics.
HOBBIES AND INTERESTS: Soccer, Racing and Porsche's.
PERSONAL PROFILE: Panayiotis Daniel is the Chief Representative at Bank Of Cyprus South Africa.

MARIA FLACK DAVISON
Commercial Attorney who is involved with the Cypriot Community in Johannesburg

PLACE OF BIRTH: Johannesburg grandfather from Nicosia
MARITAL STATUS: Single.
SCHOOLS/COLLEGE: University of Witwatersrand.
QUALIFICATIONS: BA Bachelor of Laws.
MEMBERSHIPS: Law Society of South Africa.
HONOURS/AWARDS: Best Commercial litigation in a case given by the Law Society.
HOBBIES AND INTERESTS: Reading and travel.
PERSONAL PROFILE: Maria Flack Davison is a Commercial Attorney involved with the Cypriot Community in Johannesburg.

South Africa

GREEK CYPRIOTS WORLDWIDE

ANDREAS DEMETRIOU
Chairman of Hellenic Community of Alberton

DATE OF BIRTH: 23-Aug-1952
PLACE OF BIRTH: Assia.
MARITAL STATUS: Married to Anna, Limassol, Artist (hobby).
CHILDREN: Smaragda, Beautician. Irene, High School Teacher.
SCHOOLS/COLLEGE: High School Trikomo.
PERSONAL PROFILE: Andreas Demetriou is the former Chairman of New Pan Hellenic Voice Greek Radio. He is now the Programming Director. He is also the Chairman of Hellenic Community of Alberton. Andreas owns a fruit juice factory and a franchise retailer.

MARIA DZEREFIS
Started the blood drive nine years ago to find blood donors

DATE OF BIRTH: 12-Jun-1950
PLACE OF BIRTH: Cairo Grandparents Nicosia.
MARITAL STATUS: Single.
CHILDREN: Three sons and two daughters.
SCHOOLS/COLLEGE: Sir John Adamson.
HOBBIES AND INTERESTS: Doing charity work.
PERSONAL PROFILE: Maria Dzerefis is a Human Resources Manager started the blood drive nine years ago to find blood donors. She is also a volunteer worker on the Greek Radio in South Africa.

ALGY DZEREFOS
Attorney a Refugee Lawyer based in Johanesburg

DATE OF BIRTH: 29-Aug-1977
PLACE OF BIRTH: Johannesburg Mother from Cyprus.
MARITAL STATUS: Single.
SCHOOLS/COLLEGE: University of Witwatersrand.
QUALIFICATIONS: BA LLB.
MEMBERSHIPS: Law Society of the Northern Provinces.
HONOURS/AWARDS: National Colours for Rowing.
HOBBIES AND INTERESTS: Sailing and hiking.
PERSONAL PROFILE: Algy Dzerefos is an Attorney a Refugee Lawyer based in Johannesburg.

CATHY DZEREFOS
Environment Consultant

PLACE OF BIRTH: South Africa Grandparents from Nicosia.
PERSONAL PROFILE: Cathy Dzerefos is a private environment consultant.

ARIS EFSTATHIOU
Chairman of the Greek Community in Cape Town

PLACE OF BIRTH: Cyprus.
PERSONAL PROFILE: Aris Efstathiou is the Chairman of the Greek Community in Cape Town and a Director of Ajax Football Club in Cape Town.

SAVVAS ENGLEZAKIS
President of Englezakis Group of Companies

PLACE OF BIRTH: Neo Chorion Paphos.
PERSONAL PROFILE: Savvas is the President of Englezakis Group of Companies who own property, leisure and food product companies. They also own an Ostrich Farm in Cyprus.

ARGYRIS PAPAGEORGIOU FLACK-DAVISON
Information Security programmer and analyst

PLACE OF BIRTH: Johannesburg Grandfather from Nicosia
MARITAL STATUS: Single.
SCHOOLS/COLLEGE: Mondeer High School. University of Witwatersrand.
QUALIFICATIONS: BSc.
MEMBERSHIPS: Hellenic Community of Johannesburg.
HOBBIES AND INTERESTS: Computers and General Sports.
PERSONAL PROFILE: Argyris is a Information Security programmer and analyst and involved in Cypriot Youth Groups in Johannesburg.

South Africa

ANDREAS FLOURENTZOU
Community

DATE OF BIRTH: 27-Jan-1946
PLACE OF BIRTH: Famagusta.
MARITAL STATUS: Married to Lorraine, London.
CHILDREN: Two Sons and Two Daughters.
SCHOOLS/COLLEGE: Famagusta Gymnasium. Hatfield Polytechnic.
HOBBIES AND INTERESTS: Sport.
PERSONAL PROFILE: Andreas Flourentzou is an Electronic Engineer and Chanter at the West Rand Community Church St Andrews.

COSTAS GAVRIEL
Head of Production for the South African TV Drama Generations

DATE OF BIRTH: 23-Oct-1960
PLACE OF BIRTH: South Africa Father from Lysos Mother from Goudhi.
MARITAL STATUS: Married to Natasha, South African Cypriot, Artist.
CHILDREN: Tomas, Elias.
SCHOOLS/COLLEGE: Brothers of Charity College. Pretoria Technikon.
QUALIFICATIONS: National Diploma in Film and Television Production.
PERSONAL PROFILE: Costas Gavriel has worked on numerous International productions filmed in South Africa. He is head of production on a daily drama called Generations.

DIMITRI GEORGIADES
Active Member of community of Hellenic Cypriot Association in South Africa

DATE OF BIRTH: 19-Mar-1932
PLACE OF BIRTH: Neo Chorion Paphos.
MARITAL STATUS: Married to Avgusta, Limassol, Housewife.
CHILDREN: Two sons and one Daughter.
SCHOOLS/COLLEGE: Lykeion, Limassol.
PERSONAL PROFILE: Dimitri Georgiades is involved in the community of Hellenic Cypriot Association in South Africa.

IOANNIS GEORGIOU
Active Committee Member of St Andrews Church in Johannesburg

DATE OF BIRTH: 29-Aug-1949
PLACE OF BIRTH: Fidi, Paphos.
MARITAL STATUS: Married to Christina, Tympou.
CHILDREN: Two daughters and one son.
SCHOOLS/COLLEGE: Fidi Elementary and Paphos Gymnasium.
HOBBIES AND INTERESTS: Community work, Gardening and Backgammon.
PERSONAL PROFILE: Ioannis Georgiou is an Estate Agent and Assistant Treasurer of St Andrews Church in Johannesburg.

NICOLAS GEORGIOU
Owner of One of the biggest shopping centres in South Africa the Fourways Mall

PLACE OF BIRTH: Cyprus.
PERSONAL PROFILE: Nicolas Georgiou is the owner of The Georgiou Group Property Developers. They are the owners of One of the biggest shopping centres in South Africa the Fourways Mall.

GREGORY GREGORIOU
Lecturer at Monash University, South Africa

DATE OF BIRTH: 25-Jul-1959
PLACE OF BIRTH: Johannesburg, Father from Karavas Mother from Kaimakli.
MARITAL STATUS: Married to Helen, South Africa, Teacher.
CHILDREN: George, School. Nicoletta, School.
SCHOOLS/COLLEGE: Gymnasio Kyrenia. Queen Mary College, London, Witwatersrand University and Monash University.
QUALIFICATIONS: BSc, MAP, MIT, MCSE, MCT, MCP and LCP.
MEMBERSHIPS: Uniforium Computer Society SA.
HONOURS/AWARDS: Runner up young Greek Businessman in South Africa.
HOBBIES AND INTERESTS: Movies, Theatre and Soccer.
PERSONAL PROFILE: Gregory Gregoriou lectures at Monash University South Africa.

South Africa

DR STELIOS HADJICHRISTOFIS
Orthopaedic Surgeon

PLACE OF BIRTH: Cyprus
MARITAL STATUS: Married to Nethi Zannettou, Cyprus, Doctor in Osteoporosis.
QUALIFICATIONS: FCS(SA) MMed(Wits)Orth.
HOBBIES AND INTERESTS: Football a Manchester United Fan.
PERSONAL PROFILE: Dr Stelios Hadjichristofi is an Orthopaedic Surgeon based at Bedford Garden Hospital in Johannesburg in South Africa.

GEORGE HADJIYIANNIS
Chairman of the Greek Community of East London, East Cape South Africa

PLACE OF BIRTH: Cyprus.
PERSONAL PROFILE: George Hadjiyiannis is the Chairman of the Greek Community of East London, East Cape South Africa.

COSTAS IOANNOU HASIKOS
Involved in the Church Community of South Africa

DATE OF BIRTH: 17-Dec-1946
PLACE OF BIRTH: Neapolis, Nicosia.
MARITAL STATUS: Married to Joey, South African.
CHILDREN: John, Computer Engineer. Annelize, Graphic Designer. Virtue, geobiology & Accounting Degree.
SCHOOLS/COLLEGE: Pancyprian Gymnasium.
HOBBIES AND INTERESTS: Bowling.
PERSONAL PROFILE: Costas Ioannou Hasikos involved in the Church Community of South Africa and owner of a Dry Cleaning Factory. He is also a committee member and ex President of the Dry Cleaning Association.

CONSTANDINOS IACOVOU
Community involved in Hellenic Youth Groups and Church Council in South Africa

PLACE OF BIRTH: Johannesburg, parents from Paphos and Derynia
MARITAL STATUS: Single.
SCHOOLS/COLLEGE: Alberton High School. University of South africa.
QUALIFICATIONS: BSc.
HOBBIES AND INTERESTS: Motor car racing, motor mechanics and computers.
PERSONAL PROFILE: Constandinos Iacovou a networks engineer at the University of Witwatersrand he is involved in Hellenic Youth Groups and Church Council.

MARY IOANNIDES
Co owner of the retail chain Socrati Shoes in Johannesburg

DATE OF BIRTH: 21-Mar-1952
PLACE OF BIRTH: Johannesburg, Father from Ormidia, Mother from Larnaca.
MARITAL STATUS: Married to Michael, Cyprus, Business.
CHILDREN: Natalie, Julie, Mario.
SCHOOLS/COLLEGE: Milner High Klerksdorp.
HOBBIES AND INTERESTS: Travelling and Reading.
PERSONAL PROFILE: Mary Ioannides is the co owner of Socrati Shoe Shops in Johannesburg.

MICHAEL IOANNIDES
Owns the retail chain Socrati Shoes and is actively involved with St Nektario Church in South Africa

DATE OF BIRTH: 06-Sep-1946.
PLACE OF BIRTH: Galata.
MARITAL STATUS: Married to Maria, Larnaca.
CHILDREN: Natalie, Julie, Mario.
SCHOOLS/COLLEGE: Soleas.
HONOURS/AWARDS: Super Spar of the year 2004.
HOBBIES AND INTERESTS: Sports, Travelling.
PERSONAL PROFILE: Michael Ioannides owns Socrati Shoes and involved with St Nektario Church in South Africa.

South Africa

GEORGE JACKOS
Actor appeared in the Films Navy Seals and Essex Boys

DATE OF BIRTH: 25-Nov-1957
PLACE OF BIRTH: Limassol.
MARITAL STATUS: Single.
SCHOOLS/COLLEGE: Haverstock School and E15 Drama School.
HOBBIES AND INTERESTS: Films.
PERSONAL PROFILE: Appeared on TV in "One Last Chance", "Soldier Soldier", "The Bill", "Coronation Street", "Grafters", "Sunburn", "Fools Gold", "Emmerdale", "Making Out", "Professional", "Bugs". Films include "Indiana Jones", "Navy Seals"and "Essex Boys".

KOSTANTINOS JOANNOU
Architect

DATE OF BIRTH: 04-Aug-1963.
PLACE OF BIRTH: Gauteng South Africa Parents from Paphos.
MARITAL STATUS: Married to Dr M Theologides, South Africa Parents from Cyprus, Child Specialist.
CHILDREN: Raphaella, School.
SCHOOLS/COLLEGE: University of Witwatersrand and Bond University.
QUALIFICATIONS: MBA.
PERSONAL PROFILE: architect.

ANDREAS KARAMICHAEL
Owner of Karaglen Superspar in Edenvale

PLACE OF BIRTH: Paphos.
PERSONAL PROFILE: Andreas Karamichael is the owner of Karaglen Superspar in Edenvale. active member of the Cypriot Community in South Africa.

ANGIE KOLATSIS
Fashion Designer

DATE OF BIRTH: 13-Oct-1970
PLACE OF BIRTH: Polokwane, South Africa Parents from Cyprus.
MARITAL STATUS: Married to Nicholas Kolatsis, Cypriot, Chartered Accountant.
CHILDREN: Stephania, School. Natalia, School. Lucy, Nursery.
SCHOOLS/COLLEGE: Greenside High. Wits Tech.
QUALIFICATIONS: National diploma Fashion Designer.
HOBBIES AND INTERESTS: Cooking.
PERSONAL PROFILE: Angie Kolatsis is a Fashion Designer.

NICOLAS KOLATSIS
Chief Financial Officer for a fruit exporting company. He is also involved in the Cypriot Community in South Africa

DATE OF BIRTH: 06-Dec-1962
PLACE OF BIRTH: Springs, South Africa. Father from Rizokarpasso Mother from Paphos.
MARITAL STATUS: Married to Angie, Johannesburg, Fashion Designer.
CHILDREN: Stephania, Natalia, Luca.
SCHOOLS/COLLEGE: Spring Boys High. University of South Africa.
QUALIFICATIONS: BSc CPA.
HOBBIES AND INTERESTS: Mountain Biking and Reading.
PERSONAL PROFILE: Nicolas Kolatsis is a Chief Financial Officer for a fruit exporting company. He is also involved in the Cypriot Community in South Africa.

NIKOS KRITIKOS
President of the Chamber of Commerce and Industry of Southern Africa

PLACE OF BIRTH: Marathovouno.
MARITAL STATUS: Married, Rizokarpasso.
PERSONAL PROFILE: Nikos Kritikos is President of the Chamber of Commerce and Industry of Southern Africa.

South Africa

ARCHBISHOP SERGIOS KYKKOTIS

His Eminence the Metropolitan of Good Hope South Africa

PLACE OF BIRTH: Platres 1967
SCHOOLS/COLLEGE: High School Petoula. University of Athens.
QUALIFICATIONS: Degree in Paliography.
PERSONAL PROFILE: Archbishop Sergios Kykkotis is the Metropolitan of Good Hope South Africa.

COSTA LAMBRIANOS

Owner of the property company Kalavrita Investments that developed the Midland Village Shopping Centre

PLACE OF BIRTH: Liopetri born 1935
MARITAL STATUS: Married to Elen.
CHILDREN: Mario, Family business. Andrew, Family business. Anastasia, Law lecturer.
PERSONAL PROFILE: Costas began business with his brother the late Andrew in Confectionery. They then diverted into packaging and dispensing milk and renting hand dryers. He also owns the property company Kalavrita Investments that developed the Midland Village Shopping Centre.

MAROULLA LAMBROU

Community

DATE OF BIRTH: 19-Jul-1951
PLACE OF BIRTH: South Africa Father From Kambo Mother from fidi.
SCHOOLS/COLLEGE: Yeovil Convent.
HOBBIES AND INTERESTS: Soccer.
PERSONAL PROFILE: Maroulla Lambrou is actively involved in the Cypriot Brotherhood.

PROKOMENOS LEONIDAS

Active member of the Cyprus Brotherhood in South Africa

DATE OF BIRTH: 15-Jul-1950
PLACE OF BIRTH: Lefkara.
MARITAL STATUS: Married to Melpo, Limassol.
CHILDREN: Two Daughters.
SCHOOLS/COLLEGE: Lefkara Gymnasium.
HOBBIES AND INTERESTS: Pilotta.
PERSONAL PROFILE: Prokomenos Leonidas is an active member of the Cyprus Brotherhood in South Africa. He has a dry Cleaning business.

ANDREAS LIONTARIDES

Director of Spar South Africa for 25 years, member of the International Executive Committee of Spar International Amsterdam

DATE OF BIRTH: 14-Sep-1946
PLACE OF BIRTH: Neon Chorion, Paphos.
MARITAL STATUS: Married to Maroulla, Neon Chorion, Business.
CHILDREN: Michael, Business. Chrystalo, Banking.
SCHOOLS/COLLEGE: High School. Polis, Paphos.
HONOURS/AWARDS: Mr Spar South Africa.
HOBBIES AND INTERESTS: Business.
PERSONAL PROFILE: Andreas Liontarides is the Director of Spar South Africa for 25 years, member of the International Executive Committee of Spar International Amsterdam. Former Chairman West Rand Hellenic Community and former Chairman of the Greek radio Pan Hellenic Voice.

South Africa

There was estimated at one time to be 25,000 Cypriots in South Africa now due to the recent political problems it has decreased to around 10,000 with many going back to Cyprus and other countries.

MAROULLA LIONTARIDES
Vice Chair of the Hellenic Community of West Rand

DATE OF BIRTH: 29-Aug-1950
PLACE OF BIRTH: Neo Chorion, Paphos.
MARITAL STATUS: Married to Andreas.
CHILDREN: One son and one daughter.
SCHOOLS/COLLEGE: Holys Chrysochous, Paphos.
HOBBIES AND INTERESTS: Athletics.
PERSONAL PROFILE: Maroulla Liontarides is Vice Chair of the Hellenic Community of West Rand. She has also been involved in the Family business of Spar Supermarkets.

ANDREAS MACHOS
Former Vice Chairman of the Hellenic West Rand Community

DATE OF BIRTH: 08-Jan-1940
PLACE OF BIRTH: Agros.
MARITAL STATUS: Married to Eleni, Nicosia.
CHILDREN: Three daughters.
SCHOOLS/COLLEGE: Agros Elementary.
HOBBIES AND INTERESTS: Carpentry.
PERSONAL PROFILE: Andreas Machos is the Former Vice Chairman of the Hellenic West Rand Community. He is also the owner of a Supermarket Business.

PETER MAMMOUS
Education

DATE OF BIRTH: 06-Jul-1945
PLACE OF BIRTH: Athienou.
MARITAL STATUS: Married to Maria, Greek Cypriot, Housewife.
CHILDREN: John, Marketing Manager. Chrystalla, Artist and Graphic Designer.
SCHOOLS/COLLEGE: Athienou Primary. Teachers College, Bulawayo, Zimbabwe and University of Rhodesia.
QUALIFICATIONS: Diplomas in Education and Marketing Management.
MEMBERSHIPS: Institute of Marketing Management SA.

HOBBIES AND INTERESTS: Golf, Cricket, Soccer, Rugby, Tennis Squash, Music and Photography.
PERSONAL PROFILE: Peter Mammous was a teacher. He is now a Businessman based in South Africa.

DEMETRI MANOLIS
Chief Executive of Goldplat PLC a gold mining and production company in South Africa

PLACE OF BIRTH: Cyprus.
SCHOOLS/COLLEGE: Technical University of Athens.
QUALIFICATIONS: Mining and Metallurgy Degree.
PERSONAL PROFILE: Demetri Manolis is the Chief Executive of Goldplat PLC a gold mining and production company in South Africa.

ANASTASIA LAMBRIANOU MARTALAS
Law Lecturer at the University of witwatersrand

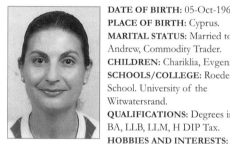

DATE OF BIRTH: 05-Oct-1968
PLACE OF BIRTH: Cyprus.
MARITAL STATUS: Married to Andrew, Commodity Trader.
CHILDREN: Chariklia, Evgenia.
SCHOOLS/COLLEGE: Roedean School. University of the Witwatersrand.
QUALIFICATIONS: Degrees in BA, LLB, LLM, H DIP Tax.
HOBBIES AND INTERESTS: Gardening, music, theatre, ballet, opera.
PERSONAL PROFILE: Lectured company law, Tax law and insolvency law, Lectured introduction to commercial law at Witwatersrand University.

ANTONIS MICHAEL
Active member of the Hellenic Cypriot Community in Johannesburg

DATE OF BIRTH: 27-Dec-1954
PLACE OF BIRTH: Fidi.
MARITAL STATUS: Married to Panayiota, Paphos.
CHILDREN: Five Daughters.
SCHOOLS/COLLEGE: Fidi Elementary.
HOBBIES AND INTERESTS: Travel.
PERSONAL PROFILE: Antonis Michael is an active member of the Hellenic Cypriot Community and has a Supermarket.

CLEO CHRISTINA NEOPHYTOU

Won a vision & Values award for being client centred which was published in the local paper (Cambridge Evening News)

DATE OF BIRTH: 23-Jul-1956
PLACE OF BIRTH: South Africa Father from Arsos Mother from Limassol.
MARITAL STATUS: Single.
CHILDREN: Nadia, Journalist, Radio 702. Matthew, Graphic Designer.
SCHOOLS/COLLEGE: Faraday Comprehensive School. Barclays International Bank Training College, Southgate Technical College, University of Witwatersrand.
QUALIFICATIONS: 7 O'Levels, Art degree, Diplomas in Fashion & Clothing, Diplomas in Flower Arranging.
HOBBIES AND INTERESTS: Reading, sewing, salsa, music.
PERSONAL PROFILE: Works for an International Law Firm ranked fifth in the world. Won a Vision & Values award for being client centred which was published in the local paper (Cambridge Evening News.).

NADIA MARIA NEOPHYTOU

Arts and entertainment journalist for Primedia Broadcasting

PLACE OF BIRTH: South Africa Father From Paphos Maternal grandparents Arsos and Kambos
SCHOOLS/COLLEGE: University of Cape Town.
QUALIFICATIONS: BA in Film, Media and Visual Studies.
HONOURS/AWARDS: The winner of the ACT Arts Correspondent Award 2007 sponsored by Distell.
PERSONAL PROFILE: As a producer for the current affairs programme 3rd Degree on etv, Nadia Neophytou has produced a number of shows about the arts. She began writing about the arts for The Big Issue magazine in her second year at Varsity, when she was also arts editor of the official student newspaper and music manager at UCT Radio. In her current position, she has found a niche as the arts and entertainment journalist for Primedia Broadcasting and broadcasts stories about arts events across the four stations. Nadia has secured a number of exclusive interviews locally and internationally ranging from celebrity international actors like Andy Garcia to musicians like Billy Joel and scooped interviews with Soweto Gospel Choir after their Grammy win.

Nadia's reports reach a total of three and a half million listeners.

COSTAS NICOLAOU

Chairman of Hellenic Cyprus Brotherhood South Africa

DATE OF BIRTH: 15-May-1944
PLACE OF BIRTH: Tymbou.
MARITAL STATUS: Married.
CHILDREN: Gregory, Business. Nicholas, Business. Michael, Business.
SCHOOLS/COLLEGE: Cyprus High School.
HOBBIES AND INTERESTS: Pilotta.
PERSONAL PROFILE:
Costas Nicolaou is the Chairman of Hellenic Cyprus Brotherhood South Africa. Also Member of Executive Council of the Federation of Hellenic Council South Africa.

STAVROS NICOLAOU

Senior Executive for Africa's Largest Pharmaceutical Company Aspen Pharmacare Holdings Ltd

DATE OF BIRTH: 24-Jun-1965
PLACE OF BIRTH: Johannesburg, Parents from Cyprus.
MARITAL STATUS: Married to Maxine.
CHILDREN: Alexeia, School. Charalambos, School.
SCHOOLS/COLLEGE: Highlands North Boys High School. University of Witwatersrand.
QUALIFICATIONS: Bachelor of Pharmacy.
HONOURS/AWARDS: Healthcare Marketer of the year Award. Executive member of the Sandton Branch of the ANC. Chairman of the Lobby Group of Cyprus. Vice President of Africa of PSEKA.
HOBBIES AND INTERESTS: Politics, Gym, Soccer, Rugby and Cricket.
PERSONAL PROFILE: Stavros Nicolaou was appointed by the SA Minister of Public Enterprise to the Board of of Directors of Transnet Ltd South Africa's, largest State owned Enterprise. Also appointed by the minister of Trade of SA to be Chairman of the Board of the State owned Airline SA Express Airways(PTY) Ltd. Stavros is employed as a Senior Executive for Africa's largest Pharmaceutical Company Aspen Pharmacare Holdings Ltd.

South Africa

ANDREAS PASCHALIDES
The Honorary President of the Cypriot Community of South Africa / South African Wrestling Champion

DATE OF BIRTH: 15-Aug-1927
PLACE OF BIRTH: Trikomo.
MARITAL STATUS: Married to Maria, Cyprus.
CHILDREN: Paschalis, Finance. Adamandia, Teacher. Angelos, Business.
SCHOOLS/COLLEGE: English School Tricomo.
HONOURS/AWARDS: Undefeated Wrestling Champion light heavyweight in South Africa. In 1956 was selected to represent South Africa in the Olympic games in Australia because of apartheid they were refused entry.
HOBBIES AND INTERESTS: Wrestling.
PERSONAL PROFILE: Andreas Paschalides is the Honorary President of the Cypriot Community of South Africa.

MARIOS PIERIDES
Consultant Psychiatrist

DATE OF BIRTH: 16-Apr-1959.
PLACE OF BIRTH: Pretoria South africa.
MARITAL STATUS: Single.
SCHOOLS/COLLEGE: University of Witwatersrand, Johannesburg.
QUALIFICATIONS: BA MBBCh MRCPsych.
MEMBERSHIPS: Member of the Royal College of Psychiatrists.
HOBBIES AND INTERESTS: Wagner and Football.
PERSONAL PROFILE: Marios Petrides is a Consultant Psychiatrist.

LOUCAS POUROULIS
Mining Entrepreneur

DATE OF BIRTH: 16-Oct-1938
MARITAL STATUS: Married to Artemis.
SCHOOLS/COLLEGE: National Technical University of Greece.
QUALIFICATIONS: Degree in Metallurgy and Engineering.
PERSONAL PROFILE: Mining Entrepreneur. Began by working as an underground manager at Anglo American Western deep levels he then went on to form the Salene group of companies which has throughout its life produced gold, platinum, diamonds, titanium and emeralds.

ARCHBISHOP JOHANNESBURG AND PRETORIA KYKKOTIS SERAPHIM
Archbishop Johannesburg and Pretoria South Africa is also the Vice President of all African Council of Churches

DATE OF BIRTH: 02-Feb-1961
PLACE OF BIRTH: Galataria.
SCHOOLS/COLLEGE: Lykeion Kykkou. University of Athens.
HOBBIES AND INTERESTS: Reading.
PERSONAL PROFILE: His Eminence Seraphim Kykkotis Greek Orthodox Archbishop Johannesburg and Pretoria South Africa is also the Vice President of all African Council of Churches, member of the CC of the South Africa Council of Churches.

VASILLIOS SILVISTRIS
Counselling Practitioner and Psychotherapist

DATE OF BIRTH: 19-Dec-1953
PLACE OF BIRTH: Johannesburg Father from Arsos Mother from Limassol.
SCHOOLS/COLLEGE: University of Pretoria, Witwatersrand, South Africa and University of Surrey.
QUALIFICATIONS: MA PhD.
MEMBERSHIPS: Royal Society of Health British Association for Counsellors and Psychotherapist.
HOBBIES AND INTERESTS: Tennis, music, travelling, reading and the arts.
PERSONAL PROFILE: Vasillis is a Counselling Practitioner and Psychotherapist based in the UK.

PROFESSOR S SOFIANOS
Professor of Physics University of South Africa

PLACE OF BIRTH: Cyprus.
QUALIFICATIONS: PhD.
PERSONAL PROFILE: Professor Sofianou is a Professor in the department of Physics in the University of South Africa.

South Africa

MICHALIS SOTERIOU
Former Chairman of Hellenic Cypriot Brotherhood of South Africa

DATE OF BIRTH: 03-Feb-1937
PLACE OF BIRTH: Larnaca.
MARITAL STATUS: Married to Stavroulla, Larnaca.
CHILDREN: One Boy and one girl.
SCHOOLS/COLLEGE: Emporikon Lykeion, Larnaca.
HOBBIES AND INTERESTS: Pillotta.
PERSONAL PROFILE: Michael Soteriou Former Chairman of Hellenic Cypriot Brotherhood of South Africa. Hes the former Chairman of SIA Export Company.

STAVROS STAVRIDES
member of the Cyprus Brotherhood of South Africa

DATE OF BIRTH: 24-Sep-1941
PLACE OF BIRTH: Trikomo.
MARITAL STATUS: Married to Yiannoulla, Ora, Larnaca.
CHILDREN: John, Andreas, Paris.
SCHOOLS/COLLEGE: High School, Trikomo.
HOBBIES AND INTERESTS: Socialising and Bush outings.
PERSONAL PROFILE: Stavros Stavrides is a member of the committee of the Cyprus Brotherhood of South Africa. Stavros owns a Supermarket.

Dr MARIA STYLIANOU
Psychologist

PLACE OF BIRTH: South Africa Father From Cyprus
SCHOOLS/COLLEGE: University of Natal, South africa and University of Liverpool.
QUALIFICATIONS: BA M. Soc and PhD.
PERSONAL PROFILE: Dr Maria Stylianou is a Research Psychologist at the University of Lancaster.

THEMI THEMISTOCLEOUS
Advisor to the South Africa Government Treasury

DATE OF BIRTH: 17-Aug-1953
PLACE OF BIRTH: Cyprus.
MARITAL STATUS: Married to Julie, Cyprus, Housewife.
CHILDREN: Harry, Junior Architect.
SCHOOLS/COLLEGE: University of Witwatersrand.
QUALIFICATIONS: B. Com.
MEMBERSHIPS: South African Institute of Chartered Accountants.
HONOURS/AWARDS: Thomas International ranked Themi in the 95th percentile worldwide in terms of logical thinking.
PERSONAL PROFILE: Themi Themistocleous as an Entrepreneur and an analyst of global trends he has created companies in fields as diverse as mining and farming. Themi is the Chairman of Indigo Cube and an adviser to the South Africa Government Treasury.

PAUL ANDREAS THEODOSIOU
Managing Director of Acucap Properties Ltd, a JSE listed property company

DATE OF BIRTH: 05-Apr-1963
PLACE OF BIRTH: Salisbury, Rhodesia(now Zimbabwe) Father Andreas from Neon Chorion.
MARITAL STATUS: Married to Gail.
CHILDREN: Samuel, Andrea.
SCHOOLS/COLLEGE: Alan Wilson High School. Rhodes University and University of Cape Town.
QUALIFICATIONS: Bachelor ofCommerce (Honours) higher National diplomain Accountancy. Chartered Accountant(SA) and MBA.
MEMBERSHIPS: SA Institute of Chartered Accountants.
HOBBIES AND INTERESTS: Cycling, classical music and reading history.
PERSONAL PROFILE: Paul Theodosiou is the Managing Director of Acucap Properties Ltd, a JSE listed property company (REIT) with assets of £450 Million.

South Africa

CHRISTOS THEOLOGIDES
Pharmacist Managing Director of a
Pharmaceutical company

DATE OF BIRTH: 04-Mar-1972.
PLACE OF BIRTH: Gauteng South Africa. Father from
Limassol Mother from Famagusta.
MARITAL STATUS: Single.
SCHOOLS/COLLEGE: Christian Brothers College and
University of Witwatersrand.
QUALIFICATIONS: Bpharm and B. A. Psychology.
HOBBIES AND INTERESTS: Tennis and Cricket.
PERSONAL PROFILE: Pharmacist Managing Director
of a Pharmaceutical company.

DR MARIA THEOLOGIDES
Child Specialist Dentist

DATE OF BIRTH: 31-Oct-1969
PLACE OF BIRTH: Gauteng
Johannesburg, Father from
Limassol. Mother from
Famagusta.
MARITAL STATUS: Married to
Kostantinos Joannou, Cyprus,
Architect, Property Developer.
CHILDREN: One Child.
SCHOOLS/COLLEGE: St
Dominics Convent. University
of Witwatersrand and Stellembosch University.
QUALIFICATIONS: B. D. S. BSc MSc.
MEMBERSHIPS: European society of anaesthetics and
Dental association of South Africa.
HOBBIES AND INTERESTS: Life Coaching and
Swimming.
PERSONAL PROFILE: Maria Theologides is a Child
Specialist Dentist, Freelance Writer, Motivational speaker,
Life Coaching and addiction Counsellor.

IOANNIS TSANGARIS
Active in the Cyprus Brotherhood,
West Rand Hellenic Community and
Rizokarpasso Association

DATE OF BIRTH: 14-Aug-1954
PLACE OF BIRTH:
Rizokarpasso.
MARITAL STATUS: Married to
Kyriacou, Kathikas.
CHILDREN: Natasa,
Optometrist. Andreas,
Accountant. Maria, Chemical
Engineer.
SCHOOLS/COLLEGE:
Rizokarpasso High School.
HOBBIES AND INTERESTS: Fishing and Hunting.

PERSONAL PROFILE: Ioannis Tsangaris is involved
with the Cyprus Brotherhood, West Rand Hellenic
Community and Rizokarpasso Association. He has a
supermarket and Restaurant Business.

DOROTHEA WILD
Community

DATE OF BIRTH: 06-Feb-1954
PLACE OF BIRTH: Lyssos.
MARITAL STATUS: Single.
CHILDREN: Elena, Mariana.
SCHOOLS/COLLEGE: Nigel
Convent.
HOBBIES AND INTERESTS:
Dancing, Pilates and Welfare
work.
PERSONAL PROFILE:
Dorothea Wild is involved with
the Hellenic Community and is in the welfare committee
of the Greek Church in Cape Town.

MARIANA WILD
Lecturer

DATE OF BIRTH: 04-Nov-1981
PLACE OF BIRTH:
Johannesburg mother from
Lyssos.
MARITAL STATUS: Single.
CHILDREN: Gabriella Zoe.
SCHOOLS/COLLEGE: Roedean
School. Stellembosch University.
QUALIFICATIONS: Music
Vocal Licentiate and Montessori
Teacher accredited.
MEMBERSHIPS: Hellenic Community.
HOBBIES AND INTERESTS: Singing, Art, Swimming,
Gardening and Cooking.
PERSONAL PROFILE: Mariana Wild is a lecturer for
Modern Montessori and course coordinator in Cape
Town.

South Africa

CHRISTOPHER YIANGOU
Industrial Engineer/Software Designer

DATE OF BIRTH: 13-Mar-1958
PLACE OF BIRTH: South Africa.
MARITAL STATUS: Single.
SCHOOLS/COLLEGE: Wits University/Sortware Designer.
QUALIFICATIONS: National Diploma in Engineering, Graduate Diploma in Engineering.
HOBBIES AND INTERESTS: Astronomy, Science and Technology, Philosophy.
PERSONAL PROFILE: Independent Industrial Engineering Consultant specializing in software solutions.

ATHENA KARSERA YIAZOU
Journalist for Cyprus Weekly

DATE OF BIRTH: 04-Oct-1977
PLACE OF BIRTH: Johannesburg Father from Famagusta.
MARITAL STATUS: Married to Vassos, Neo Chorio Kythreas, Land Registry Official.
CHILDREN: Giorgos.
SCHOOLS/COLLEGE: Houghton Primary, International school of Paphos. European University Cyprus.
QUALIFICATIONS: Associate Degree in Arts and Sciences with a specialisation in Communication studies.
MEMBERSHIPS: Member of Union of Cyprus Journalists.
HOBBIES AND INTERESTS: Scuba diving, nature, music and reading.

PERSONAL PROFILE: Athena Karsera Yiazou is a reporter at the Cyprus Weekly newspaper in Nicosia, Cyprus.

NETHI ZANNETTOU
Doctor in Osteoporosis

PLACE OF BIRTH: Cyprus
MARITAL STATUS: Married to Stelios Hadjichristofis, Cyprus, Orthopaedic Surgeon.
PERSONAL PROFILE: Nethi Zannettou is a Doctor in Osteoporosis at Bedford Gardens Hospital in Johannesburg.

It is free to nominate someone, or yourself, who deserves to be in the book, just send in the name, contact address, telephone number and email to:

Greek Cypriots Worldwide
111 St Thomas's Road, London, N4 2QJ
Telephone 0044 207503 3498

cypriotwhoswho@aol.com
www.greekcypriotsworldwide.com

South Africa

UK

ARTEMIS ACHILLEOS
Commissioned to make the bridesmaids shoes for the royal wedding of Prince Andrew and Sarah Ferguson

DATE OF BIRTH: 28-Jun-1953
PLACE OF BIRTH: Larnaca.
MARITAL STATUS: Married to Lilia, London, Fashion Designer.
CHILDREN: Nicolas, Alexis.
SCHOOLS/COLLEGE: Copeland Senior High School.
HOBBIES AND INTERESTS: Community work, film and TV.
PERSONAL PROFILE: In 1986, was commissioned to make the bridesmaids' shoes for the royal wedding of Prince Andrew and Sarah Ferguson.
Served as Chairman of the PTA at Chancellors School, Brookmans Park, Hertfordshire. Former Vice Chairman at Twelve Apostles Greek Orthodox Church, Hertfordshire and former Secretary of London branch of British Boot & Shoe Institute.

CHRIS ACHILLEOS
Conceptual artist for the film Willow directed by George Lucas

DATE OF BIRTH: 26-Sep-1947
PLACE OF BIRTH: Famagusta.
MARITAL STATUS: Single.
CHILDREN: Esther, Manageress of Gap Stores. Anna, Window Dresser.
SCHOOLS/COLLEGE: Tollington Park School. Hornsey College of Art.
PERSONAL PROFILE: Chris Achilleos was a conceptual artist for the film Willow directed by George Lucas. Has also done book illustrations for authors such as Robert Howard's book Conan.

SOTOS ACHILLEOS
Inventor/Illustrator/Designer/Time Out's Good Toy Guide Puzzle of the Year 2001

DATE OF BIRTH: 02-Sep-1955
PLACE OF BIRTH: London. Father, Andreas, from Vokolida; Mother, Eleni, from Eptakomi.
MARITAL STATUS: Married to Tanya, New Zealand.
CHILDREN: Helen, Leonida, Alexander, Lily.
QUALIFICATIONS: BA Honours in Commercial Design and Illustration.
HONOURS/AWARDS: National Association of Toy & Leisure Libraries Gold Medal for inventing reflection puzzles - Time Out's Good Toy Guide Puzzle of the Year 2001.
HOBBIES AND INTERESTS: All arts.
PERSONAL PROFILE: Trained as a Commercial Artist/Designer and has, for most of his career, worked as a Freelance Illustrator/Designer. Over the years, his work has appeared in various publications, books, toys and games. His close association with the toy business prompted him to become an inventor within this industry. He is also a painter and some of his early canvasses are on permanent. display at the Whitechapel Hospital.

ANDREAS ADAM
Professor of Interventional Radiology University of London

DATE OF BIRTH: 04-May-1951
PLACE OF BIRTH: Nicosia.
MARITAL STATUS: Married to Jane, London, Consultant Radiologist.
CHILDREN: Sophie, Clio.
SCHOOLS/COLLEGE: First Greek Gymnasium for Boys, Famagusta. Middlesex Hospital Medical School. Numerous medical societies.
QUALIFICATIONS: MB, BS Honours FRCP, FRCR, FRCS.
MEMBERSHIPS: Numerous medical societies.
HOBBIES AND INTERESTS: Current affairs and music.
PERSONAL PROFILE: Professor of Interventional Radiology University of London.

GINA ADAMOU
Former Mayor of Haringey

DATE OF BIRTH: 06-Feb-1945
PLACE OF BIRTH: Psymolophou.
MARITAL STATUS: Married.
CHILDREN: Christina, Social Worker. Andreas, Project Manager. Niki, Special Needs Teacher.
SCHOOLS/COLLEGE: Schooling in Cyprus, then North London College as a mature student for four years.
MEMBERSHIPS: Labour Party.
HONOURS/AWARDS: Award in celebration of Lifetime Achievements from Greek Cypriot Women's Organisation of Haringey.
HOBBIES AND INTERESTS: Reading.
PERSONAL PROFILE: Councillor since 1990 (Haringey Council), chairing Social Services 1993-97 and 1999-00 Ethnic Minorities Organisation, Women's Organisation and more voluntary sector organisations. Former Mayor of Harringey.

MARIOS ADAMOU
Doctor who set up a number of innovative NHS services providing free care to people with mental health problems

PLACE OF BIRTH: Limassol in 1972
MARITAL STATUS: Married to Anna, Doctor.
SCHOOLS/COLLEGE: Aristotle University of Thessaloniki, Kings College. Northumbria University, Staffordshire University, Northampton University. University of Kent.
QUALIFICATIONS: MRC psych, DOcc Med.
HONOURS/AWARDS: Scholarship from Ministry of Economics Cyprus during graduate studies.
HOBBIES AND INTERESTS: Opera, History, Art.
PERSONAL PROFILE: Doctor who set up a number of innovative NHS services providing free care to people with mental health problems in Kent. Has had links with Manic Depressive Fellowship (Patient group) and Adders (Patient group).

MOYSIS ADAMOU
President of Achna Association UK

DATE OF BIRTH: 06-Aug-1940
PLACE OF BIRTH: Achna.
MARITAL STATUS: Married to Maria Nicola.
CHILDREN: Adam, Graphic Designer. Helen, Travel Agent.
SCHOOLS/COLLEGE: Primary education.
HOBBIES AND INTERESTS: Gardening and politics.
PERSONAL PROFILE: President of Achna Association in Britain.

LORD ANDREW ADONIS
Secretary of State for Transport

DATE OF BIRTH: 22-Feb-1963
PLACE OF BIRTH: UK. Father from Yialoussa.
MARITAL STATUS: Married to Kathryn Davis.
CHILDREN: Two.
SCHOOLS/COLLEGE: Kingham Hill School, Keble College, Oxford; Christ Church, Oxford.
QUALIFICATIONS: BA 1st Class Honours Modern History, D Phil.
PERSONAL PROFILE: Member of the HQ Secretariat British Gas Corporation 1984-85. Fellow in Politics, Oxford University, 1988-1991. Financial Times Public Policy correspondent 1993-1994, The Observer 1996-98. 1987-1988 member of Oxford City Council. A member of the Prime Minister's Policy Unit since 1998, former Head of the Policy Unit. Has written five books: Parliament Today (1990), Making Aristocracy Work - the Peerage and the Political System in Brtiain 1884 to 1914 (1993), A Conservative Revolution: the Thatcher-Reagan Decade in Perspective (1994), Failure in British Government; the politics of the Poll Tax (1994), and A Class Act - the Myth of Britain's Classless Society (1997). Made a Lord and department for education and skills parliamentary secretary and Minister of Schools in London in 2005. In 2008 Lord Adonis was appointed Minister of State for Transport. In 2009 he was appointed Secretary of State for Transport.

UK

Lord Adonis is the first Greek Cypriot lord and first Greek Cypriot to hold a ministerial position in the UK

FRANCESCA PHOTIADES ADONIS
Merchandiser for Tescos

DATE OF BIRTH: 27-Aug-1974
PLACE OF BIRTH: Dhekelia. (The intention of the family was to go and live in Cyprus - as a result of the outbreak of the war in 1974 Francesca was born in the British bases).
MARITAL STATUS: Married.
SCHOOLS/COLLEGE: Parliament Hill, Islington 6th Form Centre, London Guildhall University.
QUALIFICATIONS: BA in Business Studies.
HOBBIES AND INTERESTS: Travel, reading and theatre.
PERSONAL PROFILE: Worked overseas for BHS as Assistant Merchandiser, then at Dorothy Perkins as Assistant Merchandiser in womenswear. Now works for Tesco as a merchandiser.

GEORGE ADONIS
Barrister/Legal advisor and Secretary of the Cyprus Brother hood

DATE OF BIRTH: 13-Jan-1942
PLACE OF BIRTH: Vasili.
MARITAL STATUS: Married to Irene, Scotland.
CHILDREN: Francesca, Merchandiser. Nicholas, Media.
SCHOOLS/COLLEGE: Pan Cyprian Gymnasium, Nicosia, North West London Polytechnic, Lincolns Inn, called to the Bar in 1973.
QUALIFICATIONS: Barrister at Law.
MEMBERSHIPS: Member of the Leonarisso Vassilli Association. On the Executive Committee of the National Federation of Cypriots. Member of the Anglo Cypriot Law Association.
HOBBIES AND INTERESTS: Theatre, tennis and football (Arsenal fan).
PERSONAL PROFILE: George Adonis is a Barrister of Law Chambers at the Temple specialising in Family private and Public Law and Licensing and crime. He is also the Legal advisor and Secretary of the Cyprus Brotherhood.

DR ANDREW AGAPIOU
Academic co-director of the centre for the built environment in Glasgow

DATE OF BIRTH: 26-Aug-1964
PLACE OF BIRTH: London, Father from Statos Mother from Paramytha.
MARITAL STATUS: Married to Fiona, Glasgow, Renal Nursing Sister.
SCHOOLS/COLLEGE: Holloway Boys School, Riversmead School. University of Herts and Loughborough University.
QUALIFICATIONS: PHD BSc MSc in civil engineering.
MEMBERSHIPS: He is a member of the Institution of Engineers Australia and a Chartered Professional Engineer, a member of the association of building Engineers and the Chartered Institute of Building.
HONOURS/AWARDS: Elected member of Strathclyde University senate.
HOBBIES AND INTERESTS: Travel.
PERSONAL PROFILE: Andrew is currently academic co-director of the centre for the built environment in Glasgow.

ANDREAS AGATHOU
Senior Manager of Cyprus Airways for Europe, Middle East & Gulf, USA and Canada

DATE OF BIRTH: 06-Mar-1951
PLACE OF BIRTH: Larnaca.
MARITAL STATUS: Married to Elpida, From Morphou.
CHILDREN: Evros, Anthea.
SCHOOLS/COLLEGE: American Academy. Polytechnic of Central London, London School of Economics and Cranfield College of Aeronautics.
QUALIFICATIONS: BA(Hons) MSc and Chartered Certified Accountant.
HOBBIES AND INTERESTS: Travelling, Reading, Films, Comedies, History & Politics, Documentaries, Writing and Walking.
PERSONAL PROFILE: Andreas Agathou is the Senior Manager of Cyprus Airways for Europe, Middle East & Gulf, USA and Canada. Has also served on the Cypriot Community Independant Greek Schools Committees including as Chairman of Moss Hall.

UK

ARIAN AGHABABAIE

Featured child pianist in the BBC documentary 'Teaching Today' highlighting children of talent in 1997

DATE OF BIRTH: 06-Apr-1987
PLACE OF BIRTH: London. Grandmother from Rizorkapasso. Grandfather from Koma Tou Yialou.
MARITAL STATUS: Single.
SCHOOLS/COLLEGE: Queen Elizabeth Boys, Barnet. Royal Academy of Music.
HOBBIES AND INTERESTS: A keen light aircraft pilot with interests in the RAF and NASA. Enjoys sports and martial arts.
PERSONAL PROFILE: Featured child pianist in the BBC documentary 'Teaching Today' highlighting children of talent in 1997. Played the lead child role in Peter Sondheim's Merrily We Roll Along at the Royal Academy of Music. Appeared at Children's charity concert at the Royal Albert Hall with singer Gabrielle, and Queen Mother's 100th Birthday Celebrations.

STEPHEN ALAMBRITIS

Advisor Parliamentary Affairs to the UK-wide Federation of Small Businesses

DATE OF BIRTH: 22-Feb-1957
PLACE OF BIRTH: Aradippou.
MARITAL STATUS: Married to Athanasia, Nicosia, Senior Haematologist.
CHILDREN: Maria, Andreas.
SCHOOLS/COLLEGE: Elliot School. London School of Economics.
QUALIFICATIONS: BA (Politics), MSc (Economics), MA (Business Law).
MEMBERSHIPS: National Union of Journalists, Amicus.
HOBBIES AND INTERESTS: Fulham FC, Class 1 Referee. Enjoys real ale and is a member of CAMRA.
PERSONAL PROFILE: Advisor Parliamentary Affairs to the UK-wide Federation of Small Businesses. Currently on a number of Government Task Forces at the Cabinet Office and at DFES and DEFRA. Came close to being selected by the Labour Party's National Executive Committee for a safe seat in the 1997 and 2001 General Elections. Now on the Party's official list of Parliamentary Candidates for the next General Election. He is currently the Deputy Leader of the Labour Group London Borough of Merton.

KATHY ALEXANDER

Three-time parliamentary candidate for the Liberal Party

DATE OF BIRTH: 16-Dec-1958
PLACE OF BIRTH: Myrtou.
MARITAL STATUS: Single.
SCHOOLS/COLLEGE: University of London, Birbeck and Bedford Colleges. University of Ghent, Belgium, University College London, Queen Mary & Westfield College.
QUALIFICATIONS: BA MA PhD, Diploma in Law, Postgraduate Diploma in Law, Solicitors Professional Exam.
HOBBIES AND INTERESTS: Writing, production of plays, active participation.
PERSONAL PROFILE: Three-time parliamentary candidate for the Liberal Party, first ever Cypriot candidate. Leader of the newly formed Democrat Liberal Reformist Party of United Cyprus.

THEO ALEXANDER

Partner of Bond Partners LLP, Chartered/Certified Accountants and Insolvency Practitioners

DATE OF BIRTH: 23-Jul-1976
PLACE OF BIRTH: London Father from Kato Pyrgos, Mother from Komi Kebir.
MARITAL STATUS: Married.
CHILDREN: Constantinos, Mia.
SCHOOLS/COLLEGE: Lochinver House School, Haileybury. Imperial Service College, Keele University.
QUALIFICATIONS: BA (Honours) Business Enterprise, Fellow of the Greek Institute.
HOBBIES AND INTERESTS: Sports, classical studies and economics.
PERSONAL PROFILE: After graduating in 1995 joined a medium sized accountancy practice in Finchley and quickly specialised in insolvency work. One of the founding team of Bond Partners LLP in 2004, now a corporate recovery partner in Bond Partners' London Head Office with a particular specialism in business recovery and turnarounds. Has been involved in the restructuring of major UK businesses.

UK

ALEX ALEXANDROU
Optician

DATE OF BIRTH: 23-Dec-1969
PLACE OF BIRTH: Famagusta.
MARITAL STATUS: Married to Hayley, Deal, Kent.
CHILDREN: Haris and Emily.
SCHOOLS/COLLEGE: Pancyprian Gymnasium in Nicosia; City-Islington College; City University London.
QUALIFICATIONS: Qualified Dispensing Optician & Ophthalmic Optician.
HOBBIES AND INTERESTS: Running, diving and football.
PERSONAL PROFILE: Qualified Optician for the last five years. Shop owner of Optikal Opticians with Kiki Soteri.

JAMES ALEXANDROU
Actor who appeared regularly for several years in the East Enders BBC TV Drama as Martin Fowler

DATE OF BIRTH: 12-Apr-1985
PLACE OF BIRTH: London. Grandparents from Akanthou.
MARITAL STATUS: Single.
SCHOOLS/COLLEGE: Anna Scher Theatre School.
HOBBIES AND INTERESTS: Keen basketball player, swimming (has swam at County level), football, is an Arsenal fan.
PERSONAL PROFILE: James is an actor and appeared regularly for several years in the East Enders BBC TV Drama as Martin Fowler. He has also appeared on TV in Friends Like These, Celebrity Special Live and Kicking, and Diggit. In 2007, he took acting classes at the Central School of Speech and Drama in order to "refresh his skills" James toured the UK & Norway with the British Shakespeare Company from June to September 2007. He played "Pistol" in Henry V, and Orlando in "As You Like It". In 2008 he appeared in In My Name, new play by Steven Hevey, at the Old Red Lion Theatre produced by Yaller Skunk Theatre Company.

DEMITRIS (DOUGLAS) ALEXIOU
Solicitor and former Chairman of Tottenham Football Club

DATE OF BIRTH: 24-Apr-1942
PLACE OF BIRTH: London. Father from Paphos; Mother from Akanthou.
MARITAL STATUS: Married to Shirley Wale.
CHILDREN: Mark, Katie.
SCHOOLS/COLLEGE: Eaton House Prep School, St. Paul Public School, Kings College, University of London.
QUALIFICATIONS: LLB Honours.
HOBBIES AND INTERESTS: Football, tennis, golf and collecting fountain pens.
PERSONAL PROFILE: Became a Solicitor in 1970. In 1971, he went to Gordon Dadds as Assistant Solicitor and went on to become Senior Partner. Left July 2001 and formed Alexiou, Fisher Philipps. Member of the Greek Cypriot Brotherhood. Voted one of the top three family Law Solicitors in England. Acted for Duchess of York, Sarah Brightman and Mel B. Went on Spurs Board of Directors in 1980, Chairman 1982-84, currently club Vice President.

KATIE ALEXIOU
Solicitor in the Family Department of Manches LLP

DATE OF BIRTH: 08-Mar-1977
PLACE OF BIRTH: London Paternal Grandparents born in Polis and Akanthou.
MARITAL STATUS: Married to Tobias, English.
SCHOOLS/COLLEGE: Broomfield House, Kew, The Lady Eleanor Holles School, Hampton. Brasenose College, Oxford.
QUALIFICATIONS: BA(hons) English Literature.
PERSONAL PROFILE: Katie Alexiou is a Solicitor in the Family Department of MANCHES LLP.

UK

MARK ALEXIOU

Owner of the well known night club Pangaea Nightclub

DATE OF BIRTH: 17-Jun-1975
PLACE OF BIRTH: London. Father, Douglas Alexiou, from Akanthou; Mother, Shirley, from UK.
MARITAL STATUS: Single.
SCHOOLS/COLLEGE: Stowe Public School.
HOBBIES AND INTERESTS: Films, snowboarding, DJ-ing, fast cars, football, Tottenham supporter.
PERSONAL PROFILE: Former Nightclub DJ in Metro-politan Turnmills, Icini, KBar. Owns Lunasa Bar in Kings Road Chelsea where clientele has included Kylie Minogue, Jodie Kidd, Mel B, Max Beesley, Gianfranco Zola and Jay Kay. Also owns Pangaea Nightclub in Piccadilly.

ADONIS ALVANIS

Violinist and Composer. Performed in renowned concert halls throughout Europe. Recordings for BBC, LWT

DATE OF BIRTH: 31-Jul-1965
PLACE OF BIRTH: London. Father from Nicosia.
MARITAL STATUS: Single.
SCHOOLS/COLLEGE: Westminster City School, Guildhall School of Music and Drama.
QUALIFICATIONS: AGSM, FLCM.
MEMBERSHIPS: MU, PRS, PAMRA, SPNM.
HONOURS/AWARDS: Lennox Berkeley Prize for Composition (1992).
PERSONAL PROFILE: Violinist and Composer. Performed in renowned concert halls throughout Europe. Recordings for BBC, LWT, Carlton, Virgin Records America, MCA, EMI, Sony Classical.

LOUIS DEMETRIUS ALVANIS

Concert pianist. First public performance at age nine at South Bank Centre, London. Royal Festival Hall.

DATE OF BIRTH: 21-Dec-1960
PLACE OF BIRTH: London. Father from Nicosia.
MARITAL STATUS: Married.
CHILDREN: Triplets.
SCHOOLS/COLLEGE: Royal Academy of Music, London.
QUALIFICATIONS: Dip Ram, ARCM.
HOBBIES AND INTERESTS: Classic cars. Organising exhibitions of works by contemporary painters.
PERSONAL PROFILE: Concert pianist. First public performance at age nine at South Bank Centre, London. Royal Festival Hall, concerto debut in 1981. Performs extensively in major concert halls in UK and throughout Europe, appearing with leading orchestras and conductors. Has broadcasted widely on radio and television. Commercially available CD recordings feature works of Bach, Brahms, Chopin, Schumann, Scriabin.

CHRISTAKIS AMERICANOS

Served as Chairman and Treasurer of Yialousa Association in UK. Treasurer of Twelve Apostles Church in Hertfordshire

DATE OF BIRTH: 26-Oct-1935
PLACE OF BIRTH: Yialoussa.
MARITAL STATUS: Married to Stella, Leonarisso.
CHILDREN: Maria, Sylvia, John, All Accountants.
SCHOOLS/COLLEGE: Yialousa Gymnasium, Nicosia College.
HOBBIES AND INTERESTS: Music, swimming and reading.
PERSONAL PROFILE: Consultant partner in John Alexander Ltd Accountants in Southgate. Was Chairman and Treasurer of Yialoussa Association in Uk. Treasurer of Twelve Apostles Church in Hertfordshire.

UK

It is free to nominate someone, or yourself, who deserves to be in the book, just send in the name, contact address, telephone number and email to:
Greek Cypriots Worldwide
111 St Thomas's Road London N4 2QJ
Telephone 0044 207503 3498
cypriotwhoswho@aol.com
www.greekcypriotsworldwide.com

KOULLA ANASTASI
Acting Head of Acquisitions/Co-productions. The History Channel and contributor Greek Cypriots in the UK

DATE OF BIRTH: 29-Nov-1976 **PLACE OF BIRTH:** London. Father from Kapedhes. Mother from Yialoussa. **MARITAL STATUS:** Married to Greg, London Parents from Lympia and Tympou, Accountant. **CHILDREN:** Two Children. **SCHOOLS/COLLEGE:** Southgate School. Churchill. College, Cambridge University. **QUALIFICATIONS:** MA Hons History, 4 A levels 10 GCSES. **HOBBIES AND INTERESTS:** Reading and travelling. **PERSONAL PROFILE:** Acting Head of Acquisitions/Co -productions, The History Channel Contributor to 'Greek Cypriots in the UK'.

MARIA (NÉE DEMETRIOU) ANASTASI
Deputy of Safeguarding and Quality Assurance Service in London Borough of Enfield

DATE OF BIRTH: 29-Sep-1961 **PLACE OF BIRTH:** London. Family from Voni. **MARITAL STATUS:** Married to George, Parents from Achna, Youth Centre Manager. **CHILDREN:** Pavlos, Neove. **SCHOOLS/COLLEGE:** Tollington Park School. Middlesex University, South Bank University. **QUALIFICATIONS:** B. Ed Diploma in Applied Social Studies (Postgraduate). QSW Certificate for Qualified Social Workers. **MEMBERSHIPS:** British Association of Social Workers. **HOBBIES AND INTERESTS:** Reading, cooking, watching football and spending time with family. **PERSONAL PROFILE:** Currently Deputy of Safeguarding and Quality Assurance Service in London Borough of Enfield. Was a Child Protection Advisor for LB Haringey. Previously employed by LB Barnet as a Child Protection Co-ordinator. Former Social Worker in Haringey (1988-1999), starting as a Section II funded worker specifically for the Cypriot community.

DAVID ANASTASIOU
Nominated North West Entrepreneur of the year 2004

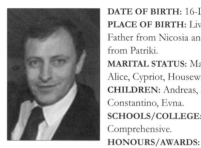

DATE OF BIRTH: 16-Dec-1962 **PLACE OF BIRTH:** Liverpool, Father from Nicosia and Mother from Patriki. **MARITAL STATUS:** Married to Alice, Cypriot, Housewife. **CHILDREN:** Andreas, Sotiris, Constantino, Evna. **SCHOOLS/COLLEGE:** Roby Comprehensive. **HONOURS/AWARDS:** Nominated North West Entrepreneur of the year 2004. **HOBBIES AND INTERESTS:** Football and Squash. **PERSONAL PROFILE:** David Anastasiou is one of the founders of the Liverpool Greek Society and a Director of the Property Company Illiad based in Liverpool.

ELIZABETH ANASTASIOU
Got to final 50 on ITV'S Pop Idol 2003

DATE OF BIRTH: 03-Oct-1985 **PLACE OF BIRTH:** London. Parents from Limassol and Rizokarpasso. **MARITAL STATUS:** Single. **SCHOOLS/COLLEGE:** Ashmole School. London Metropolitan University. **QUALIFICATIONS:** BA in Performing Arts. **MEMBERSHIPS:** Equity. **HONOURS/AWARDS:** Grade 8 Piano Award for Music at Ashmole School. **HOBBIES AND INTERESTS:** Music, Drama, Dance, Choreography, Directing. **PERSONAL PROFILE:** Elizabeth Anastasiou recently released her Debut Single written By the artist herself. Final 10 in Cypriot National for Eurovision Contest 2008, Final 50 on ITVs Pop Idol 2003, Backing Singer For Westlife, Piano Teacher to Young Children.

UK

PETER JAMES ANDREA (KNOWN AS PETER ANDRE)

Pop singer who has had several chart hits and a sell-out concert at Wembley Arena

DATE OF BIRTH: 27-Feb-1973
PLACE OF BIRTH: London. Father from Kyrenia (Harja and Ayios Amvrosios); Mother from Angastina.
MARITAL STATUS: Married to Katie Price, British, Model, Author and TV personality.
CHILDREN: Harvey step son, Junior Savva, Princess Tiaammi.
SCHOOLS/COLLEGE: Sudbury Junior School; Wembley High, London; Benowa High School, Australia.
HONOURS/AWARDS: From Smash Hits – Monaco World Music Awards.
HOBBIES AND INTERESTS: Martial arts, jet-skiing and eating.
PERSONAL PROFILE: Pop singer who has had several chart hits and a sell-out concert at Wembley Arena. Recently entered the Aussie Jungle as a contestant in I'm a Celebrity, Get Me Out of Here!, making £214, 932 for his chosen charity, the National Society for the Prevention of Cruelty to Children (NSPCC). Peter released the single Mysterious Girl, which went straight to number one for the third time round, thus ensuring him a place in The Guinness Book of Records. 300, 000 copies of the record were sold and even more money was made for the NSPCC. His single Insania went to number three in the charts. He regularly appears on TV with his wife on the Katie and Peter Show.

CHRIS ANDREA

Musician performed with his brother Peter Andre and Mikis Theodorakis

DATE OF BIRTH: 21-Jun-1963
PLACE OF BIRTH: London Father from Kyrenia Harja and Ayios Amvrosios, Mother from Angastina.
SCHOOLS/COLLEGE: Wembley High School.
HOBBIES AND INTERESTS: Soccer.
PERSONAL PROFILE: Chris has spent many years writing, recording, and performing with his brother Peter Andre and has played bouzouki for Mikis Theodorakis.

DIMITRI ANDREAS

Actor appeared on TV in The Jury, Sam's Game, The Bill, Sunburn, London's Burning,

DATE OF BIRTH: 06-Jan-1942
PLACE OF BIRTH: Rizokarpasso, Cyprus.
MARITAL STATUS: Married.
CHILDREN: Andreas, Student.
SCHOOLS/COLLEGE: Webber Douglas School of Music and Dramatic Art.
MEMBERSHIPS: Equity.
PERSONAL PROFILE: Has appeared on TV in The Jury, Sam's Game, The Bill, Sunburn, London's Burning, Casualty, Minder films, Family Money, Demob, Into the Blue, Top Secret. Founder member of Theatro Technis.

LISA ANDREAS

Singer represented Cyprus in the 2004 Eurovision Song Contest

DATE OF BIRTH: 22-Dec-1987
PLACE OF BIRTH: Chatham, Kent. maternal grandparents from Pano Lakatamia, Nicosia, Cyprus.
MARITAL STATUS: Single.
SCHOOLS/COLLEGE: Chatham Grammar School for Girls.
MEMBERSHIPS: Member of Music Union.
HOBBIES AND INTERESTS: Singing, dancing, drama, ice-skating, netball, song-writing, poetry, music and playing keyboards.
PERSONAL PROFILE: One of Lisa Andreas poems was published in the book(Celebration 2000 Northern Kent) representing young poets from around the UK. She started singing at eleven years old, and has won many talent competitions, including the Strand Festival. She has also appeared in a concert featuring Atomic Kitten, Damage and also represented Cyprus in the 2004 Eurovision Song Contest.

UK

ANTONIOS MICHAEL ANDREOU

Antonios is involved with the Hellenic Brotherhood, Manchester, and served the Church as Secretary and Chairman of the Committee

DATE OF BIRTH: 02-Apr-1947
PLACE OF BIRTH: Ormidia, Cyprus.
MARITAL STATUS: Married to Chrystalla, Larnaca, Bookkeeper.
CHILDREN: Iacovos, Costas, Michael.
SCHOOLS/COLLEGE: Hull University, Manchester Polytechnic.
QUALIFICATIONS: BSc in Mathematics. PGCE.
PERSONAL PROFILE: Antonios is involved with the Hellenic Brotherhood, Manchester, and served the Church as Secretary and Chairman of the Committee. After a short break, was appointed a Trustee of the Church.

CHRISTINA ANDREOU

Production Journalist for London Tonight at ITN (Independent Television News) on ITV 1

DATE OF BIRTH: 31-May-1976
PLACE OF BIRTH: London. Parents from Kalogrea.
MARITAL STATUS: Married to Stavros Kallis, Dhali.
CHILDREN: None.
SCHOOLS/COLLEGE: Haberdashers' Aske's Hatcham College Girls' School. Middlesex University, Westminster University.
QUALIFICATIONS: BA Honours Media, Cultural and communication Studies, Post Graduate diploma in Journalism, awarded with Merit.
MEMBERSHIPS: National Union of Journalists.
PERSONAL PROFILE: Production Journalist for London Tonight at ITN (Independent Television News) on ITV 1. Writes the news and helps put together the bulletins and programmes seen by around a million people each day.

PERICLES ANDREOU

Community

DATE OF BIRTH: 25-Nov-1942
PLACE OF BIRTH: Kontea, Cyprus.
MARITAL STATUS: Married to Elizabeth, Kontea.
CHILDREN: Soulla, Joanna, Andreas.
SCHOOLS/COLLEGE: English School, Nicosia; Commercial School, Famagusta; London College of Fashion.
HOBBIES AND INTERESTS: Sport, football (Manchester United fan) and politics/current affairs.
PERSONAL PROFILE: Pericles Andreou is the Chairman of Kontea Community Association, former member of Ashmole Greek School Parents' Association. Representative of Ekeka, and of the National Federation of Cypriots.

PETROS STELIOU ANDREOU

Ophthalmic Surgeon

DATE OF BIRTH: 08-Sep-1966
PLACE OF BIRTH: London. Parents from Koma Tou Yialou and Aradippou.
MARITAL STATUS: Married to Anita, (Father Maltese, Mother English).
CHILDREN: Joseph.
SCHOOLS/COLLEGE: Chase School for Boys. Southampton University.
QUALIFICATIONS: 3 A Levels (2 at grade A); 10 O Levels (6 at grade A). MBBS; FRCOphth.
MEMBERSHIPS: Royal College of Ophthalmologists.
HONOURS/AWARDS: Fellowship of Royal College of Ophthalmologists.
PERSONAL PROFILE: Specialist Ophthalmic Surgeon and Certified Specialist in Ophthalmology.

STELIOS ANDREW

British Artistic Team of the year 2004

DATE OF BIRTH: 31-Oct-1964
PLACE OF BIRTH: Stockwell, South London. Parents from Davlos and Trikomo.
MARITAL STATUS: Married to Nicky, Rizokarpasso, Housewife.
CHILDREN: Eleni, Demi.
SCHOOLS/COLLEGE: Norbury Manor, Robert Fielding Hairdressing College.

UK

QUALIFICATIONS: 3 O Levels. Hairdressing Honours with Distinction.

HONOURS/AWARDS: Andrew was responsible for training the team at Rush Salons, which has won the following awards: Guild Photo Stylist, 2001. British Southern Hairdresser of the Year, 2001. Master Hairdresser of the Year, 2001. British F. A. M. E Team Member, 2001 & 2002. Brit.

HOBBIES AND INTERESTS: Football and art.

PERSONAL PROFILE: Stelios Andrew is a Director and Creative Coach of Rush Hairdressers, Andrew's job is to train hairdressers to the highest standards.

ANDREW ANDREWS
World Silver Medallist and European Gold Medallist in Clay Pigeon Shooting

DATE OF BIRTH: 03-Oct-1980
PLACE OF BIRTH: London. Parents from Nicosia, Cyprus.
MARITAL STATUS: Single.
SCHOOLS/COLLEGE: Clay Pigeon Shooting Society.
HONOURS/AWARDS: GB Junior Championships, World Silver Medallist and European Gold Medallist in Clay Pigeon Shooting.

HOBBIES AND INTERESTS: Shooting and fishing.

PERSONAL PROFILE: An engineer who has won many competitions and trophies in clay pigeon shooting.

ANASIA ANGELI
Founder of the website Desperate Greek housewives

DATE OF BIRTH: 12-Jul-1968
PLACE OF BIRTH: Paphos.
MARITAL STATUS: Single.
SCHOOLS/COLLEGE: Finchley Manor Hill. Southgate College.
QUALIFICATIONS: 11 O levels Diploma in Business Studies, Diploma in Fine Art.
HOBBIES AND INTERESTS: Photography, cooking, Interior design and travelling.

PERSONAL PROFILE: Anasia Angeli found the website Desperate Greek housewives.

CHRISTOS EMILIOS ANGELIDES
Executive Director and Board member of the Next Fashion Group

DATE OF BIRTH: 27-Mar-1963
PLACE OF BIRTH: UK. Father from Nicosia, Cyprus.
MARITAL STATUS: Married to Suzanne, USA, a self-employed garment agent.
CHILDREN: Nicole-Taylor, Max Emilios.
SCHOOLS/COLLEGE: Langley School; Solihull College; Leicester Polytechnic.

QUALIFICATIONS: BA (Honours) in Business Studies (2: 1). MDIP, Marketing.

HOBBIES AND INTERESTS: Gym and golf.

PERSONAL PROFILE: Christos Angelides is a Group Product Director with the retail group Next and has been on the Main Board as an Executive Director since year 2000.

ELENA ANGELIDES
Helped to set up a Music Channel on Sky Digital

DATE OF BIRTH: 08-Feb-1985
PLACE OF BIRTH: London.
MARITAL STATUS: Single.
SCHOOLS/COLLEGE: Broomfield Secondary. Wood Street College.
QUALIFICATIONS: 10 GCSEs and 3 Alevels.
HOBBIES AND INTERESTS: Music, Theatre, Travelling, Media and Religion.

PERSONAL PROFILE: Elena has done missionary work in places like India, Russia and India. Has worked in Media since 2003 to date on TV. In 2006 she was assigned to help set up a Christian music channel on Sky TV.

UK

There is an estimated 300,000 Cypriots born in Cyprus or of Cypriot ancestry living in the UK

PROFESSOR FLOYA ANTHIAS
Professor of Sociology at Oxford Brookes University

DATE OF BIRTH: 31-May-1945
PLACE OF BIRTH: Nicosia, Cyprus. Father, Tefcros Anthias, from Kontea; Mother, Anastasia, from Aradippou.
MARITAL STATUS: Married to Ronald Ayres, Professor of Economics.
CHILDREN: Alexander, IT Specialist & Musician; Natasha, Rese.
QUALIFICATIONS: BSc in Sociology; MSc, PhD. PGCE, Sociology; ACCS.
MEMBERSHIPS: British Sociological Association.
HOBBIES AND INTERESTS: Reading, theatre and cinema.
PERSONAL PROFILE: Professor of Sociology at Oxford Brookes University. Member of the inter-university Research Committee on Cyprus. Author of numerous books and articles.

ANDREAS ANTONA
Won a coveted Michelin star and was recognised as one of Britain's finest chefs. Having previously worked at the Ritz and the Dorchester in London, Andreas now runs what was recently voted 'Best Restaurant in Birmingham'

DATE OF BIRTH: 24-Sep-1957
PLACE OF BIRTH: Cuckfield, Sussex. Parents from Achna.
MARITAL STATUS: Married to Alison, Warwickshire.
CHILDREN: Four children.
SCHOOLS/COLLEGE: Ashton House Preparatory School; Ealing College School; Ealing Technical College.
HONOURS/AWARDS: Michelin. Rosette 2000 Guide; 1999 Craft Guild of Chefs; Hotel and Restaurant Chef of the Year Award. Voted Birminghams Best Restaurant also runner up Restaurant outside of London in the Evening Standard Restaurant Awards 2008.
HOBBIES AND INTERESTS: Reading and golf.
PERSONAL PROFILE: Owner of Simpsons Restaurant in the Midlands, which has achieved the Michelin star. Committee member and former chairman of the Midlands Association of Chefs. Governor at Birmingham College of Food, Tourism and Creative Studies.

VASSILLIS ANTONAS
Psychotherapist

DATE OF BIRTH: 30-May-1974
PLACE OF BIRTH: Nicosia.
MARITAL STATUS: Single.
SCHOOLS/COLLEGE: Tasis Hellenic High School. University of La Verne Athens, South Bank University, Middlesex University.
QUALIFICATIONS: BSc Psychology Graduate Diploma Psychotherapy, MSc Psychotherapy.
MEMBERSHIPS: Hellenic Medical Society.
HOBBIES AND INTERESTS: Motor sports, diving, reading and martial arts.
PERSONAL PROFILE: Worked as a psychotherapist for the NHS for three years. Currently in Private Practice in Islington, London.

ANTONIS ANTONIADES
Director of Capital Homes Estate Agents and Valuers

PLACE OF BIRTH: born in Paphos, 1957.
MARITAL STATUS: Married.
CHILDREN: Christopher, Ariana.
SCHOOLS/COLLEGE: Southgate College.
QUALIFICATIONS: OND Business Studies.
MEMBERSHIPS: Member of the Institute of Commercial Management.
HOBBIES AND INTERESTS: Football and travel.
PERSONAL PROFILE: Antonis Antoniades is a Director of Capital Homes Estate Agents and Valuers. Also a director of Chrisaria Investments. Antonis is known for his philanthropic work.

UK

ANTONIS ANTONIADES
Served as General Manager of the Vema Newspaper

DATE OF BIRTH: 25-Feb-1929
PLACE OF BIRTH: Anaphotia.
MARITAL STATUS: Single.
CHILDREN: Melanie, Material Designer. Anthony, Business.
SCHOOLS/COLLEGE: Pancyprian Lyceum, Larnaca;. Regent Street Polytechnic, London.
QUALIFICATIONS: In Journalism.
MEMBERSHIPS: AKEL and the National Federation Of Cypriots in the UK.
HOBBIES AND INTERESTS: Writing and reading.
PERSONAL PROFILE: General Manager of Vema (Newspaper); Chair and Secretary of the Cyprus Committee of the Democratic Left.

ATHOS ANTONIADES
Inducted into 'Martial Arts Hall of Fame'

PLACE OF BIRTH: Platres, Cyprus.
MARITAL STATUS: Married to Susan Antoniades, Beauty Therapist.
CHILDREN: Helen, Marianne.
SCHOOLS/COLLEGE: Westminster University.
QUALIFICATIONS: BA (Hons), ACEA, FMAAT. 5th Dan American Kenpo.
HONOURS/AWARDS: Inducted into 'Martial Arts Hall of Fame'.
HOBBIES AND INTERESTS: Martial Arts.
PERSONAL PROFILE: Athos is a martial arts expert founder member of American Kenpo Taiji association.

GEORGE ANTONIADES
Essex Archery Champion

DATE OF BIRTH: 17-Jul-1947
PLACE OF BIRTH: Ktima, Paphos, Cyprus.
MARITAL STATUS: Single.
CHILDREN: Yolanda, Degree in Psychology. Alexander, At Bristol University.
SCHOOLS/COLLEGE: William Ellis School, Highgate;. Jesus College, Oxford.
QUALIFICATIONS: BA MA (Oxon). Solicitor of the Supreme Court.

MEMBERSHIPS: Club secretary Woodford Archery Club.
HONOURS/AWARDS: Award for bravery from High Sheriff of Essex.
HOBBIES AND INTERESTS: Classical History, archery and gardening.
PERSONAL PROFILE: Solicitor. Current Essex Archery Champion and double record-holder at 180 yards.

MARIANNE ANTONIADES
Singer in the girl group Cookie what was a support group for the Girls Aloud Tour

DATE OF BIRTH: 12-Feb-1981
PLACE OF BIRTH: London Father from Platres mother from Nicosia.
MARITAL STATUS: Single.
SCHOOLS/COLLEGE: Copthall Secondary. Barnet College and Sylvia Young Theatre School.
QUALIFICATIONS: Diploma in performing arts.
PERSONAL PROFILE: Marianne Antoniades is a singer in the girl group Cookie which was a support group for the Girls Aloud Tour.

RENO ANTONIADES
Solicitor working for Lee and Thompson, Expert Film and Television Lawyers

DATE OF BIRTH: 27-Jul-1966
PLACE OF BIRTH: London. Father, Mikis, from Davlos; Mother, Joy, from London.
MARITAL STATUS: Married to Julie Cunningham, London (Originally from Ireland).
SCHOOLS/COLLEGE: Alleyns School in Dulwich; Leicester University; London Law School.
QUALIFICATIONS: LLB (Honours).
HOBBIES AND INTERESTS: Football (Tottenham supporter), cinema and travelling.
PERSONAL PROFILE: Reno Antoniades is a Solicitor working for Lee and Thompson, expert Film and Television Lawyers.

UK

SOTOS ANTONIADES
General Secretary of the Cypriot Football League in the UK

DATE OF BIRTH: 28-Jan-1948
PLACE OF BIRTH: Limassol.
MARITAL STATUS: Married to Yianoulla.
CHILDREN: Antonis, Marina, Peter.
SCHOOLS/COLLEGE: Lanition Gymnasium, Limassol.
PERSONAL PROFILE: Sotos Antoniades is the General Secretary of the Cypriot Football League in the UK, Member of the Executive Committee of the Greek Cypriot Brotherhood. He is an Estate Agent by occupation.

ANDREAS ANTONIOU
Owner of the award winning restaurant Vrisaki Evening Standard and London Tonight award 2003

DATE OF BIRTH: 11-Jun-1943
PLACE OF BIRTH: Koma tou Yialou.
MARITAL STATUS: Single.
CHILDREN: Three.
HONOURS/AWARDS: London Weekend Award, Evening Standard Award and London Tonight Award 2003 for his restaurant presented by Jamie Oliver at the Grosvenor hotel that was televised by ITV.
HOBBIES AND INTERESTS: Driving cars and Arsenal FC.
PERSONAL PROFILE: Andreas Antoniou is the owner of Vrisaki Restaurant, North London (founded in 1981). Chairman of the Koma tou Yialou Association, UK.

ANTONIOS VARNAVAS ANTONIOU
Obstetrician/Gynaecologist

DATE OF BIRTH: 28-Oct-1967
PLACE OF BIRTH: London. Parents from Milia, Cyprus.
SCHOOLS/COLLEGE: Kings College, London; Hunterian Institute; Royal College of Surgeons; Guys & St Thomas Medical School, London.
QUALIFICATIONS: BSc PhD MBBS MRCOG.
MEMBERSHIPS: Royal College of Obstetrics & Gynaecology. British Medical Association.

HOBBIES AND INTERESTS: Travelling, scuba diving, photography, listening to jazz and Greek music.
PERSONAL PROFILE: Obstetrician/gynaecologist with special interest in keyhole surgery. Previously Senior Registrar, University College Hospital. Was President of Democratic Movement of Cypriot Students in Britain and Co-editor of Students Voice. Consultant at Newham University Hospital, London.

GEORGE ANTONIOU
Owner of Chain of Hairdressing Salons and Principal of two Hairdressing Schools in Kent

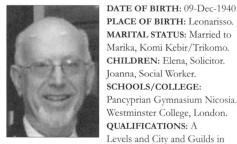

DATE OF BIRTH: 09-Dec-1940
PLACE OF BIRTH: Leonarisso.
MARITAL STATUS: Married to Marika, Komi Kebir/Trikomo.
CHILDREN: Elena, Solicitor. Joanna, Social Worker.
SCHOOLS/COLLEGE: Pancyprian Gymnasium Nicosia. Westminster College, London.
QUALIFICATIONS: A Levels and City and Guilds in Hairdressing.
MEMBERSHIPS: National Hairdressers Federation.
HOBBIES AND INTERESTS: Football and Golf.
PERSONAL PROFILE: George Antoniou is the owner of Chain of Hairdressing Salons and Principal of Two Hairdressing Schools in Kent. He is an active member of the Greek Orthodox Church in Margate and of the Leonarisso-Vasili Association.

GREGORY ANTONIOU
Councillor in the London Borough of Enfield

PLACE OF BIRTH: London. Father from Famagusta. Mother from Ayios Theodoros, Karpassia.
MARITAL STATUS: Single.
SCHOOLS/COLLEGE: Firs Farm and Winchmore Schools, Imperial College London, Hughes Hill Cambridge, University College London.
QUALIFICATIONS: BSc (Honours) ARCS, Dip. Comp. Sc, LLM. Called to the Bar March 2000 (Inner Temple).
MEMBERSHIPS: Inner Temple, Conservative Party, M.
PERSONAL PROFILE: Barrister-at-Law, Councillor in the London Borough of Enfield (elected May 2002).

UK

KATRINA ANTONIOU

Qualified for the All-England Championship Finals, in which she achieved runner-up in the Tap Section in 1999 (aged 14),

DATE OF BIRTH: 12-Jul-1985
PLACE OF BIRTH: London; grandmother from Rizokarpasso; grandfather from Famagusta.
MARITAL STATUS: Single.
SCHOOLS/COLLEGE: Rush Croft School, Epping Forest College.
QUALIFICATIONS: 10 GCSEs and 2 A Levels.
MEMBERSHIPS: British Theatre Dance Association.
HONOURS/AWARDS: Has passed many dance examinations and entered various competitions. Qualified for the All-England Championship Finals, in which she achieved runner-up in the Tap Section in 1999 (aged 14), runner-up in the Song and Dance Section in 2003, and third place.
HOBBIES AND INTERESTS: Dancing.
PERSONAL PROFILE: Now training to become a dance teacher.

MICHAEL ANTONIOU

Senior Lecturer in Molecular Genetics, GKT School of Medicine, Guy's Hospital, London

DATE OF BIRTH: 20-Feb-1955
PLACE OF BIRTH: Famagusta. Father from Komi Kebir.
MARITAL STATUS: Married to Janey, London, Mental Health Trainer.
SCHOOLS/COLLEGE: Hampstead Comprehensive School;. University of Oxford, University of Reading.
QUALIFICATIONS: BA (Oxon), Biochemistry; PhD.
HOBBIES AND INTERESTS: Light aircraft flying, transcendental meditation, organic food and farming.
PERSONAL PROFILE: Senior Lecturer in Molecular Genetics, GKT School of Medicine, Guy's Hospital, London. Helps the UK Thalassaemia Society and the Muscular Dystrophy Campaign. Biotechnology Advisor to Greenpeace, Friends of the Earth, Soil Association. Professional research interests: human gene control mechanisms; safe and efficacious gene therapy for thalassaemia and muscular dystrophy.

NICK ANTONIOU

Accountant/Treasurer Independant Greek Schools of England

DATE OF BIRTH: 04-Nov-1960
PLACE OF BIRTH: London. Parents from Rizokarpasso and Larnaca.
MARITAL STATUS: Married to Christalla, London, parents from Akaki and Aradippou.
CHILDREN: Phillipa, Miranda, Both still at school.
SCHOOLS/COLLEGE: Stationers. Barnet College, North London Polytechnic.
QUALIFICATIONS: FCCA.
HOBBIES AND INTERESTS: Football, music, gardening, travel, DIY and cars.
PERSONAL PROFILE: Accountant Partner/Director in Smith & Williamson Chartered Accountants. A regular contributor to articles on accounting, financial and taxation issues has featured in the Daily Telegraph, Evening Standard. Writes regularly for the Building Magazine and Drapers Record. Past Chairman and currently Vice Chairman of the Hellenic School of High Barnet, and Treasurer, Independent Greek Schools of England.

TONY ANTONIOU

President Omonia Youth FC, London

DATE OF BIRTH: 27-Jul-1960
PLACE OF BIRTH: London. Father from Leonarisso; Mother, Tymbou.
MARITAL STATUS: Married to Maria, father from Xylotymbou, Financial advisor.
CHILDREN: Christopher, School.
SCHOOLS/COLLEGE: Clerkenwell & St William of York.
QUALIFICATIONS: Advanced Financial Planning Certificate.
HOBBIES AND INTERESTS: Football and music.
PERSONAL PROFILE: Independent Financial Adviser at his own companyThomas Anthony Mortgage & Financial Services. Former Secretary of New Salamis and is now President of OmoniaYouth FC. Qualified Football Association Coach.

UK

ZENON ANTONIOU
Philanthropist major contributor to the UK Cypriot Community

DATE OF BIRTH: 14-Feb-1947
PLACE OF BIRTH: Peyia.
MARITAL STATUS: Married to Androulla, Kili.
CHILDREN: Demetrios, Maria, Harry.
SCHOOLS/COLLEGE: Queen Mary College University of London.
QUALIFICATIONS: BSc Economics (Honours).
MEMBERSHIPS: NAEA.
HOBBIES AND INTERESTS: Travelling, Football and Golf.
PERSONAL PROFILE: Zenon Antoniou is a Philanthropist and major supporter of several Cypriot Organisations. He is the owner of Omega Lettings which is now based in its own building Omega House in Lea Bridge Road in East London employing 25 people.

NICK APOSTOLIDES
Senior Lecturer at the University of the West of England

DATE OF BIRTH: 10-Apr-1950
PLACE OF BIRTH: London.
Father from Limassol; Mother from Platres.
MARITAL STATUS: Married to Phoebe, Nicosia.
CHILDREN: Kiki, Victoria, Michael.
SCHOOLS/COLLEGE: George Monoux, Walthamstow; Lancaster University; City University.
QUALIFICATIONS: BA Economics. MBA Finance.
HOBBIES AND INTERESTS: Football (Leyton Orient fan), sport, travel, cars and music.
PERSONAL PROFILE: Senior Lecturer at the University of the West of England (UWE). Research interest: annual general meetings.

EVANGELOS APOSTOLOU
Legal counsel for Europe, Middle East and Africa for Fujitsu Services

DATE OF BIRTH: 23-Jun-1969
PLACE OF BIRTH: London.
Father from Mandres; Mother from Moniatis.
MARITAL STATUS: Single.
SCHOOLS/COLLEGE: Holloway School, University College London, Lincolns Inn.
QUALIFICATIONS: Called to the Bar of England and Wales. Admitted as Advocate by the Cypriot Bar Association. Admitted as Solicitor of the Supreme Court.
PERSONAL PROFILE: Solicitor and Barrister. Has worked in Cyprus with Christos Pourgourides & Co. Now legal counsel for Europe, Middle East and Africa for Fujitsu Services.

SOFIA NEOPHITOU APOSTOLOU
Editor in Chief 10 Magazine

DATE OF BIRTH: 21-Dec-1965
PLACE OF BIRTH: London.
Father from Morphou; Mother from Episkopion.
MARITAL STATUS: Married to Apostolos Demos Apostolou.
CHILDREN: Zacharia.
SCHOOLS/COLLEGE: Southgate College; Middlesex University.
QUALIFICATIONS: 9 O Levels, 3 A Levels, BA Honours, Interior Design.
HOBBIES AND INTERESTS: Cinema, galleries, travel, music and theatre.
PERSONAL PROFILE: Fashion Editor of Independent Saturday Magazine, 10 Magazine, Italian Vogue and Sunday Times.

UK

In 1931 the British census recorded about a 1000 Cypriot born people living in the UK

GEORGINA ARGYROU
Presenter and newsreader for LBC 97. 3 FM and Heart 106. 2 FM, and is currently the voice of the Sky Patrol

DATE OF BIRTH: 21-Jul-1972
PLACE OF BIRTH: London. Father from Mazoto; Mother from Akanthou.
MARITAL STATUS: Married to Michael Sergeant, London, BBC Reporter.
SCHOOLS/COLLEGE: Woodford County High School. University of London.
QUALIFICATIONS: BA Radio Broadcasting Foundation; CNN Internship.
MEMBERSHIPS: Amnesty, NSPCC.
HOBBIES AND INTERESTS: Jazz, singing, theatre work and writing (currently working on a novel).
PERSONAL PROFILE: Georgina is a journalist employed as a presenter and newsreader for LBC 97. 3 FM and Heart 106. 2 FM, and is currently the voice of the Sky Patrol. Other radio work includes presenting on ITN News Direct and newsreading for LGR. TV employment includes editorial and production work (mainly foreign news at ITN, Channel Four News, the BBC and APTN). She was a reporter and assistant producer on BBC Newsround, and has also worked in the Press, including reporting for the Cyprus Mail.

GEORGE ARISTIDIS ARISTIDOU
Dental Surgeon/Lecturer

DATE OF BIRTH: 15-Jul-1971
PLACE OF BIRTH: London. Parents from Akanthou.
MARITAL STATUS: Single.
SCHOOLS/COLLEGE: St Dunstan's College, Catford. King's College School of Medicine and Dentistry, University of London; Eastman Dental Institute, University of London.
QUALIFICATIONS: 9 O Levels and 3 A Levels. BDS (Lon); MSc Prosth.
MEMBERSHIPS: British Society for the Study of Prosthetic Dentistry; British Dental Association; Angloakanthou Aid Society.
HOBBIES AND INTERESTS: Bouzouki-playing, football and basketball.
PERSONAL PROFILE: Dental surgeon, Lecturer in prosthetic dentistry.

NICHOLAS ARISTOU
Director, Business Development at the Four Seasons Hotel Hotel Limassol

DATE OF BIRTH: 21-Jan-1961
PLACE OF BIRTH: London, Father from Omodhos, Mother from Mandria.
MARITAL STATUS: Single.
CHILDREN: Leon.
SCHOOLS/COLLEGE: William Ellis. University of North London.
PERSONAL PROFILE: Nick Aristou after graduation Joined Forte Hotels as a Management Trainee at the age of 24 he became the youngest Front office manager Forte ever had in London. Through a series of promotions he became General manager at Fortes newly acquired hotel, the Balmoral in Edinburgh. After the Balmoral he returned to London as Resident Manager at the Waldorf. In late 1993 he joined Hawaii Grand Hotel in Limassol as Deputy General Manager and then subsequently was promoted to General Manager a position he held to July 2004. In September 2004 he took on the challenge of Director, Business Development at the Four Seasons Hotel Limassol reporting directly to the Chairman Mr Christos Mouskis.

DR DEMETRA ARSALIDOU
University Lecturer

DATE OF BIRTH: 06-Aug-1972
PLACE OF BIRTH: Nicosia.
MARITAL STATUS: Single.
SCHOOLS/COLLEGE: Lyceum Archbishop Makarios, Nicosia; University of Lancaster; University of Exeter.
QUALIFICATIONS: LLB (Lancaster); LLM, PhD (Exeter). Accreditation as an Associate Teacher in Higher Education (University of Exeter).
HOBBIES AND INTERESTS: Singing, gym and long walks.
PERSONAL PROFILE: Lecturer in Law at the University of Exeter. Has been contributing to the organisation 'Children in Need' for the past four years. Author of The Impact of Modern Influences on the Traditional Duties of Care, Skill and Diligence of Company Directors (published by Kluwer Law International).

UK

PAUL ARTEMI
Queen's Award for Enterprise 2000

DATE OF BIRTH: 27-Aug-1969
PLACE OF BIRTH: London.
Father from Limassol; Mother from Famagusta.
SCHOOLS/COLLEGE: Aylward.
HONOURS/AWARDS: Queen's Award for Enterprise 2000.
HOBBIES AND INTERESTS: Greek history, football and wine.
PERSONAL PROFILE: Invented the Artemi Spacemaker Hook, which is now sold in over 15 countries.

MICHAEL ARTEMIS
Educational Psychologist

DATE OF BIRTH: 28-Jan-1956
PLACE OF BIRTH: London.
Father from Xylotympou; Mother from Mazoto.
MARITAL STATUS: Single.
SCHOOLS/COLLEGE: Universities of East London, Greenwich and London; Thames Polytechnic.
QUALIFICATIONS: MSc MA BEd.
MEMBERSHIPS: Association of Educational Psychologists; National Union of Teachers;Executive member of the Hackney community and police consultative group.
HOBBIES AND INTERESTS: Sport, reading and travel, martial arts 1st dan karate and gymnastics.
PERSONAL PROFILE: Michael Artemis is Senior specialist educational psychologist and specialist consultant to behaviour support team with the LB of Hillingdon (1997-present).

SOTIRIS ASPRIS
Business/Philanthropist

DATE OF BIRTH: 29-Aug-1939
PLACE OF BIRTH: Akanthou.
MARITAL STATUS: Married to Christalla.
CHILDREN: Kyriacos, Business. Paulina, Solicitor.
SCHOOLS/COLLEGE: Akanthou Elementary and Technical School.
HOBBIES AND INTERESTS: Reading, swimming, writing and poetry.

PERSONAL PROFILE: Sotiris Aspris founded his company S Aspris and Son Ltd in the 60's to sell products from his homeland Cyprus wholesale and retail. They now sell products from Cyprus, Greece and France such as Keo products, Petrides Ouzo and Zivania, Kourtakis wines and import wines from the Albert Bichot Winery in France.

ARGYROULLA (LOULLA) ASTIN
Granada TV Woman of the Year Award, 1995

DATE OF BIRTH: 23-Jun-1951
PLACE OF BIRTH: Avgorou, Cyprus.
MARITAL STATUS: Married to Stewart Astin, Manchester, Restauranteur.
CHILDREN: Solos, Restaurant Manager. Vasos, TV Production. Stefanos, Student.
SCHOOLS/COLLEGE: Avgorou School; Salford College.
QUALIFICATIONS: Fashion Design Diploma.
MEMBERSHIPS: The Restaurant Association.
HONOURS/AWARDS: Granada TV Woman of the Year Award, 1995. Kosmos Taverna Perrier Restaurant of the year 1990. Invited to Buckingham Palace in 2008 for her services to hospitality.
HOBBIES AND INTERESTS: Cookery and travel.
PERSONAL PROFILE: Argyroulla opened the Kosmos Taverna in Manchester with her husband. The restaurant is listed in the Egon Ronay Guide, the AA Top 500 Restaurants. Loulla has appeared on TV on Eggs and Baker, This Morning, and her own series, Simply Greek. Loulla can be seen once a week on Granada Regional (The Afternoon Show) on satellite television.

GEORGE ATHANASIADES
General Secretary of Ekeka (Cyprus Refugees Association). Secretary of Desy (Democratic Rally)UK

DATE OF BIRTH: 07-Aug-1948
PLACE OF BIRTH: Trikomo.
MARITAL STATUS: Married to Andre. Marathovouno.
CHILDREN: Julie, Peter.
SCHOOLS/COLLEGE: Greek Gymnasium, Famagusta; Institute of Foreign Languages; Ecole Superieure de Journalisme.
MEMBERSHIPS: British Institute of Journalists, NUT.
HOBBIES AND INTERESTS: Writing, theatre, politics and music.

PERSONAL PROFILE: Worked with Islington Council as Chief Executive, Neighbourhood Office. General Manager of Lazari Investments Ltd. Worked for several Greek newspapers and for Cyprus Radio Broadcasting. Contributor to the Vema newspaper, and Editor-in-Chief of the newspaper Parikiakos Typos. General Secretary of Ekeka (Cyprus Refugees Association). Secretary of Desy (Democratic Rally)UK.

BISHOP ATHANASIOS OF TROPAEOU
(Nee Constantinos Kyriacou Theocharous)
Bishop

DATE OF BIRTH: 20-Nov-1943
PLACE OF BIRTH: Marathovounos, Famagusta, Cyprus.
SCHOOLS/COLLEGE: Pancyprian Gymnasium; Theological School, University of Athens.
QUALIFICATIONS: Degree in Theology.
HOBBIES AND INTERESTS: Byzantine music.
PERSONAL PROFILE: Ordinations: as a Deacon on 6. 8. 69; as a priest on 10. 8. 69; consecrated as Bishop on 12. 4. 97 (all took place in London). Based at the Greek Orthodox Church, Wood Green, London.

MICHALIS ATTALIDES
Cyprus High Commissioner in London, 1998-2000

DATE OF BIRTH: 15-Nov-1941
PLACE OF BIRTH: Cyprus.
MARITAL STATUS: Married to Alexandra Alexandrou.
SCHOOLS/COLLEGE: London School of Economics; Princeton University.
QUALIFICATIONS: BSc Econ; PhD.
PERSONAL PROFILE: Lecturer in Sociology at Leicester University, 1966-8. Sociologist, Cyprus Town and Country Planning Project, 1968-70. Military service, 1973-4. Journalist, 1974-5. Ministry of Foreign Affairs and Ambassador to France and Morocco, 1989-97. Ambassador to Spain and Portugal, 1991-5. Delegate to EU, 1995-8. High Commissioner in London, 1998-2000. Currently Permanent Secretary, Ministry of Foreign Affairs, Cyprus.

ANDREAS AUGOUSTI
Professor of Applied Physics and Instrumentation at Kingston University

DATE OF BIRTH: 17-Apr-1960
PLACE OF BIRTH: London
Father Pentayia Mother Deftera.
MARITAL STATUS: Married to Michelle, Marketing Director.
CHILDREN: Michael, Anna, Lydia, All at School.
SCHOOLS/COLLEGE: Pooles Park Primary and Stationers. Imperial College London and University of Kent.
QUALIFICATIONS: BSc PhD MBA.
MEMBERSHIPS: Associate of the Royal college of Science.
HOBBIES AND INTERESTS: Squash and reading.
PERSONAL PROFILE: Andy Augousti is a Professor of Applied Physics and Instrumentation at Kingston University. Formerly Director of three high technology companies.

ANDREA AUGOUSTIS
Chairman of St Cosmas and St Damian Greek Church, Gospel Oak

DATE OF BIRTH: 07-Mar-1925
PLACE OF BIRTH: Akanthou.
MARITAL STATUS: Married to Christalla Lefkara.
CHILDREN: Nicholas, Headteacher. Thalia, Housewife.
SCHOOLS/COLLEGE: Akanthou Elementary School.
HONOURS/AWARDS: Archon Ecumenico Patriarchiou from the Greek Orthodox Church.
HOBBIES AND INTERESTS: Church and travelling.
PERSONAL PROFILE: Came to England and went into the catering and grocery business. Agent for Metaxas for thirteen years. Chairman of St Cosmas & St Damian Greek Church (Gospel Oak) for 30 years.

UK

NICHOLAS AUGOUSTIS
Deputy Head at Sheldon Heath Comprehensive School, Birmingham

PLACE OF BIRTH: born 1950 in London. Father, Andreas, from Akanthou; Mother, Christalla, from Lefkara. **MARITAL STATUS:** Married to Jane, from Birmingham. **CHILDREN:** Eleanor, in Promotions; Melanie, BSc in Marketing, Marianna at school. **SCHOOLS/COLLEGE:** Holland Park School; Teacher Training College; Birmingham University.
QUALIFICATIONS: BPhilosophy (Education).
HOBBIES AND INTERESTS: Soccer (Tottenham supporter), and travel.
PERSONAL PROFILE: Deputy Head at Sheldon Heath Comprehensive School, Birmingham.

ANNA AVERKIOU
Business Development Executive for BBC World Service English Network and News

DATE OF BIRTH: 02-Jul-1963 **PLACE OF BIRTH:** London Father from Vavatsinia. **MARITAL STATUS:** Single. **SCHOOLS/COLLEGE:** Palmers Green High School. Woodhouse 6th Form College and London College of Fashion.
HOBBIES AND INTERESTS: travelling, scuba diving, theatre, concerts, salsa dancing, reading, theology and current affairs.
PERSONAL PROFILE: Anna Averkiou has worked in freelance editorial and production roles both in the UK and abroad. In 1990 produced a Documentary for ITV about relatives of the missing. Has worked for the BBC for the past ten years initially as a foreign news producer covering conflict zones such as Bosnia. She is now a Business Development Executive for BBC World Service English Network and News.

AVERKIOS 'ERIC' AVERKIOU
Producer/Director TV and Film

DATE OF BIRTH: 22-Aug-1973 **PLACE OF BIRTH:** Hainault, England, Father Vavatsinia Mother Dhali. **SCHOOLS/COLLEGE:** Coppice Primary School, Hainault High School. Barking College of Technology, Farnborough College of Technology, University. Of Hertfordshire. **QUALIFICATIONS:** HND. BA.
HOBBIES AND INTERESTS: Film making, foreign cinema, current affairs, a keen sport enthusiast, horse racing, football.
PERSONAL PROFILE: His short film 'First Time' A romantic comedy was filmed in Cyprus in 2 languages. English and Greek at the same time using 2 different sets of actors. The film was screened at the 2006 Cypriot Film Festival in London and the Cyprus International Film Festival in Cyprus.

FIVOS AVERKIOU
Natural British Bodybuilding Champion 2002/2004/2006

DATE OF BIRTH: 22-Aug-1968 **PLACE OF BIRTH:** Vavatsinia and Layia. **SCHOOLS/COLLEGE:** Middlesex University. **QUALIFICATIONS:** Computer Science. **HONOURS/AWARDS:** Natural British Bodybuilding Champion 2002/2004/2006. UIBBN World Championships 4th 1999, 2004, 2006. WABBA Colchester 2007 Class 2 2nd Place.
HOBBIES AND INTERESTS: Natural Bodybuilding, Strongman.
PERSONAL PROFILE: Body Building Champion.

MARIOS AVRAAM
DJ On Inspiration FM with Own Show

DATE OF BIRTH: 08-Sep-1966 **PLACE OF BIRTH:** Nikita, Morphou. **MARITAL STATUS:** Married to Maria. **CHILDREN:** Anastasis, Andreas. **SCHOOLS/COLLEGE:** Gladesmore. Middlesex University. **HOBBIES AND INTERESTS:** Football.

UK

PERSONAL PROFILE: Marios Avraam is a DJ On Inspiration FM with Own Show called the Greek.

STELLA BAXTER
BT Essence of the Entrepreneur Award 2006

DATE OF BIRTH: 09-Dec-1959
PLACE OF BIRTH: Limassol.
MARITAL STATUS: Single.
SCHOOLS/COLLEGE: Fosse High School. Leicester University.
QUALIFICATIONS: C. S. S, BA Hons Humanities, NVQ Level 4 Registered Manager Award.
MEMBERSHIPS: CERETAS Headway, UKBIF, Action on Elder Abuse, Member of the Chartered Manager Institute.
HONOURS/AWARDS: BT Essence of the Enterpreneur Award 2006, Nominated for the Queens Award for Innovation, Nominated for the Department of Health Social Care Awards 2006. Leicester Chamber of Commerce Business woman of the year Award 2008.
HOBBIES AND INTERESTS: Writing.
PERSONAL PROFILE: Created the first online booking service for live in care and support services. Disability and old age are growing concerns in the UK, and Athena Care has successfully created a much- needed service with massive potential for growth. Stella is also a Dog Show judge.

DR JOHN BEHIRI
Senior Lecturer/Associate Director, International Office

DATE OF BIRTH: 14-Sep-1956
PLACE OF BIRTH: London. Parents from Rizokarpasso.
MARITAL STATUS: Married to Martha, London.
CHILDREN: Christopher, Panayiotis.
SCHOOLS/COLLEGE: Creighton. Queen Mary, University of London.
QUALIFICATIONS: B. Eng in Material Science, PhD Fracture, Mechanics of Bone Post Doc.
MEMBERSHIPS: Institute of Materials, Institute of Bio Medical Engineers.
HOBBIES AND INTERESTS: Squash and tennis.

PERSONAL PROFILE: Senior Lecturer in Bio-Medical materials at Queen Mary's University of London, specialising in the area of synthetic replacement materials used in the body. Director of the International office as well. Nominated by the Cyprus Government to act on the creditation panel to assess higher education colleges in Cyprus.

ANGELOS BESHONGES
Chairman of Ayios Amvrosios Association

DATE OF BIRTH: 05-Dec-1954
PLACE OF BIRTH: Ayios Amvrosios. Father, Kyriakos Beshonges, teacher at English School, Nicosia.
MARITAL STATUS: Married to Michelle, (parents from Ayios Amvrosios and Ireland).
CHILDREN: Michael, Chantel.
SCHOOLS/COLLEGE: The English School, Nicosia.
HONOURS/AWARDS: Duke of Edinburgh Gold award.
HOBBIES AND INTERESTS: Shooting and tennis.
PERSONAL PROFILE: Chairman of Ayios Amvrosios Association.

ANDONEA (TONIA) MICHAEL BUXTON
TV Presenter

DATE OF BIRTH: 12-May-1968
PLACE OF BIRTH: Camden, London. Father from Larnaca; Mother from Latsia.
MARITAL STATUS: Married to Paul Buxton, Architect.
CHILDREN: Antigoni, Sophia.
SCHOOLS/COLLEGE: St Marthas Convent, Hadley Wood University of North London (UNL). University of North London.
QUALIFICATIONS: BA (Honours) Classical History & Philosophy. P. G. C. E.
MEMBERSHIPS: NSPCC, Amnesty, World Family (Child Sponsor).
HONOURS/AWARDS: A. N. B (Association of Natural Bodybuilders), South East Britain 1997.
HOBBIES AND INTERESTS: Exercise, skiing, tri athlete, alternative complementary therapics, acting, singing and dance.
PERSONAL PROFILE: She is the host of the Discovery Channel Travel & Living show My Greek Kitchen, which is aired in the UK. The show has had two series as of May 2007. Also the author of Have A Baby And Look Better Than Ever, Angel publications.

UK

ANTIGONI BUXTON
Title Winner of the British Born Cypriot Idol Competition 2008

DATE OF BIRTH: 9-Mar-1996
PLACE OF BIRTH: Born London Grandparents from Cyprus
PERSONAL PROFILE: Antigoni won the British Born Cypriot Idol Competition 2008 organised by the Leukaemia Society.

CHRISTIAN CANDY
Property Developer has articles on him regularly in the National Press

PLACE OF BIRTH: UK Mother from Cyprus
PERSONAL PROFILE: Christian and his brother Nick are property developers doing mainly luxury flats. Christian originally worked in Finance. They have been Stated by the National Media in The UK that they are changing the face of London. They Bought Chelsea Barracks for 900 million pounds and are in the process of trying to develop it into residential property.

NICK CANDY
Property Developer stated by the press that he and his brother are changing the face of London

PLACE OF BIRTH: UK Mother from Cyprus
PERSONAL PROFILE: Nick is in partnership with his brother Christian doing property development projects mainly in Chelsea and Kensington. They have been stated by the National Media in The UK that they are changing the face of London. They Bought Chelsea Barracks for 900 million pounds and are in the process of trying to develop it into residential property

DINO CHAPMAN
Artist shortlisted for the Turner prize 2003 widely considered to be one of the most important and prestigious awards for the visual arts in Europe

DATE OF BIRTH: 15-May-1962
PLACE OF BIRTH: London. Mother is Cypriot from Larnaca area, Cyprus.
SCHOOLS/COLLEGE: Ravensbourne College of Art, Royal College of Art.
QUALIFICATIONS: BA Art, MA Art.
PERSONAL PROFILE: Artist. Work shown in White Cube Gallery in London, Tokyo, Paris, New York, Toronto, in public collections such as Saatchi collection London, British Museum London, has appeared on TV Channel 4 on TV Sculpture. Dinos and Jake Chapman were shortlisted for the turner prize 2003 widely considered to be one of the most important and prestigious awards for the visual arts in Europe.

JAKE CHAPMAN
Artist, work shown in public collections such as Saatchi and the British Museum

DATE OF BIRTH: 19-May-1966
PLACE OF BIRTH: Cheltenham. Mother from Larnaca area.
SCHOOLS/COLLEGE: North East London Polytechnic, Royal College of Art.
QUALIFICATIONS: BA Honours.
HONOURS/AWARDS: shortlisted for the turner prize 2003 widely considered to be one of the most important and prestigious awards for the visual arts in Europe.
PERSONAL PROFILE: Brother of Dino Chapman. Work shown at the White Cube Gallery in Hoxton London, in Paris, New York, Tokyo, Toronto, Work shown in public collections such as Saatchi, London, British Museum, London, appeared on TV Channel 4 on TV Sculpture.

UK

CHARALAMBOS CHARALAMBIDES
Consultant Orthopaedic Surgeon

DATE OF BIRTH: 02-May-1962
PLACE OF BIRTH: Nicosia, Cyprus.
MARITAL STATUS: Married to Dr Irene Hadjikoumi, Nicosia, Consultant Paediatrician.
CHILDREN: Maria, Stavros.
SCHOOLS/COLLEGE: Graduated from Kykko's Lyceum, Nicosia and from Aristotle University Medical School, Thessaloniki, Greece.
QUALIFICATIONS: MD. FRCS, FRCS (Trauma and Orthopaedics).
MEMBERSHIPS: Fellow of the British Orthopaedic Association.
HOBBIES AND INTERESTS: Swimming, photography and clay shooting.
PERSONAL PROFILE: Consultant Orthopaedic surgeon. Honorary Senior Lecturer, University College London, Medical School. Whittington Hospital, London.

CHARALAMBOS THEODOROU CHARALAMBIDES
Barrister, Former representative of the British Hellenic Chamber of Commerce

DATE OF BIRTH: 10-Oct-1929
PLACE OF BIRTH: Moutoullas.
MARITAL STATUS: Married to Panayiota.
CHILDREN: Georgia, Theodora.
SCHOOLS/COLLEGE: Commercial School of Pedulas, Regent St Polytechnic.
QUALIFICATIONS: Called to the Bar in 1959.
HOBBIES AND INTERESTS: Snooker, poetry, reading and walking.
PERSONAL PROFILE: Barrister, London. Former representative of the British Hellenic Chamber of Commerce. Worked for the Royal Courts of Justice for nearly 20 years as a Supreme Court Associate. Since his retirement in 1984, works as an Educational Consultant representing several institutes. In 1984 established the Academy of Negotiating.

ELENITSA CHARALAMBOU
Charity Events Organiser

DATE OF BIRTH: 27-Jun-1929
PLACE OF BIRTH: Komi Kebir.
MARITAL STATUS: Married to Widow of George Charalambou, Eptakomi.
CHILDREN: Harry, Chartered Accountant. Christine, Co Director. Katia, Co Director.
SCHOOLS/COLLEGE: Komi Kebir Elementary School.
HOBBIES AND INTERESTS: Organising charity events, socialising and travelling.
PERSONAL PROFILE: Pattern cutter, running the sample departments of the House of Nicholas Bridal Co. of which she is one of the founders.

SOTIRAKIS CHARALAMBOU
Artist

DATE OF BIRTH: 07-Mar-1947
PLACE OF BIRTH: London. Father from Akanthou; Mother from Angastina.
CHILDREN: Nichola, Community worker. Martine, Art.
SCHOOLS/COLLEGE: Saint Martins School of Art, University London of Institute of Education.
QUALIFICATIONS: BA Honours Fine Art painting; PG. CE; ATC.
HOBBIES AND INTERESTS: Music, science, poetry, film and literature.
PERSONAL PROFILE: Independent Visual Artist. Has exhibited in Germany, Holland, England and USA. Works as a part-time lecturer. Work featured in newspapers and books.

UK

It is free to nominate someone, or yourself, who deserves to be in the book, just send in the name, contact address, telephone number and email to:
Greek Cypriots Worldwide
111 St Thomas's Road London N4 2QJ
Telephone 0044 207503 3498
cypriotwhoswho@aol.com
www.greekcypriotsworldwide.com

ANDREW LAMBROU CHARALAMBOUS
Parliamentary candidate, Conservative Party, for Tottenham Constituency general election 1992

DATE OF BIRTH: 12-Mar-1967
PLACE OF BIRTH: London. Parents from Episkopi, Paphos.
MARITAL STATUS: Single.
SCHOOLS/COLLEGE: Southgate Technical College, Queen Mary College, University of London, Inns of Court School of Law.
QUALIFICATIONS: Barrister at Law, LLB PhD.
MEMBERSHIPS: Member of Institute of Directors, Fellow of the Royal Society of Arts.
HOBBIES AND INTERESTS: Martial Arts.
PERSONAL PROFILE: Company Director for a successful private residential property developers in North London. Parliamentary candidate, Conservative Party, for Tottenham Constituency general election 1992. Radio presenter on LGR the Green Hour. President and Creator of Club4Climate an environmental awareness organization.

ANDY CHARALAMBOUS
Stockbroker Co Founder of the City Stockbroking firm Lewis Charles Securities Ltd

DATE OF BIRTH: 05-Oct-1971
PLACE OF BIRTH: London. Parents from Sia, Nicosia.
MARITAL STATUS: Married to Maria, Cyprus, Business owner of oxygene Ltd.
CHILDREN: Ellis, Rico, Katianna.
SCHOOLS/COLLEGE: School of St Davids, St Katherines Secondary & Sixth Form.
ACADEMIC QUALICATIONS: 9 GCSEs, 3 A Levels. ISMA (International Securities Market Association) General representative.
QUALIFICATIONS: SFA(Securities & Futures Authority) General representative.
MEMBERSHIPS: ISMA (Interrnational Securities Market Association).
HOBBIES AND INTERESTS: Football, boxing, golf, keeping fit and supporting Spurs.
PERSONAL PROFILE: Co Founder of the City Stockbroking firm Lewis Charles Securities Ltd. Sponsor of Omonia Youth Football club.

BAMBOS CHARALAMBOUS
Managing Director Parikiaki Newspaper

DATE OF BIRTH: 09-Apr-1956
PLACE OF BIRTH: Morphou.
MARITAL STATUS: Married to Soulla, a housewife, from Morphou.
CHILDREN: Elbida, George, Christopher.
PERSONAL PROFILE: Managing Director of Parikiaki Haravgi from Dec 2001. Secretary of Omonia FC (London) from 1989-2000.

BAMBOS CHARALAMBOUS
Parliamentary candidate for the Labour Party Enfield Constituency Election

DATE OF BIRTH: 02-Dec-1967
PLACE OF BIRTH: London. Parents from Kalo Chorio and Fasoulla.
MARITAL STATUS: Single.
SCHOOLS/COLLEGE: Chace Boys' School. Tottenham College; University of North London; South Bank University; Liverpool University.
QUALIFICATIONS: LLB Honours. Qualified Solicitor.
MEMBERSHIPS: Labour Party, Law Society, Enfield Law Centre.
HOBBIES AND INTERESTS: Chelsea football club, reading, politics, current affairs, cinema, the arts and walking.
PERSONAL PROFILE: London Borough of Enfield Councillor, and Councillor for Palmers Green Ward. Chair of Special Projects Security Panel, Enfield Council. Chair of Enfield Law Centre. School Governor at Eversley, St Michael at Bowes. Cabinet member of the Council. He is a Parliamentary candidate for the Labour Party Enfield Constituency Election.

UK

BAMBOS CHARALAMBOUS
Rally Driver

DATE OF BIRTH: 16-Nov-1960
PLACE OF BIRTH: Limassol.
Father was Melis Charalambous, marathon champion of Greece from 1952 to 1956.
MARITAL STATUS: Married to Katerina.
CHILDREN: Three children.
SCHOOLS/COLLEGE: Limassol Gymnasium, William Penn School in Dulwich, Southwark College, Camberwell School of Art & Craft.
HOBBIES AND INTERESTS: Rallying and football (Tottenham supporter).
PERSONAL PROFILE: Owns a printing company called The Press, printing work for ICI, Fords, BMW, Jaguar. Bambos is a Rally Driver - started 1993 won motoring News Group N Championship in 1994. Won Twyford Wood Forest Stages in 1998 & 2000. Won Bournemouth Winter Rally in 1997 in group A.

BAMBOS MICHAEL CHARALAMBOUS
Patent for novel meningitis vaccine development

DATE OF BIRTH: 30-Sep-1954
PLACE OF BIRTH: Parents from Yialoussa.
MARITAL STATUS: Married to Joy Louise, UK.
SCHOOLS/COLLEGE: Ambrose Fleming School, University of Wales.
QUALIFICATIONS: BSc Hons in Biochemistry, PhD in Biochemistry.
HONOURS/AWARDS: Discretionary Award for teaching & research.
HOBBIES AND INTERESTS: Windsurfing, cooking, gardening.
PERSONAL PROFILE: Senior Lecturer in Medical Microbiology at University College London. Published over 30 scientific papers and holds a patent for novel meningitis vaccine development.

CHRIS CHARALAMBOUS
Solicitor/Duke Of Edinburgh Award

DATE OF BIRTH: 20-Mar-1977
PLACE OF BIRTH: London Mother from Kyrenia Father from Paphos.
MARITAL STATUS: Married.
SCHOOLS/COLLEGE: St Albans School. Nottingham University and London Guildhall Law School.
QUALIFICATIONS: LLB(Honours).
MEMBERSHIPS: Law Society.
HONOURS/AWARDS: Duke Of Edinburgh Award.
HOBBIES AND INTERESTS: Travelling and experiencing other cultures.
PERSONAL PROFILE: Solicitor specialising in property law and founder and owner of the Law Firm Angel Law.

DINO CHARALAMBOUS
TV Director Richard & Judy on Channel 4 and the reality show Saturday Kitchen

DATE OF BIRTH: 02-Jul-1970
PLACE OF BIRTH: London.
Father born in Ayios Domedios, Nicosia.
MARITAL STATUS: Married.
CHILDREN: One Child.
SCHOOLS/COLLEGE: North Bridge House, London (Prep School). University College School.
HOBBIES AND INTERESTS: Sports, Music, Travelling, Reading and a Passionate Arsenal fan.
PERSONAL PROFILE: T. V. Director. Credits include, The Big Breakfast (Channel 4), GMTV, Nickelodeon, Disney Channel, Richard & Judy on Channel 4 and the reality show Saturday Kitchen. Has his own production company, Angelic Pictures.

UK

Dino Charalambous TV director credits include the big breakfast and Richard and Judy show.

HARRY CHARALAMBOUS
Semi Professional Boxer

PLACE OF BIRTH: London Father from Linou Solea
MARITAL STATUS: Married to Anna, Kornos.
CHILDREN: four kids.
SCHOOLS/COLLEGE: Finchley and Manor Hill.
HONOURS/AWARDS: Spraytech Awarded the Motor Care Key Platinum Repairers Award 2000 and 2004. Also the Body Shop magazine estimator of the year 2003.
HOBBIES AND INTERESTS: Boxing and Football.
PERSONAL PROFILE: Harry Charalambous is a Heavyweight Semi Professional Boxer as an Amateur Boxer. He had 15 fights lost 4. He is also the Managing Director of Spraytech Ltd in Edmonton which is one of the biggest accident repair centres in London.

JOHN CHARALAMBOUS
University Professor

DATE OF BIRTH: 13-Jan-1937
PLACE OF BIRTH: Nicosia.
MARITAL STATUS: Married to Elma, Canada, Compliance Manager.
CHILDREN: Alexia, Technical Development Manager.
SCHOOLS/COLLEGE: Pancyprian Gymnasium. University of London, University of Western Ontario.
QUALIFICATIONS: BSc, PhD (London).
MEMBERSHIPS: Member of Society of Chemical Industries.
HOBBIES AND INTERESTS: Gardening and preservation/restoration of old buildings.
PERSONAL PROFILE: John Charalambous is a Professor in the Chemistry department at the University of North London. Co-author of over 100 papers, books and patents. Has been Secretary/Vice President of the Greek Cypriot Brotherhood and former Secretary of National Federation of Cypriots in Great Britain. Established the Cyprus Community Centre at the University of North London in 1987 from which time has been its Director.

JOSEPHINE CHARALAMBOUS
The Founder of Broxenia. com. It is a World wide forum for Greeks to meet

DATE OF BIRTH: 01-Jun-1982
PLACE OF BIRTH: London Parents from Nicosia and Famagusta.
MARITAL STATUS: Single.
SCHOOLS/COLLEGE: City of London School for Girls. Queen Mary University of London and Inns of Court School of Law.
QUALIFICATIONS: LLB(Hons) PgDip (Bar vocational Course).
HONOURS/AWARDS: Silver and Bronze medals in the 23rd Region one Tang Soo Do Championships. Duke of Edinburgh Bronze Award. Drama Grades 1-6 from the Guild Hall School for Music and Dance.
HOBBIES AND INTERESTS: Travel, Learning Languages and Cooking.
PERSONAL PROFILE: Josephine Charalambous is the Founder of Broxenia. com. It is a world wide forum for Greeks to meet with over 1200 members hailing from five Continents. They have expanded their reach by jointly creating Love Match-Broxenia. com. Josephine is a Qualified Barrister by profession.

LOUIS CHARALAMBOUS
Leading Defamation and Human Rights Lawyer in Legal 500 and Chambers Law Firm Directories

DATE OF BIRTH: 10-Feb-1957
PLACE OF BIRTH: London Parents from Spatharikou and Ardana.
MARITAL STATUS: Married to Debbie, Director of a Childrens Charity.
CHILDREN: Anna, Studying Law. Eva, Student. Nina, Student.
SCHOOLS/COLLEGE: St Marylebourne Grammar. University of Bradford and University of Leeds.
QUALIFICATIONS: BA MA.
MEMBERSHIPS: Law Society.
HOBBIES AND INTERESTS: Photography, World Cinema and Tennis.
PERSONAL PROFILE: Louis Charalambous is a partner in the Law firm Simons Muirhead and Burton he is a leading Defamation and Human Rights lawyer in Legal 500 and Chambers Law Firm Directories.

UK

MARINOS CHARALAMBOUS
Prince of Wales Business Trust Advisor

DATE OF BIRTH: 08-Feb-1973
PLACE OF BIRTH: London.
Parents from Kalo chorio and Fasoula.
MARITAL STATUS: Married to Nancy from Portugal.
CHILDREN: One son.
SCHOOLS/COLLEGE: St Michaels at Bowes, Chase Boys, Enfield College, University of North London.
HOBBIES AND INTERESTS: Football.
PERSONAL PROFILE: Was marketing assistant at Bank of Cyprus, then head of marketing at the Popular Bank. Former head of marketing in Channel Marketing at Siemens. Involved in the Radio Marathon, Prince of Wales Trust Business advisor. Now Director of a Marketing & Design Agency.

MENELAOS (MELIS) CHARALAMBOUS
Youngest competitor in the British Rally Championship

DATE OF BIRTH: 06-Sep-1989
PLACE OF BIRTH: London
Father from Limassol Mother from London her parents from Kellaki.
MARITAL STATUS: Single.
SCHOOLS/COLLEGE: Keble and Aldenham School.
MEMBERSHIPS: Oxford Motor Club and Chelmsford Motor Club.
HOBBIES AND INTERESTS: Reading, fitness and motorsport.
PERSONAL PROFILE: Melis is the youngest competitor in the British Rally Championship (BRC) finished 10th in his second ever BRC event The Jim Clark Rally of Scotland.

MILTIS CHARALAMBOUS
Founder member of Southgate Greek School, Chairman for three years then Honorary Chairman

DATE OF BIRTH: 03-Jun-1945
PLACE OF BIRTH: Avlona.
MARITAL STATUS: Married to Charoulla, from Limassol.
CHILDREN: Katina, Solicitor. Sophia, Musician. Stylianos, Recruitment.
HOBBIES AND INTERESTS: Manchester United and Greek Music.
PERSONAL PROFILE: Founder member of Southgate Greek School, Chairman for three years then Honorary Chairman. Former Vice Chairman of Independent Greek Schools of London. Former Chairman of Twelve Apostles Greek Church Committee. Freeman of the City of London, Dress Manufacturer for thirty years, now runs his own Property Company.

PHILLIPOS CHARALAMBOUS
Businessman/Philanthropist

DATE OF BIRTH: 08-Jan-1937
PLACE OF BIRTH: St Demetrianos, Paphos.
MARITAL STATUS: Married to Katina, Rizokarpasso.
CHILDREN: One son, one daughter.
SCHOOLS/COLLEGE: Technical School, Paphos.
HOBBIES AND INTERESTS: Travel and reading.
PERSONAL PROFILE: Owned Valentina Fashion Group, producing ladieswear for multiples. Owns hotel and property business in UK & Cyprus. Does a lot of charity work and fundraising.

UK

Entrants in Greek Cypriots Worldwide have been nominated for their achievements and contributions.
It is free to nominate someone, or yourself, who deserves to be in the book, just send in the name, contact address, telephone number and email to:
Greek Cypriots Worldwide
111 St Thomas's Road London N4 2QJ
Telephone 0044 207503 3498
cypriotwhoswho@aol.com
www.greekcypriotsworldwide.com

ANDREW MICHAEL CHIALOUFAS
Educational chairman of Kingsbury High Greek school for over 20 years Co Founder of the Cyprus Wine Festival UK

DATE OF BIRTH: 26-Jul-1930
PLACE OF BIRTH: Alithinou.
MARITAL STATUS: Married to Christalla, from Omodhos.
CHILDREN: Jenny, Stella, Michael.
SCHOOLS/COLLEGE: Samuel Commercial School, Cyprus.
MEMBERSHIPS: AKEL.
HONOURS/AWARDS: Brent Council Citizenship of the year 1995.
HOBBIES AND INTERESTS: Politics.
PERSONAL PROFILE: Educational Chairman of Kingsbury High Greek school for over 20 years. General Manager of Parikiaki Newspaper from 1984 to 1995. Was a member of the main commitee of OESEKA. Co Founder of the Cyprus Wine Festival UK. Now retired living in Cyprus. Where he is Chairman of the Pan Cypriot Association of Repatriated Cypriots from England.

ANDREAS STYLIANOU CHIMONAS
Chairman of OESEKA

DATE OF BIRTH: 04-Apr-1944
PLACE OF BIRTH: Xylotympou.
MARITAL STATUS: Married to Anna, from London.
CHILDREN: Stelios, Helen.
SCHOOLS/COLLEGE: Famagusta Gymnasium, Kilburn Polytechnic, North London University, London University.
MEMBERSHIPS: Institute of Electrical Engineers.
HOBBIES AND INTERESTS: Football - Man United; Cars and DIY.
PERSONAL PROFILE: Chairman of OESEKA, Secretary of EFEPE, Chairman of Greek Parents Association, Chairman of Hazelwood Greek School.

ANGELIQUE CHRISAFIS
Journalist, Northern Ireland Correspondent for The Guardian

DATE OF BIRTH: 30-Oct-1975
PLACE OF BIRTH: London. Father from Eptakomi; Mother is English.
MARITAL STATUS: Single.
SCHOOLS/COLLEGE: Pembroke College. Cambridge University.
QUALIFICATIONS: BA Honours Modern Languages (Spanish & Portuguese) Cambridge. Post Graduate Diploma in Journalism, University of Central Lancashire.
HONOURS/AWARDS: Riley Prize for undergraduate achievement, Cambridge; Cambridge University Modern Languages prize.
HOBBIES AND INTERESTS: Writing, travel and film.
PERSONAL PROFILE: Was Northern Correspondent, then Arts Correspondent, general news reporter, now Northern Ireland Correspondent for The Guardian, which she joined in 1998. Prior to that, worked as a features writer on a Portuguese National Newspaper in Lisbon, was a voluntary worker with street kids in Mexico and a runner in special effects department of the film industry.

PETROS CHRISOSTOMOU
Artist commissioned to paint portrait of Sir Patrick Moore for National Portrait Award 2003

DATE OF BIRTH: 22-Feb-1981
PLACE OF BIRTH: London, Parents from Komi Kebir and Lythrodontas.
MARITAL STATUS: Single.
SCHOOLS/COLLEGE: Holy Trinity, St Martins School of Art.
QUALIFICATIONS: 10 GCSEs, 4 A Levels. Currently in 2nd year of BA Honours degree at St Martins.
HONOURS/AWARDS: Queens Heritage Trust Fund.
HOBBIES AND INTERESTS: Art, literature, cinematics photography and sport.
PERSONAL PROFILE: Artist exhibits frequently. Most recent one is a corporate project involving the US Law Firm Paul Hastings. Has also been commissioned to paint portrait of Sir Patrick Moore for National Portrait Award 2003. Worked to raise money for charities such as War on Want.

UK

PETER CHRISTIANSON
Founder of Greek City

DATE OF BIRTH: 26-Dec-1941
PLACE OF BIRTH: Lythrodontas.
MARITAL STATUS: Single.
CHILDREN: None.
SCHOOLS/COLLEGE: English School, Nicosia.
PERSONAL PROFILE: Founder of Greek City Music Centre. One of the first to put Greek films onto Video and DVD. First to promote Greek music in UK having managed Greek bands from the 1970s. Known in the community as 'Mr Entertainment' after the successful concerts, including one with Parios and Haris Alexiou at the Royal Albert Hall in 1986.

GEORGE CHRISTODOULIDES
Lecturer in Marketing at Birmingham University

DATE OF BIRTH: 21-Jul-1977
PLACE OF BIRTH: Limassol.
MARITAL STATUS: Single.
SCHOOLS/COLLEGE: St Peter and Paul Lyceum Limassol. Both Lancaster and Strathclyde University and University of Birmingham.
QUALIFICATIONS: BSc MSC PhD.
HOBBIES AND INTERESTS: Travelling, World Cinema, Health & Fitness, Politics and Current Affairs, Cooking and Wine.
PERSONAL PROFILE: George Christodoulides is a lecturer in marketing at Birmingham University Business School and active member of the centre for research in brand marketing.

MICHAEL D CHRISTODOULIDES
Teacher and Author. GCE Associate examiner 1971-1991

DATE OF BIRTH: 12-May-1921
PLACE OF BIRTH: Ikos, Marathassa.
MARITAL STATUS: Married to Niki. Kalopanayiotis, Housewife.
CHILDREN: Nearchos, Quantity Surveyor. Lenia, Chemistry. Maria, Computer Science.
SCHOOLS/COLLEGE: Teacher Training College.

QUALIFICATIONS: BA. DIPL.. Adolescent Development. Teacher.
HONOURS/AWARDS: Patriarchate Offico.
HOBBIES AND INTERESTS: Reading, writing and gardening.
PERSONAL PROFILE: GCE Associate examiner 1971-1991, co-founder of community organisations: Muswell Hill, Barnet. Kalopanayiotis-Ikos Association. Author of books, Regular article writing in community newspapers.

ANASTASIOS CHRISTODOULOU CBE
Founding Secretary of the Open University, Awarded the CBE for contribution to the establishment of the Open University. (Deceased)

DATE OF BIRTH: 01-May-1932
PLACE OF BIRTH: Akanthou, Cyprus.
MARITAL STATUS: Married to Joan.
CHILDREN: Two sons and two daughters.
SCHOOLS/COLLEGE: Marylebone Grammar School, Queens College, Oxford University.
HONOURS/AWARDS: CBE in 1978 for contribution to the establishment of the Open University. Honorary Doctorate from the Open University and by eight other universities in the Commonwealth. Professor of the universities of Mauritius and Surrey.
PERSONAL PROFILE: First Secretary of the Open University from 1968-80. Previously Deputy Secretary of Leeds University. Joined colonial service and spent six years in what is now called Tanzania as a District Officer and Magistrate. Was Secretary General of the Association of Commonwealth Universities form 1980-1996.

ANDREAS G. CHRISTODOULOU
Vice Chairman of the Hellenic Centre

DATE OF BIRTH: 30-Jan-1934
PLACE OF BIRTH: Makrasyka.
MARITAL STATUS: Married to Loulla, Ayios Amvrosios Kyrenia.
CHILDREN: George, Certified Accountant. Ambrose, Optician. Despina, Optometrist.
SCHOOLS/COLLEGE: Studied in Cardiff South Wales, City University London, Refraction Hospital.
QUALIFICATIONS: Ophthalmic Optician Optometrist.
HONOURS/AWARDS: Patriarchate Officialos from the Greek Orthodox Church.

UK

121

HOBBIES AND INTERESTS: Swimming, reading and socialising.
PERSONAL PROFILE: Optometrist. Former general secretary, Greek Cypriot Brotherhood, and Chairman of the Cypriot Estia of London. First secretary of the Cypriot Centre at Wood Green. Share holder & Director of LGR.

DR ARISTOPHANES CHRISTODOULOU
Radiologist

DATE OF BIRTH: 08-Feb-1962
PLACE OF BIRTH: London. Parents from Limassol.
MARITAL STATUS: Single.
CHILDREN: Andreas, Both Students. Carolina.
SCHOOLS/COLLEGE: Agios Georgios Gymnasium, Larnaca. Tottenham Technical College Middlesex Hospital Medical School.
QUALIFICATIONS: 5 A Levels. MB. BS. FRCR (1).
MEMBERSHIPS: Royal College of Radiologists.
HOBBIES AND INTERESTS: Swimming and clay shooting.
PERSONAL PROFILE: Helped to offer MRI scans to a large number of Greek Cypriots in the UK who suffered and had to wait for months, sometimes years, to have this expensive examination performed.

DAISY CHRISTODOULOU
One of the team at Warwick University to win University Challenge on TV

PLACE OF BIRTH: UK parents from Cyprus
SCHOOLS/COLLEGE: Warwick University.
PERSONAL PROFILE: Daisy was one of the Warwick University team that won the University Challenge beating Manchester University in the final year 2007.

JOHN CHRISTODOULOU
Property Developer/ Investments/ Philanthropist

DATE OF BIRTH: 24-May-1965
PLACE OF BIRTH: Nicosia.
MARITAL STATUS: Married.
SCHOOLS/COLLEGE: Creighton School.
HOBBIES AND INTERESTS: Fitness training and water sports.
PERSONAL PROFILE: Property Developer Investments Chairman of Yianis Holdings Property Investment Co. One of their investments is a freehold of Canary riverside in Canary Wharf, over 1. 1 million square feet which includes a leisure and residential complex. John is a known philanthropist in the community. One of his ambitions is to enter into politics in Cyprus.

KYRIAKOS CHRISTODOULOU
Former Lobby for Cyprus Co-ordinator

DATE OF BIRTH: 15-Aug-1957
PLACE OF BIRTH: Ayios Amvrosios.
MARITAL STATUS: Single.
CHILDREN: Two.
SCHOOLS/COLLEGE: Agios Amvrosios Gymnasium. North London College, Tottenham Tech and north London Polytechnic.
QUALIFICATIONS: BSc Statistics and Computing.
HOBBIES AND INTERESTS: Football (Arsenal Supporter).
PERSONAL PROFILE: IT Development Manager. Was Secretary and played for Ethnikos FC in Cypriot League. Former Secretary of Agios Amvrosios Association, still a commitee member. Former Lobby for Cyprus Co-ordinator.

Robert winder once reported that Haringey a part of London was the second biggest Cypriot town in the world.

LEFTERIS CHRISTODOULOU
Former Honorary Commissioner for Cyprus in Birmingham (Deceased)

DATE OF BIRTH: 18-May-1948
PLACE OF BIRTH: Lymbia.
MARITAL STATUS: Married to Anastasia Birmingham. (parents from Aradippou). Birmingham. (parents from Aradippou).
CHILDREN: One son, one daughter.
SCHOOLS/COLLEGE: University of East London.
QUALIFICATIONS: BSc in applied Microbiology.
HOBBIES AND INTERESTS: Football, (Aston Villa Fan).
PERSONAL PROFILE: Owner of a catering business and Director of a company selling holiday homes in Cyprus. Chairman of West Midlands Cypriot Association for 9 years. Committee of St Andrews Church in Birmingham. Former Honorary Commissioner for Cyprus in Birmingham.

LEONDIOS CHRISTODOULOU
Former Chairman of Yialoussa Association

DATE OF BIRTH: 23-Aug-1936
PLACE OF BIRTH: Yialoussa.
MARITAL STATUS: Married to Katerina.
CHILDREN: Four.
SCHOOLS/COLLEGE: Cyprus.
QUALIFICATIONS: Master Baker.
HOBBIES AND INTERESTS: Shooting and snooker.
PERSONAL PROFILE: Owner of Leons Patisserie. Chairman of Twelve Apostles Greek Orthodox Church for six years. Chairman of Yialousa Association for two years.

LOULLA CHRISTODOULOU
Deputy Chairwoman/Treasurer of the Greek Cypriot Brotherhood Ladies Committee 1974-1982

DATE OF BIRTH: 16-Jul-1944
PLACE OF BIRTH: Ayios Amvrosios, Kyrenia.
MARITAL STATUS: Married to A. G. Christodoulou, from Makrasyka.
CHILDREN: Three.
SCHOOLS/COLLEGE: City and East London College. Member of the Association of Dispensing of Opticians & Contact Lenses Practitioners.
QUALIFICATIONS: FADO C. L specialising in contact lenses.
HOBBIES AND INTERESTS: Reading, walking and charity work.
PERSONAL PROFILE: First Chairwoman of the Woman's Committee of the Cypriot Estia of London. Deputy Chairwoman/Treasurer of the Greek Cypriot Brotherhood Ladies Committee 1974-1982.

SAVVAS CHRISTODOULOU
Founder and proprietor of the Erotica Festival, the world's largest public adult lifestyle event, held annually at London's Olympia

DATE OF BIRTH: 20-Sep-1951
PLACE OF BIRTH: Strovolos.
MARITAL STATUS: Single.
CHILDREN: Pavlos.
SCHOOLS/COLLEGE: Stratford Grammar School, London School of Economics. Graduated 1974.
QUALIFICATIONS: BSc (Economics) Honours. ACA. Admitted to the Institute of Chartered Accountants in England & Wales in 1978.
PERSONAL PROFILE: Founder and proprietor of the Erotica Festival, the world's largest public adult lifestyle event, held annually at London's Olympia. For 18 years, operated the biggest residential care homes for the elderly in the London Borough of Havering. Over the last 20 years, has owned, managed and operated a series of nightclubs, and in addition has owned and managed small hotels in the UK and the Greek Dodecaneses islands.

UK

ANDRIANA CHRISTOFI

Appeared in commercial for Holsten Pils and appeared on Blue Peter the BBC programme

PLACE OF BIRTH: London, daughter of Varnava Christofi the Cyprus International Goalkeeper and Rita both from Famagusta.
MARITAL STATUS: Single.
SCHOOLS/COLLEGE: Edmonton Senior School, Brits Performing Arts technology School in Croydon.
HOBBIES AND INTERESTS: Gym.
PERSONAL PROFILE: Singer/Songwriter. A professional singer, sessions, performance and studios, backing singer for BoyZone, Michael Bolton. Appeared in commercial for Holsten Pils and appeared on Blue Peter on BBC 1 and performed in Wembley Arena.

APOSTOLOS CHRISTOFI

Served as President of the St Demetrios Community in Edmonton

DATE OF BIRTH: 19-Nov-1948
PLACE OF BIRTH: Analyondas.
MARITAL STATUS: Married to Irene, Analyonda. a Qualified Childminder.
CHILDREN: Maria, Teacher. Michael, IT Consultant. Andreas, Student.
SCHOOLS/COLLEGE: Analyonda Primary School, Wandsworth SecondaryLewisham Technical College. Lewisham Technical College, South Bank University.
QUALIFICATIONS: BSc BA PGCE.
MEMBERSHIPS: Member of the Institute of Electrical Engineers.
HOBBIES AND INTERESTS: Reading, swimming, charity work. Travel and theatre.
PERSONAL PROFILE: Apostolos Christofi works for a firm of Building Services Consultants as an Associate Director. Has been actively involved with the St Demetrios Community in Edmonton for the last 16 years, serving for ten of them as President of the committee.

DESPINA CHRISTOFI

Philanthropist

DATE OF BIRTH: 14-Aug-1947
PLACE OF BIRTH: Kato Pyrgos.
MARITAL STATUS: Married to Andronicos.
SCHOOLS/COLLEGE: Kato Pyrgos Elementary, Highgate Girls School.
HOBBIES AND INTERESTS: Reading, music, cooking.
PERSONAL PROFILE: Former owner of Spitiko Restaurant, now proprietor of Despina's Food Store in Arnos Grove. She is known for her philanthropic help towards schools and various charities in the community.

LUCY LOUKIA CHRISTOFI

Actress Appearances include The Bill, Road to Ithaca, Family Affairs

DATE OF BIRTH: 24-Oct-1966
PLACE OF BIRTH: London. Father from Vasili; Mother from Eptakomi.
MARITAL STATUS: Single to Engaged to Christaki Patriotis.
SCHOOLS/COLLEGE: Rose Brunford School of Speech. Drama, Royal Academy of Dramatic Art, London.
QUALIFICATIONS: BA in Drama & Theatre Studies.
MEMBERSHIPS: Equity. On the Board of Directors Theatro Technis.
HOBBIES AND INTERESTS: The arts, theatre, film, photography, literature and history.
PERSONAL PROFILE: Professional Actress, has worked in radio, theatre, film and television, both in UK and in Cyprus. Appearances include TV The Bill, Family Affairs and lead role in RIK TV series Kato Stes Teratsies. Films appaeared in Road to Ithaca, Akamas and Sea Urchin. Voice-overs in Captain Corelli's Mandolin, Mama Mia. Appeared in Theatre Macbeth, Ajax and Writing on the Wall at prominent London Theatres.

UK

NICOS CHRISTOFI
Full Professor in Environmental Biotechnology and Director of the Pollution Research Unit at Napier University in Edinburgh

DATE OF BIRTH: 26-Aug-1950
PLACE OF BIRTH: Limassol.
MARITAL STATUS: Married to Svetlana Vetchkanova, Russia.
CHILDREN: Sarah Marie, Events Organiser red Bull. Timothy, IT. Suzie, Housemaker. Jennifer, School.
SCHOOLS/COLLEGE: Sloane Grammar. Dundee University.
QUALIFICATIONS: BSC PhD.
MEMBERSHIPS: Society of General Microbiology.
HOBBIES AND INTERESTS: Travel. Gardening and Reading.
PERSONAL PROFILE: Nicos Christofi is a Full Professor in Environmental Biotechnology and Director of the Pollution Research Unit at Napier University in Edinburgh.

VARNAVAS CHRISTOFI
Footballer played in North American League with Vancouver Whitecaps, who were managed by Ferenc Puskas

DATE OF BIRTH: 23-Apr-1943
PLACE OF BIRTH: Famagusta. Father from Achna; Mother from Famagusta.
MARITAL STATUS: Married to Rita, Famagusta.
CHILDREN: Christakis, IT. Andrianna, Singer.
SCHOOLS/COLLEGE: Emporiko Lykeion, Famagusta.
MEMBERSHIPS: Cypriot Golf Society, Player of the year 1999/2000.
HONOURS/AWARDS: Represented the Cyprus National team 25 times.
HOBBIES AND INTERESTS: Golf.
PERSONAL PROFILE: Goalkeeper for six years with Salamis in Cyprus. Two years in North American League with Vancouver Whitecaps, who were managed by Ferenc Puskas. Played for Olympiakos for one year. Also played in the Cypriot League in London for Athletic United, and managed the teams Anorthosis, Dynamo and New Salamis. Also managed the Cypriot League team which won the League Cup. Former Captain of Enfield Golf Club.

CHRIS CHRISTOFIDES
Principal Education Adviser for Essex County Council

DATE OF BIRTH: 03-Dec-1950
PLACE OF BIRTH: Nicosia, Cyprus.
MARITAL STATUS: Married to Helen.
CHILDREN: Michael, Paul, Anna.
SCHOOLS/COLLEGE: Michenden Grammar School. University of Sussex.
QUALIFICATIONS: BSC PGCE.
HONOURS/AWARDS: Fellow of the Institute of Mathematics and its applications.
HOBBIES AND INTERESTS: Travel, reading and politics.
PERSONAL PROFILE: Chris is currently Principal Education Adviser for Essex County Council. Been a teacher, education adviser and inspector for the last 20 years working in a number of local education authorities in North London and now Essex.

GEORGE CHRISTOFIDES
Former President of the National Federation of Cypriots in the UK

DATE OF BIRTH: 09-Sep-1931
PLACE OF BIRTH: Apesha, Limassol.
MARITAL STATUS: Married to Yiota, Kilani.
CHILDREN: Zeza, Anna Maria, Both Barrister at Law.
SCHOOLS/COLLEGE: Limassol Gymnasium, Balham & Tooting College, Grays Inn.
QUALIFICATIONS: Fellow International Accountant and Barrister at Laws.
PERSONAL PROFILE: Barrister at Law and Business Consultant, has a practice in Cyprus with representative office in London. President of the South London Cyprus Association, and a member of the Board of Directors of Theatro Technis. was the Secretary of the Greek Cypriot Brotherhood for a number of years and for 15 years the President, of the Democratic Party of Cypriots in the UK Former President of the National Federation of Cypriots in the UK. Former Vice-Chairman of PSEKA and former President of the World Federation of Overseas Cypriots is the Honorary President of POMAK.

GEORGIOS C CHRISTOFIDES
Former Chairman of Bank Of Cyprus

DATE OF BIRTH: 04-Dec-1915
PLACE OF BIRTH: Nicosia.
MARITAL STATUS: Married to Mona, London.
CHILDREN: Christakis, Stelios, Businesses in Cyprus.
SCHOOLS/COLLEGE: Pancyprian Gymnasium and London School of Economics. Institute of Directors and RIIA.
QUALIFICATIONS: AIB.
MEMBERSHIPS: Institute of Directors and RIIA.
HONOURS/AWARDS: Awarded an Honorary Doctorate by the University of North London.
HOBBIES AND INTERESTS: Studies, participation in Conferences and Seminars.
PERSONAL PROFILE: Former Chairman Bank of Cyprus Group, later Chairman of Bank of Cyprus (London), currently Director. Served as Director-Chairman of Cyprus Employers Association.

DR GEORGE CHRISTOFINIS
Microbiologist

DATE OF BIRTH: 11-Mar-1926
PLACE OF BIRTH: Limassol.
MARITAL STATUS: Married to Annie, Denmark.
CHILDREN: Maria, Irini, Adonis.
SCHOOLS/COLLEGE: Limassol Gymnasium. Iowa State University and Oklahoma State University USA; London University.
QUALIFICATIONS: BSc PhD.
MEMBERSHIPS: Royal Society of Medicine, Society for General Microbiology.
HOBBIES AND INTERESTS: Theatre, music, politics, nature and gardening.
PERSONAL PROFILE: A Microbologist who has worked in several institutes and pharmaceutical companies, working on vaccine development and production, and on the classification of viruses. Has had work published in several scientific journals. Was President of the Union Of Cyprists in Britain and Vice President of the Federation of Cyprists in Great Britain. He is the Founder and Chairman of C G Christofides and Son Ltd Nicosia.

ANDREAS CHRISTOFOROU
Businessman/Philanthropist

DATE OF BIRTH: 03-Mar-1943
PLACE OF BIRTH: Milia.
MARITAL STATUS: Married to Kika, also from Milia.
CHILDREN: Maria, Estate Agent. Lakis, Business. Pamela, business.
SCHOOLS/COLLEGE: School in Milia.
HOBBIES AND INTERESTS: Shooting, snooker and backgammon.
PERSONAL PROFILE: Worked with Brother Michalakis who owned Milia & Co. Then started own business, Salamis & Co wine supplier. Agent for Hajipavlou Wines for 27 years. Agent for six years for Peoples Coffee Co, and ETKO for 25 years. In 1999 sold business now retired.

CHRISTIANA MARIA CHRISTOFOROU
Railton Prize for Business management (ACA paper), achieving the highest mark

DATE OF BIRTH: 21-Dec-1978
PLACE OF BIRTH: London. Father from Leonarisso; Mother from Larnaca.
MARITAL STATUS: Single.
SCHOOLS/COLLEGE: Winchmore School, Southgate Sixth Form, Brunel University.
QUALIFICATIONS: GCSEs 8As, 2Bs; A Levels ABC; BSc Mathematics & Statistics with management studies (1st class Honours). ACA (ICAEN).
HONOURS/AWARDS: Railton Prize for Business management (ACA paper), achieving the highest mark.
HOBBIES AND INTERESTS: Socialising with friends and family, drama and dance, gym, member of the St John's Ambulance.
PERSONAL PROFILE: Trainee Chartered Accountant, Price Waterhouse, Coopers.

It is free to nominate someone, or yourself, who deserves to be in the book, just send in the name, contact address, telephone number and email to:
Greek Cyprists Worldwide
111 St Thomas's Road London N4 2QJ
Telephone 0044 207503 3498
cypriotwhoswho@aol.com
www.greekcypriotsworldwide.com

CHRISTOPHER CHRISTOFOROU
One of the top 100 Estate Agents in the UK

DATE OF BIRTH: 28-May-1950
PLACE OF BIRTH: London. Parents from Sylikou and Yerakies.
MARITAL STATUS: Married to Betty, Lebanon.
CHILDREN: Nicholas, Alexis.
SCHOOLS/COLLEGE: Middlesex University.
QUALIFICATIONS: HND, BA Honours in Business Studies.
HOBBIES AND INTERESTS: Walking, travelling and skiing.
PERSONAL PROFILE: Started Christo & Co in 1983, Estate Agents, Surveyors and Valuers for pension funds, banks and building societies. One of the top 100 Estate Agents in the UK. Company does property management, lease renewals and rent reviews.

HAMBIA (HARALAMBIA) IRENE CHRISTOFOROU (nee TOFI) MBE
Awarded MBE for services to art education

DATE OF BIRTH: 27-Aug-1950
PLACE OF BIRTH: UK, Mother: Asha, Father: Komatou Yialou.
MARITAL STATUS: Married to Christopher Christoforou, UK.
CHILDREN: Anthony, History Honours graduate, University of Bristol. Chrisanthy, Geography undergraduate, University of Oxford.
SCHOOLS/COLLEGE: Tufnell Park Primary School, Shelbourne Secondary School. Hornsey College of Art, North-east London Polytechnic, North London Polytechnic.
QUALIFICATIONS: BA, Fine Art, Certificate in Education.
HONOURS/AWARDS: MBE for services to art education.
HOBBIES AND INTERESTS: Reading, painting, drawing, theatre and spending time with my family.
PERSONAL PROFILE: Art Teachers, Assistant Headteacher and an accredited Art Inspector.

ANDREAS CHRISTOU
Owner of Champion Racehorses most famous the World Globe trotting champion Phoenix Reach

DATE OF BIRTH: 15-Mar-1951
PLACE OF BIRTH: Phlasou. Soleas.
MARITAL STATUS: Married to Diane Gartlan married twice before, Company Secretary.
CHILDREN: sarah, Housewife. Antony, Business. Karen, Business. From first marriage.
SCHOOLS/COLLEGE: Quantock Public Prep School. Clarks College, Christchurch, Oxford.
PERSONAL PROFILE: Andreas Christou was originally in the fashion business now he is in horse racing and breeding he has a stud in Vale of Beaver with 15 mares and about 12 racehorses. Most famous is the 2007 stallion and world globe trotting champion Phoenix Reach he also has a property company in Cyprus.

ARTEMIS CHRISTOU
Schools and community

DATE OF BIRTH: 26-Oct-1950
PLACE OF BIRTH: Aradippou.
MARITAL STATUS: Married to Stelios Christou, a Businessman, from Nicosia, Cyprus.
CHILDREN: Christo, own Business; Toulla, Teacher.
SCHOOLS/COLLEGE: Convent For Girls, Larnaca.
QUALIFICATIONS: School Leaving Certificate. Cambridge RSA/Celta, (Certificate in English Langauge Teaching Adults).
HOBBIES AND INTERESTS: Reading.
PERSONAL PROFILE: Founding member and Secretary of Moss Hall Greek School. Founding member and Chair for 15 years of The Greek Women's Philanthropic Organisation Finchley & Barnet, Chair of The Ladies Committee of St Katherines Church in Barnet.

UK

GEORGE CHRISTOU
Programmes Director for the MA
International Politics and Europe at
Warwick University

DATE OF BIRTH: 28-Jul-1973
PLACE OF BIRTH: Strovolos,
Nicosia.
MARITAL STATUS: Married to
A Christou, British.
SCHOOLS/COLLEGE:
Sheffield University, Leeds
Metropolitan University.
QUALIFICATIONS: PhD in
Political Science, Postgraduate
Certificate in Higher Education
(PCHE), MA in International Studies, BA (HONS) in
Economics and Public Policy.
HOBBIES AND INTERESTS: Cycling, reading and cooking.
PERSONAL PROFILE: Programmes Director for
the MA International Politics and Europe at Warwick
University.

NICK (NEOCLIS) CHRISTOU
Headteacher of East Barnet Secondary
School

DATE OF BIRTH: 17-Jul-1957
PLACE OF BIRTH: Episkopi.
MARITAL STATUS: Married to
Janet, London, Teacher.
CHILDREN: Eleni, Student.
Katerina, Student.
SCHOOLS/COLLEGE:
Highgate Wood School.
University of Sussex; King's
College, University of
London.
QUALIFICATIONS: Bsc PGCE National Professional
Qualification for Headship (NPQH).
MEMBERSHIPS: Secondary Headteachers Association
(SHA), National Association of Headteachers (NAHT).
HOBBIES AND INTERESTS: Football (Tottenham),
Greek Music, reading The Guardian and the Cyprus
Weekly.
PERSONAL PROFILE: Headteacher of East Barnet
School, one of the largest Secondary Schools in Barnet
(1250 students). Previously Deputy Headteacher of
Hendon School and Head of Science at Highbury Grove.
Also Chair of Barnet Secondary Headteachers' Forum.

PAUL CHRISTOU
Footballer Paul is deaf he was on YTS at
Leeds United football club and played
for Leeds under 16s

DATE OF BIRTH: 29-Jun-1974
PLACE OF BIRTH: Limassol.
MARITAL STATUS: Married to
Panayiota, from Nicosia.
CHILDREN: Koulla.
SCHOOLS/COLLEGE: St John
Boston, Leeds Deaf School.
HONOURS/AWARDS: FA
Youth Cap.
HOBBIES AND INTERESTS:
Football and snooker.
PERSONAL PROFILE: Paul is deaf he was on YTS at
Leeds United football club and played for Leeds under
16s. He now plays and manages St Johns, a deaf club
that plays in the Cypriot football league. Works tirelessly
fundraising and organizing events for them. Paul is a
Carpenter but now works as a Chef.

RICHARD CHRISTOU
Chief Executive of ICL

PLACE OF BIRTH: born in
Cyprus, 1944.
MARITAL STATUS: Married.
CHILDREN: Two sons.
SCHOOLS/COLLEGE: Eltham
College, London, Trinity
College, Cambridge.
QUALIFICATIONS: Double first
BA Honours in Law, later an MA.
HONOURS/AWARDS: He was
Senior College Scholar and
Prizeman. Won the Lizette Bentwich Prize for law.
PERSONAL PROFILE: Christou was general legal
advisor latterly Director and General Manager of Lanitis
Bros Ltd, Cyprus, 1970 to 1974. In 1975 was Company
Secretary to STC Telecommunications Ltd. In 1990
moved to ICL as commercial and legal affairs Director.
Now Chief Executive of ICL, which is one of Europe's
leading business services companies.

UK

ANDREAS CHRYSANTHOU
Senior Lecturer, Dept of Aerospace Civil and Mechanical Engineering, University of Hertfordshire

DATE OF BIRTH: 12-Jan-1960
PLACE OF BIRTH: Nicosia.
MARITAL STATUS: Single.
SCHOOLS/COLLEGE: Imperial College.
QUALIFICATIONS: BSc (Eng) PhD ARSM DIC.
MEMBERSHIPS: Institute of Materials.
HOBBIES AND INTERESTS: Traditional Greek Dancing.
PERSONAL PROFILE: Senior Lecturer, Dept of Aerospace Civil and Mechanical Engineering, University of Hertfordshire. Vice President of The Anglo Hellenic Society of the Midlands 1993-1995.

SAVVAS CHRYSANTHOU
Co Founder of Independent Greek Schools of London, Manor Hill Greek School,

DATE OF BIRTH: 23-Jun-1949
PLACE OF BIRTH: Akaki.
MARITAL STATUS: Married to Flora, Larnaca, Housewife.
CHILDREN: Maria, Myroulla, Niki, Chrysanthos, All in Business.
SCHOOLS/COLLEGE: Pancyprian Gymnasium, Nicosia, evening classes at Fogel Academy for Design and Patterns.
HOBBIES AND INTERESTS: Reading and travelling.
PERSONAL PROFILE: Clothing Manufacturer. Involved with Independent Greek Schools of London, Manor Hill Greek School, UK Thalasssemia Society. Founder of Eleftheria Newspaper, London. Managing Director of Fosby Ladies' Clothing Manufacturers and Pomilo Ladieswear Retailers.

YIORGOS CHRYSANTHOU
Lecturer in Computer Science Department, University College London

DATE OF BIRTH: 18-Sep-1967
PLACE OF BIRTH: Nicosia.
MARITAL STATUS: Married.
SCHOOLS/COLLEGE: Queen Mary and Westfield College.
QUALIFICATIONS: BSc 1st Class Honours, Computer Science and Statistics.
HOBBIES AND INTERESTS: Cycling, climbing, DIY and interior design.
PERSONAL PROFILE: Lecturer in Computer Science Department, University College London, 1998-present. Teaching undergraduate and postgraduate courses on Computer Graphics and Virtual Environments. Has written books and published articles for numerous publications.

ALICIA SOPHIA CHRYSOSTOMOU
Lecturer at London Metropolitan University

DATE OF BIRTH: 05-May-1966
PLACE OF BIRTH: London. Father from Avgorou.
MARITAL STATUS: Single.
SCHOOLS/COLLEGE: Schoil Mhuire, Trim and Athlone Regional Technical College both in Ireland. University of North London.
QUALIFICATIONS: MSc PhD.
MEMBERSHIPS: Institute of Materials, Minerals and Mining.
HONOURS/AWARDS: Governors Award - UNL for meritorious research project.
HOBBIES AND INTERESTS: Craftwork, genealogy, travelling and exploring new countries.
PERSONAL PROFILE: Lecturer at London Metropolitan University where specialist field is in polymer engineering. Has lectured primarily in England but has also worked as a lecturer in New Zealand.

UK

It is free to nominate someone, or yourself, who deserves to be in the book, just send in the name, contact address, telephone number and email to:
Greek Cypriots Worldwide
111 St Thomas's Road London N4 2QJ
Telephone 0044 207503 3498
cypriotwhoswho@aol.com
www.greekcypriotsworldwide.com

ANDREAS CHRYSOSTOMOU
Business/Philanthropist

DATE OF BIRTH: 08-Feb-1952
PLACE OF BIRTH: Sotira.
MARITAL STATUS: Married to Niki, Famagusta.
CHILDREN: Dino, Business. Lakis, BSc Estate Management. Elena, Student.
SCHOOLS/COLLEGE: 2nd Gymnasium, Famagusta, Princeton College, Holborn, Middlesex Polytechnic, now Middlesex University.
QUALIFICATIONS: HND in Hotel Management.
HOBBIES AND INTERESTS: Tennis, swimming and basketball.
PERSONAL PROFILE: First worked in Intercontinental Hotels as a trainee Manager, then Food & Beverage Manager. Now has own Estate Agency Network Agencies in Finsbury Park. A Director of Mayfair London Properties Ltd with offices in Cyprus. Also Vice Chairman of Famagusta Association for five years. Was involved with Bowes Greek School.

ANDREAS CHRYSOSTOMOU
Businessman/Philanthropist

DATE OF BIRTH: 24-Mar-1947
PLACE OF BIRTH: Boghazi. Father from Patriki; Mother from Sphatariko.
MARITAL STATUS: Single.
CHILDREN: Lucy, Lakis, Stephanie, Alexi.
SCHOOLS/COLLEGE: Laycock.
HOBBIES AND INTERESTS: Music.
PERSONAL PROFILE: Former Chairman United Buying Services. Director Nisa Today. Former managing Director and Chairman of Venus & Co and Eurovenus, co-formed in 1972. A known Philanthropist within the Community.

EVDOKIA (Howells) CHRYSOSTOMOU
1st prize in Cypriot singing/songwriting competition in 1998, won award for best performance

DATE OF BIRTH: 03-Apr-1980
PLACE OF BIRTH: London. Father from Morphou; Mother from Pano Zodhia.
MARITAL STATUS: Married to Richard Howells.
SCHOOLS/COLLEGE: Cuffley Primary School, Chancellors School, Goffs School. Goldsmiths University.
QUALIFICATIONS: Grade 8 Piano, singing, saxophone. B. Mus.
HONOURS/AWARDS: 1st prize in Cypriot singing/songwriting competition in 1998, won award for best performance. Honoured by EKON in 1999.
HOBBIES AND INTERESTS: Singing, dancing, swimming.
PERSONAL PROFILE: Evdokia has Appeared in Theatre productions and given concerts at the Millfield Theatre. Has released 3 CDs. Evdokia is the Head of Music at Bassingbourn Village College in Herts.

MARCOS CHRYSOSTOMOU
Chairman of Cypriot Football League in the UK

DATE OF BIRTH: 09-Dec-1946
PLACE OF BIRTH: Lapithos.
MARITAL STATUS: Married to Julie, Komi Kebir, founder of Barnet Youth Club.
SCHOOLS/COLLEGE: Barnsbury Boys School. NW London Polytechnic and London School of Economics.
QUALIFICATIONS: BA MSc.
HOBBIES AND INTERESTS: Politics, social activities, arts, radio and travelling.
PERSONAL PROFILE: Marcos was a teacher at Upton House Hackney. Then a Director of G & S Formwork. Then became manager of Islington Advice Bureau. Founder Barnet Youth Club in 1975, then formed Dynamo Football Club in 1977. Secretary of the Cypriot Football League. Now Chairman. Currently Director of Citizens Advice Bureau at Haringey Council.

MIKKOS CHRYSOSTOMOU
Football Journalist

DATE OF BIRTH: 12-Dec-1946
PLACE OF BIRTH: Ayios Loukas, Famagusta.
MARITAL STATUS: Married to Catherine, London, PA.
CHILDREN: Vassos, IT Manager. Alex, Graphic Designer. Nicos, Computers.
SCHOOLS/COLLEGE: Ayios Loukas, Lykeion Famagusta, William Grimshaw, Tottenham Technical College.
QUALIFICATIONS: O Level GCE 5, A Level Maths. HND Structural Engineering.
HOBBIES AND INTERESTS: Football and all sports.
PERSONAL PROFILE: Founder of Anorthosis FC London 1975, Founder of Famagusta FC London 1988. Worked with the Cypriot League since the start 1975. Columnist with Parikiaki for several years, now with Eleftheria Newspaper.

TAKIS CHRYSOSTOMOU
Charity Worker, Gold Medal from the British Heart Foundation

DATE OF BIRTH: 29-Nov-1944
PLACE OF BIRTH: Rizokarpasso.
MARITAL STATUS: Married.
CHILDREN: Three.
SCHOOLS/COLLEGE: Primary and Secondary at Rizokarpaso and Peter St College London.
QUALIFICATIONS: Sales Rep, Silver Service Waiter and Hairdresser.
MEMBERSHIPS: Rizokarpaso Association and Kisos EDEK.
HONOURS/AWARDS: Gold medal from Rizokarpaso Association and gold, silver and bronze medals from British Heart Foundation.
HOBBIES AND INTERESTS: Reading, history, biking, travelling and gardening.
PERSONAL PROFILE: Raises money for charity by cycling from London to Brighton every year.

SALOMI COLMAN
Charity Worker, active member of many charity organisation's, disabled herself

DATE OF BIRTH: 15-Jun-1959
PLACE OF BIRTH: Paphos.
MARITAL STATUS: Married to Vernon, England, Architect and Chairman of the IF Group, charity for disabled people.
CHILDREN: Two stepsons, Oliver and, Christopher.
SCHOOLS/COLLEGE: Vale Road School. North East London College, Enfield College & Middlesex University.
QUALIFICATIONS: BA.
HOBBIES AND INTERESTS: Travelling, theatre, reading, socialising, writing short stories and poems.
PERSONAL PROFILE: Disabled - Tetraplegic due to catching/having Encephalitis. Mrs Colman is a member of various organisations/charities that deal with disabilities. ie: Haringey Community Health Council, The Haringey Joint Services Planning Team for Physical Disabilities and on the Mulitiple Sclerosis (MS) management committee.

VAS CONSTANTI
Actor Appeared on TV in The Bill and on stage in Miss Saigon and Grease

DATE OF BIRTH: 23-Apr-1967
PLACE OF BIRTH: London. Father, Kyriako from Gerani; Mother, Despo Neophytou, from Avgorou.
MARITAL STATUS: Single.
SCHOOLS/COLLEGE: Winchmore, Guildford School of Acting.
QUALIFICATIONS: Actor.
PERSONAL PROFILE: Organised Crusaids, charity midnight matinee for Rocky Horror Show, starred Robbie Williams, Shane Richie. Wrote Musical "Golden Fleece". Appeared on TV in "The Bill", in theatre in "Miss Saigon", "Grease". Film: "Road to Ithaca".

UK

RICKY CONSTANTINE
Karate British National Champion, 1967 to 1970, 1972 to 1973. (Deceased)

DATE OF BIRTH: 14-Feb-1952
PLACE OF BIRTH: Psemadismeno, Nicosia.
CHILDREN: One daughter.
SCHOOLS/COLLEGE: Camden Town Primary, North Haringey Secondary.
HOBBIES AND INTERESTS: Martial Arts.
PERSONAL PROFILE: 7th Dan in Karate WADO-RYU, European Martial Arts Champion 1970-1973, British National Champion, 1967 to 1970, 1972 to 1973. South East area national coach. Teaches Martial Arts at David Lloyd Centre Finchley.

ALEXANDROS CONSTANTINIDES
Head of Highways Department, London Borough of Haringay Council

DATE OF BIRTH: 07-Oct-1962
PLACE OF BIRTH: Limassol, Cyprus.
MARITAL STATUS: Married to Androulla from Cyprus.
CHILDREN: Christian, Natasha, Melissa, Panicos and Vasos.
SCHOOLS/COLLEGE: Edith Cavell, Westminster.
QUALIFICATIONS: MSc Transportation, Post Grad Diploma Highways, HNC Civil/Structural Engineering.
HONOURS/AWARDS: Chartered Engineer Transportation, Chartered Logistic Engineer, Incorporated Engineer, Fellow I. H. I. E.
HOBBIES AND INTERESTS: Taking my twins to Arsenal and to their football club Olympiakos. Also visiting Cyprus.
PERSONAL PROFILE: Head of Highways Department, London Borough of Haringay Council.

ANDREAS CONSTANTINIDES
Former Mayor of Enfield

DATE OF BIRTH: 25-Feb-1943
PLACE OF BIRTH: Pera Pedhi.
MARITAL STATUS: Married to Maroulla from Paleomylos.
CHILDREN: Theodhotos, Chartered Quantity Surveyor;. Joanne, IT support.
SCHOOLS/COLLEGE: Paedagogical Academy of Cyprus. Aston University, Birmingham.
QUALIFICATIONS: BSC.
HONOURS/AWARDS: Awarded Honorary Doctorate from Middlesex University.
HOBBIES AND INTERESTS: Gardening, football and backgammon.
PERSONAL PROFILE: Councillor for Enfield Council, was Mayor of Enfield. Director of Millfield Theatre and Governor of Oakthorpe School. Andreas is currently a teacher of mathematics at a secondary school.

ANTHONY GEORGE CONSTANTINIDES
Honorary Professor of Archaeology, University College London

DATE OF BIRTH: 01-Jan-1943
PLACE OF BIRTH: Acheritou.
MARITAL STATUS: Married to Pamela Maureen Bowman, an Anthropologist, from England.
CHILDREN: George, completed his PhD.
SCHOOLS/COLLEGE: Pancyprian Gymnasium. Regent Street Polytechnic, Imperial College.
QUALIFICATIONS: BSc PhD.
MEMBERSHIPS: Fellow IEE, Fellow IEEE, Fellow RSA.
HOBBIES AND INTERESTS: Reading.
PERSONAL PROFILE: Professor of signal processing; author of more than 300 learned papers and six books. Honorary Professor of Archaeology, University College London.

CHRIS CONSTANTINIDES
General Secretary of Sunday Cup Competitions in LFA

DATE OF BIRTH: 28-Jul-1940
PLACE OF BIRTH: Nicosia.
MARITAL STATUS: Married to Dora, from Nicosia.
CHILDREN: Athina, Alex, Nico Andy, Dimi and Dimitra.
SCHOOLS/COLLEGE: Pancyprian Gymnasium, Harrow Technical, Central London University.
HOBBIES AND INTERESTS: Football (Arsenal supporter), amateur radio, DIY, computers and theatre.
PERSONAL PROFILE: Works at ICL as a Senior Support Specialist teaching younger engineers in maintenance of systems. Started refereeing in 1970, joined Cypriot League in 1974 was member of management committee in various posts. General Secretary, First Cypriot on LFA Disciplinary Committee. General Secretary of Sunday Cup Competitions in LFA.

SUSIE CONSTANTINIDES
Two awards from Haringey Council Woman of the Year 1997 and 2001

DATE OF BIRTH: 07-Jun-1940
PLACE OF BIRTH: England. Father Tseri, Nicosia;Mother from Greece.
MARITAL STATUS: Single.
SCHOOLS/COLLEGE: Hornsey High School. Sorbonne University, Paris, Middlesex University, University of North London.
QUALIFICATIONS: Royal Society of Arts.
MEMBERSHIPS: Chair Cypriot Community Centre Chair Cypriot Womens League (England), Member of the Secretariat and the Executive Council National Federation of Cypriots in Great Britain.
HONOURS/AWARDS: One of the Women of the Year nominated at ceremony by Smith Kline Beecham in 1992 and 1993. Two awards from Haringey Council Woman of the Year 1997 and 2001.
HOBBIES AND INTERESTS: History, theatre, music, art, squash, archaeology and sociology.
PERSONAL PROFILE: 1972 appointed Liaison Officer, Cypriot Community for the London Borough of Haringey. 1990 Principal Race Equality Officer of Haringey. At present, working with the Cypriot elderly and disabled at the Cypriot Community Centre, Wood Green.

ACHILLEAS CONSTANTINOU
Founder and Chairman of the British Fashion & Design Protection Association

DATE OF BIRTH: 21-Apr-1948
PLACE OF BIRTH: Platres.
MARITAL STATUS: Married to Androulla.
CHILDREN: Three sons, one daughter.
SCHOOLS/COLLEGE: Arnos Secondary School, Waltham Forest Technical College, Kings College, London University.
QUALIFICATIONS: LLB (Honours).
HONOURS/AWARDS: Awarded the Shield of Haringey for his services to the Borough. In 1992, Ariella was honoured by a visit from the Princess Royal to its Wood Green headquarters in celebration of its 25th anniversary. British Apparel Export Award in 1996. Queens Award for export 1998 and UK Fashion Export Award 2008.
HOBBIES AND INTERESTS: Tennis, swimming, chess, backgammon and collectors cars.
PERSONAL PROFILE: With his late brother Aristos, founded Ariella Fashions Ltd in the Sixties. Retail shops in such locations as Carnaby Street, Oxford Street and Duke Street in London. The company now has a wholesale design and manufacturing business. He is a founder member and current director of the British Fashion Council. He is also appointed to the Board of Management of the British Knitting and Clothing Export Council (UK Fashion Exports) and Founder and Chairman of the British Fashion & Design Protection Association Achilleas is also the 'Fashion Guru' for LGR (London Greek Radio).

UK

Most of the dress factories in London in the 60's and 70's were owned by the Greek Cypriots.

ANDREA (GEORGIOU) CONSTANTINOU
Editor, English Section Parikiaki
Newspaper

DATE OF BIRTH: 09-Jun-1982
PLACE OF BIRTH: London.
Mother born in Larnaca.
MARITAL STATUS: Married
to George Georgiou, born in
Poland but raised in Ormidia,
Cyprus. journalist.
CHILDREN: One Daughter.
SCHOOLS/COLLEGE: Mount
Carmel R. C. Girls School, City
& Islington College.
QUALIFICATIONS: 11 GCSEs, 3 A Levels.
HOBBIES AND INTERESTS: Reading magazines/
newspapers, music and shopping.
PERSONAL PROFILE: English Section Editor for
Parikiaki. Also had a column entitled 'The Rumour Mill'
in Cypria in Britain magazine, and has reported the news
in English on London Greek Radio. Presented The
Entertainment programme at Parikiaki's Cyprus Wine
Festival at Alexandra Palace in 1999. Was involved in a
student exchange programme between Greek & Turkish
Cypriot youths in Cyprus, which was organised by
EKON in September 1999.

COSTAS CONSTANTINOU
Five times winners of Drapers Best
Women's Footwear Retailer and Best
Overall Retailer 2005

DATE OF BIRTH: 09-Nov-1968
PLACE OF BIRTH: London.
Father from Pervolia. Mother
from Famagusta.
MARITAL STATUS: Married
to Katerina, born in London.
(Father from Patriki. Mother
from Limassol).
CHILDREN: Marina, Andrew.
SCHOOLS/COLLEGE:
Southgate School.
HONOURS/AWARDS: Five times winners of Drapers
Best Women's Footwear Retailer and Best Overall
Retailer 2005.
HOBBIES AND INTERESTS: Football and music.
PERSONAL PROFILE: Shoe Retailer.

COSTAS M CONSTANTINOU
Professor of International Relations,
Keele University

DATE OF BIRTH: 21-Dec-1965
PLACE OF BIRTH: Nicosia.
MARITAL STATUS: Married
to Demetra, Cyprus, Senior
Officer Cyprus Chamber of
Commerce and Industry.
CHILDREN: Daphne.
SCHOOLS/COLLEGE: Kykkos
Lyceum. Keele University,
Lancaster University.
QUALIFICATIONS: BSocSc.
MA PhD.
MEMBERSHIPS: British International Studies.
HOBBIES AND INTERESTS: Basketball, Football,
Literature and Archaeology.
PERSONAL PROFILE: Costas Constantinou is a
Professor of International Relations, Keele University,
also taught at the Universities of Hull and Lancaster he
is the author of On the way to Diplomacy and States of
Political Discourse.

FRIXOS CONSTANTINOU
Film Producer. Work includes The
Devil's Men starring Peter Cushing and
Donald Pleasance, and Anna Pavlova
starring Galina Beliaeva and Peter Fox

DATE OF BIRTH: 31-Oct-1928
PLACE OF BIRTH: Lapithos.
MARITAL STATUS: Married to
Ikouko, Japan.
CHILDREN: Eroula, both
postgraduate students;.
Alexander, student. Daphne.
SCHOOLS/COLLEGE:
Lapithos Gymnasium.
MEMBERSHIPS: Member of
the British Academy.
HONOURS/AWARDS: First TV prize for
Educational series, 1997.
HOBBIES AND INTERESTS: Writing and travelling.
PERSONAL PROFILE: Film Producer. Work includes
eight educational TV series, seven feature films, Two of
them are The Devil's Men starring Peter Cushing and
Donald Pleasance, and Anna Pavlova starring Galina
Beliaeva and Peter Fox. Also 15 documentaries, and
ten animation series for children. Also co arranged the
first overseas concert of Mikis Theodorakis with Maria
Farantouri in 1966 at the then famous Saville Theatre in
London.

UK

JASON CONSTANTINOU
Surgeon

DATE OF BIRTH: 14-Jan-1972
PLACE OF BIRTH: London.
Parents from Famagusta.
CHILDREN: Thomas.
SCHOOLS/COLLEGE:
University College, London,
Medical School.
QUALIFICATIONS: MB BS BSc
MRCS.
MEMBERSHIPS: British
Medical Association, Medical
Protection Society, Royal College of Surgeons.
HONOURS/AWARDS: A number of awards at university.
HOBBIES AND INTERESTS: Tennis and travelling.
PERSONAL PROFILE: Surgeon.

GEORGE CONSTANTINOU (SECULAR NAME) ATHENAGORAS CONSTANTINOU (ecclesiastical name)
Senior Clergyman

DATE OF BIRTH: 14-Dec-1948
PLACE OF BIRTH: Anaphotia.
QUALIFICATIONS: B. D
in Theology, Kings College,
University of London,
Degree in Theology from
Athens University, Cambridge
Diploma of English Studies.
Archimandrite. Also a trained
Teacher 1970-1972 at Thomas
Huxley College of Education.
HOBBIES AND INTERESTS: A Linguist, a
Philologist, a Polyglot and a Polymath.
PERSONAL PROFILE: Senior Clergyman of the Greek
Orthodox Church. A Greek Language Teacher since
1969.

MARIO CONSTANTINOU (MATT DI ANGELO)
Appeared as Deano Wicks in the popular British Soap East Enders

DATE OF BIRTH: 06-Aug-1987
PLACE OF BIRTH: London,
Father from Cyprus, Mother
Irish.
MARITAL STATUS: Single.
SCHOOLS/COLLEGE:
Southgate School, Boden
Studios and Sylvia Young
Theatre School.
PERSONAL PROFILE: Actor
Matt has appeared in the TV
programmes "I Dream" and "Harbour Lights2. His
major breakthrough came when he appeared in "East
Enders" as Deano Wicks. He appeared in Strictly Come
Dancing (series 5) where he was runner up with partner
Flavia Cacace.

AMILIOS COSTA
Philanthropist/Accountant

DATE OF BIRTH: 21-Oct-1968
PLACE OF BIRTH: London,
Parents from Vasa Kilaniou,
Limassol, Kalo Chorio.
MARITAL STATUS:
Married to Loulla,
Lettings Negotiator.
SCHOOLS/COLLEGE:
Ashmole School, London
School of Economics.
QUALIFICATIONS: BSc
(Honours) Economics. FCA. Chartered Accountant.
HOBBIES AND INTERESTS: Watching and playing
football, keeping fit and golf.
PERSONAL PROFILE: Amilios Costa is a Chartered
Accountant and a Partner in a Firm of Chartered
Accountants He is known for his Philanthropic help.

ANTONY DANIEL COSTA
Singer with pop group Blue

DATE OF BIRTH: 23-Jun-1981
PLACE OF BIRTH: UK.
Grandparents from Famagusta
and Morphou.
MARITAL STATUS: Single.
SCHOOLS/COLLEGE: Hendon
School.
QUALIFICATIONS: Drama and
Greek GCSE (A) and (B).
HONOURS/AWARDS: Brit
Award 2002 for Best Newcomer.
HOBBIES AND INTERESTS: Football, singing,
comedy and socialising.
PERSONAL PROFILE: Young recording artist signed to
Virgin. Debut single All Rise entered the UK chart at No.
4, the second single Too Close went to No. 1. The band's
first album All Rise went on to spawn three more singles
including two No 1's. Second album, One Love went to
the top of album charts. Did duet with Elton John. Has
appeared in a leading role in Blood brothers and done his
own shows.

UK

COSTAS COSTA
TV Personality has own series

DATE OF BIRTH: 13-Jun-1968
PLACE OF BIRTH: London.
Father from Ikos Marathassa;
Mother from Ayios Sergios,
Famagusta.
MARITAL STATUS: Single.
SCHOOLS/COLLEGE: St
Mark's Secondary School,
Hammersmith and West
London College, University of
Westminster.
QUALIFICATIONS: BA (Honours) Business Studies.
HOBBIES AND INTERESTS: Learning languages
and travelling.
PERSONAL PROFILE: Comedy magician/TV
Personality, has had two TV series in Cyprus, "Costa
Costa Stis Okto"(Sigma TV) Sept 96 to Jan 98, Costas
Costa Show (PIK), Jan 00 to Jun 01. Performs regularly
in London, New York and Cyprus.

LARA COSTA
Actress appeared in West End theatre
productions

PLACE OF BIRTH: London.
Grandfather, Costa Sofocleaus
(Halouvas), born in Analyonta;
Grandmother, Maria Lazarou,
born Larnaca.
MARITAL STATUS: Single.
SCHOOLS/COLLEGE: London
Studio Centre, Elmhurst Ballet
School, Royal Ballet School.
Equity.
QUALIFICATIONS: 8 GCSEs.
HOBBIES AND INTERESTS: Reading, travel, ski-ing
and anything thats a challenge.
PERSONAL PROFILE: Actress. Has appeared in theatre
in "Bombay Dreams", "Saturday Night Fever". Appeared
on TV in Smith & Jones, Bliss, Crimewatch. TV
commercials, such as Evening Standard and Motown.

DR ZACHARIAS COSTA
Medical Private Practice Doctor

DATE OF BIRTH: 20-Feb-1925
PLACE OF BIRTH: Kontea.
MARITAL STATUS: Married to
Anastasia from Akhna.
CHILDREN: Costas, Christos,
Anna, Charalambous and
Georgia.
SCHOOLS/COLLEGE:
American Academy, Larnaca,
Lille and Bordeaux (France)
Universities.
QUALIFICATIONS: MD, FRCOG. LRCP, MRCS,
DIPVEN, MRCGP, LAH Dip, BA (Honours),
Philosophy, D. T. M (France).
HOBBIES AND INTERESTS: Studying Law with the
Open University, writing books, learning languages.
PERSONAL PROFILE: In Medical Private Practice in
North London. Was responsible for the eradication
of the killer common disease in Cyprus called Hydatid
(Echinoculus), about which he co-operated with the
French Professors Jean Jean Biquet, Debroque and
Gabren. Dr. Costa's first wife, Eleni, died of this disease
at the age of 28.

BARRY COSTAS
Senior Lecturer at University of Herts

DATE OF BIRTH: 06-Mar-1960
PLACE OF BIRTH: London
Father from Kalopsida.
MARITAL STATUS: Married
to Joan, British, Health Service
Aministrator.
SCHOOLS/COLLEGE:
Brooke House. North London
University.
QUALIFICATIONS: B. Ed and
MSc.
MEMBERSHIPS: Greek Institute and Amateur Athletic
Association.
HOBBIES AND INTERESTS: Cycling, running, football
and swimming.
PERSONAL PROFILE: Barry Costas is a Senior Lecturer
at the University of Hertfordshire. He is the President
of the South Cyprus Flyers Running Club. He has ran 17
full marathons including the Athens Olympic route.

UK

DR ALAN C. F. CROSS
Doctor specialising in Psychiatry

DATE OF BIRTH: 12-Feb-1974
PLACE OF BIRTH: London. Mother Greek Cypriot.
MARITAL STATUS: Single.
SCHOOLS/COLLEGE: Chigwell School for Boys, U C L Medical School.
QUALIFICATIONS: A Level Biology, Chemistry, Maths, General studies. Medical Doctor MBBS.
MEMBERSHIPS: G. M. C. (General Medical Council).
HOBBIES AND INTERESTS: Music, sport, drama and travel.
PERSONAL PROFILE: Doctor, specialising in Psychiatry, East London Group.

STELIOS DAMIANOU
General Manager KEO UK

PLACE OF BIRTH: Ayios Theodoros, Larnaca, Cyprus.
MARITAL STATUS: Married to Beba, from Ayios Theodoros, Larnaca.
CHILDREN: Akis, MSC, M PHIL Biochemistry Biology Food Techno.
PERSONAL PROFILE: General Manager of KEO UK.

ALKI DAVID
Film maker/Actor His most recent film is Fishtales, released in August 2007 which he co-wrote, directed and starred in. The film also stars Kelly Brook and Billy Zane

DATE OF BIRTH: 23-May-1968
PLACE OF BIRTH: Nigeria, Parents from Cyprus.
MARITAL STATUS: Married to Emma, Qualified Nurse now a make up artist.
CHILDREN: Three Children.
SCHOOLS/COLLEGE: Stowe School. Royal College of Art.
QUALIFICATIONS: Masters graduate.
PERSONAL PROFILE: Alki David stars in major films and mini series as well as writing, directing and starring in his own independent movies. His most recent film is Fishtales, released in August 2007 which he co-wrote, directed and starred in. The film also stars Kelly Brook and Billy Zane and was filmed on the Greek island of Spetses where David has a home. He is also a partner in the UK model agency ICM models. He also founded the charity organisation BIOS which works on marine conservation in Greece.

ZACH DAY
Actor Has appeared in films and TV, including Sammie & Rosie Get Laid

DATE OF BIRTH: 07-Jan-1969
PLACE OF BIRTH: London. Mother from Rizokarpasso.
MARITAL STATUS: Single.
SCHOOLS/COLLEGE: Leeds University.
QUALIFICATIONS: BA Honours English, MA Theatre Studies.
MEMBERSHIPS: Equity.
HONOURS/AWARDS: Winner of several awards, National & International for Poetry.
PERSONAL PROFILE: Actor and Poet. Has appeared in films and TV, including Sammie & Rosie Get Laid, and at the Narcissus Theatre in Macbeth, Romeo & Juliet.

ALEXIS DEMETRIADES
Wrestler Won the English Senior Championship for his weight

DATE OF BIRTH: 06-Mar-1979
PLACE OF BIRTH: London. Parents from Morphou, Cyprus.
MARITAL STATUS: Single.
SCHOOLS/COLLEGE: Hampstead Comprehensive.
HOBBIES AND INTERESTS: Cinema and travel.
PERSONAL PROFILE: Wrestler. Top athlete in the 74kg category in Freestyle Wrestling (an Olympic Sport) in England. Won the English Senior Championship for his weight.

UK

PANICOS DEMETRIADES
Professor of Financial Economics, University of Leicester

DATE OF BIRTH: 09-Jan-1959
PLACE OF BIRTH: Limassol.
MARITAL STATUS: Married to Svetlana Andrianova, a Lecturer in Economics, from Moscow.
CHILDREN: Polyvios, at school in Nicosia.
SCHOOLS/COLLEGE: Lanition, University of Essex and University of Cambridge. Econometric Society.
QUALIFICATIONS: PhD, MA, BA.
PERSONAL PROFILE: Professor of Financial Economics, University of Leicester.

ALEXIA DEMETRIOU
Actress From the age of 11-14, played the part of Janine Butcher in East Enders

DATE OF BIRTH: 25-Nov-1981
PLACE OF BIRTH: UK. Father from Nicosia, Mother from Ayios Theodoros, Larnaca.
MARITAL STATUS: Married.
SCHOOLS/COLLEGE: Coombe Girls School New Malden, Surrey. Esher College. Esher College.
QUALIFICATIONS: 9 GCSEs (C+) A Levels Sociology, Theatre Studies and History.
(BCC). CIM Certificate & Member of Chartered Institute of Marketing.
HONOURS/AWARDS: Millennium Volunteer and has a 200 Voluntary Service Award.
HOBBIES AND INTERESTS: Dancing, socializing with friends, yoga, traveling and studying Psychology.
PERSONAL PROFILE: Fundraiser for children's charity, Barnardo's. Goes to schools to tell children about the work Barnado's does. Also goes to companies to manage fundraising events. From the ages of 11-14, played the part of Janine Butcher in East Enders.

ANDREW DEMETRIOU
Leader in providing TV and Data communication systems worldwide

DATE OF BIRTH: 07-Jul-1951.
PLACE OF BIRTH: Father from Xylotympou.
MARITAL STATUS: Married to Margaret, British, Business.
CHILDREN: Ben, Company director. Kate, accounts Secretary.
SCHOOLS/COLLEGE: Woodberry Down. Havering College.
MEMBERSHIPS: Fellow member of the Society of cable television engineers.
HOBBIES AND INTERESTS: Music, photography and motor racing.
PERSONAL PROFILE: Andrew Demetriou together with his wife started the Business called SCC providing television systems in the early 70's. It has grown to become UK's leader in providing TV and Data communication systems. It has offices in Cheshunt, Guildford, Leeds and Glasgow. Organization that covers the globe employing some 100 employees. The Company also provides for charitable causes such as Children in Need and helping to provide hand tools for Village Communities.

DEMETRI DEMETRIOU
Actor appeared in the film Sea Wolf and the TV programme The Way We Live Now

DATE OF BIRTH: 15-Jun-1973
PLACE OF BIRTH: Nicosia, Cyprus.
MARITAL STATUS: Single.
SCHOOLS/COLLEGE: King's College (University of London). Drama Centre London.
QUALIFICATIONS: Law and Drama degrees.
HOBBIES AND INTERESTS: Reading, theatre, cinema, and swimming.
PERSONAL PROFILE: Actor. Appearances have included the film Sea Wolf and the TV programme The Way We Live Now.

UK

DEMETRIOS DEMETRIOU
Father and son finalists in TV Britains got talent show 2009

PLACE OF BIRTH: Born London Parents from Ayios Sergios
MARITAL STATUS: Married.
CHILDREN: One Son and Daughter, Southgate School.
SCHOOLS/COLLEGE: Went to Southgate School
PERSONAL PROFILE: Demetrios with his son Lakis were finalists in the Britains got talent show 2009 TV show with their comedy dance routine Stavros Flatley.

DIMITRIS DEMETRIOU
Former Mayor of Epping

DATE OF BIRTH: 20-Jun-1949
PLACE OF BIRTH: Lapathos.
MARITAL STATUS: Married to Vasoulla, from Labathos.
CHILDREN: George, Maria & Katerina.
SCHOOLS/COLLEGE: Tricomo Gymnasium, Hotel School in Nicosia, West Ham College, North East London Polytechnic.
QUALIFICATIONS: Diploma of Higher Education. Qualified as a teacher.
HOBBIES AND INTERESTS: Business and gardening.
PERSONAL PROFILE: Worked one and a half years as a teacher in Newham, opened a fish and Chip, Shop and several restaurants, notably Abbey Taverna in Waltham Cross, and Thatched House in Epping. Twelve years Councillor in Epping and Waltham Abbey, Mayor of Epping 1992-93, was chairman of the Planning Committee of Epping. President of Waltham Abbey Football Club in the Vauxhall League and Governor of St. Johns School in Epping.

JASON DEMETRIOU
Footballer with Leyton Orient

DATE OF BIRTH: 18-Nov-1987
PLACE OF BIRTH: Newham, London, Grand Father from Cyprus.
SCHOOLS/COLLEGE: Caterham.
HONOURS/AWARDS: Cyprus International footballer.
HOBBIES AND INTERESTS: Fishing and football.
PERSONAL PROFILE: Jason is a central midfielder playing for Leyton Orient made his league debut during the 2005/6 season aged 18 in the clash with Cheltenham and now a regular in the first team.

LOUCAS DEMETRIOU
Finance Committee member of the Cypriot Diaspora and Treasurer of the Greek Parents Association

DATE OF BIRTH: 14-Apr-1952
PLACE OF BIRTH: Galataria.
MARITAL STATUS: Married to Christina, Born in London Parents from Arminou and Yialoussa.
CHILDREN: Alexia, University. Kyriacos, University. Marcos, School.
SCHOOLS/COLLEGE: First Gymnasium of Paphos. Harrow College of Further Education and Polytechnic of North London.
QUALIFICATIONS: Seven O Levels and Four A Levels.
MEMBERSHIPS: Member of National Association of Estate Agents.
UK Association of Letting Agents and Ombudsman of Estate Agents.
HOBBIES AND INTERESTS: Photography, Travel, Football, Golf and Badminton.
PERSONAL PROFILE: Loucas Demetriou is on the Committee and Finance officer of the Cypriot Diaspora project. Also Treasurer of the Greek Parents Association and served as Chairman of Harrow Greek School.

UK

Mario Constantinou (Matt di Angelo) appeared as Deano Wicks in the popular British soap East Enders.

MADELEINE DEMETRIOU
Lecturer in European Studies at University of Kent

DATE OF BIRTH: 03-Mar-1969
PLACE OF BIRTH: Nicosia.
MARITAL STATUS: Married.
SCHOOLS/COLLEGE: University of East Anglia, Bristol University, University of Kent.
QUALIFICATIONS: BA in Economic & Social Studies; MSc in Domestic Politics and Foreign Policy; PhD Graduate School of Politics & International Relations.
HOBBIES AND INTERESTS: Yoga, drama, Cypriot Women's Bi-Communal Group, Domestic Violence Niteline.
PERSONAL PROFILE: Lecturer in European Studies at University of Kent. Formerly Political researcher in Cyprus, reporter for Cyprus Mail, and has written several publications.

MARIE-ELENI DEMETRIOU
Barrister/Co-author of References to the European Court (Sweet & Maxwell, 2002)

DATE OF BIRTH: 13-Feb-1972
PLACE OF BIRTH: UK, Father from Nicosia.
MARITAL STATUS: Single.
SCHOOLS/COLLEGE: Campion School, Athens, Greece, Oxford University.
QUALIFICATIONS: BA, BCL (Jurisprudence).
PERSONAL PROFILE: Barrister at Brick Court Chambers, specialising in European Union Law, competition law and public law. Previously worked as Referendaire to Judge Edward at the European Court of Justice. Co-author of References to the European Court (Sweet & Maxwell, 2002).

PANAYIOTIS (PETER) DEMETRIOU
Philanthropist

DATE OF BIRTH: 24-Apr-1968
PLACE OF BIRTH: London. Parents from Pomos Paphos and Ayios Sergios (Famagusta).
MARITAL STATUS: Single.
CHILDREN: One Son.
SCHOOLS/COLLEGE: Michenden School.
HOBBIES AND INTERESTS: Travel and shooting.
PERSONAL PROFILE: Owner of Demetriou & English Funeral Directors, based in Myddleton Rd, N. 22. Known for his Philanthropic help.

PROCOPIS DEMETRIOU
Articles in the Evening Standard for the work he does to keep the Cypriot Culture active in London

DATE OF BIRTH: 10-Oct-1946
PLACE OF BIRTH: Analyondas, Cyprus.
MARITAL STATUS: Single.
CHILDREN: Demitris, Zacharoulla.
HOBBIES AND INTERESTS: Football, Socialising, Music and Greek Bouzouki Music.
PERSONAL PROFILE: Procopis is an active member of AKEL Political Party in the UK, his Car Repair Garage is well known within the Cypriot Community and because of this, he has had articles written about him and his Garage in the Evening Standard. Procopis, nick-named Rouski has given his time and help to many Cypriot organizations in the UK.

SIMON DEMETRIOU
UK Poetry Society Young Poet of the Year Winner 2004

DATE OF BIRTH: 26-Apr-1986
PLACE OF BIRTH: London Parents from Famagusta.
MARITAL STATUS: Single.
SCHOOLS/COLLEGE: Dame Alice Owens School. Wadham College and University of Oxford.
QUALIFICATIONS: 11 GCSE's 5 A levels studying for a BA in English Language and Literature at Oxford.
HONOURS/AWARDS: UK Poetry Society Young Poet of the Year Winner 2004.

HOBBIES AND INTERESTS: Reading, Manchester. United, semiotics, writing, film, cooking, satire, travelling and celebrity gossip.
PERSONAL PROFILE: Simon Demetriou is a student at Oxford University.

ZAHAROULLA DEMETRIOU
Negotiating Executive for an International property developer in the city

DATE OF BIRTH: 01-Mar-1981
PLACE OF BIRTH: London, Father from Analyondas, Mother form Rizokarpasso.
MARITAL STATUS: Single.
SCHOOLS/COLLEGE: Christ Church CE School, Finchley, Woodhouse. College, Anna Sher Theatre School. University of Hertfordshire.
QUALIFICATIONS: BA LLM in International Law and Maritime Law.
HOBBIES AND INTERESTS: Active member of the drama society and performed in several musicals. currently a TV extra and has appeared on the Discovery channel in a documentary called Unexplained Air Crashes. Likes traveling.
PERSONAL PROFILE: Zaharoulla is an investment consultant for major Middle East Property Developers.

MARIA DESPINA
Actress/Singer/Dancer and Model appeared in the film Mamma Mia

DATE OF BIRTH: 11-Jun-1980
PLACE OF BIRTH: Herts Mum from Limassol.
MARITAL STATUS: Married to Ben Birchwood.
SCHOOLS/COLLEGE: Laine Theatre Arts.
HOBBIES AND INTERESTS: Dancing, singing and writing music.
PERSONAL PROFILE: Maria Despina is an Actress, has appeared in films such as Mamma Mia also appeared on Sarah Brightman's and Russell Grant Video and the Bacardi Commercial.

ELENI DIAKOU
Social Worker. Founder of Cypriot Day Centre in Islington

DATE OF BIRTH: 22-Mar-1947
PLACE OF BIRTH: Komi Kebir.
MARITAL STATUS: Married to David McCulloch, Scottish, Enviromental Health Manager.
CHILDREN: Androulla, GP. Adrian, Website Specialist.
SCHOOLS/COLLEGE: Girls Classical Gymnasium Famagusta. Dame Alice Owen's Girls' School, Loughborough College of Education.
QUALIFICATIONS: BA Social Studies and Politics.
HOBBIES AND INTERESTS: Walking, reading, visiting other countries and travelling.
PERSONAL PROFILE: Manager in Social Work. Lead in local, patchwork. Co-author of books on community social work and access to advice services. Amateur actress; set up Cypriot Day Centre in Islington, ex-Director of Theatro Technis.

DEMETRIOS ACHELLEOUS DJIALLI
Professor in Engineering at the University of Glamorgan

DATE OF BIRTH: 29-Oct-1948
PLACE OF BIRTH: Lefkoniko.
MARITAL STATUS: Married to Mary a Partner in Djialli Associates.
CHILDREN: Helena, Lawyer.
SCHOOLS/COLLEGE: Lefkoniko High School. Llandaff Technical College. Cardiff, and University of Glamorgan.
QUALIFICATIONS: Professor, BSc, CEng, MICE.
HOBBIES AND INTERESTS: Current affairs, restoration of historic buildings, classical music.
PERSONAL PROFILE: Professor of Design and Construction. Director of The Centre for Engineering Research and Environment Applications (CEREA), University of Glamorgan, South Wales.

UK

PETER DROUSSIOTIS
President, National Federation of Cypriots in the UK

DATE OF BIRTH: 21-Sep-1960
PLACE OF BIRTH: Pera Chorion Nissou, Nicosia.
MARITAL STATUS: Married to Carolyn, Yorkshire, Teacher.
CHILDREN: Isabella, Alexandra, Theodora.
SCHOOLS/COLLEGE: Terra Santa College Cyprus, Alexandra Park School London, University of Birmingham, Bar School London.
QUALIFICATIONS: LL B (Law & Politics). Barrister-at-Law of the Middle Temple.
MEMBERSHIPS: The Labour Party, Society of Labour Lawyers, Episteme, Fabian Society and Smith Institute.
HOBBIES AND INTERESTS: Family, politics & current affairs, people, the countryside, history, IT, astronomy and travelling.
PERSONAL PROFILE: President, National Federation of Cypriots in the UK. Member of Labour Party official panel of Parliamentary candidates. Former Haringey Council Executive member. President of Episteme. Chair Labour Cypriot Society. Chairman PGD Strategy, a corporate finance firm.

AGGI KOUMIS DULSON
Champion Bodybuilder

DATE OF BIRTH: 17-Jul-1961
PLACE OF BIRTH: London Parents from Larnaca.
MARITAL STATUS: Married to Jim Dulson, British, Professional Bodyguard and Gym owner.
CHILDREN: Stepson James Dulson.
SCHOOLS/COLLEGE: Hornsey High School. Southgate Technical College.
QUALIFICATIONS: Fashion Design.
MEMBERSHIPS: International Federation of Body Building.
HONOURS/AWARDS: 1st Miss Cyprus 1995 1st Gold Medallist Mediteranean Champion 1st Cyprus Open 2003 Top Ten womens World Championships Spain.
HOBBIES AND INTERESTS: Restaurants, Walking, Archaeology.
PERSONAL PROFILE: Aggi Koumas Dulson was a fashion designer now a qualified personal trainer/instructor she has her own gym in Cyprus and is a competitive body builder. She has also worked with Police against Drug abuse and organised fund raising for local Leukaemia society.

DEMETRIOS ECONOMIDES
Obstetrician & Gynecologist

DATE OF BIRTH: 14-Oct-1956
PLACE OF BIRTH: London. Parents from Lefkonico.
MARITAL STATUS: Married to Daphne Christie, of the Stakis family from Kato Drys, Scientific Editor.
CHILDREN: Margarita and Alexandra.
SCHOOLS/COLLEGE: The English School, Nicosia; Charing Cross Medical School, London.
QUALIFICATIONS: MBBS, MD. FRCOG.
MEMBERSHIPS: Royal Society of Medicine, Hellenic Medical Society.
HOBBIES AND INTERESTS: Travel, photography and shooting.
PERSONAL PROFILE: Consultant & senior lecturer obstetrician & gynecologist, Royal Free Hospital.

HERACLIS A ECONOMIDES
HSBC, Managing Director Equity Capital Markets

DATE OF BIRTH: 18-Mar-1961
PLACE OF BIRTH: Famagusta, Cyprus.
MARITAL STATUS: Married.
CHILDREN: One daughter.
SCHOOLS/COLLEGE: English School in Nicosia; Archbishop Tennysons Grammar School, Kennington; Brasenose College, Oxford University.
QUALIFICATIONS: BA in Philosophy, Politics, and Economics. Chartered Accountant.
HOBBIES AND INTERESTS: Tennis, opera and travel.
PERSONAL PROFILE: First worked with Coopers and Lybrand, now with HSBC, Managing Director Equity Capital Markets.

PAUL ECONOMIDES
Professional Boxer

DATE OF BIRTH: 19-Nov-1986
PLACE OF BIRTH: Chester parents from Kakopetria and Nicosia.
MARITAL STATUS: Single.
SCHOOLS/COLLEGE: Richard Green.
HONOURS/AWARDS: Three times National Boxing Champion in Wales. Bronze medalist in multi Nations Championships.
HOBBIES AND INTERESTS: Boxing.
PERSONAL PROFILE: Featherweight boxer turned professional in march 2008 has had four professional fights has been seen on Sky TV.

DR GEORGE JOHN EFSTATHIADES
Served as Honorary Commissioner for the Republic of Cyprus in Birmingham

DATE OF BIRTH: 23-Mar-1939
PLACE OF BIRTH: Kato-Drys.
MARITAL STATUS: Married to Antigone (Loizides), from Nicosia, Company Director.
CHILDREN: John, Consultant Engineer. Marios, Insurance. Helena, Flight Attendant.
SCHOOLS/COLLEGE: Kato Drys Primary; Pancyprian Gymnasium, Nicosia; University of Birmingham.
QUALIFICATIONS: BSc, PhD (Mechanical Engineering).
PERSONAL PROFILE: Chief Engineer, Hellenic Mining Corporation Cyprus 1966-67. Founder & Managing Director of Zet Insurances Services Ltd. Honorary Commissioner for the Republic of Cyprus in Birmingham 1981-2004.

GEORGE PETROS EFSTATHIOU
Professor of Astrophysics University of Cambridge

DATE OF BIRTH: 02-Sep-1955
PLACE OF BIRTH: London. Parents from Achna, Cyprus.
MARITAL STATUS: Single.
CHILDREN: Zoe and Peter.
SCHOOLS/COLLEGE: Somerset School, Tottenham London; Keble College, University of Oxford; Durham University.
QUALIFICATIONS: BA (1976), PhD (1979).

MEMBERSHIPS: Fellow of Royal Society, Fellow of Institute of Physics, Fellow of Royal Astronomical Society.
HONOURS/AWARDS: Maxwell medal & prize Institute of Physics 1990, Bodassaki prize for Astrophysics 1994, Bappu Medal, Astronomical Society of India 1988, Robinson prize for Cosmology, Univ Newcastle 1997.
HOBBIES AND INTERESTS: Running and playing guitar.
PERSONAL PROFILE: Assistant Director of Research, Institute of Astronomy, Cambridge. Savilian Prof of Astronomy, Univ of Oxford (1988-1997), Head of Astrophysics (1988-1994), Professor of Astrophysics University of Cambridge (1997-present).

STATHI EFSTATHIOU
Senior Lecturer, Dept of Pathology Cambridge University

DATE OF BIRTH: 15-Oct-1960
PLACE OF BIRTH: London. Parents from Achna.
MARITAL STATUS: Married to Caroline, from Cheshire, Computer Programmer.
CHILDREN: Claudia Mary and James.
SCHOOLS/COLLEGE: Southgate Comprehensive; Leeds University (undergraduate), Cambridge University (postgraduate).
QUALIFICATIONS: BSc Microbiology, PhD Virology.
MEMBERSHIPS: Society of General Microbiology.
HOBBIES AND INTERESTS: Music and guitar.
PERSONAL PROFILE: Senior Lecturer, Dept of Pathology Cambridge University. Research area - virus pathogenesis and gene therapy. Editorial Journal of Genereal Virology (1995-2000), Member of the Virus Group Committee of the Society of General Microbiology. Member of the European Society of Gene Therapy Meetings Organising Committee. Member of the SGM Herpesvirus Workshop Committee (1989-1991).

UK

143

TASSOS EFSTATHIOU
Chairman of the 41 Club Rotary Charity Organisation

DATE OF BIRTH: 24-Apr-1955
PLACE OF BIRTH: London, Parents from Lymbia.
MARITAL STATUS: Married to Gillian, Southend.
CHILDREN: Andreas, Joseph, and Alexandra.
SCHOOLS/COLLEGE: Henry Thornton School, Southbank Polytechnic.
QUALIFICATIONS: 5 GCEs, 2 A Levels, OND Building; BA, MA Architecture.
HOBBIES AND INTERESTS: Golf, Bridge, eating out and music.
PERSONAL PROFILE: Tassos is the Chairman of the 41 Club Rotary Charity Organisation. He is a Architectural Consultant, Director of a Building Company, Former Chairman of under-13s football team, and was on committee of parents for scouts in Southgate 6th group.

ANDROULLA EFSTRATIOU
Head of WHO Collaborating Centre for Reference and Research on Diptheria and Streptococcal Infections, Health Protection Agency London

DATE OF BIRTH: 03-Jul-1960
PLACE OF BIRTH: London. Parents from Famagusta and Larnaca.
MARITAL STATUS: Single.
SCHOOLS/COLLEGE: St Joseph's Convent Grammar School. City University London.
QUALIFICATIONS: BSc, PhD. SRCS, MRCPath.
MEMBERSHIPS: Royal College of Pathologists, American Society for Microbiology, Hellenic Medical Society.
HONOURS/AWARDS: Louis Pasteur Medal for Distinction in Infectious Diseases.
HOBBIES AND INTERESTS: Gardening, art and travel.
PERSONAL PROFILE: Consultant for Cyprus Ministry of Health, and Consultant for World Health Organisation and European Commission.

STRATOS EFSTRATIOU
Dentist, private practitioner and owner of a six surgery practice

DATE OF BIRTH: 04-Sep-1967
PLACE OF BIRTH: Johannesburg, South Africa. Father from Peristerona, Paphos; Mother from Nicosia.
MARITAL STATUS: Married to Chrisoula, South Africa Parents from Greece, Dentist.
CHILDREN: Nicholas and Angela.
SCHOOLS/COLLEGE: University of Witwatersrand, SA.
QUALIFICATIONS: BDS (Bachelor of Dental Surgery).
HOBBIES AND INTERESTS: Golf and squash.
PERSONAL PROFILE: Dentist, private practitioner and owner of a six surgery practice.

ANDRIA EFTHIMIOU
Voted Heroine of the Year 2007 Independent on Sunday

DATE OF BIRTH: 13-Jul-1963
PLACE OF BIRTH: London. Father from Morphou, Mother from Rizokarpasso.
SCHOOLS/COLLEGE: Camden school for girls. Middlesex Polytechnic, London School of Economics.
QUALIFICATIONS: Bsc, Msc.
HONOURS/AWARDS: Voted Heroine of the year 2007 Independent on Sunday.
HOBBIES AND INTERESTS: Singing, swimming, walking and reading.
PERSONAL PROFILE: Co-founder/ peer supporter, Terence Higgins Trust-First HIV&NGO in UK; Counsellor of HIV& drug users and their significant others, International Community of Women Living with HIV/AIDS Trustee; Founder/Director John Mordant, advocating for the health and human rights of drug users affected by blood borne disease.

DR CHRIS EFTHYMIOU
Formula One doctor at Monaco and the British Grand Prix

DATE OF BIRTH: 11-Dec-1973
PLACE OF BIRTH: Famagusta.
MARITAL STATUS: Single.
SCHOOLS/COLLEGE: Ewell Castle School, Surrey. St Bartholomews Medical School; University of London, Royal College of Surgeons.
QUALIFICATIONS: MBBS, BSc (Honours) Physiology, MRCS.
PERSONAL PROFILE: Formula One doctor at Monaco and the British Grand Prix.

IOANNIS EFTHYMIOU
Chief Exec Association of Greek Travel Agents

DATE OF BIRTH: 09-Jan-1946
PLACE OF BIRTH: Morphou.
MARITAL STATUS: Single.
SCHOOLS/COLLEGE: Greek Gymnasium, Morphou.
HOBBIES AND INTERESTS: Reading, writing, cinema and travel.
PERSONAL PROFILE: Chief Executive AGTA (UK), now generally regarded as the mouthpiece for Greek Cypriot specialist travel agents and tour operators in the UK, the number one market for Cyprus tourism.

PETROS EFTYCHIOU
Former High Commissioner for the Republic of Cyprus in the UK

DATE OF BIRTH: 25-Oct-1950
PLACE OF BIRTH: Nicosia.
MARITAL STATUS: Married.
CHILDREN: Two daughters.
SCHOOLS/COLLEGE: The English School Nicosia. American University of Beirut.
QUALIFICATIONS: BA.
HOBBIES AND INTERESTS: Sports, Football- Played for Apoel in Cyprus.
PERSONAL PROFILE: 1993 he was elected Minister of Plenipotentiary, Chief of Cabinet of the Minister of Foreign Affairs, Nicosia. In 1994 and then again in 2000, Eftychiou worked as the Ambassador of Cyprus to the State of Israel. Between these years he was the permanent representative at the UN office in Geneva, (In 1998 he was elected and served for a year as Vice President of the Economic Commission for Europe). In 2004 he was appointed High Commissioner for Cyprus in the UK to the year 2006.

SAPPHIRE ELIA
Actress Played Cossette in Les Miserables on the London stage

DATE OF BIRTH: 15-Apr-1987
PLACE OF BIRTH: UK. Maternal grandparents from Lapithos, paternal grandparents from Larnaca and Akanthou.
MARITAL STATUS: Single.
SCHOOLS/COLLEGE: Sylvia Young Theatre School since the age of eight.
QUALIFICATIONS: Honours in LAMDA acting exam.
HOBBIES AND INTERESTS: Singing, dancing and skiing.
PERSONAL PROFILE: Sapphire has performed for the Princess Royal. Filmed in American Space Camp. Performed in choir for Lady Rattlings Charity Ball, and performed many times at the Royal Albert Hall. Played Cossette in Les Miserables on the London stage, and appeared on TV in comedy awards and Fun Song Factory, East Enders and Dream Team.

PANOS ELIADES
Former Manager of Lennox Lewis the Boxing World Champion

DATE OF BIRTH: 24-Apr-1951
PLACE OF BIRTH: London. Parents from Livadhia who had the Shaftesbury Restaurant in London's West End.
CHILDREN: Christian, Eleonora.
SCHOOLS/COLLEGE: Tollington Grammar, Loughborough University.
QUALIFICATIONS: Chartered Accountant.
HOBBIES AND INTERESTS: Football, (Spurs supporter).
PERSONAL PROFILE: In 1980 formed own practice Panos Eliades & Co Chartered Accountants, specialising in liquidations. In 1991 bought contract of the boxer Lennox Lewis to manage and promote him. Director of Panix Promotions.

UK

DR C. P. ELLINAS
Civil and Structural Engineer

DATE OF BIRTH: 18-Sep-1949
PLACE OF BIRTH: Engomi, Famagusta.
MARITAL STATUS: Single.
CHILDREN: Olympia.
SCHOOLS/COLLEGE: University College London.
QUALIFICATIONS: BSc (Honours), PhD.
MEMBERSHIPS: Fellow of Institute of Civil Engineers.
PERSONAL PROFILE: Civil and Structural Engineer, Managing Director of Oil & Gas Energy at Mott McDonald Group. Has written many publications, both books and magazine contributions.

MICHAEL S ELLINAS
Managing Director of Eleftheria Newspaper

DATE OF BIRTH: 09-Apr-1957
PLACE OF BIRTH: Paphos (Houlou).
MARITAL STATUS: Married to Elissa, Paphos, teacher.
CHILDREN: Stavros, Secondary School.
SCHOOLS/COLLEGE: Lanition Gymnasium, Limassol.
QUALIFICATIONS: Law Degree (BA), University of Athens (Law).
HOBBIES AND INTERESTS: Greek Dancing.
PERSONAL PROFILE: Managing Director of weekly Greek Newspaper, Eleftheria. Also, headmaster of independent Greek Community Schools of Barnet (Manor Hill & Finchley). President of the Democratic Party of Cypriots in England (DEKO). Executive Member of the National Federation of Cypriots in the UK.

KALLY ELLIS
Florist Designer for the Vanity Fair Oscars Party in Los Angeles

DATE OF BIRTH: 09-Jun-1962
PLACE OF BIRTH: London Parents from Melanarka.
MARITAL STATUS: Married to Damian.
CHILDREN: Two, a son and daughter.
SCHOOLS/COLLEGE: Parliament Hill School. University of East Anglia.
HONOURS/AWARDS: Trendsetting award from wedding magazine in New York.
HOBBIES AND INTERESTS: Cinema, travel, food and shopping.
PERSONAL PROFILE: Kally is the founder of the florists Mcqueens whose styling and demonstrations can be seen at magazine shoots and TV shows to product launches events and interiors. McQueens are renowned as first class stylists the world over, thanks mainly to their work at the vanity fair Oscars party in LA. They have also featured in numerous TV shows including This Morning, CN news, The Richard and Judy Show and the real lives documentary Celebrity Florist.

AGAMEMNON A EPENETOS
Medical oncologist at St. Bartholomew's Hospital and a consultant in clinical oncology at The Harley Street Cancer Clinic

DATE OF BIRTH: 15-Oct-1949
PLACE OF BIRTH: Nicosia.
MARITAL STATUS: Married to Panayiota.
CHILDREN: Antoni and Kristina.
SCHOOLS/COLLEGE: Famagusta 1st Gymnasium, Glasgow University.
QUALIFICATIONS: MB. chB, FRCP, PhD.
MEMBERSHIPS: Many medical societies.
HOBBIES AND INTERESTS: Starting Biotec Companies.
PERSONAL PROFILE: Dr Epenetos is a medical oncologist at St. Bartholomew's Hospital and a consultant in clinical oncology at The Harley Street Cancer Clinic. He is a visiting Professor at Imperial College London and the School of Pharmacy London. Professor Epenetos is a member of the Board of Directors and Chairman of Alexis Biotech Ltd, Trojantec Ltd, and Lifeline Biotech Ltd. He is also the President, Director and Chief Executive of Somanta Pharmaceuticals.

UK

AKIS ERACLEOUS
Co-Founder, London Greek Radio and Kiss FM

DATE OF BIRTH: 26-Dec-1952
PLACE OF BIRTH: Famagusta.
MARITAL STATUS: Married to Julietta, London, Housewife.
CHILDREN: Emilios, Eva and Markos.
SCHOOLS/COLLEGE: Islington Green School, London.
QUALIFICATIONS: 6 grade 1 CSEs, 1 A Level Art. Certificate of Hotel and Catering Management.
MEMBERSHIPS: Equity.
HOBBIES AND INTERESTS: Football, Arsenal supporter. Watching a good movie or listening to a good album. Cycling and swimming.
PERSONAL PROFILE: Original founder of Kiss FM, a London based dance music radio station. Co-founded London Greek Radio in 1983, and was appointed General Manager in 1989 when the station obtained its legal licence. Currently owns a highly successful independent record label, Nice 'N' Ripe Records, and still presents his own show on LGR every weekday between 10am and 1pm.

HARALAMBOS EROTOCRITOU
Ran London Marathon three years in succession in aid of Marie Curie

DATE OF BIRTH: 21-Feb-1963
PLACE OF BIRTH: Pyroi.
MARITAL STATUS: Married to Janina, Romanian.
CHILDREN: Alexander, Zoe, Paris.
PERSONAL PROFILE: Haralambos Erotocritou Ran London Marathon Three years in succession in aid of Marie Curie.

DR PETROS PAVLOU EROTOCRITOU
Doctor

DATE OF BIRTH: 31-Dec-1944
PLACE OF BIRTH: Limassol.
MARITAL STATUS: Married to Sarah, England, Nurse.
CHILDREN: Paul, at medical school.
SCHOOLS/COLLEGE: Lanition Gymnasium, Limassol.
QUALIFICATIONS: MD, SIM 1973 Athens Medical School, Athens University 1980 SIM.
MEMBERSHIPS: GMC, MDU, BMA London.
HONOURS/AWARDS: 1990 Aviation Medicine.
HOBBIES AND INTERESTS: Game shooting, DIY, gardening, olive oil production and wine growing.
PERSONAL PROFILE: After qualifying, worked in hospitals until 1982 then entered general practice. Currently general practitioner in Luton. Regular attender of local Greek Orthodox church.

ANDROULLA EROTOKRITOU
Actress, TV appearances on Nickleodeon and ITV's Diggit, and Queen Mother's 100th birthday celebrations

DATE OF BIRTH: 12-Jan-1987
PLACE OF BIRTH: London (twin with a brother). Parents from Nicosia and Famagusta.
MARITAL STATUS: Single.
SCHOOLS/COLLEGE: Chesterfield Junior School, Bishop Stortford Secondary, Sylvia Young Theatre School.
HOBBIES AND INTERESTS: Swimming, reading, travel and shopping.
PERSONAL PROFILE: Actress, dancer, singer. Choreographer at both junior and secondary school productions. Performed in the Night of 1000 Voices at the Royal Albert Hall 1999 & 2000. Michael Jackson's album launch at London's Hippodrome 1998, solo spot. TV appearances on Nickleodeon and ITV's Diggit, and Queen Mother's 100th birthday celebrations.

UK

TASOS EROTOKRITOU
Former Secretary of AKEL Islington and in the Secretariat of AKEL UK

DATE OF BIRTH: 11-Sep-1934
PLACE OF BIRTH: Chloraka.
CHILDREN: Yianni, Law Graduate. Erotokritos, Engineer. Maria.
SCHOOLS/COLLEGE: Chloraka Elementary.
MEMBERSHIPS: Union of Tailors, Islington Cypriot Association and AKEL.
HOBBIES AND INTERESTS: Birds (has large aviary).
PERSONAL PROFILE: Former Secretary of AKEL Islington and in the Secretariat of AKEL UK. Former member of OESEKA Committee, and formerly on the committee of the Islington Cypriot Association. Committee member of EKA.

GEORGE EUGENIOU
Actor and Founder of Theatro Technis

DATE OF BIRTH: 14-Jun-1931
PLACE OF BIRTH: Limassol.
MARITAL STATUS: Married to Maroulla.
CHILDREN: Aris.
SCHOOLS/COLLEGE: Open University.
QUALIFICATIONS: BA in Arts.
MEMBERSHIPS: Equity.
HOBBIES AND INTERESTS: Writing plays and directing.
PERSONAL PROFILE: Formed Theatro Technis in 1957 in Camden Town. Actors that went through the Theatro were Peter Polycarpou, Demetris Andrea, Anna Savva and George Savvides. Appeared in films Moonlight with Dirk Bogarde, Riviera Touch with Morecombe and Wise, and Hungry Hill with Robert Mitchum.

MICHAEL EVANGELOU
He played the baby son of Ali and Sue Osman in the East Enders

PLACE OF BIRTH: London in 1984 Parents from Cyprus
PERSONAL PROFILE: Michael Evangelou played the Baby son of Ali and Sue Osman in East Enders.

SIMOS EVANGELOU
Lecturer in Mechanical and Electrical and Electronic Engineering at Imperial College London

PLACE OF BIRTH: Limassol
SCHOOLS/COLLEGE: Cambridge University, Imperial College.
QUALIFICATIONS: BA/M. Eng. Ph. D.
MEMBERSHIPS: Institute of Electrical and Electronics Engineers (IEEE)American Society of Mechanical Engineers (ASME).
HOBBIES AND INTERESTS: Exercise, nice food, music, travelling, riding motorcycles.
PERSONAL PROFILE: Lecturer in Mechanical and Electrical and Electronic Engineering at Imperial College London.

STELIOS EVANGELOU
Chairman of Kalogrea Association

DATE OF BIRTH: 20-Dec-1939
PLACE OF BIRTH: Kalogrea.
CHILDREN: Nicos, Insurance. Angela, banking.
SCHOOLS/COLLEGE: Kyrenia Gymnasium.
QUALIFICATIONS: Chartered Certified Accountant.
MEMBERSHIPS: Member of the Securities Institute and the British Institute of Management.
HOBBIES AND INTERESTS: Swimming, football, reading, stock market and travelling.
PERSONAL PROFILE: Former chief accountant and financial controller Bank of Cyprus UK. Now senior financial consultant. Chairman of Kalogrea Association. Chairman of St Raphael Greek Orthodox Church in Sutton, Surrey. Chairman of the Sutton Greek Language School.

UK

TONY EVANGELOU
On the shortlist for the London Restaurant Awards 2008

DATE OF BIRTH: 13-Jun-1944
PLACE OF BIRTH: Dora.
MARITAL STATUS: Married to Maria, Cyprus.
CHILDREN: Angela, Business. Koulla, Teacher.
SCHOOLS/COLLEGE: Dora Elementary. Hammersmith Day College.
HOBBIES AND INTERESTS: Cooking, Travel.
PERSONAL PROFILE: Owner of Lemonia Restaurant in Primrose Hill on the shortlist for the London Restaurant Awards 2008. Also the owner of Limani Restaurant and a Property Investment Company.

HELEN EVANS
Head Teacher Stags Lane middle School, Harrow

DATE OF BIRTH: 18-May-1954
PLACE OF BIRTH: London. Father from Agios Sergios; Mother from Ardana.
MARITAL STATUS: Single.
CHILDREN: Joanna, Thomas and Alexa.
SCHOOLS/COLLEGE: Tollington Park, Westminster College, Battersea Teachers College.
QUALIFICATIONS: Cert Ed.
MEMBERSHIPS: NAHT.
HOBBIES AND INTERESTS: Theatre and reading.
PERSONAL PROFILE: Head teacher Staggs Lane Middle School in Harrow. Maths LEA leader.

KYRIAKOS NICOS FALEKKOS
Dental Surgeon

DATE OF BIRTH: 26-May-1960
PLACE OF BIRTH: Johannesburg, South Africa. Grandparents from Kaimakli Nicosia.
MARITAL STATUS: Single.
SCHOOLS/COLLEGE: Marian College, Johannesburg.
QUALIFICATIONS: Matriculation Certificate. Bachelor of Dental Science.
MEMBERSHIPS: British Dental Health Foundation - Confederation of Dental employers, General Dental Practioners Association.

HONOURS/AWARDS: Vocational Training Trainer (Dental).
HOBBIES AND INTERESTS: Photography, computer graphics and music.
PERSONAL PROFILE: Dentist, Practice Owner, Appointed Trainer of Newly Qualified Dentists.

TAKIS FELLAS
Chairman and Managing Director of Hellenic TV

PLACE OF BIRTH: Pano Zodia
SCHOOLS/COLLEGE: Manchester University, Aston University and Surrey University.
QUALIFICATIONS: BSc Physics MSc in Nuclear reactor technology and PhD in Physics.
HOBBIES AND INTERESTS: Community work.
PERSONAL PROFILE: Takis Fellas is the Chairman and Managing Director of Hellenic TV it is a Greek language Television channel based in Harringey. It started in 1982 when cable television was first introduced in the UK. It started broadcasting in December 1990, for 3 hours, connected to just 13 homes in Camden. In a years time Hellenic TV had over a thousand subscribers in London. Broadcasting hours also increased to 17 hours with direct transmissions of the daily programs of ERT, RIK and evening programme of local productions, concerts and feature films. They have evolved through the years to a 24 hour, 7 days a week television channel.

UK

There is a Greek language TV channel and radio station in London that caters for the Cypriot community.

DINOS FLORENTZOU

Co-founded EDEK UK Political Party and was their first Chairman. Now member of Secretariat

DATE OF BIRTH: 11-Feb-1942
PLACE OF BIRTH: Agros.
MARITAL STATUS: Married to Theodoulla, Agros.
CHILDREN: One son, one daughter.
SCHOOLS/COLLEGE: Agros Elementary & High School. Borough Polytechnic now (South Bank University).
QUALIFICATIONS: City & Guilds in Electrical Engineering.
HONOURS/AWARDS: Honoured by EDEK 1986 for Services to the Party and to Cyprus.
HOBBIES AND INTERESTS: Travel, football, helping Youth & Community.
PERSONAL PROFILE: Served as Chairman of Cosmos FC. Was on Cypriot Football League's Management Committee for 12 years. In 1972, co-founded the Greek School at Streatham where he was Chairman until 1988. Chairman of Agros Association UK. Trustee of St. Nectarius Church at Battersea, now Chairman.

SERGHIS PETROU FLORIDES
Deceased
Founding Member of PEO in Cyprus

DATE OF BIRTH: 26-Jan-1903
PLACE OF BIRTH: Lapithos.
MARITAL STATUS: Married to Panayiota, Lapithos.
CHILDREN: Yiannakis, Musician. Costakis, Musician. Andreas, Taxi Driver. Petros and Nitsa, Professor and Housewife.
SCHOOLS/COLLEGE: Elementary School Lapithos.
MEMBERSHIPS: LELA AKEL Labour Party, Lapithos Association.
HONOURS/AWARDS: Honoured with AKEL Veteran's Award.
HOBBIES AND INTERESTS: Poetry and music.
PERSONAL PROFILE: Was a builder, poet, active member of the Greek Parents Association. Former Chairman of Coppetts Wood Greek School, and a founding member of the Trade Union PEO in Cyprus.

MICHELLE FOULIA

Winner of the regional Award for the HSBC new start up stars Awards

PLACE OF BIRTH: Engomi
MARITAL STATUS: Married to Andreas Constantinou, Agglisides, Business.
CHILDREN: Michalis.
SCHOOLS/COLLEGE: Yeri Elementary and Secondary.
HOBBIES AND INTERESTS: Reading, Animals.
PERSONAL PROFILE: Michelle Foulia and her Husband Andreas own the Roses Tea rooms in Heswall Wirral which has been named as one of 26 regional finalists in the Daily Express sponsored HSBC start up stars contest. They beat hundreds of competitors to get to this stage.

ANDY FRANCESCOU

Actor/Comedian As an actor has appeared in the films The Mummy and Greenwich Meantime and on TV in the Bill and Ant and Dec

PLACE OF BIRTH: London, parents from Patriki and Ayio Andronico.
SCHOOLS/COLLEGE: Holloway School, William Foster, Anna Scher. Performing Arts College.
HOBBIES AND INTERESTS: Football.
PERSONAL PROFILE: Andy has been doing stand-up comedy for over eight years including gigs from London's Kings Head to Bloomsbury Theatre and abroad in Cyprus, he has also had extensive TV appearances. As an actor has appeared in the films The Mummy and Greenwich Meantime and on TV in the Bill and Ant and Dec.

It is free to nominate someone, or yourself, who deserves to be in the book, just send in the name, contact address, telephone number and email to:
Greek Cypriots Worldwide
111 St Thomas's Road London N4 2QJ
Telephone 0044 207503 3498
cypriotwhoswho@aol.com
www.greekcypriotsworldwide.com

UK

COSTAS FRANGESKIDES
Solicitor/Active member of Lobby for Cyprus

DATE OF BIRTH: 16-Oct-1967
PLACE OF BIRTH: London. Parents from Limnia, Cyprus & Chios Greece.
MARITAL STATUS: Married to Maria, London. Parents from Neo Livadhi, Limassol and Paphos, Solicitor.
CHILDREN: Two sons.
SCHOOLS/COLLEGE: John Lyon Secondary School. University of Essex, College of Law Guildford.
QUALIFICATIONS: BA Dip of Law.
MEMBERSHIPS: Law Society.
HOBBIES AND INTERESTS: Reading, films, tennis, soccer and current affairs.
PERSONAL PROFILE: Senior Solicitor in Insurance and Reinsurance Litigation with City Law firm Holman Fenwick & Willan. Treasurer of Anglo Cypriot Lawyers Association. Active member of Lobby for Cyprus.

MARIA NICOLA FRANGESKIDES
Solicitor/Chairwoman of Anglo Cypriot Lawyers Association

DATE OF BIRTH: 02-Jan-1967
PLACE OF BIRTH: London. Parents from Neo Livadhi, Limassol and Paphos.
MARITAL STATUS: Married to Costas, London Parents from Limnia and Chios in Greece, Lawyer.
CHILDREN: Two sons.
SCHOOLS/COLLEGE: Whittingham Junior School, Henrietta Barnett, UCL London, College of Law (Chancery Lane).
QUALIFICATIONS: LLB (Honours).
MEMBERSHIPS: Law Society, London Maritime Arbitrators Association.
HOBBIES AND INTERESTS: Swimming, theatre and dancing.
PERSONAL PROFILE: A Solicitor, a Partner & Head of Commercial litigation at London Offices of a large US firm Coudert Bros, Chairwoman of Anglo Cypriot Lawyers Association.

BELINDA FRIXOU
Solicitor/Trustee of Radiomarathon (For children with special needs)

DATE OF BIRTH: 07-Jul-1955
PLACE OF BIRTH: Famagusta, Cyprus, (Parents from Yialoussa).
MARITAL STATUS: Single.
CHILDREN: Christian, at school.
SCHOOLS/COLLEGE: Liverpool Institute, London School of Economics.
QUALIFICATIONS: LLB Law. Solicitor.
MEMBERSHIPS: Law Society.
HOBBIES AND INTERESTS: Travelling, theatre and music.
PERSONAL PROFILE: Senior Partner of a firm of Lawyers in Kingsway. Was a Trustee of Radiomarathon (For children with special needs).

MICHAEL GABRIEL (Gavrilatsou)
Chairman of Kato Drys Association UK

DATE OF BIRTH: 15-Oct-1960
PLACE OF BIRTH: UK. Parents from Kato Drys.
MARITAL STATUS: Married to Mary, from Kato Drys.
SCHOOLS/COLLEGE: Hearsall Secondary School, Coventry. Tilehill College, Coventry; Lancaster University.
QUALIFICATIONS: BA Honours in International Politics, also Chartered Institute of Bankers Exams (ACIB).
HOBBIES AND INTERESTS: Football (Coventry fan), history of Greece and Cyprus and playing drums.
PERSONAL PROFILE: Bank of Cyprus Corporate Manager, Birmingham. Chairman of Kato Drys Association UK. Member of Action for Cyprus. Member of Hellenic Association of Cyprus. Active in community affairs, and provided assistance in the compilation of Greek Cypriots in the UK.

UK

ELENA GABRILATSOU
Second Assistant Director for the comedy drama dept at Granada TV

DATE OF BIRTH: 08-Aug-1976
PLACE OF BIRTH: UK, Parents from Kato Drys and Skarinou.
MARITAL STATUS: Single.
SCHOOLS/COLLEGE: Bury Grammar School Girls. Manchester Met University.
QUALIFICATIONS: BA (Honours) Creative Arts Music and Drama.
HOBBIES AND INTERESTS: Watching films and playing piano.
PERSONAL PROFILE: 2nd Assistant Director for the Comedy Drama Dept at Granada TV. Productions include Cold Feet, Royle Family and Donovan.

CATIA GALATARIOTOU
Lecturer Psychanalytic Theory, University College London

DATE OF BIRTH: 30-Jan-1955
PLACE OF BIRTH: Limassol.
MARITAL STATUS: Single.
CHILDREN: Alfred, Anna.
SCHOOLS/COLLEGE: Limassol Gymnasium. Middlesex Polytechnic, Inns of Court, Centre of Byzantine, Ottoman and Modern Greek Studies, Univeristy of Birmingham, British Institute of Psychoanalyst.
QUALIFICATIONS: BA (Honours), Humanities PhD, Byzantine Studies.
MEMBERSHIPS: Member of Cyprus Bar, Member of British Psychoanalytical Society.
HOBBIES AND INTERESTS: Art, theatre, travelling and food & wine.
PERSONAL PROFILE: Worked as a Lawyer in Cyprus. Worked as a NHS Psychotherapist at various hospitals. Currently a Psychoanalyst in private practice and a Teacher of Psychanalytic Theory, University College London.

Ivan Gazidis is the Chief Executive of Arsenal Football Club.

ANDREW GAVAS
Director of Oak Insurance Services, Philanthropist helps many community organisations

DATE OF BIRTH: 26-Nov-1953
PLACE OF BIRTH: Sydney Father from Lofos Mother from Limassol.
MARITAL STATUS: Married to Barbara.
CHILDREN: Antony, School.
SCHOOLS/COLLEGE: Brookside Secondary, Middlesborough. Tottenham College of Technology.
QUALIFICATIONS: OND Business Studies.
MEMBERSHIPS: FSA.
HOBBIES AND INTERESTS: Football arranged transfers of Daryl and Delroy to Aris and Epa in Cyprus from AEK London.
PERSONAL PROFILE: Director of Oak Insurance Services, broker to Lord Foster famous Architect of the Gherkin and other famous sites. Was contributor to Sir Charlie's Cypriot Magazine. Organised Javine UK Entry in Eurovision on tour of Cyprus and Greece. Arranged with partner A Constantinou free concerts for pre Eurovision which included Sakis and Constantinos.

STALA M GAVRIELIDES
Researcher in Economics and Political Science

DATE OF BIRTH: 22-Jul-1968
PLACE OF BIRTH: London. Father, from Nicosia; Mother, from Rizokarpasso.
MARITAL STATUS: Single.
SCHOOLS/COLLEGE: Mount Allison University, New Brunswick, Canada, McGill University, Montreal, Canada.
QUALIFICATIONS: BA Economics & Political Science, MA International Relations.
PERSONAL PROFILE: Researcher in Economics & Political Science in various universities in Canada. Researcher for Lord Avebury a Parliamentary Human Rights Group in UK.

UK

THEO GAVRIELLIDES
Trustee of London Voluntary Service Council UK and the Justice and Reconciliation Project USA(LVSC)

PLACE OF BIRTH: Born 1976 Cyprus
MARITAL STATUS: Single.
SCHOOLS/COLLEGE: Law School, London School of Economics (LSE), University of London, UK.
QUALIFICATIONS: Masters in Human Rights Law (LL. M).
MEMBERSHIPS: London Voluntary Sevice Council. British Society of Criminology, UK Member, Meditation Member UK.
PERSONAL PROFILE: Policy and Strategy Expert with Internationally recognised expertise in human rights & equalities, criminal justice and restorative justice. Head of Policy of Race on the Agenda. Trustee of London Voluntary Service Council UK and the Justice and Reconciliation Project USA.

IVAN GAZIDIS
Chief Executive of Arsenal Football Club

DATE OF BIRTH: 13-Nov-1964
PLACE OF BIRTH: Johannesburg Father from Greece maternal Grandparents from Cyprus.
SCHOOLS/COLLEGE: Oxford University.
QUALIFICATIONS: Degree in Law.
HOBBIES AND INTERESTS: Sport.
PERSONAL PROFILE: Ivan Gazidis is the Chief Executive of Arsenal Football Club. Previously the Deputy Commissioner of Major League Soccer in USA.

DR THEKLI MARIA GEE (nee KAKOULLIS)
Specialist Registrar in Medical Microbiology

DATE OF BIRTH: 29-May-1972
PLACE OF BIRTH: UK, Father: Pyla, Mother: Limnia.
MARITAL STATUS: Married to Dr Bruce Colin Gee, of Manchester, Dermatologist.
SCHOOLS/COLLEGE: Blue Coat School, Holy Child School, King Edward VI High School for Girls. Birmingham University.
QUALIFICATIONS: BSc Honours (1st class) Medical Biochemistry, MBChB with honours Medicine.
MEMBERSHIPS: British Medical Association, British Society of Antimicrobial Infection Agents and Chemotherapy.
HONOURS/AWARDS: Duke of Edinburgh's Award- Bronze, Silver & Gold.
HOBBIES AND INTERESTS: Hiking, skiing, aerobic and fitness training, swimming, tennis, badminton, theatre, photography, art and travel.
PERSONAL PROFILE: Specialist Registrar in Medical Microbiology. Currently working as registrar at the University Hospital, Queen's Medical Centre, Nottingham.

ANDREAS GEORGALLI
Appeared on TV in Stars in their eyes

DATE OF BIRTH: 10-Dec-1968
PLACE OF BIRTH: Glasgow, Scotland. Father from Ayios Serghios Famagusta, Cyprus;. Mother from Naples, Italy.
MARITAL STATUS: Married to Thalia, Paphos, Housewife.
CHILDREN: George, Anthea, Both at School.
SCHOOLS/COLLEGE: Tottenham County School. Middlesex University.
QUALIFICATIONS: Postgraduate in Environmental Studies.
MEMBERSHIPS: Dean Martin Association and Centre for Alternative Technology.
HOBBIES AND INTERESTS: Singing, gardening, travelling, human evolution, culture and mythology.
PERSONAL PROFILE: Professional tribute artist, Previously a landscape gardener. Appeared on "Stars in Their Eyes", November 2000 as Dean Martin.

UK

CHRIS GEORGALLIS
Pharmacist

DATE OF BIRTH: 25-Oct-1957
PLACE OF BIRTH: Nicosia.
MARITAL STATUS: Single.
SCHOOLS/COLLEGE: Ackland Burghley, Chelsea College, University of London, School of Pharmacy. Member of Royal Pharmaceutical Society of Great Britain, Member of Cyprus Study Circle.
QUALIFICATIONS: Degree in Pharmacy, Registered Pharmaceutical Chemist.
HOBBIES AND INTERESTS: Sport, Philately of Cyprus and photography.
PERSONAL PROFILE: Been a Pharmacist for 19 years and worked within the hospital clinical areas. Worked for the Royal Free Hospital NHS Trust.

SAVVAKIS ANDREOU GEORGALLIS
Former Editor of Haravgi in Cyprus/Co-Founder of Omonia FC in London

DATE OF BIRTH: 24-Oct-1930
PLACE OF BIRTH: Marathovounos.
MARITAL STATUS: Married to Margarita, a Housewife, from Ayios Georgios Spathariko Famagusta.
CHILDREN: Andrea, Housewife. Liza, Business.
SCHOOLS/COLLEGE: London University and Lincolns Inn.
QUALIFICATIONS: MA and Barrister At Law.
HOBBIES AND INTERESTS: Sports.
PERSONAL PROFILE: Member of committee for Omonia Football Club Nicosia. One of the Founders of Omonia Football Club London. Editor of Haravgi Newspaper from its birth in 1955 to 1969, when he came to U. K. Member of the Committee of the Youth Organisation (EDON).

MARIOS C. GEORGHIADES
Formerly Chief Accountant-Cyprus Tourism Organisation, London, School Governor Tottenhall Infants School

DATE OF BIRTH: 06-Sep-1966
PLACE OF BIRTH: Nicosia.
MARITAL STATUS: Married to Maria, London, Banking.
CHILDREN: Daniel, Harry.
SCHOOLS/COLLEGE: Kykkos A, Lyceum, Nicosia. Luton College of Higher Education, BPP Professional Training School.
QUALIFICATIONS: ACCA. AAT.
MEMBERSHIPS: Member of the Association of Martial Arts (AMA).
HONOURS/AWARDS: Chief Instructor of International Shaolin (Kung Fu) Academy. Appointed as a Chairman of International Shaolin (Kung FU) Academy-Cyprus branch.
HOBBIES AND INTERESTS: Martial arts and music (Djing).
PERSONAL PROFILE: Currently employed at Alexander Johnson & Co. a firm of Chartered Certified Accountants and Registered Auditors, as Audit Manager. School Governor at Tottenhall Infants School.

GEORGE GEORGHIOU
Actor TV work in Mind your Language, Dr In The House, Dr At Sea, Please Sir Films, Home Sweet Honeycomb with Michael Crawford

DATE OF BIRTH: 11-Nov-1948
PLACE OF BIRTH: Frenaros.
MARITAL STATUS: Married.
CHILDREN: One daughter.
SCHOOLS/COLLEGE: St Michaels in Camden, Kynaston Secondary, Kingsway College, Pheldene Stage School.
HOBBIES AND INTERESTS: Painting and making model boats.
PERSONAL PROFILE: Actor, TV work in Mind your Language, Dr In The House, Dr At Sea, Please Sir Films, Home Sweet Honeycomb with Michael Crawford. Theatre work, Zigger Zagger at Strand Theatre. Was Manager of Wyndham Picadilly and Criterion Theatres.

UK

DR MARIA GEORGHIOU
Doctor works in Accident & Emergency in London

DATE OF BIRTH: 16-Aug-1973
PLACE OF BIRTH: Nicosia. Father from Ayios Pavlos, Nicosia; Mother from Katokopia, Morphou.
MARITAL STATUS: Single.
SCHOOLS/COLLEGE: University College, London (UCL), Guys, Kings and St Thomas School of Medicine (GKT), London.
QUALIFICATIONS: MBBS, GKT, BSc (Hons) UCL. MBBS.
MEMBERSHIPS: British Medical Association, Anthony Nolan Bone Marrow Trust. Member St Sofia Cathedral Choir.
HONOURS/AWARDS: Travel Scholarship to the Amazon Region of Peru.
HOBBIES AND INTERESTS: Travelling, South America, Asia, scuba diving, Latin American dance, painting and National League Volley Ball.
PERSONAL PROFILE: Whilst at university was elected President of the UCL Cypriot Society and later the Hellenic Society of Guys and St. Thomas's School of Medicine. Currently working in Accident & Emergency in London, and planning to pursue a career in anaesthetics.

ELIKKOS GEORGIADES
Barrister/Psychotherapist/Hypnotherapist

DATE OF BIRTH: 21-Jun-1953
PLACE OF BIRTH: Engomi, Nicosia.
MARITAL STATUS: Single.
CHILDREN: Tiffany.
SCHOOLS/COLLEGE: English School, Nicosia.
QUALIFICATIONS: LNCPLicentiate Member of National Council Of Psychotherapists.
HOBBIES AND INTERESTS: Music and socialising.
PERSONAL PROFILE: Joined Scotland Yard as an Executive Officer, whilst there studied Law externally, took a degree in Law, then became a Barrister. In 1994 set up Chambers by himself as a Sole Practitioner at Bromley Chambers. Studied Graphology which is a scientific analysis of personality from handwriting. Qualified Psychotherapist and Hypnotherapist.

MICHAEL GEORGIADES
Awarded the Nokia Prize for Research Excellence in 2004 at the University of Surrey

DATE OF BIRTH: 23-Sep-1979
PLACE OF BIRTH: Lapithos.
MARITAL STATUS: Single.
SCHOOLS/COLLEGE: Kings College London, University College London, University of Surrey.
QUALIFICATIONS: MSc in Telecommunications for Industry PhD in Mobility Management for all-IP Networks, BEng Communications & Radio Engineering (First Class Honours).
MEMBERSHIPS: IET (Institute of Engineering and Technology), UK. IEEE (Institute of Electrical and Electronics Engineering.
HONOURS/AWARDS: Awarded the Nokia Prize for Research Excellence in 2004 at the University of Surrey.
HOBBIES AND INTERESTS: Guitar, Swimming, Chess, Philosphy.
PERSONAL PROFILE: Researcher at The University of Surrey.

NICOLAS GEORGIADES
President of United Cypriot Youth Organisation and Member of the AKEL Secretariat UK

DATE OF BIRTH: 17-Aug-1971
PLACE OF BIRTH: Nicosia.
MARITAL STATUS: Single.
SCHOOLS/COLLEGE: Archbishop Makarios Lyceum, Nicosia. Essex University, City Business School.
QUALIFICATIONS: BA MSc.
MEMBERSHIPS: Institute of Internal Auditors UK, British Rumanian Chamber of Commerce.
HONOURS/AWARDS: Supplier of the Year award, from a main High St Fashion retailer.
HOBBIES AND INTERESTS: Politics and sport.
PERSONAL PROFILE: Chief Operations Officer for a group of companies (one in Cyprus, one in UK and three in Romania). President of United Cypriot Youth Organisation. Ex Vice President of the National Federation of Cypriot Students in the UK. Member of the Secretariat of AKEL UK. Member of the Executive Committee of Episteme, and former member of the Executive of the National Federation of Cypriots.

UK

ACHILLEAS GEORGIOU
Enfield Councillor

DATE OF BIRTH: 19-Sep-1957
PLACE OF BIRTH: Nicosia.
MARITAL STATUS: Married.
CHILDREN: Two sons.
SCHOOLS/COLLEGE: London School Of Economics, University Of Bath.
QUALIFICATIONS: BA (Honours), DIP Econ, M. sc.
HOBBIES AND INTERESTS: Football and cycling.
PERSONAL PROFILE: Communications (Media/Public Relations), Councillor Of Enfield.

ANDREW GEORGIOU
Co Founder of Dynamo Athletic FC and Barnet Cypriot Youth Club

DATE OF BIRTH: 16-Nov-1949
PLACE OF BIRTH: Famagusta.
MARITAL STATUS: Married to Irene, UK Parents from Cyprus.
CHILDREN: Alexandra Maria, Kristina.
SCHOOLS/COLLEGE: Holloway. Southbank College.
QUALIFICATIONS: 7 GCE, s, 3 A Levels, 1 S level Building and quantity Surveying Foundation.
HOBBIES AND INTERESTS: Football, Sport, Dining and Travelling.
PERSONAL PROFILE: Andrew Georgiou is the Co Founder of Dynamo Athletic FC part of Barnet Cypriot Youth Club. Andy by profession is a Quantity Surveyor and is now an Estate Agent a Director of Des Res Properties in NW3.

ANTONIS KYRIAKOS GEORGIOU
Author and Researcher founder of first research centre for occupied Towns and Villages

DATE OF BIRTH: 14-Dec-1967
PLACE OF BIRTH: London. Father from Kalopsida Mother from Asha. Famagusta.
MARITAL STATUS: Married to Anna Maria, London (parents from Ayia Triada and Athienou).
CHILDREN: Athena.
SCHOOLS/COLLEGE: Southgate School. Kalopsida Association, Vatili Association, Lobby for Cyprus.

HOBBIES AND INTERESTS: Travel.
PERSONAL PROFILE: Formed the 1st research centre for occupied towns and villages of Cyprus. Published the book The Living Past Of Kalopsida. Hes also a contributor to the Parikiaki and Eleftheria Newspapers.

COSTAS GEORGIOU
Awarded Best British Restaurant in London by Archant group of newspapers 2006, 2007 and 2008

DATE OF BIRTH: 06-Aug-1956
PLACE OF BIRTH: Ayia Varvara.
MARITAL STATUS: Married to Lucy, Livadhia, Hairdresser.
CHILDREN: Mario, Sofie.
HONOURS/AWARDS: Winner of the retail manager of the year LEB, also managed Debenhams flagship store in Oxford Street. Best British Restaurant in London voted by the Archant Group of newspapers 2006, 2007 and 2008.
HOBBIES AND INTERESTS: Football, Chelsea fan.
PERSONAL PROFILE: Costas is a Partner and manager of Toffs Fish Restaurant in Muswell Hill, North London.

COSTAS MODESTOU GEORGIOU
Chairman of Enfield Business Assoc

DATE OF BIRTH: 12-Feb-1948
PLACE OF BIRTH: Vasili.
MARITAL STATUS: Married to Angela from Rizokarpasso.
CHILDREN: Katerina, Derby University. Andrew, Norwich University.
SCHOOLS/COLLEGE: Eastbourne College of Further Education, Bournemouth College of Technology.
HOBBIES AND INTERESTS: Walking and politics.
PERSONAL PROFILE: Teacher at Bournemouth College. Then worked at Metal Box as a Setter Engineer, where he was Chairman of TGWU section at Metal Box. Had a shoe repair shop in Palmers Green, now a Property Developer. Served as Chairman of Leonarisso-Vaslli Association for five years. Chairman of Green Lanes Business Association for last five years. Now Chairman of Enfield Business Association. Member of Lobby for Cyprus.

UK

ELENI GEORGIOU
Singer

DATE OF BIRTH: 13-Sep-1990
PLACE OF BIRTH: Nicosia.
MARITAL STATUS: Single.
SCHOOLS/COLLEGE:
Mountview School of acting,
University Aix-Marseille
(FRANCE) and Kingston
University.
QUALIFICATIONS: BA MA.
HOBBIES AND INTERESTS:
Watching live performances and
especially famous Sopranos.
PERSONAL PROFILE: Eleni Georgiou Singer and Music
Teacher has appeared in her own concert at the Hellenic
Centre, as Dido and Aeneas (Sorceress-Digby Stuart
Chapel in Roehampton), Dido and Aeneas (Sorceress-
Hampton Court), Private Concert (Gateway Studio), Vox
(Royal Albert Hall), Requiem by Mozart.

GEORGE GEORGIOU
Actor and Co-Producer played Panos in
the film Mama Mia

DATE OF BIRTH: 27-May-1978
PLACE OF BIRTH: London.
Parents from Dhali.
MARITAL STATUS: Single.
SCHOOLS/COLLEGE: Drama
Centre, London. Equity.
QUALIFICATIONS: Degree
B(A) Acting.
HOBBIES AND INTERESTS:
Dance, theatre, films, yoga and
travelling.
PERSONAL PROFILE: Actor and Co-Producer,
Credits as an actor include "Mamma Mia" the film and
"Cyranode Bergerac" at Royal Opera House. He also
runs a stage school for children.

GEORGE GEORGIOU
Solicitor partner in Lorrells Georgiou
Nicholas Solicitors. Former Chairman of
Monken Hadley Conservative Association.

DATE OF BIRTH: 08-Nov-1958
PLACE OF BIRTH: London.
Parents from Vothylakas and
Ayios Andronicos.
MARITAL STATUS: Married to
Andrea, Ayios Andronicos.
CHILDREN: Three daughters.
SCHOOLS/COLLEGE: Sir
William Collins School, Kingsway
College, Middlesex University,
Guildford Law School.
QUALIFICATIONS: BA Honours Law.
HOBBIES AND INTERESTS: Football, (Arsenal Fan).
PERSONAL PROFILE: Solicitor, Partner in Lorrells,
Georgiou Nicholas Solicitors. Former Chairman of
Monken Hadley Conservative Association.
George is also a registered Lawyer with the Football
Association.

GEORGE GEORGIOU
Award Winning Restauranter

DATE OF BIRTH: 20-Nov-1957
PLACE OF BIRTH: Ayia Varvara.
MARITAL STATUS: Married
to Kika, London parents from
Cyprus.
CHILDREN: Steven,
Christopher.
HONOURS/AWARDS: 2006
Toff's of Muswell Hill was
awarded the Best British
Restaurant in London by the
Archant group of newspapers.
HOBBIES AND INTERESTS: Avid Chelsea fan.
PERSONAL PROFILE: George Georgiou started work
at the age of 17 as accounts assistant with Pizza Express,
he worked his way up to head of finance whilst studying
an accountancy course in the evenings. After 13 years
of seeing the successful expansion of Pizza Express. He
decided not to work under the shadow of Pizza Express
founder Peter Boizot. He opened his own 2 franchises in
Staines and Muswell Hill. It was the second area that then
took him to extra heights, when along with his brother
Costas he purchased Toff's Fish and chip Shop in 1999.
George gives credit to Mr Toffali who founded Toff's
and has been his inspiration, who also won the best fish
and chip shop award.

UK

GEORGE GEORGIOU
Photographer/Picture of the year
International USA 2004

DATE OF BIRTH: 17-Jan-1961
PLACE OF BIRTH: London
Father from Marathovounos
Mother from Aradippou.
MARITAL STATUS: Married to
Vanessa.
SCHOOLS/COLLEGE: Finchley
Manor Hill School. Polytechnic
of Central London.
QUALIFICATIONS: BA.
HONOURS/AWARDS: World
Press Photo 2nd prize Art stories 2005, Flour Festival,
Greece. Picture of the year international, USA 1st prize
Spot News for Magazine, 2004 Istanbul bombings. World
Press Photo 1st prize portrait stories 2003 Serbs.
PERSONAL PROFILE: George is a photographer
his work has been published in the Sunday Times,
Independant Magazines, Newsweek.

GEORGE GEORGIOU
Accountant Partner in Chelepis Watson
and Co

DATE OF BIRTH: 13-Apr-1976
PLACE OF BIRTH: London
Father from Davlos Mother
from Rizokarpasso.
MARITAL STATUS: Married to
Kelly, English.
CHILDREN: Three sons.
SCHOOLS/COLLEGE: Ingram
High School. Southbank
University.
QUALIFICATIONS: BA
Accounting and Finance. FCCA ACA.
HOBBIES AND INTERESTS: Football and chess.
PERSONAL PROFILE: George is an Accountant and
partner in established South London Accountancy Firm
Chelepis Watson.

GEORGE A. GEORGIOU
Journalist. Has worked for Haravgi,
Radio Astra, Parikiaki, Hellenic TV,
Cypria in Britain

DATE OF BIRTH: 17-Aug-1973
PLACE OF BIRTH: Poland.
Father from Ormidia, Cyprus;
Mother from Poland.
MARITAL STATUS: Married to
Andrea Constantinou, London
Parents from Cyprus, Journalist.
CHILDREN: One Daughter.
SCHOOLS/COLLEGE:
Makarios III Lyceum in Larnaca
and the Europa College for
Journalists in Nicosia. Secretary of Omonia F. C in
London and KOPA (Cypriot football league in London).
QUALIFICATIONS: Diploma in Journalism and Public
Relations.
HONOURS/AWARDS: Award for services as district
secretary of the Edon Youth Organisation in Cyprus.
HOBBIES AND INTERESTS: Football, reading, history,
politics and philosophy.
PERSONAL PROFILE: Journalist. Has worked for
Haravgi, Radio Astra. Formerly editor at Parikiaki and
Cypria in Britain. Has travelled to Palestine for an
interview with Saeb Eracat (chief Palestinian negotiator).

GEORGE MICHAEL GEORGIOU
Project Manager for the Cypriot
Diaspora Project

DATE OF BIRTH: 10-Aug-1958
PLACE OF BIRTH: Pentayia,
Cyprus.
MARITAL STATUS: Married to
Johannah, UK, Banker.
CHILDREN: Elizabeth, Michael.
SCHOOLS/COLLEGE: Salford
University.
QUALIFICATIONS: Degree in
Advertising and Marketing.
HONOURS/AWARDS:
Millennium Awards Fellowship.
HOBBIES AND INTERESTS: Writing Ancient Greek
and Cypriot History for a weekly page in Parikiaki.
PERSONAL PROFILE: Advertising & Marketing
Consultant, Ancient Greek History Project for schools
funded by the Millennium Awards. Project Manager
for the Cypriot Diaspora Project, Fundraiser for Greek
Parents Association.

UK

GEORGIA CLARK GEORGIOU
Actress appeared on TV in Capital City

DATE OF BIRTH: 01-Aug-1957
PLACE OF BIRTH: London.
Parents from Limassol and Asha.
MARITAL STATUS: Married to Barry Wickens, a musician.
CHILDREN: Nicholas and Michael.
SCHOOLS/COLLEGE: Willesden High School, East 15, Acting School, Debdon Essex. Equity, A. I.
QUALIFICATIONS: Acting Diploma. TEFEL teacher.
HOBBIES AND INTERESTS: Reading, walking, cinema and theatre.
PERSONAL PROFILE: Actress with Theatro Technis. Has appeared with The Natural Theatre on tour, on TV in "Capital City", and in films "The Nutcracker", "Leave To Remain", and "Eleni".

IOANNIS GEORGIOU
Priest

DATE OF BIRTH: 13-Dec-1930
PLACE OF BIRTH: Dromolaxia, Larnaca.
CHILDREN: One son, one daughter.
SCHOOLS/COLLEGE: Dromolaxia Elementary School.
HOBBIES AND INTERESTS: Gardening and reading.
PERSONAL PROFILE: Priest at St Lazarus and St Andrews Church in Forest Gate, London.

KAY GEORGIOU
Solicitor won a record £10 million settlement for Zeta Graff, the former wife of Francois Graff, the heir to a diamond fortune

DATE OF BIRTH: 02-Jun-1961
PLACE OF BIRTH: London.
Parents from Aradippou and Ardana.
MARITAL STATUS: Single.
SCHOOLS/COLLEGE: Hornsey High, London University, Lancaster Gate Law School.
QUALIFICATIONS: BA Honours History and Politics.
HOBBIES AND INTERESTS: Theatre, opera and cinema.

PERSONAL PROFILE: Solicitor, own practice specialising in Family Law. won a record £10 million settlement for Zeta Graff, the former wife of Francois Graff, the heir to a diamond fortune.

KYRIAKOS SPIROS GEORGIOU
Served as Vice Chairman and Registration Secretary of the Cypriot Football League UK

DATE OF BIRTH: 20-Feb-1937
PLACE OF BIRTH: Komi Kebir.
MARITAL STATUS: Married to Panayiota, from Morphou.
CHILDREN: Spiros.
SCHOOLS/COLLEGE: Pitmans, accounts.
HOBBIES AND INTERESTS: Football, (Arsenal supporter).
PERSONAL PROFILE: Former member of Greek Parents Association. Former Chairman Komi Kebir Association. Served as Vice-Chairman and Registration Secretary of the Cypriot Football League, UK.

MICHAEL GEORGIOU
Represented England in the European Snooker Team Championship in 2005

DATE OF BIRTH: 18-Jan-1988
PLACE OF BIRTH: Gerani.
MARITAL STATUS: Single.
PERSONAL PROFILE: Michael Georgiou Represented England in the European Snooker Team Championship in 2005. He is ranked in the top 50 Snooker Player Rankings.

Michael Georgiou represented England in the European snooker team championship in 2005

UK

MYRIA GEORGIOU
Lecturer at Leeds University

DATE OF BIRTH: 15-Aug-1971
PLACE OF BIRTH: Nicosia.
SCHOOLS/COLLEGE: Panteion University, Athens. Boston University, London School of Economics and Political Science (LSE).
QUALIFICATIONS: BA, MSc, PhD.
MEMBERSHIPS: British Sociological Association, National Union Of Journalists, Athens Association Of Journalists.
HOBBIES AND INTERESTS: Travel, languages, theatre, film and reading.
PERSONAL PROFILE: Previously a journalist. Between 1989 and 1996 worked as a journalist in Athens, first for the Daily Avgi and then for Eleftherotypia, also appointed as a correspondent for CBC's Radio 3 and then for Astra. Moved to London, and between 1997 and 2000 worked as a journalist and presenter for the Greek Section of BBC World Service. Now lecturer at Leeds University.

PETER GEORGIOU
International Fencing Champion

DATE OF BIRTH: 10-Apr-1952
PLACE OF BIRTH: Wales. Father from Pano Lakatamia; Mother from Leonarisso.
MARITAL STATUS: Single.
CHILDREN: Melitsa, Hairdresser. Louis, Hairdresser. Alexander, Plant Driver.
QUALIFICATIONS: City & Guilds Certificate in Hairdressing, City & Guild Youth Trainers Award.
PERSONAL PROFILE: Hairdresser. Established the Newport Clinic of Trichology and Dermocosmetology. Was Welsh School Fencing Champion in 1966. 1968 represented Wales at the National Schoolboy Championships. 1968 received Silver Award from British Amateur Fencing Association. In 1971 represented Wales at the British Quadrangular Tournament. 1972 represented Wales at the International Tournament, Denmark. 1972 winner Welsh Men's Team Championships.

PETROS GEORGIOU
Secretary of Acheritou Football Club/ Owner of Fore Street Electrical Wholesalers/Philanthropist

DATE OF BIRTH: 22-Mar-1951
PLACE OF BIRTH: Acheritou.
MARITAL STATUS: Married to Stavroulla, Frenaros, Housewife.
CHILDREN: George, Electrician. Theodora, Student.
SCHOOLS/COLLEGE: Paddington College for Electrical Installation.
HOBBIES AND INTERESTS: Football.
PERSONAL PROFILE: Owns Electrical Wholesale Business. Secretary of Acheritou Football Club.

PETROS GEORGIOU
Publisher of Cyprus Real Estate magazine

PLACE OF BIRTH: London October 2008
SCHOOLS/COLLEGE: JKB School. London School of Printing.
HOBBIES AND INTERESTS: International current affairs, the Cyprus problem.
PERSONAL PROFILE: Petros is the publisher of "Move To Cyprus" The No 1 Cyprus Real Estate magazine.

VASOS GEORGIOU
Accountant Sage Solution Centre one of the top Sage Business Partners in London

DATE OF BIRTH: 27-Dec-1956
PLACE OF BIRTH: Birmingham. Parents from Xylophagou.
MARITAL STATUS: Married to Kika. Cypriot origin, Book Keeper.
CHILDREN: George, Andrew, Paul, Maria.
SCHOOLS/COLLEGE: Copeland School, Wembley. Central London Polytechnic.
QUALIFICATIONS: ACCA.
HOBBIES AND INTERESTS: Keep fit.

PERSONAL PROFILE: Accountant, Founder and managing Director of Anthony Lawson Ltd Chartered Certified Accountants 1995-2006. Managing Director of Alex Johnson Ltd chartered certified accountants and Lawson Ltd, Sage Solution Centre one of the top Sage Business Partners in London.

TASSOS GEORGOPOULLOS
Founder of the Xorianous Website

DATE OF BIRTH: 26-Jul-1974
PLACE OF BIRTH: Father Greece, Mother Cyprus.
MARITAL STATUS: Married to Christina born UK parents from Cyprus.
CHILDREN: Natalia.
SCHOOLS/COLLEGE: Friern Barnet College, Middlesex University.
QUALIFICATIONS: HND Computing, BSc Honours Applied Computing with Information Technology.
HOBBIES AND INTERESTS: Playing the Bouzouki, socialising, Martial arts.
PERSONAL PROFILE: Managing Director of Swift Digital Solutions Ltd in London, founder of the Xorianous website trying to unite Cypriots all around the world by Villages.

COS GEROLEMOU
Sculptor has worked for some of the world's leading sculptors including Barry Flanagan and the late Sir Eduardo Paolozzi

DATE OF BIRTH: 06-May-1959
PLACE OF BIRTH: London Parents from Limassol.
MARITAL STATUS: Married to Christalla.
CHILDREN: Two sons.
SCHOOLS/COLLEGE: Archway. Chelsea, the Central and Royal College of Art.
QUALIFICATIONS: BA RCA Dip.
HONOURS/AWARDS: Royal College of Art Angeloni Prize. Henry Moore Bursary.
HOBBIES AND INTERESTS: Visiting art galleries, music, keeping fit and travel.
PERSONAL PROFILE: Sculptor has works in private collections and has exhibited at the Royal Academy of Arts and internationally. Art facilitator for adults with mental health problems at the Chocolate Factory Studios.

ANTHONY GHOSH
Surgeon researching a new method of imaging brain activity

DATE OF BIRTH: 14-Apr-1978
PLACE OF BIRTH: Bromley UK Maternal Grandparents from Yialoussa.
MARITAL STATUS: Married to Emily, Scottish, Nurse.
CHILDREN: Daisy.
SCHOOLS/COLLEGE: The Grammar School, Limassol. Orpington College, Orpington, Kent and Dundee University.
QUALIFICATIONS: MBChB (Bachelor of Medicine, bachelor of Surgery).
MEMBERSHIPS: Member of the Royal College of Surgeons.
HOBBIES AND INTERESTS: Surfing, Martial Arts, Playing Electric and Bass Guitars.
PERSONAL PROFILE: Anthony graduated at Dundee University Medical School in 2003 and became a member of the Royal College of surgeons in 2006. He has worked in surgery and Neurosurgery in Dundee, Cambridge and Haywards Heath.
He is now researching a new method of imaging brain activity in London and aims to become a consultant neurosurgeon.
He also runs a website called ProCypriots. Net to help Cypriot students and professionals form a global network.

FILIOS A GRAMMENOPOULOS
First Chairman of the Executive Board of the Hellenic Centre UK

DATE OF BIRTH: 05-Jun-1923
PLACE OF BIRTH: Larnaca.
MARITAL STATUS: Married to Nitsa, Larnaca.
CHILDREN: Mary, Art Historian. Anthony, Architect.
SCHOOLS/COLLEGE: Pancyprian Commercial Lyceum Larnaca, American Academy, Larnaca.
QUALIFICATIONS: BA.
HONOURS/AWARDS: Order of St Mark (1st class) Patriarchate of Alexandria.
HOBBIES AND INTERESTS: Anthropology, history and. evolutionary matters.
PERSONAL PROFILE: Businessman & director of companies. Nairobi, Kenya (1948-1972). High Commissioner for Cyprus in Kenya (1974-1984) Founder member of the Hellenic Centre, London and it's first Chairman of the Executive Board 1991-1993. Council Member Hellenic Community Trust (1991 to date).

UK

ARCHBISHOP GREGORIOS of THYATEIRA & GREAT BRITAIN
(Nee Gregorios Theocharous Hadjittofi)
Archbishop of Thyateira and Great Britain

DATE OF BIRTH: 28-Oct-1928
PLACE OF BIRTH: Marathovounos, Famagusta.
SCHOOLS/COLLEGE: Lefkonikon High School, Pan-Cyprian Gymnasium, Theology University of Athens (1958).
QUALIFICATIONS: Chancellor of the Archdiocese of Thyateira & Great Britain 1965-1979; Honorary Doctorate, University of North London.
HOBBIES AND INTERESTS: Poetry, history, gardening and farming.
PERSONAL PROFILE: Deacon, 24. 06. 53; Priest 19. 04. 59, Bishop 12, 12 1970, consecrated as Bishop of Tropaiou. Elected Archbishop of Thyateira & Great Britain 16. 4. 88. Orthodox President of the Anglian & Eastern Churches Association, and the Fellowship of St Alban & St Sergius; Co-President of the Society of St John Chrysostomos, and the Council of Christians & Jews.

DR CHRISTIANA GREGORIOU
Lecturer at the University of Leeds

DATE OF BIRTH: 12-Dec-1978
PLACE OF BIRTH: Nicosia.
MARITAL STATUS: Single.
SCHOOLS/COLLEGE: Lancaster University, Nottingham University and Leeds University.
QUALIFICATIONS: BA 'MA, PhD.
MEMBERSHIPS: Associate Member of the Poetics and Linguistics Association.
HOBBIES AND INTERESTS: Cinema, Theatre and Reading.
PERSONAL PROFILE: Christiana Gregoriou is a lecturer in English at University of Leeds.

GEORGE ('KOKIS') GREGORIOU
Music Presenter and Newsreader at LGR

DATE OF BIRTH: 13-Dec-1954
PLACE OF BIRTH: Ayios Theodoros, Famagusta.
MARITAL STATUS: Married to Christalla, London (parents from Acheritou and Famagusta).
CHILDREN: Gregory, Stella.
SCHOOLS/COLLEGE: Gymnasium of Tricomo.
MEMBERSHIPS: Member of Equity, appeared on TV commercials, such as Texaco Oil and Smirnoff Vodka.
HONOURS/AWARDS: Diploma in Music Presentation and News Casting.
HOBBIES AND INTERESTS: Music, travel, sports and reading.
PERSONAL PROFILE: Director and Share Holder of LGR. Programme controller, Newsreader, Music Presenter at LGR, and producer, singer and member of the Venus Band. Appeared on New Generation Game with Jim Davidson, representing Cyprus and Greece on live TV, in the Eurovision Song Contest (sort of!) and appeared on breakfast TV's morning show. Produced 4 CDs: Ellinika Laika Tragoudia (Vols 1 and 2), Varosi Mou and To Horio Mou. Appeared on Cyprus TV, has sung with Greek singers such as Nicos Xanthopoullos and Demitris Kontolazos.

PANIKOS GREGORIOU
Secretary of Oeseka (Federation of Educational Associations of Greek Cypriots in England)

DATE OF BIRTH: 15-Aug-1951
PLACE OF BIRTH: Trikomo.
MARITAL STATUS: Married to Elizabeth, Norway, Secretary.
CHILDREN: Helen, Florist. Kate, Fashion Designer.
SCHOOLS/COLLEGE: Economic Lyceum of Tricomo, Kensington College.
QUALIFICATIONS: HND Business Studies and Accountancy.
HOBBIES AND INTERESTS: Football.
PERSONAL PROFILE: Accountant. Treasurer of North London Greek Educational Association and Secretary of Oeseka (Federation of Educational Associations of Greek Cypriots in England). Chairman of Tricomo Association UK.

YIANNIS GRIVAS
Actor/Poet (Deceased)

DATE OF BIRTH: 10-Sep-1948
PLACE OF BIRTH: Klirou, Nicosia.
MARITAL STATUS: Married to Marikou, Ayios Andronicos.
CHILDREN: Four sons, one daughter.
SCHOOLS/COLLEGE: Pancyprian Gymnasium. Equity.
HONOURS/AWARDS: Honoured by Black Cab Association for raising money for handicapped children.
HOBBIES AND INTERESTS: Acting, football, Man Utd Fan.
PERSONAL PROFILE: As an actor, appeared on TV in Into The Blue, a BT commercial. A DJ with LGR, and has written songs with Hajimike. Also was involved with Thea Theatrical Group.

DR CHRISTOS HADJICHARITOU
General Practitioner/ Honorary Commissioner for the Republic of Cyprus in Leeds

DATE OF BIRTH: 30-Sep-1946
PLACE OF BIRTH: Palouriotisa.
MARITAL STATUS: Married to Leila, England (parents from Poland).
CHILDREN: Elias, Management & Administration. Barbara Anne, Student.
SCHOOLS/COLLEGE: Pancyprian Gymnasium Nicosia. University of Athens.
QUALIFICATIONS: MD (Athens) 1971, LRCP. MRCG (London) 1979.
HOBBIES AND INTERESTS: Charity Work.
PERSONAL PROFILE: GP in Wakefield since 1982. Honorary Commissioner for the Republic of Cyprus in Leeds since 1990. Involved with Greek Orthodox Church and Community in Leeds.

GREGORY CHRISTODOULOU HADJIKYRIACOU
Accountant/Active member of Southampton Cypriot Community

DATE OF BIRTH: 27-Jan-1958
PLACE OF BIRTH: Cyprus. Parents from Marathovounos.
MARITAL STATUS: Married to Marica Michael Hannides from Southampton.
CHILDREN: Haralambia, Christodoulos.
SCHOOLS/COLLEGE: Kilburn Polytechnic.
QUALIFICATIONS: Chartered Certified Accountant.
HOBBIES AND INTERESTS: Travel.
PERSONAL PROFILE: Accountant. Active member of Southampton Cypriot Community.

GEORGE HADJIMATHEOU
Professor, London Metropolitan University

DATE OF BIRTH: 12-Jun-1943
PLACE OF BIRTH: Aradippou.
MARITAL STATUS: Married to Helen Suddards, an IT Consultant, from Britain.
CHILDREN: Chloe, Katerina, Both University Graduates.
SCHOOLS/COLLEGE: Pancyprian Lyceum, Larnaca, Pedagogical Academy, Nicosia, ASOEE, Athens; LSE, London University. Royal Economic Society; American Economic Association.
QUALIFICATIONS: BA MSc PhD.
HOBBIES AND INTERESTS: Walking, skiing, theatre and poetry.
PERSONAL PROFILE: Professor of Economics, Head of Economics, Finance and International Business Department, London Metropolitan University.

UK

Entrants in Greek Cypriots Worldwide have been nominated for their achievements and contributions.
It is free to nominate someone, or yourself, who deserves to be in the book, just send in the name, contact address, telephone number and email to:
Greek Cypriots Worldwide
111 St Thomas's Road London N4 2QJ
Telephone 0044 207503 3498
cypriotwhoswho@aol.com
www.greekcypriotsworldwide.com

ANDROULA HADJIMICHAEL
Lecturer & Coordinator in ESOL (City and Islington College)

DATE OF BIRTH: 13-Mar-1948
PLACE OF BIRTH: Yialoussa.
MARITAL STATUS: Married to Sotiris, Vasili, Engineer.
CHILDREN: Yiannis, Computing. Marios, Business.
SCHOOLS/COLLEGE: Greek Gymnasium (Yialousa), Greek Educational Institute G/B. UL Institute of Education. NATFHE.
QUALIFICATIONS: Dip Ed. MA in Education. Lecturer in ESOL.
HOBBIES AND INTERESTS: Reading and writing poetry.
PERSONAL PROFILE: Lecturer & Coordinator in ESOL (City and Islington College). Teacher of the Greek Language and Culture at the Greek Supplementary Schools in GB.

MIROULLA HADJIMICHAEL
Hammer, Cancer Fund Raising Organiser. Raised Thousands of Pounds

PLACE OF BIRTH: Komi Kebir.
MARITAL STATUS: Married to Theophanis (Fanos) Hadjimichael.
CHILDREN: Rebecca, Constantinos.
SCHOOLS/COLLEGE: Elementary.
PERSONAL PROFILE: Miroulla with her Husband Theophanous were Hammer, Cancer Fund Raising Organisers they Raised over Hundred Thousand pounds.

DIMITRI J. HADJIMINAS
Breast & Endocrine Surgeon

DATE OF BIRTH: 26-Oct-1961
PLACE OF BIRTH: Athens. Father, Yiannis from Kyrenia.
MARITAL STATUS: Married to Catherine Louise, England, Private Practice Manager.
CHILDREN: Steven. School. Alexandra, School.
SCHOOLS/COLLEGE: Athens Medical School.
QUALIFICATIONS: MBBS, MD MPhil. FRCS (Eng), FRCS (Ed), FRCS (Gen Surg).
HOBBIES AND INTERESTS: Tennis.

PERSONAL PROFILE: Breast & Endocrine Surgeon, Director of St. Mary's Breast Unit, Honorary Senior Lecturer. Chairman Harley Street Clinic Breast Unit.

DINO HADJINICOLA
Chief Executive Theoria Design Group Digital Architects

DATE OF BIRTH: 04-Dec-1976
PLACE OF BIRTH: London parents from Ayia Napa and Komi Kebir.
MARITAL STATUS: Single.
SCHOOLS/COLLEGE: Middlesex University.
QUALIFICATIONS: BA (Hons).
HOBBIES AND INTERESTS: Snowboarding, Art, Gym.
PERSONAL PROFILE: After free-lancing as a Web designer, for 8 years Dino started his own company based in UK and Cyprus 'Theoria Design Group'. It is a collective of 'digital architects' namely Web Theoria & North Digital Media. They have been working on projects for high end clients such as HSBC, IBM, Lexus, Nokia, Hewlett-Packard, Shell and many more. Inspired by minimalist design, simplicity and uncluttered spaces, their process is a balanced combination of art and science designed to empowering businesses to connect with consumers.

EVA HADJINICOLA
Head Teacher

DATE OF BIRTH: 05-Feb-1950
PLACE OF BIRTH: London. Parents from Komi Kebir, Cyprus.
MARITAL STATUS: Single.
CHILDREN: Ntinos, Graphic Design. Christopher, Animation.
SCHOOLS/COLLEGE: Shelbourne School, Holloway London; Middlesex College; Sheffield University.
QUALIFICATIONS: Cert. Ed, Dip. Ed, M. Ed.
HOBBIES AND INTERESTS: Reading and swimming.
PERSONAL PROFILE: Headteacher, Private English Primary School in Cyprus.

MARILENA LOIZIDOU HADJINICOLAOU
Senior Lecturer in Surgical Oncology at UCL/Cypriot Woman Scientist/ Academic of the year 2006

PLACE OF BIRTH: Nicosia **MARITAL STATUS:** Married to John, Famagusta, Chartered Accountant. **CHILDREN:** Leonidas. **SCHOOLS/COLLEGE:** Kykko Gymnasium for girls Nicosia (Secondary School), English School, Nicosia (Part-time, Secondary School). McMaster University, Ontario, Canada, Southampton University, UK. **QUALIFICATIONS:** BSc, MSc, PhD. **MEMBERSHIPS:** British Association of Surgical Oncology, Society of Academic & Research Surgery, Hellenic Medical Society. **HONOURS/AWARDS:** Cypriot Woman Scientist/ Academic of the year 2006. **HOBBIES AND INTERESTS:** Scuba-diving and piano. **PERSONAL PROFILE:** Non-clinical Senior Lecturer in surgical oncology (UCL) University College, London.

MARIOS HADJINICOLAOU
Lecturer, Dept. Electronic & Computer Engineering, Brunel University

PLACE OF BIRTH: Nicosia **MARITAL STATUS:** Married to Leila, Tunisia. **CHILDREN:** Gregory, Iosif. **SCHOOLS/COLLEGE:** The English School, Nicosia. **QUALIFICATIONS:** BSc (Honours), MSc, PhD. C. Eng. **HOBBIES AND INTERESTS:** Classical Music. **PERSONAL PROFILE:** Lecturer, Dept. Electronic & Computer Engineering, Brunel University.

ANDRIANA HADJI-PANAYI
Dental Surgeon

DATE OF BIRTH: 11-Sep-1944 **PLACE OF BIRTH:** Rizokarpasso. **MARITAL STATUS:** Married to Panayiotis, Rizokarpasso. **CHILDREN:** Demetri, Doctor. Christian, Project Manager. **SCHOOLS/COLLEGE:** University of Sydney, Australia, Birkbeck College, University of Kent. **QUALIFICATIONS:** Batchelor of Dental Surgery, Diploma in International Studies, Master in International Relations. Dental Surgeon. **MEMBERSHIPS:** British Dental Association, Greek Cypriot Brotherhood, Association of Rizokarpasso. **HOBBIES AND INTERESTS:** Art, music, theatre, opera, travel, current affairs & international & domestic politics. **PERSONAL PROFILE:** Practicing Dental Surgeon for 32 years.

DR DEMETRI HADJI-PANAYI
Doctor Medical Practitioner, specialising in Gynaecology

DATE OF BIRTH: 19-May-1973 **PLACE OF BIRTH:** Luton, Bedfordshire, UK. Parents from Rizokarpasso. **MARITAL STATUS:** Single. **SCHOOLS/COLLEGE:** Haberdashers, St. Mary's Medical School, Imperial College, London. **QUALIFICATIONS:** BSc Physiology. MBBS. Medical Doctor. **MEMBERSHIPS:** British Medical Association, General Medical Council. **HOBBIES AND INTERESTS:** Tennis, golf, skiing, swimming, reading & writing. **PERSONAL PROFILE:** Medical Practitioner, specialising in Gynaecology & presently conducting Research at the Royal Free Hospital in London.

UK

PANAYIOTIS HADJI-PANAYI
Honorary Chairman of Rizokarpasso Association

DATE OF BIRTH: 08-Sep-1934
PLACE OF BIRTH: Rizokarpasso, Famagusta.
MARITAL STATUS: Married to Andriana, Rizokarpasso, Dental surgeon.
CHILDREN: Demetri, Doctor. Christian, Project Manager.
SCHOOLS/COLLEGE: Rizokarpasso High School. University of Leicester, Birkbeck College, London.
QUALIFICATIONS: Dip. in Bus. Admin. Dip in Soc. Science. BA.
HOBBIES AND INTERESTS: Reading, National & International Affairs, Community Affairs, Travel, History, Cyprus.
PERSONAL PROFILE: Association of Rizokarpasso, (Honorary Chairman), Greek Cypriot Brotherhood, Cypriot Forum for Labour, Federation of Cypriots in Britain - Member of the Executive & Secretariat for over 20 yrs.

ANDROULLA HADJISIMOU
Childcare Lawyer, Greenwich Legal Services

DATE OF BIRTH: 15-Dec-1973
PLACE OF BIRTH: London. Father from Akanthou, Mother from Patriki.
MARITAL STATUS: Single.
SCHOOLS/COLLEGE: Waverley Secondary School, Croydon College, Keele University, Inns of Court School of Law, London, College of Law, London, Kings College (University of London). National Children's Bureau and Amnesty International.
QUALIFICATIONS: LLB (Honours), Law & History. Solicitor.
HOBBIES AND INTERESTS: Keep fit.
PERSONAL PROFILE: Currently working as a Childcare Lawyer for the London Borough of Greenwich's Social Services Legal Department.

MICHELLE SOTIRIS HADJISIMOU
Solicitor Recorded one of the fastest House completions from offer to completion Five and a half hours

DATE OF BIRTH: 24-Aug-1977
PLACE OF BIRTH: London. Parents from Akanthou and Patriki.
MARITAL STATUS: Single.
SCHOOLS/COLLEGE: Waverley School, Dulwich/ London, Selhurst College, Croydon, Keele University, Keele/Staffordshire. Law Society.
QUALIFICATIONS: LLB Joint Honours, Law and Politics. Legal Practice Course.
HOBBIES AND INTERESTS: Football, reading, and aerobics.
PERSONAL PROFILE: Solicitor (Conveyancer)Recorded one of the fastest House completions from offer to completion Five and a half hours. The Magazine Residential Property Investor said But for one man in Leyton, East London, last week things happened a little more quickly. From deciding to buy a £133, 000 house in Capworth Street, E10 at 11am on Friday, to picking up keys at 3. 30pm took Mr Sinan Dogan just 5 and a half hours, believed to be the fastest ever private purchase thanks to Michelle Hadjisimou.

DAKIS HAGEN
Barrister at Searle Court Lincolns Inn

DATE OF BIRTH: 02-Apr-1978
PLACE OF BIRTH: Newcastle Parents from Cyprus.
MARITAL STATUS: Single.
SCHOOLS/COLLEGE: Newcastle Royal GS Peterhouse. Cambridge University.
QUALIFICATIONS: MA (Cantab) (First class, Dip law (city univ) Barrister.
MEMBERSHIPS: Lincolns Inn, Commercial Bar Assciation.
HOBBIES AND INTERESTS: Music, History, Travel, Dinning out.
PERSONAL PROFILE: Barrister at Searle Court Lincolns inn.

GEORGE HAJIFANIS
Secretary of the National Federation of Cypriots UK (Deceased)

DATE OF BIRTH: 25-Feb-1937
PLACE OF BIRTH: Larnaca.
MARITAL STATUS: Married to Eleni.
CHILDREN: Two daughters.
SCHOOLS/COLLEGE: Studied Architecture, University of London. University of Westminster, University of Essex. Member of the Royal Institute of British Architects and the Royal Society of Arts.
HOBBIES AND INTERESTS: Books, arts, topography. Greek affairs and tennis.
PERSONAL PROFILE: George Hajifanis was the Secretary of the National Federation of Cypriots in the UK. Board of Governors of the Metropolitan University and had his own Architectural practice.

SIR STELIOS HAJI-IOANNOU
Received a Knighthood from Queen Elizabeth the 2nd for services to entrepreneurship

DATE OF BIRTH: 14-Feb-1967
PLACE OF BIRTH: Glyfada, Greece. Father from Pedhoula; Mother from Limassol.
MARITAL STATUS: Single.
SCHOOLS/COLLEGE: Doukas High School Athens. London School of Economics, City University.
QUALIFICATIONS: BSc Economics; MSc Shipping Trade & Finance.
HONOURS/AWARDS: Received a Knighthood from Queen Elizabeth the 2nd for services to entrepreneurship.
HOBBIES AND INTERESTS: Sport and travel.
PERSONAL PROFILE: Founder, ex-Chairman and shareholder of Easy Jet Airlines; owner of Easy Internet Cafes, Easy Car Hire. Founding Chairman of Cymera, the Cyprus Marine Environment Protection Association. Stelios is involved with the Stelios disabled entrepreneur award and the Stelios Scholars award.

REV FOKAS HAJILOIZIS
Reverend for Mansfield Sheffield & District Greek Orthodox Church

DATE OF BIRTH: 22-Jun-1954
PLACE OF BIRTH: Cyprus, Famagusta - Peristeronopiyi.
MARITAL STATUS: Married to Zooulla.
CHILDREN: Constantinos, Stella, Marios and Kiriaki.
SCHOOLS/COLLEGE: Gymnasium, Famagusta.
QUALIFICATIONS: Reverend.
HOBBIES AND INTERESTS: Football and swimming.
PERSONAL PROFILE: Reverend for Mansfield Sheffield & District Greek Orthodox Church.

ANDREAS ANTONIOU HAJIMICHAEL
President of the Greek Community in Margate

DATE OF BIRTH: 23-Jun-1937
PLACE OF BIRTH: Aradippou.
MARITAL STATUS: Married to Elli Louca Theodoulou, a Housewife, from Aradippou.
CHILDREN: Tony, Building Surveyor. George, Teacher. Theodoros, Student.
SCHOOLS/COLLEGE: American Academy - Cyprus, Balham & Tooting College of Commerce - London.
QUALIFICATIONS: Certified Accountant.
PERSONAL PROFILE: Restaurateur - Business in Margate since 1962, casino owner for 15 years - Property Developer - Secretary from the beginning of the formation of the Greek Community in Margate for 15 years & president for the last three years.

UK

CONSTANTIA HAJIPANAYI

Founder Member of OESEKA. Chairwoman of North London Cypriot Assoc

DATE OF BIRTH: 02-Oct-1926
PLACE OF BIRTH: Psematismenos.
CHILDREN: George, Christos, Marios.
SCHOOLS/COLLEGE: Psematismenos Elementary.
HOBBIES AND INTERESTS: Reading.
PERSONAL PROFILE: Was a Manageress in Dress Factory. In 1960 became involved in Greek Schools. Founder Member of OESEKA. Chairwoman of North London Cypriot Assoc. Member of National Federation of Cypriots Executive Committee.

MARIOS HAJIPANAYI

Team Manager and Head Coach for England National Athletics Squad for people with learning difficulties

DATE OF BIRTH: 16-Aug-1962
PLACE OF BIRTH: London. Parents from Larnaca and Psematismeno.
MARITAL STATUS: Married.
CHILDREN: Constandia.
SCHOOLS/COLLEGE: Wood Green School, Barnet College.
QUALIFICATIONS: BEC General Diploma.
HOBBIES AND INTERESTS: Athletics.
PERSONAL PROFILE: Competed in the Hammer Event for Haringey Athletics Club and the Counties of Essex and Middx under 19s. Was Haringey Athletic Coach for Shot Putt, Hammer, Javelin and Discus. Team Manager and Head Coach for England National Athletics Squad for people with learning difficulties. Also an actor: has appeared in Bridget Jones's Diary, on TV in The Bill; on stage in Cinderella and Old Time Musical; been in TV Commercials for British Telecom, Ericsson.

HARRY HAJIPAPAS

Managing Director of Cyplon Travel

DATE OF BIRTH: 21-Jul-1958
PLACE OF BIRTH: Kenya. Father from Trimiklini, Cyprus; Mother born in Tanzania of Cypriot parents.
MARITAL STATUS: Married to Debra Bennett, England, Housewife.
CHILDREN: Christos, Voula, Students.
SCHOOLS/COLLEGE: Creighton School Muswell Hill, London School of Economics.
QUALIFICATIONS: 8 O Levels, 3 A Levels, BSc (Econ), MBA (Marketing) MINSTM, Diploma (Inst. Of Marketing) MRS (Dip).
MEMBERSHIPS: Council Member of AGTA (The Assoc. of Greek Travel Agents).
HOBBIES AND INTERESTS: Reading, theatre, cinema and football.
PERSONAL PROFILE: Managing Director of Cyplon specialist tour operators to Cyprus, Greece & Dubai.

PETER HAJITTOFI

Managing Director and co-founder of Pebble Beach Systems, a world leader in the development of broadcast automation software to the TV industry

DATE OF BIRTH: 05-Aug-1956
PLACE OF BIRTH: London, parents from Eptakomi.
MARITAL STATUS: Married to Dawn.
CHILDREN: Nina.
SCHOOLS/COLLEGE: Holloway School, Islington. University of East London.
QUALIFICATIONS: BSc, MSc dynamic systems engineering.
HOBBIES AND INTERESTS: Travelling, socialising, with family and friends, current affairs, sports.
PERSONAL PROFILE: Managing Director and co-founder of Pebble Beach Systems, a world leader in the development of broadcast automation software to the TV industry.

UK

PANTELLIS HAJI-YIANNAKIS
Consultant Oncologist at Derriford
Hospital, Plymouth

DATE OF BIRTH: 13-Dec-1967
PLACE OF BIRTH: Nicosia.
MARITAL STATUS: Married to
Jane, England, Psychologist.
CHILDREN: George.
SCHOOLS/COLLEGE: English
School Nicosia, University of
Nottingham.
QUALIFICATIONS: Bmed
sci, BM, BS, MRCP, FRCR.
Specialist in Oncology.
HOBBIES AND INTERESTS: Tennis, gym and travelling.
PERSONAL PROFILE: Consultant Oncologist at
Derriford Hospital, Plymouth.

DR SOTIRIS HAMILOS
Dental Surgeon

DATE OF BIRTH: 20-Mar-1945
PLACE OF BIRTH: Gypsos.
MARITAL STATUS: Married to
Diana from UK.
CHILDREN: Marcos, Banker.
Michael, Political Editor for the
guardian Unlimited Web Site.
Anna, Policy advisor for CABE.
SCHOOLS/COLLEGE:
Lefkoniko Gynasium, Kingston
College, London University.
QUALIFICATIONS: Dentist.
HOBBIES AND INTERESTS: Photography, Bridge,
gardening and travelling.
PERSONAL PROFILE: Retired Orthodondist had Dental
practice in Croydon. Chairman of GYPSOS friendly
Association.

DAVID HANDS
Filmed and edited over 700 news stories
for major broadcasters such as the
BBC, ITN

DATE OF BIRTH: 22-Apr-1969
PLACE OF BIRTH: London
Mother from Kontea.
MARITAL STATUS: Single.
SCHOOLS/COLLEGE:
Acropolis High School Nicosia.
KTEE Nicosia, Frederick
Polytechnic Nicosia.
MEMBERSHIPS: Board
member of Kontea Heritage
Foundation.

Honourable board member of ICFFCY (International
Children's Film Festival of Cyprus
HOBBIES AND INTERESTS: Motorcycle riding,
Wildlife Conservation, Scuba diving, Classic Cars.
PERSONAL PROFILE: Director of Photography/Editor/
Producer. Partner and Director in Crewhouse Media Ltd.
David has filmed and edited over 700 news stories in
Africa, Europe and the Middle East for major broadcasters
such as the BBC, ITN, Associated Press, ZDF, RTL etc.
He also filmed documentaries in East Africa, Egypt and
Cyprus, and also Directed and Produced two Crewhouse
Media documentaries and a Cyprus bi-communal
documentary for UNDP. He also works as a professional
photographer for selected publications and for the
Internet. He works as a volunteer teaching film making to
children with the Weaving Mill and ICFFCY.

ANTHONY HANNIDES
Appeared in the Live Finals of the UK's
biggest TV Talent show the X-Factor in
2005

DATE OF BIRTH: 12-Mar-1987
PLACE OF BIRTH: London
Father from Southampton his
Grandfather from Koma tou
Yialou Mother from Famagusta.
MARITAL STATUS: Single.
SCHOOLS/COLLEGE: Shirley
Junior and Thornden Secondary.
HONOURS/AWARDS: MTV
Baselounge Winners.
HOBBIES AND INTERESTS:
Football, Gym and watching Dvds.
PERSONAL PROFILE: Anthony is part of the Vocal
Group 4TUNE who Appeared in the Live Finals of the
UK's biggest TV Talent show the X-Factor in 2005. They
toured Europe for two years currently recording their
first Album. They have also worked with the Princes
Trust. Helped raise money for several charities too
including Childline and Breast Cancer.

UK

JOHN MICHAEL HANNIDES
Councillor

DATE OF BIRTH: 25-Nov-1963
PLACE OF BIRTH: Southampton. Parents from Koma-Tou-Yialou.
MARITAL STATUS: Married to Athanasia, London, Bank Official.
CHILDREN: Michael John, toddler.
SCHOOLS/COLLEGE: Richard Taunton College/ University of Wolverhampton. Member of the Employment Consultants Institute.
QUALIFICATIONS: Honours Degree.
HOBBIES AND INTERESTS: Sport, cinema and current affairs.
PERSONAL PROFILE: Recruitment Consultant. Elected Local Councillor - Southampton City Council since 1994.

MICHAEL HANNIDES
Appeared in the Live Finals of the UK's biggest TV Talent show the X-Factor in 2005

DATE OF BIRTH: 06-Jun-1984
PLACE OF BIRTH: Southampton. Father from Southampton, Grandfather from Koma Tou Yialou Mother from Famagusta.
MARITAL STATUS: Single.
SCHOOLS/COLLEGE: Shirley Junior, Bellemoor Boys School and Thornden Secondary. Barton Peveril College.
HONOURS/AWARDS: MTV Base Lounge Winners.
HOBBIES AND INTERESTS: Singing/Songwriting, Playing Football and Gym.
PERSONAL PROFILE: Michael is part of the Vocal Group 4TUNE who Appeared in the Live Finals of the UK's biggest TV Talent show the X-Factor in 2005. They toured Europe for two years currently recording their first Album. They have also worked with the Princes Trust. Helped raise money for several charities too including Childline and Breast Cancer.

NICHOLAS MICHAEL HANNIDES
Solicitor and President of Greek Orthodox Church community of St. Nicolas, Southampton

DATE OF BIRTH: 05-Nov-1958
PLACE OF BIRTH: Southhampton. Parents Koma-Tou-Yialou.
MARITAL STATUS: Married to Denise, England, Housewife.
CHILDREN: Nicholas, Marika, Michael, and Haralambia.
SCHOOLS/COLLEGE: Shirley Junior School/Bellemoor Secondary/Richard Tauntons College - Southampton. Cardiff University. Law Society.
QUALIFICATIONS: 10 O Levels, 5 A Levels, LLB. Law Finals.
HOBBIES AND INTERESTS: Sports, mainly football - Runs Son's Team, Church/Community Affairs.
PERSONAL PROFILE: Solicitor and President of Greek Orthodox Church community of St. Nicolas, Southampton (last four years). Father - "George" Hannides. (First Cypriot resident in Southampton).

DEMOS HAPESHIS
Formerly chairman of Potters Bar Independent Greek School, Part of Katsouris Brothers and Fresh Foods

DATE OF BIRTH: 21-Jun-1951
PLACE OF BIRTH: Nicosia, Cyprus.
MARITAL STATUS: Married to Angela.
CHILDREN: Stephano, Adam, Mario.
SCHOOLS/COLLEGE: Famagusta Grammar School for Commerce West. London College Business, Thames University.
QUALIFICATIONS: BA in Business.
HOBBIES AND INTERESTS: Watching football especially Arsenal, Playing snooker and table-tennis, reading and dining out.
PERSONAL PROFILE: Part of Katsouris Bros. and Fresh Foods, worked with cousins Tony and Panikos to expand business. Dealing in daily operations and running transport and sales. He also helps with various charities and church. Formerly chairman of Potters Bar Independent Greek School.

UK

JASMINE HARMAN
Presenter on the channel 4 programme A place in the sun

PLACE OF BIRTH: London Mother from Cyprus
PERSONAL PROFILE: For ten years Jasmine worked in the health and fitness industry in the UK and abroad. In 2000 she was head hunted for a post in Portugal where she lived for three and a half years. She began writing for local English language publications and presented on local radio stations Kiss FM. Harman returned to the UK and after a single approach was auditioned and got the job of presenting on the channel 4 programme A place in the sun, she has presented 5 series of the spin off show A place in the sun : Home or away. She is currently working on her fifth series for the channel. She has also presented items on GMTV's LK Today and the Travel Channel and has become a member of the beauty counsel at Tesco where she has been developing a new range of luxurious spa products.

KATIA DAVID HARMANDA MBE
Awarded MBE for Services to Anglo Greek Relations and to the Community at Large

DATE OF BIRTH: 04-Feb-1967
PLACE OF BIRTH: London. Parents from Kozani, Greece and Ayios Andronicos, Cyprus.
MARITAL STATUS: Married to Chris Harmanda, Acheritou, Businessman.
CHILDREN: Lucy, Eleni, both students.
SCHOOLS/COLLEGE: Hellenic College of London.
QUALIFICATIONS: BSc, MBA.
HONOURS/AWARDS: Awarded MBE for Services to Anglo Greek Relations and to the Community at Large.
HOBBIES AND INTERESTS: Photography.
PERSONAL PROFILE: Katia was with LGR from the pirate days 1984-2006, Chairman of Manor Hill Greek School and The Independent Greek Schools in London from 1992-2004. She was a Governor at various Schools in Barnet, a elected Councillor and Member of the Cabinet and Chairman of planning between 1998-2006. Since receiving her MBE Katia left LGR and Barnet Council to concentrate on her work as a Magistrate and her business commitments. Katia sits as Chairman of the court in Highgate, Wood Green and Highbury & Islington since 1996. She also co runs Home and Away Estates with her husband Chris Harmanda selling properties and investments abroad and property lettings and management in the UK. Katia is also Chairman of Praxis Investment Fund based in Cyprus.

TAKIS HARMANDA
Co Founder of London Greek Radio

DATE OF BIRTH: 12-Jan-1959
PLACE OF BIRTH: Acheritou.
MARITAL STATUS: Married to Katia Harmanda, London Parents from Greece and Cyprus, Former Councillor.
CHILDREN: Two daughters.
SCHOOLS/COLLEGE: Holloway School, Dean College.
QUALIFICATIONS: Bsc in Marketing.
HOBBIES AND INTERESTS: Football, boxing and travel.
PERSONAL PROFILE: Saw need of Greek Radio Station and Co founded London Greek Radio in 1983. Among the founders of Acheritou Assoc. Vice Chair of Hadley Wood Conservative Assoc. Known for his wide Charity work. He is now the Managing Director of Home and Away Estates selling properties and investments abroad and property lettings and management in the UK. They also manage their own family property portfoilio.

NICHOLAS DEMOS HARRIS
Headmaster

DATE OF BIRTH: 02-Nov-1944
PLACE OF BIRTH: Famagusta.
MARITAL STATUS: Married to Christine, UK, Teacher.
CHILDREN: Elena Christina, Fashion.
SCHOOLS/COLLEGE: Battersea College of Education, Roehampton. Institute of Education, London University.
QUALIFICATIONS: Certificate of Education, Batchelor of Education.
MEMBERSHIPS: National Union of Teachers - Teachers' Benevolent Fund - NAHT (National association of Headteachers).
HOBBIES AND INTERESTS: Reading, Greek culture, history and religion, football, wildlife conservation and gardening.
PERSONAL PROFILE: Nicholas Harris is a Headmaster in Camden and President of Greek Orthodox Community of St. Athanasios, Cambridge from 1990 to date.

UK

DEMIS HASSABIS
Chess Master, Mind Sports Olympiad Champion, Computer Games Designer

DATE OF BIRTH: 27-Jul-1976
PLACE OF BIRTH: London. Grandparents from Famagusta.
SCHOOLS/COLLEGE: Cambridge University.
QUALIFICATIONS: Double First, BA Honours, Computer Science.
HONOURS/AWARDS: Chess Master, four times Mind Sports Olympiad Champion.
HOBBIES AND INTERESTS: Games, Chess and diplomacy.
PERSONAL PROFILE: Was Chairman & Chief Executive Officer and Creative Director of Elixir. Broke into industry age 17 when co-created Theme Park with Peter Molyneux at Bullfrog. Taught himself to play chess at four years old, became chess Master at twelve and was highest ranked player of his age in the world. Won over 20 medals in total at the 1998/99/2000 Mind Sports Olympiads, including prestigious overall title, He has left the games industry switching to cognitive neuroscience research.

DR REBECCA HATJIOSIF
Doctor, General Practitioner, Muswell Hill

DATE OF BIRTH: 20-Sep-1955
PLACE OF BIRTH: Nottingham, England. Father from Strovolos, Nicosia; Mother from Davlos.
MARITAL STATUS: Single.
CHILDREN: Andreas, Maria.
SCHOOLS/COLLEGE: Loughborough Girls High School. Leeds University.
QUALIFICATIONS: MBCHB. DRC0G. FPC (Bachelor of Medicine & Surgery Diploma of Obstetrics & Gynaecology, Family Planning Cert).
MEMBERSHIPS: British Medical Assoc. Hellenic Medical Soc. Referral Advisor to Haringey Primary Care Trust.
HOBBIES AND INTERESTS: Reading, golf, travel, art theatre and music.
PERSONAL PROFILE: General Practitioner, Muswell Hill, Member of Ladies Committee - Cypriot Estia.

DIMITRIS HATZIARGYROU
Deputy High Commissioner of Cyprus to the UK

DATE OF BIRTH: 07-Aug-1960
PLACE OF BIRTH: Larnaca.
MARITAL STATUS: Married to Elpida from Greece.
CHILDREN: Alexandros.
SCHOOLS/COLLEGE: Queens College of City University (New York). Columbia University (New York), European Security and Defence College (EU).
QUALIFICATIONS: BA MA Diploma in European Security and Defence.
HOBBIES AND INTERESTS: Reading, Chess and various sports.
PERSONAL PROFILE: A career officer in the diplomatic service. Has served as vice consul in New York, at the Cyprus Permanent Mission in New York in charge of the Third Committee (Human Rights, Social and Humanitarian), as a UN desk chief in the Political Department in Nicosia, as European Correspondent of Cyprus, as Coordinator for CFSP and ESDP (European Foreign and Defence Policy), as REFLEX Coordinator (external policies of the EU) and as a Director of the Minister's Office. He is currently the Deputy High Commissioner of Cyprus to the UK.

CONSTANTINOS KAMEL HAWA
Award from Archbishop & President of Cyprus Makarios III Re-Charitable Donations

DATE OF BIRTH: 15-Nov-1933
PLACE OF BIRTH: Kato Polemidia.
MARITAL STATUS: Married to Androulla, Limassol, Housewife.
CHILDREN: Stelios, Fashion Designer. Zoe, Teaching Assistant.
SCHOOLS/COLLEGE: Commercial Academy of Cyprus.
HONOURS/AWARDS: Award from Archbishop & President of Cyprus Makarios III Re-Charitable Donations.
HOBBIES AND INTERESTS: Football.
PERSONAL PROFILE: Member of Cyprus Brotherhood.

LUCY HAYCOCK
Served as Mayor of Scarborough

DATE OF BIRTH: 08-May-1943
PLACE OF BIRTH: Famagusta.
MARITAL STATUS: Married to Ted Haycock.
CHILDREN: Elaine, Lecturer. Solette, Marketing. Nicholas.
SCHOOLS/COLLEGE: Attended College in Cyprus to GCSE level.
HOBBIES AND INTERESTS: Flower arranging, cooking and community work.
PERSONAL PROFILE: Borough Councillor for 18 yrs. Mayor 2001-2002 Scarborough Borough Council.

DR ELAINE HAYCOCK-STUART
Lecturer, Dept of Nursing Studies, University of Edinburgh

DATE OF BIRTH: 04-Mar-1964
PLACE OF BIRTH: El Adem, Libya. Mother from Famagusta.
MARITAL STATUS: Married to Dr. Neil Stuart, English, University Lecturer.
CHILDREN: Alethea (Elithia) Stuart.
SCHOOLS/COLLEGE: Scarborough Sixth Form College, University of Edinburgh.
QUALIFICATIONS: PhD Social Science. RGN, RM, DipHV.
HONOURS/AWARDS: Churchill Fellow (1996).
HOBBIES AND INTERESTS: Gardening, sailing and exercise.
PERSONAL PROFILE: Lecturer, Dept Nursing Studies, University of Edinburgh.

GEORGIA HAYHOE
President of the Greek School Committee in Northampton

DATE OF BIRTH: 14-Aug-1962
PLACE OF BIRTH: Nicosia.
MARITAL STATUS: Married to Mark Regional Investment Manager, Bristol, Regional Investment Manager.
CHILDREN: Francesca, Anthony.
SCHOOLS/COLLEGE: HTI Nicosia 1980-83 High School 1974-80.
QUALIFICATIONS: HND Civil Engineering.

HOBBIES AND INTERESTS: Painting, learning Spanish, keeping fit, working at Northampton Greek School.
PERSONAL PROFILE: President of the Greek School Committee in Northampton.

IRINI GERMANACOS HENDERSON
Councillor and Cabinet Member Milton Keynes Council

DATE OF BIRTH: 14-Mar-1942
PLACE OF BIRTH: Limassol.
MARITAL STATUS: Married to Euan Scott Henderson, Professor of IET - Open University.
CHILDREN: Christopher, Senior Manager, Boots UK. Anna, Manager.
SCHOOLS/COLLEGE: Pancyprian Gymnasium, Guys Hospital School of Physiotherapy, Open University.
QUALIFICATIONS: Diploma in Physiotherapy, BA - Open University. Chartered Physiotherapist, State Registered Physiotherapist.
MEMBERSHIPS: Justice of the Peace, also a Liberal Democrat Councillor for Newport Pagnell.
HOBBIES AND INTERESTS: Opera, reading, theatre, gardening and family.
PERSONAL PROFILE: Leader of the Opposition Newport Pagnell Council. Now cabinet member for Liberal Democrats administration running Milton Keynes Council. Chair of Age Concern Milton Keynes for many years. Member of many local Community groups, School Governor etc.

UK

Three female councillors in the H section alone Katia Harmanda, Lucy Haycock and Irini Germanicos Henderson.

GREEK CYPRIOTS WORLDWIDE

DAVID HESSAYON OBE
In 1999 he received a Guinness World Record Award as 'Britain's best-selling living author of the 1990s'

PLACE OF BIRTH: Born 1928 Broughton, UK Father from Cyprus
MARITAL STATUS: Married.
CHILDREN: Two children.
SCHOOLS/COLLEGE: Salford grammar. Leeds University and Manchester University.
QUALIFICATIONS: PhD.
HONOURS/AWARDS: OBE for writing a record-breaking series of gardening books. Awarded the 1993 Gardening Book of the Year Award from the Garden Writers Guild and received the first-ever Lifetime Achievement 'Oscar' at the National British Book Awards. In 1999 he received a Guinness World Record Award as 'Britain's best-selling living author of the 1990s'.
PERSONAL PROFILE: Was Managing Director of Pan Brittanica Industries the makers of Baby Bio. From the age of 5 he would help his Cypriot Father Jack a watchmaker to cultivate a few colourful reminders of the Country he had left behind. Dr David Hessayon initiated a major innovation in gardening publications in 1959 with the first of his Gardening Expert guides. These best-selling guides have had an unparalleled influence on gardening over the past 50 years. There are over 47 million copies in print.

TONY HJIHANNAS
Former Middleweight Wrestling World Champion

DATE OF BIRTH: 03-Feb-1941
PLACE OF BIRTH: Ayia Marina Skyloura, Nicosia.
MARITAL STATUS: Married to Suzanna from Ayia Marina.
CHILDREN: Joseph, Andrew, Marina.
HOBBIES AND INTERESTS: Shooting.
PERSONAL PROFILE: DHKO Committee Member in UK.
Worked as a Mechanic then Dress Manufacturer. Was a Wrestling Professional until 1990, regular on TV; Middle East Champion, Middleweight World Champion. Was Walker and Southgate Greek School Chairman, and one of the founders & Chairman of the Maronites Assoc. in UK.

ANDREW HUBBARD
Classical Pianist

DATE OF BIRTH: 19-Apr-1966
PLACE OF BIRTH: Tricomo.
MARITAL STATUS: Single.
SCHOOLS/COLLEGE: Bedford School, The Royal Academy of Music London.
QUALIFICATIONS: 9 O Levels, 3 A Levels, GRSM Honours. LRAM.
MEMBERSHIPS: Musicians Union.
HONOURS/AWARDS: Harry Fargeon Prize.
HOBBIES AND INTERESTS: Cookery, travel, cats, the arts.
PERSONAL PROFILE: Classical Pianist and Musician. Gives regular performances all over Europe.

GEORGE IACOVOU
Politics

PLACE OF BIRTH: Peristeronopiyi in 1938
MARITAL STATUS: Married to Jennifer.
CHILDREN: Four Children.
SCHOOLS/COLLEGE: Famagusta Gymnasium. Boston University, Birkbeck College, University of London, Imperial College, London and University of London.
QUALIFICATIONS: Bsc MSc MA.
HONOURS/AWARDS: Grand Cross of Merit with sash and star of the Federal Republic of Germany. The Grand Cross of the Order of the Phoenix of the Hellenic Republic. The Honorary Professorship of the State University of Donetsk, Ukraine.
PERSONAL PROFILE: Mr George Iacovou was High Commissioner for Cyprus in the United Kingdom in year 2006/7. In 1998 he reached the final round in the Cyprus Presidential Elections. He has served as Minister of Foreign affairs in Cyprus for Three terms. He is also well known for the rehabiliatation of Greek Cypriot Refugees and for persons of Greek origin living in the former Soviet Union. George Iacovou is presently in Cyprus and is the Presidential Commissioner.

UK

AKIS NEOKLIS IOANNIDES
Chairman of St Eleftherius Church in Leyton

DATE OF BIRTH: 23-Aug-1939
PLACE OF BIRTH: Pedhoula.
MARITAL STATUS: Married to Maroulla, Lefkara.
CHILDREN: Yiannis, George, Evangelos.
SCHOOLS/COLLEGE: Pedhoula Gymnasium; College of Aeronautical and Automobile Engineering, London.
HOBBIES AND INTERESTS: Helping the community, family life and travel.
PERSONAL PROFILE: Owner of a manufacturing company producing edible food carriers supplying restaurants and hotels, based in Ponders End, Middlesex. Chairman and Trustee of St Eleftherious Church in Leyton. Trustee of St Nicholas Educational Trust. General Secretary of the Association of Greek Orthodox Communities of GB.

COSTAS IOANNIDES
University Lecturer

DATE OF BIRTH: 10-Feb-1948
PLACE OF BIRTH: Nicosia.
MARITAL STATUS: Married to Cleopatra, Greece, Retail.
CHILDREN: Alexandros, Marios, Anna, All three are students.
SCHOOLS/COLLEGE: Pancyprian Gymnasium, Dudley Technical College, University of Liverpool, University of Surrey.
QUALIFICATIONS: BSc, PhD, DSc.
HONOURS/AWARDS: American Association for Cancer Research - recognition of work in the field of cancer.
HOBBIES AND INTERESTS: Music and theatre.
PERSONAL PROFILE: Published more than 250 papers in scientific journals. Edited eight scientific books. University Lecturer.

GEORGE IOANNIDES
Partner of Bond Partners LLP, Chartered/ Certified Accountants and Insolvency Practitioners/Promoted the American Comedian Jimmy "SuperGreek" Santis in his debut UK tour in January 2008;

DATE OF BIRTH: 15-Apr-1967
PLACE OF BIRTH: London. Father from Pedhoulas; Mother from Lefkara.
MARITAL STATUS: Single.
CHILDREN: Pavlos and Anthony.
SCHOOLS/COLLEGE: Whittingham School, London, Friern Barnet Grammar School, London. Southgate College, London, Hatfield Polytechnic, (Now Hertfordshire University).
HOBBIES AND INTERESTS: Greek Music, football and travelling.
PERSONAL PROFILE: George spent 12 years in Lloyd's of London, then set up his own consulting company in 1999 and then merged his business with Bond Partners in 2004.
Past Chairman of the Greek Orthodox Youth Association, Wood Green;Represented UK Greek youth at the Conference of Migrant Greek youth, Athens, 1984; Promoted the American Comedian Jimmy "SuperGreek" Santis in his debut UK tour in January 2008

KIKI OLYMPIOS IOANNIDES
General Secretary of the Democratic Party in the UK

DATE OF BIRTH: 23-Sep-1955
PLACE OF BIRTH: Nicosia.
CHILDREN: Constantine, Miltiades, Elena, All University graduates.
SCHOOLS/COLLEGE: American Academy Nicosia.
QUALIFICATIONS: BSc.
HOBBIES AND INTERESTS: Politics.
PERSONAL PROFILE: General Secretary of the Democratic Party in the UK, member of the Executive of the National Federation of Cypriots in GB. Programme manager for the United States and Arab Open Universities.

UK

ANDREAS IOANNOU
Treasurer Pentayia Association; Owner of Aroma Patisserie/Philanthropist

DATE OF BIRTH: 03-Aug-1951
PLACE OF BIRTH: Pentayia.
MARITAL STATUS: Married to Maria, London Parents from Cyprus, Pastry Chef.
CHILDREN: Angela, Anna, Both University graduates.
SCHOOLS/COLLEGE: Borehamwood College.
QUALIFICATIONS: 11 O levels and Diploma in Computer Engineering. Food Hygiene Certificate.
MEMBERSHIPS: Pentayia Association.
HOBBIES AND INTERESTS: Travelling and football.
PERSONAL PROFILE: Owner of Aroma Patisserie and Treasurer of the Pentayia Association.

ANDREAS ELIA IOANNOU
Chairman of St John the Baptist Greek School. On the committee of EFEPE

DATE OF BIRTH: 06-Oct-1950
PLACE OF BIRTH: Neo Chorion Kythreas, Nicosia.
MARITAL STATUS: Married to Dimitra, Gastria.
CHILDREN: Eliana, Solicitor. Ioannis, Student. Christiana, student.
SCHOOLS/COLLEGE: Pancyprian Gymnasium.
QUALIFICATIONS: Chartered Accountant.
HOBBIES AND INTERESTS: Shooting, Tottenham Football Club.
PERSONAL PROFILE: Accountant. Chairman of St John the Baptist Greek School. On the committee of EFEPE.

CONSTANTINOS ELIA IOANNOU
Vice President of London Society of Chartered Accountants

DATE OF BIRTH: 21-Jun-1956
PLACE OF BIRTH: Neon Chorion Kythreas.
MARITAL STATUS: Married to Florentia, Achna, Bio Chemist.
CHILDREN: Christina, Marina, Elias, Elina.
SCHOOLS/COLLEGE: Technical School of Nicosia. Kingsway College for Further Education, North London University.

QUALIFICATIONS: Chartered Accountant (FCA).
MEMBERSHIPS: Fellow of Institute of Chartered Accountants in England & Wales. Committee member of North London Society of Chartered Accountants - Chairman 1998-2000. Vice President of London Society of Chartered Accountants.
HOBBIES AND INTERESTS: Reading, walking, cinema, golf, nature watch and travelling.
PERSONAL PROFILE: Accountant and Governor of All Saints Primary (CofE) School in Whetstone. Governor of St. John the Baptist Greek School. Treasurer of St. John the Baptist Church in London N8.

CONSTANTINOS S. IOANNOU
Principal Lecturer in Structures & Design University of East London

DATE OF BIRTH: 23-Feb-1949
PLACE OF BIRTH: Yerolakkos.
MARITAL STATUS: Married to Stella, Famagusta, Bio chemist.
CHILDREN: Savvas, Microbiologist. Christos, Student. Elena, Student.
SCHOOLS/COLLEGE: Willesden College of Technology; Queen Mary College, Imperial College, Univ of London.
QUALIFICATIONS: B. Sc (Eng), M. Sc (Structr. Eng), DIC (Diploma of Imperial College).
HOBBIES AND INTERESTS: Philatelism, history, classical music, aviation and traditional Greek music.
PERSONAL PROFILE: Principal Lecturer in Structures and Design at University of East London.

DEMETRA (YIAKOUMI) IOANNOU
Director of Haringey Racial Equality Council

DATE OF BIRTH: 12-Dec-1962
PLACE OF BIRTH: London. Father, Andreas Yiakoumi from Komi Kebir; Mother, Loukia from Eptakomi.
MARITAL STATUS: Single.
CHILDREN: Lucy, Mario.
SCHOOLS/COLLEGE: High Cross Tottenham, CRE Post entry training at Liverpool University.
HOBBIES AND INTERESTS: Football, (Tottenham fan) and most sports.
PERSONAL PROFILE: Director of Haringey Racial Equality Council.

UK

GEORGE IOANNOU
Ninth best selling artist in the UK 2005

DATE OF BIRTH: 22-Oct-1974
PLACE OF BIRTH: Croydon
Grandfather from Yialoussa,
Grandmother from Maroni.
MARITAL STATUS: Single.
SCHOOLS/COLLEGE: St
Josephs College, London.
QUALIFICATIONS: A-level Art
and performing Arts.
HONOURS/AWARDS: Ninth
best selling artist in the UK 2005.
HOBBIES AND INTERESTS: Acting, Boxing and Clay
Pigeon Shooting.
PERSONAL PROFILE: George Ioannou is an Artist
and is a pioneer of Iconic/Cult artwork some of his
collectors include Michael Caine Sven Goran Eriksson
Roman Abramovich and many others. Also Raised £35k
for The Bobby Moore Fund for cancer research, through
donations of his art work.

JOHN IOANNOU
Actor played Bartholomew in Franco Zefferellis Jesus of Nazareth

DATE OF BIRTH: 27-May-1949
PLACE OF BIRTH: Nicosia.
MARITAL STATUS: Single.
SCHOOLS/COLLEGE: City
of Bath Boys School. Webber-
Douglas Academy of Dramatic
Art.
QUALIFICATIONS: A level
Spanish and French.
MEMBERSHIPS: Equity.
HONOURS/AWARDS: Watson
trophy for Solo Acting The de Reyes Memorial Trophy
for verse speaking (Bath mid Somerset Festival).
PERSONAL PROFILE: Actor played Bartholomew in
Franco Zefferellis Jesus of Nazareth. Has played on TV
in The Bill and Londons Burning.

JOHN IOANNOU
Semi Finalist in the Entrpreneur of the year Awards 2000 from Ernst & Young

DATE OF BIRTH: 15-Feb-1961
PLACE OF BIRTH: Nicosia.
MARITAL STATUS: Married to
Anna, Akaki.
CHILDREN: Three Children.
SCHOOLS/COLLEGE:
American Academy Larnaca.
Barnet College and Southbank
University.
QUALIFICATIONS: BSc MSc.
MEMBERSHIPS: Institute of
Electrical and Electronic Engineers.
HONOURS/AWARDS: Best subnotebook of the year
2002 Award from PC Advisor. Voted one of the 50
fastest growing IT Companies by Deloitte Touche.
Directors of AJP were semi finalists in the Entrepreneur
of the year Awards 2000 from Ernst & Young.
HOBBIES AND INTERESTS: Basketball, Football,
Squash and Music.
PERSONAL PROFILE: Co founder of AJP Computers
PLC also own AJP Investments Ltd.

KOULLA IOANNOU
On the advisory body of Wandsworth Education Committee

DATE OF BIRTH: 08-Dec-1952
PLACE OF BIRTH: London,
father from Khirokitia, Mother
from Lefkara.
CHILDREN: John, Andrew, Harry.
SCHOOLS/COLLEGE:
Alperton High School Wembley.
QUALIFICATIONS: O and A
levels. Diploma in Sociology.
Various community work
certificates.
HOBBIES AND INTERESTS: Family, art, history and
gardening.
PERSONAL PROFILE: Community Worker. At present
manager of Camden Cypriot Womens Organisation.
Served on Parent Committees and on Governing bodies
of two schools in South London and remains on the
advisory body of Wandsworth Education Committee.

UK

KYRIAKOS IOANNOU
Chairman of Trypimeni Association

DATE OF BIRTH: 13-Sep-1936
PLACE OF BIRTH: Tripimeni.
MARITAL STATUS: Married to Flori London Parents from Eptakomi.
CHILDREN: John, Tony, Loulla.
SCHOOLS/COLLEGE: English School Nicosia, Morphou Teacher Training College.
HOBBIES AND INTERESTS: Shooting and gardening.
PERSONAL PROFILE: Chairman of Trypimeni Association. Teacher in Cyprus for 19 yeras. Came to England in 1975, was relief teacher at Mandeville Secondary in Edmonton, then two years in Civil Service. Teaches Greek in Greek Schools in London. In 1988 became a supply teacher for primary schools, and from 1993 teacher at Lea Valley Primary School.

PETER IOANNOU
Voted one of the fastest 50 growing IT Co's by Deloitte Touche

DATE OF BIRTH: 15-Feb-1961
PLACE OF BIRTH: Nicosia.
MARITAL STATUS: Married to Yiota, Athienou.
CHILDREN: Three children.
SCHOOLS/COLLEGE: American Academy Larnaca; St Marys Hendon, Barnet College, South Bank University.
QUALIFICATIONS: BSc Honours Electronics, MSc Information Technology.
MEMBERSHIPS: Member of Institute of Electrical & Electronic Engineers.
HONOURS/AWARDS: 2000 award, Deloitte Touche.
HOBBIES AND INTERESTS: Reading, football and family.
PERSONAL PROFILE: Founder AJP Computers PLC with brother John, also own property investment co AJP Investments Ltd, AJP Computers won best subnotebook of the year 2002 Award from PC Advisor. Was voted one of the fastest 50 growing IT Co's by Deloitte Touche. Won award for notebooks at the PC Direct Hits Awards (1992, 98, 99 & 2000), also Special Achievement Award for Business 1997. Directors of AJP were semi-finalists in the Entrepreneur of the Year Awards 2000 from Ernst & Young.

YUSUF ISLAM (FORMERLY KNOWN AS CAT STEVENS BORN STEVEN GEORGIOU)
Singer/Songwriter

DATE OF BIRTH: 21-Jul-1948
PLACE OF BIRTH: London Father from Cyprus, Mother Swedish.
MARITAL STATUS: Married to Fauzia.
CHILDREN: Five Children.
SCHOOLS/COLLEGE: St Joseph Primary School. Hammersmith Art School.
HONOURS/AWARDS: 2004 Man For Peace Award. 2007 Mediterranean Prize for Peace. 2007 Ivor Novello Award for Outstanding Song Collection as well as other numerous awards not mentioned.
PERSONAL PROFILE: As Cat Stevens singer / songwriter he sold over 60 million albums worldwide classics like Peace Train, Wild World and the First Cut is The Deepest. Many famous singers have performed his songs like Dolly Parton and Rod Stewart. Cat converted to Islam in 1977. The following year he adopted his Muslim name Yusuf Islam and left his music career to devote himself to educational and philanthropic causes in the Muslim Community. In 2006 he returned to pop music with an album entitled An Other Cup.

CHRYSI JACOB (nee Koussertari)
Senior Lecturer in the Fashion Department at University of the Arts London

DATE OF BIRTH: 14-Nov-1943
PLACE OF BIRTH: Yialoussa.
MARITAL STATUS: Married to Christopher Jacob, British, Computer Manager.
CHILDREN: Maria, Web Designer. Joanna, Computer Manager.
SCHOOLS/COLLEGE: College for the Garment Trade, Central St Martins College of Art and Design.
QUALIFICATIONS: Certificate in Dressmaking, National Diploma in Dress Design, Certificate in Tailoring.
HONOURS/AWARDS: Painting in watercolours, foreign travel, international politics, gardening, music and theatre.
PERSONAL PROFILE: Senior Lecturer in the Fashion Department at University of the Arts London since 1967. Has taught many fashion icons such as Professor Katherine Hamnett, Professor John Galliano CBE, Francesca Versace, Hussein Chalayan MBE and Arkchadius.

Uk

CHRIS JOANNIDES
Councillor in the London borough of Enfield, the youngest elected councillor in the Greek Cypriot Community

DATE OF BIRTH: 24-May-1978
PLACE OF BIRTH: London, Father from Neo Livadhi, Morphou, Mother Ayios Sergios, Famagusta.
MARITAL STATUS: Single.
SCHOOLS/COLLEGE: Highgate Wood School. Enfield College and University. College London.
QUALIFICATIONS: BA Honours, Modern History.
HOBBIES AND INTERESTS: Politics, History, Adventure and Cultural Holidays.
PERSONAL PROFILE: Joined family business St Raphael's Integrity Care Homes Ltd in 2000. In 2001 he set up Integrity Care Ltd providing specialist care services for adults with mental health and substance abuse problems. In 2006 he was elected councillor in the London borough of Enfield, the youngest elected councillor in the Greek Cypriot Community.

EFTYCHIA STROUTHOU JOANNIDES
President Ayios Sergios Association

DATE OF BIRTH: 06-Mar-1942
PLACE OF BIRTH: Ayios Sergios Famagusta.
MARITAL STATUS: Married to Phivos, Paphos, Businessman.
CHILDREN: Costas, Graphic designer. Christos, Councillor and Care Manager.
SCHOOLS/COLLEGE: Greek Gymnasium Famagusta. Hadassah University Israel and Moorfields Eye Hospital, London.
QUALIFICATIONS: BSc in Science Psychology.
HOBBIES AND INTERESTS: Housewife.
PERSONAL PROFILE: Ayios Sergios President, Care Manager and Lecturer at Middlesex University.

PHIVOS JOANNIDES
Director and Co Founder of St Raphaels Integrity Care Homes Ltd

DATE OF BIRTH: 29-Jan-1943
PLACE OF BIRTH: Neo Livadhi, Paphos.
MARITAL STATUS: Married to Eftychia, Ayios Sergios, registered Nurse.
CHILDREN: Costas, Graphic Designer. Chris, Local Authority Councillor.
SCHOOLS/COLLEGE: Morphou Gymnasium. Barnet College.
QUALIFICATIONS: Two A levels, HND in Hotel and Catering Management. NVQ Level in 4 in Registered Managers Award in Care.
MEMBERSHIPS: Tottenham Conservative Party Association.
HOBBIES AND INTERESTS: Gardening and Walking.
PERSONAL PROFILE: Phivos Joannides is a Residential Care provider for people with mental health and learning disabilities since 1985. Director and Co-Founder of St Raphaels Integrity Care Homes Ltd.

DR STELIOS CONSTANTINOU JOANNIDES
Doctor-Gerontology, Geriatrics

DATE OF BIRTH: 23-Jan-1946
PLACE OF BIRTH: Kaimakli.
MARITAL STATUS: Married to Veronica Donnelly from Ireland.
CHILDREN: Costas, Lecturer. Stavros, Healthcare. Titania, Teacher.
SCHOOLS/COLLEGE: Pancyprian Gymnasium Nicosia, UCL London, Bristol Royal Infirmary, Watford General, Great Ormond Street Hospital, Surrey, Herts & Leeds Universities. Fellow of the Royal Society of Health; Member of Archaeology Society, Herts.
QUALIFICATIONS: MBCHA MPhil PhD DTMed.
MEMBERSHIPS: Fellow of the Royal Society of Health; Member of Archaeology Society, Herts.
HOBBIES AND INTERESTS: Reading, antiques, history, backgammon and photography.
PERSONAL PROFILE: Has written books, articles and essays in many medical magazines. Founder member and Secretary of Kaimakli Association.

UK

COSTAS ANDREOU JOANNOU
Accountancy, Shipping and General
Insurance

DATE OF BIRTH: 22-Feb-1956
PLACE OF BIRTH: Ayios
Epiktitos.
MARITAL STATUS: Married to
Shalina, Mauritius.
CHILDREN: Andrea from
previous marriage, just
completed her BA in English.
Panayiota from previous
marriage, Studying for a
BA in criminology. Shania
Stepdaughter, Primary School.
SCHOOLS/COLLEGE: Kyrenia Gymnasium, Tottenham
College of Technology, London School of Economics.
QUALIFICATIONS: BSc Honours in Management
Science. Chartered Certified Accountant. FCCA.
MEMBERSHIPS: Fellow of the Chartered Association
of Certified Accountants. Baltic Exchange.
HONOURS/AWARDS: Commendation from the
National Guard of the Republic of Cyprus for
outstanding service. Honoured by the Democratic
Rally(UK) for long and outstanding service.
HOBBIES AND INTERESTS: Travelling, Swimming,
writing, reading, golf and walking.
PERSONAL PROFILE: Practising as an Accountant and
currently Vice Chairman and shareholder in Kounnis
and Partners Plc. Also a Director and shareholder in
Kounnis Insuforce Plc and Founder and Chairman of
CAJ Holdings Plc and Ocean Shipping Plc.

MARY JOANNOU
Senior Lecturer in English at Anglia
Ruskin University in Cambridge

DATE OF BIRTH: 06-Sep-1947
PLACE OF BIRTH: London.
MARITAL STATUS: Single.
SCHOOLS/COLLEGE:
Highbury Hill High School.
Manchester, Hertfordshire,
Cambridge University.
QUALIFICATIONS: BA, MA, PhD.
MEMBERSHIPS: National
Convenor of the Women's
History Network.
HONOURS/AWARDS: Holder of the Fleur Cowles
Research Fellowship at the University of Texas.
HOBBIES AND INTERESTS: History, cinema, walking.
PERSONAL PROFILE: Senior Lecturer in English at
Anglia Ruskin University in Cambridge Since 1993.

CHRIS JOSEPH
Philanthropist

DATE OF BIRTH: 31-Aug-1945
PLACE OF BIRTH: Larnaca.
MARITAL STATUS: Married to
Maria.
CHILDREN: Eleanor, Desi,
Andrew, Bobbie.
SCHOOLS/COLLEGE:
St Georges, Larnaca.
MEMBERSHIPS:
Thalassaemia Society UK.
HONOURS/AWARDS: From
various charities.
HOBBIES AND INTERESTS: Gym, travelling and
socialising.
PERSONAL PROFILE: Owner of the Desilu Group of
Companies. Fashion, properties, hotels. Helped many
organisations along with his late brother Costas.

MARIA JOSEPH
President of Hadley Wood Cockfosters
Conservatives

DATE OF BIRTH: 06-Mar-1947
PLACE OF BIRTH: Ayios
Amvrosios.
MARITAL STATUS: Married to
Chris, a Hotelier, from Larnaca.
CHILDREN: Eleanor, Desi,
Andrew, Bobbie.
SCHOOLS/COLLEGE:
Barnsbury Central.
MEMBERSHIPS: Conservative
Party, Thalassaemia Society,
Greek Women's Philanthropic Society, St Katherines
Church.
HOBBIES AND INTERESTS: Politics, charities,
travelling and grandchildren.
PERSONAL PROFILE: Studied and worked in
hairdressing then fashion. Chaired Conservatives in
Hadleywood/Cockfosters. Currently president. Maria
helps many organisations and charities.

UK

CHRISTODOULUS KACOURIS
Accountant/Treasurer/player of London Nigerians Rugby Union Club

DATE OF BIRTH: 10-Jan-1973
PLACE OF BIRTH: London. Parents from Famagusta.
MARITAL STATUS: Single.
SCHOOLS/COLLEGE: Merchant Taylor's School; Queen Mary & Westfield, University of London; Lancaster University. FCMA (Fellow of Chartered institute of Management Accountants).
QUALIFICATIONS: GCSEs/A Levels/ BSc (Honours) Mathematical Sciences/ MBA. Chartered Management Accountant.
HOBBIES AND INTERESTS: Sport (Especially Rugby).
PERSONAL PROFILE: Financial Controller at City Bank. Treasurer/player of London Nigerians Rugby Union Club.

HELEN KACOURIS
Deputy Head Teacher of Secondary School

DATE OF BIRTH: 16-Apr-1963
PLACE OF BIRTH: London. Parents from Famagusta.
SCHOOLS/COLLEGE: Peterborough St Margarets School for Girls; Hughes Hall, Cambridge Univerity.
QUALIFICATIONS: GCEs, O Levels, A Levels, BA (Honours), English/Education.
HOBBIES AND INTERESTS: Sport, travel, theatre and singing.
PERSONAL PROFILE: Secondary School Deputy Head teacher.

Zoe Kakolyris was invited to Buckingham palace by Princess Anne where the National Autistic Society presented to the Princess Royal "on the slopes" a picture painted by Zoe in recognition of her work with the society.

ZOE KAKOLYRIS
Is an Artist who is deaf was invited to Buckingham Palace by Princess Anne where the National Autistic Society presented to the Princess Royal 'On the Slopes' picture painted by Zoe in recognition of her work with the society

DATE OF BIRTH: 16-Dec-1976
PLACE OF BIRTH: London. Father, Panayiotis, owner of Bevelynn food products, from Athens. Mother, Artemis, from Nicosia.
SCHOOLS/COLLEGE: Royal National Institute for the Deaf.
QUALIFICATIONS: 1 GCSE, Maths.
MEMBERSHIPS: Royal National Institute for the Deaf.
HONOURS/AWARDS: Invited to Buckingham Palace by Princess Anne where the National Autistic Society presented to the Princess Royal 'On the Slopes' picture painted by Zoe in recognition of her work with the society.
PERSONAL PROFILE: As a result of strong antibiotics given for strong colds when Zoe was six months old she became deaf although it was not until two and a half years later that the deafness was properly diagnosed. It was not until Zoe was twenty four that the Asperger Syndrome she also suffers from was recognised. Zoe produces extraordinary artwork, full of humour and vitality.

MICHAEL KAKOULLIS
Optometrist/Lecturer to the final year students of Aston University, Vision Sciences Department

DATE OF BIRTH: 26-Nov-1943
PLACE OF BIRTH: Pyla.
MARITAL STATUS: Married to Soula (née Seridou), a non-practising Physiotherapist, from Limnia Village, Famagusta.
CHILDREN: Thekli, Registrar in Medical Microbiology. Irene, University Graduate. Alexander, Junior Doctor.
SCHOOLS/COLLEGE: Primary School of Pyla, American Academy, Larnaca, Aston College, Birmingham, Aston University.
QUALIFICATIONS: BSc Honours in Optometry and Vision Sciences. FBOA, FDMC, DCLP.
PERSONAL PROFILE: Michael works with his brother Costa in their family group of practices and as a part time tutor/lecturer to the final year students of Aston University, Vision Sciences Department.

UK

AGATHA KALISPERAS
Director of the Hellenic Centre

DATE OF BIRTH: 06-Apr-1946
PLACE OF BIRTH: Nicosia.
MARITAL STATUS: Single.
CHILDREN: Costas, Leandros,
Both investment Bankers.
SCHOOLS/COLLEGE:
Pancyprian Gymnasium,
Nicosia, London University,
Surrey University. Institute of
Personnel Management.
QUALIFICATIONS: BSc
(Honours) Psychology, MSc Tourism Management.
HOBBIES AND INTERESTS: Opera, theatre, travel
and Bridge.
PERSONAL PROFILE: Director of The Hellenic
Centre for four years Jan 1997-Jan 2001. Reappointed as
Director in April 2003. Justice of the Peace since 1994.
School Governor since 2002.

ANDREAS NICOLAS KALISPERAS
President of North London Greek
Educational Association

DATE OF BIRTH: 18-Feb-1939
PLACE OF BIRTH: Leonarisso.
MARITAL STATUS: Married to
Maroulla, Ayios Elias, famagusta,
Teacher.
CHILDREN: Militsa, Skevi,
Nicholas.
SCHOOLS/COLLEGE:
Rizokarpasso Greek
Gymnasium. Laura College,
Clapton E5.
QUALIFICATIONS: Cyprus Certificate Of Education,
English, Maths and Geography.
PERSONAL PROFILE: 1970-2000 owned own company
making tents and caravan awnings. From 1995 has been
working for Haringey Council in the social services
department as an emergency response officer dealing
with the elderly and special needs. He is the President of
the North London Greek Association running 10 Greek
Community Schools in North london. Vice-President of
OESEKA.

MARIO KALLI
Actor appeared on TV in The Bill, Lock
Stock, Second Sight, Casualty

DATE OF BIRTH: 24-Feb-1966
PLACE OF BIRTH: London.
Parents from Yialoussa and
Lefkoniko.
MARITAL STATUS: Married
to Jenny. Father from Paphos.
CHILDREN: Natasha and
Daniella.
SCHOOLS/COLLEGE: Bognor
Regis Comprehensive School.
Academy of Live and Recorded Arts.
PERSONAL PROFILE: Professional actor since 1987.
Appeared in plays in the Sheffield Crucible, Edinburgh
Theatre Royal. Appeared on TV in The Bill, Lock Stock,
Second Sight, Casualty. In Commercial for W. H. Smith
with Nicholas Lyndhurst.

MICHAEL KALLI
Footballer Represented England
Universities in the Great Britain Games
in 2001

DATE OF BIRTH: 24-Jun-1980
PLACE OF BIRTH: London.
Grandparents from Yialoussa,
Leonarisso.
MARITAL STATUS: Married to
Tania, Italian/English, Project
Manager.
SCHOOLS/COLLEGE: St.
Andrews, Ashmole. University
of Luton.
QUALIFICATIONS: BA
Honours in Politics.
HONOURS/AWARDS: Eight caps for England
University football team.
HOBBIES AND INTERESTS: Football Tottenham FC,
Goalkeeper and socialising.
PERSONAL PROFILE: Played football for Wingate
Finchley FC, Enfield, and Cheshunt. Has represented
Britain against the National Game Eleven. Played
for Watford, Portsmouth, Cambridge, Liverpool and
Southend Youth. Represented England Universities in
the Great Britain Games in 2001. He is in charge of 8 of
the ten biggest media agencies in the UK.

GEORGE KALLIS
Chairman of St John the Baptist Greek Orthodox Church

DATE OF BIRTH: 13-Mar-1929
PLACE OF BIRTH: Labathos.
MARITAL STATUS: Married to Maroulla.
CHILDREN: Jack, Antonis, both accountants. Panayiotis, Heart Surgeon.
HOBBIES AND INTERESTS: Politics, Anorthosis FC.
PERSONAL PROFILE: Involved with St. John the Baptist Greek Church Wightman Road, 18 years treasurer, then Chairman. Member of Labathos Association.

PANAYIOTIS KALLIS
Consultant Cardiac Surgeon

PLACE OF BIRTH: Lapathos, 1959
MARITAL STATUS: Married to Sophia, London (parents from Karavas).
CHILDREN: Georgio.
SCHOOLS/COLLEGE: William Ellis School. University College Hospital, Medical School.
QUALIFICATIONS: BSc (Honours) MB BS (Honours) FRCS MS.
MEMBERSHIPS: Fellow of the Royal College of Surgeons, British Cardiac Society.
HOBBIES AND INTERESTS: Tennis and golf.
PERSONAL PROFILE: Consultant Cardiac Surgeon at the Middlesex Hospital. Also based at Harley St, London.

Dr YIANNIS KALLIS
Gastroenterology Specialist Registrar at St Marys Hospital, London

DATE OF BIRTH: 08-Feb-1974
PLACE OF BIRTH: Mannheim, Germany, Father from Karavas.
MARITAL STATUS: Married.
SCHOOLS/COLLEGE: Highgate School, London. Trinity College, Cambridge.
QUALIFICATIONS: MA Honours Medical Science. MB Bchir(Distinction).
HOBBIES AND INTERESTS: Travelling, Diving and Photography.
PERSONAL PROFILE: Yiannis is a Gastroenterology Specialist Registrar at St Marys Hospital, London.

Author of Medical Textbooks for Junior Doctors and contributes research articles to scientific journals.

EVI KALODIKI
Research Fellow On Vascular Surgery

DATE OF BIRTH: 10-Jan-1956
PLACE OF BIRTH: Nicosia.
MARITAL STATUS: Single.
SCHOOLS/COLLEGE: Larnaca High School. University of Athens, Medical School, University of Athens, Imperial College, London.
QUALIFICATIONS: MD. BA PhD, DIC Diploma Of Imperial College. Certificate in Vascular Surgery, Diplom.
MEMBERSHIPS: Surgical Research Society of GB and Ireland, European Society for Vascular Research, Hellenic Medical Society, UK.
HOBBIES AND INTERESTS: Reading, theatre and travelling.
PERSONAL PROFILE: Research Fellow on vascular surgery; involved in cultural (non-political) activities.

ALEXANDRA KALYMNIOS
Film Director, Directed episodes for Channel 4's teen soap Hollyoaks

DATE OF BIRTH: 08-Jan-1980
PLACE OF BIRTH: London. Father from Piraeus, Greece; Mother, from Kaimakli.
MARITAL STATUS: Single.
SCHOOLS/COLLEGE: Latymer School. Bournemouth University.
QUALIFICATIONS: BA (Honours) Television and Video Production, 2: 1.
MEMBERSHIPS: Member of the British Academy of Television and Film (BAFTA).
HONOURS/AWARDS: Awarded funding for script More than a Job's Worth from Enfield Film Council. Best New Director Award, Greenwich Film Festival.
HOBBIES AND INTERESTS: Travelling, music, art, dance, theatre, film, video, sport and physical training.
PERSONAL PROFILE: Television researcher at the BBC. Over the past six years directed and produced short films, professional corporate videos, written and directed for the Children's BBC programme Stitch Up. Completed director training programme in Children's BBC Drama. Directed episodes for Channel 4's teen soap Hollyoaks.

UK

MARIA (nee Tsianidou) KALYMNIOS
Co Ordinator of primary and secondary schools (Head of bilingual & home school project in Barnet

DATE OF BIRTH: 23-Jan-1951
PLACE OF BIRTH: Kaimakli.
MARITAL STATUS: Married to Dr Kalymnios, Greece, University Lecturer.
CHILDREN: Triada, Lawyer. Harilaos, University graduate in Physics and Astrophysics. Alexandra, TV and Film producer.
SCHOOLS/COLLEGE: Tollington Park School. Hull University.
QUALIFICATIONS: MA in Education, Certificate in Education.
HOBBIES AND INTERESTS: Arts, Music, Sport and Travel.
PERSONAL PROFILE: Teacher in mainstream schools advisory and support teacher, Co Ordinator of primary and secondary schools (Head of bilingual & home school project in Barnet). Secretary of the North London Greek Educational Association (voluntary).

TRIADA KALYMNIOS
Solicitor in Trowers & Hamlins Dispute Resolution and Litigation department and writes for various legal publications

DATE OF BIRTH: 10-Apr-1975
PLACE OF BIRTH: Beverley, Yorkshire, England. Father from Greece; Mother from Kaimakli.
MARITAL STATUS: Single.
SCHOOLS/COLLEGE: Belmont Junior school, London; Latymer Secondary School; University of Sussex (plus one year Law School in London).
QUALIFICATIONS: Bachelor of Law with Honours LLB European Commercial Law with French. Diploma de Droit Francais; Law Society BAC 1 + 11 - Russian.
HONOURS/AWARDS: Grade V in violin and piano; Grade III in flute.
HOBBIES AND INTERESTS: Scuba diving, sailing, snowboarding and music. Travelled extensively (one year travelling around the world) including USA, Asia, Australia and Europe.
PERSONAL PROFILE: Solicitor in Trowers & Hamlins Dispute Resolution and Litigation department and writes for various legal publications.

TRYFON KALYVIDES
Architect, MIPIN European building award 2006

DATE OF BIRTH: 09-Aug-1960
PLACE OF BIRTH: Kyrenia (father) Larnaca (Mother).
MARITAL STATUS: Married to Helen, UK.
CHILDREN: Efthymia, Niki, Emilia.
SCHOOLS/COLLEGE: Birmingham School of Architecture. Westminster University.
QUALIFICATIONS: BA Dip Arch, MA RIBA.
HONOURS/AWARDS: BDA commercial building award 2002, Best small commercial building award 2003, MIPIN European building award 2006.
HOBBIES AND INTERESTS: Art & Design, Photography, World Travel.
PERSONAL PROFILE: Tryfon owns an Architectural Practice, The Kalyvides Partnership with offices in Camden Town. External postgraduate tutor of architecture at The Polytechnic of North London.

DR ANDREAS DEMETRI KANARIS
Honorary Commissioner for the Republic of Cyprus in Manchester

DATE OF BIRTH: 23-May-1928
PLACE OF BIRTH: Piyi.
MARITAL STATUS: Married to Vivi from Greece.
CHILDREN: Antigoni, Demetris, Maria, Leonidas and Vera.
SCHOOLS/COLLEGE: Pancyprian Gymnasium, Manchester University.
QUALIFICATIONS: BSc, PhD.
HOBBIES AND INTERESTS: Travel, reading and community affairs.
PERSONAL PROFILE: Instructor of Physics at Manchester University. Several research publications in physics journals. Honorary Commissioner for the Republic of Cyprus in Manchester since 1980. Former Chairman of Hellenic Brotherhood in Manchester and Greek Orthodox Community of Manchester.

UK

PETROULA KANETI-DIMMER
Actress/Writer, TV & Film Credits, The Bill, East Enders, Mile High

DATE OF BIRTH: 11-Apr-1974
PLACE OF BIRTH: Yialoussa Cyprus.
MARITAL STATUS: Married to N. Paul Dimmer, British, Painter and Decorator.
CHILDREN: Nicholas Alexander Kaneti-Dimmer.
SCHOOLS/COLLEGE: Highbury Fields Secondary School. Westminster Kingsway College of Performing Arts.
QUALIFICATIONS: BTEC National Diploma in The Performing Arts.
MEMBERSHIPS: Equity. Citizens Commission on Human Rights. Narconon (Drug Education and Rehabilitation Charity).
HOBBIES AND INTERESTS: Acting, Reading, Writing comedy, Sketches, Film and Television, Various charity work.
PERSONAL PROFILE: TV & Film Credits, The Bill, East Enders, Mile High. Theatre & Tours, Helped the Citizens Commision on Human Rights.

COSTAS KAOUNIDES
Co Founder and First General Secretary of Omonia FC, Cyprus

DATE OF BIRTH: 06-Aug-1924
PLACE OF BIRTH: Assia.
MARITAL STATUS: Married to Beatrice, born in New York, Cypriot origin.
CHILDREN: Lakis, Lecturer. Carolina, Journalist. Monica, Housewife.
SCHOOLS/COLLEGE: Executive Committee of Cypriot football league in England for several years.
PERSONAL PROFILE: Co founder and first General Secretary of Omonia FC, Cyprus. Also, co founder of Omonia Fc London and Honorary President. Journalist for Haravgi, Cyprus, for several years and now journalist for Parikiaki Newspaper, London.

LAKIS KAOUNIDES
Director, Technology Management and Innovation Queen Mary University

DATE OF BIRTH: 04-Sep-1948
PLACE OF BIRTH: Nicosia.
MARITAL STATUS: Single.
SCHOOLS/COLLEGE: Tollington Grammar School. Birmingham, Essex and Oxford.
QUALIFICATIONS: BSc. BComm and MA.
MEMBERSHIPS: Materials Panel. Fellow Institute of Nano Technology UK.
HOBBIES AND INTERESTS: Classical Music, Film Making, Greek History, space research and politics.
PERSONAL PROFILE: Lakis Kaounides is Director, Technology Management and Innovation Department of Materials at Queen Mary University, London. Was previously a senior consultant and International expert to the United Nations in the area of advanced materials and their strategic implications for developing economies.

DR COSTAS I. KARAGEORGHIS
Senior Lecturer at Brunel University

DATE OF BIRTH: 15-Sep-1969
PLACE OF BIRTH: London. Parents from Anaphotia.
MARITAL STATUS: Married to Tina Suzanne, Kent.
CHILDREN: Anastasia, Lucia, Both at School.
SCHOOLS/COLLEGE: Langley Park School. Brunel University, United States Sports Academy (Daphne, Alabama).
QUALIFICATIONS: PhD MSc BA.
MEMBERSHIPS: British Olympic Association Psychology Advisory Group.
HONOURS/AWARDS: 1998 BASES Prize for Best Sport Psychology Presentation at Annual Conference. Awarded in excess of £200, 000 in research funding as principal investigator.
HOBBIES AND INTERESTS: Athletics, music and international politics.
PERSONAL PROFILE: Senior Lecturer at Brunel University (2000 to present). Secretary of Greek School at St Mary's Cathedral, Camberwell.

UK

ODYSSEAS KARAGEORGIS
Chairman of Lefkonico Association

DATE OF BIRTH: 28-Oct-1933
PLACE OF BIRTH: Lefkoniko.
MARITAL STATUS: Married to Jovanka.
CHILDREN: Kyriakos, Economics graduate. Alexander, University student. Christopher, still at School.
SCHOOLS/COLLEGE: Lefkoniko High School;Famagusta Gymnasium;. Battersea College of Advanced Technology (graduated in 1958) Affiliated to London University, later Surrey University.
QUALIFICATIONS: Dip Electrical Engineering, Chartered Electrical Engineer; MIEE.
HOBBIES AND INTERESTS: Reading, volleyball, athletics; Famagusta Gymnasium 400m record-holder.
PERSONAL PROFILE: First worked with GEC specializing in microwave equipment, then joined Research and Development Laboratories of STL (Standard Telephone Labs); and later on Fibre Optics at STL. Worked on the automatic landings of aircraft, and classified and NASA Projects specialising on Aircraft Horn Aerials. Was a founder member of EFEKA, and Secretary of the Hellenic Society, University of London, 1956-58. Chairman of EFEKA 1958-60. Current Chairman of Lefkoniko Association UK. Director of the renowned Greek restaurant Elyzee in London's West End.

ANDREAS KARAISKOS
Architect Acted as concept architect for the refurbishment of Wembley Arena

DATE OF BIRTH: 14-Aug-1968
PLACE OF BIRTH: London Father from Strovolos Mother from Pera Orinis.
MARITAL STATUS: Married to Antoinette, Irish, Housewife and Designer.
CHILDREN: Kealan, Orin.
SCHOOLS/COLLEGE: Whitmore High School. Birmingham City University.
QUALIFICATIONS: BA MA ARCH PG DIP. ARCH.
MEMBERSHIPS: Royal Institute of British Architects.
HONOURS/AWARDS: Entry Shortlisted and Published in the far Eastern International Digital Architectural Design Award 2000.
HOBBIES AND INTERESTS: Sports, design, art music and food.
PERSONAL PROFILE: Andreas karaiskos is at Hok Sport Architecture has worked principally on stadia and arenas. Acted as concept architect for the refurbishment of Wembley Arena. Andreas has been significantly involved with the new Emirates Stadium.

HELEN KARAMALLAKIS
Lecturer at the London School of Fashion

DATE OF BIRTH: 20-Mar-1962
PLACE OF BIRTH: London. Father from Nicosia, mother from Ora.
MARITAL STATUS: Married to Michael Davis, Teacher.
CHILDREN: Twins: Katerina and Christopher, Sophia.
SCHOOLS/COLLEGE: Winchmore School. London University, Chelsea College, Oxford University, Keble College.
QUALIFICATIONS: 7 O Levels, 3 A Levels, BSc Biology. PGCE Science Education.
HOBBIES AND INTERESTS: Film, music, cooking, eating out, gardening and the environment.
PERSONAL PROFILE: Teacher, previous posts at Manor Hill School, East Barnet; Queen Elizabeth Boys; then Winchmore School. Now teaches science to beauty therapy students at the London School of Fashion.

MILTON KARAMANIS
Junior Tennis Player road to Wimbledon semi finalist 2005

DATE OF BIRTH: 09-Jun-1992
PLACE OF BIRTH: London, Parents from Davlos, Trikomo and Rizokarpasso Syngrassis.
MARITAL STATUS: Single.
SCHOOLS/COLLEGE: Highgate Boys School.
MEMBERSHIPS: Lawn Tennis Association UK.
HONOURS/AWARDS: Middlesex County Champion 2004, Ellesse Open under 14s Champion 2006, Ellesse Open Men's Division Champion 2006.
HOBBIES AND INTERESTS: Tennis, Football, Golf and Music.
PERSONAL PROFILE: Milton Karamanis is a tennis player, some of his achievements are Road to Wimbledon Semi - Finalist 2005. Represents Middlesex in under 14s and is a member of the County cup team UK finalists 2006.

NICHOLAS KARANICHOLAS
Year 2000 World Champion Kumite Fighting

DATE OF BIRTH: 26-Oct-1986
PLACE OF BIRTH: London. Father from Kato Varosi; Mother from Limassol.
MARITAL STATUS: Single.
SCHOOLS/COLLEGE: Loyola Prep School. Davenant Foundation Sports College.
QUALIFICATIONS: Bronze Prize in National (UK) Maths test at 13.
HONOURS/AWARDS: 2000 World Championship at Glasgow, and the 2001 London Youth Games at Crystal Palace.
HOBBIES AND INTERESTS: Football, rugby, dance, shooting, drumming, drama and music.
PERSONAL PROFILE: Kumite-Fighting, Kata-Exhibition of Style. Won several awards, both National and Junior Championships for that style.

ELENI KARAOLI
Education Co-ordinator

DATE OF BIRTH: 28-Sep-1950
PLACE OF BIRTH: Famagusta.
MARITAL STATUS: Married to Christaki an Office Manager at Big K Charcoal Merchants.
CHILDREN: Stylianos, Louis.
SCHOOLS/COLLEGE: Famagusta Girls Gymnasium, Alexandra Park. The Institute of Linguists, North London Schools Network.
QUALIFICATIONS: BEd Teaching qualification.
HOBBIES AND INTERESTS: Theatre, Greek music and travel.
PERSONAL PROFILE: Examiner for the Institute of Linguists. Head of Greek at the centre of Bilingualism, Chair of Co-ordinating Committee for GCSE and A Level Greek. Teacher and Head Teacher of Finchley Independent Greek School 1994-1999. Monthly column in Eleftheria Newspaper, Co-ordinator of European School Projects and International Links Officer.

ANDREAS CHRISTOU KARAOLIS
Executive Secretary of the National Federation of Cypriots and Greek Cypriot Brotherhood

DATE OF BIRTH: 20-Dec-1939
PLACE OF BIRTH: Morphou, Cyprus.
MARITAL STATUS: Married to Mary, London Parents from Rizokarpasso, Head Teacher.
CHILDREN: Christos, Gregory, George.
SCHOOLS/COLLEGE: Morphou primary and Gymnasium. Pedagocical Academy of Cyprus.
QUALIFICATIONS: Qualified teacher status both in Cyprus and the UK BA Classical Greek.
MEMBERSHIPS: Theatro Technis, Greek Teachers Association and numerous others.
HONOURS/AWARDS: Barnet Civic Award in recognition of service to the Borough of Barnet.
HOBBIES AND INTERESTS: Politics, reading, football, chess and backgammon.
PERSONAL PROFILE: Executive Secretary, National Federation of Cypriots and Greek Cypriot Brotherhood. Teacher at Manor Hill Greek School, 1991 – present. Initiated the twinning of Morphou with Barnet, 1995. GCSE Examiner for modern Greek for the University of London Examinations Board.

CHRISTOS KARAOLIS
President of the World Organisation for Young Overseas Cypriots(NEPOMAK)

DATE OF BIRTH: 29-Apr-1984
PLACE OF BIRTH: London Parents from Morphou, Rizokarpasso and Sisklipos.
MARITAL STATUS: Single.
SCHOOLS/COLLEGE: Queen Elizabeth Boys School. Trinity College, University of Oxford.
QUALIFICATIONS: Bar Vocational Course, Inns of Court School of Law, Jurisprudence BA(Hons).
MEMBERSHIPS: Grays Inn, NEPOMAK, Greek Cypriot Brotherhood.
HONOURS/AWARDS: Prince of Wales Scholar, Grays Inn. Colin Nicholls QC Prize for Criminal Law Moderations.
HOBBIES AND INTERESTS: Current Affairs, Politics, Long Distance running, youth affairs and chess.
PERSONAL PROFILE: Christos Karaolis is President of the World Organisation for Young Overseas Cypriots(NEPOMAK). He is a Barrister by occupation.

UK

MARY KARAOLIS
Head Teacher of Ravenscroft Comprehensive School, Barnet

DATE OF BIRTH: 04-May-1947
PLACE OF BIRTH: London Father from Sysklipos Mother from Rizokarpasso.
MARITAL STATUS: Married to Andreas, Morphou, Executive Secretary of the National Federation of Cypriots.
CHILDREN: Christos, Barrister. Gregory, Cambridge University Graduate. George, Student at LSE.
SCHOOLS/COLLEGE: Morpeth Comprehensive School. University of London and LSE.
QUALIFICATIONS: BeD, MA National Professional qualification for Headship.
MEMBERSHIPS: Member of the Greek Cypriot Brotherhood, Member of the Association of School and College Leaders. National Association of Head Teachers and Member of Barnet Executive Committee.
HONOURS/AWARDS: Barnet civic award in recognition of service to the borough of Barnet.
HOBBIES AND INTERESTS: Politics, reading, walking. gardening, chess, backgammon and cooking.
PERSONAL PROFILE: Head Teacher of Ravenscroft School Barnet. President of the Association of Rizokarpasso in Britain.

COSTAS KARAVIAS
Joint Managing Director of Task Systems a leading Office Furniture Design Company based in Central London

DATE OF BIRTH: 31-Jul-1955
PLACE OF BIRTH: Kyrenia.
MARITAL STATUS: Married to Voulla from Nicosia.
CHILDREN: Nadia, Stephanos, Anthia.
SCHOOLS/COLLEGE: Kalogeras, Wood Green School. Southgate College.
HOBBIES AND INTERESTS: Tennis, Manchester United Supporter and travel.
PERSONAL PROFILE: Costas Karavias sold his Furniture and IT company WHG in 1997. Started Task Systems a leading Office Furniture Design Company based in Central London that employs 60 staff.

JOSEPH KARAVIOTIS
Treasurer and director of the Sadler's Wells Theatre Appeal Fund Ltd

PLACE OF BIRTH: Cyprus 1942
SCHOOLS/COLLEGE: North Western Polytechnic.
QUALIFICATIONS: Degree in Business Studies Qualified as a financial accountant.
PERSONAL PROFILE: Joseph Karaviotis was originally Finance director of Sadlers Wells Theatre then Treasurer and director of the Sadler's Wells Theatre Appeal Fund Ltd. He was also the Director of New Sadlers Wells Opera. He was also the Director of Productions for the Noel Coward Estate.

PETROS KARAYIANNIS
Reader in Molecular Virology, Imperial College of Science, London

DATE OF BIRTH: 31-Jul-1951
PLACE OF BIRTH: Famagusta.
MARITAL STATUS: Married to Maria, Kyrenia.
CHILDREN: Nicholas, Computer Programmer. Stiliana, Hotel guest relations manager. Georgios, Student.
SCHOOLS/COLLEGE: 1st Gymnasium for Boys, Famagusta, Cyprus. Waltham Forest Technical College, University of Liverpool.
QUALIFICATIONS: BSc and Ph. D in microbiology.
MEMBERSHIPS: Fellow of the Institute of Biomedical Sciences, Fellow of the Royal College of Pathologists.
HOBBIES AND INTERESTS: Swimming, gardening and stamp collecting.
PERSONAL PROFILE: Petros Karayiannis Research work interests are. concerned with the study of molecular biology of the hepatitis viruses. He is Patron of the Leukaemia society UK. Served as president of the Hellenic Medical Society and Episteme.

UK

SAVVAS KARAYIANNIS
Chairman of Kingston Greek Orthodox Church

PLACE OF BIRTH: Mandres - Famagusta, 1926
MARITAL STATUS: Married to Vassiliki, Khirokitia.
CHILDREN: Akis, Banker. John, Architect.
SCHOOLS/COLLEGE: Lefkonico High School, University of London Goldsmith College.
QUALIFICATIONS: Teacher's Certificate.
PERSONAL PROFILE: Voluntary work and contribution for the advancement of political, Social Welfare and Educational aims of the Hellenic Community in the UK. Chairman of Kingston Greek Orthodox Church.

TASSOS GEORGIOU KARAYIANNIS
Professor of Engineering at South Bank University

DATE OF BIRTH: 24-Jan-1957
PLACE OF BIRTH: Kato Zodhia.
MARITAL STATUS: Married to Elena, Kato Zodia, Banking.
CHILDREN: George.
SCHOOLS/COLLEGE: The English School, Nicosia; City University, London; The University of Western Ontario, Canada.
QUALIFICATIONS: BSC (Honours) PhD.
MEMBERSHIPS: Institute of Mechanical Engineers.
HOBBIES AND INTERESTS: Greek Literature and tennis.
PERSONAL PROFILE: Professor of Engineering, Head of Division of Environmental, Energy and Building Services Engineering South Bank University.

MICK KARN
(Real Name Anthony Michaelides)
Part of the well known Rock Band Japan

DATE OF BIRTH: 24-Jul-1958
PLACE OF BIRTH: Nicosia.
PERSONAL PROFILE: Mick Karn is a musician multi-instrumentalist and songwriter most noted as the bassist for the 1980's art rock band Japan. Was invited by Peter Townsend to join him in a super group to celebrate the engagement of Prince Charles and Lady Diana at the Princes Trust Gala Performance.

KYRIACOS GARY KARSA
Head of Youth Academy at Wycombe Wanderers Football Club

DATE OF BIRTH: 15-Sep-1961
PLACE OF BIRTH: London. Father from Rizorkarpasso; Mother from Peristeropiyi.
MARITAL STATUS: Married to Bobbie, a Pre-school Teacher, (parents from Kontea).
CHILDREN: Rebecca, George, Both at School.
SCHOOLS/COLLEGE: Highbury Grove Comprehensive School, 1972-1978, Southgate Technical College, Central College for Physical Recreation. College of North East London. The Football Association Coaches Association.
QUALIFICATIONS: 5 O Levels, English Language, English Literature, Maths, Art, Modern Greek. FA Advance. Coaching Licence UEFA 'A' Coaching Award.
HOBBIES AND INTERESTS: Football and sport development in general. Reading and writing.
PERSONAL PROFILE: Previously with Barnet FC and Charlton Orient FC, Now in charge of the Youth Academy of Wycombe Wanderers.

MICHAEL KASHIS
Secretary of EDEK UK

DATE OF BIRTH: 16-Jul-1940
PLACE OF BIRTH: Neo Chorio Kythrea, Cyprus.
MARITAL STATUS: Married to Maria, Cyprus, ex-Consular Officer.
CHILDREN: Kypros, Teacher. Costas, Banking. Agathoclis, Solicitor.
SCHOOLS/COLLEGE: Elementary Neochorio, Pancyprian Gymnasium, Nicosia. Teachers' Training College Cyprus, University of Edinburgh.
QUALIFICATIONS: Diploma, University of London - MA Phil. Teacher/Headteacher/Advisory Teacher, Chief Examiner Greek Language, ULEAC.
MEMBERSHIPS: National Federation of Cypriots in UK.
HOBBIES AND INTERESTS: Literature, gardening, Byzantine music.
PERSONAL PROFILE: Secretary of POED (Teachers Trade Union, Cyprus) 1973-1980. Secretary of EDEK UK. Vice President of the National Federation of Cypriots in the UK.

UK

FATHER IACOVOS KASINOS
Priest at Greek Orthodox Church of St. Nicolas, Liverpool

DATE OF BIRTH: 10-Jun-1940
PLACE OF BIRTH: Ypsonas Limassol.
MARITAL STATUS: Married to Irini from Lefkara.
CHILDREN: Two sons and one daughter.
SCHOOLS/COLLEGE: Limassol Greek Gymnasium Lanition.
HOBBIES AND INTERESTS: Religion and gardening.
PERSONAL PROFILE: Started as Deacon at Liverpool then Theological school in Cyprus for one year. Later ordained Priest at Greek Orthodox Church of St. Nicolas, Liverpool.

SIMON KASSIANIDES
Appears in the new James Bond Movie Quatum of Solace as the Villain Yusef

PLACE OF BIRTH: UK my Father from Greece, Mother from Cyprus.
HONOURS/AWARDS: Represented Cyprus at Kick Boxing.
PERSONAL PROFILE: Simon appears in the new James Bond Movie Quatum of Solace as the Villain Yusef. He has also appeared in the film The Edge of Love with Keira Knightley and Sienna Miller. Simon has also appeared in many TV dramas including the Fixer, The Passion, Spooks, Love Soup and Ultimate Force.

DR GEORGE KASSIANOS
General Practitioner Bracknell. Appeared on TV, Watchdog, BBC News, Sky News, Debates on BBC2

DATE OF BIRTH: 30-Sep-1948
PLACE OF BIRTH: Lyssi, Famagusta.
MARITAL STATUS: Married to Karen, Born Canada Parents British, Nurse.
CHILDREN: Alexis, Nicholas, Julian, All Students.
SCHOOLS/COLLEGE: Nicosia Gymnasium, Zographos Grammar, Athens. Lodz Medical Academy Poland.

QUALIFICATIONS: MD LRCS FRCGP, MILT, DRCOG, LRCP.
MEMBERSHIPS: Primary Cave Cardio-vascular Society.
HONOURS/AWARDS: Doctor of the year Award, British Migraine Association.
HOBBIES AND INTERESTS: Reading, gardening and music.
PERSONAL PROFILE: General Practitioner Bracknell. Appeared on TV, Watchdog, BBC News, Sky News. Appeared in the Daily Telegraph, Independent, written several books. Editor of Audit General Practice Journal. Hon Secretary British travel Health Association.

COSTAS KATSANTONIS
Professional Boxer British Southern Area Light Welter Champion

DATE OF BIRTH: 16-Oct-1970
PLACE OF BIRTH: London. Father from Limassol, Cyprus; Mother from England (parents from Famagusta and Paralimni).
CHILDREN: Marcus and Elysia.
SCHOOLS/COLLEGE: Firs Farm Primary School, Winchmore Secondary School.
HONOURS/AWARDS: Twice Middlesex & Regional Area Junior Champion (amateur). British Southern Area Light Welter Champion (professional).
PERSONAL PROFILE: Professional Boxer.

DR NIKI KATSAOUNI
Cultural Counsellor for the Cyprus High Commission in London

PLACE OF BIRTH: Famagusta
SCHOOLS/COLLEGE: Bedford College, London University, Sorbonne, Paris and Athens University.
QUALIFICATIONS: BA(HONS) in Psychology. Doctorate with Distinction on the Philosophy of Art and Political Science.
MEMBERSHIPS: One of the founding members of 'Women walk home' a movement which broke peacefully and dynamically the Turkish military line dividing Cyprus since the 1974 Turkish invasion. Member of the board of the National Theatre of Cyprus.
HONOURS/AWARDS: John Dalton Medal European Geophysical Society. Distinguished Mcknight University Professor University of Minnesota.
PERSONAL PROFILE: Niki Katsaouni is the Cultural Counsellor for the Cyprus High Commission in London. She worked as Editor in Chief and as managing Director

of magazines Cosmopolitan and Vogue (Greek Editions) in Athens. Had her own programme on the State radio in Greece(ERT) and on TV and Radio in Cyprus.

CHRISTINE KATSOURIS
Journalist covering Oil & Politics for Energy Intelligence GP Publishers

DATE OF BIRTH: 15-Apr-1955
PLACE OF BIRTH: London. Father from Komi Kebir. Mother from Ireland.
MARITAL STATUS: Married to Neil Wilson, a Journalist, from the UK.
CHILDREN: Franklin Christopher John, at Primary School.
SCHOOLS/COLLEGE: London University (School of Oriental & African Studies). Subscription to Amnesty International.
QUALIFICATIONS: MA (History), BA (History & Politics).
HOBBIES AND INTERESTS: Travel, cycling, swimming, reading, cinema and African issues.
PERSONAL PROFILE: Currently a Journalist covering Oil & Politics for Energy Intelligence GP Publishers. Formerly Speechwriter/Press Officer at World Bank, writer at UN, Former Risk Analyst at London Forfeiting Co. Former Writer at Middle East Economic Digest. Voluntary work: Rosendale Play Centre (for kids of working mothers).

PANIKOS KATSOURIS
Founding director of Katsouris Fresh Foods Ltd, Filo pastry Ltd and Wine and Mousaka Restaurants

DATE OF BIRTH: 27-May-1950
PLACE OF BIRTH: Komi Kebir.
MARITAL STATUS: Married to Diana, Armenian from Iran.
CHILDREN: Alexander.
SCHOOLS/COLLEGE: Eftakomi Elementary, Famagusta Gymnasium. Southampton University.
HOBBIES AND INTERESTS: Golf, Photography and Skiing.
PERSONAL PROFILE: In 1974 Panikos joined the family business Katsouris Brothers Ltd importers of Cypriot and Greek food products. With their Cypressa label they have expanded to become a household name within the Cypriot and UK community. He is a founding director of Katsouris Fresh Foods Ltd, Filo pastry Ltd and Wine and Mousaka Restaurants.

CHRISTOS KAVALLARES MBE
Awarded MBE for work in Race Relations

DATE OF BIRTH: 10-Oct-1935
PLACE OF BIRTH: Lapithos, Cyprus.
MARITAL STATUS: Married to June Hedley, Newcastle, Housewife.
CHILDREN: Kypros, Engineer. Christina, Stylist. Marios, Software.
QUALIFICATIONS: School Certificate, Intermediate Electronics.
HONOURS/AWARDS: Gold Medal London Borough Haringey awarded Two Mayoral Cerificates of Merit. MBE for work in Race Relations.
HOBBIES AND INTERESTS: Sailing, skiing, theatre and politics.
PERSONAL PROFILE: Self employed electronic engineer, was Haringey Race Equality Council Chair, Haringey Cypriot Organisation Vice Chair Was Home Office Advisor for six years in race relations and community affairs.

STAVROS KAZACOS
Deputy Head Teacher of Ernest Bevin School in Tooting

DATE OF BIRTH: 31-Jul-1948.
PLACE OF BIRTH: Acheritou.
MARITAL STATUS: Married to Donna, British.
CHILDREN: Leon, Alexander, Lara, Georgios.
SCHOOLS/COLLEGE: Famagusta Practico Gymnasium. Kings College, London.
QUALIFICATIONS: BA PGCE.
HONOURS/AWARDS: Greek Music and Culture.
PERSONAL PROFILE: Stavros Kazacos is the Deputy Head Teacher of Ernest Bevin School in Tooting.

UK

The first generation of Cypriots in the UK were involved in the catering industry as kitchen staff and waiters in the restaurants and hotels by the late 60's some realised their dreams and owned cafés and restaurants.

ANDREW KAZAMIA

Actor best known for his eight years playing the leading role of Nick Georgiades in ITV's highly successful London's Burning

DATE OF BIRTH: 09-Dec-1952
PLACE OF BIRTH: Famagusta.
MARITAL STATUS: Married to Frances, Theatre Designer.
CHILDREN: Dino, Alex, Both at School.
SCHOOLS/COLLEGE: Wilsons School, Central School of Speech & Drama.
PERSONAL PROFILE: Andrew as an actor, has worked in theatre. On TV he has appeared in award winning series (Inspector Morse, Widows), but is best known for his eight years playing the leading role of Nick Georgiades in ITV's highly successful London's Burning. His directing work has included a double bill of his own one-act plays for The Royal Shakespeare Company His writing credits include original single films for both the BBC and Channel 4, Andrew's award-winning short film, Gooseberries Don't Dance (starring Ian Holm) was selected to launch the British Short Film Festival, as well as screenings in New York and Los Angeles as part of the British 'New Directors' programme.

ELLENA KIKI

Picture Researcher at the Times and on various children's magazines at the BBC

DATE OF BIRTH: 02-Apr-1973
PLACE OF BIRTH: London, parents from Eptakomi.
MARITAL STATUS: Single.
SCHOOLS/COLLEGE: Great Yarmouth High School, Great Yarmouth College of Higher Education, Norwich School of Art, Cleveland College of Art, London College of Printing.
QUALIFICATIONS: Design, HND BTEC in Design Communications (advertising fashion & Editorial Photography). Postgraduate Diploma in Photojournalism.
HONOURS/AWARDS: Winner of Portrait Photography Award in a competition arranged by Cosmopolitan Magazine in 1996.
HOBBIES AND INTERESTS: Photography, travel and art.
PERSONAL PROFILE: Freelance Picture Researcher at the Times and on various children's magazines at the BBC.

JOHN KIKI

Artist

DATE OF BIRTH: 09-May-1943
PLACE OF BIRTH: Eptakomi.
MARITAL STATUS: Married to Mary from Eptakomi.
CHILDREN: Ellena, Media. Antonia, Art.
SCHOOLS/COLLEGE: Camberwell Art College, Royal Academy Schools.
PERSONAL PROFILE: Artist. Paintings in major collections include Chantry Bequest, National Gallery of Wales. The Saatchi collection Gallop Finland Siemens PLC.

MARIA KIKILLOU

Chair of Leonarisso Vasili Association

DATE OF BIRTH: 12-May-1965
PLACE OF BIRTH: Famagusta.
CHILDREN: Alexandria, University. Daniella, School.
PERSONAL PROFILE: Maria Kikillou is the Chair of Leonarisso Vasili Association.

CARY KIKIS

Champion Snooker Player

DATE OF BIRTH: 18-Aug-1973
PLACE OF BIRTH: Great Yarmouth. Parents from Eptakomi and Limnia.
MARITAL STATUS: Single.
SCHOOLS/COLLEGE: Caister High.
PERSONAL PROFILE: Played snooker from the age of twelve. Turned professional at 17 played against Ronnie O'Sullivan, Mark Williams. Breaking into top 100 players in the World. Had to give up Snooker at the age of 19 because diagnosed with ME - now cured. Has own health business called KIKI Ltd based in Great Yarmouth specialising in mail order nutritional products.

UK

GEORGE KILLIKITAS
Football Secretary & Director of Haringey Football Club

DATE OF BIRTH: 24-Aug-1950
PLACE OF BIRTH: England. Parents from Achna.
MARITAL STATUS: Married.
CHILDREN: Anastasia and Panayiota.
SCHOOLS/COLLEGE: St Mary Magdalenes School. Barnsbury Boys.
HOBBIES AND INTERESTS: Football, (Arsenal Fan).
PERSONAL PROFILE: Co Founder of Achna FC. Keen member of Achna Association, Secretary & Director of Haringey Football Club.

CHARILAOS KITROMILIDES
Awarded Haringey Shield for services to the Community

DATE OF BIRTH: 27-Aug-1916
PLACE OF BIRTH: Nicosia.
MARITAL STATUS: Married to Julia.
CHILDREN: Yiannis, University Lecturer. Nadia, Self Employed.
SCHOOLS/COLLEGE: Pancyprian Gymnasium. Didaskalio, Morphou Teachers College, Westminster College.
QUALIFICATIONS: Teacher's Certificate, Social Science.
HONOURS/AWARDS: Haringey Shield and Cross from Archdiocese of Thyateira and GB.
HOBBIES AND INTERESTS: Gardening, walking and reading.
PERSONAL PROFILE: One of the founders of the Academy Social Club, Parents Guidance Centre, Oak Leaf Club. Teacher, Social Worker.

ALEXANDER KLEANTHOUS
Employment and commercial litigation solicitor

DATE OF BIRTH: 10-Jul-1965
PLACE OF BIRTH: Newcastle. Father from Limassol.
MARITAL STATUS: Single.
SCHOOLS/COLLEGE: Merchant Taylors School Northwood, Brasenose College Oxford.
QUALIFICATIONS: BA Oxford. Solicitor.
MEMBERSHIPS: Law Society.
HOBBIES AND INTERESTS: Military History.
PERSONAL PROFILE: Alex Kleanthous is an employment and commercial litigation solicitor with Gannons Law Firm.

ANDREAS KLEANTHOUS
President of Philia Association

DATE OF BIRTH: 08-Jul-1942
PLACE OF BIRTH: Philia.
MARITAL STATUS: Married to Sotiroulla, London, (Father from Eptakomi, Mother from Komi Kebir).
CHILDREN: Helen, Olivia, Areti, Chris.
SCHOOLS/COLLEGE: Completed 6th Form High School in Nicosia.
QUALIFICATIONS: Telecom Technician's course, Southgate College.
HOBBIES AND INTERESTS: Shooting, gardening and DIY.
PERSONAL PROFILE: Was Manager with BT for many years. Parent Governor with Broomfield School for four years. President of Philia Association.

ANTHONY KLEANTHOUS
Chairman of Barnet FC and on the Board of Directors of the Football League

DATE OF BIRTH: 26-Nov-1966
PLACE OF BIRTH: London. Father, Andreas, from Limassol; Mother, Anna, from Rizokarpasso.
MARITAL STATUS: Married.
SCHOOLS/COLLEGE: St Aloyisius, Hornsey.
PERSONAL PROFILE: At the age of 20 was youngest licensee to operate a Shell petrol station. The founder of NAG Telecom, which became the second largest mobile phone retailer in the UK while he was a chief executive. At 28 became the youngest football league chairman and owner of Barnet FC. At 32 became chairman of Service Direct PLC where he merged Samsung Telecom UK with Zoo Internet Enterprize to become the largest independent suppliers and maintainers of telephone systems in the UK. Chairman of Triton Europe who are one of the largest manufacturers in the world, manufacturing media products in the Far East. Tony was also voted in as League 2 Representative to the Football League of Directors in 2008.

UK

COSTAS PHOTIOS KLEANTHOUS
Chairman of the Hellenic Community Trust Council, London

DATE OF BIRTH: 15-Jun-1938
PLACE OF BIRTH: Limassol.
MARITAL STATUS: Married to Valerie Anne, Newcastle Upon Tyne, Solicitor.
CHILDREN: Alexander, Solicitor. Anthony, Business Manager.
SCHOOLS/COLLEGE: Lanition Gymnasium, Limassol; Hackney Downs Grammar School, London; Sir John Cass College (now Guildhall University).
QUALIFICATIONS: BSc Mathematics.
HOBBIES AND INTERESTS: Antiques, history, environment, international and community affairs, theatre and music.
PERSONAL PROFILE: Has antiques business with brother Chris in Portobello Road. Chairman of Portobello road Antiques Dealers and Director of the National Association of Art & Antique Dealers. Has served as Vice-Chairman of the Greek Cypriot Brotherhood, and the Federation of Cypriots in the UK and Overseas. Co-founder and Chairman of the Hellenic Community Trust Council, London. In Cyprus, Chairman of both the Luona Foundation and Terra Cypria conservation and countryside projects.

NIKIFOROS (NICK) KLEANTHOUS
Received the Queen's Award for export achievement

DATE OF BIRTH: 09-Feb-1951
PLACE OF BIRTH: Paleomylos Troodos.
CHILDREN: Zoe, BSc in Psychology; Natasha, at Sheffield Uni.
SCHOOLS/COLLEGE: Clissold Park School.
HOBBIES AND INTERESTS: Golf, shooting and music.
PERSONAL PROFILE: Was in the Garment Industry from 1970. Formed the company called KACY Ltd, women's tailoring manufacturers. It grew into a substantial size, employing 30 people and subcontracting to companies employing several hundred people. In 1993, received the Queen's Award for export achievement. The company ceased trading in 1997 when Nick retired; it still exists, though its only activity is to rent out its properties.

TAKIS KLEANTHOUS
Former Secretary of KLN Football Club and Results Secretary of Cypriot Football league in UK. Owner of Big K Charcoal Merchants

DATE OF BIRTH: 28-Jul-1950.
PLACE OF BIRTH: Kampia, Nicosia.
MARITAL STATUS: Married to Vivian.
CHILDREN: Alex, Business. Melina, Student.
SCHOOLS/COLLEGE: Friern Barnet County School. Cypriot Golf Society.
HOBBIES AND INTERESTS: Golf and football (Tottenham Fan).
PERSONAL PROFILE: Former Secretary of KLN Football Club and Results Secretary of Cypriot Football league in UK. Owner of Big K Charcoal Merchants with premises in North London and Kings Lynn. Suppliers to Waitrose, John Lewis, Homebase, Petrol Stations and Restaurants.

MYRNA Y KLEOPAS
Former High Commisioner for the Republic of Cyprus in the UK

DATE OF BIRTH: 23-Aug-1944
PLACE OF BIRTH: Nicosia.
MARITAL STATUS: Married to Yiangos P Kleopas.
CHILDREN: Kleopas, Sophia.
SCHOOLS/COLLEGE: Studied Law at Grays Inn, London.
HOBBIES AND INTERESTS: Reading, the arts, swimming, walking.
PERSONAL PROFILE: Practised law in Cyprus. 1977-1979. Served as Legal Advisor on Human rights to the ministry of foreign affairs. April 1980-1986, served as Counsellor at the Cyprus High Commission, London. In 1981, also appointed Consul-General and then year 2000 to 2004 was High Commissioner. Was Ambassador in Italy and China for Cyprus. Myrna is also the Chair of the UN Committee against Torture.

UK

MARIOS KOMBOU

Appeared in the leading role in Jailhouse Rock at the Piccadilly Theatre, London,

DATE OF BIRTH: 27-Feb-1965
PLACE OF BIRTH: London. Father born in Pentayia, Mother from Rizokarpasso.
MARITAL STATUS: Single.
SCHOOLS/COLLEGE: Rhodes Avenue Junior, Alexandra Park Secondary, Waltham Forest College, Alan International Hairdressing Academy, ALRA Drama School.
QUALIFICATIONS: Hairdressing Diploma, three year Acting and Musical Theatre Degree.
HONOURS/AWARDS: Only UK Elvis Presley Tribute Act to have been officially endorsed by Elvis's first cousin, Donna Presley.
HOBBIES AND INTERESTS: Football (Salamina & Cypriot Football League, representative Goalkeeper for many years), golf, skiing and music.
PERSONAL PROFILE: Actor and singer. Voted in the Top 5 Elvis Tribute Artists in the world at the Images of Elvis Contest, Memphis, USA 2000/2001. Mario appeared in the leading role in Jailhouse Rock at the Piccadilly Theatre, London, in 2004.

VASSOS KONI

Chairman of Elliniki Kypriaki Estia in Birmingham

DATE OF BIRTH: 02-Jan-1964
PLACE OF BIRTH: London. Parents from Ayios Theodoros and Kambia.
MARITAL STATUS: Married.
CHILDREN: Kyri, Andreas.
SCHOOLS/COLLEGE: Salisbury School in Edmonton.
QUALIFICATIONS: ACIB (Associate of Chartered Institute of Bankers} MBA, CEMAP, CEFA.
HOBBIES AND INTERESTS: Football, cinema and reading.
PERSONAL PROFILE: Chairman of Elliniki Kypriaki Estia in Birmingham since march 2005, formerly Area Manager of Bank of Cyprus in Birmingham between 1993-2004. Financial Advisor and Director of Thomas Anthony Financial Services.

PETER NICANDROS KONIOTES

TV Snooker Referee

DATE OF BIRTH: 19-Apr-1933
PLACE OF BIRTH: London. Father Leandros Koniotes from Konia Paphos.
MARITAL STATUS: Married to Iris, London, Hairdressing.
CHILDREN: Tina, Photographic Industry. Anita, Full time Mother.
SCHOOLS/COLLEGE: Tottenham County School, Pitmans College.
QUALIFICATIONS: RSA Advanced Bookkeeping, Shorthand & Typing, Business studies. GCSE Modern Greek 1997.
HOBBIES AND INTERESTS: Snooker, quizzes, DIY, fitness and antiques.
PERSONAL PROFILE: Owner of two Snooker Clubs, active snooker Referee at many TV Tournaments 1975/92. Now retired. Helped local Advocacy Group. Raised money for Cancer Research by swimming.

PHILLIP ROY KONIOTES

Built the largest tricycle in the world, 24 seats, to raise money for charity, in Guinness Book Of Records 1998

DATE OF BIRTH: 13-May-1949
PLACE OF BIRTH: London. Father from Konia Paphos.
MARITAL STATUS: Married to Linda Valerie (née King), Personal Assistant.
SCHOOLS/COLLEGE: Belmont Secondary Modern, Tottenham County, Tottenham Technical College.
QUALIFICATIONS: 4 GCE, A Levels, HND & Endorsements Structural Engineering.
HOBBIES AND INTERESTS: Scuba diving, cycling, travel to Polar regions.
PERSONAL PROFILE: Director of Normanshire Building Co Ltd. Owner of office buildings. Support Cystic Fibrosis Trust. Built the largest tricycle in the world, 24 seats, to raise money for charity, in Guinness Book Of Records 1998. Gives talks on Artic dog sledding, scuba diving and travel.

UK

MARIA (AGHABABAIE) KORIPAS
Opera Performer

DATE OF BIRTH: 08-Sep-1957
PLACE OF BIRTH: London.
Father from Koma Tou Yialou;
Mother from Rizokarpasso.
MARITAL STATUS: Married
to Hassan Aghababaie, Iran,
Sculptor.
CHILDREN: Arian, Nikian.
SCHOOLS/COLLEGE: Star
Cross School, Laban Centre
London.
PERSONAL PROFILE: Performed in over 20 major
productions with the English National Opera as dancer
and actress. Also danced in Parsifal (Royal Opera)
and Le Boheme (Royal Albert Hall). Her work for the
BBC includes WOZZEC with the English National
Opera. Wives and Daughters and the film Verdi with
the English National Opera. In 1998 Maria created the
Performance Studies Dance Programme for Birkbeck
College, Univesity Of London and continues her work as
educator and director of these courses.

CHAS K. KOSHI
Produced the music score For Sky TV's
new Agatha Christie movie

DATE OF BIRTH: 03-Feb-1962
PLACE OF BIRTH: London.
Parents from Nicosia.
MARITAL STATUS: Single.
CHILDREN: Sophia,
Christopher, Theo, All at School.
SCHOOLS/COLLEGE:
Haringey Junior Stationers.
Tottenham Technical College,
Royal Trinity Music College.
QUALIFICATIONS: A Levels in
Art and Technical Drawing/Pianoforte Grades, 1, 2, 3, 4, 5.
MEMBERSHIPS: MCPs, Pamra Musician's Union.
PERSONAL PROFILE: Musical Pop Producer/
Songwriter, plays in the Greek Cypriot band Spartacus.
Working with Yioryos, Yusuf Islams son latest Album
and produced the music score for Sky Tvs new Agatha
Christie movie.

NICOS KOTSIAMANIS
Sculptor works include a colossal
bronze statue of Archbishop Makarios
for the precinct of Archbishops Palace,
Nicosia

DATE OF BIRTH: 29-Jul-1946
PLACE OF BIRTH: Morphou.
MARITAL STATUS: Married to
Veronica.
CHILDREN: Charalambous,
Computers. Alexandros,
Student.
SCHOOLS/COLLEGE: East
Ham Polytechnic, Byam Show
School of Art. Royal Society of
British Sculptors.
QUALIFICATIONS: Dip in Art & Design; LDN
Certificate in Art; Postgraduate in Art.
HONOURS/AWARDS: Gold Cross of Thyateira.
HOBBIES AND INTERESTS: Theatre, politics and
athletics.
PERSONAL PROFILE: President of the Morphou
District Association. Former Secretary to the National
Federation of Cypriots. Sculptor and painter. Has had
exhibitions in Cyprus, London, Athens, USA, Mansfield.
Notable works include a colossal bronze statue of
Archbishop Makarios for the precinct of Archbishops
Palace, Nicosia. Also statue of President Kennedy for the
Kennedy Centre in Boston.

KLEANTHIS GEORGIOU KOTSIOFIDES
Artist

DATE OF BIRTH: 04-Nov-1939
PLACE OF BIRTH: Larnaca.
MARITAL STATUS: Married to
Christina, Egypt, Housewife.
CHILDREN: George, Journalist.
John, Retail.
SCHOOLS/COLLEGE:
Commercial Lyceum of
Pedhoulas and Anotati
Emporiki, Athens.
PERSONAL PROFILE: Worked
for the Bank of Cyprus (London) Ltd as Manager of
the main branch at Charlotte Street. Wrote a specialist
Glossary of Business Terms (English-Greek, Greek
English) Dictionary- Art exhibition at Gallery K and
shortlisted for the Bank Of Cyprus Art Award 1993.
Joint painting exhibition with Renos Lavithis at the
Hellenic Centre London.

UK

CONSTANTINA KOULLA
Creative Director at Eve Magazine

DATE OF BIRTH: 01-Oct-1969
PLACE OF BIRTH: London. Father from Rizokarpasso; Mother from Gerani.
MARITAL STATUS: Single.
SCHOOLS/COLLEGE: Southall School for Girls, Woodhouse Sixth Form College, Middlesex University.
QUALIFICATIONS: 9 O Levels, 3 A Levels. BA (Honours) Graphic Design.
HOBBIES AND INTERESTS: Music and travel.
PERSONAL PROFILE: Creative Director at Eve Magazine, BBC Worldwide.

JASON KOUMAS
Professional Footballer plays for Wigan FC in The Premiership

DATE OF BIRTH: 25-Sep-1979
PLACE OF BIRTH: Wrexham. Parents from Paralimni.
MARITAL STATUS: Single.
SCHOOLS/COLLEGE: Mosslands.
QUALIFICATIONS: 6 GCSEs. Professional Footballer.
MEMBERSHIPS: P. F. A Professional Football Association.
HONOURS/AWARDS: Echo Player of the Year, Tranmere Player of the Year and Top Goal Scorer. Welsh International.
HOBBIES AND INTERESTS: Snooker and golf.
PERSONAL PROFILE: Welsh International, was playing for West Bromwich Albion. Transferred from Tranmere Rovers, reportedly for £2 million then transferred to Wigan for 6 Million Pounds where he now plays. Does charity work for children's hospitals.

NINOS KOUMETTOU
Treasurer and Executive Member of the National Federation of Cypriots in UK

DATE OF BIRTH: 04-Oct-1952
PLACE OF BIRTH: Kormakitis, near Kyrenia.
MARITAL STATUS: Married to Aliki.
CHILDREN: Yiannis, Marita and Vasilia.
SCHOOLS/COLLEGE: English School, Nicosia.
QUALIFICATIONS: Chartered Accountant FCA.
HOBBIES AND INTERESTS: Shooting, swimming and football.
PERSONAL PROFILE: Chairman of Independent Greek Schools of London. Former Chairman of Union of Independent Maronites in UK. Treasurer and Executive Member of the National Federation of Cypriots in UK. Founder member of the Association of Cypriot Qualified Accountants.

IACOVOS KOUMI
Chief Executive of Bank of Cyprus UK

DATE OF BIRTH: 02-Apr-1957
PLACE OF BIRTH: London Father from Sotira, Mother from Achna.
MARITAL STATUS: Married to Fiona.
CHILDREN: Sophia, Alexander.
SCHOOLS/COLLEGE: Wood Green School. University of Warwick.
QUALIFICATIONS: First Class Honours Degree in Mathematics.
HOBBIES AND INTERESTS: Football, Reading and Cypriot Culture.
PERSONAL PROFILE: Iacovos Koumi is an experienced banking and finance professional currently Chief Executive of Bank of Cyprus UK. Trustee of Exposure Organisation Ltd a registered charity that gives young people a voice. Helped his brother Andreas, author of The Cypriot to research and publish the novel.

UK

MAGGIE (MARGARET) KOUMI
Founding Editor, 'Hello' Magazine

DATE OF BIRTH: 15-Jul-1942
PLACE OF BIRTH: London, England. Father from Kilanemos ; Mother from Koma Tou Yialou.
MARITAL STATUS: Married to Ramon Sola, Spanish, Artist.
SCHOOLS/COLLEGE: Buckingham Gate, Victoria, London SW1.
QUALIFICATIONS: GCEs in English Language, Literature, French, Shorthand and typing.
HONOURS/AWARDS: None personally, but Media Awards for Magazine.
HOBBIES AND INTERESTS: Reading (and tidying up!).
PERSONAL PROFILE: Former Editor of 'Hello' Magazine. Previous Positions: Editor 19 Magazine. Managing Editor: Practical Parenting, Practical Health.

PETER KOUMIS
Architect/Partner in the Architectural Practice Vivendi Architects

DATE OF BIRTH: 12-Sep-1973
PLACE OF BIRTH: London Father from Leonarisso, Mother From Komi Kebir.
MARITAL STATUS: Single.
SCHOOLS/COLLEGE: Southgate. De Montford University and Southbank University.
QUALIFICATIONS: BA, DIP ARCH.
HOBBIES AND INTERESTS: Football, Travelling and films.
PERSONAL PROFILE: Peter Koumis is a Partner in the Architectural Practice Vivendi Architects who work with major property companies.

DEMETRIOUS KOUNNIS
Accountant/Philanthropist

DATE OF BIRTH: 30-Jun-1939
PLACE OF BIRTH: Kalopsida, Famagusta.
MARITAL STATUS: Married to Evelyn from Isle of Wight.
CHILDREN: Gary and Constandinos.
SCHOOLS/COLLEGE: Famagusta Gymnasium, Chiswick College.
HONOURS/AWARDS: Fellow of the International Accountants, Fellow of the Authorised and Public Accountants.
HOBBIES AND INTERESTS: Swimming and business.
PERSONAL PROFILE: Started Kounnis Freeman Accountants in 1961. Chairman now in Kounnis and Partners PLLC. Formed Kounnis Brokers in 1970 and owns Kounnis Group PLC Property Co.

NICK KOUNOUPIAS
Coordinator for the Lobby of Cyprus

DATE OF BIRTH: 01-Jan-1963
PLACE OF BIRTH: London. Father from Klirou; Mother from Akanthou.
MARITAL STATUS: Single.
CHILDREN: Sophia, Alexander.
SCHOOLS/COLLEGE: St Pauls School, London. Queen Mary College, London University.
QUALIFICATIONS: LLB (Honours). Solicitor.
MEMBERSHIPS: Amnesty International.
HOBBIES AND INTERESTS: Music, European literature and human Rights.
PERSONAL PROFILE: Solicitor specialising in copyright law. Presently employed by the MCPS/PRS Music Alliance as the head of litigation and anti-piracy operations. These bodies are music industry collecting societies responsible for the collection of royalties on behalf of songwriters and music publishers whenever their songs are exploited. Nick is the Coordinator for the Lobby of Cyprus.

Maggie Koumi is the founding editor of Hello Magazine

CHRISTOS KOUPPARIS
Accountant, Ex-Chairman of EKEKA

DATE OF BIRTH: 14-Feb-1926
PLACE OF BIRTH: Lefkoniko.
MARITAL STATUS: Married to Elizabeth from Achna.
CHILDREN: Eroulla, Interior Designer. Katie, Computer Operator.
SCHOOLS/COLLEGE: Lefkoniko High School; Foulks Lynch, Tooting Broadway College, London.
QUALIFICATIONS: Chartered Certified Accountant.
MEMBERSHIPS: British Institute of Management, Certified and Corporate Accountants.
HOBBIES AND INTERESTS: Reading and studying, Cypriot Community Problems.
PERSONAL PROFILE: Accountant - had practice in London for 30 years. Founding member and ex Chairman of. EKEKA. General Secretary of the National Cypriot Committee 1952-1959. Chairman of the Repatriated Cypriots 1991-1996 in Cyprus. Published a book - 50 Years of Contribution for the Cypriot Cause.

DR LUKE KOUPPARIS
General Practitioner

DATE OF BIRTH: 05-Jan-1971
PLACE OF BIRTH: London. Parents (Lefkonico).
MARITAL STATUS: Single.
SCHOOLS/COLLEGE: St. Bartholomews Hospital Medical School.
QUALIFICATIONS: BSc MBBS FRCA, DFFP, MRCGP.
HOBBIES AND INTERESTS: IT.
PERSONAL PROFILE: General Practitioner.

SIMON KOUPPARIS
Secretary of Lefkoniko Association, and in the Executive Committee of the National Federation of Cypriots

DATE OF BIRTH: 23-Mar-1941
PLACE OF BIRTH: Lefkoniko.
MARITAL STATUS: Married to Linda from London.
CHILDREN: Luke, Anaesthetist; Anthony, Surgeon.
SCHOOLS/COLLEGE: High School Lefkoniko, University of North London.
QUALIFICATIONS: BSc (Honours) Dip. Arch (UNL).
MEMBERSHIPS: Royal Institute of British Architects (RIBA).
HOBBIES AND INTERESTS: Golf, swimming, walking, reading and politics.
PERSONAL PROFILE: Architect with own practice called Koupparis Associates in Kentish Town. Secretary of Lefkoniko Association, and in the Executive Committee of the National Federation of Cypriots. Also Vice-Chairman of the Democratic Rally in UK.

KYRIAKOS KOUREAS
Youngest player to represent Cyprus at Football

DATE OF BIRTH: 06-Sep-1947
PLACE OF BIRTH: Famagusta. Father from Yialloussa; Mother from Limassol.
CHILDREN: One son.
SCHOOLS/COLLEGE: Famagusta Gymnasium.
HONOURS/AWARDS: 36 International Caps for Cyprus.
HOBBIES AND INTERESTS: Football, basketball and swimming.
PERSONAL PROFILE: Footballer, played for New Salamis in Cyprus Ethnikos and Olympiakos in Greece. Also represented American All Stars. Youngest player to represent Cyprus, played in European Cup Games, played in UEFA against Spurs in the Cypriot Football League in UK, managed the League team, New Salamis and Anorthosis.

UK

ANDREW KOUROUSHI
Secretary of Omonia Youth UK

DATE OF BIRTH: 28-Feb-1969
PLACE OF BIRTH: Ayios Andronikos.
MARITAL STATUS: Married.
PERSONAL PROFILE: Omonia Youth Football Club Under 18's Manager & Hon. Club Secretary.

MARIOS KOUSOULOU
Labour Councillor for 4 years and Labour Group leader for one year

DATE OF BIRTH: 10-Oct-1952
PLACE OF BIRTH: Lefkoniko.
MARITAL STATUS: Married to Janet, Enfield, Lecturer.
CHILDREN: Stuart, Retail. Emma, Student.
SCHOOLS/COLLEGE: St Davids Hornsey. Tottenham College of Technology, University of North London.
QUALIFICATIONS: LLB and degree in Building. MCIOB.
MEMBERSHIPS: Institute of Builders, Institute of Clerk of Works.
HOBBIES AND INTERESTS: Squash player.
PERSONAL PROFILE: Chief Clerk of Works, Haringey Council. Labour Councillor for 4 years and Labour Group leader for one year. Constituency Chairman for two years, Press Officer for four years. Justice of the Peace - Magistrate since 1990.

NICOLA KOUSSERTARI
Singer

DATE OF BIRTH: 24-Nov-1984
PLACE OF BIRTH: Cyprus.
MARITAL STATUS: Single.
SCHOOLS/COLLEGE: Bohunt School, Southampton University.
QUALIFICATIONS: BA Music Degree, National Diploma Vocals.
HONOURS/AWARDS: Excellence in Music.
HOBBIES AND INTERESTS: music, singing and dancing, some sport.
PERSONAL PROFILE: Nicola recorded the song Who am I and appeared in the New Years Festival in Nicosia has helped out at the Orpthus Centre, people with disabilities helping to put on a show. Also works as a promoter putting on gigs.

CHRISTOS KOUTSOFTAS
Chairman of Aradippou Association

DATE OF BIRTH: 11-Aug-1960
PLACE OF BIRTH: Aradippou, Cyprus.
MARITAL STATUS: Married to Maria, Cyprus, Legal secretary.
CHILDREN: Andrea, Demetris.
SCHOOLS/COLLEGE: Makarios III Secondary School, Larnaca, Cyprus.
QUALIFICATIONS: Graduate of Classical Studies (was awarded a University Scholarship).
MEMBERSHIPS: Member of the Board of The Cypriot Community.
HOBBIES AND INTERESTS: Reading travelling, sport and socialising.
PERSONAL PROFILE: President of the Aradippou Association also responsible for a memorial service for Cypriot war heroes, which is conducted in August every year.

GEORGE KOUTTOUKIS
Top Student McGraw Hill Economics Award Indiana University, Pennsylvania 1991

DATE OF BIRTH: 20-May-1968
PLACE OF BIRTH: Zodia.
MARITAL STATUS: Married to Maria, Ergates.
CHILDREN: Chrysostomos, Panayiota.
SCHOOLS/COLLEGE: Indiana University of Pennsylvania and Louisianna State University.
QUALIFICATIONS: BA, BSc MSc.
MEMBERSHIPS: ARLA, UKALA.
HONOURS/AWARDS: Top Student McGraw Hill Economics Award Indiana University, Pennsylvania 1991.
HOBBIES AND INTERESTS: Football, Reading.
PERSONAL PROFILE: George Kouttoukis is a Director of Property Centre (London)Ltd in Southgate.

UK

IOANNIS-METAXAS MENICOU KOUVAROS
Honorary President, Limnia Association

DATE OF BIRTH: 11-Feb-1941
PLACE OF BIRTH: Limnia.
MARITAL STATUS: Married to Victoria, Gypsos, Teacher.
CHILDREN: Menicos, accountant. Elena, Student.
SCHOOLS/COLLEGE: Famagusta Gymnasium, Kingsway College, Hackney College, Elephant & Castle College.
HONOURS/AWARDS: Democratic Rally for long service to the party. Medal for participation in the EOKA struggle 1955 and 1959 awarded by the President of the Republic of Cyprus.
HOBBIES AND INTERESTS: Football, swimming and politics.
PERSONAL PROFILE: Limnia Association. Honorary President of the Limnia Association Member of the Secretariat of the National Federation of Cypriots.

MENICOS IOANNIS KOUVAROS
Served as Youth President of the World Federation of Overseas Cypriots and member of the Secretariat of the National Fed of Cypriots UK

DATE OF BIRTH: 29-Mar-1978
PLACE OF BIRTH: London. Parents from Limnia and Gypsou.
MARITAL STATUS: Single.
SCHOOLS/COLLEGE: L. S. E. Queen Mary College.
QUALIFICATIONS: B. Sc. MSc.
HOBBIES AND INTERESTS: Current affairs. Impressionist and post-impressionist art, tennis and long distance running.
PERSONAL PROFILE: Associate at Pricewaterhouse Coopers. Menicos served as Youth President of the World Federation of Overseas Cypriots and member of the Secretariat of the National Fed of Cypriots UK also been Youth secretary of both Gypsos and Limnia Associations.

PHOTOS KOUZOUPIS
Chairman of Hazelwood Greek School. Member of the Executive Committee of the Greek Parents Association

DATE OF BIRTH: 14-May-1954
PLACE OF BIRTH: Famagusta.
MARITAL STATUS: Married to Chrisanthi.
CHILDREN: Three sons and three daughters.
SCHOOLS/COLLEGE: 1st Gymnasium, Famagusta. Willesden College. University College London.
QUALIFICATIONS: BSc in Architecture.
HOBBIES AND INTERESTS: Reading Music and football.
PERSONAL PROFILE: Former Secretary of OESEKA, Organiser Secretary of Akel, Member of the Secretariat of the National Federation of Cypriots UK. Chairman of Hazelwood Greek School. Member of the Executive Committee of the Greek Parents Association. Executive Member of the Enfield Cypriot Association.

ALKIS KRITIKOS
Actor Appeared on TV in The Cuckoo Waltz with Diane Keen, and The Adventures of Sherlock Holmes with Jeremy Brett

PLACE OF BIRTH: Limassol.
MARITAL STATUS: Single.
SCHOOLS/COLLEGE: Lanition Gymnasium Limassol, Isleworth Polytechnic, Drama School Delyon in Richmond.
MEMBERSHIPS: Equity & Directors Guild of GB.
HOBBIES AND INTERESTS: Music.
PERSONAL PROFILE: Actor, Director at Several Theatres all over the UK. Appeared on TV in The Cuckoo Waltz with Diane Keen, and The Adventures of Sherlock Holmes with Jeremy Brett. Also appeared in Connie with Stephanie Beacham, and in the James Bond film For Your Eyes Only with Roger Moore.

UK

ANDREW KROKOU
Labour party chair of Hornsey and Wood Green Labour Party

DATE OF BIRTH: 28-Oct-1947
PLACE OF BIRTH: Camden. Parents from Eptakomi.
MARITAL STATUS: Married to Angela Greatley, UK, former leader of Haringey Council.
CHILDREN: Thomas, Leisure. Katherine, Student.
SCHOOLS/COLLEGE: Newcastle University, London University.
QUALIFICATIONS: BA. MA. (Urban Education). PGCE.
MEMBERSHIPS: Trustee Tottenham Grammar School Foundation. NUT Labour party.
HOBBIES AND INTERESTS: Opera, reading and Tottenham Hotspur.
PERSONAL PROFILE: Assistant HeadTeacher, Member Haringey Council 1971-1978, Chair of Finance Committee, re-elected May 2002, Chair of Alexandra Palace and Park Trustees. Chair of Governors Somerset School and Labour party chair of Hornsey and Wood Green Labour Party, Chair of Haringey Labour party local government committee.

NICHOLAS KTORI
Assistant Director in Corporate Finance at Ernst & Young, Birmingham

DATE OF BIRTH: 23-Apr-1967
PLACE OF BIRTH: London. Parents from Rizokarpasso.
MARITAL STATUS: Married to Sarah from Birmingham, a Chartered Accountant.
SCHOOLS/COLLEGE: K. E. VI Camphill Boys, Birmingham, Sheffield University.
QUALIFICATIONS: BA (Honours) Economics and Statistics. Chartered Accountant.
HOBBIES AND INTERESTS: Football, current affairs and travel.
PERSONAL PROFILE: Assistant Director in Corporate Finance at Ernst & Young, Birmingham. Specialising in Private Equity Transactions.

THEO KYPRI
British Trampoline Champion

PLACE OF BIRTH: London. Father from Ormidhia; Mother from Palekythron.
MARITAL STATUS: Single.
SCHOOLS/COLLEGE: Highbury Grove.
QUALIFICATIONS: 2 O levels, 2 CSEs.
MEMBERSHIPS: Member of Register of British Stunt Performers.
HONOURS/AWARDS: Winner of Sports Personality of the Year Award in Islington.
HOBBIES AND INTERESTS: Reading, backgammon, guitar and music.
PERSONAL PROFILE: Former British Trampoline Champion 8th in the World Championships. Holder of ten national titles. Represented Cyprus at the 1999 World Trampoline Championships. Professional Stunt Performer in The Film & TV Industry for five years, credits include: Tomb Raider, Mortal Kombat, 102 Dalmations, Harry Potter and Entrapment.

ERMIS KYPRIANOU
President St Barnabas Church in Wood Green

DATE OF BIRTH: 14-May-1939
PLACE OF BIRTH: Dhali Village, Nicosia.
MARITAL STATUS: Married to Maria from Rizokarpaso, Famagusta.
CHILDREN: Nicos, Helen, Cypriella, All Company Directors.
SCHOOLS/COLLEGE: Emporikon Lykeion, Nicosia.
QUALIFICATIONS: Fellow Hotel & Catering Institute.
MEMBERSHIPS: Institute of Directors, Confederation of British Industry, Essex Chamber of Commerce.
HOBBIES AND INTERESTS: Reading and Religious Studies.
PERSONAL PROFILE: President St Barnabas Church in Wood Green. Owner of Heybridge Hotel, Essex for a number of years.

UK

KYPROS KYPRIANOU
Chairman of Omonia Youth Football Club/Chief Executive Officer of Ryman Group Ltd

PLACE OF BIRTH: London parents from Kornos
MARITAL STATUS: Married.
CHILDREN: Three sons.
SCHOOLS/COLLEGE: Alexandra Park. City University.
QUALIFICATIONS: BSc in Acturial Science. ACIB (Qualified Banker).
HOBBIES AND INTERESTS: Football, especially watching his sons play.
PERSONAL PROFILE: Played Football in the Cypriot League UK. Played and captained Omonia and the League team. Also played for AEL and New Salamis. Chairman of Omonia Youth Football Club. Former Bank of Cyprus (UK) Departmental Head of Corporate Banking. Now Chief Executive Officer of Ryman Group Ltd.

LOUKIS KYPRIANOU
Magician

DATE OF BIRTH: 15-May-1931
PLACE OF BIRTH: Analyondas.
MARITAL STATUS: Married to Sophie, Alexandria, Egypt.
CHILDREN: Antony, Travel. Kypro, Driving Instructor. Ted, Essential Safety Products.
SCHOOLS/COLLEGE: Commercial School of Samuel. The Magic Circle of England.
QUALIFICATIONS: O and A Levels in English.
HONOURS/AWARDS: Honourable Citizen of St Pancras.
HOBBIES AND INTERESTS: Football.
PERSONAL PROFILE: Magician, Member and co-Founder of St Andrews Greek Church and School and of St Michael Church and School of Hendon. General Secretary of Cyprus Brotherhood Association in the 60s. Involved with Greek Cypriot Football League with club Anemos, and was also a member of the Committee of the Greek Cypriot Football League in the UK.

ROBERT KYPRIANOU
Chief Executive Officer of AXA Framlington and Head of Securities Investment Management of AXA IM

PLACE OF BIRTH: Parents from Trikomo and Ayios Georgios, Famagusta.
CHILDREN: four boys.
SCHOOLS/COLLEGE: William Ellis. Oxford University.
QUALIFICATIONS: MA in Philosophy, Politics and Economics.
MEMBERSHIPS: Member of the Advisory Board of the Global Fixed Income Institute and of the Bank of Englands Fixed Income Committee.
HOBBIES AND INTERESTS: Seafood, science fiction and Liverpool FC.
PERSONAL PROFILE: Robert Kyprianou is the Chief Executive Officer of AXA Framlington and Head of Securities Investment Management of AXA IM.

ANDREW KYRIACOU
Pop Artist Drummer & Vocalist for 80s' pop band Modern Romance who had several top 10 hits

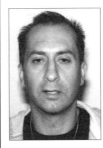

DATE OF BIRTH: 18-Apr-1958
PLACE OF BIRTH: London. Father from Assia, Mother from Rizokarpasso.
MARITAL STATUS: Single.
CHILDREN: Stephanie and Natalie.
SCHOOLS/COLLEGE: William Foster School.
QUALIFICATIONS: O Levels and CSEs.
HONOURS/AWARDS: Gold & Silver Discs for Record Sales, including no 1's.
HOBBIES AND INTERESTS: Arsenal Season Ticket Holder, Reading, Current Affairs, playing with his children, Films & Music.
PERSONAL PROFILE: Drummer & Vocalist for 80s' pop band Modern Romance. Currently Gigging with new line-up of Modern Romance. Session work includes: Boy George, Angie Gold, John Themis, Craig McGlaughlin, David Austin, also a drummer with the Spartacus.

UK

ANDREW KYRIACOU
Secretary of SOLEA Association in UK/
Senior Engineering Specialist with Bechtel

DATE OF BIRTH: 26-Oct-1958
PLACE OF BIRTH: London. Parents from Petra, Soleas and Skarinou, Larnaca.
MARITAL STATUS: Married to Ekaterini, an Optometrist, from Ktima.
CHILDREN: Demetrios, Marios and Sotirios.
SCHOOLS/COLLEGE: The English School, Nicosia, Finchley Manor Hill, Barnet College, Aston University.
QUALIFICATIONS: BSc, MSc Chemical Engineering.
HOBBIES AND INTERESTS: Collects antiquarian books about Cyprus, and Byzantine music.
PERSONAL PROFILE: Senior Engineering Specialist with Bechtel, Secretary of Solea Association in the UK.

ARTEMI KYRIACOU
Invited by the British Council to hold masterclasses in photography in Kiev (ukraine) and to represent Creative UK at the yearly held European Day

DATE OF BIRTH: 23-Apr-1969
PLACE OF BIRTH: Famagusta.
MARITAL STATUS: Married.
CHILDREN: One Child.
SCHOOLS/COLLEGE: South Manchester College, Mid-Chesire College, Blackpool & Fylde College.
QUALIFICATIONS: British Institute of Professional Photographers PQE, HND, Photography.
HOBBIES AND INTERESTS: Food, Cooking, Walking, Travelling.
PERSONAL PROFILE: Company director of Gustoimages Ltd incorporating Gusto Gallery since 1999. In 2005 was invited by the British Council to hold masterclasses in photography in Kiev (ukraine) and to represent Creative UK at the yearly held European Day.

EKATERINI KYRIACOU
Optometrist

DATE OF BIRTH: 31-Mar-1963
PLACE OF BIRTH: Ktima.
MARITAL STATUS: Married to Andrew Kyriacou, London(father from Petra, Mother from Skarinou). Chemical Engineer.
CHILDREN: Demetrios, Mario, Sotirios.
SCHOOLS/COLLEGE: Rokesly Junior School, Hornsey High School For Girls, City University.
QUALIFICATIONS: BSc. MC Optom.
MEMBERSHIPS: Member of the British College of Optometry.
HOBBIES AND INTERESTS: Swimming and walking.
PERSONAL PROFILE: Optometrist.

GEORGE KYRIACOU
Founder of Gallery K/Sculptor

DATE OF BIRTH: 13-Mar-1940
PLACE OF BIRTH: Exo-Metochi, Nicosia.
MARITAL STATUS: Married to Maria (Ritsa), kakopetria, Art.
CHILDREN: Panikos, Diplomat. Andreas, Marine Inspector. Lefkos, Architect. Eleni, student.
SCHOOLS/COLLEGE: Chelsea School Of Art, Sorbonne, Paris Polytechnic Of Central London.
QUALIFICATIONS: Teacher, Sculptor, Art Administrator.
MEMBERSHIPS: Hellenic Centre (Steering Committee, Chairman 1988-1992).
HOBBIES AND INTERESTS: Art collecting, including studio ceramics.
PERSONAL PROFILE: Participated in the Liberation Of Cyprus against British Colonial Rule 1955-1959, arrested and detained as political prisoner. Co founder of the Political Party Disy. Was an Art Teacher in secondary education and worked. as a Cultural Officer at the Ministry of Education and Culture. Director of Gallery K in Hampstead.

UK

KYRIAKOS KYRIACOU
Solicitor

DATE OF BIRTH: 07-Jan-1969
PLACE OF BIRTH: London.
Parents from Nikitari.
MARITAL STATUS: Married to
Maria, a Teacher.
SCHOOLS/COLLEGE:
Riverston School, Erith College,
University of London.
QUALIFICATIONS: LL. B
(Honours) Solicitor.
MEMBERSHIPS:
Commonwealth Lawyers Association.
HOBBIES AND INTERESTS: Writing fiction and poetry.
PERSONAL PROFILE: Partner in Langshaw Kyriacou
Solicitors. Has had a number of High Profile cases
reported in the Press, including The Times, Evening
Standard, Private Eye. Also interviewed for Business
Monthly and Law Society Gazette re: Lawyer in the news.

DR PANAYIOTIS KYRIACOU
Assistant Dean, Senior Lecturer,
Programme Director in Bio Medical
Engineering at the University of London

DATE OF BIRTH: 09-Jan-1969
PLACE OF BIRTH: Famagusta,
Cyprus.
SCHOOLS/COLLEGE: Medical
College St. Bartholomews
Hospital. University of London,
University of Western Ontario,
Canada.
QUALIFICATIONS: BESc, MSc,
PhD, CEng, CSci, CPhys, MIPEM,
MIET, SMIEEE, MInstP.
MEMBERSHIPS: Chair of the Physiological
Measurement group, Member of Science, Engineering
and Technology.
HONOURS/AWARDS: Project Report, Certificate of
Merit Awarded by MDS Health Group Ltd, Semi-finalist
Project Thesis Presentations.
HOBBIES AND INTERESTS: Reading, Cooking and
Gardening.
PERSONAL PROFILE: Assistant Dean, Senior Lecturer,
Programme Director in Bio Medical Engineering at the
University of London.

PAUL KYRIACOU
Youngest ever Mayor of London Borough
of Southwark

PLACE OF BIRTH: Born 1973
in London Mother from Ayios
Amvrosios
SCHOOLS/COLLEGE: St
Francis Xavier. Vauxhall College
and Southbank University.
HONOURS/AWARDS: Freedom
of the City of London.
HOBBIES AND INTERESTS:
Sports, socialising, motoring and
fine dining.
PERSONAL PROFILE: City Councillor 2002 to date
Cabinet member and Mayor of Southwark.

RITSA KYRIACOU
Founder of Gallery K

PLACE OF BIRTH: Kakopetria.
MARITAL STATUS: Married to
George Kyriacou, Exo Metochi,
Sculptor.
CHILDREN: Lefkos, Architect.
Eleni, Student.
QUALIFICATIONS: Dip
in Modern Art, DIP in fine
Decorative Art.
HOBBIES AND INTERESTS:
Reading and travelling.
PERSONAL PROFILE: One of the founding members
of The Hellenic Centre, member of the Hellenic
Community Trust, Member of the Womens Committee
of Estia. Was curator of exhibitions at the Hellenic
Centre. Co founder of Gallery K in Hampstead and in
Cyprus. Published books about Art.

Approximately 300 part
time Greek schools operate
in the UK.

UK

SOPHIA KYRIACOU

Broadcast Graphic Designer for the BBC. Programmes to date include 10 o'clock News, Weekend Watchdog, Healthcheck

DATE OF BIRTH: 12-Mar-1969
PLACE OF BIRTH: London. Father from Phlasou; Mother from Livadhia.
MARITAL STATUS: Single.
SCHOOLS/COLLEGE: Skinners Company's School For Girls, Camberwell College of Art, Central St Martins College of Art & Design.
QUALIFICATIONS: BA. MA.
HONOURS/AWARDS: High Commendation in 1993 by the Royal Society of Arts for her short animated film A Different Point Of View which was screened in the National Film Theatre.
HOBBIES AND INTERESTS: Music, Produces own dance music. Squash and socialising.
PERSONAL PROFILE: Broadcast Graphic Designer for the BBC. Programmes to date include 10 o'clock News, Weekend Watchdog, Healthcheck, World Liquid News. Redesigned the entire Liquid News Programme on BBC3. Other titles include The Teaching Awards, In Stephen's Name (Black Britain Special), Flying Gardener, Crimewatch.

ALEC KYRIAKIDES

Microbiologist/Member of the Advisor Committee on the Microbiological Safety of Food (ACMSF),

DATE OF BIRTH: 29-Jan-1965
PLACE OF BIRTH: South Shields, County Durham. Father and Grandparents from Pano Deftera.
MARITAL STATUS: Married to Susan, a Teaching Assistant, from Southend-on-Sea.
CHILDREN: Amelia and Oliver.
SCHOOLS/COLLEGE: Shoeburyness Comprehensive School, Surrey University.
QUALIFICATIONS: BSc (Honours) Microbiology.
MEMBERSHIPS: Member of the Institute of Food Science and Technology (MIFST).
HOBBIES AND INTERESTS: Book writing, football and decorating.
PERSONAL PROFILE: Head of Product Safety for Sainsbury's Supermarkets Ltd, Member of the Advisor Committee on the Microbiological Safety of Food (ACMSF), Author of books on E. coli, Listeria, Salmonella and Clostridium Botulinum.

JOHN KYRIAKIDES

Trustee of Radio Marathon, Director LGR

DATE OF BIRTH: 13-Jun-1944
PLACE OF BIRTH: Famagusta.
MARITAL STATUS: Married to Helen, UK Cypriot, Housewife.
CHILDREN: Pamela, Lisa, alexander, All at School.
SCHOOLS/COLLEGE: Lyceum in Famagusta, Norwood Technical College, London.
QUALIFICATIONS: Certificate in Radiotelegraphy, Certificate in Telecoms & Electronics.
MEMBERSHIPS: Federation of Small Business.
HONOURS/AWARDS: 1st Class Marine Prize in Radio Telegraphy.
HOBBIES AND INTERESTS: Gardening, radio, and electronics telecoms.
PERSONAL PROFILE: Property Developer. Chairman of SAEA; Society of Children with Special Needs. Ex-Chairman of first Multi -ethnic Radio Station in Britain (Spectrum Radio). Director of London Greek Radio. Trustee of Radio Marathon Body. Ex Governor of Hawkswood School for Deaf Children. Also publisher of the Greek Directory.

ROBERT KYRIAKIDES

Solicitor/Author of the books Master Conman (Head Press) and A Concise Guide to Energy in the United Kingdom

DATE OF BIRTH: 24-Jul-1949
PLACE OF BIRTH: London. Grandparents from Kato Amiandos.
MARITAL STATUS: Married to Patricia Johnson, England, Nurse.
CHILDREN: Matthew, Richard, Both Students.
SCHOOLS/COLLEGE: George Greens Grammar School. Manchester University, Liverpool College of Law.
QUALIFICATIONS: LLB Solicitor.
MEMBERSHIPS: Cypriot Golf Society, International Solar Energy Society.
HOBBIES AND INTERESTS: Golf, cricket and writing.
PERSONAL PROFILE: Foundation Governor George Green's School, Solicitor and Senior Partner, Kyriakides & Braier, Chief Executive Genersys plc. Author of the books Master Conman (Head Press) and a Concise Guide to Energy in the United Kingdom.

JASON KYRIAKIDES (AKA JASON KAYE)
Quoted as being Prince Williams Favourite DJ

DATE OF BIRTH: 19-Feb-1969 **PLACE OF BIRTH:** London. Grandparents from Limassol. **MARITAL STATUS:** Single. **SCHOOLS/COLLEGE:** Southgate School. **QUALIFICATIONS:** 6 O Levels. **HONOURS/AWARDS:** Ms Dynamite- Morgan's Spiced UK Garage Awards 2001. **HOBBIES AND INTERESTS:** Watching and playing football. **PERSONAL PROFILE:** Jason Kaye club DJ and promoter. Recently quoted as being Prince William's favourite DJ. As co-promoter of Garage Nation, one of the most successful Garage club nights, he has promoted club nights in the UK, and a CD compilation series produced by Sony Music. Jason also co-owns Social Circles, an indie record label that promotes and produces UK Dance Music. The highly acclaimed track 'BOO' reached No 12 in the UK charts in June 2001.

COSTAS KYRIAKOU
Honorary Chairman of the St John Greek Orthodox Church in Hackney

DATE OF BIRTH: 20-Jun-1922 **PLACE OF BIRTH:** Komi Kebir. **MARITAL STATUS:** Married to Ioanna, from Patriki. **CHILDREN:** John, Civil Engineer. Varnava, Engineer. Kaliopi, Housewife. **PERSONAL PROFILE:** Worked as a Mechanic, now retired. Honorary Chairman of the St John Greek Orthodox Church in Hackney.

JOHN KYRIAKOU
Footballer

DATE OF BIRTH: 10-Sep-1987 **PLACE OF BIRTH:** London. Parents from London. Grandparents from Gerani and Ayia Varvara Nicosia. **HOBBIES AND INTERESTS:** Snooker, computers and music. **PERSONAL PROFILE:** Footballer, right back, was a professional at Tottenham Football Club Academy. Represented Middlesex at District Level. Also played for AEL in Cyprus.

KYRIAKOS KYRIAKOU
Fashion Designer/Celebrity clients

DATE OF BIRTH: 18-Dec-1972 **PLACE OF BIRTH:** London. Father from Pachna; Mother from Agios Loucas, Famagusta. **MARITAL STATUS:** Married. **SCHOOLS/COLLEGE:** St. Davids & St. Katherines School Hornsey, Southgate College. **PERSONAL PROFILE:** Ladies Wear Designer. Celebrity clients: Victoria Beckham, Tracy Shaw, Amanda Holden. Specialist in Corsetry. Seven years in business the Company is called Kyri.

MARIOS KYRIAZIS
Anti-Ageing Physician and Author

DATE OF BIRTH: 11-Mar-1956 **PLACE OF BIRTH:** Larnaca. **MARITAL STATUS:** Married to Stella from London. **CHILDREN:** Neoclis, at school. **SCHOOLS/COLLEGE:** Larnaca Gymnasium, University of Rome, University of London. **QUALIFICATIONS:** MD, MSc, BA, CBiol. Diploma in Geriatric Medicine. **MEMBERSHIPS:** Member of the Institute of Biology. **HOBBIES AND INTERESTS:** Medical History. **PERSONAL PROFILE:** Founder of the British Longevity Society. Anti-Ageing Physician and Author.

GEORGE KYTHREOTIS
Architect Partner in Vivendi Architects

DATE OF BIRTH: 14-Apr-1965 **PLACE OF BIRTH:** London, Grandparents from Kyrenia and Larnaca. **MARITAL STATUS:** Married to Barbro from Finland. **CHILDREN:** Gregorios, Eleni. **SCHOOLS/COLLEGE:** University of Westminster. **QUALIFICATIONS:** BA (Hons) DIP ARCH. **HOBBIES AND INTERESTS:** Films, walking dog. **PERSONAL PROFILE:** Partner in the Architectural Practice Vivendi Architects who work with major property companies.

UK

MARIOS PAMBOS LAMBIS
Barrister/Has been involved in high profile cases such as the Iraqi hijacking, appeals involving human rights and matters of disclosure

DATE OF BIRTH: 18-Nov-1964
PLACE OF BIRTH: Islington, London. Father from Ayia Fyla, Limassol; Mother from Polemidhia, Limassol.
MARITAL STATUS: Single.
SCHOOLS/COLLEGE: International School of London; Sussex University; City University.
QUALIFICATIONS: BA (Honours); Diploma in Law. Bar Vocational Course.
MEMBERSHIPS: Middle Temple, Liberty, Amnesty International, Anglo-Cypriot Lawyers Association; European Lawyers Association.
HOBBIES AND INTERESTS: Cinema, swimming and travel.
PERSONAL PROFILE: Barrister of ten years calling, specialising in criminal cases. Has been involved in high profile cases such as the Iraqi hijacking, appeals involving human rights and matters of disclosure.

PHOTIS LAMBRIANIDES
Chairman of Kalavasos Village/ Commercial Director of Olympic Holidays

DATE OF BIRTH: 27-Sep-1950
PLACE OF BIRTH: Kalavasos.
MARITAL STATUS: Married to Georgina from London. (parents from Kalavasos and Tochni).
CHILDREN: Apostolos and Elena.
SCHOOLS/COLLEGE: American Academy, Larnaca; University of Wales.
QUALIFICATIONS: BSc (Honours) Economics. Professional Certified Accountant.
HOBBIES AND INTERESTS: Travelling, walking, hiking, tennis and gardening.
PERSONAL PROFILE: Commercial Director of Olympic Holidays, major tour operator for Greece and Cyprus. Chairman of Kalavassos Village Association UK. Was on the committee of Moss Hall Greek School.

CHRISTOFIS LAMBROU
Former Vice Chairman OESEKA

DATE OF BIRTH: 23-Sep-1934
PLACE OF BIRTH: Achna.
MARITAL STATUS: Married.
CHILDREN: Four sons, one daughter.
MEMBERSHIPS: AKEL.
HOBBIES AND INTERESTS: Politics and football.
PERSONAL PROFILE: Vice Chairman of Greek Parents' Association; Secretary OESEKA for eight years; Vice Chairman OESEKA for four years.

LAMBROS LAMBROU
Solicitor/Contributor to the Arsenal Football Club Programme

DATE OF BIRTH: 07-Apr-1964
PLACE OF BIRTH: London. Parents from Achna and Kontea.
MARITAL STATUS: Married to Nadia, England.
CHILDREN: Two daughters.
SCHOOLS/COLLEGE: City University; Wolsey Hall, Oxford; Greenwich University.
QUALIFICATIONS: BA (Honours) Sociology; MA in Communications Policy.
HOBBIES AND INTERESTS: Golf, following Arsenal.
PERSONAL PROFILE: Former editor of the English Section of Parikiaki newspaper. Was London correspondent for Cyprus Weekly, and currently writes articles in the Arsenal Football Programme. Now a Solicitor and Senior Partner with YVA Solicitors.

RENOS G LAVITHIS
Artist/Designer

DATE OF BIRTH: 25-Oct-1944
PLACE OF BIRTH: Paphos, Cyprus.
MARITAL STATUS: Married to Anna, Manchester, Theatre.
CHILDREN: Niki, Theatre/ Dance.
SCHOOLS/COLLEGE: Gymnasium of Paphos); Ealing School of Art; London College of Printing.
QUALIFICATIONS: Degree in Graphic Design; postgraduate course in Typographic Design.
HOBBIES AND INTERESTS: Arts, Travelling, Golf, Books and photography.

PERSONAL PROFILE: Owner of a design/advertising/ publishing company, working for the Daily Mail from 1974 till retirement. Major occupation now is painting, including Greek themes and images. His works can be seen at the House of Lords, in private collections and Banks. Has exhibited regularly in London and Herts.

CHRISTO LAZARI
Member of the Radiomarathon Children in Need Committee/Businessman

DATE OF BIRTH: 20-May-1946
PLACE OF BIRTH: Dora.
MARITAL STATUS: Married to Maria, Dora, Company Director.
CHILDREN: Leonidas, BA Honours Economics. Nicholas, BA Honours Economics MA Property Law and Valuation. Andrie, LLB Honours. MA Property Law and Valuation.
HOBBIES AND INTERESTS: Reading.
PERSONAL PROFILE: Owner of a property company. Member of the Radiomarathon Children in Need Committee.

ATHANASIS LAZARIDES
Honorary Commissioner for the Republic of Cyprus for Bristol

DATE OF BIRTH: 19-Dec-1961
PLACE OF BIRTH: Bristol. Father from Rizokarpasso; Mother from Trikomo.
MARITAL STATUS: Married to Natalie Scott.
CHILDREN: Pavlos and Konstantino, both studying in Nicosia.
SCHOOLS/COLLEGE: Henbury School, Bristol; Birmingham Polytechnic.
QUALIFICATIONS: BA Honours Business Studies.
MEMBERSHIPS: Member of the Federation of Recruitment & Employment Services.
HOBBIES AND INTERESTS: Travel.
PERSONAL PROFILE: UK Business Development Director for Randstad Employment Bureau, the third largest employment business in the world. Honorary Commissioner for the Republic of Cyprus for Bristol, South West and South Wales. President of the Greek Orthodox Community of Bristol.

STEPHEN LAZARIDES
Photo editor of several magazines and the owner of an Art gallery in Soho well known for displaying the artists Banksy's work he is also the manager of Banksy the well known artist

DATE OF BIRTH: 03-Sep-1969
PLACE OF BIRTH: Bristol. Father from Famagusta; Mother English.
SCHOOLS/COLLEGE: Brimsham Green School. Bristol Filton Technical. College; Newcastle Polytechnic.
QUALIFICATIONS: BA Honours Media Studies.
HOBBIES AND INTERESTS: Loud music, collecting. books and graffitti.
PERSONAL PROFILE: Founder of PYMCA. a photo-library of British youth culture. Photo-editor of several magazines. The owner of an Art gallery in Soho well known for displaying the artists Banksy's work who he is the manager of.

UK

Banksy is a well known graffiti artist born in Bristol who has been able to keep his real identity secret. His manager is Stephen Lazarides of Greek Cypriot origin.

DEMETRIS LAZAROU
Member of Central Committee of AKEL (Cyprus)

DATE OF BIRTH: 05-Oct-1954
PLACE OF BIRTH: Marathovounos, Cyprus.
MARITAL STATUS: Married to Eleftheria, a Housewife, born in London.
CHILDREN: Miranda, nursery nurse. Lefteris, recruitment officer.
SCHOOLS/COLLEGE: Technical School, Famagusta; Hendon College, London; University of London.
QUALIFICATIONS: Diploma in Community Studies. In Youth Work.
MEMBERSHIPS: Various Cypriot organisations; political and professional organisations.
HOBBIES AND INTERESTS: Football and politics.
PERSONAL PROFILE: General Secretary of Ekon; 1991-99: Organising Secretary of AKEL in Great Britain. 1990-2000: Member of Central Committee of AKEL (Cyprus).

TONY LAZAROU
Former Chairman of Enfield FC

DATE OF BIRTH: 04-Apr-1956
PLACE OF BIRTH: UK. Father from Kaimakli; Mother from Yialloussa.
MARITAL STATUS: Married.
SCHOOLS/COLLEGE: Tollington Park School, Winchmore Hill; Turnford College.
HOBBIES AND INTERESTS: Football and reading.
PERSONAL PROFILE: Worked for Adam Kennedy, becoming their Managing Director. Former Chairman of Enfield Football Club.

CHRISTOFOROS LAZOU
Scientific Research

DATE OF BIRTH: 10-May-1942
PLACE OF BIRTH: Achna.
MARITAL STATUS: Married to Elizabeth Yeats.
CHILDREN: Two sons.
SCHOOLS/COLLEGE: Technical Polytechnic, Nicosia; University of London.
QUALIFICATIONS: BSc in Mathematics & Physics.

PERSONAL PROFILE: University career of over 20 years in leading edge computing, providing technical services for large-scale applications in cosmology, climate. aerospace, medicine and many other fields of scientific research. Currently runs HiPerCom Ltd, specialising in high-performance computing. Has written widely in scientific/technical journals and is best known for his book Supercomputers and their use, published in three editions by Oxford Universtity Press.

GEORGE LEFTERI
Financial Director, London Greek Radio/Member of the Executive Committee DYSY UK

DATE OF BIRTH: 05-Dec-1952
PLACE OF BIRTH: Famagusta.
CHILDREN: Two sons, one daughter.
SCHOOLS/COLLEGE: First and Second Gymnasium, Famagusta; Hammersmith & West London College; Middlesex University.
QUALIFICATIONS: HND and Post-Graduate in Business Studies. Fellow of the Financial Accountants.
HOBBIES AND INTERESTS: Travel, swimming, pool and snooker.
PERSONAL PROFILE: Financial Director of London Greek Radio. Former Chairman of Anorthosis FC, and former Governor of Tottenhall School. Chairman of Walker School PTA. Member of the Executive Committee DYSY UK.

LEONIDAS LEONIDOU
Chairman of EKEKA, the Federation of Cypriot refugees in the UK

DATE OF BIRTH: 13-Oct-1947
PLACE OF BIRTH: Ayios Theodoros, Famagusta.
MARITAL STATUS: Married to Anne-Marie, London (parents from Constantinople).
CHILDREN: Four sons.
SCHOOLS/COLLEGE: Famagusta Gymnasium; Athens University; University of Wales.
QUALIFICATIONS: Degree in Physics; MSc in Electronics and computing.
HOBBIES AND INTERESTS: Writing and research.

PERSONAL PROFILE: Founder of the website for the Greek Cypriot community called Nostos. com. Author of the book Ayios Theodoros Karpasias, and of the biography of General Grivas (2 volumes). Chairman of EKEKA, the Federation of Cypriot Refugees in the UK. Chairman of Ayios Theodoros Association UK. Teaches Greek at several Greek schools. While at primary school during British rule with his mother in hospital and his father a Political prisoner he sent a letter to the Cyprus Governor Sir Hugh Foot pleading for his father's release which received wide media publicity.

KRISTIAN LEONTIOU

Singer/ Songwriter recorded the single Story of my Life and the album Someday Soon, they both entered the music charts

DATE OF BIRTH: 01-Jan-1982
PLACE OF BIRTH: London. Father, Leonti from Ayios Andronicos Karpassi; Mother Paraskevoulla from Ayios Amvrosios.
MARITAL STATUS: Single.
SCHOOLS/COLLEGE: Hatch End School.
HOBBIES AND INTERESTS: Karate, bikes and snooker.

PERSONAL PROFILE: Kristian is black belt in Karate. Played snooker and rode bikes to a semi professional level. Went to South London, played his demo to a management company who then declined him. As he was leaving he bumped into Mike Sault of Warner Chappell (publishers of Dido and Artful Dodger) who heard Kristians song through the office wall and realised that the youngster had one of the best voices he had ever heard. Recorded the single Story of my Life went to no 9 and the album Someday Soon went to no 13, in the charts. Uncomfortable with the music and image he was pressured into presenting, Leontiou broke away from the pop scene and embarked on forming a new indie Band called One Eskimo and an album was released in March 2008.

ANASTASIOS PAUL LEVENTIS OBE

Chairman of the AG Leventis Foundation

DATE OF BIRTH: 19-May-1941
PLACE OF BIRTH: Ghana.
MARITAL STATUS: Married.
CHILDREN: Three.
SCHOOLS/COLLEGE: In England and France.
HONOURS/AWARDS: Honoured with the award of Commander of the order of the British Empire (OBE) in the Queen's Birthday Honours List of 2004. Also honoured with the award of order of Madarski Konnik by the President of Bulgaria in 2004. He was appointed Officer of Order of the Federal Republic, Nigeria in 2002.

PERSONAL PROFILE: He is on the Board of Directors on Leventis Group Companies in Nigeria and is also a Director of Leventis Group International Companies which have investments worldwide. He supervises Leventis group activities in Nigeria. A. P. Leventis is Chairman of the A. G Leventis Foundation. He is a Founder Trustee of the Nigerian Conservation Foundation; Honorary Vice-President of BirdLife International; a Fellow of the Royal Geographical Society; until recently, for seven years, a member of the Board of Trustees of the Brazilian Atlantic Rainforest Trust. A P Leventis was accredited Honorary Commissioner for the Republic of Cyprus to Nigeria by the Government of the Republic of Cyprus on 04 April 1990.

The first Radiomarathon in the UK took place in 1993 with the cooperation of the London Greek Radio (LGR) and Laiki Bank UK. This is an organisation helping people with special needs.

CONSTANTINE LEVENTIS
Former Chairman of the Trustees of the AG Leventis Foundation (Deceased)

DATE OF BIRTH: 19-Apr-1938
PLACE OF BIRTH: Larnaca.
MARITAL STATUS: Married to Edmee.
CHILDREN: Anastasis, Businessman. Louisa, Administrator. George, Student.
SCHOOLS/COLLEGE: Harrow School and Clare College, Cambridge.
QUALIFICATIONS: MA in Classics. MA in Political Science.
HONOURS/AWARDS: Honorary Doctorate from the University of Ghana; Honorary Fellowships from the University of North London and Royal Holloway College, London; Taxiarchis tou Tagmatos tou Foinika, Hellenic Republic; Commandeur de l'Ordre des Arts et des Lettres, French Rep.
PERSONAL PROFILE: Was Company Director. Chairman of the Trustees of the AG Leventis Foundation. From 1979, Ambassador and Permanent Delegate of Cyprus to UNESCO. Member of the Council of the University of Cyprus. Member of the Board of the Bank of Cyprus. Member of the Council of Europa Nostra.

EDMEE LEVENTIS (nee VASSILIADES)
Former Chairwoman of the Board of Governors, Hellenic College

DATE OF BIRTH: 20-Feb-1945
PLACE OF BIRTH: Paphos.
MARITAL STATUS: Married to Constantine Leventis.
CHILDREN: Anastasis, Anastasis, Businessman. Louisa, Louisa, Administrator. George, George, Student, Oxford University.
SCHOOLS/COLLEGE: Pancyprian Gymnasium (Phaneromeni), Nicosia. University of Rome, La Sapienza.
QUALIFICATIONS: MA, Political Science.
MEMBERSHIPS: Anglo-Hellenic League; Caryatids, British Museum; Cypriot Estia of London; Greek Cypriot Brotherhood; Hellenic Centre; Hellenic Foundation; Lykion ton Hellinidon (London Lyceum of Greek Women); Hellenic Society of Professional People and Scientists in Great Britain.
PERSONAL PROFILE: Full-time voluntary worker. Former Chair and present member of the Board of Governors of the Hellenic College. Former Chairwoman of the Executive Board of the Hellenic Trust. Member of the Board of the Anglo-Hellenic League; Member of the Board of the Hellenic Foundation.

MARTHA LEWIS
Singer/Actress and Part of the creative partnership Martha & Eve, who have a number of TV, radio and theatre shows to their credit

DATE OF BIRTH: 20-Jun-1962
PLACE OF BIRTH: London. Parents from Larnaca and Famagusta.
MARITAL STATUS: Single.
SCHOOLS/COLLEGE: Middlesex University.
QUALIFICATIONS: BA Honours in Performing Arts.
PERSONAL PROFILE: Actress, vocalist, composer. Part of the creative partnership Martha & Eve, who have a number of TV, radio and theatre shows to their credit. They have released their third album, and recent performances include various festivals throughout Europe. Martha composes, arranges and performs work for the nine-piece orchestra Cafe Aman, and has also written and composed work for film and TV. She has appeared on TV in Daytime Live, Birds of a Feather, Mid-life, Edinburgh Nights, Middlemarch and other programmes.

BAMBOS LIASIDES
Creator of the first SMS information services for BT Cellnet and Vodafone

DATE OF BIRTH: 22-Oct-1955
PLACE OF BIRTH: London. Parents from Labathos and Komi Kebir.
MARITAL STATUS: Single.
CHILDREN: Charlie, Isabelle.
SCHOOLS/COLLEGE: Dame Alice Owens; Marketing Centre for Business Studies.
QUALIFICATIONS: Certificate and Diploma in Marketing.
MEMBERSHIPS: Member of the Chartered Institute of Marketing.
HONOURS/AWARDS: He was appointed an expert reviewer by the European Commission on a 20mecu project.
HOBBIES AND INTERESTS: Ancient history and food.
PERSONAL PROFILE: Creator of the first SMS information services for BT Cellnet and Vodafone. Bambos founded Brainstorm one of the first mobile applications service providers later sold to Opera Telecom. His previous background included business development and corporate marketing. He has lectured at Henley Management College and is a visiting fellow at the London School of

Economics. Appointed to the Technology and Innovation Committee of the Confederation of British industry to advise on industrial policy and research funding.

NICOS LIPSOS
Member of the Central Committee of DEKO in Cyprus

DATE OF BIRTH: 25-Apr-1950
PLACE OF BIRTH: Kato Zodia.
MARITAL STATUS: Married to Kyriaki, Nicosia, Teacher.
CHILDREN: Elena, Yioda.
SCHOOLS/COLLEGE: West Ham Polytechnic and Kilburn Polytechnic.
QUALIFICATIONS: Accountancy, International Management and property management and Investment.
MEMBERSHIPS: Fellow of the Chartered Management Institute(FCMI) and Fellow member of the Association of Accounting Technician(FMAAT). ARLA and UKALA.
HOBBIES AND INTERESTS: Politics, travelling and socialising.
PERSONAL PROFILE: Nicos Lipsos is an active member of DEKO and member of the Central Committee in Cyprus. He is also a Director of the Property Centre (London)Ltd.

NEOPHYTOS LOIZIDES
Education

PLACE OF BIRTH: Kathika
SCHOOLS/COLLEGE: University of Pennsylvania, Central European University, Harvard University and University of Toronto.
QUALIFICATIONS: BA MA and PhD.
PERSONAL PROFILE: Former lecturer at Princeton University, now based at Queens University Belfast.

Bambos Liassides creator of the first sms information services for BT Cellnet and Vodafone

NICK 'POWER' LOIZIDES
Pioneer of the Ayia Napa Club Scene

DATE OF BIRTH: 23-May-1959
PLACE OF BIRTH: London. parents from Nicosia and Asha.
MARITAL STATUS: Married to Koulla, Cyprus, Housewife.
CHILDREN: Michelle, Dion, Angela, Kia and Mike.
SCHOOLS/COLLEGE: Seven Sisters Junior School; St Davids C of E Secondary School. Tottenham College of Technology.
HOBBIES AND INTERESTS: Music production, computing and radio presenting.
PERSONAL PROFILE: Businessman in the entertainment industry. Pioneer of the Ayia Napa clubscene, and the person who kicked-started Ayia Napa's current popularity. Former owner of the now defunct Music Power Group of record stores in London. Former radio presenter with London Kiss 100 FM, and several other radio stations. Presents shows on Unknown FM 108 in London Energy FM in Cyprus and Dance FM 106. 7 in Tenerife. Also employed as a Lecturer at North Herts College teaching City Guilds courses in Electrical Installations.

PETER LOIZOS
Professor of Anthropology and BBC TV Documentary Film Producer

DATE OF BIRTH: 17-May-1940
PLACE OF BIRTH: Argaki.
MARITAL STATUS: Married.
SCHOOLS/COLLEGE: Cambridge, Harvard, Pennsylvania and LSE.
QUALIFICATIONS: PhD.
MEMBERSHIPS: European Association of Social Anthropologists.
HOBBIES AND INTERESTS: Photography, Literature, British and Ottoman Imperial History and British Social History.
PERSONAL PROFILE: Peter is a Emeritus Professor of Anthropology based at London School of Economics. He has worked for BBC TV as a documentary film producer, for Oxfam and Save the children fund also for the UK's Department for International Development as a consultant.

UK

ANDREAS LOIZOU
Director, Financial Times Knowledge

DATE OF BIRTH: 13-Dec-1964
PLACE OF BIRTH: London.
Father's family from Ayia Triada, Yialousa, Cyprus; Mother's family from Zurich, Switzerland.
MARITAL STATUS: Married to Monica Hernanz from Madrid, Spain.
SCHOOLS/COLLEGE: Chatham House Grammar School, Ramsgate, Kent; University of Leeds; London Institute.
QUALIFICATIONS: BA (First Class Honours) in English; MA in Media Strategy. Chartered Accountant.
PERSONAL PROFILE: Director, Financial Times Knowledge.

ANDROS LOIZOU
Lectures Philosophy at the Centre for Professional Ethics, University of Central Lancashire,

DATE OF BIRTH: 02-Jun-1941
PLACE OF BIRTH: London.
Father from Komi Kebir; Mother from Koma tou Yialou.
MARITAL STATUS: Married to Moira, Bolton, Teacher.
CHILDREN: Sophia, Stav, Nicholas, All three children are students.
SCHOOLS/COLLEGE: Bedford School, Bedford, University College London, London School of Economics (1983-4).
QUALIFICATIONS: BA MSc, PhD.
MEMBERSHIPS: Society for Greek Political Thought.
HOBBIES AND INTERESTS: Music plays piano and sings for a choral society. Has a keen interest in politics and current affairs.
PERSONAL PROFILE: Andros Loizou teaches philosophy at the Centre for Professional Ethics, University of Central Lancashire. Has published two books on the nature of time, an edited collection of papers on Greek ethical and political thought, and some papers on Plato's Republic.

PROFESSOR GEORGHIOS LOIZOU
Professor in Computer Science

DATE OF BIRTH: 07-Apr-1937
PLACE OF BIRTH: Livadhia, Larnaca, Cyprus.
MARITAL STATUS: Married to Diane, London, HR manager.
CHILDREN: Suzanne, Finance. Melanie, Sales and Marketing. Michael, Accountant.
SCHOOLS/COLLEGE: Elementary School, Livadhia, Larnaca, Pancyprian Commercial Lyceum Larnaca, Teacher Training College, Morphou. University of London.
QUALIFICATIONS: BA Postgraduate Diploma in Numerical Analysis; PhD.
MEMBERSHIPS: British Computer Society; IEEE Computer Society.
HOBBIES AND INTERESTS: Ancient history, politics, travel and theatre.
PERSONAL PROFILE: Emeritus Professor and Head of School of Computer Science & Information Systems at Birkbeck College, University of London. Author of A Guided Tour of Relational Databases and Beyond.

KATHERINA MARIA LOIZOU
Director of Sheffield International Documentary Festival

DATE OF BIRTH: 07-Mar-1961
PLACE OF BIRTH: London.
Father from Ayia Triad, Yialousa; Mother from Zurich, Switzerland.
MARITAL STATUS: Single.
CHILDREN: Alexander.
SCHOOLS/COLLEGE: London College of Printing; University College, London; Clarendon House Grammar School, Ramsgate.
QUALIFICATIONS: MA in Documentary; BA (Honours) Geography; 9 O Levels, 3 A Levels.
MEMBERSHIPS: Royal Television Society; Women in Film and Media.
PERSONAL PROFILE: Director since 1996 of Sheffield International Documentary Festival, one of the UK's premier media events.

UK

LINDA LOIZOU
Actress. TV credits include The Satirist and Two Deaths

DATE OF BIRTH: 31-May-1956
PLACE OF BIRTH: London. Parents from Paphos and England.
MARITAL STATUS: Single.
SCHOOLS/COLLEGE: North London Academy of Speech and Drama; Chickenshed Theatre Co.
QUALIFICATIONS: BTech in Performing Arts.
MEMBERSHIPS: Equity.
HOBBIES AND INTERESTS: Learning languages; computers.
PERSONAL PROFILE: Actress, singer and dancer. TV credits include The Satirist and Two Deaths; theatre roles include Aladdin and Cinderella. Linda has been put forward for a part in the third Silence of the Lambs film in Hollywood.

LOUIS LOIZOU
Young Entrepreneur 2003 Who's Who

DATE OF BIRTH: 29-Jun-1972
PLACE OF BIRTH: London Parents from Limassol.
MARITAL STATUS: Married to Anita, British.
CHILDREN: Johnny, Paul.
SCHOOLS/COLLEGE: Ashmole.
HONOURS/AWARDS: Young Entrepreneur 2003 Who's Who.
PERSONAL PROFILE: Louis Loizou started work with British Aerospace PLC as an Avionics Engineer, then was the Chief Executive of the Restaurant Chain Bar Meze from 1994 to 2004 and former owner of Molos Restaurant. 2009 sees him launching his biggest restaurant the Carob Tree in Highgate.

LOUIS LOIZOU
Trustee and former Chairman, Twelve Apostles Church, Hertfordshire member of Hertfordshire Black and Ethnic Minorities Committee

DATE OF BIRTH: 11-Jan-1946
PLACE OF BIRTH: Komi Kebir.
MARITAL STATUS: Married to Liz. Kiti.
CHILDREN: Flora, Teacher. Zoe, Production Manager for ITN. Chris, Leisure.
SCHOOLS/COLLEGE: Holloway School. University of Wales.
QUALIFICATIONS: BA Economics and History.
HOBBIES AND INTERESTS: Opera, skiing and football (Spurs and Barnet fan).
PERSONAL PROFILE: Trustee and former Chairman of the Twelve Apostles Church in Hertfordshire. Member of the Welwyn Hatfield Ethnic Minorities Committee and Hertfordshire Black and Ethnic Minorities Committee.

LOUIS LOIZOU
Management Official in the Food Standard Agency

DATE OF BIRTH: 02-Oct-1972
PLACE OF BIRTH: London Parents from Cyprus.
MARITAL STATUS: Married to Androulla, Cyprus.
CHILDREN: Alexandros, Christiana.
SCHOOLS/COLLEGE: Bacons. South Bank University.
QUALIFICATIONS: BA(hons) Political Studies.
HOBBIES AND INTERESTS: Gym, Greek Music and Politics.
PERSONAL PROFILE: Louis Loizou has progressed from being a Policy Officer to management position within the Food Standards Agency. He also helps organise events for the Greek Youth of St Mary's Orthodox Church.

UK

GREEK CYPRIOTS WORLDWIDE

LUCY LOIZOU
Family Law Solicitor led a complex child abduction case that was reported in the National press in August 2005

DATE OF BIRTH: 28-Jul-1980
PLACE OF BIRTH: UK Father from Ayios Andronicos, Mother from Yialoussa.
MARITAL STATUS: Single.
SCHOOLS/COLLEGE: Ricards Lodge High School. Esher College, Kingston University.
MEMBERSHIPS: Chair of Young surrey Resolution.
HOBBIES AND INTERESTS: Golf, Greek Music and Dance.
PERSONAL PROFILE: Family Law Solicitor led a complex child abduction case that was reported in the National press in August 2005.

SOZOS LOIZOU
Principal Clinical Scientist in Rheumatology

DATE OF BIRTH: 01-May-1942
PLACE OF BIRTH: Larnaca.
MARITAL STATUS: Single.
SCHOOLS/COLLEGE: Stoneham Grammar, Reading; Kings College London; Royal Postgraduate Medical School.
QUALIFICATIONS: BSc, MSc, PhD, DMS.
HONOURS/AWARDS: Invitation to the Buckingham Palace Garden Party by HM the Queen, in recognition of his services to British science and to the Royal Postgraduate Medical School.
HOBBIES AND INTERESTS: Reading, theatre, art, walking and swimming.
PERSONAL PROFILE: Principal Clinical Scientist in Rheumatology at Imperial College of Medicine, Hammersmith Hospital. Has published several scientific papers. Was invited as a visiting scientist by the World Health Organisation Immunology Laboratories in Venezuela. In March 2000, he was Visiting Professor to the Italian Institute of medical research in Milan.

The Cypriot football league formed in 1973 based in London consists of 24 teams and hoping to grow.

STAVROS LOIZOU
Managing Director, Lewis Charles Securities/Sponsors of Omonia Youth

DATE OF BIRTH: 10-Oct-1964
PLACE OF BIRTH: London. Father from Larnaca; Mother from Limassol.
MARITAL STATUS: Married to Joanne Allen, London, Housewife.
CHILDREN: Jessica Sophia, Sophia Isabella.
SCHOOLS/COLLEGE: Highgate School; City University Business School.
QUALIFICATIONS: 10 O Levels, 3 A Levels; BSc (Honours) Banking & International Finance.
HOBBIES AND INTERESTS: Sport and travel.
PERSONAL PROFILE: Managing Director of Lewis Charles Securities (private client stockbrokers). Formerly Managing Director of SFS stockbrokers. Previously Manager of Strategic Trading Group at Fuji Bank Limited (London).

ZOE MORRIS (nee) LOIZOU
Production Director ITN Factual

DATE OF BIRTH: 22-Apr-1976
PLACE OF BIRTH: London Father Louis from Komi Kebir and Mother Liz from Kiti.
MARITAL STATUS: Married to James Morris.
CHILDREN: Sofia.
SCHOOLS/COLLEGE: Haberdashers Aske. University College of London.
QUALIFICATIONS: BA (Honours) French and German.
HOBBIES AND INTERESTS: Travelling and Sculpture.
PERSONAL PROFILE: Zoe is the Production Director of ITN Factual.

ANTONY LOUCA
Member of governing body of Mid-Kent College (15 000 students)

DATE OF BIRTH: 24-Feb-1946
PLACE OF BIRTH: Kaimakli, Nicosia, Cyprus.
MARITAL STATUS: Married to Ann, a Housewife, from Maidstone, Kent.
CHILDREN: Athos Christian, Andrea, Christian.
SCHOOLS/COLLEGE: Pancyprian Gymnasium, Nicosia; City of London University.

UK

216

QUALIFICATIONS: Chartered Certified Accountant.
MEMBERSHIPS: Fellow of the Association of Chartered Certified Accountants.
HOBBIES AND INTERESTS: Skiing, football and snooker.
PERSONAL PROFILE: Senior Partner of Louca & Co. Member of governing body of Mid-Kent College (15,000 students).

LOUCA ANDREAS LOUCA
Lecturer at Imperial College London in the Department of Civil & Environmental Engineering

DATE OF BIRTH: 30-Jun-1962
PLACE OF BIRTH: London. Father from Khirokitia; Mother from Ayios Sergios, Famagusta.
MARITAL STATUS: Married to Niki Louca, a secretary (father from Ayios Nikolaos; Mother from Styllous).
CHILDREN: Elaine and Andrea.
SCHOOLS/COLLEGE: Thames Polytechnic; University of Surrey; Imperial College London.
QUALIFICATIONS: BSc (Honours), MSc, DIC, PhD.
MEMBERSHIPS: Graduate Member – Institute of Civil Engineers, Institution of Structural Engineers.
HOBBIES AND INTERESTS: Scuba diving and keeping fit.
PERSONAL PROFILE: Lecturer at Imperial College London in the Department of Civil & Environmental Engineering.

DR LOUCAS LEFTERIS LOUCA
General Practitioner

DATE OF BIRTH: 15-Sep-1958
PLACE OF BIRTH: Peristerona/Piyi.
MARITAL STATUS: Married to Rachel, Sheffield.
CHILDREN: Sophia, Serena, Zara.
SCHOOLS/COLLEGE: Strettford Grammar School Manchester. Manchester Medical School.
QUALIFICATIONS: MBCLB MRCGP DRCOG.
HOBBIES AND INTERESTS: Music, History and Squash.
PERSONAL PROFILE: General Practitioner in Nottingham.

STAVROS LOUCA
Actor appeared on TV in Casualty, Family Affairs, The Human Body. Film work includes Wicked and Dangerous Neighbours, Phases of Life

DATE OF BIRTH: 12-Jul-1980
PLACE OF BIRTH: London. Parents from Pyla and Lapathos.
MARITAL STATUS: Single.
SCHOOLS/COLLEGE: Langham; Mountview Theatre School; Chickenshed Theatre; Theatro Technis.
QUALIFICATIONS: BTech in Performing Arts.
MEMBERSHIPS: Equity.
HOBBIES AND INTERESTS: Bingo.
PERSONAL PROFILE: Actor, singer and dancer. Has appeared on TV in Casualty, Family Affairs, The Human Body. Film work includes Wicked and Dangerous Neighbours, Phases of Life. Stage work: A Taste of Honey, Cinderella in Boots. Also appeared in an Alliance & Leicester commercial. He is also a casting agent in Directors Cut Revolver 2004 and Xmas Chopra Town.

DR MARIA LUCA
Head of the School of Psychotherapy and Counselling at Regent's College

DATE OF BIRTH: 27-Mar-1956
PLACE OF BIRTH: Lymbia.
MARITAL STATUS: Single.
CHILDREN: Andros, Psychologist. Kyriacos, Businessman.
SCHOOLS/COLLEGE: Primary school Lympia, KASA Secondary School in Larnaca and the Anglo-French School Pallari in Nicosia. City University and Middlesex University.
QUALIFICATIONS: MA in Psychotherapy & Counselling, BA (Honours) Social Science. PhD Psychotherapeutic Studies.
MEMBERSHIPS: The Society for Psychotherapy Research.
HOBBIES AND INTERESTS: Greek traditional and ballroom dancing; theatre and classical music; traditional Greek-Cypriot and Middle Eastern cooking.
PERSONAL PROFILE: Head of the School of Psychotherapy and Counselling at Regent's College. Clinical Psychotherapist at St Ann's Hospital in Haringey, and Clinical Supervisor & Consultant at Newham General Hospital. External examiner for Surrey University's undergraduate courses in Counselling. Has published various articles in scientific journals of psychoanalysis and psychotherapy.

UK

ANDREAS SYMEON LYSANDROU

Awarded Gold Disc featuring himself Victoria Beckham and Dane Bowers (Out of Your Mind), which reached number two in the charts

DATE OF BIRTH: 25-Jul-1970
PLACE OF BIRTH: England. Father from Ayios Andronikos; Mother from Piyi.
MARITAL STATUS: Single.
SCHOOLS/COLLEGE: Montem Primary School; George Orwell Secondary School.
HONOURS/AWARDS: Gold disc, featuring him Victoria Beckham and Dane Bowers (Out of Your Mind), which reached number two in the charts.
HOBBIES AND INTERESTS: Cars.
PERSONAL PROFILE: Director of Ice Cream Records. Also Head of A&R, and a freelance record producer and songwriter. Occasionally presents shows on various radio stations. To date, has been involved with six records that have reached the national charts.

EVE MAKIS

Winner of Booksellers International Book of the Year Award

DATE OF BIRTH: 29-Mar-1967
PLACE OF BIRTH: Nottingham Parents from Kaimakli.
MARITAL STATUS: Married to Tasos, Tricomo, Business Formerly a Professional Footballer in Cyprus.
SCHOOLS/COLLEGE: West bridgford School. Leicester University.
QUALIFICATIONS: BA NCTJ (National Council For Training Of Journalist).
HONOURS/AWARDS: Winner of Booksellers International Book of the Year Award.
PERSONAL PROFILE: Eve Makis is an author currently signed to Transworld Publishing- a division of the Random House Group, Two novels so far published. Eat drink and be married and The Mother in Law. She is probably the first to have published a Cypriot mainstream novel about the Cypriot Community/History. So far 30, 000 copies sold and book translated into four languages including Greek.

DR ANDREAS MAKRIS

Consultant & Senior Lecturer in Oncology

DATE OF BIRTH: 07-Jan-1961
PLACE OF BIRTH: Nicosia.
MARITAL STATUS: Married to Andrea, Wales, GP.
CHILDREN: Thomas, Catherine.
SCHOOLS/COLLEGE: Yerolakkos Elementary School; English School, Nicosia; Raynes Park High School; Oxford & Sheffield Universities.
QUALIFICATIONS: MA, MB, CHB, MRCP, FRCR, MD.
HOBBIES AND INTERESTS: AFC Wimbledon.
PERSONAL PROFILE: Currently at Mount Vernon Hospital as Consultant & Senior Lecturer in Oncology, specialising in Treatment of Breast and Bowel Cancer.

DR MICHAEL MAKRIS

Consultant & Senior Lecturer in Haemotology

DATE OF BIRTH: 15-Jul-1959
PLACE OF BIRTH: Yerolakkos.
MARITAL STATUS: Married to Martina, Ireland.
SCHOOLS/COLLEGE: English School Nicosia. Raynes Park High School. Oriel College Oxford, University of London, London Hospital Medical College. MBBS.
QUALIFICATIONS: BA Physiological Sciences.
HOBBIES AND INTERESTS: Photography, walking computers and football (Sheffield Wednesday).
PERSONAL PROFILE: Worked at one London Hospital as Junior Doctor. Two years at Morriston Hospital, Swansea. 1987 till now at Royal Hallamshire Hospital Sheffield as Senior Lecturer in Haemotology & Consultant Haemotologist.

MICHALIS MALLOURIS

Chairman of Hellenic Brotherhood, Manchester

DATE OF BIRTH: 25-Nov-1962
PLACE OF BIRTH: Nicosia.
MARITAL STATUS: Married to Anna, Ayia Varvara, Banking.
CHILDREN: Andrea, Elena, Christalla.
SCHOOLS/COLLEGE: Woodberry Down Secondary. Kingsway College, Nottingham, University of Surrey.

UK

QUALIFICATIONS: BSc (Honours) Applied Chemistry, PhD Bioinorganic Chemistry.
MEMBERSHIPS: Hellenes Scientists of Manchester Soc.
HONOURS/AWARDS: European Sales Person of the Year, 1996 & 97, World Wide Sales Achievements, 8th & 12th 1996 & 97 respectively.
HOBBIES AND INTERESTS: Most sports, cooking, travelling, reading, painting and share dealing.
PERSONAL PROFILE: Business Manager at Buckman Lab Ltd, UK involved with Greek Church in Manchester, Church warden, Hellenic Brotherhood, Manchester Chairman.

STELIOS MAMAS
Deputy Mayor, Royal Borough of Kingston

DATE OF BIRTH: 05-Apr-1934
PLACE OF BIRTH: Astromeritis.
MARITAL STATUS: Single.
SCHOOLS/COLLEGE: Kingston College, Kingston Poly, Ruskin College Oxford.
QUALIFICATIONS: Social Science Diploma. Chartered Secretary & Diploma in Municipal Admin.
HOBBIES AND INTERESTS: Politics and arts.
PERSONAL PROFILE: In local Government for 35 years & Local Councillor for 33 years. Presently Deputy Mayor, Royal Borough of Kingston. 2002-2003.

ANDREAS MARCOU
Actor appeared on TV, Dangerman, Casualty, The Bill, Coronation St, London's Burning

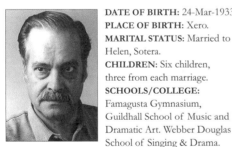

DATE OF BIRTH: 24-Mar-1933
PLACE OF BIRTH: Xero.
MARITAL STATUS: Married to Helen, Sotera.
CHILDREN: Six children, three from each marriage.
SCHOOLS/COLLEGE: Famagusta Gymnasium, Guildhall School of Music and Dramatic Art. Webber Douglas School of Singing & Drama.
MEMBERSHIPS: Equity.
HONOURS/AWARDS: 1st prize for Drama at Theatre for Humanity.
HOBBIES AND INTERESTS: Acting profession.

PERSONAL PROFILE: One of the founders of Theatro Technis. Active member in the Theatrical and Cultural life of the Community since 1951. Appeared on TV, Dangerman, Casualty, The Bill, Coronation St, London's Burning. Films include Cool of the Day with Jane Fonda, Peter Finch and Angela Lansbury.

HARRY MARCOU JP
Appointed to be a "Justice of the Peace" for the Commission Area of Hereford & Worcester

DATE OF BIRTH: 07-Dec-1955
PLACE OF BIRTH: Galini, Nicosia.
MARITAL STATUS: Married to Krinoula, Galini, Hairdresser.
CHILDREN: Nicholas, Markos.
SCHOOLS/COLLEGE: Pitmaston Secondary, Birmingham. Hall Green Tech College, City & Guilds, (metal body repairs).
HONOURS/AWARDS: 1998 - Appointed to be a "Justice of the Peace" for the Commission Area of Hereford & Worcester.
HOBBIES AND INTERESTS: Cyprus and its national political problem, religion, golf, shooting (Game) and gardening.
PERSONAL PROFILE: S/E Gaming Machine Operator & Joint Salon Proprietor, Founder Member of "Action for Cyprus" (Midlands), Member of Community Organisations ie. Church Committee. Member of St Andreas, Birmingham.

MARCOS A MARCOU
Former Chairman Eptakomi Association Marcos was featured in the Daily Telegraph after buying 290 acre Sherbourne Farm in Warwickshire

DATE OF BIRTH: 22-Feb-1955
PLACE OF BIRTH: Eptakomi, Cyprus.
MARITAL STATUS: Single.
CHILDREN: Andreas and Despina.
SCHOOLS/COLLEGE: Eptakomi, Pancyprian Gymnasium, Nicosia, Central Hotel School, Nicosia.
HOBBIES AND INTERESTS: Travel, nature, reading and sports.
PERSONAL PROFILE: Former chairman of Eptakomi Association. Owner of Marcos Trimmings. Marcos was featured in the Daily Telegraph after buying 290 acre Sherbourne Farm in Warwickshire.

UK

MARKOS CHRISTOFIS MARCOU
General Dental Practitioner

DATE OF BIRTH: 26-Dec-1972
PLACE OF BIRTH: UK. Father Ayios Elias; Mother Koma Tou Yialou.
MARITAL STATUS: Single.
SCHOOLS/COLLEGE: Enfield Grammar School, United, Medical & Dental Schools (Guy's Dental School).
QUALIFICATIONS: Bachelor of Dental Surgery (BDS). 3 A Levels (Maths, A; Chemistry, B; Physics, B).
MEMBERSHIPS: British Dental Assoc. - General Dental Council.
HOBBIES AND INTERESTS: Eating out, playing football, film/cinema, dancing, news and current affairs and travelling the world.
PERSONAL PROFILE: General Dental Practitioner for five years, in North London, treating a large part of the Greek Community.

YIOLA MARCOU
Oncologist at St. Barts Hospital

DATE OF BIRTH: 08-Jan-1970
PLACE OF BIRTH: Paralimni.
MARITAL STATUS: Single.
SCHOOLS/COLLEGE: Paralimni Gymnasium, Athens Medical School.
HOBBIES AND INTERESTS: Reading, swimming and cycling.
PERSONAL PROFILE: 1995 started work at Medway Hospital, Gillingham as a medic. Six months at North Middlesex Hospital. Since 1997 Oncologist at St. Barts Hospital.

ARIS GEORGIOS MARCOULLIDES
Dental Surgeon

DATE OF BIRTH: 27-Feb-1948
PLACE OF BIRTH: Larnaca.
MARITAL STATUS: Married to Christine, London (parents from Famagusta).
CHILDREN: Nadia, Solicitor.
SCHOOLS/COLLEGE: William Ellis Schoo. Royal Dental Hospital, University of London.
QUALIFICATIONS: BDS (Lond); LDSRCS (Eng).
HOBBIES AND INTERESTS: Travelling to the more remote and interesting parts of the world. Food and wine.

PERSONAL PROFILE: Qualified as a Dentist in 1971. Has been in private practice since 1984. In 1988, opened the Cannon Hill Clinic, a private, multi-disciplinary healthcare centre in North London.

ANDREAS MARKIDES
Led many major projects including the redevelopment of Hounslow town centre and the establishment of a new settlement in Northamptonshire

DATE OF BIRTH: 08-Mar-1959
PLACE OF BIRTH: Kyra Morphou, Nicosia.
MARITAL STATUS: Married to Kay Swift, Stoke on Trent, Teacher.
CHILDREN: Eleni, Nike, Stephanie, Alexander, All at School.
SCHOOLS/COLLEGE: The English School Nicosia, Felsted School. Essex.
QUALIFICATIONS: BSc (Honours), MSC. CEng, MICE, FIHT.
MEMBERSHIPS: Member of the Institute of Civil Engineers.
HOBBIES AND INTERESTS: Football, tennis and literature.
PERSONAL PROFILE: Director at Colin Buchanan and Partners whom he joined in 1994. He is involved in the design and supervision of infrastructure works. His specialist traffic expertise includes traffic impact studies for new development proposals, highway design and expert witness at Planning Inquiries. He has led many major projects including the redevelopment of Hounslow town centre and the establishment of a new settlement in Northamptonshire.

ANDREAS MARKIDES
Musician/Bandleader (Deceased)

DATE OF BIRTH: 02-Jun-1923
PLACE OF BIRTH: Limassol.
MARITAL STATUS: Married to Iro, a housewife, from Xeros Cyprus.
CHILDREN: Peter, hairdresser. Helen, housewife.
SCHOOLS/COLLEGE: Limassol Gymnasium.
QUALIFICATIONS: A. Mus. LCM London College of Music.
MEMBERSHIPS: Musicians Union, Performing Right Society.

UK

HONOURS/AWARDS: Honorary member of Musicians Union, awarded for continous membership of the Union since 1947.
HOBBIES AND INTERESTS: Reading and sports.
PERSONAL PROFILE: Musician, Bandleader, Composer, Arranger & Music Teacher.

CONSTANTINOS MARKIDES
Professor at London Business School

DATE OF BIRTH: 24-Nov-1960
PLACE OF BIRTH: Nicosia.
MARITAL STATUS: Single.
SCHOOLS/COLLEGE: Boston University Harvard University.
QUALIFICATIONS: BA, MA MBA, DBA Doctorate in Business Studies.
MEMBERSHIPS: Member of the Academic Board of the Cyprus International Institute of Management.
HOBBIES AND INTERESTS: Football, tennis and theatre.
PERSONAL PROFILE: Author of three books. Fellow of the World Economic Forum of Davos, Non-Executive Director of Amathus (UK) Ltd. Associate Editor of the European Management Journal. Professor at London Business School.

DEMETRIS MARKOU MBE
1992 John Major recommended him for an MBE which was awarded to him in 1992 for Political & Charitable work

DATE OF BIRTH: 07-Feb-1944
PLACE OF BIRTH: Nicosia.
CHILDREN: Marcus, Journalist. Andrea, Computer programmer. Contantinos, Chartered Surveyor.
SCHOOLS/COLLEGE: Economics Gymnasium, Nicosia. 1962 Handsworth Technical College. Handsworth Technical College. Aston University.
QUALIFICATIONS: O & A Levels. FCA Chartered Accountant.
HONOURS/AWARDS: MBE.
HOBBIES AND INTERESTS: Skiing and politics.

PERSONAL PROFILE: 1970 opened own Practice in Birmingham called Marcus & Co. Helped the Greek Church in Birmingham & the ESTIA. Officer of the Conservative Party occupying many posts over 25 yrs. 1992 John Major recommended him for an MBE which was awarded to him in 1992 for Political & Charitable work. He is also a Director of several private and public companies.

MARCUS MARKOU
Managing Director for www. businessesforsale.com, a global website for buying and selling small and medium sized businesses

DATE OF BIRTH: 21-Jan-1971
PLACE OF BIRTH: Sutton Coldfield, Birmingham. Father, Demetrious, from Nicosia; Mother Christalla, born in Birmingham.
MARITAL STATUS: Married to Victoria.
SCHOOLS/COLLEGE: Eversfield School, Solihull, Bloxham School, Banbury, Birmingham University, University College London, London Academy of Music & Dramatic Art.
QUALIFICATIONS: 7 O Levels, 4 A Levels, BA Honours in Modern History and Political Science (2: 1), MA Legal & Political Theory. Diploma in Classical Acting.
PERSONAL PROFILE: Journalist - launched, edited and wrote for magazine industry. Currently writing regular column for Management Today. Managing Director for www. businessesforsale. com a global website for buying and selling small and medium sized businesses.

NADIA MARKS
writer/journalist works on a freelance basis for national newspapers and magazines

PLACE OF BIRTH: Nicosia
MARITAL STATUS: Married to Graham Marks.
CHILDREN: Leo, Pablo.
SCHOOLS/COLLEGE: Harrow School of Arts.
PERSONAL PROFILE: Nadia Marks worked on many mainstream magazines starting with Cosmopolitan was instrumental in launching the Magazines Company and Nadia is now a writer /journalist works on a freelance basis for national newspapers and magazines.

MICHAEL MATSOUKAS
Creative Designer Parikiaki Newspaper

DATE OF BIRTH: 04-Apr-1940
PLACE OF BIRTH: Palechori.
MARITAL STATUS: Married to Katerina, a Housewife.
CHILDREN: Marina, Georgoulla.
SCHOOLS/COLLEGE: London School of Printing & Commercial School Samuel - Cyprus.
PERSONAL PROFILE: Creative Designer Vema Newspaper now for Parikiaki Newspaper.

NICHOLAS CHRISTOPHER MAVROMATIS
Higher Scientific Officer, Government Operational Research Group

DATE OF BIRTH: 26-Dec-1974
PLACE OF BIRTH: Aberystwyth, Wales. Father from Larnaca.
MARITAL STATUS: Single.
SCHOOLS/COLLEGE: Penglais School, Aberstwyth. University of Oxford, (St. Peter's College) University of Kent.
QUALIFICATIONS: MA. (Oxon), MSc (Kent).
MEMBERSHIPS: London Mathematical Society, Operational Research Society, UK.
HOBBIES AND INTERESTS: Violin, football, karate and astronomy.
PERSONAL PROFILE: Was a Statistics Tutor, University of Wales, Aberystwyth 1997. Now a Higher Scientific Officer, Government Operational Research Group. Committee member: Young Operational Researchers Society, UK.

PANAYIOTIS MAVROMATIS
Director and trustee of the Haringey Legal & Financial Advice Centre

DATE OF BIRTH: 31-Jul-1946
PLACE OF BIRTH: Larnaca.
MARITAL STATUS: Married to Maria, Cypriot.
CHILDREN: Christina, Eva.
SCHOOLS/COLLEGE: St Marylebone C of E School, Tollington Park School. Liverpool University.
QUALIFICATIONS: BSc (Hons) Mathematics, Statistics & Computer Science.

MEMBERSHIPS: Deko and Larnaca Association.
HOBBIES AND INTERESTS: Chess, Bridge, Mycology.
PERSONAL PROFILE: Chartered Accountant in private practice in Mayfair. Founder member and trustee of St Catherine's Greek Orthodox Church, Warden of St Bartholomew's Greek Orthodox Church for 10 years. Director and trustee of the Haringey Legal & Financial Advice Centre. Past president Rotary Club of Paddington.

VASSILI C. MAVROMATIS
Professor in Mathematics, University of Wales, Aberystwyth

DATE OF BIRTH: 24-Sep-1944
PLACE OF BIRTH: Larnaca.
MARITAL STATUS: Married to Anastasia, Plymouth Father from Famagusta, Hotel Management.
CHILDREN: Nicholas, Civil Service. Christine, Musician.
SCHOOLS/COLLEGE: St. Marylebone School, Owen's School. Cambridge University, London University.
QUALIFICATIONS: MA (Cambridge) MSc, PhD. (London).
MEMBERSHIPS: FIMA (Fellow of Institute of Maths, & its Applications).
PERSONAL PROFILE: Professor in Mathematics, & Director of Postgraduate Studies, Maths, Dept. University of Wales, Aberystwyth.

CHRISTIANA MAVRON
Musician Violinist who has had performances with Kayne West, Brit Awards, special performances for HRH The Prince of Wales, HRH Prince Philip

DATE OF BIRTH: 08-Nov-1978
PLACE OF BIRTH: Aberystwyth, Wales. Father from Larnaca.
MARITAL STATUS: Single.
SCHOOLS/COLLEGE: The Purcell School of Music, London, The Guildhall. School of Music and Drama, The Royal Welsh College of Music and Drama.
QUALIFICATIONS: MMus BMus.
HONOURS/AWARDS: First prize winner, CAVATINA Chamber Music.

PERSONAL PROFILE: Violinist who has had performances with Kayne West, Brit Awards and Apollo Theatre, Katherine Jenkins Albert Hall, Recordings on Alex Park 'Honesty' and Judie Tsuk 'End of the Beginning Albums. Extra player with the BBC national Orchestra of Wales, Educational work and recitals throughout UK and Europe with Mavron Quartet, Special performances for HRH The Prince of Wales, HRH Prince Philip.

DR VASSILLIS MAVROU
Chairman of Union of Cypriots in the UK (EKA)

PLACE OF BIRTH: Famagusta.
MARITAL STATUS: Single.
SCHOOLS/COLLEGE: CTL Academy, Famagusta, Greenwich University, Guildhall University, City University. Guildhall University and City University.
QUALIFICATIONS: BA Political Economics. MA Politics, Doctorate in Sociology.
HOBBIES AND INTERESTS: Politics, community work, reading, karate, dancing and travel.
PERSONAL PROFILE: Research Assistant for the MP Jeremy Corbyn, was Senior project officer for social housing for the London Borough of Hackney as well as senior race relations officer for the same borough. Has written many articles for Haravgi Cyprus and Parikiaki in London. Now the owner of a lettings Agency called Varosi Lettings. He is also the Chairman of Union of Cypriots in Britain (EKA).

ANTHONY GEORGE MELAS
2 MOBO Awards, 1 Brit Award, 1 UK G Award I Smash Hits Award

DATE OF BIRTH: 14-May-1982
PLACE OF BIRTH: Norwich Parents from Ayia Marina Skyllouras.
MARITAL STATUS: Single.
SCHOOLS/COLLEGE: American Acadamy, Larnaca. Middlesex University and Berklee College of Music.
QUALIFICATIONS: A levels in Accounting, Economics, Law and Modern Greek.
MEMBERSHIPS: PRS-MCPS. World Waterpark Association.
HONOURS/AWARDS: BPI Certified Platinum Sales Award to recognise over 300, 000 sales in the UK.

2 MOBO Awards, 1 Brit Award, 1 Uk G Award I Smash Hits Award.
HOBBIES AND INTERESTS: Cars, Football, gadgets, Video Games and Boxing.
PERSONAL PROFILE: Anthony AKA Sniper is both a producer and rapper he has performed with Memphis Bleek and Freeway, 50 Cent Akon and Julian Marley. He produced and remixed the Cassius Henry single The One featuring Freeway and Kanye West. Anthony. He is one of the members of Solid Crew whose album "They Dont Know" went Platinum in 2001. His production company La Familia Entertainmentis home to up and coming producers including Merzerio his protegeand home to large scale concerts and parties worldwide in association with Twice as nice from Jay Z. Anthony is involved also in the family business which includes Europes largest themed waterpark Waterworld as well as the night clubs Black and White and Club Ice and Napa Radio. www. snipermusic. com.

LOUKIS MELEAGROS
Consultant Surgeon - North Middlesex University Hospital

DATE OF BIRTH: 10-Jun-1953
PLACE OF BIRTH: Nicosia.
MARITAL STATUS: Married to Lynn, Leeds, Hospital Manager.
CHILDREN: Evie, Yiannis, Kerynia, All the children are students.
SCHOOLS/COLLEGE: Kykkos Pancyprian Gymnasium - Nicosia, Haberdashers' Aske's School - UK, University College - London, St. George's Hospital Medical School - London.
QUALIFICATIONS: BSc, MBBS, FRCS, MD.
MEMBERSHIPS: Assoc of Surgeons of GB and Ireland, British Soc of Gastroenterology.
HOBBIES AND INTERESTS: Swimming, keep fit/walking, Greek music, Blues, Jazz music, fooball, athletics and theatre.
PERSONAL PROFILE: Consultant Surgeon - North Middlesex University Hospital, Specialist Surgeon in Abdominal/Intestinal Diseases. Laparoscopy & Endoscopy & Hernia Surgery, Medico-legal Expert.

UK

ANDREAS MENELAOU
Chairman of Anglisides Association, UK

DATE OF BIRTH: 10-Jan-1932
PLACE OF BIRTH: Perivolia, Larnaca.
MARITAL STATUS: Married to Christalla, Anglisides.
CHILDREN: Three children.
SCHOOLS/COLLEGE: Perivolia Elementary School.
MEMBERSHIPS: MBIM (Member of British Institute of Management); ACI (Associate of the Institute of Commerce); Cyprus Philatelic Society.
HOBBIES AND INTERESTS: Reading, antiques, stamp collecting, antique books and travel.
PERSONAL PROFILE: Chairman of Anglisides Association UK. Former Secretary of Haringey Cypriot Association.

CHRISTIANA KOUFETTA MENICOU
Researcher at University of Nottingham

DATE OF BIRTH: 08-Aug-1974
PLACE OF BIRTH: Famagusta.
MARITAL STATUS: Married to Michalis Menicou.
SCHOOLS/COLLEGE: University of Cyprus (undergraduate), University of Sheffield (postgraduate).
QUALIFICATIONS: B. Ed. in Primary Education, Ph. D. in Science Education. Piano Diploma.
MEMBERSHIPS: European Assoc. for research in Learning and Instruction.
HOBBIES AND INTERESTS: Music, swimming and photography.
PERSONAL PROFILE: Research Associate, Centre for Research in Development, Instruction and Training, (Credit Centre), Department of Psychology, University of Nottingham.

GEORGE MENICOU
Telecommunications

DATE OF BIRTH: 28-Feb-1932
PLACE OF BIRTH: Limnia Famagusta.
MARITAL STATUS: Married to Angela Georgiou, Phlamoudi, Housewife.
CHILDREN: Nicolas, Maria, Adonis.
SCHOOLS/COLLEGE: Famagusta Gymnasium, City University of London.
QUALIFICATIONS: (Dip. EE) Charter Engineer (C. Eng).
MEMBERSHIPS: Fellow of The Institute of Electrical Engineers (FIEE).
HOBBIES AND INTERESTS: Gardening, computing and television.
PERSONAL PROFILE: Senior Telecommunication Consultant with ITT. Participated in the Development of the 1st Digital Telephone Exchange in the world. Now retired. Has a number of patents for basic inventions in telecommunications.

KYL MESSIOS
Actor, Stage work includes Disney's the Lion King and the film 55 degrees North

DATE OF BIRTH: 20-Jan-1977
PLACE OF BIRTH: London, Father from Kalopsida.
MARITAL STATUS: Married to Andrea, England, Trusts Manager.
SCHOOLS/COLLEGE: Southgate School. Birmingham University & Lamda.
QUALIFICATIONS: BA Drama Theatre Arts (2: 1 Honours) 3 A Levels, 9 GCSEs.
HONOURS/AWARDS: National Youth Music Theatre.
HOBBIES AND INTERESTS: Theatre, Film, Football Charity Organisations.
PERSONAL PROFILE: Stage work includes Disney's the Lion King, Cinderella, Union St, Swallow Song. TV and Film work includes Peep Show, Doctors, 55 Degrees North, the trial of Tony Blair, Whistleblowers and Daybreak.

UK

CHARILAOS K METTIS
Teacher, Journalist/Head of Greek Section at the Greek Archdiocese in GB

DATE OF BIRTH: 23-Jan-1934
PLACE OF BIRTH: Philia (Morphou).
MARITAL STATUS: Married to Stella, Dromolaxia, Dress Designer.
CHILDREN: Anna, Teacher. Kyriacos, Teacher.
SCHOOLS/COLLEGE: Pancyprian Gymnasium (Nicosia), University of Athens, London University.
QUALIFICATIONS: Degree in Literature and History.
HONOURS/AWARDS: Ecumenical Patriarchate "Teacher Officio".
HOBBIES AND INTERESTS: Reading and writing.
PERSONAL PROFILE: Head of Greek Section at the Greek Archdiocese in GB, Author of articles and books on history & education of Greeks in GB.

ANDREW MICHAEL
Managing director of Quiss technology PLC a specialist IT outsourcing organisation based in London and Staffordshire

DATE OF BIRTH: 30-Nov-1960
PLACE OF BIRTH: London.
MARITAL STATUS: Married to Maria, Achna, Housewife.
CHILDREN: Alex, Anthony.
SCHOOLS/COLLEGE: John Kelly. Harrow College.
QUALIFICATIONS: TEC Cerificate- Electronic Engineering.
HOBBIES AND INTERESTS: Rifle Shooting, Golf, Reading, Travelling.
PERSONAL PROFILE: Managing director of Quiss technology PLC a specialist IT outsourcing organisation based in London and Staffordshire.

CHRISTINE (nee Chrisoulla Georgiou Leventis) MICHAEL
Estate Agent and Developer serving the North London Community for 32 years

PLACE OF BIRTH: Rizokarpasso
MARITAL STATUS: Married.
CHILDREN: Sandra, BA Business Studies. Nicholas, BSc Management Science, MSc Risk Management and CIMA.
QUALIFICATIONS: GCE O levels, Diploma in Commerce, Business Studies and Economics.
MEMBERSHIPS: Fellow Member of the National Association of Estate Agents.
HOBBIES AND INTERESTS: Cooking, entertaining, socialising, reading, travelling and interior design.
PERSONAL PROFILE: Christine owns and runs Michael Wright Estate Agents based in Cockfosters for 32 years serving the North London Community.

DOULLA MICHAEL
Chair of Bowes Greek School and Member of the Secretariat of the Federation of Greek-Cypriot Educational Associations of England (OESEKA)

DATE OF BIRTH: 15-Apr-1957
PLACE OF BIRTH: London. Father, Antonis Yiakoumi, from Leonarisso; Mother, Maria Tsioupra, from Komi Kebir.
MARITAL STATUS: Married to Andy Michael, Famagusta, Businessman.
CHILDREN: Vasillia, Sussex University Graduate, Assistant Producer/ production manager for News Network International. Anthony, Brighton University. Christopher, Middlesex University.
SCHOOLS/COLLEGE: Tollington Park School, Tottenham Technical College.
HOBBIES AND INTERESTS: Silversmithing and travelling.
PERSONAL PROFILE: Chair of Bowes Primary School PTA, Chair of Bowes Greek School, Member of the Secretariat of the Federation of Greek-Cypriot Educational Associations of England(OESEKA).

UK

EFSTATHIOS MICHAEL
Solicitor, including acting for Carlton and Granada in their widely reported successful action against the Football League

DATE OF BIRTH: 09-Jul-1971
PLACE OF BIRTH: London. Father from Xylotymbou; Mother from Prastion, Morphou.
MARITAL STATUS: Single.
SCHOOLS/COLLEGE: Bancroft's School, Woodford Green, 1982-89. Worcester College, Oxford University 1989-92.
QUALIFICATIONS: MA (Law) (Oxon). Law Society Finals.
HOBBIES AND INTERESTS: Sport (especially football), travel and music.
PERSONAL PROFILE: Partner in Law Firm, Slaughter and May. Specialises in Commercial Litigation, Arbitration and Dispute Resolution, including acting for Carlton and Granada in their widely reported successful action against the Football League.

GEORGE MICHAEL
Businessman involved with the North Middlesex Club and the Pavilion

DATE OF BIRTH: 09-Oct-1957
PLACE OF BIRTH: Petra, Soleas.
MARITAL STATUS: Married to Chryso, Larnaca.
CHILDREN: Olga, Zoe, Evagoras.
SCHOOLS/COLLEGE: Grammar School, Nicosia. Boreham Wood College.
QUALIFICATIONS: Business Studies OND.
HOBBIES AND INTERESTS: Sports.
PERSONAL PROFILE: George is a director of George London Letting's and is also involved with North Middlesex Cricket Club and the Pavilion. George is the son of Evagoras one of the first Greek Cypriot Estate Agents in the UK. the agents were called Chandler Fox and MIchael.

GEORGE STEPHANOS MICHAEL
President of Greek Community in Weston Super Mare/Accountant

DATE OF BIRTH: 21-Nov-1952
PLACE OF BIRTH: Ardana Famagusta.
MARITAL STATUS: Married to Christina, Xylophagou, Retail.
CHILDREN: Stephanos, Laura, Yiangos, Savvas.
SCHOOLS/COLLEGE: Agricultural Gymnasium - Morphou, Weston Super Mare Technical College, Aston University, Birmingham.
QUALIFICATIONS: BSc (Hons) Maths and Computer Science.
MEMBERSHIPS: ACCA.
HONOURS/AWARDS: Best Science Student in 1974 Weston Super-Mare Technical College.
HOBBIES AND INTERESTS: Christian religion, hiking, walking, football and athletics.
PERSONAL PROFILE: Own Accountancy Practice, President of Greek Community in Bristol for Weston Super Mare. Treasurer of Citizens' Advice Bureau for South West Region.

HAMBIS (MITCHELL) MICHAEL
Chairman of Khirokitia Association UK

DATE OF BIRTH: 03-Mar-1920
PLACE OF BIRTH: Khirokitia.
MARITAL STATUS: Married to Maroulla, Ora.
CHILDREN: Michael, Andy, Irene.
SCHOOLS/COLLEGE: Chirokitia Elementary School.
MEMBERSHIPS: AKEL, General & Municipal Workers Union, Communist Party GB.
HONOURS/AWARDS: National Federation of Cypriots in GB for several years of National & Community work. Medal from AKEL for 50 years membership.
HOBBIES AND INTERESTS: Gardening, walking, reading and TV.
PERSONAL PROFILE: Former Editor of Vema Newspaper, Member of the Secretariat of the London District Committee of the Communist Party of GB and Secretary of the Committee. Chairman of the Fleet Leaseholders and Tenants' Association in Camden. Chairman of Chirokitia Association UK.

UK

KERRY MICHAEL
Owner of Weston Super Mare Pier

PLACE OF BIRTH: Parents from Cyprus
HOBBIES AND INTERESTS: Rally Driving.
PERSONAL PROFILE: Kerry Michael is the owner of Weston Super Mare Pier and owns hotels and Restaurants on the sea front there. Was also the owner of the Regency Group, a warranty insurance company which he has since sold.

MICHAEL MICHAEL
Board Member of Mercia Institute of Enterprise, Connect Midlands Investment Committee and Birmingham Future/Accountant

DATE OF BIRTH: 12-Apr-1972
PLACE OF BIRTH: Birmingham. Father from Vasili, Leonarisso; Mother from Limassol.
MARITAL STATUS: Single.
SCHOOLS/COLLEGE: King Edward School Birmingham, Oxford University.
QUALIFICATIONS: BA (Honours) in Geography. Chartered Accountant.
MEMBERSHIPS: Securities Institute.
HOBBIES AND INTERESTS: Business, golf, keep-fit, football, (Arsenal fan), socialising and travel.
PERSONAL PROFILE: Corporate Finance Partner with Friend LLP, a niche firm of professional advisors. Also Board Member of Mercia Institute of Enterprise, Connect Midlands Investment Committee and Birmingham Future.

MICHAEL MICHAEL CBE
CBE {Commander of the Order of the British Empire} for services to Customs and Excise

DATE OF BIRTH: 02-Apr-1941
PLACE OF BIRTH: Hertfordshire, Father from Aradippou, Mother from Larnaca.
MARITAL STATUS: Married to Christina, England, Retired Secretary.
CHILDREN: Christopher, Nicholas, David.
SCHOOLS/COLLEGE: Waverly Grammar School, Birmingham, Sheffield. University, Inns of Court School of Law.
HONOURS/AWARDS: CBE {Commander of the Order of the British Empire} for services to Customs and Excise.
HOBBIES AND INTERESTS: Reading, rambling, foreign travel.
PERSONAL PROFILE: He was a government lawyer for HM Customs & Excise in London he handled both criminal and civil cases either as advocate or instructing solicitor in all courts including cases before the House of Lords, the European Court of Justice and the European Court of Human Rights. In 1989 and 1990 he was loaned to the Republic of Cyprus for 8 weeks to draft the Republic's secondary VAT legislation.

MICHAEL MICHAEL
Cyprus Intenational Football Player

DATE OF BIRTH: 21-Apr-1947
PLACE OF BIRTH: Famagusta.
MARITAL STATUS: Married to Mary, Aradippou.
CHILDREN: Tony, Fitness manager. Katerina, Salon Technician. Stavrou, Business.
SCHOOLS/COLLEGE: Lykeion Famagusta. Technical School Athens.
HONOURS/AWARDS: Played for the Cyprus National Football Team.
HOBBIES AND INTERESTS: Football, Souvla.
PERSONAL PROFILE: Michael as a Footballer played for the Cyprus National Team and New Salamis in Cyprus. In England played For Aekon In the Cyprus League UK. Currently the Vice Chairman of The Cypriot Football League in the UK. He is a partner in the Family Fish and Chip Shop Business.

MICHAEL COSTAS MICHAEL
Councillor, Cardiff County Council

DATE OF BIRTH: 29-Sep-1952
PLACE OF BIRTH: Lymbia Nicosia.
MARITAL STATUS: Married to Joyce, a Hairdresser, from Cardiff, Wales.
CHILDREN: Jordan, James, Zoe.
SCHOOLS/COLLEGE: Kitchener Rd Primary School, Severn Rd, Canton Cardiff, & Market Rd Comprehensive School.
MEMBERSHIPS: Labour Party since 1983, Greek Cypriot Assoc. Fabians, Assoc. of Labour Councillors.
HOBBIES AND INTERESTS: Sports, politics and environment.
PERSONAL PROFILE: Hairdresser. Elected as Councillor for Cardiff County Council in April 97, Deputy Chair Economic Development 98, Elected 99 Executive Member Environment with responsibility for Highways, Parks Cemetarys, waste Control, Street Cleaning, Recycling. Worked with Fairwater Sports Trust on Sportlot Bid. Worked with Greek Cypriot Association to access Lottery funding for a new community hall in Cardiff.

NEOPHYTOS MICHAEL
Totally blind writes poems received letters of thanks from the Queens of the UK, Sweden, Holland, Denmark & Belgium for poems sent to them on different occasions

DATE OF BIRTH: 20-Jan-1946
PLACE OF BIRTH: Petra.
MARITAL STATUS: Married to Eleni from Sykhari.
SCHOOLS/COLLEGE: Solea Gymnasium, Xeros Technical School.
HOBBIES AND INTERESTS: writing and music.
PERSONAL PROFILE: Was a qualified Electrician but had problems with vision so became a receptionist in Nicosia General Hospital. Came to England in 1974, did Rehabilitation training for the Blind for three months with RNIB training in Engineering. Worked as a Tool Operator for five year, then Royal London Society for the Blind in Engineering until 1998. Registered partially blind in 1979 and totally blind in 1997. Has written poems entitled Darling I Love You, My Sweet Lady I Adore You, Baby You're a Dream, Everything For You My Love. Received letters of thanks from the Queens of the UK, Sweden, Holland, Denmark & Belgium for poems sent to them on different occasions.

VASILIA MICHAEL
Assistant Producer/ Production manager for News Network International

DATE OF BIRTH: 17-Jun-1983
PLACE OF BIRTH: London, Father from Famagusta, Mother from London Maternal Grandparents from Vasili and Komi Kebir.
MARITAL STATUS: Single.
SCHOOLS/COLLEGE: Bowes Primary School, Broomfield Secondary School. Sussex University.
QUALIFICATIONS: Politics BA.
HOBBIES AND INTERESTS: Cinema, music, writing songs, going to concerts, meeting new people, visiting new places, current affairs and documentaries.
PERSONAL PROFILE: Assistant Producer/ production manager for News Network International Ltd, a production company focusing on making programmes on security and defence, the environment, ethics and religion. Previously Vasilia has been a researcher on various projects at ITN Factual, producing documentaries for the Discovery Channel and National Geographic. Has also written articles for the Greek Rich List 2007 and 2008.

ALEX MICHAELIDES
lecturer at the London School of Economics

DATE OF BIRTH: 24-Jan-1969
PLACE OF BIRTH: Nicosia.
MARITAL STATUS: Married to Argyro, Cyprus, Equity research analyst.
CHILDREN: Sofia.
SCHOOLS/COLLEGE: Harvard University and Princeton.
QUALIFICATIONS: BA PhD.
HOBBIES AND INTERESTS: Football.
PERSONAL PROFILE: Alex Michaelides is a lecturer at the London School of Economics.

UK

ANDREW MICHAELIDES
DJ & Radio Presenter

DATE OF BIRTH: 25-May-1979
PLACE OF BIRTH: London.
Parents from Famagusta, Son
of George, Journalist for
Parikiaki Newspaper and Photini
Michaelides.
MARITAL STATUS: Married.
SCHOOLS/COLLEGE:
Kingsbury High School, Harrow
Weald College, West Herts,
Watford.
QUALIFICATIONS: HND & BA in Media Production
Management.
HOBBIES AND INTERESTS: Music and dining out.
PERSONAL PROFILE: A top DJ on LGR presents
New Generation Wednesday 10 - 12am, Drivetime Show
Thursday 4 - 6pm.

CHRISTOPHER MICHAELIDES
Councillor, Bridgend County Borough
Council

PLACE OF BIRTH: Barry, South
Wales. Father, Michael, from
Pedhoulas
MARITAL STATUS: Married.
CHILDREN: Three daughters.
SCHOOLS/COLLEGE:
Gladstone Rd Secondary
Modern, Barry, S. Wales,
Llandaff Polytechnic.
QUALIFICATIONS: An
approved driving instructor.
PERSONAL PROFILE: Formed The Bettws Amenities
Society (1990-01), which raised over 1 & 1/2 £million for
community projects in village of Bettws, Bridgend, which
is an area of social deprivation. Its population approx 3,
000. Founder & President of The Bridgend & Valleys
Railway Co. (1985-01) Member of the Garw Community
Council (1983-01). Cabinet Member responsible for
Educ, Leisure, and Community Services, Bridgend
County Borough Council, Chairman of Glamorgan
Archives, Committee Member of the Board of the Arts
Council for Wales.

GEORGE MICHAELIDES
Journalist

DATE OF BIRTH: 01-Feb-1951
PLACE OF BIRTH: Famagusta.
MARITAL STATUS: Married to
Photini.
CHILDREN: Vasos, Works in Job
Centre. Andreas, Radio Presenter.
SCHOOLS/COLLEGE:
Famagusta Gymnasium.
MEMBERSHIPS: AKEL Party.
HOBBIES AND INTERESTS:
All sports, especially football.
PERSONAL PROFILE: Worked as a Jounalist with
Verna Newspaper from 1974 - 85, now with Parikiaki
Newspaper. Also a presenter for LGR & Hellenic TV.
Secretary of New Salamis Football club.

GEORGE PANOS MICHAELIDES
Councillor Howlands in Welwyn Hatfield
Borough Council. Accountant

DATE OF BIRTH: 09-Aug-1952
PLACE OF BIRTH: Nicosia.
MARITAL STATUS: Married to
Stavroulla.
CHILDREN: Two.
SCHOOLS/COLLEGE: English
School Nicosia, North London
University.
QUALIFICATIONS: BA
Accountancy. Chartered
Certified Accountant.
HOBBIES AND INTERESTS: Football
(Tottenham & Barnet fan) and politics.
PERSONAL PROFILE: George Michaelides is the
Elected Local Councillor with the Conservative Party in
the Howlands Ward of Welwyn, Hatfield Constituency.
Was treasurer of Cypriot Football League from 1977-
85. Former Chairman of Potters Bar Greek School,
Chairman of Independent Greek Schools of UK.
Was first Chairman of Assoc. of Cypriot Qualified
Accountants for two years. President of the Association
of Chartered Certified Accountants, North London
District Society. Partner in ALG Chartered Certified
Accountants in North London.

UK

MICHAEL MICHAELIDES
Founder Partner at Bond Partners LLP/
The Company help several community
organisation's

DATE OF BIRTH: 22-Dec-1969
PLACE OF BIRTH: London
Parents from Athienou and
Sikopetra.
MARITAL STATUS: Single.
SCHOOLS/COLLEGE:
Winchmore School. Emile
Woolf College.
QUALIFICATIONS: FCCA Cert
PFS.
HOBBIES AND INTERESTS:
Greek current affairs (Greece and Cyprus), fitness
training, sports, reading, film and music.
PERSONAL PROFILE: Michael Michaelides is a
founding partner of Bond Partners LLP. which now has
several offices around the UK and associated offices
abroad. Focus: Working with owner managed businesses.
The company helps several community organisation's.

OMIROS MICHAELIDES
Chairman of Yerakies Association
& Chairman of the Greek Orthodox
Church in Newcastle

DATE OF BIRTH: 19-May-1935
PLACE OF BIRTH: Yerakies.
MARITAL STATUS: Married.
CHILDREN: One son, three
daughters.
SCHOOLS/COLLEGE:
Yerakies Elementary;Pedhoula
Gymnasium.
HOBBIES AND INTERESTS:
Work and travel.
PERSONAL PROFILE: Came
to England in 1953, did National Service in British Army
for two years, had Hairdresser, Coffee Bar, Restaurant
& Nightclub, Casino in Surrey. 1967 opened Casino in
Newcastle was Director in Pleasurama Casinos Division.
Now owns the Banqueting Halls Assembly Rooms
in Newcastle. Chairman of Yerakies Assoc. UK &
Chairman of the Greek Orthodox Church in Newcastle.

PROFESSOR PANTELEIMON MICHAELOUDIS
Musician gave an exclusive performance
for the Queen and Prince of Denmark
and their representatives at the British
Ambassador's residence in Denmark

DATE OF BIRTH: 07-Mar-1966
PLACE OF BIRTH:
Famagusta. Father, Michalakis,
former Principal Conductor
of the Famagusta Municipal
Band.
MARITAL STATUS: Single.
SCHOOLS/COLLEGE: Royal
College of Music.
QUALIFICATIONS: DIP RCM,
ARCM.
HOBBIES AND INTERESTS: Sports and reading.
PERSONAL PROFILE: Taught six years at the Royal
College of Music, now busy recording and performing
in concerts and touring. He has given concerts in many
international Guitar Festivals and appeared on Radio
and TV. Gave an exclusive performance for the Queen
and Prince of Denmark and their representatives at the
British Ambassador's Residence in Denmark.

CHRISTOS KALLONAS MICHAELS
Co Founder of Sound Films. First film
produced by them was "Hibernation",
the international multi award winning
short by John Williams

DATE OF BIRTH: 30-May-1970
PLACE OF BIRTH: London.
Father, George, from Larnaca;
Mother, Antigoni Kallonas,
from Latsia.
MARITAL STATUS: Single.
SCHOOLS/COLLEGE: Lochinver
House School, (Junior School),
St. Albans, (Senior School), Leeds
University (Degree), Kings College,
London (Post Grad Diploma).
QUALIFICATIONS: LLB. LSF.
MEMBERSHIPS: Law Society, New Producers Alliance.
HOBBIES AND INTERESTS: Film making, acting and
Greek dancing.
PERSONAL PROFILE: Co Founder of Sound Films.
First film produced by them was "Hibernation", the
international multi award winning short by John Williams.
He joined in 2006 from Mel Gibson's Icon UK Group,
where for several years he was in charge of business
affairs UK, Australia and internationally. Christos is also
a partner of leading entertainment law firm of Lee &
Thompson.

UK

REV ANDREAS MICHAILIDIS
Greek Orthodox Priest of the Church Virgin Mary in Nottingham

DATE OF BIRTH: 07-Dec-1937
PLACE OF BIRTH: Lefka.
MARITAL STATUS: Married to Alkmini, Greece.
CHILDREN: Anastasios, killed in accident in Greece;. Eleni, Student. Menelaos, Monk. Michael and Eftychia, Business and Student.
SCHOOLS/COLLEGE: Pancyprian Gymnasium Nicosia, Columbia University USA, University of Athens, University of Thessaloniki.
HOBBIES AND INTERESTS: Writing books & poems. One has been published (The Lexicon of Byzantine Music).
PERSONAL PROFILE: Greek Orthodox Priest of the Church Virgin Mary in Nottingham. Former teacher and translator in Cyprus and Thessaloniki, Greece, Teaches translation for MA in Linguistics as a visiting lecturer at the University of Sheffield. Also responsible for the Greek schools of Nottingham and Derby.

LEFKOS MIDDLETON
Vice President & Worldwide Head of the Medical Genetics Division Glaxo Kline

DATE OF BIRTH: 21-Dec-1950
PLACE OF BIRTH: Nicosia.
MARITAL STATUS: Married to Georgia, Nicosia.
CHILDREN: Theodore, George, Constantinos, All three are Students.
SCHOOLS/COLLEGE: Pancyprian Gymnasium, Louis Pasteur University in Strasbourg, France.
HONOURS/AWARDS: Awarded the European Federation of Neurological Societies Investigator Award in 1994 & the Italian Caetano Conte Academy Prize in 1996.
HOBBIES AND INTERESTS: music, theatre and travel.
PERSONAL PROFILE: Joined GlaxoSmith Kline R&D in 1999, based in London. In 1990, founded the Cyprus Institute of Neurology and Genetics. He identified two new diseases and mapped genes of four diseases in the Mediterranean region. Served as Nicosia Municipal Councillor from 1985-1990.

HELEN CHRISTA MIKELLIDES
Chiropodist/Sang as a backing singer in the Group Neos Kosmos for the Eurovision Song Contest in Cyprus

DATE OF BIRTH: 23-Dec-1970
PLACE OF BIRTH: UK. Father from Nicosia; Mother from Famagusta.
MARITAL STATUS: Single.
SCHOOLS/COLLEGE: Bishop Douglas Secondary, Southgate College, University of Westminster, Leaf Hospital, School of Podiatric Medicine, University of Brighton. Pancyprian Gymnasium.
QUALIFICATIONS: BSc (Honours) Podiatry. State Registered Chiropodist/Podiatrist.
MEMBERSHIPS: Society of Chiropodists and Podiatrists.
HOBBIES AND INTERESTS: Singing, playing accordion, summer concerts on the lawn. Learning violin and in Gospel choir.
PERSONAL PROFILE: Sang as a backing singer in the Group Neos Kosmos for the Eurovision Song Contest in Cyprus. Part of a Greek Dancing Group that performed on the Generation Game in February 2002. Chiropodist with her own practice.

ANDREAS MIKKIDES
Former Mayor of Haringey (Deceased)

DATE OF BIRTH: 15-Feb-1932
PLACE OF BIRTH: Kythrea.
MARITAL STATUS: Married to Eleni, Pano Lakatamia.
CHILDREN: Ioakim, Christa, Eraclis.
SCHOOLS/COLLEGE: Pancyprian Gymnasium.
HOBBIES AND INTERESTS: Poetry published an Anthology Photini Orizontes and two books entitled "Three Stories look like Fairy Tails" and "Pages of my Life".
PERSONAL PROFILE: Was an active member of the Labour movement and took part in many demonstrations including ban the bomb, against the war in Vietnam and against the apartheid regime of South Africa. Elected as Councillor at Haringey Borough in 1982, Deputy Mayor 1985 and 1986 then Mayor. Was the first Cypriot Mayor in Britain.

UK

ANNA MINA
Secretary and Vice-President for the Greek School in Brent

PLACE OF BIRTH: London. Parents from Nicosia.
MARITAL STATUS: Married to Costakis, London Parents from Cyprus.
CHILDREN: Paul, Christopher, Andreas.
SCHOOLS/COLLEGE: Maria Grey.
QUALIFICATIONS: Cert Ed. Dip Ed.
HONOURS/AWARDS: Brent Citizenship Award 2002.
HOBBIES AND INTERESTS: Reading, Photography, writing poetry and gardening.
PERSONAL PROFILE: Secondary School Teacher of English & Special Needs. English Co-ordinator, Learning Mentor Volunteer on the Committee of the "Association of Cypriots Brent & Harrow" - Secretary and Vice-President for the Greek School in Brent.

KATERINA MINA
Operatic Soprano

DATE OF BIRTH: 06-Feb-1975
PLACE OF BIRTH: Limassol.
MARITAL STATUS: Married to Dimitris Melas, Greece, Banker.
SCHOOLS/COLLEGE: Gymnasium in Cyprus. Guildhall School of music and drama.
QUALIFICATIONS: BMUS(Hons) PGDip (opera). Diploma of Licentiateship in singing performance.
MEMBERSHIPS: London ambassador for "Alkionides UK" charity dedicated to providing financial assistance to poor families and young children who need medical treatment in the UK.
HONOURS/AWARDS: Prize winner in two International singing competitions the 1st Concorso Vocale Internationale Di Music Sacra in Rome and the 7th Julian Gayarre International singing competition in Spain.
HOBBIES AND INTERESTS: Dancing, reading, meditation and cooking.
PERSONAL PROFILE: Operatic Soprano sang in many famous venues, made her debut with the New Moscow Opera sang major roles with British Youth Opera, English Touring opera and Polish National Opera.

DR MINAS GEORGE MINA
Former Honorary Secretary of National Federation of Cypriots/Teacher/Lecturer

DATE OF BIRTH: 21-Sep-1953
PLACE OF BIRTH: Makrasyka, Famagusta.
MARITAL STATUS: Married to Katey, London (parents from Cyprus). Lawyer.
SCHOOLS/COLLEGE: American Academy, Larnaca, Kingsway-Princeton College, London. Kings College, London.
QUALIFICATIONS: BSc Ph. D.
MEMBERSHIPS: Institute of Clinical Research.
HOBBIES AND INTERESTS: Politics, world & social affairs and swimming.
PERSONAL PROFILE: Teacher/Lecturer. Scientific Research for many years at Univ, currently also training in Medical Diagnostics, General Secretary of Organisation of Relatives of missing Cypriots (UK). Former honorary Secretary of National Federation of Cypriots and member of other community Organisations.

MICHAEL MINAS
Artist/Production Designer/Art Director for Joseph & the Amazing Technicolor Dreamcoat for the Really Useful Group

DATE OF BIRTH: 14-Aug-1942
PLACE OF BIRTH: Morphou.
MARITAL STATUS: Married to Jacqueline, London, Lecturer.
CHILDREN: Miraphora, Graphic Artist.
SCHOOLS/COLLEGE: Greek Gymnasium Morphou, Hornsey College of Art & Crafts.
QUALIFICATIONS: National Diploma in Design (NDD), Studied Painting.
HOBBIES AND INTERESTS: Writing.
PERSONAL PROFILE: 1967-78 Scenic Designer Thames Television. 1977-96 Five solo exhibitions of his paintings as well as selected group exhibitions Television Work: Design & Art Direction: Orchestra C4 with Sir George Solti & Dudley Moore Operalia- with Placido Domingo for Televisa, Mexico, Royal College of Art and Chelsea College of Art.
Art Director for Joseph & the Amazing Technicolor Dreamcoat for the Really Useful Group. The Three Tenors, Christmas in Vienna 2000 for Sony.

UK

GEORGE MICHAEL MISHELLIS
Former Chairman of Manor Hill Greek School

DATE OF BIRTH: 20-Mar-1940
PLACE OF BIRTH: Larnaca.
MARITAL STATUS: Married to Antigoni, Latsia.
CHILDREN: Andonea Buxton, TV Presenter. Christos, Solicitor. Mishellis, Media.
SCHOOLS/COLLEGE: American Academy Larnaca.
QUALIFICATIONS: Designer - Pattern Cutter.
MEMBERSHIPS: Greek Brotherhood.
HOBBIES AND INTERESTS: Fishing and Arsenal Fooball Club.
PERSONAL PROFILE: Previous business: Manufacturer of Ladies Clothing - Ladies Hairdressing - Hotelier & now Landlord/Property Owner. Helped to create the Independent Greek School's in London. Chairman to Manor Hill School for six years.

DR CONSTANTINOS MISSOURIS
Consultant Cardiologist

DATE OF BIRTH: 23-Dec-1959
PLACE OF BIRTH: Zodhia, Nicosia.
MARITAL STATUS: Single.
SCHOOLS/COLLEGE: The English School Nicosia, St George's Hospital Medical School, London.
QUALIFICATIONS: BSc, MBBs, MD, MRCP.
MEMBERSHIPS: Numerous National & International Societies.
HOBBIES AND INTERESTS: Poetry and classical reading.
PERSONAL PROFILE: Consultant Cardiologist, Heatherwood & Wexham Park Hospital & Royal Brompton Hospital, London.

COSTAS MORFAKIS
Managing Partner of Bond Partners LLP, Chartered/Certified Accountants and Insolvency Practitioners Past Chairman of the Institute of Chartered Accountants Small Practitioners Group of Central London

DATE OF BIRTH: 08-May-1963
PLACE OF BIRTH: Finchley. Father from Ayios Georgious Kyrenia; Mother, Amygdalia, Greece.
CHILDREN: Adam and Zoe.
SCHOOLS/COLLEGE: The Grammar School, Nicosia, Arnos School, Southgate. Polytechnic of North London now London Metropolitan University.
QUALIFICATIONS: FCA, FCCA, FCMA, MARBP.
MEMBERSHIPS: Past Chairman of Institute of Chartered Accountants, small practitioners group of Central London.
HOBBIES AND INTERESTS: Classic cars and martial arts.
PERSONAL PROFILE: After graduating in 1986 trained within a medium sized accountancy practice in Finchley, became a partner in 1995 and in 2004 co founded Bond Partners which now has several offices around the UK and associated offices abroad. Auditor of Greek & Greek Cypriot Community of Enfield Charity.

THANOS MORPHITIS
Deputy Director of Education, Islington

DATE OF BIRTH: 05-Mar-1954
PLACE OF BIRTH: London. Father from Morphou;Mother from Athens.
MARITAL STATUS: Married.
CHILDREN: Five.
SCHOOLS/COLLEGE: William Ellis School. University of Hull.
QUALIFICATIONS: BA (Honours). Qualified Youth Worker.
PERSONAL PROFILE: Deputy Director of Education, Islington.

UK

GEORGE MOUKTARIS
Accountant/Secretary of Lobby for Cyprus

DATE OF BIRTH: 25-May-1951
PLACE OF BIRTH: Famagusta.
MARITAL STATUS: Married to Christalleni, Dherynia.
CHILDREN: Anastasis, Christina, Stavri.
SCHOOLS/COLLEGE: 1st & 2nd Gymnasium Famagusta; West Norwood Tech College.
QUALIFICATIONS: Chartered Accountant.
HOBBIES AND INTERESTS: Sailing, diving and shooting.
PERSONAL PROFILE: Has own accountancy practice in Edgware called Mouktaris & Co. Chairman of Famagusta Assoc. Chairman of Hellenic School of the Holy Cross, and Secretary of Lobby for Cyprus.

ANTHOULLA MOUSIKOU
President of the Greek School of Ayia Marina and Panayia Chryseleousa of Stoke-on-Trent

DATE OF BIRTH: 23-Nov-1960
PLACE OF BIRTH: Famagusta.
MARITAL STATUS: Married to Panayiotis, Oroklini, Business.
CHILDREN: Spyroulla, All Students. Evangelos, Constantinos, Georgios.
SCHOOLS/COLLEGE: Ardana 1st School, Tricomo High School, Naseby Secondary School, Birmingham.
HOBBIES AND INTERESTS: Reading, photography, listening to music, cooking and travelling.
PERSONAL PROFILE: President of the Greek Orthodox Ladies Auxillary Society of Stoke-on-Trent in 1997-98, also currently President of the Greek School of Ayia Marina and Panayia Chryseleousa of Stoke-on-Trent.

GEORGE K. MOUSKAS
Managing Director of Shipping Company Zela Shipping Co, Ltd/on the Council of the Trust of Archbishop of Thyateira & GB

DATE OF BIRTH: 14-Jul-1953
PLACE OF BIRTH: London. Parents from Famagusta and Nicosia.
MARITAL STATUS: Married to Mary Vavlitis in 1975. (parents from villages Vavla & Kato Drys).
CHILDREN: Elli, University of London Graduate. Kyriacos, Reading French at London University. Zela, Student.
SCHOOLS/COLLEGE: Finchley Catholic Grammar School then read Law at Ealing College London.
QUALIFICATIONS: BA (Honours) Law.
MEMBERSHIPS: Baltic Exchange, Lloyds of London.
HOBBIES AND INTERESTS: Watching football, playing tennis and snow skiing.
PERSONAL PROFILE: Managing Director of Shipping Company Zela Shipping Co, Ltd, established in 1963. Currently on the Council of the Trust of Archbishop of Thyateira & GB, which overlooks all Ecclesiastical matters in UK.

KYRIACOS MOUSKAS
Shipowner/built a new hospital wing in Voula-Athens, which comprised eleven operating theatres. This was opened in February 2001 by the Greek Minister of Health. (Deceased)

DATE OF BIRTH: 25-Nov-1917
PLACE OF BIRTH: Famagusta.
MARITAL STATUS: Married to Zela Loukiades, from Nicosia, Cyprus.
CHILDREN: Zenon, Gloria, George.
SCHOOLS/COLLEGE: Gymnasium High School, Famagusta, Cyprus.
MEMBERSHIPS: Baltic Exchange since 1955.
HONOURS/AWARDS: Made 'Archonta' by Patriarch of Constantinople in 1968.
HOBBIES AND INTERESTS: His work and family.
PERSONAL PROFILE: Shipowner since 1957, becoming the first Greek Cypriot shipowner. Helped to build Greek school at St Andrews Church, Kentish Town, and helped financially many other Greek schools in the UK. Also built a new hospital wing in Voula-Athens, which

comprised eleven operating theatres. This was opened in February 2001 by the Greek Minister of Health. Kyriacos Mouskas was one of the founders of the Church of St John the Baptist in Wightman Road.

KYRIACOS Z MOUSKAS
Cited in the Who's Who of Britains Young Business Elite 2003

DATE OF BIRTH: 04-Jul-1971 **PLACE OF BIRTH:** London Parents Zenon and Helen from London Grandparents from Famagusta, Nicosia, Dhali and Larnaca Grandfathers Mouskas Founder of Zela Shipping And Pittas Founder of Pittas Pastries. **MARITAL STATUS:** Married to Marianna, Nicosia, daughter of Irene Checkley MBE, Lady Mountbattens right hand Lady and Solon Christodoulides Importer of Pharmaceuticals.
CHILDREN: Zen, Irene, Both at School.
SCHOOLS/COLLEGE: Hereward House Prep School in St Johns Wood, Bloxham School in Oxford and Aldenham School in Elstree. United States International University.
QUALIFICATIONS: BSc in International Business.
MEMBERSHIPS: Baltic Exchange.
HONOURS/AWARDS: Cited in the Whos Who of Britains Young Business Elite 2003.
HOBBIES AND INTERESTS: Sports, Weight Training, Football, Car Rallies. Particpated in the 4x4 AA Cyprus Rally in 1995 as a co driver and finished 8th. Collector of Classic and Exotic Cars.
PERSONAL PROFILE: Kyriacos is a Director of Zela Shipping a company operating capesize vessels which are the largest dry cargo ships in the World. Also a Director of Kenville Properties and Pittas Properties that invest in Commercial and Residential Properties. He is also one of the founders of Starcomm Telecoms.

MARY MOUSKAS JP
Justice of the Peace at Barnet Magistrates Court also Chairperson of Cancer Research UK Totteridge Society

DATE OF BIRTH: 07-Jan-1956 **PLACE OF BIRTH:** London Father from Vavla, Mother from Kato Drys.
MARITAL STATUS: Married to George, London Parents from Famagusta and Nicosia, Managing Director of Zela Shipping Co Ltd.
CHILDREN: Elli, London University graduate in Sociology is now a Teacher. Kyriacos, London University graduate in French and Management and Internal Auditing. Zela, at school.
SCHOOLS/COLLEGE: South Hampstead High School For Girls. London School of Economics.
QUALIFICATIONS: BSc Sociology.
HOBBIES AND INTERESTS: Reading, theatre, watching Tottenham Hotspur with her Husband.
PERSONAL PROFILE: Mary Mouskas is a Justice of the Peace at Barnet Magistrates Court and also Chairperson of Cancer Research UK Totteridge Society.

ZENON MOUSKAS
Co-founder of Zela Shipping Co Ltd. Member of the Council of the Greek Shipping Cooperation Committee

DATE OF BIRTH: 02-Aug-1941 **PLACE OF BIRTH:** London. Father from Famagusta; Mother from Nicosia.
MARITAL STATUS: Married to Helen Pittas, born in London (father from Dhali, Mother from Larnaca).
CHILDREN: Zela, Housewife. Kyriacos, Shipping Company Director.
SCHOOLS/COLLEGE: Crest Nursery School, Wessex Gardens Primary School, Clarks College Grammar School.
QUALIFICATIONS: FICS AIARS.
MEMBERSHIPS: Baltic Exchange, Lloyds of London.
HOBBIES AND INTERESTS: Sports, Church, Charities.
PERSONAL PROFILE: Co-founder of Zela Shipping Co Ltd. Member of the Council of the "Greek Shipping Co-operation Committee". Trustee & Council Member of the Church of "The Holy Cross & St. Michael"Golders Green.

UK

HARRY MOUSKIS
Managing Director of an Architectural Visualisation Company

DATE OF BIRTH: 13-Aug-1977
PLACE OF BIRTH: London. Parents from Kaimakli and London.
MARITAL STATUS: Married to Olga.
CHILDREN: Leonida.
SCHOOLS/COLLEGE: Queen Elizabeth Boys' School, Bournemouth University.
QUALIFICATIONS: BSc in Production Design & Manufacture, MA in Digital Entertainment Systems.
HOBBIES AND INTERESTS: Computers, films and music.
PERSONAL PROFILE: Harry Mouskis is the Managing Director of a architectural visualisation company in North London called V-real who are specialists in producing high quality photorealistic computer generated images and animation. Clients ranging from Architects, Developers, Housing Associations, Marketing Agencies, Product Designers and Estate Agents.

JOHN MOUSKIS
Secretary of The Greek Parents Association and of the Cypriot Diaspora Committee

DATE OF BIRTH: 08-Jun-1948
PLACE OF BIRTH: Kaimakli.
MARITAL STATUS: Married to Loulla, London (parents from Dromolaxia).
CHILDREN: Andrew, Bournemouth University. Harry, Business. Jason, Student.
SCHOOLS/COLLEGE: Pancyprian Gymnasium in Nicosia.
QUALIFICATIONS: Accountant.
HOBBIES AND INTERESTS: Greek Music, socialising, walking and theatre.
PERSONAL PROFILE: Partner in the Accountancy Practise G. George Associates in Wood Green. Chairman of Queenswell Greek School, Secretary of Greek Parents Association, Functions Organizer for OESEKA.

JOHN MICHAEL MOUSKOS
Mountaineer has summited Mont Blanc and Mount Elbrus Europe's highest Mountain

DATE OF BIRTH: 13-Mar-1964
PLACE OF BIRTH: London.
MARITAL STATUS: Single.
SCHOOLS/COLLEGE: Paddington Green, Crookham Court, Christchurch. Polytechnic of North London.
QUALIFICATIONS: BA Hons, Dip Arch Hons Architecture RIBA.
MEMBERSHIPS: Greek Mountaineering Federation.
HOBBIES AND INTERESTS: Mountaineering, writing poetry, film making.
PERSONAL PROFILE: Mountaineer in 2006 he summited Mont Blanc and Mount Acconcagua in Argentina(the highest mountain in the Southern Hemisphere). Crossed the Alps from Argentiere in France to Zermatt in Switzerland. In 2007 summited Mount Elbrus in Russia Europe's highest mountain. RIK made a film about him called Breathe Me. In 2004 founded the Breathing Life Trust working in partnership with Great Ormond Street Hospital and the Cyprus Government to open the Breathing Life Lung Centre in Nicosia Cyprus in 2009.

KYRIAKOS MOUSTOUKAS
Chairman of Liverpool Greek Society

DATE OF BIRTH: 27-Jul-1962
PLACE OF BIRTH: Liverpool. Parents from Lefkara.
MARITAL STATUS: Married to Panayiota.
CHILDREN: Georgia, Christopher, Nikolaos, Dimitris.
SCHOOLS/COLLEGE: Quarry Bank Comp School, Liverpool, Lancaster University.
QUALIFICATIONS: BSc (Honours) 2. 1, Physics with Electronics. Financial Planning Certificate Parts 1, 2, 3.
MEMBERSHIPS: MLIA (Dip) (Member of Life Insurance Ass.).
HOBBIES AND INTERESTS: Greek music, Greek dancing, ballroom dancing and Bouzouki.
PERSONAL PROFILE: Financial Adviser with Zurich Advice Network; Founder Member & Chairman of Liverpool Greek Society; Greek Church of St. Nicholas (formerly Committee Member).

PATRICK MYLES
Recipient of the Society of London Theatre New Producer Bursary Award in 2006

PLACE OF BIRTH: Cyprus in 1979 Irish Father Mother Cypriot
SCHOOLS/COLLEGE: Bristol Old Vic Theatre School.
HONOURS/AWARDS: Recipient of the Society of London Theatre New Producer Bursary Award in 2006.
PERSONAL PROFILE: Patrick Myles is an actor producer as an actor has appeared in Planespotting, the Bill and Red Thursday. He co produced the play Glengarry Glen Ross at the Apollo Theatre Shaftesbury Avenue starring Jonathan Pryce.

MICHAEL JOHN MYLONAS
Barrister (Ladbroke Grove Inquiry - Lead Counsel)

DATE OF BIRTH: 11-Jun-1966
PLACE OF BIRTH: England. Mother from Amiandos.
MARITAL STATUS: Single.
SCHOOLS/COLLEGE: Eton College, University of Buckingham, Bar School (London).
QUALIFICATIONS: LLB (Honours), BAR.
MEMBERSHIPS: International BAR Association, Professional Negligence Bar Association. Personal Injury Bar Association. Hurlingham Polo Association.
HONOURS/AWARDS: Scholarship, Grays Inn; Scholarship - Inns of School of Law.
HOBBIES AND INTERESTS: Polo, sailing, skiing and motor racing.
PERSONAL PROFILE: Barrister specialising in medical negligence and major disaster litigation. (Ladbroke Grove Inquiry - Lead Counsel).

GEORGE MYRISTIS
Played football in Cyprus, for Pezoporikos & the National Team of Cyprus (1955-58) Owns Myristis the bed linen Business

DATE OF BIRTH: 23-Apr-1937
PLACE OF BIRTH: Livadhia, Larnaca.
MARITAL STATUS: Married to Annika, Larnaca.
CHILDREN: Panicos, Margarita.
SCHOOLS/COLLEGE: Graduated Commercial Lyceum Larnaca.
QUALIFICATIONS: 5 O Levels.
PERSONAL PROFILE: Consultant in Men's Outdoor clothing - 39 years experience & still going. Also in the Bedlinen Business for 30 yrs as a Manufacturer. Played football in Cyprus, for Pezoporikos & the National Team of Cyprus (1955-58).

JASON NEARCHOU
President of Greek Community in Coventry

DATE OF BIRTH: 16-Dec-1958
PLACE OF BIRTH: Limassol.
MARITAL STATUS: Married to Olga, Coventry (parents, Cypriot).
CHILDREN: Christian, Petros, Stefanos, Panayiota.
SCHOOLS/COLLEGE: Limassol Gymnasium.
QUALIFICATIONS: Registrar.
HOBBIES AND INTERESTS: Horse riding, swimming and reading.
PERSONAL PROFILE: President of Greek Community of Coventry and of Midlands Festival Communities.

UK

CHRISTOS DEMOS NEOCLEOUS
Solicitor

DATE OF BIRTH: 28-Sep-1961
PLACE OF BIRTH: London. Parent Dora Limassol and Mandres Famagusta.
MARITAL STATUS: Single.
CHILDREN: Two sons.
SCHOOLS/COLLEGE: Sir William Collins School. City & East London College, Chelmsford University, College of Law, Lancaster Gate.
QUALIFICATIONS: A levels, LLB Degree.
HOBBIES AND INTERESTS: Go karting, clay shooting, race cars, skiing and D. I. Y.
PERSONAL PROFILE: Joined Solicitors Kenneth Shaw & Co in 1981 as a trainee; now Equity Owner in the same practice but now called Christos Wybrew.

EKATERINA (KAT) NEOCLEOUS
Singer/Radio Presenter

DATE OF BIRTH: 27-May-1982
PLACE OF BIRTH: London, Mother and Father from Aradippou.
MARITAL STATUS: Single.
SCHOOLS/COLLEGE: Winchmore Secondary School, Enfield. University of Westminster, Harrow.
QUALIFICATIONS: BA Honours Commercial Music.
HONOURS/AWARDS: Awarded Scholarship for participation in the 'Westminster Voices' Gospel Choir (2003 & 2004).
HOBBIES AND INTERESTS: Performing, music, theatre, dancing, literature, watching Wimbledon.
PERSONAL PROFILE: Singer/Songwriter. Sings both in Greek and English. Has performed extensively, venues include Theatre Royal Drury Lane, The Royal Albert Hall, Alexandra Palace, Lock 17. Recorded with the Royal Philharmonic Orchestra for Shirley Thompson's New Nation Rising EP released in 2004. Has also collaborated with Fusing Naked Beats and appears on their 2006 album 'Outer Prospective'. Stagework as an actress includes roles in Midsummer Nights Dream, Twelfth Night, Our Country's Good, and Mill on The Floss, appeared in music video 'Johnny Teardrop' by Edwyn Collins. Radio presenter has her own show on London Greek Radio.

MARIANNA NEOFITOU
Actress Appeared in the film Harry Potter No. 2

DATE OF BIRTH: 23-Jun-1989
PLACE OF BIRTH: UK. Father from Kalavasos, Mother from Peristeronopiyi.
MARITAL STATUS: Single.
SCHOOLS/COLLEGE: Sylvia Young Theatre School.
HOBBIES AND INTERESTS: Singing, dancing, reading and writing songs.
PERSONAL PROFILE: Has appeared on TV in Watchdog and Eastenders and various commercials in the UK and abroad. Appeared in the film Harry Potter No. 2 "Chamber of Secrets"and had a role in the West end show Chitty Chitty Bang Bang at the London Palladium. Other credits include Captain Corellis mandolin, BBC, Eastenders, Disney channel, Duets with Lil Romeo on ITV. "Silver Birch House"at the Arcola Theatre and "Broken"Channel 4 award winning short film 2007.

ANDREW NEOPHYTOU
Director of Travelmania a travel company that is a major help to community organisations. Finalist in the category for small leisure offline agency of the year 2007 at the agent achievement awards

DATE OF BIRTH: 31-May-1963
PLACE OF BIRTH: London Parents from Paphos and Akanthou.
MARITAL STATUS: Married to Paula, Hair Stylist.
CHILDREN: Anna Maria, Stavroulla, Helen.
SCHOOLS/COLLEGE: William Penn. Hotel and Travel Training College.
QUALIFICATIONS: O and A levels and Blue Riband college Diploma in Travel and Tourism.
HONOURS/AWARDS: Finalist in the category for small leisure offline agency of the year 2007 at the agent achievement awards.
HOBBIES AND INTERESTS: Travelling.
PERSONAL PROFILE: Andrew Neophytou is a Director of Travelmania Ltd continually helping community organisations.

CHRIS NEOPHYTOU
Presidential candidate for the Cyprus elections 2008

DATE OF BIRTH: 29-May-1950
PLACE OF BIRTH: Famagusta.
MARITAL STATUS: Married.
CHILDREN: N. Neophytou, G. Neophytou.
SCHOOLS/COLLEGE: East London University.
QUALIFICATIONS: BSc Applied Economics.
HOBBIES AND INTERESTS: Swimming, sailing, diving, cinema, fishing and shooting.
PERSONAL PROFILE: Chairman of Caretower Ltd. One of the Founders and First president of the Church of The Twelve Apostles. Was a Presidential candidate for the Cyprus elections 2008.

ELEFTHERIA MARIA NEOPHYTOU
Senior Lecturer, Metropolitan University

DATE OF BIRTH: 02-Apr-1958
PLACE OF BIRTH: Prodromi, Paphos.
MARITAL STATUS: Married to Charalambos Tsakalotos, Greece, Management Accountant.
CHILDREN: Leonidas.
SCHOOLS/COLLEGE: Yerbury Primary School and Shelburne Girls School. Kingsway College, University of Essex, Garnet College & Birkbeck College(University of London).
QUALIFICATIONS: BA MA PGCE.
HOBBIES AND INTERESTS: Languages, cultures, travel, music and art.
PERSONAL PROFILE: Eleftheria Maria Neophytou is a Senior Lecturer, Department of Education, London Metropolitan University.

JOHN NEOPHYTOU
Managing Director of Travelmania, Finalist in the category for small leisure off line agency of the year 2007 at the agent achievement awards

DATE OF BIRTH: 03-Sep-1965
PLACE OF BIRTH: London Father from Paphos mother from Akanthou.
MARITAL STATUS: Married to Helen.
CHILDREN: Nicholas, George, Christina.
SCHOOLS/COLLEGE: William Penn. South London College.
QUALIFICATIONS: 7 O levels 2 A levels. Diploma in the Blue Riband Course for travel and tourism.
HONOURS/AWARDS: Finalist in the category for small leisure off line agency of the year 2007 at the agent achievement awards.
HOBBIES AND INTERESTS: Movies, travelling and dining out.
PERSONAL PROFILE: John Neophytou is the Managing Director of Travelmania which was formed in 1988. The company is well known for its help towards the community.

SPYROS NEOPHYTOU
Former Chairman of Manor Hill Greek School and was on the committee of Independent Greek Schools

DATE OF BIRTH: 26-Jun-1951
PLACE OF BIRTH: Ayios Theodoros, Famagusta.
MARITAL STATUS: Married to Christine, London (parents from Komi Kebir).
CHILDREN: Johnathan, Stockbroker. Melanie, Teacher.
QUALIFICATIONS: Studied Aeronautical engineering at Delta College Athens and Hatfield Polytechnic.
HOBBIES AND INTERESTS: Keep fit, squash and tennis.
PERSONAL PROFILE: Former Chairman of Manor Hill Greek School and was on the committee of Independent Greek Schools. Sales Manager of Cyprus Airways UK.

UK

SPYROS J NEOPHYTOU
Director of Bank of Cyprus (London) Ltd. Director - Bank of Cyprus (Channel Islands) Ltd

DATE OF BIRTH: 19-Apr-1944
PLACE OF BIRTH: Paphos, Cyprus.
MARITAL STATUS: Married to Angela.
CHILDREN: Barbara, Marianna.
SCHOOLS/COLLEGE: Graduate of Paphos Greek Gymnasium.
QUALIFICATIONS: 1972 - Associate Member of the Institute of Chartered Accountants in England and Wales. 1979 - Fellow of the Institute of Chartered Accountants in England and Wales.
MEMBERSHIPS: Council Member of the Cyprus-British Chamber of Commerce and Industry.
HONOURS/AWARDS: Gold Cross of the Archdiocese of Thyateira.
HOBBIES AND INTERESTS: Golf.
PERSONAL PROFILE: Director of Bank of Cyprus (London) Ltd. Director - Bank of Cyprus (Channel Islands) Ltd. Former General Manager Bank of Cyprus(London)Ltd.

TONY NEOPHYTOU
London Greek Radio Broadcaster

DATE OF BIRTH: 26-Aug-1973
PLACE OF BIRTH: London. Parents from Limassol.
SCHOOLS/COLLEGE: George Orwell Secondary, Islington 6th form Centre, University of North London.
QUALIFICATIONS: BSc Honours Politics.
PERSONAL PROFILE: Tony is a Broadcaster on London Greek Radio and writes a column for the Parikiaki newspaper.

ZINA NEOPHYTOU
Travel Distribution Director BBC Worldwide Global Channels

DATE OF BIRTH: 28-Feb-1973
PLACE OF BIRTH: London Father From Larnaca Mother from Nicosia.
MARITAL STATUS: Single.
SCHOOLS/COLLEGE: Finchley Manor Hill School. London Guildhall University and Le Mireil University, Toulouse, France.
QUALIFICATIONS: BA Honours Degree in French with a Spanish minor.
HOBBIES AND INTERESTS: Skydiving, Travelling, Cooking, Salsa Dancing, Shopping, Theatre and Literature.
PERSONAL PROFILE: Zina Neophytou is Travel Distribution Director BBC Worldwide Global Channels she works very closely with many travel organisations including Pacific Asia Travel Association where she is on the Executive Committee.

ROBERT NEWMAN
Comedian appeared with David Baddiel, Hugh Dennis and Steve Punt (among others)this was the regular quartet in the BBC radio and TV programme The Mary Whitehouse Experience

DATE OF BIRTH: 07-Jul-1964
PLACE OF BIRTH: London Father from Cyprus.
SCHOOLS/COLLEGE: Cambridge University.
PERSONAL PROFILE: Robert Newman is an Impressionist who appeared with David Baddiel, Hugh Dennis and Steve Punt (among others)this was the regular quartet in the BBC radio and TV programme The Mary Whitehouse Experience. He and Baddiel then followed this up with their own series Newman and Baddiel in pieces. His latest solo work has been A history of Oil and the History of the World Backwards.

ANDY NICHOLAS
Head Teacher Lea Valley School

DATE OF BIRTH: 25-Jun-1952
PLACE OF BIRTH: Larnaca.
MARITAL STATUS: Married to Helen, Larnaca.
CHILDREN: two sons and one daughter.
SCHOOLS/COLLEGE: Gayhurst Primary School, Hackney, St Davids School, Hornsey, All Saints Teachers Training College.
HOBBIES AND INTERESTS: Vintage cars and family.
PERSONAL PROFILE: First post teacher at Chesterfield Junior School in Enfield. Then went to Coleridge School as a Senior Teacher, followed by Lea Valley School in 1985 as Deputy Headteacher, then Headteacher with 500 Pupils. Ofsted Inspector for Primary Schools. Magistrate with Haringey.

JACK NICHOLAS
Operations Manager UK Holiday Inn Hotel Group

DATE OF BIRTH: 01-Feb-1955
PLACE OF BIRTH: London. Parents from Komi Kebir.
MARITAL STATUS: Married to Helen, London, Parents from Neo Chorio Kythreas, Retail.
CHILDREN: Joanna, Christina.
SCHOOLS/COLLEGE: Middlesex Polytechnic.
QUALIFICATIONS: Higher National Diploma in Hotel & Catering; Management.
MEMBERSHIPS: Fellow of the Hotel & Catering Institute Management Association.
HONOURS/AWARDS: Hotel of the Year Award, 1987.
HOBBIES AND INTERESTS: Playing golf, watching Arsenal, cricket and rugby.
PERSONAL PROFILE: Was General Manager of the Holiday Inns at Newcastle and Cardiff, and of the London Marriott, Swiss Cottage. Joined Premier in October 1999 as Director of Operations for London and in March 2000 was promoted to Operations Manager UK. Now responsible for the day-to-day operation of 22 hotels - 15 Express by Holiday Inn Hotel, 4 Howard Johnson Hotels and 3 Days Inn Hotels. Whilst in Cardiff was on the Committee of the RNIB South Wales Looking Glass Appeal and helped raise £100, 000 in twelve months for the centre in Cardiff. One of the founding members of The Komi Kebir Football Club.

KYPROS NICHOLAS
Chairman of the Greek Orthodox Communities of Great Britain/Solicitor

DATE OF BIRTH: 12-Nov-1937
PLACE OF BIRTH: Khirokitia.
MARITAL STATUS: Married to Maria.
CHILDREN: Yiota, Stella, Nicholas.
SCHOOLS/COLLEGE: English School, Nicosia. Inns of Courts School of Law, College of Law, Guildford.
QUALIFICATIONS: Solicitor, formerly Barrister at Law.
HONOURS/AWARDS: Freeman of the City of London 1983. Honorary Chief Enyoma in Nigeria, 1985. Director of the Iwuanyanwu F. C in Nigerian football league. Former Governor of the University of East London.
HOBBIES AND INTERESTS: Tennis, swimming and Arsenal.
PERSONAL PROFILE: Senior Partner of the practice Nicholas & Co. President of the Greek Orthodox Church in Edmonton, London and Chairman of the Greek Orthodox Communities of Great Britain. Trustee of the Archdiocese of Thyateira & G. B. Solicitor to the Archdiocese of Thyateira & G. B and formerly to the Cyprus Relief Fund. Trustee of the Cardiovascular Disease & Research Trust (CDER).

NICHOLAS CHRISTOPHER KYPROS NICHOLAS
Solicitor Partner in Nicholas & Co solicitors active in supporting community organisations

DATE OF BIRTH: 30-Jun-1971
PLACE OF BIRTH: UK. Parents from Khirokitia, Cyprus.
MARITAL STATUS: Married to Katrina, English/Armenian.
CHILDREN: Adam.
SCHOOLS/COLLEGE: Bethany Davis College of East Anglia, University of North London, Southbank University.
QUALIFICATIONS: BA Honours.
HOBBIES AND INTERESTS: Football (Arsenal fan), rugby and general Sport.
PERSONAL PROFILE: Solicitor, Partner in Nicholas & Co Solicitors who are active in supporting community organisations.

UK

STEVEN NICHOLAS

Chairman and Director of Tiuta PLC a specialist company in providing short term property finance

DATE OF BIRTH: 08-Oct-1958
PLACE OF BIRTH: UK, Parents from Ayios Amvrosios.
MARITAL STATUS: Married to Eleni, from Yerolakkos.
CHILDREN: Three sons.
SCHOOLS/COLLEGE: William Collins School. Kingsway College, Middlesex Poly, College of Law Guildford.
QUALIFICATIONS: BA Honours in Law.
MEMBERSHIPS: Cypriot Golf Society.
HOBBIES AND INTERESTS: Spurs, golf, squash and Bouzouki.
PERSONAL PROFILE: Solicitor. Former Senior Partner in Georgiou Nicholas Solicitors. Chairman of Tiuta PLC a specialist company in providing short term property finance.

YIACOUMIS NICHOLAS

Formed the Company Nicholas Bros in 1948, making bridal wear, known all over the world. Known for his philanthropic work within the community

PLACE OF BIRTH: Komi Kebir 1925
MARITAL STATUS: Married to Pepa, Yialloussa.
CHILDREN: Nick, Chris, Nina, Julie Eleni.
SCHOOLS/COLLEGE: Komi Kebir Elementary School.
HOBBIES AND INTERESTS: Gardening, reading, politics.
PERSONAL PROFILE: Served in the Cyprus Regiment of the British Army. Formed the Company Nicholas Bros in 1948, making bridal wear, known all over the world. Known for his philanthropic work within the community.

THEODORA NICKSON

Vice Principal at John Kelly Girls' Technology College

DATE OF BIRTH: 31-Aug-1956
PLACE OF BIRTH: Kingsbury, London. Father from Skylloura; Mother from Skarinou.
MARITAL STATUS: Single.
CHILDREN: Peter, Teacher. Maria, Media. Elena, School.
SCHOOLS/COLLEGE: Downer Grammar School, Edgware. University of Nottingham.
QUALIFICATIONS: MA, BEd Honours, Cert ED.
HOBBIES AND INTERESTS: Reading, theatre, Cinema and walking.
PERSONAL PROFILE: Theodora Nickson is the Head Teacher of Bishops Hatfield Girls School in Hertfordshire.

CONSTANTINOS NICOLA

Consultant Civil Engineer, spent four years in East Africa designing and supervising water supply, airports and infrastructure related projects

DATE OF BIRTH: 20-Aug-1946
PLACE OF BIRTH: Nicosia, Cyprus.
MARITAL STATUS: Married to Nitsa, Nicosia, Lettings consultant.
CHILDREN: Steven Louissa, Louissa.
SCHOOLS/COLLEGE: Upton House. Kingston University.
QUALIFICATIONS: BSc Civil Engineering.
MEMBERSHIPS: Member of the Institute of Civil Engineering, Member of the Institute of Highway and Transportation Engineers.
HOBBIES AND INTERESTS: Photography, Golf and football.
PERSONAL PROFILE: Early employment included working as a civil servant for the Department of the Environment involved in the design and construction of Kent's M25 motorway section. Later he worked on infrastructure design for major international building projects with a firm of consultants. He was subsequently appointed to work in Kenya and spent four years in East Africa designing and supervising water supply, airports and infrastructure related projects. Returned to England in late 1980 and has since worked for a major international construction group where he has coordinated the management of a variety of energy related worldwide contracts.

GEORGE NICOLA
London's Perfect Portion Winner 2009.
Seafish Fryers Quality Award 2008

DATE OF BIRTH: 12-Jul-1973
PLACE OF BIRTH: London
Father from Ayia Triada, Mother from Ayios Dometios.
CHILDREN: Demetri.
SCHOOLS/COLLEGE: American Acadamy, Larnaca.
MEMBERSHIPS: National Federation of Fish Fryers.
HONOURS/AWARDS: London's perfect portion winner 2009. Seafish fryers quality award 2008.
HOBBIES AND INTERESTS: Fishing, biking and reading.
PERSONAL PROFILE: George is the proprietor of the award winning George's Fish and Souvlaki bar in South Woodford.

YIANOULLA NICOLA
Author of the book Holly Blue

DATE OF BIRTH: 05-Apr-1959
PLACE OF BIRTH: Cyprus.
MARITAL STATUS: Married to Nicholas, Cypriot, London Cabby.
CHILDREN: Christyanna, Kiri.
SCHOOLS/COLLEGE: Arnos Grove. Waltham Forest.
QUALIFICATIONS: Diploma in Fashion Design.
HOBBIES AND INTERESTS: reading, painting and socialising.
PERSONAL PROFILE: Author of the book Holly Blue published in 2008.

PROFESSOR ANDREAS NICOLAIDES
Professor of Vascular Surgery

DATE OF BIRTH: 17-Oct-1938
PLACE OF BIRTH: Nicosia.
MARITAL STATUS: Married to Lala, Nicosia.
CHILDREN: Nicolas, Banker. Savvas, IT.
SCHOOLS/COLLEGE: Pancyprian Gymnasium, Nicosia, Guys Hospital Medical School, London.
QUALIFICATIONS: MBBS LRCP MRCS. FRCS MS.
MEMBERSHIPS: Fellow of the Royal College of Surgeons (England and Edinburgh).
HONOURS/AWARDS: Awarded the Jacksonian prize by the Royal College of Surgeons England in 1972 for his work on the prevention of venous thromboembolism.
HOBBIES AND INTERESTS: Wildlife photography.
PERSONAL PROFILE: Emeritus Professor of Vascular Surgery at the Imperial College School of Medicine (St Mary's Hospital) and Director of the Irvine Laboratory for Cardiovascular Investigation and Research from 1983-2000. He is Editor-in-Chief of International Angiology and is on the Editorial Board of many vascular journals. He. is an examiner for MS and PhD degrees for London University. Now the Medical Director of the Cyprus Institute of Neurology and Genetics. He is co-author of over 400 original papers and editor of fourteen books.

ANNA NICOLAIDES
Textile Artist and Designer/2002Charles Henry Foyle Trust -Award for Stitched Textiles

DATE OF BIRTH: 24-Nov-1943
PLACE OF BIRTH: Birmingham
Father from Avgorou.
MARITAL STATUS: Married to Metaxas, Gastria, Restaurateur.
CHILDREN: Nicolas, Senior Corporate Analyst. Andrew, Property Developer. Matthew, Property Developer. Jason and Marianna, Head Teacher and Curriculum Manager.
SCHOOLS/COLLEGE: Bath Spa University.
QUALIFICATIONS: BA (Hons) Textiles and Fine Art.
HONOURS/AWARDS: Bath Spa University Fellowship Award 2002 Charles Henry Foyle Trust -Award for Stitched Textiles.
HOBBIES AND INTERESTS: Literature, World Travel, Art History, Short Story Writing and Theatre.
PERSONAL PROFILE: Anna Nicolaides is a Textile Artist and Designer exhibit all over the UK including Royal West of England Academy. She also lectures in Textiles.

ANTONIS NICOLAIDES
Commonwealth Games Gold Medallist 2002

PLACE OF BIRTH: London
HONOURS/AWARDS: Commonwealth Games Gold Medallist, skeet (pairs). Commonwealth Games bronze medallist skeet (individual) 2002.
PERSONAL PROFILE: Antonis Nicolaides is a Shooting Champion representing Cyprus.

243

JASON NICOLAIDES
Head Teacher of Walliscote Primary School

PLACE OF BIRTH: UK Parents from Gastria and Avgorou
PERSONAL PROFILE: Jason Nicolaides is the Head Teacher of Walliscote Primary School, in Weston Super Mare.

PROFESSOR KYPROS NICOLAIDES
Obstetrician & Gynaecologist/Regularly gives TV interviews. The head of the biggest foetal medicine research centre in the world

DATE OF BIRTH: 09-Apr-1953
PLACE OF BIRTH: Limassol.
MARITAL STATUS: Single.
CHILDREN: Erodotos, Despina.
SCHOOLS/COLLEGE: Paphos Primary, English School, Nicosia, Kings College, London.
QUALIFICATIONS: BSc in Bio-Chemistry, MBBS in Medicine Professor in Foetal Medicine.
HONOURS/AWARDS: Ian Donald Gold Award of the International Society of Ultrasound in Obstetrics and Gynaecology, Eric Salling award of the World Association of Perinatal Medicine.
HOBBIES AND INTERESTS: Reading, classical and Greek music.
PERSONAL PROFILE: Pioneer of new methods of diagnosing abnormalities and correcting of the Foetus. is based at Kings College Hospital. Formed the charity of Foetal Medicine Foundation. Promoting research and training internationally. He has been in over 1000 scientific and national publications. Regularly gives TV interviews. The head of the biggest foetal medicine research centre in the world. President of the Cypriot Students Association and, member of the National Federation of Cypriots in the 1970's.

ANDREAS NICOLAOU
Solicitor, Vice President of the Democratic Party of Cyprus in the UK (Deceased)

DATE OF BIRTH: 25-Sep-1932
PLACE OF BIRTH: Achna.
MARITAL STATUS: Married to Vera, Laxis.
CHILDREN: Constantina, Helena, Susanna.
SCHOOLS/COLLEGE: Achna Elementary School, Famagusta Gymnasium, Council of Legal Education and College of Law.
QUALIFICATIONS: Barrister at Law, Solicitor.
MEMBERSHIPS: The Law Society.
HONOURS/AWARDS: Honoured by the Co Patriarch of Constantinople for services to the Greek Orthodox Church.
HOBBIES AND INTERESTS: Football and athletics, classical and Greek music.
PERSONAL PROFILE: Solicitor (own office, A Nicolaou & Co). Chairman All Saints Greek Orthodox Church. Vice President of the Democratic Party of Cypriots in England. Legal advisor to the Greek Orthodox Church in GB. Shareholder in LGR.

REV ECONOMOS GEORGIOS NICOLAOU
Parish Priest Bristol. 1st Chairman of Eptakomi Association

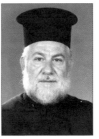

DATE OF BIRTH: 28-Sep-1941
PLACE OF BIRTH: Eptakomi.
MARITAL STATUS: Married to Christalleni from Eftakomi.
CHILDREN: Nicos, Sotiroulla, Andreas and Angela.
SCHOOLS/COLLEGE: Lanition Gymnasium, Limassol, Theological School, Nicosia.
MEMBERSHIPS: Eftakomi Association. Honorary member of Hellenic Society Bristol.
HONOURS/AWARDS: Silver Cross of the Archdiocese of Thyateira of Great Britain.
HOBBIES AND INTERESTS: Stamp collection (Cyprus), Coin collection (Cyprus) and gardening.
PERSONAL PROFILE: Parish Priest Bristol. Was 1st Chairman of Eptakomi Association.

UK

LORA NICOLAOU
Architect/Urban Designer/Senior Lectureship at Oxford Brookes University

DATE OF BIRTH: 05-Mar-1957
PLACE OF BIRTH: Nicosia.
MARITAL STATUS: Single.
SCHOOLS/COLLEGE: Palourgiotissa & Acropolis Gymnasium, Nicosia; National Technical University of Athens; Bartlett School of Architecture - University College, London; Oxford Brookes University.
QUALIFICATIONS: Diploma in Architecture, MSc in Advanced Architectural Studies, MA in Urban Design.
MEMBERSHIPS: Member of Urban Design Group UK.
HOBBIES AND INTERESTS: Swimming and walking.
PERSONAL PROFILE: Director of Development Planning at DEGW plc, London.

MARIA K NICOLAOU
Chair of The Leukaemia Society

DATE OF BIRTH: 09-Sep-1961
PLACE OF BIRTH: London. Father from Pano Arodhes, Paphos; Mother from Athienou.
MARITAL STATUS: Married to Savvas, London Father from Famagusta; Mother from Rizakarpasso). Structural Engineer.
CHILDREN: Twins: John Christopher and Georgia Penny.
SCHOOLS/COLLEGE: Trinity House School for girls, Kingsway Princeton College.
QUALIFICATIONS: O Levels. YCSW & National Certificate in Supported Housing.
MEMBERSHIPS: Chartered Institute of Housing.
HOBBIES AND INTERESTS: Travel, reading and charity work.
PERSONAL PROFILE: Scheme Manager for Sheltered Housing for Cypriots. Chair of The Leukaemia Society.

NEOPHYTOS NICOLAOU
Organising Secretary AKEL Section in Great Britain

DATE OF BIRTH: 11-Dec-1946
PLACE OF BIRTH: Erimi.
MARITAL STATUS: Married to Evoulla, from Limassol.
CHILDREN: One son and two daughters.
SCHOOLS/COLLEGE: Lanition Gymnasium, Limassol. Pitmans London.
MEMBERSHIPS: AKEL, National Fereation of Cypriots, EKA.
HOBBIES AND INTERESTS: Gardening.
PERSONAL PROFILE: Former General Manager of Parikiaki Newspaper. Vice Chair of Association of Cypriots in Enfield. Organising Secretary AKEL Section in Great Britain.

NICHOLAS VENEDI NICOLAOU
Regional Finance Governor for London Unison

DATE OF BIRTH: 19-Jun-1960
PLACE OF BIRTH: London. Father from Kalopsida: Mother from Kyrenia.
MARITAL STATUS: Married to C Perez, Spanish, Teacher.
CHILDREN: Andalucia, at school in Sevillia in Spain.
SCHOOLS/COLLEGE: Cardinal Manning Catholic School, Kensington.
QUALIFICATIONS: BA (Honours) Degree Politics & Economics. M. I. L (Institute of Linguists).
HOBBIES AND INTERESTS: Politics, current affairs, travelling, socialising, sport.
PERSONAL PROFILE: Regional Finance Governor for Unison since 1998 - membership in London of 150, 000 - nationally 1. 4 million. Also Chair of London Unison Diversity Forum.

UK

NICK NICOLAOU
Consultant Gynaecologist at Hillingdon Hospital

DATE OF BIRTH: 23-Jun-1953
PLACE OF BIRTH: London. Parents from Vokolida and Lefkara.
MARITAL STATUS: Married to Eve.
CHILDREN: Erini, Soteri, Katerina.
SCHOOLS/COLLEGE: Guys Hospital Medical School.
QUALIFICATIONS: BSc (Honours) Biochemistry; MD; BS; FRCOG; LAW HBSc (Honours).
HOBBIES AND INTERESTS: Computers, skiing, rugby and football (Chelsea supporter).
PERSONAL PROFILE: Consultant Gynaecologist at Hillingdon Hospital. Senior Gynaecologist at University of London. Examiner of University of London. Former President of Hellenic Medical Society. Junior Vice President of Royal Society of Medicine. UCAS screener for Imperial Medical School.

DR NICOS NICOLAOU
Lecturer, Imperial College, London

DATE OF BIRTH: 14-Apr-1974
PLACE OF BIRTH: Nicosia, Cyprus.
MARITAL STATUS: Single.
SCHOOLS/COLLEGE: The English School, Nicosia Cyprus, University of Bristol, University of Cambridge, Imperial College, London.
QUALIFICATIONS: BSc (First class hons) in Economics, M. Phil. in Economics, Ph. D in Management.
HONOURS/AWARDS: Selected for inclusion in Who's Who in Science and Engineering, Principal's Award for Teaching Excellence, 2006, Awarded the Psion Prize for the best doctoral thesis completed in 2004, Admitted to the status Fellow of the Cambridge Commonwealth Society, A.
HOBBIES AND INTERESTS: Wine – tasting, Formula 1 racing.
PERSONAL PROFILE: Lecturer in Entrepreneurship, Imperial College London.

ALEXIS NICOLAS
Footballer Played with Chelsea - Full squad member

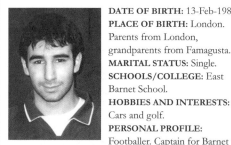

DATE OF BIRTH: 13-Feb-1983
PLACE OF BIRTH: London. Parents from London, grandparents from Famagusta.
MARITAL STATUS: Single.
SCHOOLS/COLLEGE: East Barnet School.
HOBBIES AND INTERESTS: Cars and golf.
PERSONAL PROFILE: Footballer. Captain for Barnet District and Middlesex, was with Arsenal from ten to sixteen years old. Joined and played for Aston Villa reserves & youth. Played with Chelsea - Full squad member appeared for first team. Cyprus Under-21 International. Also played for Brighton.

NICKY NICOLAU
Footballer Played Professionally for Arsenal under 19's and reserves

DATE OF BIRTH: 12-Oct-1983
PLACE OF BIRTH: London. Father from Pano Zodia, Morphou; Mother from Ireland.
MARITAL STATUS: Single.
SCHOOLS/COLLEGE: Highams Park, E17.
HOBBIES AND INTERESTS: Pool and Snooker.
PERSONAL PROFILE: Played Professionally for Arsenal under 19's and reserves. Originally began as a left winger, now a left back. He played for Southend F. C on loan season 2003-4, then back to Arsenal. Was back at Southend, helped them get promoted between 2004/2005. Also played for Swindon and Hereford now playing for Barnet.

LUKE NICOLI
Journalist News Editor for Shoot and Match Magazine

DATE OF BIRTH: 31-Oct-1972
PLACE OF BIRTH: Hitchin, GrandParents from Patriki.
MARITAL STATUS: Married to Tanya, Baldock, Herts, Housewife.
CHILDREN: One Child.
SCHOOLS/COLLEGE: Noble School. North Herts College.
QUALIFICATIONS: 10 GCSE's, 3 A Levels, NCTJ Accredited in Journalism.

UK

MEMBERSHIPS: Member of the Football Writers' Association.
HONOURS/AWARDS: EMAP Sports News Editor of the year 1999, IPC News Editor Highly Commended 2000.
HOBBIES AND INTERESTS: Football. Golf, Tennis and DIY.
PERSONAL PROFILE: Luke Nicoli started his sports journalism career at Match magazine as news editor in 1994, before taking up a similar role at Shoot magazine in 1998. He was then made deputy at Shoot before turning freelance in 2000. Luke has also Written for the Daily star, Express, Total football, Worlds soccer, Maxim, Loaded, The Voice, Golf Monthly and Boxing News. Reported on Football matches for the Sunday Mirror also writes for the News of the World, Zoo and Shoot. He has participated on BBC Five Live programme, co wrote the Wayne Rooney Annual has written books on Sunderland Football Club the World Cup and Prince William.

MARINA NORRIS
Head of Development Arts Council England, South East

DATE OF BIRTH: 19-Aug-1971
PLACE OF BIRTH: London Mother from Paphos.
CHILDREN: Partner has son Joshua, student.
SCHOOLS/COLLEGE: Royal Naval School. City University.
QUALIFICATIONS: BA MA.
HOBBIES AND INTERESTS: Theatre, Travel and Films.
PERSONAL PROFILE: Marina Norris works as Head of Development Arts Council England, South East in this role she is responsible for leading the work on education and learning, diversity and audience development across the South East Region.

VASILIS OLYMBIOU
Chairman of Greek School in Maidstone District

DATE OF BIRTH: 16-Jan-1948
PLACE OF BIRTH: Kyrenia.
MARITAL STATUS: Married to Thelma, Famagusta, Secretary.
CHILDREN: Niki, Both students. Andreas.
SCHOOLS/COLLEGE: Pancyprian Gymnasium, Nicosia, Aristotelion university, Salonica.
HOBBIES AND INTERESTS: Travel, reading, sport and politics.
PERSONAL PROFILE: Worked in a shipping company for 23 years. Has held the position of Chairman, Vice Chairman and Treasurer in the Greek community of Maidstone & District, and has been Chairman of the Greek school since 1992.

MARIOS OLYMPIOS
Chairman of Education for the Institute of Cost and Executive Accountants and then Chairman of the Institute for two years

DATE OF BIRTH: 16-Jul-1944
PLACE OF BIRTH: Lymbia Nicosia.
MARITAL STATUS: Married to Chrystalla, Alamino, secretary.
SCHOOLS/COLLEGE: Primary and High School in Lymbia, Commercial l Lykion Nicosia. East London University.
QUALIFICATIONS: Msc with distinction, Finance Accountancy and Management.
HONOURS/AWARDS: Received an award for being an active member of EOKA 1955/59. Award from Lymbia for financial support to the Association.
HOBBIES AND INTERESTS: Athletics, travelling, music, reading Football.
PERSONAL PROFILE: Own practice since 1983 as Accountant, Mortgage Advisor and Financial Advisor. From 1984 to 1995 owned fast food businesses in four different locations. Chairman of Education for the Institute of Cost and Executive Accountants and then Chairman of the Institute for two years. Visiting Lecturer at Guildford College teaching. international business and finance.

MELIS ANTONIS OURRIS
Owner and Managing Director of Ourris Residential Homes, former president of the Ayios Serglos Famagusta Association

PLACE OF BIRTH: Ayios Sergios, Famagusta.
MARITAL STATUS: Married to Tasoula, Peristeronopiyi.
CHILDREN: Antonis, Estate Agent. Tom, Business. Elena, Solicitor.
SCHOOLS/COLLEGE: Educated in Cyprus.
HOBBIES AND INTERESTS: Community work as hobbies.
PERSONAL PROFILE: Treasurer and former president of the Ayios Sergios Famagusta Association. Owner and Managing Director of Ourris Residential Homes, Anastasia Lodge and Autumn Gardens residential home for the elderly. and Ourris properties Ltd.

UK

TONY OURRIS
Owner of Anthony Webb Estate Agents/ Committee of the Green Lanes Business Association

DATE OF BIRTH: 28-Aug-1972
PLACE OF BIRTH: London
Father from Ayios Sergios
Mother from Peristeronopiyi.
MARITAL STATUS: Married to
Vasoulla, London Parents from
ayios Andronicos.
CHILDREN: Harry, Anastasia.
SCHOOLS/COLLEGE: Enfield
Grammar. DeHaviland College
Boreham Wood.
HOBBIES AND INTERESTS: Bouzoukia and Music.
PERSONAL PROFILE: Tony Ourris is the owner of
Anthony Webb Estate Agents based in Palmers Green
from 1990 which was opened by the MP Stephen Twiggit
is one of the leading Estate Agents in the Area. He is
also involved in the family busines's of Anastasia Lodge
and Autumn Gardens Care Homes he is also on the
Committee of the Green Lanes Business Association.

ELENI PALAZIDOU
Chair of Maanyelka Charity helping to build hospitals in Somalia

DATE OF BIRTH: 01-Nov-1947
PLACE OF BIRTH: Nicosia.
MARITAL STATUS: Single.
SCHOOLS/COLLEGE:
Pancyprian Gymnasium of
Nicosia. The Medical. Academy
of Sofia.
QUALIFICATIONS: MD, PhD,
MRCP, FRCPSYCH.
HOBBIES AND INTERESTS:
History (in particular
Byzantinology), antiques, travelling.
PERSONAL PROFILE: Consultant Psychiatrist
in the NHS in London with a special interest in
Psychopharmacology and the treatment of Mood
Disorders {Bipolar disorder and Depression}. Has been
involved in the setting up of a Charity, Maanyeelka Burao
{which she Chairs} which aims to help build Hospitals
and develop mental health service in Somaliland
{Northern Somalia}.

ANDRONICOS PALLIKAROS
President of the church and school of St Mamas Church in Bedford

DATE OF BIRTH: 09-Oct-1936
PLACE OF BIRTH: Gypsos.
MARITAL STATUS: Married to
Margarita from Lefkara.
CHILDREN: One son, two
daughters.
SCHOOLS/COLLEGE:
Lefkoniko High School, Tricomo
High School, Acton College.
HOBBIES AND INTERESTS:
Community affairs.
PERSONAL PROFILE: Teacher at the All Saints Greek
Church at Camden Town. Secretary of the Committee
of the All Saints Church in Camden Town. Was Also
Secretary of the Committee of St Nicholas Church in
Shepherds Bush. One of the Founders and President of
the St Charalambous Church in Luton and Presdent of
St Mamas in Bedford.

ZAKOS PALLIKAROS
Champion Bodybuilder Mr Cyprus Grand Prix Bodybuilding contest 2006

DATE OF BIRTH: 06-Apr-1970
PLACE OF BIRTH:
Rizokarpasso.
MARITAL STATUS: Single.
CHILDREN: One Child.
SCHOOLS/COLLEGE:
Holloway School. Royal Free
Medical School.
QUALIFICATIONS: BSc Hons
in medicinal chemistry, PhD in
Steroid Biochemistry.
MEMBERSHIPS: Member of the Royal Society of
Chemistry.
HONOURS/AWARDS: Won the international IFBB Mr
Cyprus Grand Prix Bodybuilding contest 2006.
HOBBIES AND INTERESTS: Keeping fit.
PERSONAL PROFILE: After 9 years of working as
a scientist in a laboratory doing research in new drug
development, he decided to follow his dream and open
his own Gym.

UK

LILY VARKARIS PANAGI
Media Agent some of her notable successes are Valerie Singleton and John Noakes

PLACE OF BIRTH: Famagusta. **CHILDREN:** Zacharias, Company Director (Telecoms). **SCHOOLS/COLLEGE:** Highbury Hill High School for Girls; St Martins School of Art. **QUALIFICATIONS:** Diploma in Art & Design Teaching Diploma. **MEMBERSHIPS:** On the Board of Agents Association of Great Britain.
HOBBIES AND INTERESTS: Tennis, dancing, gardening, history and reading.
PERSONAL PROFILE: TV presenters' agent Lili Panagi, has over 25 years experience in representing clients in the entertainment industry. Amongst her most noted successes - Alan Titchmarsh, John Stapleton, Bob Holness, Valerie Singleton, Pam Rhodes, Diana Moran and John Noakes.
Volunteer for the British Red Cross (20 years).

BARRY PANARETOU
Senior Lecturer in Molecular Genetics at King's College London

DATE OF BIRTH: 12-Jul-1967 **PLACE OF BIRTH:** London, parents both from Rizokarpasso, Cyprus. **MARITAL STATUS:** Single. **SCHOOLS/COLLEGE:** Christ Church School, London, Woodhouse Sixth Form. College, London, Queen Mary University of London, University College London.
QUALIFICATIONS: B. Sc {Hons} Biochemistry, PhD Biochemistry.
PERSONAL PROFILE: Senior Lecturer in Molecular Genetics at King's College London(KCL). Prior to joining KCL, Barry was a postdoctoral research associate at Unilever Research, the MRC Laboratory for Molecular Cell Biology.

NICK PANAY
Consultant Gynaecologist Queen Charlotte's & Chelsea Hospital, London

DATE OF BIRTH: 26-Mar-1963 **PLACE OF BIRTH:** London. Father from Ayios Amvrosios;. Mother from Limassol. **MARITAL STATUS:** Married to Justine, a General Practitioner, from England. **CHILDREN:** Isabelle and Thomas. **SCHOOLS/COLLEGE:** Creighton School, Muswell Hill, University College, London. Royal College of Obsygynae, Royal Society of Medicine (Council), British Menopause Society.
QUALIFICATIONS: BSc, MBBS.
HOBBIES AND INTERESTS: Tennis, golf, sailing and skiing.
PERSONAL PROFILE: Consultant Gynaecologist, Queen Charlotte's & Chelsea Hospital, London.

ANDREA PANAYI
Publisher/Editor of Close Up Magazines Ltd

DATE OF BIRTH: 26-Jul-1974 **PLACE OF BIRTH:** London, Father from Akanthou, Mother from Kalo Chorio. **MARITAL STATUS:** Married. **CHILDREN:** Two Children. **SCHOOLS/COLLEGE:** Southgate School. Barnet College. **PERSONAL PROFILE:** Andrea is the Publisher/Editor of Close Up Magazines Ltd.

UK

CHRISTOPHER PANAYI
Actor Appeared in Othello at the Royal Opera House in Covent Garden. Appeared in the film The Krays

DATE OF BIRTH: 10-Oct-1970
PLACE OF BIRTH: London. Parents from Famagusta.
SCHOOLS/COLLEGE: Holloway School, Arts Educational Drama School, Anna Schers Drama School, North London College Performing Arts Council.
QUALIFICATIONS: Drama Diploma, Salsa Teacher/Drama.
MEMBERSHIPS: Equity.
HONOURS/AWARDS: Trophy for Best Stage Fight at Drama School, Shot Putt Winner at school.
HOBBIES AND INTERESTS: Acting.
PERSONAL PROFILE: Actor. Appeared in Othello at the Royal Opera House in Covent Garden. Appeared in the film The Krays, and the TV Commercial for Malborough Cigarettes.

PROFESSOR GABRIEL PANAYI
Professor of Rheumatology at Guys Kings and St Thomas School of Medicine, Guys Hospital, London SE1

PLACE OF BIRTH: Kato Drys, Larnaca.
MARITAL STATUS: Married to Alexandra, (parents from Yialousa).
CHILDREN: Stavros, Lawyer. Alexander, Student.
SCHOOLS/COLLEGE: Royal Grammar School, Lancaster, University of Cambridge.
HONOURS/AWARDS: Awarded many honours, including Heberden Orator of the British Society of Rheumatology.
HOBBIES AND INTERESTS: Reading especially Greek poetry, painting and gardening.
PERSONAL PROFILE: Professor of Rheumatology at Guys Kings and St Thomas School of Medicine, Guys Hospital, London SE1. Presently President British Society of Rheumatology. Has written or edited several books on Rheumatology as well as contributing chapters in books and review articles.

JAMES PANAYI
Footballer played for the 1st team at Watford FC. under Graham Taylor

DATE OF BIRTH: 24-Jan-1980
PLACE OF BIRTH: Hammersmith, London. Father from Achna.
SCHOOLS/COLLEGE: St Ignatius Tottenham, Bishops Douglas School.
HOBBIES AND INTERESTS: Football and golf.
PERSONAL PROFILE: Signed 01. 07. 88, played for the 1st team at Watford FC. under Graham Taylor.

PANICOS PANAYI
Professor of European History De Montford University

DATE OF BIRTH: 18-Oct-1962
PLACE OF BIRTH: London Mother and Father from Lymbia and Mitseron.
MARITAL STATUS: Married to Mundeep Panayi.
SCHOOLS/COLLEGE: Stationers. Polytechnic of North London and University of Sheffield.
QUALIFICATIONS: BA History Ph. D.
MEMBERSHIPS: Fellow of the rotal Historical Society.
HOBBIES AND INTERESTS: Supporting Chelsea.
PERSONAL PROFILE: Professor of European History De Montford University has also published 13 books on the same topic.

SIMOS PANAYI
Organised Cypriot film festival's in London in 2007, 8 and 9

DATE OF BIRTH: 17-Apr-1980
PLACE OF BIRTH: London, Father from Derynia, Mother from Gerani.
MARITAL STATUS: Single.
SCHOOLS/COLLEGE: Grafton Primary School, St Alyousius College. Barnet. College London College of printing, {now known as London College of. Communication}.
QUALIFICATIONS: HND BA Marketing and Advertising.
HOBBIES AND INTERESTS: Enjoy keeping fit, music and cinema.

UK

PERSONAL PROFILE: Collaborated and hosted 'Something In between', a subsidiary event in conjunction with the Wood Green Jazz Jam, performed by local musicians. Organised Cypriot film festival in London in 2007. The festival profiled 10 critically acclaimed, award winning short films, music videos and documentaries from the best writers, directors and producers from the community.

VASILLIS PANAYI
Actor/Radio Presenter

DATE OF BIRTH: 17-Apr-1952
PLACE OF BIRTH: Sykhari.
SCHOOLS/COLLEGE: Stanisiavsky Drama School, Cyprus, Birmingham School of Speech, Training and Dramatic Art.
HOBBIES AND INTERESTS: Cinema, snooker and shopping.
PERSONAL PROFILE: Actor and Radio presenter for LGR. Appeared in Theatre Habeus Corpus, Once a Catholic. On TV Boon, Birds of a Feather, Soldier, Soldier, The Bill. Film: Sleeping with the Fishes with Ewan McGregor. Did voice-over for Captain Corelli's Mandolin.

ALEXANDROS PANAYIDES
Principal conduct of a number of high profile matters, including disputes arising from the 9/11 terrorist attacks and in relation to the construction of Wembley Stadium

DATE OF BIRTH: 01-Feb-1971
PLACE OF BIRTH: Bonn, Germany parents from Ktima, Paphos.
MARITAL STATUS: Married to Marianna, Athens.
CHILDREN: Anastasis.
SCHOOLS/COLLEGE: Westminster School, London / Oxford University/ the. College of Law.
QUALIFICATIONS: BA/MA Hons.
HOBBIES AND INTERESTS: Reading, Scuba-diving.
PERSONAL PROFILE: An equity partner in the firm Clifford Chance LLP, specialising in international litigation, arbitration and dispute resolution. Clifford Chance LLP is the world's largest law firm. Principal conduct of a number of high profile matters, including disputes arising from the 9/11 terrorist attacks and in relation to the construction of Wembley Stadium.

ANDREAS PANAYIOTOU
Property Developer and Essex Amateur Boxing Champion

DATE OF BIRTH: 09-Jan-1966
PLACE OF BIRTH: Mile End, London. Father from Klonari, Limassol, Mother from Kalo chorio, Larnaca.
CHILDREN: Two sons, three daughters.
SCHOOLS/COLLEGE: Wellington Way, Bow; King Harold, Waltham Abbey.
HONOURS/AWARDS: Essex Amateur Boxing Champion (Middleweight).
HOBBIES AND INTERESTS: Boxing and training.
PERSONAL PROFILE: As a youngster, was a keen amateur now a property developer and investor. Owns Ability Developments, Ability Investments and Ability Air. Owns and charters private jets and Ability Shipping, which charters ships. He has adopted a change of direction focusing on Hotels bought the Liverpool Hilton Premier Inn Glasgow the old Stakis Hotel in Dunblane and a Hotel complex in Sicily.

DONATELLA PANAYIOTOU
Model/Actress appeared on TV in Celebrity Fear Factor UK Loose women and young posh and loaded

PLACE OF BIRTH: London Father from Famagusta
PERSONAL PROFILE: Model and Actress appeared on TV in Celebrity Fear Factor UK Loose women and young posh and loaded.

UK

ELEFTHERIOS PANAYIOTOU
Director of Costain International LTD

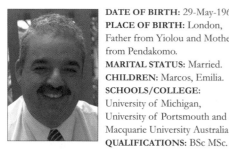

DATE OF BIRTH: 29-May-1961
PLACE OF BIRTH: London, Father from Yiolou and Mother from Pendakomo.
MARITAL STATUS: Married.
CHILDREN: Marcos, Emilia.
SCHOOLS/COLLEGE: University of Michigan, University of Portsmouth and Macquarie University Australia.
QUALIFICATIONS: BSc MSc.
MEMBERSHIPS: Chartered Director.
HOBBIES AND INTERESTS: Travelling, Chess, Stamp Collecting and Reading.
PERSONAL PROFILE: Eleftherios Panayiotou is a director of Costain International LTD based in London.

JAKE PANAYIOTOU
Night Club Owner of exclusive Wellington Club in Knightsbridge, which boasts Mick Jagger, Bono, Mick Hucknall and Kate Moss as founder members

DATE OF BIRTH: 06-Nov-1953
PLACE OF BIRTH: Famagusta.
MARITAL STATUS: Married to Irene, London, Business.
CHILDREN: Kelly, Media. Christian, Business. Jake Junior.
SCHOOLS/COLLEGE: Ackland Burghley-Tufnell Park.
HOBBIES AND INTERESTS: Football.
PERSONAL PROFILE: Jake's dreams of becoming a professional football player with Arsenal were shattered after two serious injuries, sustained whilst playing for their youth team. He then went on to find success with his own company. In 1985 he opened Browns Night Club in Covent Garden, which was to become a haven for the stars, including Jack Nicholson, Madonna, Freddie Mercury and Prince.

In October 2002, he opened the doors to the exclusive Wellington Club in Knightsbridge, which boasts Mick Jagger, Bono, Mick Hucknall and Kate Moss as founder members.

MIROFORA PANAYIOTOU
Assistant Director of the Doctor Series on TV

DATE OF BIRTH: 29-May-1977
PLACE OF BIRTH: Northolt, Middlesex. Parents from Ardana, Famagusta.
MARITAL STATUS: Single.
SCHOOLS/COLLEGE: Sutton Coldfield Girls School, Warwick University.
QUALIFICATIONS: BA in Film & Literature.
HOBBIES AND INTERESTS: Photography writing and jogging.
PERSONAL PROFILE: Scriptwriter - made a short film Vince and Johnny. Also works in Traffic Link, provides travel news to BBC News. assistant Director of the Doctor Series on TV.

KYRIACOS PANAYIOTOU AKA Jack PANOS
Horse Breeder

DATE OF BIRTH: 23-Apr-1936
PLACE OF BIRTH: Patriki.
CHILDREN: George Kyriacos, Aka George Michael, Singer/ Songwr.
SCHOOLS/COLLEGE: Patriki Elementary School, English High School Tricomo, Cyprus.
QUALIFICATIONS: English Lower & Higher. Restaurateur & now an Equine Breeder.
HOBBIES AND INTERESTS: Shooting and horse racing.
PERSONAL PROFILE: Horse breeding (thoroughbreds) Kyriacos supports numerous charities.

George Michael (George Kyriacos Panayiotou) singer/ songwriter sold over 85 million records.

UK

GEORGE KYRIACOS PANAYIOTOU AKA GEORGE MICHAEL
Singer/Songwriter sold over 85 million records

DATE OF BIRTH: 25-Jun-1963
PLACE OF BIRTH: London
Father from Patriki.
SCHOOLS/COLLEGE:
Kingsbury High School.
HONOURS/AWARDS: The
Faith Album received a Grammy
for best album in 1998. Two
Ivor Novello Awards for
songwriter of the year and
International hit of the year
for Faith. In 1996 voted Best British Male at the MTV
Europe Awards and the BRITS, and at the Ivor Novello
Awards he was awarded the title of song writer of the
year for the third time.
PERSONAL PROFILE: Singer /Songwriter formed
the group Wham with Andrew Ridgeley and they had
string of top ten hits together having their final concert
at Wembley Stadium in an emotional farewell in front
of 72, 000 people. First Solo single came in 1984 with
Careless Whisper. In 2006/7/8 George did the 25 Live
Tour through Europe and America. He was the first artist
to perform live at the newly renovated Wembley Stadium.
George sang on the Band Aid Charity song donated the
songs from Last Christmas by Wham to Band Aid and
the proceeds from the single Dont let the sun go down
on me were divided among 10 different charities for
children, aids and education.

CHRISTOPHER JAMES PANTELI
Journalist, Ilford Recorder

DATE OF BIRTH: 02-Apr-1978
PLACE OF BIRTH: London.
Parents from Larnaca.
SCHOOLS/COLLEGE: Canon
Palmer High School, Ilford,
Essex.
QUALIFICATIONS: A
Level Media Studies, English
Lanaguage, Photogaphy.
Currently studying for a
Journalism Diploma.
HOBBIES AND INTERESTS: Enjoys all genres of music
and film and is currently writing his first novel.
PERSONAL PROFILE: Journalist, Ilford Recorder.
Sponsored by Archant on Journalism Diploma Course.

LOU PANTELI
Football Association Referee, first woman to officiate at the new Wembley Stadium

PLACE OF BIRTH: London
parents from Akanthou
MARITAL STATUS: Single.
SCHOOLS/COLLEGE:
Woodberry Down School.
QUALIFICATIONS: A Levels.
MEMBERSHIPS: Writers Guild
of Great Britain.
NEW PRODUCERS ALLIANCE.
HONOURS/AWARDS: Winner
Odysseus Audience Choice at
the London Greek Film Festival 2008.
Nominated Best Short at the Waterford Film Festival
Ireland 2008.
Lou is a Football Association referee she was the first
woman to officiate at the new Wembley Stadium. Her
involvement in developing the women's football game
was honored with a 10 year service award from the
Middlesex County FA.
HOBBIES AND INTERESTS: Sport.
PERSONAL PROFILE: Lou is a scriptwriter previously
employed as a business writer for Nat West. In 2008 she
wrote and directed her first short film titled an unsuitable
boy.
Lou regards one of her football career highlights as
being instrumental in developing women's football in the
deprived areas of North London through a partnership
with the Metropolitan Police.

DR STAVROS PANTELI
Writer/Lecturer/Historian (Deceased)

DATE OF BIRTH: 01-Apr-1947
PLACE OF BIRTH: Phlasou.
MARITAL STATUS: Married to
Floria, London Parents from
Famagusta, Counsellor.
SCHOOLS/COLLEGE:
Kingsway, Kilburn, Lincoln's
Inn, ASU London University.
QUALIFICATIONS: BSc (Econ),
ACI, PhD.
HOBBIES AND INTERESTS:
Sports, reading and community care.
PERSONAL PROFILE: Lecturer and Writer. Historian.
Author of twelve books, general history and biographies.
Was active member of various Cypriot organisations,
National Federation, Solea, Morphou. Founder and
co-ordinator of the First Cypriot All England Musical
Festival (1984-86), in aid of children with special needs
and Kings College Hospital. Was a regular contributor to
London Greek Radio with two weekly programme slots:
'Your own view' and 'Book review'.

UK

MICHAEL LEONIDA PANTELIDES
Urological Surgeon in Bolton

DATE OF BIRTH: 12-Dec-1953
PLACE OF BIRTH: Athienou.
MARITAL STATUS: Married to Kathy, a Physiotherapist, from Manchester.
CHILDREN: Nicholas, All Students. Helen, Andrew, Christopher.
SCHOOLS/COLLEGE: Elementary School Athienou, English School, Nicosia. Manchester University.
QUALIFICATIONS: MD FRCS.
MEMBERSHIPS: British Medical Association, Royal College of Surgeons, British Association of Urological Surgeons.
HOBBIES AND INTERESTS: Music. Enjoys classical music, popular" Greek and Cyprus folk music. Plays the Violin Fervent Bolton Wanderers Supporter.
PERSONAL PROFILE: Specializes in Urological Surgery. Has published around 20 papers in peer reviewed journals. Appointed Consultant Urologist at Bolton in 1992.

ANDREA CHRISTOFI PAPADIMITRI
Runs London Marathon and other runs to raise money for charity, such as Leukaemia, Thallassaemia Children in Need, Radio Marathon

DATE OF BIRTH: 29-Nov-1938
PLACE OF BIRTH: Leonarisso.
MARITAL STATUS: Married to Anastasia, Peristerona.
CHILDREN: Three sons.
SCHOOLS/COLLEGE: Leonarisso Elementary.
HOBBIES AND INTERESTS: Long distance running, wrestling, boxing and farming.
PERSONAL PROFILE: Fish & Chip shop owner. Charity Worker. Runs London Marathon and other runs to raise money for charity, such as Leukaemia, Thallassaemia Children in Need, Radio Marathon. Runs 70 miles per week. Has used up to 36 pairs of running shoes!.

IRENA PAPADOPOULOS
Professor of Transcultural Health & Nursing

DATE OF BIRTH: 01-Oct-1950
PLACE OF BIRTH: Famagusta.
MARITAL STATUS: Married to Costas, Morphou, Hairdressing and Property developer.
CHILDREN: Panikos, Fitness Instructor. Chris, Psychologist.
SCHOOLS/COLLEGE: Royal College of Nursing, London University, Open University, University of North London. RCN (Royal College of Nursing), Public Health Alliance, EPISTEME.
QUALIFICATIONS: BA, MA (Ed), PhD. RGN, RM, NDN Cert, DN, DipNEd.
MEMBERSHIPS: RCN (Royal College of Nursing), Public Health Alliance, EPISTEME.
HOBBIES AND INTERESTS: Reading, writing, socialising and travel.
PERSONAL PROFILE: Professor of Transcultural Health & Nursing. Head of Research Centre for Transcultural Studies in Health, Middlesex University. Co-Founder and ex-Chief of Directors, Greek and Greek Cypriot Community of Enfield. Co-Author of one book & Editor of three others.

LINDA PAPADOPOULOS
Psychologist. Also contributing editor of Cosmopolitan magazine and appears regularly on TV and radio to comment on psychosocial matters

DATE OF BIRTH: 03-Feb-1971
PLACE OF BIRTH: Toronto, Canada. Parents from Limassol.
MARITAL STATUS: Married to Theo Pitsillides, Limassol, Investment Banker.
SCHOOLS/COLLEGE: York University, Surrey University, City University.
QUALIFICATIONS: BA (Hons), MSc, PhD. CPsychol. (Chartered Psychologist), AFBPS (Associate Fellow of the British Psychological Society).
MEMBERSHIPS: British Psychological Society; All Parliamentary Group on Dermatology.
HONOURS/AWARDS: Awarded a Readership in Psychology (one of the youngest in the country); Nominated for the BPS annual prize in Counselling Psychology.
HOBBIES AND INTERESTS: Writing, travelling and diving.
PERSONAL PROFILE: Course Director of the MSc in

Counselling Psychology at London Guildhall University - also holds a research grant. Linda sits on the editorial board of three academic journals and has authored three books and numerous research/academic articles. Has a private practice where she sees patients clinically. Also contributing editor of Cosmopolitan magazine and appears regularly on TV and radio to comment on psychosocial matters.

MARIO PAPADOPOULOS
Musical Director Oxford Philomusica

DATE OF BIRTH: 20-Dec-1954
PLACE OF BIRTH: Limassol.
MARITAL STATUS: Married to Anthie, Nicosia.
CHILDREN: Michael, Stella.
SCHOOLS/COLLEGE: English School, Nicosia, City Univ.
QUALIFICATIONS: Dr of Musical Arts.
PERSONAL PROFILE: Musical Director of the Oxford Philomusica appointed orchestra in residence at the University of Oxford. In October 2002 the Orchestra was lauched with a concert at the Barbican. As a recognition of their work the orchestra was honoured at a reception at 10 Downing Street in April 2002 hosted by Cherie Blair. Appeared in Paris at Salle Gaveau, Athens, Queen Elizabeth Hall London. Mario has directed the London Mozart Players, The Royal Philarmonic Orchestra. He conducted the Magic Flute, Trovatone, the Marriage of Figaro, with the Greek National Opera.

NICOS PAPADOPOULOS
Journalist, Newscaster London Greek Radio

DATE OF BIRTH: 28-Jul-1952
PLACE OF BIRTH: Nicosia.
MARITAL STATUS: Married to Maria, Karavas.
CHILDREN: Elena, George.
SCHOOLS/COLLEGE: English College, Cyprus, ABC College, Athens, St Patricks College, London.
QUALIFICATIONS: Journalism, Public Relations, Marketing, Advertising.
MEMBERSHIPS: Cyprus Journalist Union, The Chartered Institute of Journalists, 41 Club and Leukaemia Society.
HOBBIES AND INTERESTS: Travelling, swimming and tennis.
PERSONAL PROFILE: Journalist. Columnist of Anthropina at Eleftheria Newspaper. News Editor and Newscaster, London Greek Radio.

RENOS KLITOU PAPADOPOULOS
Professor at the Centre for Psychoanalytic Studies of the University of Essex

DATE OF BIRTH: 17-Feb-1947
PLACE OF BIRTH: Limassol.
MARITAL STATUS: Married to Nina, South Africa, University Lecturer.
CHILDREN: Olga and Michelle.
SCHOOLS/COLLEGE: Pancyprian Gymnasium, Nicosia. University of Belgrade; University of Capetown.
QUALIFICATIONS: PhD Chartered Clinical Psychologist with the British Psychological Society. Analytic Psychologist (Jungian Psychoanalsyt).
MEMBERSHIPS: Member of the International Association for Analytical Psycholology. Registered member of the United Kingdom Council for Psychotherapy.
HOBBIES AND INTERESTS: Cycling, reading and watching soccer (Arsenal supporter).
PERSONAL PROFILE: Professor at the Centre for Psychoanalytic Studies of the University of Essex, Consultant Clinical Psychologist at the Tavistock Clinic, Family Therapist and training and supervising Jungian analyst.

SOLON PAPADOPOULOS
Winner of three Royal Television Society awards. Nominated for BAFTA award and winner of Merit award for San Francisco Film Festival

DATE OF BIRTH: 14-Feb-1961
PLACE OF BIRTH: London, Father Sykopetra, Mother Tire.
MARITAL STATUS: Married to Lyn, British.
SCHOOLS/COLLEGE: Campion Grammar, Liverpool Polytechnic (John. Moores University).
QUALIFICATIONS: Degree in Marine Engineering.
HONOURS/AWARDS: Winner of three Royal Television Society awards. Nominated for BAFTA award and winner of Merit award for San Francisco Film Festival.
HOBBIES AND INTERESTS: Film and TV, enjoying the great outdoors.
PERSONAL PROFILE: Creative Director of film production company Hurricane Films. Directed a feature film 'Under The Mud', working with a group of teenagers who wrote the piece in collaboration with Hurricane Films – completed in 2006.

ANDREAS PAPAEVRIPIDES
Chairman of Democratic Rally UK

DATE OF BIRTH: 24-Apr-1952
PLACE OF BIRTH: Kato Pyrgos Tyllirias.
MARITAL STATUS: Married to Katerina, Ayios Theodoros, Larnaca, Secretary.
CHILDREN: Constantinos, Alexandros.
SCHOOLS/COLLEGE: Gymnasium Morphou, Hackney Technical College. Chelsea College, London School of accountancy.
QUALIFICATIONS: BSc Economics.
MEMBERSHIPS: Fellow of the Institute of Financial Accountants, Member of the British Institute of Management.
HONOURS/AWARDS: Commendation from National Guard of Cyprus for outstanding service in 1972. Honoured by National Union of Cypriots in England.
HOBBIES AND INTERESTS: Politics, history, football and shooting.
PERSONAL PROFILE: Accountant with own practice. Vice-President of the National Federation of Cypriots in Great Britain, President of the National Union of Cypriot Students in England (E. F. E. K. A.) during 1979/1980 and Non-Executive Director of the Enfield Community Care NHS Trust from 1992-1998. General Secretary of Kato Pyrgos Tyllirias Association since. Vice-Chairman "Conservatives For Cyprus". General Secretary of the Cypriot football League in England from 1975 to 1981.

ANDREAS PAPAGEORGI
Head of Energy & Economics, National Grid Co

DATE OF BIRTH: 06-Feb-1949
PLACE OF BIRTH: Koma tou Yialou.
MARITAL STATUS: Married to Maria, Kakopetria, Housewife.
CHILDREN: Christina, Demetris, Marianna, All Students.
SCHOOLS/COLLEGE: Pancyprian Gymnasium, Kykkou. Woolwich College for Further Education, Catford College, Southampton University, Reading University.
QUALIFICATIONS: BSc Economics, MA Business Economics.
MEMBERSHIPS: International Institute of Energy Economics.
HOBBIES AND INTERESTS: Reading, swimming and politics.

PERSONAL PROFILE: Head of Energy & Economics, National Grid Company. Chairman of Prospectives Group, Chairman of EuroG Group of Experts, Eurelectric, President of Greek School of Coventry, member of Action for Cyprus Midlands.

DR GEORGE PAPAGEORGIOU
Senior Research Associate for National Institute for Medical Research UK

DATE OF BIRTH: 22-Aug-1957
PLACE OF BIRTH: Anaphotia.
MARITAL STATUS: Married to Alexandra, London, Solicitor.
CHILDREN: Xanthy, Eleni, Vasiliki, Constantia.
SCHOOLS/COLLEGE: Larnaca Gymnasium. Queen Mary College, University of London, Loughborough University.
QUALIFICATIONS: MSc, PhD, EurChem, CChem MRSC.
MEMBERSHIPS: American Chemical Society, Royal Society of Chemistry.
HOBBIES AND INTERESTS: Gardening, current affairs, and trying to teach his daughters the Greek language.
PERSONAL PROFILE: Senior Research Associate for National Institute for Medical Research UK.

GEORGE MICHAEL PAPAGEORGIS
Barrister/Head of Chambers

DATE OF BIRTH: 28-Sep-1947
PLACE OF BIRTH: Leonarisso, Famagusta.
MARITAL STATUS: Married to Elizabeth Jane, England, Housewife.
CHILDREN: Michael, Students. Sophia.
SCHOOLS/COLLEGE: Greek Gymnasium for Boys, Famagusta, Middle Temple, London.
QUALIFICATIONS: Barrister-at-Law.
HOBBIES AND INTERESTS: Theatre.
PERSONAL PROFILE: Has been practising for over 20 years from 2 Kings Bench Walk, Temple, London. Was The Head of Chambers for over four years. Member of Anglo-Cypriot Lawyers Association.

JOHN PAPALOIZOU
Professor of Mathematical Physics at Cambridge University

DATE OF BIRTH: 04-May-1947
PLACE OF BIRTH: Yialoussa, Cyprus.
MARITAL STATUS: Married to Elaine from the UK.
CHILDREN: Edward.
SCHOOLS/COLLEGE: Quintin School, University College, London, and. University of Sussex.
QUALIFICATIONS: DPhil University of Sussex.
HONOURS/AWARDS: Fellow of Royal Society, Brouwer award of American Astronomical Society, Institute of Physics.
HOBBIES AND INTERESTS: Gardening.
PERSONAL PROFILE: Professor at University of Cambridge Centre for Mathematical Sciences Department of Applied Mathematics and Theoretical Physics.

PROFESSOR JOHN KYROS PAPALOIZOU
Deputy Chairman of KOPA and member of KOPA Management Committee/ Chartered Surveyor

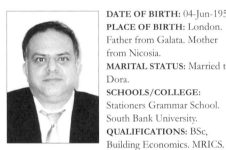

DATE OF BIRTH: 04-Jun-1958
PLACE OF BIRTH: London. Father from Galata. Mother from Nicosia.
MARITAL STATUS: Married to Dora.
SCHOOLS/COLLEGE: Stationers Grammar School. South Bank University.
QUALIFICATIONS: BSc, Building Economics. MRICS.
MEMBERSHIPS: Royal Institute of Chartered Surveyors, Quantity Surveying Division. Accredited domestic energy assessor and Hips provider.
HOBBIES AND INTERESTS: Football, tennis golf and music.
PERSONAL PROFILE: Director of Letting and Property Management Company, Thomas Properties. Secretary and Chairman of Greek Football Team Neos Asteras 1970s-1980s. Former Deputy Chairman and member of KOPA Management Committee.

TASOS PAPALOIZOU
Chartered Accountant/Philanthropist always helping community organisations

DATE OF BIRTH: 02-May-1962
PLACE OF BIRTH: London. Father from Galata; Mother from Nicosia.
MARITAL STATUS: Married to Yasmin, born in London (parents from India).
CHILDREN: Thomas, Natasha, Alexander.
SCHOOLS/COLLEGE: Friern Barnet Grammar School, Barnet College, University of North London. ICAEW.
QUALIFICATIONS: BA (Honours). Chartered Accountant.
HOBBIES AND INTERESTS: Football (played for Neos Asteras 1970s-1980s). All forms of sport, travel, cinema and theatre.
PERSONAL PROFILE: Chartered Accountant in own practice, also Director and Shareholder of a Property Company.

FREDOS PAPANGELOU
Professor of Mathematical Statistics at the University of Manchester

DATE OF BIRTH: 07-Oct-1939
PLACE OF BIRTH: Limassol.
MARITAL STATUS: Married to Elizabeth, Greece.
CHILDREN: Aris, Markos.
SCHOOLS/COLLEGE: University of Athens.
QUALIFICATIONS: PhD.
HOBBIES AND INTERESTS: Music and history.
PERSONAL PROFILE: Former Professor of Mathematical Statistics at the University of Manchester. Now Professor Emeritus. Was member of the Interim Governing Board of the University of Cyprus and of the Preparatory Committee of Cyprus University of Applied Sciences and Arts.

UK

ELIAS PAPANICOLA
Proprieter of SOS Catering Equipment and Engineering/Philanthropist

DATE OF BIRTH: 11-Oct-1953
PLACE OF BIRTH: Limassol.
MARITAL STATUS: Married to Maria, Famagusta.
CHILDREN: John, Georgina, Apostolos.
SCHOOLS/COLLEGE: Emporikon, Limassol.
HOBBIES AND INTERESTS: Football.
PERSONAL PROFILE: Elias Papanicolas is the proprieter of SOS Catering Equipment Engineering established 1980 first in Queens Road they now situated in a larger premises 6000 square feet in Billet Road, Walthamstow. Elias is known for his philanthropic help in the community.

THEODOULOS PAPANICOLA
Senior Partner of Bond Partners LLP, Chartered/Certified Accountants and Insolvency Practitioners also Lecturer on Insolvency

DATE OF BIRTH: 03-Mar-1949
PLACE OF BIRTH: Vokolida. London. Parents from Aradippou and Larnaca.
MARITAL STATUS: Married.
CHILDREN: Three daughters and Two Step Daughters.
SCHOOLS/COLLEGE: Credon School for Boys. Westminster College.
QUALIFICATIONS: FCA, FCCA, FABRP, MCI, ARB. Licenced Insolvency Practitioner.
MEMBERSHIPS: Member of the Chartered Institute of Arbitrators and Members of the Institute of Chartered Accountants Cyprus.
HOBBIES AND INTERESTS: Cooking, Swimming and Classical Music.
PERSONAL PROFILE: Theodoulos Started his first Practice in 1974. In 1993 they merged with another firm until 2004 then breaking away and setting up Bond Partners LLP.
Past Chairman of the Institute of Chartered Accountants Small Practitioners Group of Central London, past President of the ACCA North London Members Panel and served on R3 Courses and Education Committee. He also lectures on Insolvency

CHRISTOPHER PAPANICOLAOU
Law/Partner in International Law Firm Jones Day

DATE OF BIRTH: 1-Sept-1966
PLACE OF BIRTH: London, Father born in Vokolida.
SCHOOLS/COLLEGE: Southgate Comprehensive, London, Birmingham. University.
QUALIFICATIONS: LL. B. Hons 1988, Upper Second, The College of Law Lancaster Gate (Law Society Finals 1989, First Class Honours).
HOBBIES AND INTERESTS: Keen follower of Tottenham Hotspur FC.
PERSONAL PROFILE: Partner in International Law Firm Jones Day.

NICOS ANDREA PAPANICOLAOU
One of the first Cypriot Solicitors with own practice in the UK

DATE OF BIRTH: 23-Jun-1932
PLACE OF BIRTH: Vokolida.
MARITAL STATUS: Married to Lilia, London, Office Manager.
CHILDREN: Andreas, Solicitor. Christopher, Solicitor. Thessa, Teacher.
SCHOOLS/COLLEGE: Famagusta Gymnasium, Grays Inn.
QUALIFICATIONS: Barrister At Law. Solicitor.
PERSONAL PROFILE: Retired Solicitor. One of the first Cypriot Solicitors with own practice in the Uk.

CHRYSOSTOMOS PAPAPAVLOU
Chairman of Labithos & Karavas Association

DATE OF BIRTH: 27-Jan-1937
PLACE OF BIRTH: Lapithos.
MARITAL STATUS: Married to Elsa, Denmark, Nurse.
CHILDREN: Nicholas, Chartered Surveyor.
SCHOOLS/COLLEGE: Lapithos Gymasium & Primary School, Regent Street Polytechnic.
QUALIFICATIONS: O. N. C. H. N. C Electrical & Electronic Engineering.
HOBBIES AND INTERESTS: DIY, travelling, languages, French, German and Danish.

UK

PERSONAL PROFILE: Now retired. Former Field Service Engineer with Lansing Forklifts. Member of the Committee Cypriot Community Centre, Wood Green. Chairman of Lapithos & Karavas Association. Former Chairman at Community Centre Edison, Chairman of Greek Parents Association of Rokesley School, Crouch End for many years.

THEO PAPAPAVLOU
Accountant/Treasurer of EDEK UK

DATE OF BIRTH: 06-Oct-1947
PLACE OF BIRTH: Panayia, Paphos.
MARITAL STATUS: Married to Penny, British, Book Keeper.
CHILDREN: Michael, BA Hons in History, MSc in IT. Helen, BA Hons.
SCHOOLS/COLLEGE: Panayia Elementary, Paphos Gymnasium. Waltham Forest College.
QUALIFICATIONS: AM. Inst. CM.
MEMBERSHIPS: Associate member of Association of Certified Public Accountants and Commitee member of the London Region of the Association of Certified Public Accountants.
HOBBIES AND INTERESTS: Travelling, Music, History, Food and Wine.
PERSONAL PROFILE: Theo has been a practising Accountant since 1978 now a Consultant with Kounnis and Ptnrs Plc. Founder of Theo & Co Accountants and Auditors, Omega Financial Services and Paps Enterprises. He is also the treasurer of EDEK UK.

DR ELLI PAPAPHOTI
Founder and Director of the Educational Institute of Great Britain - 1990-1995

PLACE OF BIRTH: Koma Tou Yialou.
MARITAL STATUS: Married to Photis, Akanthou, Banking.
CHILDREN: Anastasia, Banking. Angelika, Accountant.
SCHOOLS/COLLEGE: Famagusta Gymnasium, Nicosia Teachers College, London University.
QUALIFICATIONS: Associate of the Institute of Education, Academic Diploma in Education, M. A. Education, PhD.
MEMBERSHIPS: Member of the Greek Educational Society (based in Athens), Member of K. E. S. (Educational Council of the Archdiocese of Thyateira and Great Britain).

HOBBIES AND INTERESTS: Reading, listening to Greek music, theatre, Greek dancing, gardening, socialising and travelling.
PERSONAL PROFILE: Founder and Director of the Educational Institute of Great Britain (1990-1995). An institute educating Greek teachers, teaching in the Greek Schools in UK. Education Counsellor of the Cyprus High Commission. Education Counsellor of the Archdioces of Thyateria and Great Britain.

ANNA PAPAPHOTIS
Finalist in the category for small leisure off line agency of the year 2007 at the agent achievement awards

DATE OF BIRTH: 05-Oct-1969
PLACE OF BIRTH: London Father from Akanthou Mother from Patriki/Komi Kebir.
MARITAL STATUS: Single.
CHILDREN: Dimitri, Nicholas.
SCHOOLS/COLLEGE: Barnsbury Girls. Hotel and Travel Training College.
QUALIFICATIONS: 9 O Levels, Diploma in Travel and Tourism.
MEMBERSHIPS: ABTA IATA ATOL AGTA.
HONOURS/AWARDS: Finalist in the category for small leisure off line agency of the year 2007 at the agent achievement awards.
HOBBIES AND INTERESTS: Travelling, socialising and keeping fit.
PERSONAL PROFILE: Anna Papaphotis is Sales and Marketing Director of Travelmania who are known for their help towards the community.

PHOTIS SAVVAS PAPAPHOTIS
President of St Marys Church Camberwell

DATE OF BIRTH: 25-Feb-1925
PLACE OF BIRTH: Akanthou.
MARITAL STATUS: Married to Sousanna deceased, Akanthou.
CHILDREN: Maria Allsop, Interior Designer.
SCHOOLS/COLLEGE: Primary School of Akanthou Village.
HOBBIES AND INTERESTS: Reading, walking and socialising.
PERSONAL PROFILE: President of St Marys Greek Orthodox Church, Camberwell, Former President of Anglo-Akanthou Aid Society. Restaurateur.

DEMOS PAPASAVVAS
Partner in Deloitte & Touche LLP

DATE OF BIRTH: 12-Jan-1956
PLACE OF BIRTH: Nicosia.
SCHOOLS/COLLEGE: The English School, Nicosia, The London School of. Economics.
QUALIFICATIONS: BSc Econ (stats).
HOBBIES AND INTERESTS: Bridge, tennis and skiing.
PERSONAL PROFILE: Partner in Deloitte & Touche LLP.

GEORGE PAPASAVVAS
Consultant Rheumatologist Brighton and Sussex University Hospitals NHS Trust

DATE OF BIRTH: 24-Sep-1954
PLACE OF BIRTH: Nicosia.
MARITAL STATUS: Married to Yiola, Cypriot.
CHILDREN: Elena, Student. Philip, Student.
SCHOOLS/COLLEGE: English School Nicosia and Taunton School. London Hospital Medical College.
QUALIFICATIONS: MB BS FRCP.
MEMBERSHIPS: Royal College of Physicians, British Society for Rheumatology.
HOBBIES AND INTERESTS: Greek Music and Football.
PERSONAL PROFILE: George Papasavvas is a Consultant Rheumatologist Brighton and Sussex University Hospitals NHS Trust.

GLYKERIS PAPASPYROU
Founder Member of Greek Orthodox Community of Hastings

DATE OF BIRTH: 15-Jul-1923
PLACE OF BIRTH: Ayia Triada, Famagusta.
MARITAL STATUS: Married to Kiki Deceased, Famagusta.
CHILDREN: One son, four daughters.
SCHOOLS/COLLEGE: AKEL.
HONOURS/AWARDS: Honoured by the Greek Orthodox Church.
HOBBIES AND INTERESTS: Travelling and reading.
PERSONAL PROFILE: Hotel Owner in Hastings. One of the Founder members of Camden Greek School. Founder member of Greek Orthodox Community of Hastings and Chairman for 25 years.

THASIS PAPATHANASIOU
Involved with South London Community Greek Schools. One of the founders of OESEKA and ESEKA

DATE OF BIRTH: 29-May-1929
PLACE OF BIRTH: Aradippou.
MARITAL STATUS: Married.
CHILDREN: Three daughters.
HOBBIES AND INTERESTS: Football, (Fulham Supporter).
PERSONAL PROFILE: Involved with South London Community Greek Schools one of the founders and Chairman of OESEKA and ESEKA. One of the Founders of Hammersmith and Fulham Council of Racial Equality for six years Chairman. One of the Founders and Former Chairman of the Aradippou Association UK.

NICOS PAPAVASILIOU
Footballer signed for Newcastle United in 1993 First Greek Cypriot to play in the Premiership

DATE OF BIRTH: 31-Aug-1970
PLACE OF BIRTH: Cyprus.
HONOURS/AWARDS: Cyprus International Footballer.
PERSONAL PROFILE: Nicos signed for Newcastle United FC when Kevin Keegan was manager for 120, 000 from Anorthosis. He made his Newcastle debut against Tottenham on August the 14th 1993.

PETER PANAYIOTIS PAPHIDES
Journalist for Time Out, Guardian and The Times

DATE OF BIRTH: 18-Jul-1969
PLACE OF BIRTH: Birmingham. Father from Kyrenia; Mother from Nea Kifisia in Athens.
MARITAL STATUS: Married to Caitlin Moran, London, Columnist for The Times Newspaper.
CHILDREN: Theodora.
SCHOOLS/COLLEGE: Cottersbrooke Infant and Primary School, Yardley's Secondary School, St David's University College, Lampeter.
QUALIFICATIONS: 5 O Levels, 4 A Levels, Second Class Honours Degree in Philosophy.

UK

MEMBERSHIPS: AA, The Ramblers Association.
HONOURS/AWARDS: My Salsa Dip has often been declared "The best this side of Holloway Road".
HOBBIES AND INTERESTS: Chips, babies, bidding for rare acid folk vinyl on eBay, driving around the North-West coast of Scotland.
PERSONAL PROFILE: Journalist. Writes in Time Out. Guardian and the Times.

THEO PAPHITIS
Business and Football

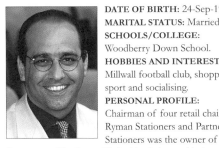

DATE OF BIRTH: 24-Sep-1959
MARITAL STATUS: Married.
SCHOOLS/COLLEGE: Woodberry Down School.
HOBBIES AND INTERESTS: Millwall football club, shopping, sport and socialising.
PERSONAL PROFILE: Chairman of four retail chains Ryman Stationers and Partners Stationers was the owner of Contessa and La Senza. Under his chairmanship he has translated ailing businesses to successful ones. As well as retail he has a passion for football was chairman of Millwall FC for eight years during which the club enjoyed its most illustrious period in its history including promotion to the first division and FA Cup Final appearance and European competition. Recently salvaged the company Red Letter Days out of administration and appears on the BBC programme Dragons' Den as a dragon. He has also written the book Enter the Dragon.

ZOE PAPHITIS
Actress/Model appeared in Dream Team on Sky One

DATE OF BIRTH: 30-Sep-1981
PLACE OF BIRTH: Lambeth, London; father from Limassol.
MARITAL STATUS: Single.
SCHOOLS/COLLEGE: Claremont Fan Court School, Esher.
QUALIFICATIONS: GCSEs (Maths, English, Drama, Music) A Level Drama.
HONOURS/AWARDS: Grade 5 singing, Grade 3 piano.
HOBBIES AND INTERESTS: Singing, playing saxophone, theatre and football.
PERSONAL PROFILE: Actress/Model. Model: Lingerie for La Senza and Contessa. Actress: Appeared in Dream Team (Sky One); The Goal (BBC Worldwide).

CHRISTOS PARASKEVA
Professor of Experimental Cancer and University Lecturer

DATE OF BIRTH: 03-Dec-1952
PLACE OF BIRTH: London. Father from Lefkoniko and Mother from Angastina.
MARITAL STATUS: Married to Doris who is Swiss.
CHILDREN: Nicole, Graduate. Andrea, Student.
SCHOOLS/COLLEGE: Manchester University, Oxford University.
QUALIFICATIONS: BSc and D Phil.
PERSONAL PROFILE: Christos Paraskeva is a Professor of Experimental Cancer and University Lecturer. Director of Experimental Oncology, Director of Cancer Research UK Colorectal cancer research group, Bowel Cancer Research (prevention and new treatments).

JANET PARASKEVA
Civil Service Commissioner, 1st Chief Executive of the Law Society

DATE OF BIRTH: 28-May-1946
PLACE OF BIRTH: Newport, Gwent. Parents from Neta.
MARITAL STATUS: Single.
CHILDREN: Amanda Hunt, Suzanne Paraskeva.
SCHOOLS/COLLEGE: Newport & Hastings High School, Worcester College of Education, Open University.
QUALIFICATIONS: Cert Ed, BA.
HONOURS/AWARDS: Robert Schuman Silver Medal.
HOBBIES AND INTERESTS: Golf, riding and gardening.
PERSONAL PROFILE: Janet was appointed the first Civil service Commissioner on Jan 2006 and in November 2007 the first chair of the child maintenance and enforcement commission. She is also on the board of Britains serious organised crime Agency. First Chief Executive of the Law Society for England and Wales. Director England, National Lottery Charities Board, 1995-2000. Chief Executive, National Youth Agency, 1991-1995. Director, National Youth Bureau, 1988-1991. HM Inspector of Schools, Department of Education and Sciences 1983-1988. Served as a member of the Youth Justice Board at the Home Office and as a magistrate for eight years. Janet is also the Head of the new Olympic Lottery Distributor. The body's key role will be to ensure proper, timely and effective distribution of Lottery money and to fund the provision of facilities, services and functions required for the staging of the London 2012 Summer Olympics & Paralympic Games.

UK

PARASKEVAS (BARRY) PARASKEVA
Surgeon at Imperial College School of
Medicine

DATE OF BIRTH: 29-Dec-1969
PLACE OF BIRTH: London.
Father from Makrasyka; Mother
from Eptakomi.
MARITAL STATUS: Married to
Rebcecca, London. Doctor.
CHILDREN: Sophia.
SCHOOLS/COLLEGE: Henry
Compton School, Fulham, St
Mary's Hospital Medical School,
London.
QUALIFICATIONS: BSc (Honours)-Physiology-1st Class,
PhD-Molecular Biology of Tumour Metastasis. MBBS
(Honours).
MEMBERSHIPS: Fellow of the Royal College of
Surgeons of England-FRCS (Eng).
HONOURS/AWARDS: Queen's Award for Higher
Education 2000, Imperial College Award for Teaching
excellence in Surgery.
HOBBIES AND INTERESTS: Byzantine art.
PERSONAL PROFILE: Surgeon-St Mary's Hospital
London and Lecturer in surgery at Imperial College
School of Medicine.

MICHAEL PARASKOS
Lecturer University of Leeds in Fine Art

DATE OF BIRTH: 08-Sep-1969
PLACE OF BIRTH: Anaphotia.
MARITAL STATUS: Married to
Emma.
SCHOOLS/COLLEGE:
University of Leeds and
University of Nottingham.
QUALIFICATIONS: BA English
Literature and History of
Art, MA History of Art, PhD
History of Art.
HONOURS/AWARDS: The Hargreaves Award.
PERSONAL PROFILE: Michael is a regular writer on
Art, Culture and Politics, for newspapers, magazines and
academic journals in Britain and Cyprus. He has written
several introductions to books on art and literature,
including introductions to Herbert Read's 'To Hell with
Culture' and ' Naked Warriors'. Until 2001 was Head of
Art History for Fine Art at the University of Hull, and
now a part-time lecturer in the University of Leeds Fine
Art. Also UK-based Director of Programmes for the
Cyprus College of Art. Also editor of 'ArtCyprus' an
Anglo-Cypriot art newspaper published by the Cyprus
College of Art.

RICHARD PARPERIS
Headteacher

DATE OF BIRTH: 09-Aug-1953
PLACE OF BIRTH: London.
Father from Achna.
MARITAL STATUS: Married to
Linda, London.
CHILDREN: Victoria Demetra,
Law.
SCHOOLS/COLLEGE:
Ackland Burghley, London,
Balls Park College,
Hertford, The University of
Hertfordshire, Leicester University.
QUALIFICATIONS: BEd, MBA, NPQH.
MEMBERSHIPS: Area Rep for the Hertfordshire
Association of Secondary Headteachers (HASSH),
member of SHA (Secondary Head's Association).
HOBBIES AND INTERESTS: Travel, reading and
education.
PERSONAL PROFILE: Secondary School Headteacher
(11-18 Comprehensive) in Hertfordshire. Started teaching
in 1974 and between 1981 and 1991 taught in Haringey,
North London. In conjunction with the local Education
Authority and the Cyprus High Commission, strove to
introduce Modern Greek onto the Curriculum at the
school.

DOROS PARTASIDES
Photographer/Film Making/
Documentaries

PLACE OF BIRTH: Ayii
Omoloyites, Nicosia.
MARITAL STATUS: Married to
Vera, Larnaca.
CHILDREN: Constantine,
Solicitor. Marianna, Journalist.
SCHOOLS/COLLEGE:
Technical School, Nicosia.
QUALIFICATIONS: Diploma,
Royal College of Art. AFIAP.
HONOURS/AWARDS: Gold
and silver medal of AFIAP.
HOBBIES AND INTERESTS: Football, golf, walks,
cinema and art.
PERSONAL PROFILE: Film making/Documentaries,
Photographer and Historian, published three books,
served on the Committee of The Greek Cypriot
Brotherhood.

PAS PASCHALI
Development Editor for the Guardian and Observer

DATE OF BIRTH: 26-May-1956
PLACE OF BIRTH: Hammersmith, London. Father born in Achna; Mother born in Komi Kebir.
MARITAL STATUS: Single.
SCHOOLS/COLLEGE: Latymer Upper School, Hammersmith/ The City University.
QUALIFICATIONS: BSc Actuarial Science. AIA (Associate of the Institute of Actuaries).
HOBBIES AND INTERESTS: Painting (oil on canvas), the arts, cinema, photography and architecture, walking (including several national trails, such as the 193-mile Coast to Coast), Italy (having travelled it extensively, exploring its cities and culture).
PERSONAL PROFILE: Development Editor for the Guardian and Observer - commissions and edits special supplements for both newspapers. Has been in publishing since 1982, during which time has co-founded an arts magazine, edited two lifestyle magazines, been arts editor for a regional newspaper and a section editor for the Evening Standard.

CHRISTAKIS PASCHALIDES
President of Yialousa Association UK

DATE OF BIRTH: 20-Sep-1939
PLACE OF BIRTH: Yiallousa.
MARITAL STATUS: Married to Maria from London (parents from Khirokitia and Dohni).
CHILDREN: Two sons, one daughter.
SCHOOLS/COLLEGE: English School, Nicosia, called to the English Bar Nov 1964.
HOBBIES AND INTERESTS: Travelling.
PERSONAL PROFILE: 1964, Legal Advisor to Inland Revenue in Cyprus, 1971, worked as Barrister, 1975, Bank of Cyprus Legal Advisor then Assistant General Manager and Acting General Manager in 1986. Now has own Solicitors office in Grays Inn Road, London and associate offices in Nicosia. President of Yialoussa Association UK.

MICHAEL PASTOU
Professional Cage fighter appears on Sky TV

DATE OF BIRTH: 19-Oct-1981
PLACE OF BIRTH: London Father from Athienou, Mother from Trikomo.
MARITAL STATUS: Single.
SCHOOLS/COLLEGE: Bishops Stortford.
HOBBIES AND INTERESTS: Keeping Fit, Martial Arts.
PERSONAL PROFILE: Michael Pastou is a Professional Cage fighter appears on Cage Rage on Sky TV. Cage Fighting consists of Mixed martial arts combining techniques from different disciplines like wrestling and boxing. There are few rules making it as true to real fighting as possible. The cage is there for safety - to stop the fighters falling out of the ring.

THEODOROS PASTOU
Chairman of Omonia Football Club (London) and Athienou Association UK

DATE OF BIRTH: 18-Feb-1951
PLACE OF BIRTH: Athienou.
MARITAL STATUS: Married to Georgia Mela, Trikomo.
CHILDREN: Panayiotis, Architect. Michael, Cagefighter. Katerina.
SCHOOLS/COLLEGE: American Academy, Larnaca.
QUALIFICATIONS: Certified Accountant.
HOBBIES AND INTERESTS: Football, Omonia Othello Athienou, West Ham, athletics, music and dancing.
PERSONAL PROFILE: Accountant partner in Family Accountancy Practice T Pastou and Co based in Palmers Green. Chair Omonia FC London, Chairman of Athienou Association and Member of the Secretariat AKEL UK.

UK

ELEFTHERIA XENOPHON PATSALOS
Vice Chair Person of Deloitte & Touche UK

DATE OF BIRTH: 22-May-1954
PLACE OF BIRTH: Aradippou.
MARITAL STATUS: Married to Professor Phillip Patsalos, Pano Lefkara, Neurologist.
CHILDREN: Nicolas, Maria.
SCHOOLS/COLLEGE: American Academy, Larnaca, London School of Economics, City University.
QUALIFICATIONS: BA Economics. MBA Financial Accounting and Marketing.
HOBBIES AND INTERESTS: Jogging, dance, music and reading.
PERSONAL PROFILE: Vice Chair person, Senior Partner and Global head of Tax Deloitte & Touche UK. Member of Cypriot Qualified Accountants Association.

PROFESSOR PHILIP N PATSALOS
Director of Pharmacology and Therapeutics at the National Hospital for Neurology and Neurosurgery

DATE OF BIRTH: 01-Apr-1952
PLACE OF BIRTH: Pano Lefkara.
MARITAL STATUS: Married to Eleftheria, Aradippou, International Tax Advisor.
CHILDREN: Nicolas, Maria.
SCHOOLS/COLLEGE: Holloway School, Reading University, University of London.
QUALIFICATIONS: Msc in Neurochemistry, FRCPath, PhD. Doctorate from University of London.
HOBBIES AND INTERESTS: Travel, writing and football, (Arsenal Fan).
PERSONAL PROFILE: Professor of Clinical Pharmacology at the Institute of Neurology, University College London.

LEDA PATTICHI
President of Democratic Rally UK Ladies Branch/Secretary of The St Andrews Greek Ladies Charity Organisation

DATE OF BIRTH: 02-May-1943
PLACE OF BIRTH: Lefkoniko.
MARITAL STATUS: Married to Melis, Lefkoniko, Baker.
CHILDREN: Kyriakos, Property Developer. Louis, accountant. Miranda, Solicitor. Odysseas, Accounts.
SCHOOLS/COLLEGE: Lefkoniko High School, College for Social Workers, Athens.
QUALIFICATIONS: High School Diploma.
MEMBERSHIPS: President of Democratic Rally (UK) Ladies Branch.
HOBBIES AND INTERESTS: International cooking and cake making.
PERSONAL PROFILE: Receptionist/Carer for elderly mothers. Secretary of The St Andrews Greek Ladies Charity Organisation, The Hellenic Central Fund Raising Committee, Events Organiser of The Lefkonico Association, National Federation of Cypriots in Britain and Trustee of The St Andrews Greek Cathedral.

ANDY PAUL
Singer sang the 1984 Eurovision Song Contest entry for Cyprus

DATE OF BIRTH: 18-Sep-1957
PLACE OF BIRTH: Limassol.
MARITAL STATUS: Married to Argentina, Moldova, Nurse.
CHILDREN: Suzan, Lisa, Joanne, Nicola and Nicolas.
MEMBERSHIPS: Equity.
HOBBIES AND INTERESTS: Computer and his children.
PERSONAL PROFILE: Sang the 1984 Eurovision Song Contest entry for Cyprus.

The first Greek orthodox church in the UK was formed in Soho in 1677 there is now over 100 churches in the UK.

UK

PAVLOS PAVLIDES
Assistant Vice President, JP Morgan Chase & Co

DATE OF BIRTH: 12-Sep-1972
PLACE OF BIRTH: Nicosia.
MARITAL STATUS: Single.
SCHOOLS/COLLEGE: Falcon School, Nicosia, The Latymer School, City University, London.
QUALIFICATIONS: B. Sc (Honours) M. Sc.
MEMBERSHIPS: Was Member of the Secretariat of the National Federation of Cypriots in Great Britain.
PERSONAL PROFILE: Assistant Vice President, JP Morgan Chase & CoPrevious positions: First elected President of The National Union of Cypriot Students in the UK. Founding member of Kypros Net Ltd, an internet organisation servicing the overseas Cypriot Communities.

SAVVAS PAVLIDES
Head of Cyprus Educational Mission in the UK

DATE OF BIRTH: 23-Jun-1946
PLACE OF BIRTH: Kyrenia.
MARITAL STATUS: Married to Eleni, Kyrenia, Teacher.
CHILDREN: Pavlos, Banking. Mary, Chartered Accountant. Rena, Law. Gloria, Social Studies.
SCHOOLS/COLLEGE: Pancyprian Gymnasium, Nicosia, Pedagogical Academy, Athens University, University of Reading.
QUALIFICATIONS: MA; BA in Education. Teacher Training Diploma (Pedagogical Academy of Cyprus);.
MEMBERSHIPS: Pancyprian Greek Teachers Organisation (POED).
HOBBIES AND INTERESTS: Singing, swimming, travelling, poetry, reading and writing.
PERSONAL PROFILE: Football Player/Referee; Member of Pancyprian Refugee Organisation Committee;Head Teacher of Greek Community Schools in Kuwait, UAE and UK; Commandos Ex-servicemen Officer and first Chairman of the Association; Head of Cyprus Educational Mission.

CHRIS PAVLO
Actor/Writer/Wrote and performed in the BBC2 award-winning comedy, The Harringham Harker

DATE OF BIRTH: 06-Jun-1967
PLACE OF BIRTH: London. Father from Famagusta; Mother from Larnaca.
MARITAL STATUS: Single.
SCHOOLS/COLLEGE: Ambrose Fleming Secondary School, Webber Douglas Academy.
HOBBIES AND INTERESTS: Football and sports.
PERSONAL PROFILE: Actor/Writer. Performed on TV in The Bill and EastEnders, Wendys House. Appeared in the films Jeremiah and Strong Language. Appeared in Shakespeare Tours. Regular at the Edinburgh Festival. Wrote and performed in the BBC2 award-winning comedy, The Harringham Harker.

ANTONIS PAVLOU
Chairman of Greek Cypriot Orthodox Community in Leeds

DATE OF BIRTH: 02-Feb-1944
PLACE OF BIRTH: Larnaca.
MARITAL STATUS: Married to Dimitra.
CHILDREN: Two sons, one daughter.
SCHOOLS/COLLEGE: Elementary School, Ayii Vavatsinia.
HOBBIES AND INTERESTS: Swimming and travel.
PERSONAL PROFILE: Businessman, Chairman of Ayii Vavatsinia Assoc UK. Chairman of Greek Cypriot Orthodox Community in Leeds.

UK

CRITON PAVLOU
Independent Consultant in Obstetrics and Gynaecology

DATE OF BIRTH: 23-Jan-1941
PLACE OF BIRTH: St Neots Hunts. Father from Dora; Mother from Rizokarpasso.
MARITAL STATUS: Married to Joy from the UK. Married to Costas Christou, also a Solicitor, from Tricomo.
CHILDREN: James, Film Industry. Lucy, Child Physiotherapy.
SCHOOLS/COLLEGE: St Clement Danes Grammar School, Middlesex Hampstead Medical School.
QUALIFICATIONS: MB BS FRCS Ed, FRCOG.
MEMBERSHIPS: British Fertility Society, Hellenic Society, British Society of Cervical Pathology & Colposcopy, British Society of Gynaecological Endoscopy.
HOBBIES AND INTERESTS: Golf, travel, gardening and DIY.
PERSONAL PROFILE: Independent General Consultant Obstetrics and Gynaecology.

PAUL PAVLOU
Former Senior Corporate Manager at BNP Paribas Cyprus

DATE OF BIRTH: 26-Sep-1954
PLACE OF BIRTH: London Father from Alethriko, Mother from Lefkara.
MARITAL STATUS: Single.
CHILDREN: Zoe, Studying Law at Sheffield University. Vasilia, American Academy Larnaca.
SCHOOLS/COLLEGE: Holloway.
QUALIFICATIONS: 5 O levels, The Chartered Institute of Bankers-Associate ACIB.
HOBBIES AND INTERESTS: Current Affairs, travel, sport, keep fit, music, theatre and socialising.
PERSONAL PROFILE: Paul Pavlou was a customer services manager at eight different branches of Barclays Bank in the UK, Branch Manager at Barclays Offshore Banking in Nicosia and Limassol, Branch Manager HSBC Bank in Limassol. Senior Corporate Manager at BNP Paribas Cyprus Ltd Limassol. Paul is now a Consultant with Headlands International-Overseas Property Company-Larnaca.

PAUL PAVLOU
Barrister Leads the Chambers Ancillary Relief Group and regularly holds seminars all over England

DATE OF BIRTH: 24-Dec-1970
PLACE OF BIRTH: Trikomo.
MARITAL STATUS: Single.
CHILDREN: One Child.
SCHOOLS/COLLEGE: Cann Hall London, University of London.
QUALIFICATIONS: LLB(Hons).
MEMBERSHIPS: Family Law Bar Association Anglo-Cypriot Lawyers Association.
HOBBIES AND INTERESTS: Fitness, Food&Wine, Travel, Eastern Mediterranean Politics my daughter.
PERSONAL PROFILE: Paul Pavlou is a Barrister writes articles on family law. Leads the Chambers Ancillary Relief Group and regularly holds seminars all over England.

SAVVAS PAVLOU
Asian and Greek Rich list

DATE OF BIRTH: 14-Apr-1970
PLACE OF BIRTH: London Father from Strovolos, Nicosia Mum from Lysos Paphos.
MARITAL STATUS: Married to Sandra, London Parents From Cyprus, Recruitment Consultant.
SCHOOLS/COLLEGE: Elthorne High School and Drayton Manor High School. London College of Printing and Leicester Polytechnic.
QUALIFICATIONS: BA(Hons) Graphic Design.
HOBBIES AND INTERESTS: Football.
PERSONAL PROFILE: Savvas Pavlou is a graphic designer has worked with the Asian and Greek Rich list, Creative Designer and co publisher of the Greek Rich list. He is also a Director of Hudge Design Studio.

UK

STEL PAVLOU

Wrote and co-produced the feature film The 51st State starring Samuel L Jackson and Robert Carlyle

PLACE OF BIRTH: UK in 1970. Father from Rizokarpasso, Mother, English. **SCHOOLS/COLLEGE:** Chatham Grammar School for Boys. Liverpool University. **QUALIFICATIONS:** BA. **HOBBIES AND INTERESTS:** Travel, genaeology, tennis, athletics, formula1, reading and painting.

PERSONAL PROFILE: Stel Pavlou has written two best selling and international best selling novels. Decipher and Gene. Wrote and co-produced the feature film The 51st State starring Samuel L Jackson and Robert Carlyle. Features in Elemental along side Sir Arthur C Clarke a science fiction anthology in aid of Save the Children Asian Tsunami Fund. Writes short stories for Dr Who at Big Finish productions.

DR ANDREAS PELENDRIDES

General Practitioner

DATE OF BIRTH: 28-Oct-1930 **PLACE OF BIRTH:** Pelendri. **MARITAL STATUS:** Married to Radka Christova, Bulgaria. **CHILDREN:** Dr Helen Pelendrides, General Practitioner. **SCHOOLS/COLLEGE:** Medical School, Sofia, Bulgaria. The Society of Apothecaries of London.

QUALIFICATIONS: MD, LMSSA. MA (Byzantine Studies), University of London-Royal Holloway College. **HONOURS/AWARDS:** MA. **PERSONAL PROFILE:** Publication of Two Byzantine Books. General Practitioner.

DR HELEN PELENDRIDES

General Practitioner on three sites in North London (East Finchley, Finchley Central & Wood Green

DATE OF BIRTH: 16-May-1961 **PLACE OF BIRTH:** Sofia, Bulgaria. Father from Cyprus; Mother from Bulgaria. **MARITAL STATUS:** Married to Nicholas Durden, a Medical Doctor, from Finchley London. **CHILDREN:** Andrew and Marie, both at school. **SCHOOLS/COLLEGE:** South Hampstead High School for Girls London, University of London, Guys Hospital. **QUALIFICATIONS:** MB, BS, DRCOG. University of London, Guys Hospital. **HOBBIES AND INTERESTS:** Skiing, keep fit and modern literature.

PERSONAL PROFILE: General Practitioner on three sites in North London (East Finchley, Finchley Central & Wood Green).

PETER PENTAYIOTIS

Freelance Photographer for the community newspapers

DATE OF BIRTH: 07-Dec-1948 **PLACE OF BIRTH:** Pentayia. **MARITAL STATUS:** Single. **CHILDREN:** Natalie. **MEMBERSHIPS:** Member of the Committee of Pentayia Association, UK. **HOBBIES AND INTERESTS:** Shooting and golf. **PERSONAL PROFILE:** Freelance Photographer, works mainly with Parikiaki and Eleftheria Newspapers.

UK

Stel Pavlou wrote and co produced the feature film the 51st state starring Samuel Lee Jackson and Robert Carlyle

MINOS PERDIOS
National Team Coach of the St Kitts & Nevis Football Association during the FIFA World Cup 2002 qualifying campaign

DATE OF BIRTH: 18-Jun-1967
PLACE OF BIRTH: London. Parents from Larnaca and Achna.
MARITAL STATUS: Married to Lucia Alexander, Leeds.
CHILDREN: Olivia.
SCHOOLS/COLLEGE: American Academy, Larnaca. Davis College, City University, University of Sheffield.
QUALIFICATIONS: BSc. Actuarial Science and Social Statistics, MSc. Sports Coaching and Exercise Science. UEFA B' Licence.
MEMBERSHIPS: FA Coaches Association.
HOBBIES AND INTERESTS: Football, tennis and reading sports autobiographies.
PERSONAL PROFILE: National Team Coach of the St Kitts & Nevis Football Association during the FIFA World Cup 2002 qualifying campaign, Youth Coach at Leeds United Football Club, General Manager at Haringey Borough Football Club, and Omonia FC London, Football in the Community Coach at Luton Town football Club. Minos is the Deputy Head at Ravenscroft School in Barnet.

BOBBY PERICLEOUS
Leukaemia Charity Fund Raiser

DATE OF BIRTH: 31-Dec-1956
PLACE OF BIRTH: London. Father Pantelli Savva from Alethrico; Mother Loiza from Famagusta.
MARITAL STATUS: Married.
CHILDREN: Mario, Panteli.
SCHOOLS/COLLEGE: Alexandra Park School.
HOBBIES AND INTERESTS: Walking, socialising, cooking and fundraising.
PERSONAL PROFILE: Chairwoman of Eleni Pericleous Trust Fund which raises money for Leukaemia to be distributed between Royal Free Hospital and Great Ormond Street Hospital. Was Social Secretary of Potters Bar Greek School.

CHRISTINE PERICLEOUS
Psychotherapist in the Cygnet Clinic a private Psychiatric Hospital

DATE OF BIRTH: 19-Aug-1955
PLACE OF BIRTH: Ayia Varvara, Nicosia.
MARITAL STATUS: Single.
CHILDREN: Mary-Louise, University Graduate.
SCHOOLS/COLLEGE: Winchmore Secondary, Southgate College.
QUALIFICATIONS: Psychoanalytic Psychotherapist.
HOBBIES AND INTERESTS: The arts, theatre, art galleries and hiking.
PERSONAL PROFILE: Former Secretary of the Thalassaemia Society UK. Then worked for Arbours Crisis Centre a residential setting for people with emotional distress. During this time began Psychotherapy training. Currently works as a Psychotherapist in the Cygnet Clinic a private Psychiatric Hospital.

LEONIDAS PERIKLEOUS
Chairman of the Greek Cypriot Orthodox Community in Leicester

DATE OF BIRTH: 12-Mar-1943
PLACE OF BIRTH: Dora, Limassol.
MARITAL STATUS: Married to Androulla from Limassol.
CHILDREN: One son, one daughter.
SCHOOLS/COLLEGE: Elementary School.
HOBBIES AND INTERESTS: Working and travel.
PERSONAL PROFILE: Chairman of the Greek Cypriot Orthodox Community in Leicester.

ALEXANDROS PETRIDES
Music Journalist & Disc Jockey writes in the Sun and Guardian

DATE OF BIRTH: 11-Aug-1964
PLACE OF BIRTH: London. Father from Amiandos; Mother from England.
MARITAL STATUS: Single.
SCHOOLS/COLLEGE: Newport Rd, Leyton, Monkswalk School, Boreham Wood College.
HOBBIES AND INTERESTS: Football and skateboarding.

PERSONAL PROFILE: DJ, in clubs all over the world and radio known as Alex P. Kiss FM and own show on MTV called Medonism. Writes articles in major papers: Guardian, Sun. Four compilation albums that sold over 150, 000 copies each, new album called Speculates. Has done work for Jay Kay, Jamiroquai. Owns Velvet Underground Night Club in Charing Cross.

ANDREAS PETRIDES
Stunt Co-ordinator/Stunt Performer appeared in James Bond films, Gladiator, Braveheart

DATE OF BIRTH: 11-Nov-1967
PLACE OF BIRTH: Father from Amiandos; Mother from England.
MARITAL STATUS: Single.
SCHOOLS/COLLEGE: Monks Walk, Welwyn Garden City.
HOBBIES AND INTERESTS: Adventure sports and walking.
PERSONAL PROFILE: Stunt Co-ordinator and Stunt Performer. Has done work in films such as the last four James Bond films, Gladiator, Braveheart, Star Wars, The Borrowers. TV work includes Casualty, Merlin and The Professionals.

PETROS PETRIDES
Executive Director of LGR

DATE OF BIRTH: 06-Feb-1943
PLACE OF BIRTH: Lincoln, UK. Greek Cypriot Parents.
MARITAL STATUS: Married to Androula, Famagusta, Company Director.
CHILDREN: Anthony, Both in Business. Eugenios.
SCHOOLS/COLLEGE: Greek Gymnasium of Famagusta, London University, Toronto University.
QUALIFICATIONS: B. Sc (Eng), P. Eng, AMIEE.
MEMBERSHIPS: Institute of Electrical Engineers.
HONOURS/AWARDS: Honorary Citizen of the City of Minneapolis, USA, Who's Who in the World (1984-1985).
HOBBIES AND INTERESTS: Fishing, hunting and travelling.
PERSONAL PROFILE: Founder and Chairman of the Plus Group of Companies with trading and investment activities in several countries. Shareholder and first chairman of London Greek Radio, Vice Chairman of Cypriot Estia of London.

ARCHIMANDRITE THEOPHANIS PETROU
High Priest

DATE OF BIRTH: 06-Jan-1942
PLACE OF BIRTH: Kythrea.
CHILDREN: Pierre, Police Press Executive Officer. Marino, Manager.
SCHOOLS/COLLEGE: High Commercial Lyceum, Nicosia.
QUALIFICATIONS: High Priest.
HOBBIES AND INTERESTS: Religion and gardening.
PERSONAL PROFILE: High Priest. Available to Greek Communities throughout the UK.

MARIO PETROU
Consultant Cardiac Surgeon

DATE OF BIRTH: 20-Jul-1964
PLACE OF BIRTH: London. Father from Kythrea; Mother from Kyrenia.
MARITAL STATUS: Married to Elizabeth from London.
SCHOOLS/COLLEGE: Hackney Downs Comprehensive School, Kingsway Princeton College, University College and Middlesex School of Medicine.
QUALIFICATIONS: PhD Cardiac Surgery; Bsc in Neuroscience. MBBS, frcs (CTH).
HONOURS/AWARDS: William Henry Rean Prize for the most promising Young Doctor. Mc Cormack Medal 2001.
HOBBIES AND INTERESTS: Classical Music, Snooker.
PERSONAL PROFILE: Consultant Cardiac Surgeon, Royal Brompton Hospital, London.

UK

PETROS PETROU
Active member of the Radio Marathon Committee

PLACE OF BIRTH: Ayia Phyla, Limassol.
MARITAL STATUS: Married to Nina.
CHILDREN: Carmelina.
Business.
SCHOOLS/COLLEGE: North London Polytechnic.
HOBBIES AND INTERESTS: Football and travel.
PERSONAL PROFILE: Petros Petrou has a property development business and also owns the Red Pepper Restaurant in Cockfosters. He is also a active member of the Radio Marathon Committee.

COSTAKIS PETROUIS
Hon Consul of the Republic of Cyprus in Birmingham and West Midlands

DATE OF BIRTH: 31-Dec-1949
PLACE OF BIRTH: Kiti.
MARITAL STATUS: Married to Eftychia.
CHILDREN: Melanie, Christina.
SCHOOLS/COLLEGE: Pancyprian Gymnasium Larnaca.
QUALIFICATIONS: Fellow Member of Institute of Financial accountants.
HOBBIES AND INTERESTS: Football, walking and travelling.
PERSONAL PROFILE: Hon Consul of the Republic of Cyprus in Birmingham and West Midlands. Self employed accountant, active member of Birmingham Community. Secretary of Church Committee of Apostolos Andreas Cathedral.

DR CONSTANTINOS N PHELLAS
Senior Lecturer in Sociology

DATE OF BIRTH: 24-Jun-1961
PLACE OF BIRTH: Nicosia.
MARITAL STATUS: Single.
SCHOOLS/COLLEGE: University of Essex, University of Warwick, City University.
QUALIFICATIONS: BSc, MSc, MSc, PhD. Taxation Accountant.
MEMBERSHIPS: Institute of Taxation.
HONOURS/AWARDS: Funding from the Government on HIV/AIDS research.
HOBBIES AND INTERESTS: Sports, music and theatre.

PERSONAL PROFILE: Senior Lecturer in Sociology. Published a book on Greek Cultural and Sexual Identities. Area of research: Sexuality, Ethnicity, Culture, Public Health and Health Promotion. He has published extensively on the above-mentioned areas.

CHRYS PHILALITHES
Appeared in the Guardian National Paper as one of 50 women to watch 2003

DATE OF BIRTH: 08-Dec-1971
PLACE OF BIRTH: London. Father from Limassol. Mother from Peyia, Paphos.
MARITAL STATUS: Single.
QUALIFICATIONS: BA, MBA.
HONOURS/AWARDS: Dean's Honours List – University of Toronto. Campaign Magazine – Faces To Watch, 2003. The Guardian – 50 Women to Watch, 2003.
HOBBIES AND INTERESTS: Music, Film, dance and Scuba Diving.
PERSONAL PROFILE: Chrys is a founding member of Espotting Media. As Marketing Director of Espotting, Chrys is responsible for group-wide marketing strategy and execution. Prior to Espotting, Chrys was New Business Manager at WCRS, one of the UK's Top 20 Advertising Agencies.

ANDREAS PHILIOTIS
Chairman of the Greek Cypriot Association of Hammersmith and Fulham 1986-2003

DATE OF BIRTH: 02-Sep-1952
PLACE OF BIRTH: Nicosia, Cyprus.
MARITAL STATUS: Married to Patricia, Ireland of Polish Descent.
CHILDREN: Anastasios, Alexandros, Theodoros, Leandros.
SCHOOLS/COLLEGE: The English School, Nicosia Cyprus, University. Tutorial College, South East London College.
QUALIFICATIONS: Business management, Certified Public Accountant.
HOBBIES AND INTERESTS: Collector of Sporting Memorabilia, Stamp and Coin Collecting.
PERSONAL PROFILE: Chairman of the Greek Cypriot Association of Hammersmith and Fulham 1986-2003. Representing the community on the council for Racial Equality, Education Committee, Police Consultative Committee.

UK

PANICO PHILIPOU
Chief Executive World Design and Trade former managing director of Diesel UK and USA

PLACE OF BIRTH: London Father Petros from Yialoussa, Mother May from Ireland. **MARITAL STATUS:** Married to Jessica. **CHILDREN:** Petros, Leonidas, Electra. **SCHOOLS/COLLEGE:** Sir William Collins School, London University. **QUALIFICATIONS:** BA Econ & Politics. Chartered Certified Accountant. **HOBBIES AND INTERESTS:** Football (Arsenal Fan), music and stamp collecting. **PERSONAL PROFILE:** Chief Executive of the Fashion Company World Design trade with brands sonneti and Firetrap. Was Managing Director of Diesel UK and USA, one of the world's leading fashion and design streetwear Co's.

DR GEORGE PHILIPPOU
Cardiac Surgeon

DATE OF BIRTH: 08-Oct-1939 **PLACE OF BIRTH:** Nicosia. **MARITAL STATUS:** Married to Dr Anna, Sofia, Medical Doctor. **CHILDREN:** Elena, Administration Manager. Maria, Beautician. **SCHOOLS/COLLEGE:** Pancyprian Gymnasium, Nicosia, Medical University, Sofia. **QUALIFICATIONS:** MD, MB, BS. Cardiac Surgeon. **MEMBERSHIPS:** BMA, MDU. **HOBBIES AND INTERESTS:** Squash, tennis and reading. **PERSONAL PROFILE:** Cardiac Surgeon.

PAUL PHILIPPOU
Lecturer University of Dundee

DATE OF BIRTH: 31-Oct-1963 **PLACE OF BIRTH:** London. Father from Ayios Sergios, Mother from the UK. **MARITAL STATUS:** Married to Mary Alexander, Perth, Trade Unions. **CHILDREN:** Cora, Leah, Rosa. **SCHOOLS/COLLEGE:** University of London, University of Liverpool. **QUALIFICATIONS:** Msc, Bsc (Eng); ACGI in Aeronautical Engineering. PGCE. **HOBBIES AND INTERESTS:** Astronomy, gardening, poetry, philosophy and left wing and local history. **PERSONAL PROFILE:** Teaches at Perth High School and the University of Dundee. Also Associate Lecturer at the Open University whilst in London. Previously Social Security Spokesperson for the Scottish Socialist Party. Labour Party candidate in Fulham for 1994 local goverment elections.

ANDROS PANAYIOTIS PHOULI
Chairman of Rush Group of Salons British artistic team of the year 2004

DATE OF BIRTH: 22-Mar-1967 **PLACE OF BIRTH:** London. Father from Achna, Mother from Odhou. **MARITAL STATUS:** Married to Angelina, Kontea, Housewife. **CHILDREN:** Panayiotis. **SCHOOLS/COLLEGE:** Purley High, Robert Fielding Hairdressing School. **HONOURS/AWARDS:** Rush have won the following awards: British Southern Hairdresser of the Year, 2001. British newcomer of the year 2003. British Artistic Team of the year 2004 these are just some of the hairdressing awards. Business Director of the year 2008 from the British Hairdressing Business Awards. **HOBBIES AND INTERESTS:** Football, shooting and family. **PERSONAL PROFILE:** Chairman of Rush Group of Salons.

UK

AKIS PHYLAKTIS
Chartered Architect/On the board of the Hellenic Community Trust and founding member of the Hellenic Centre

DATE OF BIRTH: 21-Aug-1948
PLACE OF BIRTH: Cyprus.
MARITAL STATUS: Married to Kate, Nicosia, Professor of Finance at Cass Business School, London.
CHILDREN: Alexandra, George, Both University graduates.
SCHOOLS/COLLEGE: Kykko Gymnasium, English School Nicosia. University of Westminster and Bartlett School of Architecture.
QUALIFICATIONS: MSc DipArch.
MEMBERSHIPS: Royal Institute of British Architects (RIBA), Member Association of Project Management (MAPM), Institute of Directors (IoD).
HOBBIES AND INTERESTS: Travel, walking, trekking, photography and wine.
PERSONAL PROFILE: Akis Phylaktis is an Architect and Project Manager, Director of Wilson Phylaktis Architects and Project Managers (rail infrastructure, underground stations, commercial and residential project work). He is also on the board of the Hellenic Community Trust and founding member of the Hellenic Centre.

KATE PHYLAKTIS
Professor of International Finance, City University Business School, London

DATE OF BIRTH: 20-Aug-1951
PLACE OF BIRTH: Nicosia.
MARITAL STATUS: Married to Akis Phylaktis, Architect.
CHILDREN: Alexandra, George, Both University graduates.
SCHOOLS/COLLEGE: Pancyprian Gymnasium Phaneromeni. Brunel University, London School of Economics, City University.
QUALIFICATIONS: BSc (Econ), MSc (Econ), PhD Banking and Finance.
MEMBERSHIPS: American Finance Association. Finacial Management Association.
HOBBIES AND INTERESTS: Wine tasting and Trekking.
PERSONAL PROFILE: Kate Phylaktis is currently a Professor of International Finance and Director of the Emerging Markets Group at Sir John Cass Business School. She has acted as a consultant to various companies and public bodies including the Commonwealth Secretariat, the Ministry of Education of Greece, the Hellenic Capital Market Commission.

She is currently a consultant to the Cyprus University of Technology. She has published in finance and economics journals. She has also written four books.

NICOLAS PIERE
Film Director

DATE OF BIRTH: 17-Mar-1980
PLACE OF BIRTH: Merseyside
Father from Koma Tou Yialou
Mother from Khirotikia.
MARITAL STATUS: Single.
SCHOOLS/COLLEGE: Great Sankey High School. University of Manchester.
QUALIFICATIONS: BA Joint Honours TV production(media studies) & Business Studies.
HOBBIES AND INTERESTS: Travelling, Spear Fishing and Astronomy.
PERSONAL PROFILE: Nicolas Piere is a film Director his first professional short film was entitled The Greek man from Pakistan. This was a quirky comedy about a British born Greek Cypriot who constantly receives racial abuse for being mistaken as Pakistani.

PAUL PIERIDES
Solicitor

DATE OF BIRTH: 22-Jun-1948
PLACE OF BIRTH: London.
Father from Astromeriti; Mother from Kefalonia, Greece.
MARITAL STATUS: Married to Miroulla, Limassol.
CHILDREN: Maria.
SCHOOLS/COLLEGE: Kingston Grammar School, University College, Oxford.
QUALIFICATIONS: BA Honours Law, MA Honours Law.
HOBBIES AND INTERESTS: Architecture.
PERSONAL PROFILE: Solicitor specialising in Property Law and Conveyancing. Partner in Gordon Dadds Solicitors.

DR KYPROS PILAKOUTAS
Lecturer Sheffield University

DATE OF BIRTH: 17-Feb-1961
PLACE OF BIRTH: Trachonas, Nicosia.
MARITAL STATUS: Married to Teresa, Portugal, Civil Engineer.
CHILDREN: Georgios, Leonora, Mariana, All three at School.
SCHOOLS/COLLEGE: The English School Nicosia, University of London.
QUALIFICATIONS: BSc (Eng), ACGI, PhD.
HONOURS/AWARDS: Medal of Iasi Technical University, Romania.
HOBBIES AND INTERESTS: Travelling, Greek music and dance, mental games, gardening and football.
PERSONAL PROFILE: University Lecturer at Sheffield University. Visiting Professor - Iasi TU Romania, 2001.

CHRIS PISHIRI
Chartered Surveyor Partner in Jon Christopher Chartered Surveyors

DATE OF BIRTH: 08-Sep-1969
PLACE OF BIRTH: London. Son of Andrico from Komi Kebir, former owner of Cronos Electronics; Mother Koulla from Komi Kebir.
MARITAL STATUS: Married to Gina, London (parents are from Frenaros and Aglantsia).
CHILDREN: Twins, Andreas & Klair; Kerri.
SCHOOLS/COLLEGE: Ashmole School, Westminster University.
QUALIFICATIONS: Bsc in Estate Management. Chartered Surveyor.
MEMBERSHIPS: Member of the Royal Institute of Chartered Surveyors.
HOBBIES AND INTERESTS: Football, Arsenal Fan.
PERSONAL PROFILE: Partner with brother Jon in Chartered Surveyors Jon Christopher in Finchley who carry out property valuations and surveys for banks and lending institutions. Philanthropist.

JON PISHIRI
Assessor for the Royal Institution of Chartered Surveyors

DATE OF BIRTH: 22-Sep-1968
PLACE OF BIRTH: London. Father Andrico, previous owner of Cronos Electronics from Komi Kebir; Mother, Koulla, from Komi Kebir.
MARITAL STATUS: Married to Anna Stratis, parents from Akanthou and Troullous.
CHILDREN: Andrianna, Helena, George.
SCHOOLS/COLLEGE: Ashmole School, University of Westminster.
QUALIFICATIONS: BSc in Estate Management. Chartered Surveyor.
MEMBERSHIPS: Associate and member of the Royal Institute of Chartered Surveyors.
HOBBIES AND INTERESTS: Sports, reading, football, (Arsenal Fan).
PERSONAL PROFILE: Partner with brother Chris in Jon Christopher Chartered Surveyors. Assessor for the Royal Institution of Chartered Surveyors.

CHRISTINA PISHIRIS
Journalist, Televisual Trade Magazine & C21

DATE OF BIRTH: 04-Feb-1974
PLACE OF BIRTH: London. Parents from Komi Kebir.
MARITAL STATUS: Single.
SCHOOLS/COLLEGE: West Twyford Primary, Ellen Wilkinson, Sussex University.
QUALIFICATIONS: BA English.
HOBBIES AND INTERESTS: Reading, cinema and internet.
PERSONAL PROFILE: Freelance Journalist, Televisual Trade Magazine & C21. Scriptwriter, written short films.

UK

CHRISTOPHER ANTONIOU PISSARIDES
Professor of Economics LSE Nominated for a Nobel Prize in 2007

DATE OF BIRTH: 20-Feb-1948
PLACE OF BIRTH: Nicosia.
MARITAL STATUS: Married to Francesca, Italy, Economist.
CHILDREN: Antony, Miranda.
SCHOOLS/COLLEGE: Eleneion (elementary), Pancyprian Gymnasium (Secondary School), both in Nicosia. Essex University, London School of Economics.
QUALIFICATIONS: BA, MA, PhD all in Economics.
MEMBERSHIPS: Royal Economic Society, Econ-ometric Society, European Economic Association.
HONOURS/AWARDS: Nominated for a Nobel Prize in 2007.
HOBBIES AND INTERESTS: Economics, gardening and cooking.
PERSONAL PROFILE: Currently a Professor of Economics at the LSE. Has written two books a consultant at the World Bank, the European Commission and a member of the Mone-tary Policy Committee of the Central Bank of Cyprus.

KYRIACOS PITSIELIS
Businessman Director and Chairman of The Penridge Banqueting Suite

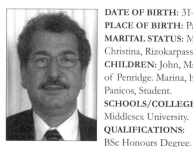

DATE OF BIRTH: 31-Aug-1950
PLACE OF BIRTH: Palechori.
MARITAL STATUS: Married to Christina, Rizokarpasso.
CHILDREN: John, Manager of Penridge. Marina, housewife. Panicos, Student.
SCHOOLS/COLLEGE: Middlesex University.
QUALIFICATIONS: BSc Honours Degree.
Engineer in Computers.
HOBBIES AND INTERESTS: Politics and golf.
PERSONAL PROFILE: He was a policeman in Cyprus. Came to the UK in 1971 to study. Worked for five years in the computer industry and then began his catering business. Now Director and Chairman of The Penridge Banqueting Suite also has a property company in Cyprus Committee Member and Co-founder of St Demetrius Church in Edmonton. Member of the Palechori village Association UK.

JOHN PITTALIS
Accountant/Non Executive Director of Cyprus Development Bank

DATE OF BIRTH: 29-Mar-1960
PLACE OF BIRTH: London. Father from Ayios Ioannis, Agros; mother from Agros.
MARITAL STATUS: Married to Sally.
CHILDREN: Kyriacos, Alexi and Xenia.
SCHOOLS/COLLEGE: Lyndhurst House Prep, Clifton College, London School of Economics.
QUALIFICATIONS: B. Sc (Econ). Chartered Accountant, FCA.
HOBBIES AND INTERESTS: Football, tennis and most sports.
PERSONAL PROFILE: Partner in family accountancy practice. Also Non Executive Director of Cyprus Development Bank Played for PAOK in Cypriot League UK.

MAGDA PITZORI
Chairwoman, Midlands Cypriot Festival

DATE OF BIRTH: 13-Nov-1950
PLACE OF BIRTH: Troulli.
MARITAL STATUS: Married to Yiannis, Rizokarpasso.
CHILDREN: Three.
SCHOOLS/COLLEGE: Lykeion Larnaca.
HOBBIES AND INTERESTS: Community work.
PERSONAL PROFILE: Chairwoman of the Greek School in Leicester, Chairwoman of the Midlands Cypriot Festival.

UK

MARY PLANT
Artist

DATE OF BIRTH: 28-Dec-1943
PLACE OF BIRTH: Famagusta.
MARITAL STATUS: Married to Guy Hetherington, London, Artist.
SCHOOLS/COLLEGE: Chelsea School of Art, London.
MEMBERSHIPS: IAA (International Association of Art Unesco Paris), EKATE (Cyprus Chamber of Fine Arts).
HONOURS/AWARDS: Morland Lewis Scholarship, GLA Grant, Bank of Cyprus Award prize-winner.
HOBBIES AND INTERESTS: The study of Literature & Archaeology.
PERSONAL PROFILE: Works as a full-time Artist and has exhibited widely. Works in many private and Public Collections, including The Leventis Foundation, London, The Bank of Cyprus, London, The Cyprus Popular Bank, London, Cultural Service, Ministry of Education Cyprus.

ANDY POLYCARPOU
Footballer scored the goal when Southend beat Watford 1-0 to play Liverpool in the next round of the FA Cup in 1978

DATE OF BIRTH: 15-Aug-1958
PLACE OF BIRTH: London. Father, Fanos, from Styllos; Mother, Smyrni, from Komi Kebir.
CHILDREN: Serena and Sophia.
SCHOOLS/COLLEGE: Wood Green School.
HOBBIES AND INTERESTS: Football and antiques.
PERSONAL PROFILE: Professional Footballer, played for Southend, Cambridge Utd, Cardiff City then Norwich. Scored the goal when Southend beat Watford 1-0 to play Liverpool in the next round of the FA Cup in 1978. Now owner of an interior furniture shop in Windsor.

EVE POLYCARPOU
Actress/Singer part of the Duo Donna and Kebab with Martha Lewis

DATE OF BIRTH: 28-Aug-1955
PLACE OF BIRTH: Brighton. Father from Korfi, Limassol; Mother from Kakopetria.
MARITAL STATUS: Single.
SCHOOLS/COLLEGE: St Angela's Convent School, Southgate College, New College School of Speech & Drama.
HOBBIES AND INTERESTS: Tennis, swimming, and walking.
PERSONAL PROFILE: Actress appears in Donna & Kebab with Martha Lewis. Appeared on TV & stage, one woman show, Eve in the Beginning. Did Big Fat Xmas at the Bloomsbury Theatre. Appeared on TV in Inspector Morse, The Bill and Forth Farm. Music Teacher in Primary School. Lectures at Southwark College and directed and devised for them a play at the Soho Theatre.

MICHAEL POLYCARPOU
President of Greek Cypriot Association of South Wales

DATE OF BIRTH: 25-Aug-1940
PLACE OF BIRTH: Famagusta.
MARITAL STATUS: Married to Eleni, Cheltenham, Retired Senior Midwife.
CHILDREN: Two Sons.
SCHOOLS/COLLEGE: English High School in Famagusta, Manchester Technical College, Pontypridd University, Barry College of Further Education.
QUALIFICATIONS: Electrical Engineer.
HONOURS/AWARDS: Member of Race Equality Council.
HOBBIES AND INTERESTS: Charities & community, works on behalf of the underprivileged, gardening & horticulture and computing.
PERSONAL PROFILE: Greek Ethnic Minority Health Advocate for Cardiff Social Services. President of The Greek Cypriots Association of South Wales, Director of Multicultural Cross Roads in Cardiff.

UK

PETER POLYCARPOU
Actor famous for playing Chris Theodopoulopoudos in the BBC sitcom Birds of a Feathers

DATE OF BIRTH: 31-Mar-1957
PLACE OF BIRTH: Brighton. Father from Korfi; Mother from Kakopetria.
MARITAL STATUS: Single.
SCHOOLS/COLLEGE: Tottenhall Primary, Southgate Comprehensive, Holmwood School for Boys, Sutton Valance School for Boys, Brighton Polytechnic, Middlesex University.
HONOURS/AWARDS: LRAM in Mime (Licensorship of The Royal Academy of Music); City and Guilds in Web Design.
HOBBIES AND INTERESTS: Makes models and puts ships in bottles; keen cricketer; playing the piano; running marathons for charity; maintaining his own website at www. polycarpou. com.
PERSONAL PROFILE: Original cast member of Les Miserables at the Barbican & Palace Theatre's, taking over the role of Thenadier. Phantom in Andrew Lloyd Webber's Phantom of the Opera at Her Majesty's Theatre. Childcatcher in Chitty Chitty Bang Bang. Kabaret. He created the role of John in the Blockbuster Miss Saigon at the Theatre Royal, and played Chris. Theodopoulopoudos in the BBC TV sitcom, Birds of a Feather. Appeared as Domingo Mercante in EVITA, with Madonna starred opposite Michelle Collins as Yiannis in Sunburn for BBC TV. Guest star for ITV's The Bill. Has given one-day workshops in several schools on the Les Miserables Schools edition.
Keen supporter and fundraiser for the Anthony Nolan Trust, for which he has run several London Marathons. Patron of the UK Thalassaemia Society. Peter made his own short film called Mad George, written by himself and starring Peter and another Cypriot actor, George Jackos.

DORA POOLE
Executive Member of Greek Parents Association

DATE OF BIRTH: 20-Jan-1953
PLACE OF BIRTH: Lymbia.
MARITAL STATUS: Married to Martin, London, Plumbing Engineer.
CHILDREN: Stephanie, Marketing. Laura, student.
SCHOOLS/COLLEGE: Tottenham Technical College.
QUALIFICATIONS: City & Guilds Certificate in Hairdresing.

MEMBERSHIPS: Member of OESEKA, Executive member of Greek Parents Association, G. P. A. position held Events Secretary.
HOBBIES AND INTERESTS: Helping to maintain our Cypriot Greek Education and Culture.
PERSONAL PROFILE: Member of St Mary's GPA Greek School of Cheshunt, held the post of Chairperson for five years on the Parents Committee.

GEORGE PORNARIS
Active member of charity organisations/ philanthropist

DATE OF BIRTH: 27-May-1967
PLACE OF BIRTH: Asha.
MARITAL STATUS: Married to Emilia, Cypriot, Studying Interior design.
CHILDREN: Christopher, Andrew.
SCHOOLS/COLLEGE: Brondesbury and Kilburn. Institute of Financial Services.
QUALIFICATIONS: Certificate in Mortgage Advice and Practice.
HOBBIES AND INTERESTS: reading, fly fishing, football and history.
PERSONAL PROFILE: George Pornaris came to England as a refugee and opened his first business at 23 is a Mortgage Consultant and has helped in funding the new church at St Panteleimon and an active member of Cancer research and cruelty to children.

MICHAEL GEORGIOU POUMPOURIS
Vice Chairman of Greek Parents Association

DATE OF BIRTH: 01-Nov-1941
PLACE OF BIRTH: Palechori.
MARITAL STATUS: Married to Helen, Korfi, Travel Agent.
CHILDREN: Marios, Chartered Building Surveyor. Alice, Buyer.
SCHOOLS/COLLEGE: Elementary School, Palekhori; Nicosia Technical Institute, Nicosia.
QUALIFICATIONS: GCE O Level English & Maths, GCE A Level Modern Greek.
MEMBERSHIPS: Has been a member of the Greek Parents Association (GPA) since 1978. For a number of years has been an active committee member of Enfield Cypriot Association, previously as Secretary and now as Treasurer.
PERSONAL PROFILE: Travel Agent. Former Chairman of Hazelwood Greek School Parents Association. Vice Chairman of Greek Parents Association.

ANTONITSA POURGOURIDES
Dental Surgeon

DATE OF BIRTH: 27-Jul-1960
PLACE OF BIRTH: Komi Kebir.
MARITAL STATUS: Single.
SCHOOLS/COLLEGE: Woodhouse Grammar School, N. Finchley. University College London Dental School.
QUALIFICATIONS: LDS. RCS (Eng), BDS (London).
MEMBERSHIPS: BDA (British Dental Association), WID (Women in Dentistry).
HOBBIES AND INTERESTS: Travel, cookery, reading and languages.
PERSONAL PROFILE: Dental Surgeon working in General Practice.

EMILIA POURGOURIDES
General Practitioner

DATE OF BIRTH: 14-May-1938
PLACE OF BIRTH: Avgorou.
MARITAL STATUS: Married to Kyriacos, Eptakomi, Doctor.
CHILDREN: Christina, Consultant Psychiatrist. Effie, Haemotologist. Panos, Solicitor.
SCHOOLS/COLLEGE: Famagusta Greek Gymnasium, Medical School, Athens University.
HOBBIES AND INTERESTS: Archaeology and plants.
PERSONAL PROFILE: Practicing GP. Helped in Old Age Homes while in Cyprus.

KYRIACOS POURGOURIDES
General Practitioner

DATE OF BIRTH: 13-Mar-1940
PLACE OF BIRTH: Eptakomi.
MARITAL STATUS: Married to Emilia, Famagusta, Doctor.
CHILDREN: Christina, Consultant Psychiatrist. Effie, Haemotologist. Panos, Solicitor.
SCHOOLS/COLLEGE: Famagusta Greek Gymnasium. Birmingham University, Medical School.
QUALIFICATIONS: ChB LRCP MRCS.
HOBBIES AND INTERESTS: Current affairs and politics.
PERSONAL PROFILE: Practicing GP.

DR PANICOS POUTZIOURIS
Director of Postgraduate Programmes at the Manchester Science Enterprise Centre

DATE OF BIRTH: 04-Dec-1963
PLACE OF BIRTH: Aradippou.
MARITAL STATUS: Married.
SCHOOLS/COLLEGE: American Academy, Larnaca, University of Nottingham.
QUALIFICATIONS: BA MBA, PhD in Economics, Management-Finance.
MEMBERSHIPS: Board member of Institute for Small Business Affairs (UK).
HOBBIES AND INTERESTS: Poetry, Musical & Cultural Festivals.
PERSONAL PROFILE: Director of Postgraduate Programmes at the Manchester Science Enterprise Centre. Lectures, publishes and advises on entrepreneurship, small business management and family firms.

PANAYIOTIS ANDREAS POYIADZIS
Accountant/Committee Member, Secretary, Treasurer of the Cypriot Golf Society UK

DATE OF BIRTH: 25-Jan-1951
PLACE OF BIRTH: Famagusta.
MARITAL STATUS: Married to Stella (née Hanna), Famagusta.
CHILDREN: Demetra, Alexi, Antoni.
SCHOOLS/COLLEGE: Upton House Secondary School in Hackney, Southgate Technical College for A' Levels and Hendon College of Technology for HND Business Studies.
QUALIFICATIONS: HND in Business Studies. Fellow Member of Association of Accountants Technicians.
MEMBERSHIPS: A member of Enfield Golf Club and Cypriot Golf Society.
HOBBIES AND INTERESTS: Golf, reading and listening to music and travelling.
PERSONAL PROFILE: An accountant with own practice PAP & CO in North London. Was Vice Chairman of Hazelwood Greek School and. Co-opted Governor of Hazelwood English School. Committee Member, Secretary, Treasurer and Captain of the Cypriot Golf Society UK.

ARISTIDES GEORGE PRATSIDES
Osteopath

DATE OF BIRTH: 25-Sep-1957
PLACE OF BIRTH: London. Parents from Morphou.
MARITAL STATUS: Married to Chryso, London Cypriot Parents, Business.
CHILDREN: Adonis, Joanna.
SCHOOLS/COLLEGE: Wembley High School, Harrow Technical College, University of Herts, British School of Osteopathy, London.
QUALIFICATIONS: BSc.
MEMBERSHIPS: General Osteopathic Council.
HOBBIES AND INTERESTS: Music, cinema, football, watching his children's development.
PERSONAL PROFILE: Registered Osteopath. Has own practice, involved in NHS work and with local general practice.

DR CHRYSOSTOMOS PRODROMOU
Senior Staff Scientist at the Institute of Cancer Research

DATE OF BIRTH: 20-May-1962
PLACE OF BIRTH: London. Father from Syngrassi; Mother from Limnia.
MARITAL STATUS: Married to Natalia, Russia, research scientist.
CHILDREN: Nicholas. Sophia.
SCHOOLS/COLLEGE: Stationers Company. Chelsea College, Queen Mary College.
QUALIFICATIONS: BSc, PhD.
MEMBERSHIPS: British Sub-Aqua Club.
HONOURS/AWARDS: Dive Leader.
HOBBIES AND INTERESTS: Surfing, sub-aqua diving, weight training and classic cars.
PERSONAL PROFILE: Senior Staff Scientist at the Institute of Cancer Research. Internationally recognised for research into HSP90 (Heat Shock Protein 90).

HAMBIS PRODROMOU
Honorary President of the Cypriot Football league

DATE OF BIRTH: 29-May-1941
PLACE OF BIRTH: Acheritou.
MARITAL STATUS: Married to Margaret, from Larnaca.
CHILDREN: Two sons, two daughters.
SCHOOLS/COLLEGE: Emporiko Lykeon, Famagusta;. Teachers College in Athens.
PERSONAL PROFILE: Worked with Greek Schools as Teacher, Secretary of Greek Parents Association. Was a Journalist with Vema Newspaper later Editor of Parikiaki Newspaper. In 1975 was a co founder of The Cypriot Football League in the UK where he was Chairman for 20 years. He was formally elected as Honorary President of the Cypriot Football league.

PETER PRODROMOU
Head of Aerodynamics, Mclarens Formula One Racing Cars in 2006 he was recruited by Red Bull

DATE OF BIRTH: 14-Jan-1969
PLACE OF BIRTH: London. Father from Kontea; Mother from Trikomo.
MARITAL STATUS: Married to Salima, GP.
CHILDREN: One son, one daughter.
SCHOOLS/COLLEGE: Ashmole School, Imperial College, London University.
QUALIFICATIONS: BENG in Aeronautical Engineering; MSc in Computational Fluid, Dynamics & Structural Mechanics.
HOBBIES AND INTERESTS: Football and motor racing.
PERSONAL PROFILE: Was Head of Aerodynamics at Mclarens Formula One Racing Cars. At the start of 2006 he was recruited by Red Bull racing as chief aerodynamicist.

It is free to nominate someone, or yourself, who deserves to be in the book, just send in the name, contact address, telephone number and email to:
Greek Cypriots Worldwide
111 St Thomas's Road London N4 2QJ
Telephone 0044 207503 3498
cypriotwhoswho@aol.com
www.greekcypriotsworldwide.com

PRODROMOS PRODROMOU
Deputy Headteacher

DATE OF BIRTH: 16-May-1954
PLACE OF BIRTH: London.
Father from Kontea; Mother
from Trikomo.
MARITAL STATUS: Married
to Agnes, Ireland, Airline
Personnel.
CHILDREN: Natasha,
Alexander, Both University
Students.
SCHOOLS/COLLEGE:
Ashmole School, Southgate N. 14, Middlesex University.
QUALIFICATIONS: 4 A Levels (Maths, Physics, Zoology,
Art). BEd (Honours) Maths/Education.
MEMBERSHIPS: Association of Maths Teachers.
HOBBIES AND INTERESTS: Sport, keeping fit and
travel.
PERSONAL PROFILE: Present Post Director of Post 16
Education, Deputy Headteacher at King Solomon High
School, Ilford.

XENOPHON SOCRATES PROTOPAPAS
President of the Greek Orthodox
Community of Barnet (Holy Cross & St
Michaels

DATE OF BIRTH: 14-Feb-1947
PLACE OF BIRTH: Nicosia.
MARITAL STATUS: Married to
Zoe, Larnaca, Solicitor.
CHILDREN: Socrates,
Chrysanthos.
SCHOOLS/COLLEGE: Kilburn
Polytechnic, Ealing School
of Law, The College of Law,
London.
QUALIFICATIONS: BA in Law.
HOBBIES AND INTERESTS: Greek/Cypriot
community affairs, the Cyprus Question, theatre, politics
and world affairs.
PERSONAL PROFILE: Senior partner in Protopapas
Solicitors. President of the Greek Orthodox Community
of Barnet (Holy Cross & St Michaels), Member of
the Hellenic Community Trust. Positions previously
held: Vice Chairman Democratic Rally UK, Member
of the Secretariat of the Federation of Greek Cypriot
Organisations, Member of the Hellenic Centre Executive
Committee.

ZOE PROTOPAPAS
Chair of the Independent Greek Schools
of England/Solicitor

DATE OF BIRTH: 14-Feb-1959
PLACE OF BIRTH: Nicosia.
MARITAL STATUS: Married to
Xenophon, Ayios Andronicos,
Solicitor.
CHILDREN: Socrates,
Chrysanthos.
SCHOOLS/COLLEGE: South
Bank University, London; Inns of
Court School of Law, London.
QUALIFICATIONS: BA Law.
HOBBIES AND INTERESTS: Greek education and
other matters concerning the Greek Community in the
UK. Theatre, politics and world affairs.
PERSONAL PROFILE: A partner in Protopapas Solicitors,
specialising in Commercial Property. Chair of the
Independent Greek Schools of England, Treasurer of
EFEPE, Vice Chair of Woodhouse Greek School, Trustee
of the Hellenic Educational Establishment, Trustee of
St. Cyprian's Greek Orthodox Denominational School,
Member of the Hellenic Community Trust.

GEORGE PSARIAS
Restaurateur, owns the Olive Tree
Greek Restaurant in Leeds/Guinness
Book of Records longest Kebab 1990

DATE OF BIRTH: 10-Jul-1948
PLACE OF BIRTH: Philousa,
Chrysochous, Paphos.
MARITAL STATUS: Married to
Vasoulla, Avgorou.
CHILDREN: Vicki, Filmaker.
Solos, Business.
SCHOOLS/COLLEGE: Greek
Lyceum, Larnaca American
Academy, Larnaca Holloway
School, London. University of
Bradford and University of Leeds.
QUALIFICATIONS: B. Sc MBA.
HONOURS/AWARDS: Guiness Book Of Records
Longest Kebab 1990 (325 metres), Guiness Book of
Records, Biggest milkshake 17, 425 Litres 1999. Yorkshire
Evening Post Best Restaurant of the Year Award 2006.
HOBBIES AND INTERESTS: Walking, swimming, wining
and dining, football matches, a keen Arsenal Supporter.
PERSONAL PROFILE: Restaurateur, owns the Olive
Tree Greek Restaurant in Leeds, West Yorkshire with
wife Vasoulla. Have been listed in the Good Food Guide,
Post Restaurant of The Year. Radio appearances: BBC
Radio Leeds, BBC Radio 4, LGR "Recipe of The Day,
appearances included Yorkshire Television, BBC 2 Food
& Drink, BBC 2 Money Programme, Sky UK Food.

UK

VICKI PSARIAS
Independent Film and Television Producer and Director Channel 4 Talent Award 2007

DATE OF BIRTH: 16-Nov-1980
PLACE OF BIRTH: Leeds, England. Father from Philousa Chrysochous Paphos; Mother from Avgorou Famagusta.
MARITAL STATUS: Married to Peter Broadbent, England, software developer.
SCHOOLS/COLLEGE: Leeds Girls High. Notre Dame Sixth Form College Leeds, Goldsmiths (University of London).
QUALIFICATIONS: BA in Media & Communications; MA in Screen Drama.
HONOURS/AWARDS: Channel 4 talent award 2007 best film maker for short film Rifts and Broken which she wrote and directed. Finalist Kodak film Awards 2007 for best film and cinematographer -broken. Awarded Finalist Daily Mail young Enterprising Brit Awards.
HOBBIES AND INTERESTS: Film making, writing and painting.
PERSONAL PROFILE: Vicki is a Film maker recent commissions include directing promos for the English National Opera and London Fashion Week. Vicki is also the Editor of the film and Festivals magazine.

DEMETRIOS PSILLOS
Animation for Nigella Lawson's TV Shows- Nigella Bites & Forever Summer with Nigella

DATE OF BIRTH: 27-Dec-1967
PLACE OF BIRTH: London, Father Liopetri, Mother Leonarisso.
MARITAL STATUS: Single.
SCHOOLS/COLLEGE: Alexandra Park School, Fortismere School. Middlesex Polytechnic.
QUALIFICATIONS: 7 O Levels, BA Hons Fashion.
HONOURS/AWARDS: Pegasus Exxon Award for most influential artist at the 48th Spoleto Festival, Italy 2005.
PERSONAL PROFILE: Animation for Nigella Lawson's TV Shows- Nigella Bites & Forever Summer with Nigella. Two years working with International Designer, John Galliano.

ANDREAS RIALAS
Chief Executive Officer Argo Capital Management

DATE OF BIRTH: 08-Jun-1967
PLACE OF BIRTH: Nicosia.
MARITAL STATUS: Married.
CHILDREN: Two Children.
SCHOOLS/COLLEGE: English School Nicosia. Queen Mary University of London.
QUALIFICATIONS: LLB Qualified Barrister.
PERSONAL PROFILE: Andreas Rialas after working as a Barrister he went into Banking working for the London forfeiting Co and Deutsche Bank. He is now the Chief Executive Officer for Argo Capital Management. Andreas has also been appointed by the Cyprus Government for attracting asset management in Cyprus.

ORESTIS ROSSIDES
Director of the Cyprus Tourism Organisation, London

DATE OF BIRTH: 09-May-1953
PLACE OF BIRTH: Budapest Hungary. Father, Iacovos, from Famagusta, Mother, Milka, from Vissinia, Greece.
MARITAL STATUS: Single.
SCHOOLS/COLLEGE: Pancyprian Gymnasium, Nicosia. Washington State University.
QUALIFICATIONS: BA MA.
HONOURS/AWARDS: Held the National Cyprus record for discus throw 1976-2000. Still holds the National Cyprus record for the Hammer throw since 1981.
PERSONAL PROFILE: Occupation: Director, office of the Cyprus Tourism Organisation in London from 1989 to date. Career progression: Lecturer in Economics, Washington State University, 1977-1979. Economics officer, Ministry Of Finance, Cyprus 1980. Tourist Officer, Cyprus Tourism Organisation, 1981-1988.

UK

DEMETREOS SOCRATES ROUSSOUNIS
Actor appeared in films Snatch, Tomb Raider

DATE OF BIRTH: 08-Apr-1968
PLACE OF BIRTH: Hastings. Parents from Pano, Arodhes.
MARITAL STATUS: Single.
SCHOOLS/COLLEGE: Middlesex University, Lee Strasberg Institute New York.
QUALIFICATIONS: BA Econ & Geography.
HOBBIES AND INTERESTS: Soccer, pubs and reading.
PERSONAL PROFILE: Actor. Performances include films The World is not Enough, Snatch, Tomb Raider, Hot Gold, Road to Ithaca (in Cyprus). TV work: The Bill, Lee Evans So What Now. Stage work: A View From the Bridge.

DR SOCRATES HERCULES ROUSSOUNIS
Consultant Paediatrician

DATE OF BIRTH: 30-Aug-1937
PLACE OF BIRTH: London. Father from Arodhes and Mother from Arsos, Limassol.
MARITAL STATUS: Married to Lucy, Cyprus, Teacher.
CHILDREN: Alexander, Eracles, Stephen.
SCHOOLS/COLLEGE: Howardian High School, Cardiff. King's College, St George's Hospital Medical School London.
QUALIFICATIONS: MBBS MRCP FRCPCH.
MEMBERSHIPS: British Paediatric Neurology Association. Fellow of the Royal College of Physicians, Fellow of the Royal College of Paediatrics and Chief Health).
HOBBIES AND INTERESTS: Golf and photography.
PERSONAL PROFILE: Consultant in Pediatric Neurology at St. James's University Hospital, Leeds. Many publications on Child Development, Epilepsy and Cerebral Palsy. Last five years helped pioneer development of clinical use of Botulinum Toxin, a new treatment for spasticity for children with Cerebral Palsy and other movement disorders. Also visiting consultant Red Cross Home For Sick children Limassol Cyprus.

COS SAKKAS
Winner of London Hairdresser of the year at the British Hairdressing Awards, 2008

DATE OF BIRTH: 11-Sep-1972
PLACE OF BIRTH: Kyrenia.
MARITAL STATUS: Single.
SCHOOLS/COLLEGE: Finchley Catholic School.
HONOURS/AWARDS: Winner of British Newcomer of the year 1999 at the British Hairsdressing Awards.
- Finalist at the British Hairdressing Awards, 2005
- Finalist at the British Hairdressing Awards, 2004
- Finalist at the British Hairdressing Awards, 2003
- Winner of London Hairdresser of the year at the British Hairdressing Awards, 2008
HOBBIES AND INTERESTS: Art, fashion travelling and indoor climbing.
PERSONAL PROFILE: International artistic director with Toni and Guys.

PROFESSOR PHILLIP SAMOUEL
Professor of Business Economics

DATE OF BIRTH: 15-Dec-1947
PLACE OF BIRTH: Larnaca.
CHILDREN: Paul, James, Irene.
SCHOOLS/COLLEGE: Enfield College of Technology. London School of Economics, Imperial College, Henley Management College.
QUALIFICATIONS: BA (Soc Sc), MSc (Econ), MSc (Man Sc), DBA.
MEMBERSHIPS: FRSA, FIMgt.
HOBBIES AND INTERESTS: Farming.
PERSONAL PROFILE: Professor of Business Economics, Owner of Ladyland Farm, the Living Classroom.

UK

MARIA SAMPSON
Deaf since birth this fact has made her more determined to succeed to being a Clinical Psychologist

DATE OF BIRTH: 09-Jan-1986
PLACE OF BIRTH: London Father from Ormidia Mother UK.
SCHOOLS/COLLEGE: Aylward School. Kingston University.
QUALIFICATIONS: 10 GCSE's 3 A levels BSc (Honours).
MEMBERSHIPS: British Psychological Society.
HOBBIES AND INTERESTS: Walking, gym, reading, psychology, motorbikes photography and socialising.
PERSONAL PROFILE: Maria Sampson has been deaf since birth through her parents devotion is able to verbally communicate to an extremely high standard this fact has made her more determined to succeed to being a Clinical Psychologist. At present, she works as a Clinical Studies officer for the UK Mental Health Research Network which covers 60% of the population England.

PAUL ANGELO SAMPSON
TV Presenter ITV, Dial A Date

DATE OF BIRTH: 25-Aug-1978
PLACE OF BIRTH: London. Parents from Larnaca.
MARITAL STATUS: Single.
SCHOOLS/COLLEGE: University College School, Hampstead, Sussex University.
QUALIFICATIONS: 3 A Levels, BA Honours in Politics.
HOBBIES AND INTERESTS: Music and football.
PERSONAL PROFILE: T. V. Presenter (ITV, Dial A Date). Series Producer (Dial A Date). Producer (D-A-D and ITV, The Dance Years). Development Executive, Hewland International.

SAMPSON SAMPSON
One of the youngest 6th Dan in Europe and in history of British Judo Council

DATE OF BIRTH: 17-Feb-1960
PLACE OF BIRTH: Ormidia.
MARITAL STATUS: Married to Karen, UK, Housewife.
CHILDREN: Maria, Andrianna, Sampson.
SCHOOLS/COLLEGE: Pakeman Primary, Tollington Park, City and East London College.
QUALIFICATIONS: 3 O Levels, 5 GCSEs, 1 A Level. Teachers Diploma in Judo and teachers certificate. Certificate in Hairdressing.
HONOURS/AWARDS: Has 324 medals 300 of them are gold. Sportsman of Year for two years 1974/75.
HOBBIES AND INTERESTS: Judo, kendo, karate, goshin jutsu, martial arts, gymnastics, athletics and fitness training.
PERSONAL PROFILE: Youngest 3rd Dan Black belt in Judo in the world at the age of 16. 2nd person ever to reach 5th Dan contests grade in British Judo Council's history. Youngest 5th Dan in Europe and in history of British Judo Council. National & British Kata Champion 15 years running, and still holds the title. Also trains the Cypriot Olympic team in preparation for major international tournaments which involves world and Olympic categories. Has helped under-privileged children and disabled children using Judo to help further their ability, mentally and physically. Now a 6th Dan.

GEORGE SANDAMAS
Lecturer of Psychology at Middlesex University

DATE OF BIRTH: 23-Jun-1964
PLACE OF BIRTH: London Father from Kontea, Mother from Kalo chorio.
MARITAL STATUS: Married to Claire, London, Senior Researcher at the Tavistock Institute.
SCHOOLS/COLLEGE: Queen Elizabeth Boys School. Oxfordshire Technical College and Middlesex University.
QUALIFICATIONS: HND. BSc. PGDip. PhD.
MEMBERSHIPS: British Psychological Society.
HOBBIES AND INTERESTS: Fly Fishing, Golf, Cycling, Guitar and Tottenham Football Club.
PERSONAL PROFILE: George Sandamas is a Lecturer of Psychology at Middlesex University he has also had research published in areas of Mental Health and Cognitive Psychology. He also taught A level Psychology at the Henrietta Barnett School in Hampstead Garden Suburb while completing his PhD.

UK

MARK SANDAMAS
Runner-up in Snowdonia Marathon, Winner of several fell-races and half-marathons

DATE OF BIRTH: 02-Dec-1966
PLACE OF BIRTH: Kontea.
MARITAL STATUS: Married to Gilly from England.
CHILDREN: Leah, Natasha, Kirsty.
SCHOOLS/COLLEGE: Wallington High School. Liverpool John Moores University.
QUALIFICATIONS: BSc (Hon) Sports Science 2: 1.
HOBBIES AND INTERESTS: Cycling, Fell running, Triathlon, Mountain-biking, outdoor pursuits.
PERSONAL PROFILE: Built up Pennine Events into major cycling and health event organising company. Organise major patrician events such as Pedal for Scotland, British Cyclosportive, Liverpool-Chester bike ride. Runner-up in Snowdonia Marathon, Winner of several fell-races and half-marathons, First Newcomer in Three Peaks Fell race, Top-ten places in several triathlons.

PETER SANDAMAS
Co Founder Chairman & Secretary of the Cypriot Golf Society

DATE OF BIRTH: 02-Apr-1947
PLACE OF BIRTH: Kontea.
MARITAL STATUS: Married to Connie, London, Housewife.
CHILDREN: Tony, Brian, Both Heating engineers.
SCHOOLS/COLLEGE: Kontea Primary School, Lykeion of Famagusta.
MEMBERSHIPS: Cypriot Golf Society, Kontea Association, Muswell Hill Golf Club, CORGI, HVCA.
HOBBIES AND INTERESTS: Golf, travel and grandchildren.
PERSONAL PROFILE: One of the Founders, and former Chairman and Secretary of the Cypriot Golf Society. Won the Bank of Cyprus Captains Cup in 1999. Partner with sons in Plumbing Supplies and Gas Installations Company.

ANDREW SAVVA
Chairman of the Old Chomelians Football Club/Director of an Investment Company

DATE OF BIRTH: 02-Mar-1964
PLACE OF BIRTH: London Father from Alethrico Mother from Famagusta.
MARITAL STATUS: Single.
SCHOOLS/COLLEGE: Highgate School.
HOBBIES AND INTERESTS: Football and Golf.
PERSONAL PROFILE: Andy Savva is the Chairman of the Old Chomelians Football Club. He played football in the Cypriot League UK for Anorthosis, Athletic and Paok. In Golf he won the 50th Anniversary Bank of Cyprus golf competition. He is the director of Next Step Care Management that teaches 15 to 18 year olds essential life skills and in dependent living. Also a Director of Tiuta PLC Finance Company.

ANNA SAVVA
Actress on TV appeared in The Chief, London's Burning, Minder

PLACE OF BIRTH: UK. Father from Kiti, Mother from Pera Orinis.
QUALIFICATIONS: LAMADA, London Academy of Dramatic Art.
MEMBERSHIPS: Equity.
HONOURS/AWARDS: Best Actress, Time Out nomination for her performance as Frida in Frida & Diego.
HOBBIES AND INTERESTS: Salsa dancing.
PERSONAL PROFILE: Actress: Appeared on T. V. ;. The Chief, London's Burning, Minder. Theatre; Frida Diego, Carmen, Midsummer Night Dream. Worked on Radio 4.

UK

ELEFTHERIOS SAVVA
Mayor of Enfield 2009/10

DATE OF BIRTH: 19-Sep-1946
PLACE OF BIRTH: Ayia Anna, Larnaca.
MARITAL STATUS: Married to Androulla, a Professional Carer, from Inia Paphos.
CHILDREN: Chrissy, workforce development co-ordinator.
HOBBIES AND INTERESTS: Rotarian, raises money for charity.
PERSONAL PROFILE: Mayor of Enfield. A professional foster carer for children of home abuse with behavioural and other complex problems. Trustee of Saint Demetrius Church in Edmonton. Assistant Co-ordinator of the Association of the Greek Orthodox Communities of Great Britain. School Governor of Edmonton County School and Bush Hill Park Primary Schools.

GEORGE SAVVA
'Best Greek Restaurant' by the Archant Food & Drinks Awards 2007

DATE OF BIRTH: 11-Nov-1946
PLACE OF BIRTH: Dromolaxia.
MARITAL STATUS: Married to Stavroulla.
CHILDREN: Melanie, Teacher. Petros, Restaurant Owner.
SCHOOLS/COLLEGE: Primary School in Cyprus.
HONOURS/AWARDS: Awarded 'Best Greek Restaurant' by the Archant Food & Drinks Awards 2007 presented by the famous chef Aldo Zili The glitzy gala dinner, at the Radisson SAS Hotel in Portman Square, London W1.
PERSONAL PROFILE: George Savva is the owner of the Award winning Apollonia Restaurant based in Gants Hill in Ilford.

GEORGE SAVVA MBE
Former Mayor of Enfield

DATE OF BIRTH: 26-Sep-1949
PLACE OF BIRTH: Lefkara.
MARITAL STATUS: Married to Eleni, from Kalopsida.
CHILDREN: Tasos, Fitness Instructor. Costakis, Student. Marios, Student. Andreas, Student.
SCHOOLS/COLLEGE: Holloway School. London College of Fashion.
MEMBERSHIPS: Labour Party.
HONOURS/AWARDS: MBE for services to the community and London Borough of Enfield.
HOBBIES AND INTERESTS: Gardening, badminton and football.
PERSONAL PROFILE: Councillor in the London Borough of Enfield. Served as a Deputy Mayor in 1994/1995 and a Mayor in 1995/1996. One of the founders of the Lefkara Association. Has helped towards the establishment of the community centre in Edmonton.

GREGORY SAVVA
Footballer played for the Cyprus National Team

DATE OF BIRTH: 14-Aug-1955
PLACE OF BIRTH: Pera Orinis.
MARITAL STATUS: Married to Marina, Ireland.
CHILDREN: Harry, Louis, Lydia, Marcus.
SCHOOLS/COLLEGE: Croydon Secondary Technical School.
QUALIFICATIONS: City & Guilds Hotel & Catering. FPC1, FPC2, FPC3.
HONOURS/AWARDS: Cyprus footballer of the year 1975. Athlete of the year 1975. Captain of National team. 20 caps for Cyprus National Team.
HOBBIES AND INTERESTS: Golf, all sports.
PERSONAL PROFILE: Financial advisor. Qualified Chef. Played football for Omonia Nicosia, Olympiakos in Greece, and Cyprus national team.

The Cyprus wine festival that takes place every year at Alexandra palace in London is attended by thousands who come to relish the Cypriot products.

HELEN SAVVA
Florist ;known for her active contributions to charities such as Thalassaemia and Leukaemia

DATE OF BIRTH: 03-Jul-1971
PLACE OF BIRTH: London Parents from Aradippou.
MARITAL STATUS: Married to Savvakis, Cypriot, Businessman.
CHILDREN: Georgia, Marianna, Stephanie.
SCHOOLS/COLLEGE: Capel Manor College.
HOBBIES AND INTERESTS: walking and travel.
PERSONAL PROFILE: Helen Savvas is a florist who is known for her active contributions to charities such as Thalassaemia and Leukaemia. She has her own florist shop in Cockfosters.

MARIA SAVVA
Author of the books Coincidences and a Time to Tell

DATE OF BIRTH: 19-Mar-1970
PLACE OF BIRTH: London Father from Nicosia Mother from Akanthou.
MARITAL STATUS: Single.
SCHOOLS/COLLEGE: Hornsey School for Girls. Barnet and Southgate Colleges and Middlesex University.
QUALIFICATIONS: 8 O levels, 3 A levels LLB(Hons).
MEMBERSHIPS: Law Society.
HONOURS/AWARDS: Sweet and Maxwell Law Prize 1990.
HOBBIES AND INTERESTS: Writing, reading, music, comedy, travel, TV and film.
PERSONAL PROFILE: Maria Savva is the Author Of the books Coincidences and a Time to Tell and is a Solicitor specialising in Conveyancing.

MARIOS SAVVA
President of Greek Cypriot Shooting Association/Property Developer

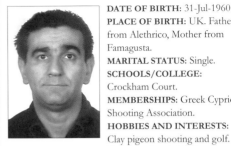

DATE OF BIRTH: 31-Jul-1960
PLACE OF BIRTH: UK. Father from Alethrico, Mother from Famagusta.
MARITAL STATUS: Single.
SCHOOLS/COLLEGE: Crockham Court.
MEMBERSHIPS: Greek Cypriot Shooting Association.
HOBBIES AND INTERESTS: Clay pigeon shooting and golf.
PERSONAL PROFILE: Chairman Greek Cypriot Shooting Association (65 members). Helps Leukaemia charities. Property Developer.

MARY SAVVA
Actress TV work includes The Bill. Films: Treasure Island, Road to Ithaca

DATE OF BIRTH: 04-Nov-1972
PLACE OF BIRTH: Croydon. Father from Pera Orinis.
MARITAL STATUS: Single.
SCHOOLS/COLLEGE: Riddlesdown High School, Croydon, Italia Conti Theatre School.
QUALIFICATIONS: 6 GCSES. 3 year Performing Diploma. A. I. S. T. D qualified teacher of dance, modern, jazz and tap.
MEMBERSHIPS: Equity.
PERSONAL PROFILE: Appeared on Stage in The Golden Land; Goodbye Girl; Rocky Horror Show. TV work includes The Bill. Films: Treasure Island, Road to Ithaca.

MIKE SAVVA
Gynaecologist and Obstetrician

DATE OF BIRTH: 01-Jan-1957
PLACE OF BIRTH: Aradippou.
MARITAL STATUS: Married to Jane.
CHILDREN: Two sons.
SCHOOLS/COLLEGE: Holloway School. London Hospital Medical College.
QUALIFICATIONS: MBBS, FRCOG.
HOBBIES AND INTERESTS: Greek & Cypriot history and football, Arsenal.
PERSONAL PROFILE: Gynaecologist, Consultant at Kings College Hospital. Former President of Hellenic Medical Society. Vice President of the Royal Society of Medicine-Section of Obstetrics and Gynaecology.

NICK SAVVA
Greyhound Trainer Owner of dog 'Tom's the Best', who won the English Derby in 1997

DATE OF BIRTH: 27-Apr-1934
PLACE OF BIRTH: Rizokarpasso.
MARITAL STATUS: Married to Natalie, London.
CHILDREN: Liza, Nicola.
PERSONAL PROFILE: Dog racing and breeding full time since 1967. Owner of dog 'Toms the Best', who won the English Derby in 1997 and Irish Derby in 1998. 'West Mead Chic' won the Oaks in 1990. Most of the classics won by his own home bred dogs.

SAVVAS SAVVA
Director of Property Company. Philanthropist, Greek School, Churches, Leukaemia/Freedom of the City of London

DATE OF BIRTH: 06-Nov-1957
PLACE OF BIRTH: London. Father from Alethrico;. Mother from Famagusta.
MARITAL STATUS: Married to Maria, London.
CHILDREN: Ellis, Helena.
SCHOOLS/COLLEGE: Highgate Public, Tottenham Technical.
HONOURS/AWARDS: Freedom of the City of London.
HOBBIES AND INTERESTS: Football, golf, reading.

PERSONAL PROFILE: Director of Property Company. Philanthropist, Greek School, Churches, Leukaemia. Played for Anorthosis and Cypriot Football League Team in the UK. Also Captain of the Cypriot Golf Society 2009/10.

THOMAS SAVVA
General Manager UK and Ireland Olympic Airlines

DATE OF BIRTH: 10-Aug-1944
PLACE OF BIRTH: Paliometocho.
MARITAL STATUS: Married to Emilia, Limnia, Director General of a Travel Agency.
CHILDREN: Christine, Supervisor of a Travel agency.
SCHOOLS/COLLEGE: Premier Commercial Lyceum, Nicosia. City of London Polytechnic and University of North London.
QUALIFICATIONS: Degree in Chartered Institute of Transport.
MEMBERSHIPS: Institute of Logistics and Transport.
HOBBIES AND INTERESTS: Travel, Football and Politics.
PERSONAL PROFILE: Thomas Savva is General Manager UK and Ireland of Olympic Airlines and Director of the Board of Airlines Representatives UK.

PETER SAVVAS
Police Long Service and Good Conduct Medal and Queens Golden Jubilee Medal

DATE OF BIRTH: 17-Feb-1956
PLACE OF BIRTH: London Father from Droushia, Mother Monagrouli.
MARITAL STATUS: Married to Maria, Hairdresser.
CHILDREN: from first marriage, Portfolio Manager Royal Bank of Scotland. Nicholas, Nanny. Andrea.
SCHOOLS/COLLEGE: Sir William Collins.
QUALIFICATIONS: Certifcate in Education, Post 16 Education and training. Metropolitan Police Trainer, Various Police Driving Qualifications.
HONOURS/AWARDS: Queens Golden Jubilee Medal, Police Long Service & Good Conduct Medal. Commendation for Professionalism in dealing with the murder of Brigadier Saunders in Athens during a Terrorist attack.
HOBBIES AND INTERESTS: Football.

UK

PERSONAL PROFILE: Peter Savva has been in the police Force for 26 years. He is also a co founder Met Police Service Greek Staff association.

DINO SAVVIDES
Former Detective Inspector Police

DATE OF BIRTH: 26-Jan-1951
PLACE OF BIRTH: Guinea (West Africa) Parents from Cyprus.
MARITAL STATUS: Married.
CHILDREN: Clare, Christopher, Nicholas.
SCHOOLS/COLLEGE: American Academy, Cyprus, London University.
QUALIFICATIONS: Electronics, Diploma in Management.
HONOURS/AWARDS: Numerous Commendations in The Police Service, Security Observer, Athens Olympics.
HOBBIES AND INTERESTS: Keep-fit, swimming.
PERSONAL PROFILE: Dino first had his Own manufacturing company (Television) and own company importing beauty products then moved into the Police Service, last position held as Detective Inspector – Wembley.

GEORGE SAVVIDES
Actor

DATE OF BIRTH: 24-Aug-1954
PLACE OF BIRTH: Famagusta.
SCHOOLS/COLLEGE: Greek Gymnasium, Famagusta. Middlesex Polytechnic, Welsh. College of Music and Drama.
QUALIFICATIONS: BA. Advanced certificate in Drama Stage Management and Design.
HOBBIES AND INTERESTS: From 91-93 a judge for the London Fringe Theatre Awards-Awarded best judge for both years.
PERSONAL PROFILE: Film and drama critic for Parikiaki. Parts in the TV September Song, Harem and Touching Evil. Films include The Fool, Memories of Midnight, Britannia Hospital and Red Thursday and Bigga than ben Theatre Battle of Green Lanes and King Oedipus.

NIKOS SAVVIDES
Singer songwriter, Performing Musician

DATE OF BIRTH: 08-Aug-1953
PLACE OF BIRTH: London from one week old lived in Famagusta till 1973.
SCHOOLS/COLLEGE: Willesden College of Technology, East London Polytechnic and Thames Polytechnic.
QUALIFICATIONS: Dip(Hons) Arch RIBA.
MEMBERSHIPS: Royal Institute of British Architects and Architects Registration Board.
HOBBIES AND INTERESTS: Music, Reading, Films, Fishing and Sports.
PERSONAL PROFILE: Nikos Savvides is a Qualified Architect runs his own practice. He is a singer songwriter, Performing Musician has produced several CDs of his own songs. A notable one is the anthem he produced recently for Anorthosis Famagusta football club.

PANOS SAVVIDES
Actor appeared in the Bill, London Burning and Queen of the East

PLACE OF BIRTH: London Parents from Famagusta
MARITAL STATUS: Single.
CHILDREN: Demetri, Panayiota.
SCHOOLS/COLLEGE: Friern Barnet Grammar School and the London School of Acting.
MEMBERSHIPS: Equity. Formerly President of the Hastings Greek Community.
HOBBIES AND INTERESTS: Tennis, Scuba Diving, Horse riding and his Children.
PERSONAL PROFILE: Panos is an Actor and entrepreneur. He is the founder of the Woodlands Theatre Company and is currently involved in film production and at Theatro Technis. TV credits are The Bill, London's Burning, Queen of the East. Appeared in theatre in cant pay wont pay. and the Inheritors.

UK

SAVVAS TOUMAZIS SAVVIDES
Teacher in elementary schools in Cyprus. Formed Othello Football Club in Famagusta which became a member of the Cypriot league

DATE OF BIRTH: 13-Feb-1930
PLACE OF BIRTH: Komi Kebir.
MARITAL STATUS: Married to Niki, Ayia Triada.
CHILDREN: Tom, TV Presenter. Yianno, Komi Kebir Football Club Captain. Katerina, Teacher. Eleni, Teacher.
SCHOOLS/COLLEGE: Famagusta Gymnasium, Teachers Training College Morphou, University of Athens.
HOBBIES AND INTERESTS: Football and politics.
PERSONAL PROFILE: Teacher in elementary schools in Cyprus. Formed Othello Football Club in Famagusta which became a member of the Cypriot league. In 1964 came to England where he was involved in the garment industry, until retirement. Involved with Komi Kebir football club Manager for several years. Active member of Komi Kebir Association.

STEPHANY SAVVIDES
National Champion in Traditional Kung Fu sets in 2004-2007

DATE OF BIRTH: 13-Jul-1979
PLACE OF BIRTH: London Parents from Trikomo and Arnadi.
MARITAL STATUS: Married to Daniel, British.
SCHOOLS/COLLEGE: Henrietta Barnett. British College of Naturopathy.
QUALIFICATIONS: BSc (Hons) Osteopathic Medicine.
HOBBIES AND INTERESTS: Kung Fu, Gymnastics, Kickboxing, plays piano and sings and learning guitar.
PERSONAL PROFILE: Stephany Savvides is an Osteopath with her own Clinic she also teaches martial arts to adults and children also involved in a stunt school and was fire co ordinator for several years and has worked in TV and Film's in this capacity in front of and behind the camera.

TOM SAVVIDES
Reporter at Meridien TV

DATE OF BIRTH: 06-Mar-1969
PLACE OF BIRTH: London. Father from Komi Kebir. Mother from Ayia Triada.
MARITAL STATUS: Single.
SCHOOLS/COLLEGE: Caterham High School, Ilford;. Portsmouth Polytechnic.
QUALIFICATIONS: BA Honours in French and German. Postgraduate diploma in Broadcast Journalism.
HOBBIES AND INTERESTS: Tennis and DIY.
PERSONAL PROFILE: Taught English at University in Paris for three years. Then worked in local radio stations as a presenter and reporter, Thames FM, County Sound Radio. Also reported for News Direct 97. 3 FM. Currently at Meridian TV as a TV Reporter on Meridian tonight and Thames Valley tonight.

DORA SCHOLARIOS
Lecturer at Strathclyde University

PLACE OF BIRTH: Glasgow. Parents from Larnaca.
MARITAL STATUS: Married to James Malley, Pittsburgh, USA.
SCHOOLS/COLLEGE: Hutchesons Grammar School, Glasgow, University of Glasgow, George Washington University, USA.
QUALIFICATIONS: PhD. Industrial/Organisational Psychology. M. Phil Industrial/Organisational Psychology. MA Psychology.
HOBBIES AND INTERESTS: Fitness training and Greek dancing.
PERSONAL PROFILE: Senior University Lecturer in Organisational Analysis at University of Strathclyde, Glasgow. Has written in several publications. Involved with the youth community of St. Lukes Greek Church in Glasgow.

NICOS SCHOLARIOS
Chairman of the Scotland Volleyball Association

DATE OF BIRTH: 21-Jul-1958
PLACE OF BIRTH: Famagusta.
MARITAL STATUS: Married to Christine, Cardross, Scotland.
CHILDREN: Katerina, Andrew & Peter (twins).
SCHOOLS/COLLEGE: Hutcheson's Grammar School, Glasgow University.
QUALIFICATIONS: Graduated with Honours, LLB (Hons), NP, Solicitor.
HOBBIES AND INTERESTS: Soccer, volleyball and athletics.
PERSONAL PROFILE: Chairman of the Scotland Volleyball Association for two years and vice-chairman for four years.

NINA SEBASTIANE
TV and Radio Presenter hosting Speedway Grand Prix and also Blue Eskimo Challenge for Channel 4

DATE OF BIRTH: 15-Nov-1969
PLACE OF BIRTH: London. Parents, Cypriot.
MARITAL STATUS: Single.
SCHOOLS/COLLEGE: Toronto & London.
HOBBIES AND INTERESTS: Skiing, snowboarding, golf, motorbikes, walking and reading.
PERSONAL PROFILE: Currently hosting Speedway Grand Prix and also Blue Eskimo Challenge for Channel 4. Other projects include Ski America for the Travel Channel for which Nina produced, directed and hosted. A fluent Greek speaker, she has also read the Greek News in English for LGR.

DEMETRIS SERGI
Liverpool. Justice of the Peace

DATE OF BIRTH: 07-Aug-1945
PLACE OF BIRTH: Maroni.
MARITAL STATUS: Married to Maro, Paphos, Housewife.
CHILDREN: Christella, Michael, Antonia.
SCHOOLS/COLLEGE: Pershore House Private School, Hollings University College, Manchester.
QUALIFICATIONS: HND Business Studies and Management.

HOBBIES AND INTERESTS: Travelling.
PERSONAL PROFILE: Company director and owner of property company and catering organisation. Treasurer of Greek Orthodox Church of St. Nicholas, Liverpool. Justice of the Peace.

MARO SERGI
Former Chairwoman of Greek School

DATE OF BIRTH: 12-Dec-1953
PLACE OF BIRTH: Paphos, Cyprus.
MARITAL STATUS: Married to Demetris.
CHILDREN: Christell, Michael, Antonia.
SCHOOLS/COLLEGE: Richard Cobden, Star Cross.
HOBBIES AND INTERESTS: Computers.
PERSONAL PROFILE: Former Chairwoman of Greek School, St Nicholas Church, in Liverpool, served for twenty three years.

EVRIDIKI SERGIDES
Barrister

DATE OF BIRTH: 01-Feb-1977
PLACE OF BIRTH: London. Father from Limassol, Mother from Linou.
MARITAL STATUS: Single.
SCHOOLS/COLLEGE: Highbury Fields Secondary School, Woodhouse College. Queen Mary and Westfield College. Queen Mary and Westfield College, University College London.
QUALIFICATIONS: Law Degree and Masters. Bar Vocational Qualifications - 'very competent'.
MEMBERSHIPS: The Honourable Society of Inner Temple.
PERSONAL PROFILE: After completing Bar school entered into a 12 month Criminal Pupillage at six Gray's Inn Square. Qualified as a Barrister.

UK

DR JOHN (YIANNI) SERGIDES
Doctor/Surgeon

DATE OF BIRTH: 24-May-1975
PLACE OF BIRTH: London.
Father from Limassol, Mother from Linou/Soleas.
MARITAL STATUS: Single.
SCHOOLS/COLLEGE: Highgate Senior, Royal Free Hospital. Royal College of Surgeons.
QUALIFICATIONS: GCSEs, A Levels, MBBS, BSE.
HOBBIES AND INTERESTS: Football and cars.
PERSONAL PROFILE: Doctor/Surgeon.

MARINA SERGIDES
Barrister, she regularly gives seminars on all housing matters and Anti Social Behaviour Orders throughout England

DATE OF BIRTH: 05-Jul-1978
PLACE OF BIRTH: London.
Father from Limassol, Mother from Linou.
MARITAL STATUS: Single.
SCHOOLS/COLLEGE: Highbury Fields Secondary School, Woodhouse College. Queen Mary and Westfield College.
QUALIFICATIONS: Law Degree LLB.
MEMBERSHIPS: The Honourable Society of Inner Temple.
HOBBIES AND INTERESTS: Art, galleries and travelling.
PERSONAL PROFILE: Barrister. Work with Amnesty International. Recently joined Lobby for Cyprus. She regularly gives seminars on all housing matters and Anti Social Behaviour Orders throughout England.

MARY SERGIDES
Headteacher Vicars Green Primary School in Ealing

DATE OF BIRTH: 24-Jan-1951
PLACE OF BIRTH: London, Father born in Yeri, Mother born in Aglanjia-Nicosia.
MARITAL STATUS: Married to George, Cyprus.
CHILDREN: Alex, Sophia, Both at University.
SCHOOLS/COLLEGE: John Kelly Girls' School. Wall Hall College of. Education.

QUALIFICATIONS: 2 GCE A' Levels, 10 GCE O' Levels. National Professional Qualification for Headship.
HOBBIES AND INTERESTS: Reading, gardening, theatre.
PERSONAL PROFILE: Headteacher, Vicars Green Primary School in Ealing.

NITSA SERGIDES
Head Teacher a 'Beacon' Primary School

DATE OF BIRTH: 03-Feb-1951
PLACE OF BIRTH: Linou.
MARITAL STATUS: Married to George, Limassol, Civil Engineer.
CHILDREN: Vicky, Barrister. Yiannis, Doctor. Marina, Barrister.
SCHOOLS/COLLEGE: Starcross and St. Gabriel's.
QUALIFICATIONS: English Diploma. Bilingualism Diploma.
DEGREE IN EDUCATION AND PSYCHOLOGY OF CHILDREN WITH SPECIAL NEEDS.
PERSONAL PROFILE: Head Teacher of a 'Beacon' Primary School. Investor in People. Presented to the Queen for high achievements in education. Chair of St. John & St. Anthony church in Westbourne Rd for ten years. Greatest achievements are her three children.

SERGIOS SERGIOU
In charge of CYTA UK Ltd in London

DATE OF BIRTH: 02-Feb-1963
PLACE OF BIRTH: Eptakomi.
MARITAL STATUS: Married to Jill, UK, Nurse.
CHILDREN: Andonis, School.
SCHOOLS/COLLEGE: Great Yarmouth Secondary. Norwich City College and Plymouth Polytechnic.
QUALIFICATIONS: BSc Electronics and Communications engineering.
PERSONAL PROFILE: Sergios Sergiou is in charge of CYTA UK Ltd in London owned by CYTA/ATYK in Cyprus that offer cheap telephone services to Cypriot Consumers and Businesses in the UK. Sergios is also the Vice Chairman of Eptakomi Association UK.

UK

DR ANDREAS N. SERGIS
Lecturer, Tutor, Research Scientist

DATE OF BIRTH: 11-May-1960
PLACE OF BIRTH: Nicosia.
MARITAL STATUS: Married to Stella, Limassol, Civil Servant.
CHILDREN: Andrea, Sophia.
SCHOOLS/COLLEGE: Southwark College, University of Greenwich, London.
QUALIFICATIONS: BSc PhD, Chartered Chemist, CChem, MRSC, Cert-Ed (FE), ATP.
MEMBERSHIPS: Professional member of the Royal Society of Chemistry and Society of Chemistry and Industry.
HOBBIES AND INTERESTS: Swimming, karate. (coaches students) and chess.
PERSONAL PROFILE: Lecturer, tutor and Research Scientist. Set up a private tuition centre. The centre offers courses at key stages 1-4, GCSE A Level, BSc, MSc and PhD Level. Governor of two Local Schools.

CONSTANTINOS SHIATIS
Solicitor/Consultant

DATE OF BIRTH: 04-Feb-1965
PLACE OF BIRTH: London. Family from Sia.
MARITAL STATUS: Married to Katherine, American, Teacher.
SCHOOLS/COLLEGE: Exeter College, Oxford University, College of Law Guildford, Insead Business School, France.
QUALIFICATIONS: MA. MBA.
HOBBIES AND INTERESTS: Winetasting, classical, opera, jazz music, theatre, art, hiking, squash, tennis and history.
PERSONAL PROFILE: Consultant Solicitor. Former Director, Telecoms Team, GE Capital. Previously principal banker, EBRD, London.

ANDRONIKOS COSTANTINOS SIDERAS
Managing Director Dinos & Sons Continental Foods also Board of Directors Haringey Business Development Agency

DATE OF BIRTH: 29-Mar-1962
PLACE OF BIRTH: London. Father from Kontea ; Mother from Peyia.
MARITAL STATUS: Married to Kyriacoulla, London, Secretary.
CHILDREN: Costantina, Vasili, Constantino, Students.
SCHOOLS/COLLEGE: Alexandra Park Secondary, Tottenham College of Technology, Middlesex University.
QUALIFICATIONS: 10 O Levels, 3 A Levels.
MEMBERSHIPS: Board of Directors Haringey Business Development Agency.
HONOURS/AWARDS: Pork Product of the Year award 1999.
HOBBIES AND INTERESTS: Football, badminton, shooting, swimming, karate, cooking dancing and travelling.
PERSONAL PROFILE: Managing director Dinos & Sons Continental Foods Ltd. Donates regularly to charities, churches and Cypriot community organisation's.

DINOS GEORGIOU SIDERAS
Founder of Dinos & Sons Contributes to cancer research, children with special needs, Akel Party, orphans around the world

DATE OF BIRTH: 26-Oct-1932
PLACE OF BIRTH: Kontea, Famagusta.
MARITAL STATUS: Married to Aspasia, Peyia.
CHILDREN: Andronikos Marios. Charoulla, Marios.
SCHOOLS/COLLEGE: High School Famagusta. Commercial School Limassol, Pitmans college, London.
MEMBERSHIPS: Haringey Cypriot Association. Cypriot Community Centre.
HONOURS/AWARDS: Highly commended, Pork Product of the Year award 1999.
HOBBIES AND INTERESTS: Swimming, walking, reading, writing.
PERSONAL PROFILE: Own business since 1960. Meat manufacturers imports, exports, nationwide distribution of Cypriot halloumi and cheese products. Contributes to cancer research, children with special needs, Akel Party, orphans around the world.

UK

LOUIS GEORGIOU SIDERAS
Director of Care Aspirations / Philanthropist

DATE OF BIRTH: 28-Sep-1938
PLACE OF BIRTH: Kontea, Famagusta.
MARITAL STATUS: Married to Eleni, Kalopsida, Co director.
CHILDREN: George, Physiotherapist. Renos, Chartered Accountant. Demetrios, Lecturer.
SCHOOLS/COLLEGE: Primary and two years at English High School, Famagusta.
MEMBERSHIPS: AKEL Party, Institute of Advanced Motorists, Road Haulage Association.
HOBBIES AND INTERESTS: Swimming, abseiling, scuba diving, fishing, skiing, walking, cycling, hunting and private air pilot.
PERSONAL PROFILE: Own Transport Haulage business for 16 years. Residential care provider for people with learning disabilities for 16 years. Co. Director. Donations to Cyprus Community Centre, Cancer Research, Water Aid, Help the Aged, Orphans and AKEL.

MARIOS SIDERAS
Production Director for his family business Dinos and Sons. Donates regularly to charities, churches and Cypriot community organisations

DATE OF BIRTH: 15-Sep-1964
PLACE OF BIRTH: London. Father from Kontea, Famagusta; Mother from Peyia.
MARITAL STATUS: Married.
SCHOOLS/COLLEGE: Alexandra Park School. St. Barnabas & Hazelwood Greek Schools, Southgate College of Technology.
QUALIFICATIONS: 7 O Levels. OND in Electrical, Electronic Engineering. HND Electrical Engineering.
HOBBIES AND INTERESTS: Swimming, volleyball, badminton, go karting, shooting, model building and DIY.
PERSONAL PROFILE: Production Director for his family business Dinos and Sons. Donates regularly to charities, churches and Cypriot community organisations.

RENOS SIDERAS
Accountant/Runs a Successful Healthcare company/Philanthropist

DATE OF BIRTH: 04-Nov-1963
PLACE OF BIRTH: London. Father from Kontea, Famagusta; Mother from Kalopsida.
MARITAL STATUS: Married to Elaine, London.
CHILDREN: Louis, Maria, Pavlos.
SCHOOLS/COLLEGE: Alexandra Park School, Tottenham College.
QUALIFICATIONS: Association of chartered certified accountants, Association of accounting technicians. Private pilot license.
MEMBERSHIPS: ACCA, MAAT.
HOBBIES AND INTERESTS: Flying, five-a-side football and shooting.
PERSONAL PROFILE: Qualified Accountant, qualified Pilot. Joined family business fulltime in 1992 and now runs a successful Healthcare Company.

SOCRATES SOCRATOUS
Vice Chairman of LFA Referees Committee

DATE OF BIRTH: 26-Oct-1938
PLACE OF BIRTH: Cairo, Egypt. Father from Peyia, Mother from Greece.
MARITAL STATUS: Married to Niki, Tsada, Housewife.
CHILDREN: Charalambos, Both Managers. Savas.
SCHOOLS/COLLEGE: High School in Cairo, Staffordshire Technical College.
MEMBERSHIPS: Council Member of London Football Association. Member of the FA.
HONOURS/AWARDS: 15 & 25 year awards as referee. Awaiting 35 year award. 20 years as London Football Association Councillor.
HOBBIES AND INTERESTS: All sports, football, travel, reading & current affairs.
PERSONAL PROFILE: Founder Member of KOPA/ Football Referee Assessor & Examiner/ Vice President Hendon & District Football League. Vice Chairman of LFA Referees Committee. Member of the Golders Green Greek Church Community.

UK

ANDREW SOFOCLEOUS
Martial Arts Expert/World record holder of Roof Tile Breaking in two mins 1997

DATE OF BIRTH: 14-Dec-1960
PLACE OF BIRTH: London, father from Polemi, mother from Akanthou.
MARITAL STATUS: Married to Tatiana, London, (parents from Peyia).
CHILDREN: Athena, Sophia.
SCHOOLS/COLLEGE: Highbury Grove Secondary.
QUALIFICATIONS: 6 O Levels, 3 A Levels. Master of Wing Chun Kung Fu for 24 years.
HONOURS/AWARDS: World record holder of Roof Tile Breaking in two mins 1997. World Record Breaker of fastest hands on Wing Chun Wooden Man 1990. 1983 European Open Fight Champion.
PERSONAL PROFILE: Master Andrew Sofos, Martial Arts expert. Also helps Thalasaemia Society, Great Ormond Street Hospital (CLAPA), Whizz Kidz.

PANY SOFOCLEOUS
Club Champion at both Hoddesdon Kart Club and Kimbolton Kart Club

DATE OF BIRTH: 06-May-1993
PLACE OF BIRTH: London. Father from Morphou Mother from Greece.
MARITAL STATUS: Single.
SCHOOLS/COLLEGE: Hendon Secondary School.
PERSONAL PROFILE: Pany is Club Champion at both Hoddesdon Kart Club and Kimbolton Kart Club. His goal is to race for a formula one team.

MARIO SOFRONIOU
Lyric Tenor/Doctor

PLACE OF BIRTH: Swindon Father from Morphou Mother from Pissouri
MARITAL STATUS: Single.
SCHOOLS/COLLEGE: University of Wales and Trinity College of Music.
QUALIFICATIONS: Mmus also graduated as a Doctor.
PERSONAL PROFILE: Mario Sofroniou is a Lyric Tenor has appeared as Don Jose in Bizets Carmen with Goldsmith University and Le Chevalier de la Force in Poulencs Dialogues des Carmelites with TCM Opera. Mario is a Doctor by occupation and continues to practice in South Wales specialising in Otolaryngology and Emergency Medicine.

CHARALAMBOS MICHAEL SOPHOCLIDES
President of the Federation of Cypriots Overseas

DATE OF BIRTH: 02-Aug-1937
PLACE OF BIRTH: Nicosia, Cyprus.
CHILDREN: Michael, Jenny, Tony.
SCHOOLS/COLLEGE: English School Nicosia. London and Liverpool University.
HONOURS/AWARDS: Archon of the Greek Orthodox Patriarchate of Constantinople.
HOBBIES AND INTERESTS: Collector of Antiquarian books and maps that include references to Cyprus. Also collects old Leica cameras, old fountain pens. Likes wide range of music.
PERSONAL PROFILE: Founder member of Amersham and Chesham Lions Club. Greek Cypriot Brotherhood - President since 1989 - and served as President of Federation of Cypriots in the UK. Now President of Federation of Cypriots Overseas. Vice President of SAE Council of Overseas Hellenes with particular responsibility on Cypriot Affairs since 1999. He is the Managing director of Joannou & Paraskevaides UK.

KIKI (KYRIACI) SOTERI
Optometrist/President of N London Association of Optometrists

DATE OF BIRTH: 19-Feb-1974
PLACE OF BIRTH: London. Father from Ardhana; Mother from Trikomo.
MARITAL STATUS: Married to Dr Bipen Patel.
SCHOOLS/COLLEGE: Henrietta Barnett, Hampstead, City University London.
QUALIFICATIONS: BSc Honours Optometry. College of Optometrists Membership examinations.
MEMBERSHIPS: 1999-2001 President of N London Association of Optometrists. Since 1998 member of the Hellenic Medical Society. Since 2000 member of the National Federation of Cypriot Youth (NFCY).
HOBBIES AND INTERESTS: Live music, Greek & English, rock, folk etc.
PERSONAL PROFILE: Ophthalmic Optician. Owner of Optikal Opticians in Finchley Central, London.

UK

MARIOS SOTERIADES
Creative Designer Parikiaki Newspaper

DATE OF BIRTH: 14-Sep-1944
PLACE OF BIRTH: Nicosia.
MARITAL STATUS: Married to Elli, Nicosia, Hairdresser.
CHILDREN: Nicholas, Anna-Maria, Alexander.
SCHOOLS/COLLEGE: Samuel's Commercial School, Nicosia.
MEMBERSHIPS: AKEL.
HOBBIES AND INTERESTS: Music.
PERSONAL PROFILE: Creative designer for Parikiaki Newspaper.

MIA SOTERIOU
Actress/Composer/TV work includes Holby City, Sunburn, Absolutely Fabulous, Smith & Jones, Eastenders

PLACE OF BIRTH: London. Parents from Styllos and Phlasou.
SCHOOLS/COLLEGE: Lady Margaret School. Wadham College, Oxford University, Royal College of Music.
QUALIFICATIONS: BA (Oxon) in English Language & Literature.
MEMBERSHIPS: Equity, Musicians Union, PRS.
HONOURS/AWARDS: Sony Awards for radio work.
HOBBIES AND INTERESTS: History, medieval & traditional music and football.
PERSONAL PROFILE: Actress, Musician, Composer, Singer. Child prodigy classical pianist, gave up at 17 to go to university. TV work includes Holby City, Sunburn, Absolutely Fabulous, Smith & Jones, Eastenders. Films include Topsy Turvy, Secrets and Lies. Stage work includes Lennon (West End). Music includes composing for theatre in the West End, National, RSC, BBC Radio and TV.

PHAEDIAS SOTERIOU MBE
MBE for services to the Police and Cypriot Community

DATE OF BIRTH: 27-Mar-1941.
PLACE OF BIRTH: Morphou.
MARITAL STATUS: Married.
CHILDREN: One son, a Professional Model, one daughter, a Sty.
SCHOOLS/COLLEGE: American Academy Larnaca, Lanition Gymnasium. Honorary Member of the UK Thalassaemia Society.
HONOURS/AWARDS: MBE for services to the Police and Cypriot Community on the 12th June 1999 in Birthday Honours List.
HOBBIES AND INTERESTS: Charity work and gardening.
PERSONAL PROFILE: When he first came to England he was a mechanic then became a Policeman for 31 years in Leyton, Special Patrol Group and CID. 1st Cypriot Police Officer.

SOTOS SOTIRIOU
FHM Retailer of the Year runner up in 2000 & 2001

DATE OF BIRTH: 08-Dec-1951
PLACE OF BIRTH: London. Parents from Prastion near Famagusta.
MARITAL STATUS: Single.
CHILDREN: Jordan, Jack and Charlotte.
SCHOOLS/COLLEGE: Clarkes College.
QUALIFICATIONS: Degree in Technical Building.
HONOURS/AWARDS: FHM Retailer of the Year runner up in both 2000 and 2001.
HOBBIES AND INTERESTS: Scuba diving, water & snow skiing and martial arts.
PERSONAL PROFILE: Menswear retail shop owner/buyer. Helps local schools, Scout groups, various charities.

CHARALAMBOS SOZOU
Professor of Mathematics at Imperial College

DATE OF BIRTH: 24-Apr-1937
PLACE OF BIRTH: Tochni, Larnaca.
MARITAL STATUS: Married to Maria, Pighi, Retired Lecturer.
CHILDREN: Sozos, Teacher. Demetris, Research Fellow LSE.
SCHOOLS/COLLEGE: Pancyprian Commercial Lyceum. Chelsea College of Advanced Technology, Queen Mary College London.
QUALIFICATIONS: BA Honours Mathematics; PhD.
HOBBIES AND INTERESTS: Education, history, politics and economics.
PERSONAL PROFILE: Teacher in Cyprus and an Assistant Lecturer in Mathematics at the City University (London). In 1965 was appointed Lecturer in Applied Mathematics at the University of Sheffield, where he was promoted to Senior Lecturer, Reader and in 1983 Professor of Applied Mathematics. Retired in 1998 and is now a visiting Professor of Mathematics at Imperial College.

PETER SPYRIDES
Won £500,000 on "Who Wants to be a Millionaire?"

DATE OF BIRTH: 16-Nov-1967
PLACE OF BIRTH: London. Father from Gypsos.
MARITAL STATUS: Married to Catherine, a full time mother, from New Zealand.
CHILDREN: Emma.
SCHOOLS/COLLEGE: Forest School, Snaresbrook E17.
QUALIFICATIONS: 4 A Levels, 10 O Levels.
HOBBIES AND INTERESTS: Cooking, reading crime fiction, computer games. Arsenal season ticket holder.
PERSONAL PROFILE: Bank office manager for Entergy-Kock Trading Ltd (Energy Trading company). Won £500, 000 on "Who Wants to be a Millionaire?".

ANDREAS SPYROU
Former Chairman of New Salamis FC (UK) (Deceased)

DATE OF BIRTH: 30-Nov-1932
PLACE OF BIRTH: Nicosia.
MARITAL STATUS: Married to Dora, from Famagusta.
CHILDREN: Spiros, Partner Andrews Shipping and Andrews Travel. Nico, Partner Exclusive Golf Tours. Chris, Telephone Sales.
SCHOOLS/COLLEGE: English High School, Famagusta.
MEMBERSHIPS: FFA and BIFA.
HOBBIES AND INTERESTS: Football (Manchester Utd fan).
PERSONAL PROFILE: In Cyprus played for New Salamis for six years. Owned Andrews Shipping and Andrews Travel. Was Chairman of New Salamis FC UK for several years.

COSTAS SPYROU
Managing Director of Star Lettings Investment Companies that have been active supporters to community organisations for many years

DATE OF BIRTH: 01-May-1957
PLACE OF BIRTH: Famagusta.
MARITAL STATUS: Married to Christina.
CHILDREN: Theodosia, University. Angela, School.
SCHOOLS/COLLEGE: Lanition Gymnasium Limassol. University of Athens and University of North London, University of Westminster and LSE.
QUALIFICATIONS: BA Economics and Diploma in Accountancy MBA and MSc in Business Administration.
HOBBIES AND INTERESTS: Gym and Tennis.
PERSONAL PROFILE: Costas Spyrou is the Managing Director of Star Lettings Investment Companies that have been active supporters to community organisations for many years.

UK

MARIA SPYROU
Chair of Greek Cypriot Women's Organisation of Haringey

PLACE OF BIRTH: Avgorou.
MARITAL STATUS: Married to Spyros, Cyprus, Engineering.
CHILDREN: Anthony, Katerina, Both University Graduates.
HOBBIES AND INTERESTS: Reading, cooking, Poetry and writing.
PERSONAL PROFILE: Chair of Greek Cypriot Women's Organisation of Haringey. Member of the Radio marathon-special needs children commitee. Chair of Avgorou Association in the UK. An advisor on legal matters at the Citizens advice bureaux. LGR, presenter on a monthly live programme and a weekly update on the latest changes in benefits and other issues.

SOULLA SPYROU
Wrote the book how to learn the Greek Alphabet

DATE OF BIRTH: 30-Apr-1957
PLACE OF BIRTH: London. Parents from Cyprus.
MARITAL STATUS: Married to Andreas, BT Engineer.
CHILDREN: Alexis, Pascalis, Kristofer, Stefanos, all Students.
SCHOOLS/COLLEGE: Ambler Primary, Highbury Hill High Girls Grammar, Birmingham University, Teacher Training.
QUALIFICATIONS: Open University degree in Social Sciences (BA), Practitioner's certificate in reflexology. Wrote the book how to learn the Greek Alphabet.
HOBBIES AND INTERESTS: Reading, pottery, sports, painting, dance, theatre, classical studies and travel.
PERSONAL PROFILE: Recently worked as supply teacher in Edmonton. Committee member of F. A. C. E. (Familites of Autistic Children Embrace), organising leisure activities and raising money.

SPYRAKIS SPYROU
Director of Andrews Shipping and Philanthropist

DATE OF BIRTH: 25-Jan-1955
PLACE OF BIRTH: Famagusta.
MARITAL STATUS: Married to Debbie, London parents from Cyprus, Partner in Travel agency.
CHILDREN: Andreas, First two in family business. Kristy, Gabriella at school. Gabriella.
SCHOOLS/COLLEGE: Arnos School. Southgate College.
QUALIFICATIONS: HND Business Studies.
MEMBERSHIPS: BIFA.
HOBBIES AND INTERESTS: Football and travelling.
PERSONAL PROFILE: Spyrakis Spyrou is a director of Andrews Shipping that has been serving the community for 40 years not just business wise but also philanthropically.

HELEN STAFFORD
Theatrical/Film Agent

DATE OF BIRTH: 28-Feb-1957
PLACE OF BIRTH: Nicosia.
MARITAL STATUS: Married to Graham, England, Computers.
SCHOOLS/COLLEGE: Archway School. New College of Speech & Drama.
QUALIFICATIONS: Diploma in Dramatic art.
MEMBERSHIPS: Equity, Licensed Agent since 1991.
HOBBIES AND INTERESTS: Music and films.
PERSONAL PROFILE: Theatrical/Film Agent, Actors/ actresses in many West End musicals and also films and TV. Casting Director for films shot in Cyprus.

UK

SIR REO STAKIS
Knighted by Queen Elizabeth the 2nd.
(Deceased)

DATE OF BIRTH: 13-Mar-1913
PLACE OF BIRTH: Kato Drys.
MARITAL STATUS: Married to Annitsa, Lefkara.
CHILDREN: Rena; Ridi; Niki; Stassia; Andros; Evros.
SCHOOLS/COLLEGE: American Academy Larnaca.
HONOURS/AWARDS: 1986 Honorary Degree Doctor of Law from Strathclyde University. 1991 Honorary Degree Doctor of Arts from Napier University. Knighted by Queen Elizabeth the 2nd.
HOBBIES AND INTERESTS: Shooting.
PERSONAL PROFILE: Former chairman of Stakis Hotels and Casinos. Philanthropist.

ZENON STAVRINIDES
Associate Lecturer in Philosophy,
University of Bradford

DATE OF BIRTH: 22-May-1945
PLACE OF BIRTH: Nicosia.
MARITAL STATUS: Single.
SCHOOLS/COLLEGE: The English School Nicosia. King's College London, Trinity Hall Cambridge, University of Leeds.
QUALIFICATIONS: BA (London), M. Phil (Cambridge), PhD (Leeds).
MEMBERSHIPS: The Philosophical Society of England, Aristotelian Society, Association for Cypriot, Greek & Turkish Affairs, AUT.
HOBBIES AND INTERESTS: Reading works of literature and history, listening to music and cinema.
PERSONAL PROFILE: Associate Lecturer in Philosophy, University of Bradford.

ROULLA STAVRINOU
Education Consultant for Haringey
Education authority

DATE OF BIRTH: 19-Sep-1963
PLACE OF BIRTH: Moscow. Father, Kyriacos Tsioupras, from Komi Kebir; Mother, Pola, from Lymbia.
MARITAL STATUS: Married to Thiso. London parents from Cyprus.
CHILDREN: Pola and Stelios.
SCHOOLS/COLLEGE: Ashmole School, Middlesex University.
QUALIFICATIONS: BEd Bachelor in Education.
HOBBIES AND INTERESTS: Salsa, travel and martial arts.
PERSONAL PROFILE: Taught at St Aidans School then at Earlsmead School, Tottenham. Was an ethnic minority achievement coordinator now education consultant for Haringey Education Authority.

HARALAMBOS STAVROU
Finalist in the Whitbread Entrepreneur
Awards 1996

DATE OF BIRTH: 24-Oct-1974
PLACE OF BIRTH: London, Father Mandres, Mother Rizokarpasso.
MARITAL STATUS: Single.
SCHOOLS/COLLEGE: Westminster, Thames Valley and Birbeck.
QUALIFICATIONS: BA MSc.
HONOURS/AWARDS: Finalist in the Whitbread Entrepreneur Awards 1996.
HOBBIES AND INTERESTS: Keen Arsenal Fan and Art.
PERSONAL PROFILE: Director and Co Founder of Beyond Certainty LTD set the company up in 2002.

UK

Entrants in Greek Cypriots Worldwide have been nominated for their achievements and contributions.
It is free to nominate someone, or yourself, who deserves to be in the book, just send in the name, contact address, telephone number and email to:
Greek Cypriots Worldwide
111 St Thomas's Road London N4 2QJ
Telephone 0044 207503 3498
cypriotwhoswho@aol.com
www.greekcypriotsworldwide.com

STEF STEFANOU OBE

In 2007 he was given the OBE for his services to the Construction Industry and also an honorary Doctorate by the University of Westminster

PLACE OF BIRTH: Born in 1941 Egypt Father from Peyia Mother from Ktima.
MARITAL STATUS: Married.
SCHOOLS/COLLEGE: London University.
MEMBERSHIPS: Deputy Chairman of Construct (after 12 years on the Chair 1993-2005), Board Member of SpeCC, the registration scheme, Chairman of Constructionarium and Member of the Construction Skills Network Observatory for the Yorkshire and Humber areas. Founder Board Member of the Movement for Innovation (a government body).
HONOURS/AWARDS: Fellow of the Institution of Civil Engineers. In 2005 the Dundee International Congress awarded him the Concrete Sector Gold Medal. In 2007 he was given the OBE for his services to the Construction Industry and also an honorary Doctorate by the University of Westminster.
PERSONAL PROFILE: Stef started working life with Peter Lind, Fairweather and Holst (now Vinci) before joining Doyle Plc in 1972, initially as Construction Manager before becoming Managing Director in 1975. As principal shareholder since 1976 he developed the business to its current form over a 30 year period.

STELIOS HARALAMBOS STEFANOU OBE

Officer British Empire (OBE)/. Honorary Doctorate from Westminster University

DATE OF BIRTH: 06-Nov-1952
PLACE OF BIRTH: Ismailia, Egypt. Father from Peyia, Cyprus; Mother from Ktima, Cyprus.
MARITAL STATUS: Married to Susie, English.
SCHOOLS/COLLEGE: Tiffin Boys School, Kingston, Surrey. Imperial College, London.
QUALIFICATIONS: BSC Chemistry, Associate of the Royal College of Science. Fellow of Institute of Directors.
MEMBERSHIPS: Royal Automobile Club.
HONOURS/AWARDS: Officer British Empire (OBE). Honorary Doctorate from Westminster University.
HOBBIES AND INTERESTS: Photography, food and tennis.
PERSONAL PROFILE: Stelios Stefanou is the Former

Chief Executive of Accord Plc (the company formed in 1999 following the de-merger of the John Doyle Group). Accord was recently sold to the Enterprise Group. From 1987 to 1999 he was Chief Executive of John Doyle Group. Prior to joining John Doyle Group, he had held senior positions at Esso (UK) and Johnson Matthey. He is a Fellow of the Institute of Directors and was Chairman of the CBI Local Government Panel, a member of the CBI Public Services Strategy Board, a member of the DTLR Best Value Evaluation Panel and a member of the Bank of England Regional Advisory Panel. Stelios is now in the process of starting the Stefanou foundation.

EUGENIOS STYLIANIDES

Chairman of Southwark Cypriot Day Centre funded by Southwark Council

DATE OF BIRTH: 09-Mar-1930
PLACE OF BIRTH: Ktima, Paphos.
MARITAL STATUS: Married to Stella, Lazania.
CHILDREN: George, Accountant. Akis, Films. Marios, BBC Producer.
SCHOOLS/COLLEGE: Greek Gymnasium, Paphos. Regent Street Polytechnic.
QUALIFICATIONS: Accountant.
HOBBIES AND INTERESTS: Football (Arsenal fan) and Cricket (Surrey Fan).
PERSONAL PROFILE: One of the founders and Chairman of DOEK FC. Treasurer and Vice Chairman of the Cypriot League. Chairman of Paphos Association. Chairman of Southwark Cypriot Day Centre funded by Southwark Council. Trustee of St Marys Church in Camberwell and Secretary of the Committee of the Church. Was School Governor at Warwick Park School, Peckham.

HELENA P STYLIANIDES

Woodcarver, Sculptor, Tutor

DATE OF BIRTH: 17-Apr-1960
PLACE OF BIRTH: Carshalton, Surrey. Father's from Gourri, Mother's family from Morphou.
MARITAL STATUS: Married to Brian, Upminster, Musician.
CHILDREN: Lukas, Christos, Rhea, Simone.
SCHOOLS/COLLEGE: Hinchley Wood Secondary, Epsom School of Art & Design, Brighton Polytechnic, Chelsea School of Art & Design.
QUALIFICATIONS: BA. MA in Fine Art.

UK

HOBBIES AND INTERESTS: Travel, world music, cinema, reading and gardening.
PERSONAL PROFILE: Helena has produced major public sculptures sited in Cumbria, Essex, London & Skyros Island in Greece. Numerous art projects & workshops for community groups. Teaches picture framing, Greek and Creative Woodcarving.

MARIOS STYLIANIDES
British Academy Television Award for Best Comedy Programme 2008

DATE OF BIRTH: 09-Dec-1963
PLACE OF BIRTH: London Father from Ktima and Mother from Lazania.
MARITAL STATUS: Single.
SCHOOLS/COLLEGE: Exeter University.
QUALIFICATIONS: Degree in Media Studies.
HONOURS/AWARDS: British Academy Television Award for Best Comedy Programme 2008 for Fone jacker.
PERSONAL PROFILE: Marios is Editor comedy for Hat Trick Productions was Executive Producer on "Worst Week Of My Life" and on Hat Trick's first foray into adult animated comedy, Bromwell High, co-produced with Decode Entertainment. Prior to joining Hat Trick, Mario worked as a Comedy Producer at BBC Television for five years, producing numerous shows, including "Dead Ringers", before moving on to produce "V Graham Norton" for So Television. Mario began his career at London Weekend Television.

ANDREAS STYLIANOU
Accountant/Director of Kounnis & Partners PLC/Captain of Cypriot Golf Society 2004/2005

DATE OF BIRTH: 16-Sep-1950
PLACE OF BIRTH: Ayios Sergios.
MARITAL STATUS: Married to Maria, Akanthou.
CHILDREN: Koulla, Christopher, Both Students.
MEMBERSHIPS: Chartered Accountant ACA, Institute of Chartered Accountants.
HOBBIES AND INTERESTS: Golf, football, socialising and travelling.
PERSONAL PROFILE: Director of Kounnis & Partners PLC. Captain of Cypriot Golf Society, 2004/2005.

ANDROULLA STYLIANOU
Founder Member of the Leukaemia Society UK

DATE OF BIRTH: 25-Nov-1955
PLACE OF BIRTH: London. Parents from Aradippou.
MARITAL STATUS: Married to Erodotos. Kapedes.
CHILDREN: Mario, Theodoros, Theodosia.
SCHOOLS/COLLEGE: Ackland Burghley, College of North East London.
QUALIFICATIONS: O & A Levels. Diploma in Business and Marketing.
PERSONAL PROFILE: One of the founder members of the Leukaemia Society. Worked very hard to help create awareness within our community and encourage people of Greek and Turkish Cypriot origin to register as potential bone marrow donors.

CHRISTAKIS STYLIANOU
Honorary President Assia Association

DATE OF BIRTH: 05-Mar-1938
PLACE OF BIRTH: Assia.
MARITAL STATUS: Married to Christalla, Livadia.
CHILDREN: Two daughters.
SCHOOLS/COLLEGE: Assia Elementary School. AKEL.
HOBBIES AND INTERESTS: Politics and reading.
PERSONAL PROFILE: One of the founders of Assia Association and Chairman for several years, now honorary President. Was involved in the Greek Parents Association for years. One of the founders of the Cypriot Estia of North London.

UK

CHRISTODOULOS STYLIANOU
Secretary of AKEL in Britain. Manager of the Cypriot Community Centre

DATE OF BIRTH: 21-Jan-1943
PLACE OF BIRTH: Avgorou.
MARITAL STATUS: Married to Katerina, Paphos.
CHILDREN: Maria, Maths Teacher. Eleni, University Lecturer.
SCHOOLS/COLLEGE: Elementary in Cyprus.
HOBBIES AND INTERESTS: Reading, Writing and Football (Manchester United fan).
PERSONAL PROFILE: Former Chairman of Bowes Greek School. Former Chairman of OESEKA. Secretary of AKEL in UK. Manager of Cypriot Community Centre in Wood Green.

DR ELENI STYLIANOU
Lecturer at the University of Nottingham

DATE OF BIRTH: 04-Dec-1962
PLACE OF BIRTH: London. Father from Avgorou; Mother from Paphos.
MARITAL STATUS: Married.
SCHOOLS/COLLEGE: North Harringey Infants & Juniors; Alexandra Park School; Royal Holloway & Bedford College; University of London, University of Wales College of Medicine.
QUALIFICATIONS: (2. 1 Honours) BSc Biochemistry, PhD Biochemistry.
HOBBIES AND INTERESTS: Having fun with family and friends, entertaining, cooking, gardening, interior design, walking, reading, current affairs, cinema, theatre, listening to all kinds of music.
PERSONAL PROFILE: University lecturer at the University of Nottingham. Lead own research team interested in understanding the basis of inflammatory diseases eg Rheumatiod Arthritis and Asthma.

STELLAKIS (STILKS) STYLIANOU
Author appeared on programme on channel 5 TV that was just based on Stellakis

DATE OF BIRTH: 21-Jul-1958.
PLACE OF BIRTH: Nicosia.
MARITAL STATUS: Married to Sheena.
CHILDREN: Five Daughters.
SCHOOLS/COLLEGE: Eaglesfield.
HOBBIES AND INTERESTS: Judo, Wrestling and Weightraining.
PERSONAL PROFILE: Stellakis Stylianou has a published autobiography called Stilk's the Hardest Bouncer in Britain, he has also appeared on TV Channel 5 on Kate Kray's series Hard Barstard's one of the programme's was just on Stellakis.

THEO STYLIANOU
Appeared on ITV London as a success story

DATE OF BIRTH: 13-Oct-1979
PLACE OF BIRTH: London Father from Kapedhes Mother from Aradippou.
MARITAL STATUS: Single.
SCHOOLS/COLLEGE: Broomfield School.
HOBBIES AND INTERESTS: Cooking, Football.
PERSONAL PROFILE: Theo Stylianou founded Simply Catering with the guidance and assistance of the Princes Trust, with this help. Theo gained the opportunity to use his banqueting skills as part of a team who prepared and served Christmas lunch in December 2003 to Prince Charles and Prince William at St James Palace. Theo has appeared on The BBC News and recently been on ITV London as a success story, was nominated for The Barclay's Trading Places Award 2006.

UK

Entrants in Greek Cypriots Worldwide have been nominated for their achievements and contributions.
It is free to nominate someone, or yourself, who deserves to be in the book, just send in the name, contact address, telephone number and email to:
Greek Cypriots Worldwide
111 St Thomas's Road London N4 2QJ
Telephone 0044 207503 3498
cypriotwhoswho@aol.com
www.greekcypriotsworldwide.com

MARIA STYLIANOU-TUTON
Teacher/Also on Parents Committee of Ashmole School

DATE OF BIRTH: 25-Feb-1965
PLACE OF BIRTH: London. Father from Avgorou; Mother from Paphos.
MARITAL STATUS: Married to Karl Tuton, Hull, Teacher.
CHILDREN: Christos and Matheos.
SCHOOLS/COLLEGE: Alexandra Park School, Avery Hill College, Thames Polytechnic.
QUALIFICATIONS: BEd (Honours) 1st class in Mathematics.
HOBBIES AND INTERESTS: Keeping fit, reading, pilates and running.
PERSONAL PROFILE: Teacher at Copthall School as head of Mathematics. Also on Parents Committee of Ashmole School.

PHOTIS STYLLIS
Director of Delphi Food Products producers of chilled dips, salads and Mediterranean specialities/Philanthropist

DATE OF BIRTH: 08-May-1947
PLACE OF BIRTH: Akanthou.
MARITAL STATUS: Married to Georgia, Anglatsia.
CHILDREN: Stavros, Business. marie, Business. Cleo, Student.
SCHOOLS/COLLEGE: Nicosia.
HOBBIES AND INTERESTS: Gym, Football, reading and travelling.
PERSONAL PROFILE: Photis Styllis is a Director of Delphi Food Products producers of chilled dips, salads and Mediterranean specialities. known for his philanthropic work.

ANDRE SYMEOU
Psychologist

PLACE OF BIRTH: Northampton, parents from Exometochi Cyprus.
SCHOOLS/COLLEGE: Northampton Schools, graduated in London.
QUALIFICATIONS: BSc. Dip. P. Psy. C. Degree in Psychology & Physiology. Studied abnormal psychiatry at post graduate and professionally qualified in Psychotherapy (Cognitive-Behavioural).
MEMBERSHIPS: Professional Psychotherapy Centre.
HOBBIES AND INTERESTS: Phobias.
PERSONAL PROFILE: Psychologist. Guest on several national TV Shows/Phone-ins with BBC Radio. Featured in ITV documentary about phobias.

ANDREAS SYRIMIS
Consultant Practitioner

DATE OF BIRTH: 17-Aug-1960
PLACE OF BIRTH: Cyprus.
SCHOOLS/COLLEGE: British School of Osteopathy, University of Westminster.
QUALIFICATIONS: BSc Osteopathy, BSc Medical Herbalism, MSc Complementary Medicine.
PERSONAL PROFILE: Consultant Practitioner, Medical Lecturer, Health-Care Advisor on LGR.

MARIOS TAKOUSHIS
Musician credits on TV and short feature films. Such as St Trinians, Fish Tales and the TV Margaret Thatcher the Long Walk To Finchley

DATE OF BIRTH: 13-Jan-1980
PLACE OF BIRTH: Nicosia, Cyprus.
SCHOOLS/COLLEGE: Berklee College of Music, Conservatoire National Superieur de Musique de Lyon.
QUALIFICATIONS: BA Arts.
MEMBERSHIPS: The MCPS-PRS Alliance.
HOBBIES AND INTERESTS: Cinema.
PERSONAL PROFILE: Composer and jazz pianist with performances on numerousCD's, compositional/orchestrational credits on TV and short feature films. Such as St Trinians, Fish Tales and the TV Margaret Thatcher the Long Walk To Finchley.

UK

ANDREAS TAMBOURIDES
Council Mayor Barnet 2005/2006

DATE OF BIRTH: 02-Jun-1946
PLACE OF BIRTH: Engomi.
MARITAL STATUS: Married to Joanna, Lincoln, Secretary.
CHILDREN: Alexandros, Aristos.
SCHOOLS/COLLEGE: Elementary & High, Cyprus.
QUALIFICATIONS: City & Guilds Electronics.
MEMBERSHIPS: Conservative Party, North London Enterprise Club.
HONOURS/AWARDS: CYBC. Play award 1st prize, Cyprus.
HOBBIES AND INTERESTS: Writing, producing and directing plays.
PERSONAL PROFILE: Andreas was editor of two community newspapers, Ellinikos Typos and Parikiaki Simerini and a radio presenter for Spectrum radio Now a self-employed businessman. Vice Chairman (voluntary) of the North London Enterprise Club which helps local unemployed or redundant people to start their own business, and trains and assists local self-employed people. In 1997 was elected Conservative Councillor for Brunswick Park Ward in the Borough of Barnet Governor of Moss Hall Junior School and Osidge Junior School. Council Mayor Barnet 2005-2006.

GEORGE TARDIOS
Actor and Writer created and established the first joint BBC TV/Poetry Society National Poetry Competition

DATE OF BIRTH: 03-Apr-1944
PLACE OF BIRTH: London. Father from Famagusta; Mother from Morphou.
MARITAL STATUS: Married to Christine, Guernsey, Teacher.
SCHOOLS/COLLEGE: Rolle College, Devon. Exeter University, Lancaster University.
QUALIFICATIONS: Cert. Ed, BEd.
HOBBIES AND INTERESTS: Literature, cinema, theatre and travel.
PERSONAL PROFILE: Director of the Arvon Foundation's residential creative writing centre in Devon and created and established the first joint BBC TV/ Poetry Society National Poetry Competition, now in its 29th year.
Also judged the BBC2 South Bank Show Poetry Competition. Actor appeared in theatre, including Hamlet, Rules of the Game. Films include African Rainbow, Hard Men. TV work: Hollyoaks and Stanley's

Footsteps where he spent three years retracing on foot Hm Stanleys journey in 1871 in his search for David Livingstone. Also teaches at the London Actors workshop.

PROFESSOR SAVVAS A TASSOU
Professor and Head of Department of Mechanical Engineering at Brunel University

DATE OF BIRTH: 30-Sep-1953
PLACE OF BIRTH: Kalopanayiotis.
MARITAL STATUS: Married to Maria, Nicosia, Housewife.
CHILDREN: Michelle, Alexis, Andreas, All Students.
SCHOOLS/COLLEGE: Technical School, Nicosia, Polytechnic of Central London.
QUALIFICATIONS: BSc PhD MBA CEng MIMechE MCIBSE.
HOBBIES AND INTERESTS: DIY, home improvements and travel.
PERSONAL PROFILE: Currently Professor and Head of Department of Mechanical Engineering at Brunel University. Has previously held posts of Research Assistant at the Polytechnic of Central London and Lecturer at the University of Westminster Author of over 120 technical papers in Journals.

PARIS TEKKIS
Consultant Colorectal Surgeon St Marys Hospital and St Marks Hospital

DATE OF BIRTH: 15-Nov-1968
PLACE OF BIRTH: Nicosia.
MARITAL STATUS: Married to Persephone, Nicosia, Lawyer currently housewife.
CHILDREN: Nicholas, Maria, Stefanos.
SCHOOLS/COLLEGE: English School Nicosia. University of London and University of Nottingham Medical School.
QUALIFICATIONS: FRCS. MD. Bm. BS. B. Med. Sci.
HONOURS/AWARDS: Award for excellence 2005. Department of Bio Surgery and surgical Technology, St Marys Campus, Imperial College London.
PERSONAL PROFILE: Paris Tekkis is a Clinical Senior Lecturer at the Imperial College London. An Honorary Consultant Colorectal Surgeon St Marys Hospital and St Marks Hospital. Also an Associate Editor for the journal Diseases of the Colon and Rectum.

ROBBIE TELFER
Actor

DATE OF BIRTH: 21-May-1969
PLACE OF BIRTH: London. Grandmother from Amargeti.
MARITAL STATUS: Single.
SCHOOLS/COLLEGE: Salford University, London Academy of Performing Arts. ACADEMIC QUALIFICAIONSBA in Spanish & French, Diploma in Acting. Salford University, London Academy of Performing Arts. ACADEMIC QUALIFICAIONSBA in Spanish & French, Diploma in Acting.
HOBBIES AND INTERESTS: Private Teacher of Spanish, French and Greek.
PERSONAL PROFILE: Actor (main profession), Appeared on TV in Hot Pursuits, a commercial for Coco Chanel. Appeared in films The Cat, Stage Nightout, Gasping, Entertaining Strangers and Wildfire.

STELIOS TERALLI
President of Greek Orthodox Church of Stoke on Trent

DATE OF BIRTH: 17-Sep-1963
PLACE OF BIRTH: Aradippou.
MARITAL STATUS: Married to Helen, Cyprus.
CHILDREN: Louise and Andrea, both at school.
SCHOOLS/COLLEGE: School (Aradippou), High School and University (Thessaloniki Greece).
QUALIFICATIONS: A Levels.
HOBBIES AND INTERESTS: Golf, piano and football.
PERSONAL PROFILE: Shop owner, President of Greek Orthodox Church of Stoke on Trent since 1991.

THEKLA TERALLI
Chairwoman of the Sheffield Greek School

DATE OF BIRTH: 28-Dec-1969
PLACE OF BIRTH: Newmarket, Suffolk. Parents from Aradippou.
MARITAL STATUS: Married to Andreas, Arradippou, Fish & Chip shop owner.
CHILDREN: Eleni, Maria and Michaela, all at school.
SCHOOLS/COLLEGE: Aelfgar Secondary School.

HOBBIES AND INTERESTS: Travelling, shopping, dancing, Greek and English music and writing plays.
PERSONAL PROFILE: Chairwoman of the Sheffield Greek School. Member of the Ladies Church Commitee in Mansfield.

JOHN THEMIS
Musician Grammy Nomination 1999

DATE OF BIRTH: 13-Oct-1954
PLACE OF BIRTH: Melbourne, Australia. Father from Astromeritis; Mother from Zodia.
MARITAL STATUS: Married to Catherine, Ireland, accounts.
CHILDREN: Emily, James, Katerina.
SCHOOLS/COLLEGE: Grammar school Nicosia. Institute of Marketing.
QUALIFICATIONS: BSc in Marketing & Management.
MEMBERSHIPS: MCPS/PRS Associate Member.
HOBBIES AND INTERESTS: Music.
PERSONAL PROFILE: John wrote No 1 hit What Took You So Long for Emma Bunton; Wrote top 10 hit for Kylie Minogue Please Stay. Has played on albums for George Michael, Dido, Rod Stewart and Gabrielle. Has appeared on many TV Shows, Top Of the Pops, Lottery Show, Aspel, The Word, Tonite with Jay Leno in America.

NICOLAS THEMISTOCLI
Banking General Manager and Chief Executive, Landesbank Baden-Wurttberg London Branch

DATE OF BIRTH: 27-Mar-1961
PLACE OF BIRTH: London, Father Pachna, Mother Kontea.
MARITAL STATUS: Married to Alexandra from Germany.
CHILDREN: Maximilian, Helena.
SCHOOLS/COLLEGE: Raines Foundation Grammar, London, Aston. University, Birmingham.
QUALIFICATIONS: BSC Combined Honours Business Administration and Computer Science.
HOBBIES AND INTERESTS: Golf, chess skiing.
PERSONAL PROFILE: General Manager and Chief Executive, Landesbank Baden-Wurttberg London Branch.

UK

THEOCHARIS THEOCHARI

Cited as a leading individual for shipping finance in The Legal 500 2004 edition

PLACE OF BIRTH: Famagusta
MARITAL STATUS: Married to Anne Elizabeth, UK.
SCHOOLS/COLLEGE: Arnos School. The London School of Economics. University of London.
QUALIFICATIONS: LLB Honours, Solicitor of the Supreme Court of England and Wales.
HONOURS/AWARDS: Legal Business Shipping and Transport Lawyer of the Year, Lloyd's List Shipping Lawyer of the Year.
Cited as a leading individual for shipping finance in The Legal 500 2004 edition
HOBBIES AND INTERESTS: Sport, current affairs.
PERSONAL PROFILE: Senior partner and Global Head of Shipping of leading City Law Firm Norton Rose. Founder member of Anglo Cypriot Solicitors Association.

DR PANTELI THEOCHAROUS

Senior Scientist

DATE OF BIRTH: 16-Jan-1968
PLACE OF BIRTH: London. Father from Kato Pyrgos: Mother from Phlasou.
MARITAL STATUS: Married to Demetra.
CHILDREN: One son.
SCHOOLS/COLLEGE: 1997-2001, Royal Free and University College Medical School (Royal Free Campus), University of London, 1992-1994 University of Westminster, London, 1988-1991 King's College, University of London, 1979-1987, School of St. David & St Katherine, London.
QUALIFICATIONS: Ph. D. M. Sc.
MEMBERSHIPS: Fellow of the Institute of Biomedical Science.
HOBBIES AND INTERESTS: Greek dancing, theatre and music.
PERSONAL PROFILE: Current Profession: Senior Scientist, Cell Biology Group. Associate Head, ONYVAX Limted, St George's Hospital Medical School.

EVANTHIS THEODORIDES

Teacher, Former Chairman of the Leukaemia Society

DATE OF BIRTH: 15-Jun-1940
PLACE OF BIRTH: Kalo Chorio, Limassol.
MARITAL STATUS: Married to Chrysanthi, Akaki, Housewife.
CHILDREN: Anna, Solicitor. Stalo, education.
SCHOOLS/COLLEGE: Primary Kalo Khorio, Limassol, Higher Commercial Lyceum, Nicosia, University of London.
QUALIFICATIONS: BA (London). PGCE (London) in Teaching History.
MEMBERSHIPS: The Leukaemia Society (U. K.) and Enfield Art Circle.
HOBBIES AND INTERESTS: Travel, gardening, drawing and painting.
PERSONAL PROFILE: Teacher, Head of History Dept in a comprehensive school for seven years, company director in the clothing trade for 17 years. Chairman of The Leukaemia Society (UK), from 1994 to 2002 on a voluntary basis.

OLYMPIA THEODOROU

Partner in Greek city. Contributor to Parikiaki Newspaper

DATE OF BIRTH: 15-Feb-1954
PLACE OF BIRTH: Hendon. Parents from Vavatsinia and Vavla.
MARITAL STATUS: Married to Steve, Architectural Photographer.
CHILDREN: Kristina, Assistant Film Editor. Anastasia, Student. Stefanos, Student.
SCHOOLS/COLLEGE: Whitfield Comprehensive.
HOBBIES AND INTERESTS: Music from classical to blues.
PERSONAL PROFILE: Partner in Greek city. Contributor to Parikiaki Newspaper and had own programme on LGR.

UK

DR ANDREW THEODOSSI
Consultant Gastroenterologist

DATE OF BIRTH: 14-Sep-1947
PLACE OF BIRTH: Polis, Paphos.
MARITAL STATUS: Married to Anne, East Grinstead, Nurse.
CHILDREN: Alexander, Anthony and Stephen.
SCHOOLS/COLLEGE: Sloane Grammer School, Chelsea University College, London, St George's Hospital Medical School London.
QUALIFICATIONS: MD, FRCP.
MEMBERSHIPS: Royal College Physicians, London, British Society Gastroenterology, Royal Society Medicine.
HOBBIES AND INTERESTS: Soccer and philosophy in medicine.
PERSONAL PROFILE: Consultant Gastroenterologist, Mayday Hospital, Croydon.

CHRIS THEODOSSIADES
Top Renault Dealer in the UK for three years

DATE OF BIRTH: 17-Jul-1947
PLACE OF BIRTH: Limassol.
MARITAL STATUS: Married to Pamela, London.
CHILDREN: Demetris, Business. Glen, Business. Zoe, Student.
SCHOOLS/COLLEGE: Daneford Modern, Finsbury Park.
MEMBERSHIPS: Member of the Round Table. Masonic Lodge.
HONOURS/AWARDS: Top Renault Dealer in the UK for three years.
HOBBIES AND INTERESTS: Gardening, travel, car racing and football (Arsenal supporter).
PERSONAL PROFILE: Trained as an automotive technician and opened a chain of petrol stations. In 1985 began to franchise new cars Renault, Fiat, Alfa Romeo, Lancia, Citroen. Expanded to own Theoco in North London, (properties and motor) and motor claims company Accident Assist Direct PLC.

GEORGE THEODOULOU
Chairman of Assia Village Association UK/Member of the National Federation of Cypriots UK Secretariat

DATE OF BIRTH: 02-Apr-1955
PLACE OF BIRTH: Assia, Cyprus.
MARITAL STATUS: Married to Kyri, Achna.
CHILDREN: Anthea, Teacher. Sofokli, Structural Engineer. Chris, Working in Family Business.
SCHOOLS/COLLEGE: In Cyprus.
MEMBERSHIPS: Chairman of Assia Village Association UK, Vice Chairman of the Omonia football club UK, member of the Secretariat AKEL UK and member of the National Federation of Cypriots Secretariat.
HOBBIES AND INTERESTS: Politics and football.
PERSONAL PROFILE: George has a Building Construction Company. He extended the Cypriot Community Centre in Wood Green, has built new homes in Islington and flats in Enfield. Renovated the National Heritage Public House The Salisbury. Has Also had the privilege of being invited to Number 10 Downing St to meet the Prime Minister, Tony Blair.

MICHAEL THEODOULOU
Journalist The Times

DATE OF BIRTH: 27-Jun-1959
PLACE OF BIRTH: Tipperary, Republic of Ireland. Father from Goudhi, Paphos, mother from Tipperary.
MARITAL STATUS: Married to Rachel, England, Journalist.
CHILDREN: Lauren, Nicholas, Grace.
SCHOOLS/COLLEGE: Ravenswood School for Boys, Kent. Exeter University, Warwick University.
QUALIFICATIONS: 2: 1 Honours degree in English Literature and Postgraduate Certificate in Education.
HOBBIES AND INTERESTS: Reading fiction and history, visiting Victorian gothic revival churches in England, walking in the Akamas, gardening, bridge football.
PERSONAL PROFILE: Working life began as a teacher in England In 1984 moved to Cyprus and spent three years teaching at the English School in Nicosia. In 1987 helped launch a magazine called Cyprus Life and began freelance journalism for British newspapers and radio, including The Times, The Observer, The Express and IRN. Apart from Cyprus, covers the Middle East, specialising in Iran and Iraq.

UK

ANDY THRASYVOULOU
Chief Executive of My Hotels Award winning Hospitality Brand

DATE OF BIRTH: 15-Mar-1963
PLACE OF BIRTH: London, Parents from Cyprus.
MARITAL STATUS: Married to Vasso.
CHILDREN: Stephanos, Yiannis, Athena.
SCHOOLS/COLLEGE: Highgate School. University of Westminster.
QUALIFICATIONS: RIBA.
MEMBERSHIPS: YPO Young Presidents Organisation.
HOBBIES AND INTERESTS: Travel and Meditation.
PERSONAL PROFILE: Andy is now the CEO as well as founder and principal shareholder of the myhotels Group, comprising three trading hotels with a further two under development and taking on new projects.

CHRIS TIMOTHEOU
Managing Director of Tims Dairy

DATE OF BIRTH: 30-Jun-1957
PLACE OF BIRTH: London. parents from Cyprus.
MARITAL STATUS: Married to Christine, London Parents from Achna and Komi kebir.
CHILDREN: Nicola, Law. Natalie, Teacher.
SCHOOLS/COLLEGE: Arnos Grove.
MEMBERSHIPS: JDC and The National Trust.
HOBBIES AND INTERESTS: Playing/watching football and keeping fit.
PERSONAL PROFILE: Managing Director of Tims Dairy Ltd, founded in the late 1940s, producing and supplying the local Cypriot Community with natural yoghurt and desserts. He took over the business with his brother, Peter, in the 1970s and they have continually expanded to its present location in the outskirts of London.

MARTINOS TIRIMO
Musician Composed film score Odyssey

DATE OF BIRTH: 19-Dec-1942
PLACE OF BIRTH: Larnaca.
MARITAL STATUS: Married to Mione.
CHILDREN: One son, one daughter.
SCHOOLS/COLLEGE: Bedales School with Cyprus Goverment Scholarship. Royal Academy.
HONOURS/AWARDS: Prizewinner International Beethoven Competition Vienna 1965. Winner Geneva International Piano Competition 1972. Silver Disc 1988, Gold disc 1994 for recording of Rachmaninov's 2nd concerto and Paganini Rhapsody.
HOBBIES AND INTERESTS: Chess, reading and badminton.
PERSONAL PROFILE: Conducted performances of La Traviata with singers and musicians from La Scala Milan at Cyprus Opera festival 1955. Concerto performance as well as recitals worldwide. Radio & TV appearances worldwide. Composed film score Odyssey. Recordings include Brahms Piano Concertos, Chopin Concertos, Shuberts Piano Sonatas. The Olympic Commitee of Athens 2004 appointed him Artistic director for several projects for the cultural Olympiad.

STELIOS TJIRKALLI
Founding member of the Independent Greek School of Finchley, where he has served as Treasurer and Vice Chairman, Vice Chairman of St Katherines Greek Orthodox Community in Barnet

DATE OF BIRTH: 19-Jun-1956
PLACE OF BIRTH: Bulawayo, Zimbabwe. Father, Andreas, from Dhikomo; Mother, Eleni Pastou, from Athienou.
MARITAL STATUS: Married to Tasoulla, Nicosia, accounts.
CHILDREN: Andreas, Harry, Marios.
SCHOOLS/COLLEGE: American Academy Larnaca, North London University.
QUALIFICATIONS: Chartered Certified Accountant Certificate.
HOBBIES AND INTERESTS: Football, travelling and sailing.
PERSONAL PROFILE: Founding partner of Andrew, Steale an accounting and auditing practise in Mayfair, London, Former Chairman of Athienou Association in UK, founding member of the Independent Greek School of Finchley, where he has served as Treasurer and Vice Chairman, Vice Chairman of St Katherine's Greek Orthodox Community in Barnet.

UK

TASOULLA TJIRKALLI

Chairwoman of the Greek Womens Philanthropic Association Of Finchley and Barnet

DATE OF BIRTH: 02-Dec-1958
PLACE OF BIRTH: Nicosia.
MARITAL STATUS: Married to Stelios, Zimbabwe Parents from Cyprus, Accountant.
CHILDREN: Andreas, Harry, Marios.
SCHOOLS/COLLEGE: The Lapithos and Soleas Gymnasiums. Studied Economics in Greece and also qualified as a Beautician.
QUALIFICATIONS: Economics and Beautician.
HOBBIES AND INTERESTS: Travelling, reading, swimming and helping other people.
PERSONAL PROFILE: Accounts manager at Andrew Steale an accounting & auditing practise in the West End. First Chairperson of the Mothers Committees Of The Independent Greek School Of Finchley. Chairperson of The Greek Womens Philanthropic Association of Finchley and Barnet.

ALEX TOFALIDES

Winner and Gold Medalist in the under 16 Boys Foil Fencing at the British Youth Championship Finals 2009

DATE OF BIRTH: 19-Dec-1993
PLACE OF BIRTH: London Father from Nicosia, Mother English.
MARITAL STATUS: Single.
HONOURS/AWARDS: Winner and Gold Medalist in the under 16 Boys Foil Fencing at the 2009 British Youth Championship Finals.
HOBBIES AND INTERESTS: Fencing, Football and Socialising.
PERSONAL PROFILE: Alex is the top under 17 cadet foilist and has been selected to represent Great Britain at the European International Cadet Tournament in France March 2009 and is also due to be selected for the World Championships in Belfast in April 2009.

LOUIS ANDREAS TOFALIDES

Assistant General Manager at the Bank of Cyprus (London) Ltd

DATE OF BIRTH: 30-Jan-1957
PLACE OF BIRTH: Nicosia.
MARITAL STATUS: Married.
CHILDREN: One son, one daughter.
SCHOOLS/COLLEGE: The English School, Nicosia, The London School of Economics (University of London).
QUALIFICATIONS: BSc. (Econ). Fellow of the Chartered Institute of Bankers.
HOBBIES AND INTERESTS: Football, theatre, classical music and sailing.
PERSONAL PROFILE: Assistant General Manager, Banking, Bank of Cyprus (London) Ltd.

DR KYPROS TOFALLIS

Author, Lecturer

DATE OF BIRTH: 27-Dec-1943
PLACE OF BIRTH: Styllos, Famagusta.
MARITAL STATUS: Married to Katerina, Kato Deftera, Teacher.
CHILDREN: Christopher, Deputy Head. Elli, Teacher. Aristos, Computer Programmer.
SCHOOLS/COLLEGE: Commercial Lyceum, Famagusta; Barnsbury School. North Western Polytechnic and University of London.
QUALIFICATIONS: BA, MA, PhD.
MEMBERSHIPS: Fellow of the Institute of Linguists, Fellow of the Royal Society of Arts.
HOBBIES AND INTERESTS: Reading, politics, history, literature, travel and theatre.
PERSONAL PROFILE: Lecturer in Modern Greek Studies at North London College and University of North London. Greek Chief Examiner of the Institute of Linguists for 20 years. He was Examiner and Moderator for the University of London and the University of Cambridge. Founder and Director of the Greek Institute. He has also contributed many articles to the Greek and British press. He has also published several books including A History of Cyprus from the Ancient Times to the Present. Currently Headmaster of St Marys Greek School in Cheshunt.

UK

DR ZANNETOS TOFALLIS
Chairman of Styllos Association UK.
Chairman of Barnet Cypriot Association.
1st Managing Director of LGR

DATE OF BIRTH: 26-Jan-1938
PLACE OF BIRTH: Styllos.
MARITAL STATUS: Married.
CHILDREN: One son, Chris.
Two grandchildren.
SCHOOLS/COLLEGE: Styllos
Elementary, English High
School. Famagusta, University
Of London.
QUALIFICATIONS: BA Greek
Studies, PhD Greek Studies.
HONOURS/AWARDS: FIL Fellow of Institute of Linguists.
HOBBIES AND INTERESTS: Reading and Travel.
PERSONAL PROFILE: Journalist at Vema, Parikiaki
newspaper and several Greek Journals. Lecturer in Greek
Studies at several Universities, Schools. Presently Greek
Translator 1st Managing Director of LGR. Chairman
of Styllos Association UK. Chairman of Barnet Cypriot
Association.

SOPHIA TOUMAZIS
Director of PR Consultancy, tpr,
whose clients include Channel 4 and
Associated Press

DATE OF BIRTH: 27-Apr-1960
PLACE OF BIRTH: London.
Father from Komi Kebir;
Mother from Kalavasso, (former
proprietors of La Primavera
Restaurant in Golders Green).
MARITAL STATUS: Married to
Andros Epaminondas.
CHILDREN: Christoforos and
Electra.
SCHOOLS/COLLEGE: The
Mount School, London. Southgate College, Warwick
University.
QUALIFICATIONS: 2: I Philosophy and Literature,
Warwick University; PGCE English and Drama.
HOBBIES AND INTERESTS: Film, writing, cooking and
walking.
PERSONAL PROFILE: Director of PR Consultancy, tpr,
whose clients include Channel 4 and Associated Press.
Contributor to both Greek Cypriots in the UK and
Worldwide.

TOM TOUMAZIS
Chief Commercial Officer of the
Endemol Group

DATE OF BIRTH: 06-Jun-1961
PLACE OF BIRTH: London.
Father from Komi Kebir;
Mother from Kalavasso, (former
proprietors of La Primavera
Restaurant in Golders Green).
MARITAL STATUS: Married to
Helen.
CHILDREN: Christopher,
Gabriel and Stephanie.
SCHOOLS/COLLEGE: Friern
Barnet Grammar School, Woodhouse, Barnet, Southbank
University, Harvard Business School.
MEMBERSHIPS: BAFTA, Royal Television Society,
SOLUS Club.
HOBBIES AND INTERESTS: Golf and film.
PERSONAL PROFILE: Was Managing Director of
Eurosport, then UK Managing Director of EMAP
Advertising. Was working for Walt Disney Television
International as Head of Buena Vista International TV.
Now Chief Commercial officer of the Endemol Group.

AKIS CHRYSOSTOMOS TOUMAZOS
Proprieter of the Banqueting Hall Trios in
Palmers Green and Genzos Restaurant
in East Finchley/Philanthropist

DATE OF BIRTH: 24-Mar-1959
PLACE OF BIRTH: Plymouth
Father from Milia Mother from
Famagusta.
MARITAL STATUS:
Married to Maria, From lysi,
Cyprus.
CHILDREN: Florenzos, Student
University of Nottingham. Fotis,
Student London School of
Economics.
SCHOOLS/COLLEGE: Chace Boys.
HOBBIES AND INTERESTS: Golf and Travel.
PERSONAL PROFILE: Akis Toumazos is the Proprieter
of the Banqueting Hall Trios in Palmers Green and
Genzos Restaurant in East Finchley. He Is also the
Captain of the Cypriot Golf Society Akis was also
involved with Ethnikos Football Club In the UK as a
player and Committee member.

ANDROS TOWNSEND
Won five caps for England Under 16's Football Team

DATE OF BIRTH: 16-Jul-1991
PLACE OF BIRTH: London Mother Cypriot origin her parents from Limassol.
MARITAL STATUS: Single.
SCHOOLS/COLLEGE: Rushcroft School.
HONOURS/AWARDS: Won five caps for England Under 16's Football Team.
HOBBIES AND INTERESTS: Formula One and Cricket.
PERSONAL PROFILE: Andros Townsend is England international under 16 left-sided midfielder/winger who was a regular in the Tottenham Under-18 squad in 2006-07. Joined Spurs academy full time 2007/2008.

PETROS TREZOS
Honorary Chairman of St Peters & Paul Church in Bristol

DATE OF BIRTH: 26-Jan-1917
PLACE OF BIRTH: Lefkoniko.
MARITAL STATUS: Married to Kyriaki, Tripimeni.
CHILDREN: Stella, Loulla and Maria. Seven Grandchildren, sev.
HONOURS/AWARDS: Honoured by the Greek Orthodox Church for services to the church & Bristol community.
HOBBIES AND INTERESTS: Golf and gardening.
PERSONAL PROFILE: Restauranteur and Fish &Chip shop owner. One of the founders of St Peter & Paul Church in Bristol, Honorary Chairman of the church.

GEORGE ANTONIOU TRIMIKLINIOTIS
Executive member of Brent Youth and Community Service Council Commitee

DATE OF BIRTH: 27-Sep-1926
PLACE OF BIRTH: Pera-pedi.
MARITAL STATUS: Married to Vassiliki, Greece.
CHILDREN: Maria, Vicky, antony.
SCHOOLS/COLLEGE: Willesden College of Technology.
QUALIFICATIONS: ONC and HNC in Building.
MEMBERSHIPS: AKEL.
HONOURS/AWARDS: Nominated by Brent Community Relations Council for a community service award in the early nineties.
HOBBIES AND INTERESTS: Politics, reading and theatre.
PERSONAL PROFILE: A structural engineer with the GLC. Former Chairman of the Cypriot Community Association of Brent. Executive Member of Brent Community Relations Council, involved in the running of the local Greek school in Brent.

IOANNIS TRITEOS
Chairman of Kato Pyrgos, Tyllirias UK Association. Chair of Governors of St Barnabas Greek Community School

DATE OF BIRTH: 01-Mar-1949
PLACE OF BIRTH: Kato Pyrgos.
MARITAL STATUS: Married to Androulla, Korakou, Teacher.
CHILDREN: Stelios, Eliana, Alexandros.
SCHOOLS/COLLEGE: Kato Pyrgos, Tyllirias Elementary, Kykkos Gymnasium. Isleworth Polytechnic and Chelsea College of Aeronautical Engineering.
QUALIFICATIONS: HND in Mechanical Engineering, Aeronautical Engineering Diploma.
HOBBIES AND INTERESTS: Sports activities, gardening, travelling, entertaining and current affairs.
PERSONAL PROFILE: Chairman of Kato Pyrgos, Tyllirias UK Association. Former Chair of Governors of St Barnabas Greek Community School, North London. One of the founders and the first chairman of A. G. T. A (U. K) and a member of the Committee.

UK

DR GERA MARIA TROISI
Senior Lecturer in Environmental Toxicology

DATE OF BIRTH: 26-Jul-1970
PLACE OF BIRTH: London. Mother from Trikomo.
MARITAL STATUS: Single.
SCHOOLS/COLLEGE: Chamberlayne Road School Burlington Danes School, The London Oratory School.
QUALIFICATIONS: BSc Honours Aquatic Biology & Ecology, PhD in Environmental Toxicology.
MEMBERSHIPS: British Toxicology Society. Society for Marine Mammology, European Cetacean Society.
HONOURS/AWARDS: British Toxicology Society. Society for Marine Mammology, European Cetacean Society.
HOBBIES AND INTERESTS: Music, travel and conservation.
PERSONAL PROFILE: Senior Lecturer (Environmental Toxicology), Kingston University. And a consultant environmental toxicologist. Director of Wildlife & Human Toxicology Unit, a UK government and charity funded research group based at Kingston University.

MICHAEL TRYPHONIDES
High Technology International Design Consultant/Local Authority Appointed School Governor

DATE OF BIRTH: 14-Oct-1950
PLACE OF BIRTH: Sinaoros, Nicosia.
MARITAL STATUS: Married to Effi, London (father from Leonarisso; mother from Aradippou).
CHILDREN: Andrea, All University Graduates. Nicholas, Helena.
SCHOOLS/COLLEGE: University College London.
QUALIFICATIONS: BSc in Electronic Engineering, MIEE, CEng.
HOBBIES AND INTERESTS: Football (Tottenham supporter), swimming and socialising.
PERSONAL PROFILE: Managing Director Of design consultancy Quartet Technology LTD - Consultants in high technology electronic design. Governor at Latymer School for ten years, local authority appointed Governor. Was Governor at Hadleywood Primary School, also for 27 years has been teaching Maths, Physics and Electronics.

LOUCAS TSANGARIDES
Chairman of Pedhoulas Assoc in UK

DATE OF BIRTH: 11-Nov-1937
PLACE OF BIRTH: Pedhoulas.
MARITAL STATUS: Married to Stavroula, Margate Parents from Yialoussa.
CHILDREN: Lara, Computer Analyst. Mariana, Fashion Buyer. Joanna, Teacher. Neophytos, Student.
SCHOOLS/COLLEGE: Institute of Chartered Ship Brokers.
QUALIFICATIONS: Member of the ICSB.
HOBBIES AND INTERESTS: Football.
PERSONAL PROFILE: Ex Managing Director of Troodos Shipping & Trading Ltd, Chairman of the Association of Pedhoulas in UK. Served as Chairman of St Barnabas Greek Church at Wood Green.

KYRIACOS TSAPARELLI
Magician

DATE OF BIRTH: 11-Sep-1955
PLACE OF BIRTH: London. Mother from Famagusta; Father from Yialoussa.
MARITAL STATUS: Married to Maria, (father from Deftera, mother from Lythrodontas).
CHILDREN: Louis, Natalya.
SCHOOLS/COLLEGE: George Elliot School, Finchley; Woolverstone Hall, Ipswich. East Anglia University; Thames Polytechnic.
QUALIFICATIONS: BSc.
MEMBERSHIPS: Magic Circle.
HOBBIES AND INTERESTS: Music Grade 6 in Piano & Cello.
PERSONAL PROFILE: A magician. In Cyprus has performed on RIK TV with presenter Irene on "Efharisto Savatobrado!. Now running a entertainment and promotion company. Jobs include taking a team of entertainers to Monte Carlo to play alongside Stevie Wonder and Kool and the Gang.

UK

LOUIS TSAPARELLI
Future Chef 2007 London Regional Final winner

DATE OF BIRTH: 28-Nov-1991
PLACE OF BIRTH: London Grandparents from Fathers side Yialoussa and Famagusta and Mothers side Deftera and Lythrothondas.
MARITAL STATUS: Single.
SCHOOLS/COLLEGE: Norfolk House Prep School, Muswell Hill Highlands and Enfield.
HONOURS/AWARDS: Future Chef 2007 London Regional Final winner Piano Grade 5 and Music Theory Grade 5.
HOBBIES AND INTERESTS: Computing, Films and Music.
PERSONAL PROFILE: Louis Tsaparelli still at school enjoys being a chef for Team dinners at Hazelwood Tennis Club.

GEORGE TSAVELLAS
General Surgeon

DATE OF BIRTH: 06-Jun-1965
PLACE OF BIRTH: London. Father from Miliou, Mother from Neo Chorio, Paphos.
SCHOOLS/COLLEGE: Winchmore School, Charing Cross & Westminster Medical School, University of London. University of London.
QUALIFICATIONS: BSc FRCS.
MEMBERSHIPS: British Medical Association.
PERSONAL PROFILE: George Tsavellas is a Consultant Surgeon at the East Kent NHS Trust and is based at The Queen Elizabeth. The Queen Mother and Kent and Canterbury Hospitals. His private practice is based in Canterbury, Margate and Hythe.

ANGELOS TSIAKLIS
Footballer

DATE OF BIRTH: 02-Oct-1989
PLACE OF BIRTH: Nicosia.
MARITAL STATUS: Single.
HONOURS/AWARDS: Part of Manchester City's FA Youth Cup winning side 2008.
PERSONAL PROFILE: Angelos Tsiaklis is a Midfield footballer signed by Manchester City currently on loan with Wrexham FC.

FOTINI TSIOUPRA
Secretary of Komi Kebir Association/ Member of the Executive Committee of the Cypriot community centre Wood Green

DATE OF BIRTH: 04-May-1965
PLACE OF BIRTH: London. Father, Takis Tsioupras (deceased, was Chairman of OESEKA), from Komi Kebir; Mother, Maritsa, from Zodia, was chairwoman of Cypriot Womens League.
SCHOOLS/COLLEGE: Exeter University, Middlesex University.
QUALIFICATIONS: BA History & Politics, Diploma in Social Work.
HOBBIES AND INTERESTS: Photography and equal opportunities.
PERSONAL PROFILE: Senior Probation Officer in London Probation Area. Secretary of Komi Kebir Asociation, Member of the Executive Committee of the Cypriot community centre Wood Green, Member of the Cypriot Womens League.

UK

GNOSOULLA LEWIS TSIOUPRA

Named in Chambers Law Directory in 2002 as one of the country's top ten in-house employment lawyers

DATE OF BIRTH: 14-Dec-1967
PLACE OF BIRTH: London; father Takis Tsioupras (deceased, was Chairman of OESEKA), from Komi Kebir; Mother, Maritsa, from Zodhia.
MARITAL STATUS: Married to Dewi Lewis, Wales, University Lecturer.
CHILDREN: Christoforos, Maritsa.
SCHOOLS/COLLEGE: Latymer School, Surrey University, Law College Lancaster Gate. Surrey University, Law College Lancaster Gate.
QUALIFICATIONS: BSc Russian & Law. Solicitor.
HONOURS/AWARDS: Named in Chambers Law Directory in 2002 as one of the country's top ten in-house employment lawyers.
HOBBIES AND INTERESTS: Travel & politics.
PERSONAL PROFILE: Joined city firm Baker & Mckenzie, specialising in employment law from 1992 to 1999. Now an in-house employment lawyer for United Business Media PLC. Board member of Novas Overtures, a charity working with the homeless, refugees, asylum seekers, victims of domestic violence and people with drug, alcohol and mental health problems.

LOUIZA TSIOUPRA

Costume Designer for the National Cypriot Theatre/Drama Teacher

DATE OF BIRTH: 03-Aug-1976
PLACE OF BIRTH: London. Father, Kyriacos, from Komi Kebir; Mother, Pola, from Lymbia.
MARITAL STATUS: Single.
SCHOOLS/COLLEGE: Ashmole School. Middlesex University, London College of Printing, University of Wales.
QUALIFICATIONS: BA Hons in Theatre Studies specialising in Design. PGCE Certificate in Education.
HONOURS/AWARDS: Awards from AKEL, Cypriot Women's League, Morphou District Association, National Federation of Cypriots in Great Britain and Haringey Council.
HOBBIES AND INTERESTS: Travelling, theatre, acting and designing. Politics, travel and grandchildren!.

PERSONAL PROFILE: Was costume assistant for White Horse Theatre Co in Germany and Costume designing for National Cypriot Theatre in Cyprus. Now a Drama Teacher at a Secondary School in North London.

MARITSA (nee Hassabis) TSIOUPRA

Honorary Chair Woman of Cypriot Womens League

DATE OF BIRTH: 10-Nov-1927
PLACE OF BIRTH: Pano Zodia.
MARITAL STATUS: Married to Takis Tsioupra (Deceased), Komi Kebir.
CHILDREN: Eddie Michael, Performing Rights Society. Des Michael, Performing Rights Society. Fotini Tsioupra, Senior Probation Officer. Gnosoulla Tsioupra, Solicitor.
MEMBERSHIPS: AKEL Commitee member.
HONOURS/AWARDS: Awards from AKEL, Cypriot Womens League, Morphou District Association, National Federation of Cypriots in Great Britain and Haringey Council.
HOBBIES AND INTERESTS: Politics and Travel.
PERSONAL PROFILE: Founder member formerly Chair person now Honorary Chairwoman of Cypriot Womens League. Former Committee member of the following organisations Ethnic minorities joint consultative Haringey Council, Cypriot Community Centre, National Federation of Cypriots, Hazelwood Greek School, Morphou District Association and also Zodhia Association.

POLA TSIOUPRA

Chairwoman of Lymbia Association UK

DATE OF BIRTH: 09-May-1941
PLACE OF BIRTH: Lymbia.
MARITAL STATUS: Married to Kyriacos Tsioupras.
CHILDREN: Stavroulla, Both Teachers. Louiza.
SCHOOLS/COLLEGE: Pancyprian Academy, Nicosia.
HOBBIES AND INTERESTS: Dancing, Greek Schools and women's rights.
PERSONAL PROFILE: Was a businesswoman with a florist shop for several years. Chairwoman of Lympia Association. In secretariat of National Federation of Cypriots. Was Chairwoman of Ashmole Greek School. Member of Cypriot Womens League OESEKA, and Greek Parents Association.

KYRIACOS LOIZOU TSIOUPRAS
Former Newspaper Editor, General Manager of LGR and Co Founder of the Cyprus Wine Festival UK

DATE OF BIRTH: 18-Dec-1932
PLACE OF BIRTH: Komi Kebir Village, Famagusta district, Cyprus.
MARITAL STATUS: Married to Pola Christoforou, Lymbia.
CHILDREN: Stavroulla, Both Teachers. Louiza.
SCHOOLS/COLLEGE: Elementary school, Komi Kebir; Famagusta Gymnasium;. London School of Economics and Political Science.
QUALIFICATIONS: BSc Economics (Honours).
MEMBERSHIPS: Served as member of the Executive Council of the National Federation of Cypriots in the UK as well as Secretary for the same organisation. Also former Vice President of the World Co-ordinating Committee Justice for Cyprus. Member of the Komi Kebir association.
HOBBIES AND INTERESTS: Politics, reading and travelling.
PERSONAL PROFILE: Sub-editor Haravgi daily newspaper, Nicosia, editor to Vema weekly newspaper, London; editor, Parikiaki weekly newspaper, London and General Manager London Greek Radio, London. Also Co Founder of the Cyprus Wine Festival UK. and Secretary of the Radio Marathon Committee UK

EVANGELIA TTOFI
Researcher in Medical Genetics

DATE OF BIRTH: 17-Nov-1981
PLACE OF BIRTH: London, Father from Eptakomi, Mother from Rizokarpasso.
MARITAL STATUS: Single.
SCHOOLS/COLLEGE: St Anne's Catholic High School for Girls, London. The. Latymer School, London. Exeter College, University of Oxford, Girton College.
QUALIFICATIONS: MBiochem, Molecular and Cellular.
HONOURS/AWARDS: Achieved an IQ of 161 on the Mensa test. Prize for the best GSCE grades in the school year.
HOBBIES AND INTERESTS: Live music, reading, languages, travel, science issues in society and public health.
PERSONAL PROFILE: After studying for an undergraduate degree at the University of Oxford (Exeter College), she moved to Cambridge Institute for Medical Research at the University of Cambridge (Girton College) where she is currently pursuing a PhD in Medical Genetics. She has published her research in peer-reviewed journals as well as registering for a patent with colleagues.

COSTAS TZIAMBAZIS
Former Chairman of Cypriot Estia, Birmingham

DATE OF BIRTH: 12-Apr-1945
PLACE OF BIRTH: Aradippou.
MARITAL STATUS: Married to Androulla, London, (parents from Aradippou and Assia).
CHILDREN: Elia, Doctor. Athos, Accounts. Constantine, Student.
SCHOOLS/COLLEGE: Pancyprian Gymnasium, Larnaca Lyceum.
MEMBERSHIPS: Greek Cypriot ESTIA, Birmingham.
HOBBIES AND INTERESTS: Poetry (writing), culture, music and choir singing.
PERSONAL PROFILE: Former Chairman, Greek Cypriot ESTIA twice. Was also Chairman of Culture Society for four years in Birmingham.

PETER SAVVAS VANEZIS OBE
Professor of Forensic Medicine and Science

DATE OF BIRTH: 11-Dec-1947
PLACE OF BIRTH: Nicosia.
MARITAL STATUS: Married to Maria, Limassol, Research Assistant.
CHILDREN: Andrew, Edinburgh University. Frosini, Student.
SCHOOLS/COLLEGE: Wanstead High School. Bristol University.
QUALIFICATIONS: MB, CHB, MD, PHD, FRCPATH, FRCP (Glasgow), DMJ.
MEMBERSHIPS: All major Forensic Societies, plus BMA, Rsm.
HONOURS/AWARDS: OBE.
HOBBIES AND INTERESTS: Golf and painting.
PERSONAL PROFILE: Regius Professor of Forensic Medicine & Science & Head of Department, University of Glasgow. Director: Human Identification Centre, Centre for International Forensic Assistance. Honorary Consultant in Forensic Medicine to: The Government of the Republic of Cyprus, The Medico-Legal Institute, Santiago Chile, The British Armed Forces.

UK

PETER KOSTA (PANAYIOTIS KOSTA VARDAKIS - LEGAL NAME)
Actor has appeared on TV in Sunburn, Family, One Last Chance

DATE OF BIRTH: 22-Mar-1949
PLACE OF BIRTH: Avgorou.
SCHOOLS/COLLEGE: Hengrove School, Bristol, Filton High School, Bristol, The Rose Bruford College of Speech and Drama, London.
QUALIFICATIONS: Rose Bruford College Diploma (RBC Dip).
MEMBERSHIPS: British Actors Equity, Directors Guild of G. B, Green Room Club, Players Theatre Club, Cyprus Actors Union.
HOBBIES AND INTERESTS: Cinema, travel and food.
PERSONAL PROFILE: Actor and Director. Member of Equity Council, Save London Theatres Campaign, International Campaign for Artists' Freedom. Has appeared on TV in Sunburn, Family, One Last Chance.

RONIS VARLAAM
Film Maker and Artist documentaries for Channel 4, including The Enthusiasts and Well You Didn't

DATE OF BIRTH: 07-May-1946
PLACE OF BIRTH: Nicosia.
MARITAL STATUS: Single.
SCHOOLS/COLLEGE: Terra Santa College Nicosia, London Film School.
HOBBIES AND INTERESTS: Photography, travel and reading.
PERSONAL PROFILE: Film Maker and Artist. Produced and directed a number of documentaries for Channel 4, including The Enthusiasts and Well You Didn't. Was also co-Director for Green Line, a documentary on Cyprus for Channel 4. Has exhibited work at the Alsager Gallery, Manchester Metropolitan University and various other galleries.

DR AMANDA VARNAVA
Consultant Cardiologist at St Marys Hospital Paddington

DATE OF BIRTH: 08-Jan-1965
PLACE OF BIRTH: Plymouth, UK, Father from Famagusta, Mother English.
MARITAL STATUS: Married to Anthony Turnbull, England, food and drinks editor of the Times.
SCHOOLS/COLLEGE: City of London Girls School, Oxford University and. St Bartholomew's Hospital.
QUALIFICATIONS: MA, MBBS, MRCP, MD.
HONOURS/AWARDS: Gold Medal, Finals, St Bartholomew's Hospital, MRC research grant.
HOBBIES AND INTERESTS: Former School Governor Notting Hill Prep School.
PERSONAL PROFILE: Consultant cardiologist, has established a regional service for patients with Inherited Cardiac Diseases at St Marys Hospital Paddington. International reputation in Inherited Cardiac Diseases with publications in leading medical journals and lectured at international meetings.

CHRISTAKIS KYRIACOS VARNAVIDES
General Medical Practitioner

DATE OF BIRTH: 09-Jul-1945
PLACE OF BIRTH: Nicosia.
MARITAL STATUS: Married to Andrea, Leeds, Nurse.
CHILDREN: Kyriacos, Police Officer. Charis, University Graduate.
SCHOOLS/COLLEGE: Leeds University.
QUALIFICATIONS: BSc (Hons) Physiology. M. B. ch. B. Dip Obst. RCOG. FRCGP.
MEMBERSHIPS: Fellow of the Royal College of General Practitioners.
HOBBIES AND INTERESTS: Photography, dermatology, plays Badminton (badly), also when the mood takes, writes poetry (also badly).
PERSONAL PROFILE: General Medical. Practitioner. Examiner for Membership of the Royal College of General Practitioners. Chairman of The Greek School, Leeds, Author of numerous Medical Papers.

ELLI VARNAVIDES
Organiser of Sothebys Auctions

DATE OF BIRTH: 21-May-1979
PLACE OF BIRTH: London, Grandparents from Paphos, Famagusta and Kato Drys.
MARITAL STATUS: Married to Andreas.
SCHOOLS/COLLEGE: Ucl and Columbia University (New York).
QUALIFICATIONS: BA MA.
HOBBIES AND INTERESTS: Travel, Visiting art galleries and exhibitions and Opera.
PERSONAL PROFILE: Works at Sotheby's London, a specialist in Contemporary and Modern Art, currently training to become an auctioneer Organises 6 auctions per year, Worked on high- profile single - owner sales such as The Collection of Jean Yves Mock and the collection of Gordon Watson.

LAMBROS KLEANTHIS VARNAVIDES
Managing Director of Shipping at the Royal Bank of Scotland

DATE OF BIRTH: 01-Jul-1949
PLACE OF BIRTH: London. Father, Professor Panayiotis, from Paphos; Mother, Despina, from Famagusta.
MARITAL STATUS: Married to Katie, London, (parents from Kato Drys).
CHILDREN: Elli. Art.
SCHOOLS/COLLEGE: Latymer Upper School, Hammersmith, University College London, London School of Economics.
QUALIFICATIONS: BSc & MSc in Economics, M. Phil.
HOBBIES AND INTERESTS: Opera, reading and travel.
PERSONAL PROFILE: Joined Williams & Glyns Bank in 1974 as a Shipping Analyst. Now Managing Director of Shipping at The Royal Bank of Scotland.

DR LYSANDROS VARNAVIDES
Researcher in Molecular Haemotology

DATE OF BIRTH: 14-Apr-1941
PLACE OF BIRTH: Neta.
MARITAL STATUS: Married to Eleni, Achna.
CHILDREN: Andreas, Alexia.
SCHOOLS/COLLEGE: Chiswick Polytechnic, Chelsea College, University College Hospital (London).
QUALIFICATIONS: BSc Chemistry and Physiology, MSc in Bio-chemistry, PhD in Bio-chemistry (London).
HOBBIES AND INTERESTS: Reading and Byzantine music.
PERSONAL PROFILE: Principal clinical scientist (prenatal diagnosis, Molecular Haemotology) at Kings College Hospital, London.

PHIL VASILI
BAFTA (Short film drama) 2006. Award

DATE OF BIRTH: 01-Jul-1956
PLACE OF BIRTH: London, grandfather- Marathovounos.
MARITAL STATUS: Single.
CHILDREN: Andrea, Fionoulla, Alexander, Louisa.
SCHOOLS/COLLEGE: Essex University, Cambridge University, Greenwich.
QUALIFICATIONS: BA Hons (Sociology), M. Phil (Criminology), PGCE (Further Education).
HONOURS/AWARDS: BAFTA (Short film drama) 2006 as the Executive Producer of the film Antonio's Breakfast, which tells the story of a young boy who cares for his disabled father.
HOBBIES AND INTERESTS: Football, writing, film, politics.
PERSONAL PROFILE: Writer, tutor, football coach and London Scout for Birmingham City FC.

UK

ANDREAS VASILIOU
Managing Director of Amathus (UK) Ltd and Business Development Director for the Aphrodite Hills Resort in Cyprus

DATE OF BIRTH: 25-Jan-1948
PLACE OF BIRTH: Saranti.
MARITAL STATUS: Married to Maria, Lemithou.
CHILDREN: Ifigenia, Sales. Andriani, Artist.
SCHOOLS/COLLEGE: Agros Apeitium Gymnasium.
QUALIFICATIONS: Fellow of Institute of Travel and Tourism.
MEMBERSHIPS: I. T. T. (Institute of Travel & Tourism).
HONOURS/AWARDS: Cyprus Tourism Organisation, November 2000.
HOBBIES AND INTERESTS: Golf and travelling.
PERSONAL PROFILE: Andreas Vasiliou is the Managing Director of Amathus (UK) Ltd and Business Development Director for the Aphrodite Hills Resort in Cyprus. Served as AGTA Chairman 1998-2002.

ANDRIANI VASILIOU
Artist

DATE OF BIRTH: 27-Jan-1982
PLACE OF BIRTH: London. Parents from Saranti and Lemithou.
MARITAL STATUS: Single.
QUALIFICATIONS: BA Honours Fine Art.
HOBBIES AND INTERESTS: Music and travelling.
PERSONAL PROFILE: Artist exhibited in Nicosia Cyprus, Gallery K, Central St Martins, and Vinopolis, London. In Nicosia, 2002, she exhibited her works at the Lions home, an organisation that cares and protects underprivileged and bereaved children in Cyprus. All profits from the sale of paintings were donated to this foundation.

MARIA VIGAR
Writer of Dramas for Radio 4 The Nets and Morning Story

PLACE OF BIRTH: Nicosia.
MARITAL STATUS: Married.
CHILDREN: Athos, James.
SCHOOLS/COLLEGE: The English School, Nicosia.
QUALIFICATIONS: MA Text & Performance -Kings College London. Cert in Education & Professional Training for the Theatre.
MEMBERSHIPS: Fellow RSA; Equity; Amnesty International.
PERSONAL PROFILE: Actress, Teacher, Drama Director (Radio/Theatre). Writer (Radio Drama; Stage Plays)The Nets and Morning Story for Radio Four. Community Development & Fundraising for local Hospice Care. Founder member of the Beckenham and West Wickham Amnesty International Group and now co-Chair.

ANTONIS G VIOLARIS
Consultant Cardiologist

DATE OF BIRTH: 30-Jan-1961
PLACE OF BIRTH: Father and Mother from Paphos.
MARITAL STATUS: Married.
CHILDREN: Three daughters.
SCHOOLS/COLLEGE: Stationers, Sheffield University, ERASMUS University Rotterdam, Netherlands.
QUALIFICATIONS: MB, ChB, MD, Phd, FRCP.
MEMBERSHIPS: Fellow of the Royal College of Physicians of London. Member of the British Cardiac Society.
HOBBIES AND INTERESTS: Work and family.
PERSONAL PROFILE: Consultant Cardiologist at North West London Hospitals. Written several books. Works at St Marys Hospital, Paddington.

UK

GLAFKOS P. VIOLARIS
Honorary President of Paphos Association in England. Secretary of St John the Baptist Greek Orthodox Church in Haringey

DATE OF BIRTH: 13-Sep-1934
PLACE OF BIRTH: Paphos.
MARITAL STATUS: Married to Maroulla, Paphos.
CHILDREN: Antonios, Cardiologist. Salome, Charity. Patroklos, Electronic Engineer. Katerine and Christodoulos, Both Optometrist.
SCHOOLS/COLLEGE: Gymnasium of Limassol, Teacher Training College, Morphou.
QUALIFICATIONS: BA.
MEMBERSHIPS: Folklore Society, England; Labour Party.
HONOURS/AWARDS: Notarios, Officio of Ecumenical Patriarchade.
HOBBIES AND INTERESTS: Folklore, history, journalism, reading, and writing books.
PERSONAL PROFILE: Worked as primary teacher in Cyprus. Member of the First Cyprus Education Mission 1969-1972, teacher at Stationers Company School. Honorary President of Paphos Association in England. Secretary of St John the Baptist Greek Orthodox Church in Haringey.

SIMON VITSAIDES
Appeared in the Live Finals of the UK's biggest TV Talent show the X-Factor in 2005

DATE OF BIRTH: 11-Jan-1983
PLACE OF BIRTH: Southampton Father from Marathovouno, Maternal Grandfather from Koma tou Yialou.
MARITAL STATUS: Single.
SCHOOLS/COLLEGE: Shirley Junior, Bellemoor Secondary. Tauntons College.
HONOURS/AWARDS: MTV Baselounge Winners.
HOBBIES AND INTERESTS: Singing, Gym, Cinema and eating out.
PERSONAL PROFILE: Simon is part of Vocal Group 4TUNE who appeared in the Live Finals of the UK's biggest TV Talent show the X-Factor in 2005. They toured Europe for two years currently recording their first Album. They have also worked with the Princes Trust. Helped raise money for several charities too including Childline and Breast Cancer.

MICHAEL CHRISTOS VOTSIS
Solicitor Partner in YVA Solicitors sponsors of the Cypriot Football League in the UK

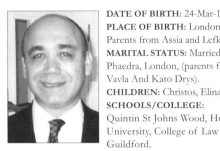

DATE OF BIRTH: 24-Mar-1951
PLACE OF BIRTH: London. Parents from Assia and Lefkara.
MARITAL STATUS: Married to Phaedra, London, (parents from Vavla And Kato Drys).
CHILDREN: Christos, Elina.
SCHOOLS/COLLEGE: Quintin St Johns Wood, Hull University, College of Law Guildford.
QUALIFICATIONS: LLB (Honours).
HOBBIES AND INTERESTS: Football (Chelsea Supporter).
PERSONAL PROFILE: Solicitor. Formed own practice in 1975 called Michael Votsis & Co. In 1995 merged with Yanakas to form YVA Solicitors.

ANTONAKIS NIKOLAS VOUROU
School Governor, Former Secretary of EKEKA and Komi Kebir Association

DATE OF BIRTH: 05-May-1955
PLACE OF BIRTH: London. Father from Rizokarpasso; Mother from Komi Kebir.
MARITAL STATUS: Married to Caroline, London, Local Government Officer.
CHILDREN: Panayiota, Nicolas.
SCHOOLS/COLLEGE: Wood Green School, Polytechnic of North London.
QUALIFICATIONS: HND.
HOBBIES AND INTERESTS: Flying and travelling. Art, photography, film, theatre, gardening and reading.
PERSONAL PROFILE: An Events Programmer and Co-ordinator. Governor of three schools. Involved with various charitable organisations. Former Secretary of Komi Kebir Association, and EKEKA Association.

UK

ELIZABETH (nee Louca) WHINCOP
Head Teacher Walker Primary School

DATE OF BIRTH: 23-Feb-1956
PLACE OF BIRTH: London
Parents from Khirokitia.
MARITAL STATUS: Married to
Simon, england, Teacher.
CHILDREN: Luke, School.
SCHOOLS/COLLEGE: Holy
Trinity Primary School and
Haverstock Secondary School.
QUALIFICATIONS: 4 GCSE A
levels, 8 GCE O levels 2CSEs.
Certificate of Education, Batchelor of Education.
HOBBIES AND INTERESTS: Art, Photography, Film,
Theatre, gardening and reading.
PERSONAL PROFILE: Worked as a primary school
teacher at Bowes and Galliard Schools for seven years.
Moved to Haringey to become an English advisory
teacher working in a range of schools across the
borough. Became a deputy head in 1988 at Holy trinity
School in Hampstead. First Head Teacher post was at
Christ Church CE School in Regents Park for 10 years
before taking up current post as the Head of walker
Primary School in Southgate in London January 2001.

RENOS EVRYVIADES WIDESON
Photographer/Retired Head of BBC Head of Film operations

DATE OF BIRTH: 12-Dec-1920
PLACE OF BIRTH: Larnaca.
MARITAL STATUS: Married to
Mary, Nicosia.
CHILDREN: Angelos Civil
Engineer, Architect. Odysseus,
Civil Engineer.
SCHOOLS/COLLEGE:
Pancyprian Commercial Lyceum,
Larnaca.
HOBBIES AND INTERESTS:
Photography, painting, woodwork, sailing, languages.
In younger days, football, tennis, swimming and water
skiing etc.
PERSONAL PROFILE: 1960-1977 retired as BBC TV's
Head of Film Operations. Publications: Cyprus in
Picture 1952, Portrait of Cyprus 1955, Cyprus, Images
of a Lifetime 1992. Photographic Exhibitions: Nicosia,
Larnaca, London, Copenhagen.

MONICA CONSTANTINOU WILLIAMS
Owner of Hellenic Book Shop specialising on Greece and Cyprus

DATE OF BIRTH: 29-Dec-1940
PLACE OF BIRTH: England,
Parents from Limassol and
Nicosia.
MARITAL STATUS: Married to
Fred Williams, Publisher.
CHILDREN: Alison Richards,
Andrew Stoddart.
SCHOOLS/COLLEGE:
Paddington and Maida Vale
Grammar School, City of
London Business School.
QUALIFICATIONS: Business Studies.
HOBBIES AND INTERESTS: Theatre, dance and travel.
PERSONAL PROFILE: Bookseller specialising on Greece
and Cyprus, 36 years, every aspect, huge range of books.

TOM WILLIAMS
Professional footballer currently plays for Wycombe Wanderers

DATE OF BIRTH: 08-Jul-1980
PLACE OF BIRTH: London,
Mother from Lefkoniko.
HONOURS/AWARDS: Cyprus
International Winner of the
PFA Fans Player of The Month
Award.
PERSONAL PROFILE: Tom
Williams began his professional
career with West Ham United
in April 2000 when he joined
the club from Walton and Hersham for a fee of £40,
000. He went on loan to Peterborough United in march
2001 without having made a senior debut the move
was made permanent in the summer, he then moved to
Birmingham City for £350, 000 he made four first team
appearances has since played for QPR, Peterborough
again, Barnsley, Gillingham, Swansea City Wycombe
Wanderers. Now back at Peterborough.

UK

NINA WILLS
Headteacher Stag Lane First School
Harrow

DATE OF BIRTH: 01-Oct-1964
PLACE OF BIRTH: Eptakomi.
MARITAL STATUS: Married to
John Will, British, Social Worker.
CHILDREN: Maria.
SCHOOLS/COLLEGE: Copthall
Secondary School. Roehampton
Institute of Higher Education.
QUALIFICATIONS: B. Ed
NPQH.
PERSONAL PROFILE: Nina
has been a teacher since 1988 working in primary schools
in areas of high social deprivation. She has worked as
part of management teams transforming schools with
serious weaknesses into very good schools. She is now
Head Teacher of Stag Lane First School Harrow.

DR CHRYSOULA KYPRIANOU WORRALL
Psychologist/Psychoanalyst

DATE OF BIRTH: 01-Oct-1939
PLACE OF BIRTH: Karavas.
MARITAL STATUS: Single.
CHILDREN: Adrian, Psychologist.
Alexis, Multi Media Artist.
QUALIFICATIONS: BA. MA.
PhD.
MEMBERSHIPS: British
Psychologist Society, UKCP-
United Kingdom Council of
Psychotherapy.
HOBBIES AND INTERESTS: Arts, travel, trekking and
walking.
PERSONAL PROFILE: Former Lecturer in Educational
Psychology at Hertfordshire University. Works privately
as a Counselling Psychologist and Psychoanalyst.

LITSA WORRALL
Chief Executive for the Greek and Greek
Cypriot Community of Enfield

DATE OF BIRTH: 10-Aug-1955
PLACE OF BIRTH: Achna.
MARITAL STATUS: Married to
Martin, England. Civil Servant.
CHILDREN: Stephanie, School.
QUALIFICATIONS: City &
Guilds NVQ level 1 & IIT.
HOBBIES AND INTERESTS:
Drama, local theatre, painting.
PERSONAL PROFILE: Litsa
is a co founder member of
the Greek and Greek Cypriot Community of Enfield
assisting the Greek speaking community with homecare,
counselling, information, advice and social activities.

CLEO NICOLAIDOU WRIGHT
Management Consultant and University
Lecturer

DATE OF BIRTH: 28-Jan-1962
PLACE OF BIRTH: Limassol.
MARITAL STATUS: Married
to Dr Jim Wright, England,
Enviroment.
SCHOOLS/COLLEGE: 1st
Gymnasium, Limassol, The
American College in Athens,
Greece, San Francisco State
University, USA and Henley
Management School, UK.
QUALIFICATIONS: BA, MA, MBA.
MEMBERSHIPS: Membership of the Association
of MBAs (AMBA); Referee for SYSTEM (Swedish
Technology & Education Journal);.
HOBBIES AND INTERESTS: Long distance running,
cross-country cycling, travelling and playing bridge.
PERSONAL PROFILE: Worked in universities for twelve
years as a Lecturer (Kuwait University), Senior Trainer
(Exeter University,) and Operations Manager (University
of Surrey). More recently has worked as a management
consultant and interim manager mainly within the Public
Sector in the UK.

UK

Entrants in Greek Cypriots Worldwide have been nominated for their
achievements and contributions.
It is free to nominate someone, or yourself, who deserves to be in the book, just
send in the name, contact address, telephone number and email to:
Greek Cypriots Worldwide
111 St Thomas's Road London N4 2QJ
Telephone 0044 207503 3498
cypriotwhoswho@aol.com
www.greekcypriotsworldwide.com

GEORGE WRIGHT
Reporter

DATE OF BIRTH: 15-Feb-1974.
PLACE OF BIRTH: London. Grandparent from Famagusta.
MARITAL STATUS: Single.
SCHOOLS/COLLEGE: Davenant Foundation School, Essex, Royal Holloway College, (London University).
QUALIFICATIONS: A Levels, Degree in Classical Studies. Journalism Diploma.
HOBBIES AND INTERESTS: Jazz and world music.
PERSONAL PROFILE: Reporter, London Evening Standard.

ALEXANDROS NICHOLAS XENOFONTOS
Composer of the theme music for the Film My Big Fat Greek Wedding

DATE OF BIRTH: 03-Oct-1974
PLACE OF BIRTH: London. Father from Ayia Varvara (Lefkosia); Mother from Akanthou.
MARITAL STATUS: Single.
SCHOOLS/COLLEGE: City Polytechnic, London Guildhall University, Newham Academy of Music.
QUALIFICATIONS: BA.
MEMBERSHIPS: PRS/MCPS, PPL.
HOBBIES AND INTERESTS: Sea fishing, shooting and athletics.
PERSONAL PROFILE: Composer, musician. Set up own record label, Feelgood Records 2000, releasing primarily his own Dance Music, debut release I Can Make You having commercial radio play on Mainstream Radio Stations. Wrote theme and other music for Hollywood Film My Big Fat Greek Wedding.

ELEFTHERIA A XENOPHONTOS
Chairwoman of Neo Chorio Committee UK

DATE OF BIRTH: 15-Feb-1956
PLACE OF BIRTH: Neo Chorio, Paphos.
MARITAL STATUS: Married to Andreas, Nicosia, Business.
CHILDREN: Xenia.
SCHOOLS/COLLEGE: Paddington College, North London College, Stanmore College, Greek Educational Institute of GB, Open University. Paddington College, North London College, Stanmore College, Greek Educational Institute of GB, Open University.
QUALIFICATIONS: HND Business Studies, Diploma in teaching Greek as a foreign language, BA (Honours).
MEMBERSHIPS: Royal Academy of Art.
HOBBIES AND INTERESTS: Visiting museums and galleries, drama, theatre, music, reading and sports such as badminton and swimming.
PERSONAL PROFILE: Chair of Neo Chorio committee. The Association has funded the opening of a health care clinic for the elderly in the Village.

MARINA YANNAKOUDAKIS
Conservative Member of the European Parliament, London Region

DATE OF BIRTH: 16-Apr-1956
PLACE OF BIRTH: Parents from Nicosia and Rizokarpasso.
MARITAL STATUS: Married to Zacharias, Company Director.
CHILDREN: Stephanie, Chartered Accountant. Basil, Student. Lefteris, Student.
SCHOOLS/COLLEGE: Beckenham Convent. Brunel University and open University.
QUALIFICATIONS: BSc (Hons) Government, Politics and Modern History. MA Education.
HOBBIES AND INTERESTS: Family, Local History, Sculpture.
PERSONAL PROFILE: Marina Yannakoudakis is a Councillor in the London Borough of Barnet. In June 2009 she became a Conservative MEP.

NICOS YENIAS
Chairman of Marathovounos Association

DATE OF BIRTH: 10-Mar-1948
PLACE OF BIRTH: Marathovounos.
MARITAL STATUS: Married to Agapi, Kaimakli.
CHILDREN: Olga, lives in Russia.
SCHOOLS/COLLEGE: Marathovouno Elementary, Lykeion Famagusta. AKEL.
HOBBIES AND INTERESTS: Sports and politics.
PERSONAL PROFILE: Car Mechanic/Panel Beater. Went to Moscow 1971-1973 studying Social Science. Went back to Cyprus 1973 then to England 1975. Chairman of Marathovouno Association, member of Secretariat AKEL UK. Member of EKO and National Federation of Cypriots.

ANTONAKIS YEROLEMOU
Chairman Radio Marathon Committee UK/Co Founder of Katsouris Fresh Foods and Cypressa

DATE OF BIRTH: 13-Jul-1942
PLACE OF BIRTH: Komi Kebir.
MARITAL STATUS: Married to Barbara, the Mayor of Ealing.
MEMBERSHIPS: Chairman Radio Marathon Committee UK. Member of Greek Cypriot Brotherhood, Komi Kebir Association. Greek Orthodox Archbishop Trust, the Hellenic Centre, and Cyprus British Chamber of Commerce.
HOBBIES AND INTERESTS: Music, reading and travelling.
PERSONAL PROFILE: Joined Family business Katsouris Bros in 1964 transforming them into successful specialist importers of Cypriot and Greek products in the UK. this was due to the creation of the Cypressa brand. Together with his family they opened the Wine and Mousaka Restaurants and then Katsouris Foods. Today Katsouris Fresh Foods Ltd employs more than 1600 people and are successful independent chilled food manufacturers. Its client base includes Marks and Spencer, Sainsburys, Tesco, Waitrose, Morrisons and Somerfields. They formed Filo Pastry Ltd the biggest Filo Producer in the UK. Also took control of Sahib Foods ethnic chilled food supplier to the multiples. Katsouris Fresh foods has since merged with Bakkavor Group Iceland.

MILTOS YEROLEMOU
Actor Mikey in BBC TV Comedy Hubbub

DATE OF BIRTH: 24-Jan-1968
PLACE OF BIRTH: London. Parents from Ayios Theodoros, Larnaca.
MARITAL STATUS: Single.
SCHOOLS/COLLEGE: Eastbourne Sixth Form College. De Montfort University, Leicester.
QUALIFICATIONS: BA Honours degree.
MEMBERSHIPS: Equity, Screenwriters Guild.
HONOURS/AWARDS: 1985, Eastbourne Herald Award for Best Actor Nicely Nicely Johnson, Guys and Dolls. 1986, Eastbourne Herald Award for Best Actor in Bottom In, Midsummer Nights Dream 1996, Manchester Evening Standard Nomination for Supporting Actor in Animal Crackers.
PERSONAL PROFILE: Actor/Director. Founder member/performer in Might and Main Theatre Company 1991-1996, Royal Shakespeare Theatre 1998-2000, Mikey in BBC TV Comedy Hubbub 1996-2001.

GEORGE YEROSIMOU
Assistant Headteacher at St Johns in Epping

DATE OF BIRTH: 21-Aug-1955
PLACE OF BIRTH: London. Grandparents from Akanthou.
MARITAL STATUS: Married to Loulla, from London (father from Akanthou, mother from Mandres).
CHILDREN: Michael, Recruitment. Elizabeth, Nurse. Matthew, School.
SCHOOLS/COLLEGE: St Clement Danes Grammar School, Borough Road College, University of London, The Open University, The Institute of Education.
QUALIFICATIONS: BA, MA, NPQH, Cert Ed.
MEMBERSHIPS: Naht-National Association of Head Teachers.
PERSONAL PROFILE: Deputy Headteacher at a comprehensive school in Epping. Class I Football Referee. Has refereed in KOPA for 20 years. Played for DOEK, Atlas & Cosmos. Chairman/School Co-ordinator of Caterham Greek School for ten years. Chairman/Secretary of Redbridge Greek Community Association.

PANAYIOTIS YIACOUMI
Chairman of the Greek Parents Association. Secretary of the Cypriot Diaspora Committee

DATE OF BIRTH: 02-Feb-1952
PLACE OF BIRTH: Gypsos.
MARITAL STATUS: Married to Yianoulla, (parents from Ayios Amvrossio and Prodromi).
CHILDREN: Eva, Kyriacos, Lia.
SCHOOLS/COLLEGE: Gypsou Primary, Centre of Higher Studies in Famagusta, Harrow College of Further Eduacation, City University, Open University.
QUALIFICATIONS: 9 O Levels, 4 A Levels, Honours degree in Economics & Political Science.
HOBBIES AND INTERESTS: Family, reading, politics, history, music, travel and sports.
PERSONAL PROFILE: General Secretary of Gypsos Association. Member and Chairman of Greek Parents Association. Magistrate in the Middlesex commission area, adjudicating at Uxbridge Magistrates Court and Isleworth Crown Court. Secretary of the Cypriot Diaspora Committee UK.

UK

ANTONIS YIAKOUMI

Former Chairman of the Greek Parents Association and General Manager of Parikiaki Newspaper. Also Co Founder of the Cyprus Wine Festival UK

DATE OF BIRTH: 07-Aug-1924
PLACE OF BIRTH: Vasili, Leonarisso.
MARITAL STATUS: Married to Maria Tsioupra, Komi Kebir.
CHILDREN: Michael, Editor of Greek Cypriots Worldwide. Doulla, Chair of Bowes Greek School. Louis, Editor of Motor Magazines.
SCHOOLS/COLLEGE: Elementary School Vasilli. AKEL.
HONOURS/AWARDS: Honoured for 50 years service to AKEL.
HOBBIES AND INTERESTS: Reading, politics and football.
PERSONAL PROFILE: Shoemaker in Famagusta. Served in British Army 1943-45. Came to UK in 1952. Was a restaurant owner then manager of Parikiaki newspaper from 1977 to 1990. Ex-Chairman of the Greek Parents Association and in the Secretariat of AKEL UK for several years. Also Co Founder of the Cyprus Wine Festival UK.

LOUIS YIAKOUMI

Publisher of Automotive Logistics Magazine

DATE OF BIRTH: 04-Aug-1962
PLACE OF BIRTH: London Father from Vasili, Leonarisso Mother from Komi Kebir.
MARITAL STATUS: Married to Andry, London Father from Yialoussa mother from Leonarisso, Classroom Assistant at Osidge School.
CHILDREN: Antony, Studying at Nottingham University. Pedro, School. Katerina, School.
SCHOOLS/COLLEGE: Ambler School and Highbury Grove School.
HOBBIES AND INTERESTS: Football and Reading.
PERSONAL PROFILE: Louis Yiakoumi is the Publisher of Automotive Logistics Magazine and a committee member of Leonarisso/Vasili and Suburbs Association.

MARIA YIAKOUMI

Sub Editor of the Greek Rich List and Researcher of the book Greek Cypriots Worldwide

DATE OF BIRTH: 22-Oct-1986
PLACE OF BIRTH: London, Grandparents from Vasili, Leonarisso/Komi Kebir and Ayios Athanasios Limassol.
MARITAL STATUS: Single.
SCHOOLS/COLLEGE: Southgate School, Sylvia Young Theatre School. Form Southgate School Sixth Form College and University of Hertfordshire.
QUALIFICATIONS: BA (Hons) Philosophy. Guildhall School of Music and Drama, speech and Drama Exams
HOBBIES AND INTERESTS: Drama, Fashion, research, making jewellery and handmade cards.
PERSONAL PROFILE: Sub-editor for the Greek Rich list and a Researcher and sub editor for the book Greek Cypriots Worldwide. Was a researcher and logger at ITN Factual. Raised money for charity by taking part in Cancer Research's race for life.

MICHAEL YIAKOUMI

Compiler of the book Greek Cypriots Worldwide

DATE OF BIRTH: 08-Aug-1955
PLACE OF BIRTH: London. Father, Antonis, from Vasilli, Leonarisso; Mother, Maria (née Tsioupra) from Komi Kebir.
MARITAL STATUS: Single.
CHILDREN: Maria, University Graduate BA (Hons) in Philosophy. Dimitri, Publishing.
SCHOOLS/COLLEGE: Ambler Primary, Holloway Secondary. Tottenham College.
QUALIFICATIONS: 9 O Levels and 1 A Level. Football Association Level 1 Coach.
HOBBIES AND INTERESTS: Football and travel, extensively travelled around the World in one year to complete the Greek Cypriot Who's Who Worldwide visited USA, Asia, Australia, Africa and Europe.
PERSONAL PROFILE: Compiler of the books Greek Cypriots in the UK and Greek Cypriot's Worldwide. Also Co Publisher of the Greek Rich List. From college he worked in a L'Loyd's insurance underwriting syndicate, then for the advertising section of the Parikiaki newspaper. He has also owned a Ladieswear business, manufacturing, wholesale and retail. Co founder of PAOK and Komi Kebir football club that play in the Cypriot League in the UK. He was a member of the

Parent Teachers Committee's at Southgate Greek School and Trent Primary School in Barnet.

CONSTANTINOS YIANGOU
Consultant in General Surgery and Surgical Oncology

DATE OF BIRTH: 28-Aug-1961
PLACE OF BIRTH: Nicosia.
SCHOOLS/COLLEGE: Pancyprian Gymnasium, Nicosia. St Mary's Hospital Medical School, University of London.
QUALIFICATIONS: BSC (Honours), MB, BS (Honours). FRCS, FRCS (Gen Surg).
MEMBERSHIPS: The British Medical Association.
HONOURS/AWARDS: Norman Plummer Memorial Prize Award by Charing Cross Hospital in March 1995. Ronald Payen Prize awarded by the British Association of Surgical Oncology in November 1995. Named in the list of leading experts in the field of Breast Cancer, by The Times.
HOBBIES AND INTERESTS: Music, motor racing and the history of Cyprus in the 20th Century.
PERSONAL PROFILE: Consultant at Queen Alexandra & Bupa Hospitals Portsmouth. Honorary Senior Lecturer Academic Department & Surgery, Ports-mouth Uni. Research interests are diagnosis and treatment of Breast and thyroid cancers.

CHRISTOPHER YIANNAKAS
Solicitor also a committee member of the Cypriot Football League in the UK

DATE OF BIRTH: 30-Apr-1963
PLACE OF BIRTH: London. Parents from Kilani and Lefkara.
MARITAL STATUS: Married to Xenia.
SCHOOLS/COLLEGE: Friern Barnet Grammar, Highgate School, Middlesex University.
QUALIFICATIONS: 12 O Levels, 3 A Levels, LLB Honours Law. Solicitor.
MEMBERSHIPS: Law Society and Solicitors Family Law Association.
HONOURS/AWARDS: Accredited specialist in Family Law with the Law Society Family Law Panel and resolution.
HOBBIES AND INTERESTS: Football, squash, world war II history.
PERSONAL PROFILE: Chris Yannakas regularly advises at the CAB at the High Court, Family Division and the CAB in Haringey. He is also a committee member of the Cypriot Football League in the UK.

PAUL YIANNAKAS
Solicitor Former Chairman and Secretary of the Cypriot Football League in London

DATE OF BIRTH: 12-Jan-1937
PLACE OF BIRTH: Kilani.
MARITAL STATUS: Married to Maria, London parents from Lefkara.
CHILDREN: Chris, Solicitor. Katerina, Housewife.
SCHOOLS/COLLEGE: Limassol Gymnasium, Bradford College, Law Society School.
HOBBIES AND INTERESTS: Football, Byzantine music church chanter.
PERSONAL PROFILE: Solicitor at one of the first practices in the Cypriot community. Former Chairman and Secretary of the Cypriot Football League in London. Served the Football League for 26 years. Acting Chairman and treasurer of School of Byzantine music. Chairman of Kilani Association. Trustee and Committee member of Holy Cross of St Michael in the Goldens Green Church. Chairman of Islington Cypriot Community Centre.

SOF YIANNAKAS
Fixture Secretary of the KOPA League and Club Secretary of AC Varosi

DATE OF BIRTH: 23-Dec-1986
PLACE OF BIRTH: London, parents from limassol.
MARITAL STATUS: Single.
SCHOOLS/COLLEGE: The Latymer School, the London School of Economics.
QUALIFICATIONS: BSc Accounting and Finance.
HOBBIES AND INTERESTS: Enjoy reading novels and journals, drawing, playing football and travelling.
PERSONAL PROFILE: Having studied Accounting and Finance at the LSE he will be joining Deutsche Bank in 2008 in the Global Banking Division. Currently, Fixture Secretary of the KOPA League and Club Secretary of AC Varosi.

UK

FATHER ANASTASIOS YIANNI
Priest at the Gospel Oak Greek
Orthodox Church

DATE OF BIRTH: 14-Dec-1929
PLACE OF BIRTH: Troullous,
Larnaca.
MARITAL STATUS: Married to
Angela, Limassol.
CHILDREN: One daughter.
SCHOOLS/COLLEGE:
Troullous Elementary, Cotwins
College, London.
HOBBIES AND INTERESTS:
Reading.
PERSONAL PROFILE: Father Anastasios is the Priest at
the Gospel Oak Greek Orthodox Church.

LEON YIANNI
Actor appeared on TV in The Bill and
October. Stage: A Song at Twilight, The
Kitchen

DATE OF BIRTH: 15-Jan-1965
PLACE OF BIRTH: London.
Father from Arsos; Mother from
Limassol.
MARITAL STATUS: Single.
SCHOOLS/COLLEGE:
Islington Green School, Drama
Centre.
QUALIFICATIONS: Diploma
in Acting.
MEMBERSHIPS: Member of
Green Peace and Amnesty International.
HOBBIES AND INTERESTS: Reading and gardening.
PERSONAL PROFILE: Actor appeared on TV in The
Bill and October. Stage: A Song at Twilight, The Kitchen.

SIMEOS DIMITRIOS YIANNIKARIS
Attended the Queen's garden party
in 2004 in recognition for children's
charity work

DATE OF BIRTH: 19-Apr-1962
PLACE OF BIRTH: London.
Parents from Limassol.
MARITAL STATUS: Married
to Maria Nicolaides, London
Parents from Cyprus, Bridal
designer.
CHILDREN: Andreas Simeos,
Natassa Georgina.
SCHOOLS/COLLEGE:
Southgate College.
QUALIFICATIONS: PCO Knowledge of London.

HONOURS/AWARDS: Probably the 1st Greek Cypriot
to take part in the Lord Mayors Show, representing the
Charity in 1997 and 2008. Attended the Queen's garden
party in 2004 in recognition for children's charity work.
HOBBIES AND INTERESTS: Reading, travel, sci-fi film,
and charity.
PERSONAL PROFILE: Committee member and
treasurer of The London Taxi Drivers Fund for Underprivileged Children.

MARIA YIANNIKARIS (nee NICOLAIDES)
Award Winning Bridal Designer

DATE OF BIRTH: 15-Oct-1957
PLACE OF BIRTH: UK, Father
from Nicosia, Mother from
Yerolakos.
MARITAL STATUS: Married to
Simeos Dimitrios Yiannikaris,
London Tax Driver.
CHILDREN: Andrea Simeos,
Natassa Georgina.
SCHOOLS/COLLEGE:
Alexandra Park School.
University of the Arts London.
HONOURS/AWARDS: Three times winner at British
Bridal Awards.
HOBBIES AND INTERESTS: Travel, reading, writing,
cinema and film.
PERSONAL PROFILE: Professional Designer since 1979
established specialist bridal co Mirror Mirror Couture in
1989 with partner Jane Freshwater. Continues to dress
celebrity clientele. Is regularly asked to contribute to
bridal articles in the press and specialist publications.

NICHOLAS YIANNOULOU
Chairman Eptakomi Association.

DATE OF BIRTH: 27-Jul-1958
PLACE OF BIRTH: Born in
London parents from Eptakomi
MARITAL STATUS: Married
Helen
CHILDREN: 3 Children
SCHOOLS/COLLEGE: Hackney
Free and Parochial School.
HOBBIES AND INTERESTS:
Chess Football
PERSONAL PROFILE:
Chairman Eptakomi Association

ANDREAS YIASOUMI
President of Hellenic Brotherhood in Manchester

DATE OF BIRTH: 12-Jun-1947
PLACE OF BIRTH: Peristeronopiyi.
MARITAL STATUS: Married to Elene Photiou from Peristeronopiyi.
CHILDREN: Costas, Actuary. Thomas, Chartered Accountant.
SCHOOLS/COLLEGE: Grammar School of Lefkonico, Famagusta.
MEMBERSHIPS: Hellenic Brotherhood Manchester.
HOBBIES AND INTERESTS: Gardening, Football, Game Shooting.
PERSONAL PROFILE: President of Hellenic Brotherhood for 8 years, also a trustee. Restaurant Owner and Property Developer.

GEORGE YIASOUMI
Actor Appeared in films such as Swept Away, The Man Who Cried, The Borrowers, Greystoke

DATE OF BIRTH: 19-Apr-1959
PLACE OF BIRTH: London, parents from Achna, Famagusta.
MARITAL STATUS: Married.
SCHOOLS/COLLEGE: Local Comprehensive, E. 15 Acting School.
HOBBIES AND INTERESTS: Photography.
PERSONAL PROFILE: Actor. TV, Sam Game, Lock Stock, Indiana Jones Chronicles, The Bill and others. Theatre: Vanitas Splendide and others. TV commercials: Daewoo, Pizza Hut, Nike, Twix and others.

OURANIOS ANDREAS YIASOUMIS
Owner of Higrade Computers, manufacturers of PCs

DATE OF BIRTH: 12-Mar-1961
PLACE OF BIRTH: Nicosia.
MARITAL STATUS: Married to Dali, Russia.
CHILDREN: Marios, Nicholas.
SCHOOLS/COLLEGE: University of Westminster.
QUALIFICATIONS: BSc Computer Science.
HOBBIES AND INTERESTS: Football, supports Liverpool but has a box at Tottenham.
PERSONAL PROFILE: Owner of Higrade Computers, manufacturers of PCs in Barking, Essex. employs over 200 people.

GREGORY ZACHARIA
Former Chairman, Cypriot Estia

DATE OF BIRTH: 10-Oct-1943
PLACE OF BIRTH: Aradippou.
MARITAL STATUS: Married to Maritsa, Aradippou.
CHILDREN: Three sons, two daughters.
HOBBIES AND INTERESTS: Traditional music and pillotta.
PERSONAL PROFILE: Owns a Fish and Chip Shop business. Chairman of Cypriot Estia for two years and a member. Chairman of St Triada Greek School in Birmingham. Member of the Secretariat of the National Federation of Cypriots in the UK. Representative of the Aradippou Association in the Midlands. DYSY representative of the Midlands and Member of the local Education Authority in Staffordshire.

JULIE ZACHARIA
Author Traditional Greek Cooking from Cyprus and Beyond

DATE OF BIRTH: 06-Dec-1947
PLACE OF BIRTH: Vokolida.
MARITAL STATUS: Married to George, Eptakomi.
CHILDREN: Peter, Chrysanthos, Andreas, Pamela.
HOBBIES AND INTERESTS: Cooking and swimming.
PERSONAL PROFILE: Julie is a Housewife but wrote the book Traditional Greek Cooking from Cyprus and Beyond.

UK

TASOS ZACHARIADES
News Editor London Greek Radio

DATE OF BIRTH: 06-May-1945
PLACE OF BIRTH: Morphou.
MARITAL STATUS: Married to Sophia, Famagusta.
SCHOOLS/COLLEGE: Cyprus Secondary School, College of Journalism, London.
MEMBERSHIPS: National Union Of Journalists, served as President of Enosis Apodimon Morphou.
HOBBIES AND INTERESTS: Theatre, reading and travel.
PERSONAL PROFILE: Journalist, News Editor London Greek Radio, London Correspondent Cyprus Weekly Newspaper.

CHRISTOS ZAVROS
Journalist & Writer

DATE OF BIRTH: 01-Apr-1925
PLACE OF BIRTH: Tseri.
MARITAL STATUS: Married to Maria, Cyprus, Housewife.
CHILDREN: Nicos, Shoe Machinist. Erini, works for Bank Of Cyprus. Lakis, Computers in Australia. Helen, Teacher.
SCHOOLS/COLLEGE: School in Tseri, Nicosia.
QUALIFICATIONS: Journalist.
MEMBERSHIPS: AKEL, EKA, LELA.
HONOURS/AWARDS: From AKEL 50 years membership, from Trade Union of Printers in Cyprus, 40 years membership from National Federation of Cypriots in Britain and from LELA.
HOBBIES AND INTERESTS: Politics.
PERSONAL PROFILE: Journalist with Parikiaki newspaper. Has written seven books. Former Secretary of AKEL UK.

AFXENDIS DEMETRI ZEMENIDES
Chartered Engineer served as Governor for Portsmouth Polytechnic

DATE OF BIRTH: 26-Feb-1930
PLACE OF BIRTH: Komi Kebir.
MARITAL STATUS: Married to Josephine, London.
CHILDREN: Debora, Christopher, Both solicitors.
SCHOOLS/COLLEGE: Northampton Engineering College.
QUALIFICATIONS: B. Sc (Engineering). Chartered Engineer.
HOBBIES AND INTERESTS: Travel, family and photography.
PERSONAL PROFILE: Sealectro Ltd 1961-1990, started as General Manager and became Director (1963), Managing Director (1980-1990). Started Portsmouth Engineering Training Association (now PETA Ltd) in 1969 and served as Governor for some years for Highbury Technical College (Portsmouth), then Portsmouth Polytechnic till retirement in 1990. Trustee for New Theatre Royal, Portsmouth for six years.

DEMETRIOS COSTA ZEMENIDES
Served as Vice Chairman of the Cypriot Estia of London/Accountant

DATE OF BIRTH: 08-Jun-1951
PLACE OF BIRTH: Nicosia, Parents born and lived in Komi Kebir.
MARITAL STATUS: Married to Lenia, Oikos Marathasa, Holds degrees in Industrial Chemistry, History and European Humanities.
CHILDREN: Sophie, Doctor. Michael, Doctor.
SCHOOLS/COLLEGE: Komi Kebir Elementary School, Famagusta Technical School. London School of Accountancy, Kings College, London and South Bank University.
QUALIFICATIONS: Chartered Certified Accountant.
MEMBERSHIPS: Chartered Management Institute. Associate Member of the Royal College of Medicine
HOBBIES AND INTERESTS: Travel, poetry, painting. shooting and scuba diving.
PERSONAL PROFILE: Demetrios completed the accountancy exams in minimum possible time of two and a half years while working with Goodman Lawrence & Co which he became a partner now principal. Holds several Directorships in the UK and Cyprus. Served as Vice Chairman of the Cypriot Estia of London and committee member of the Cypriot Brotherhood and the National Federation of Cypriots in the UK. Demetrios is a master Clinical Hynotherapist/Psychotherapist and a master scuba diving instructor.

MICHAEL ZEMENIDES
Doctor Senior House Officer (Surgery)
Luton and Dunstable General Hospital

DATE OF BIRTH: 18-Jun-1980
PLACE OF BIRTH: London
Father from Nicosia grew up
in Komi Kebir, Mother from
Nicosia.
MARITAL STATUS: Single.
SCHOOLS/COLLEGE: St
Mary's Convent, Lyndhurst
School, St Paul's School.
University College/Medical
School London.
QUALIFICATIONS: BSc (Hons) in Clinical Immunology
MB BS (London).
HOBBIES AND INTERESTS: Basket Ball (trained
coach), Football, Scuba Diving and travelling.
PERSONAL PROFILE: Michael Zemenides is a Doctor
Senior House Officer (Surgery) Luton and Dunstable
General Hospital.

PANICOS ZEMENIDES
Chairman of Komi Kebir Association

DATE OF BIRTH: 04-Apr-1959
PLACE OF BIRTH: Komi
Kebir.
MARITAL STATUS: Married
to Helen, London, Father
from Kalopsida Mother from
Rizokarpasso, accountant.
CHILDREN: Andrea, Angela,
Both studying law at Cambridge
University.
SCHOOLS/COLLEGE: St
Davids and St Katherine School, Hornsey; University of
North London, London School of Accountancy.
QUALIFICATIONS: Chartered Certified Accountant.
HOBBIES AND INTERESTS: Squash and reading.
PERSONAL PROFILE: An Accountant - worked in
practice for 27 years. Now has own practice OMG
Chartered Certified Accountants based in Woodford
London E18. Chairman of Komi Kebir Association. On
parents committee of Finchley Greek School for five
years, Treasurer for two years, Vice Chairman for two
years.

SOPHIE ZEMENIDES
Doctor has a post as an Academic
Clinical Fellow in Clinical Immunology
at Oxford University

DATE OF BIRTH: 27-Jun-1979
PLACE OF BIRTH: London
Father from Nicosia grew up in
Komi Kebir Mother from Nicosia.
MARITAL STATUS: Single.
SCHOOLS/COLLEGE: St
Marys Convent and Channing
School. University College of
London and Oxford University.
QUALIFICATIONS: BSc (Hons)
in Tumour Biology MB BS
(London), MSc(Clinical Immunology). MRCP(England).
Diploma in Law and Medical Ethics (Edinburgh).
MEMBERSHIPS: Member of the Royal College of
Physicians.
HOBBIES AND INTERESTS: Rowing, Fencing, Scuba
Diving, Flying and Travelling.
PERSONAL PROFILE: Sophie Zemenides is a Academic
Clinical Fellow in Clinical Immunology at Oxford
University. Carried out research in cancer (Imperial College,
Eastman Dental College and Mount Vernon Cancer
Centre) and Heart and Lung Transplantation (Harefield
Hospital); carried out several Audits (Watford General,
Barnet General, Mount Vernon Cancer Centre and
Harefield Heart and Lung Transplantation Hospital). Has
several publications and presented at international level.

ANTHONY ZENIOS
Director CIL International Ltd

DATE OF BIRTH: 11-Oct-1942
PLACE OF BIRTH: London.
Father born in Kontea.
MARITAL STATUS: Married to
Ray Rachel Zenios, Alexandria,
Egypt, Independent Financial
Advisor.
CHILDREN: Jonathan David
Zenios, MD at Barclay Capital.
Natalie Desiree Zenios,
Housewife.
SCHOOLS/COLLEGE: Ambler Primary 1950-1954,
William Ellis 1954-1961, London School of Economics
1961-1964.
QUALIFICATIONS: BSc (Econs).
MEMBERSHIPS: British Philatelic Federation, Jaguar
Drivers Club.
HOBBIES AND INTERESTS: Bridge, philately, wine,
football, food, literature and music.
PERSONAL PROFILE: Company Director, City
Industrial Ltd, CIL International Ltd, CIL involved in
major charitable works via The Morris Charitable Trust.

UK

PANAYIOTIS ZENIOU
British Decathlon Champion

DATE OF BIRTH: 07-Feb-1953
PLACE OF BIRTH: Ormidia, Larnaca.
MARITAL STATUS: Married.
CHILDREN: Mixed race children. His son's (Adam) Godfather is, Daley Thompson.
SCHOOLS/COLLEGE: Archway Secondary, Kings Way F. E, North London University.
QUALIFICATIONS: Certificate in Education. Sports Coaching Qualification in ten sports.
MEMBERSHIPS: Life Member of NL Athletes Club.
HONOURS/AWARDS: Islington Sportsman of the Year.
HOBBIES AND INTERESTS: My children.
PERSONAL PROFILE: Lecturer at the College of N. E London. Great Britain Junior International, 1972, Great Britain Senior International, 1984. Vets International 1993-1996 European Bronze medallist (Decathlon). Captain of Great Britain European Cup 1977. British International in two sports, decathlon and bobsleigh. Competed for Cyprus 1978 & 1982 Commonwealth Games. Held record for GB appearances in Decathlon (25). British Decathlon Champion 1975, 1977, second on three occasions. Competed for Great Britain from 1972-1996 provided the Athletics Tournament for EKON.

ALEXANDROS ZENON
High Commissioner for the Republic of Cyprus in the UK

DATE OF BIRTH: 28-Jan-1953
PLACE OF BIRTH: Limassol.
MARITAL STATUS: Married to Aliki Pascali.
CHILDREN: One Daughter from previous marriage.
SCHOOLS/COLLEGE: Larnaca Lyceum. Athens University, Sorbonne University.
QUALIFICATIONS: Degree in Law and Diploma of the International Institute of Public Administration. Paris.
HOBBIES AND INTERESTS: Cycling, photography and reading.
PERSONAL PROFILE: Has held several positions most recent have been Ambassador to The Netherlands also to Italy, Switzerland, Malta and San Marino. He was Permanent Secretary, Ministry of Foreign Affairs, Nicosia. Presently.
High Commissioner for the Republic of Cyprus in the UK.

DR GEORGE M. ZINTILIS
Chartered Civil & Mechanical Engineer

DATE OF BIRTH: 28-Sep-1952
PLACE OF BIRTH: Nicosia.
MARITAL STATUS: Married to Jennifer, Australian, Company Director.
CHILDREN: Andonella.
SCHOOLS/COLLEGE: Pancyprian Gymnasium Nicosia, University College, London.
QUALIFICATIONS: BSc (Eng) Honours, PhD. Chartered Civil & Mechanical Engineer.
MEMBERSHIPS: MICE, MIMeehe, FEANI, ETEK (Cyprus), American Academy of Forensic Sciences, Expert Witness Institute, Society of Expert Witnesses.
HOBBIES AND INTERESTS: Reading, history, astronomy, films and driving.
PERSONAL PROFILE: Consulting Engineer, worked in Hong Kong, Australia and UK. Set up his own consulting firm (ZACE) in 1993. Part-time University Lecturer. Delivers short specialist courses for Architects and Engineers. Published articles and technical papers overseas.

ANDREAS MICHAEL ZISSIMOS
Scientist/Lecturer

DATE OF BIRTH: 08-Sep-1972
PLACE OF BIRTH: Famagusta.
MARITAL STATUS: Married to Andry, Kormakiti, Advertising.
SCHOOLS/COLLEGE: Kykkos Lyceum, Cyprus, University of North London.
QUALIFICATIONS: PhD Chemistry, BSc (Hons).
MEMBERSHIPS: Royal Society of Chemistry.
HOBBIES AND INTERESTS: Keen sportsman, likes writing and continental cinematographer.
PERSONAL PROFILE: Research Fellow at University College, London; 1996-1999, Visiting Lecturer, University Of North London. Scientist currently working in drug discovery and development in collaboration with various pharmaceutical companies. Has published various scientific articles in scientific journals. Represented Cyprus in various meetings (Commonwealth Youth Meeting Manchester 1997, youth and student festival in Cuba 1996).

CHRIS VAKIS ZISSIMOS
Councillor with Haringey Council for 20 years. Created the Islington Advice Centre for Cypriots

DATE OF BIRTH: 01-Jan-1922
PLACE OF BIRTH: Famagusta.
MARITAL STATUS: Married.
CHILDREN: One son, a Reseacher at university.
SCHOOLS/COLLEGE: Famagusta Elementary and Gymnasium, University of London, studied Economics.
HOBBIES AND INTERESTS: Reading.
PERSONAL PROFILE: Was a Teacher. Has worked a lot with the community. Councillor with Haringey Council for 20 years. Co created the Islington Advice Centre for Cypriots.

A. K. ZIVANARIS
Hotelier/Director of Middlesborough FC in the 1980s

DATE OF BIRTH: 01-Mar-1942
PLACE OF BIRTH: Lefkara.
MARITAL STATUS: Married.
CHILDREN: Theano, Business.
SCHOOLS/COLLEGE: University of Hull.
QUALIFICATIONS: B. Sc (Econ) Honours.
MEMBERSHIPS: Institute of Directors, CBI.
HOBBIES AND INTERESTS: Music, reading and sport.
PERSONAL PROFILE: Chairman and Managing Director of Lincoln Group. Member of Variety Club of Great Britain. Was a Director of Middlesborough FC in the 1980s.

ALEX ZORBAS
Actor Television: has appeared in waking the dead, the Bill, Plane Spotting and Casualty

DATE OF BIRTH: 16-Oct-1973
PLACE OF BIRTH: London. Father from Limassol; Mother from Lefkada, Greece.
MARITAL STATUS: Single.
SCHOOLS/COLLEGE: Mountview Theatre School.
HOBBIES AND INTERESTS: Music, Greek dancing, croupier, painting, football, skiing and tennis.
PERSONAL PROFILE: Actor. Television: has appeared in waking the dead, the Bill, Plane Spotting and Casualty. Stage: Sexual Perversity In Chicago, Street Scene, When Five Years Pass, Blood Wedding, Greenland, Metamorphosis, The Seagull. Commercial: Cellnet Corporate Film.

It is free to nominate someone, or yourself, who deserves to be in the book, just send in the name, contact address, telephone number and email to:

Greek Cypriots Worldwide
111 St Thomas's Road, London, N4 2QJ
Telephone 0044 207503 3498

cypriotwhoswho@aol.com
www.greekcypriotsworldwide.com

UK

USA

DIAMANDO AFXENTIOU
Associate Professor in Economics

PLACE OF BIRTH: Cyprus
SCHOOLS/COLLEGE: West Virginia University and City University of New York.
QUALIFICATIONS: BS MA PhD.
PERSONAL PROFILE: Diamando Afxentiou is an Associate Professor in the Department of Economics, School of Management at the New York Institute of Technology.

IRENE AFXENTIOU
Performing arts co ordinator at St Cloud State University

PLACE OF BIRTH: Parents from Cyprus.
PERSONAL PROFILE: Irene Afxentiou is a Performing arts co- ordinator at St Cloud State University, Minnesota.

CHARLES AGAPIOU
Owner of the Rolls Royce and Bentley Dealership in Hollywood

PLACE OF BIRTH: Eptakomi.
SCHOOLS/COLLEGE: Acland Burghley.
PERSONAL PROFILE: Charles ended up in the USA via England he is the owner of the Rolls Royce and Bentley Dealership in Hollywood.

MARIANA AGATHOKLIS
Publicist for MTV Networks

DATE OF BIRTH: 08-Jun-1981
PLACE OF BIRTH: Famagusta.
MARITAL STATUS: Single.
SCHOOLS/COLLEGE: Dulaney High School. Boston University.
QUALIFICATIONS: BS.
MEMBERSHIPS: Public Relations Society of America, Alpha Phi Fraternity. Golden Key International Honour Society. Greek Orthodox Philoptohos Society.
HONOURS/AWARDS: Boston University College of Communication 2003 Blue Chip Award.
HOBBIES AND INTERESTS: Travel, Movies, Music and Dancing.

PERSONAL PROFILE: Mariana Agathoklis is a publicist for MTV Networks.

DEMETRIS AGROTIS
Vice President and General Manager of BEI Duncan Electronics

PLACE OF BIRTH: Cyprus.
MARITAL STATUS: Married.
CHILDREN: Four Daughters.
SCHOOLS/COLLEGE: University of Dayton and Ohio State University.
QUALIFICATIONS: Doctorate in Electrical Engineering, Master of Science Degree in Engineering Management and Batchelors degree in Electrical Engineering.
PERSONAL PROFILE: Dr Demetris Agrotis is Vice President and General manager of BEI Duncan Electronics who are a leader in supplying major automotive and heavy equipment manufacturers with a variety of contacting and non contacting sensors.

MICHAEL ALEXIOU
Fellow of the American Academy of Otolaryngology Head and Neck Surgery

PLACE OF BIRTH: USA Parents from Cyprus
SCHOOLS/COLLEGE: Trueman State University and University of Kansas.
QUALIFICATIONS: BA and MD.
MEMBERSHIPS: Fellow of the American Academy of Otolaryngology Head and Neck Surgery.

PERSONAL PROFILE: Michael Alexiou is in private practice in Harrisonburg, Virginia. His clinical interest focus on Endoscopic sinus surgery, skin cancer excision and repair, hearing disorders and hearing restoration surgery.

ANASTASIS ANASTASIADES
Vice President Pan Cyprian Association

DATE OF BIRTH: 18-Dec-1936.
PLACE OF BIRTH: Neon Chorio, Cyprus.
MARITAL STATUS: Married to Diane.
CHILDREN: Stavros, Accountant.
SCHOOLS/COLLEGE: Youngstown State University.
QUALIFICATIONS: BSBA, MBA.
MEMBERSHIPS: AHI, AHEPA Pinellas Chapter, Pancyprian Society(currently VP).
PERSONAL PROFILE: Anastasis is the Vice President of the Pancyprian Society and an Accountant by occupation.

USA

ATHOS ANASTASIADES
Cardiologist

DATE OF BIRTH: 22-Feb-1946.
PLACE OF BIRTH: Nicosia.
SCHOOLS/COLLEGE: University of Athens.
PERSONAL PROFILE: Cardiologist at Deaconess Hospital in New Jersey.

CHRISTOPHER ANASTASIOU
Enviromental Specialist in the Florida Department of Enviromental Protection

PLACE OF BIRTH: Cyprus.
QUALIFICATIONS: MSc Biological Sciences.
PERSONAL PROFILE: Chris Anastasiou is an Enviromental Specialist in the Florida Department of Enviromental Protection.

ELENI ANASTASIOU
Lecturer in English at Pittsburgh University

PLACE OF BIRTH: London Parents from Larnaca.
PERSONAL PROFILE: Eleni Anastasiou is a Lecturer in English at Pittsburgh University.

HARRY ANASTASIOU
Faculty Member of the Conflict Resolution Graduate Program and of International Studies

PLACE OF BIRTH: Cyprus.
SCHOOLS/COLLEGE: University, Cincinatti, Ohio, Free University of Amsterdam and University of Toronto.
QUALIFICATIONS: BA MA PhD.
PERSONAL PROFILE: Harry Anastasiou is a Faculty Member of the Conflict Resolution Graduate Program and of International Studies at the Portland State University. Has published many articles on peace and conflict issues.

MARIA ANASTASIOU
Vice President of the Hellenic Society Paideia of South Carolina

DATE OF BIRTH: 12-Mar-1976
PLACE OF BIRTH: Cyprus.
MARITAL STATUS: Married.
CHILDREN: One son.
SCHOOLS/COLLEGE: University of North Carolina and University of South Carolina.
QUALIFICATIONS: BA in Economics and International Studies, MA in International Studies.
PERSONAL PROFILE: Maria has been working at the Walker Institute for the last six years and has taught International Relations Theory and Contemporary US Foreign Policy in the department of Political Science. She has also taught Modern Greek at the Greek Orthodox Church in Columbia for three years and is currently the Vice President of the Hellenic Society Paideia of South Carolina.

ANDREAS ANAYIOTOS
Associate Professor at the Department of Bio Medical Engineering at the University of Alabama

PLACE OF BIRTH: Cyprus 1961
SCHOOLS/COLLEGE: Boston University and Georgia Institute of Technology.
QUALIFICATIONS: BS MS PhD.
MEMBERSHIPS: Pi Tau Sigma in Mechanical Engineering.
HONOURS/AWARDS: John Shortfall Award for outstanding ASME Faculty Advisor in 1997.
PERSONAL PROFILE: Andreas Anayiotou is an Associate Professor at the Department of Bio Medical Engineering at the University of Alabama.

USA

PHILIOS ANGELIDES
Senior Vice President at Alpha
Corporation

DATE OF BIRTH: 01-Jun-1959
PLACE OF BIRTH: Famagusta.
MARITAL STATUS: Married to
Alicia.
CHILDREN: Two children.
PERSONAL PROFILE: Philios
Angelides is Senior Vice
President at Alpha Corporation
an engineering construction
consulting company.

ALEXANDROUS ANTONIOU
Director of Educational Programs for the
National Swimming Pool Foundation

DATE OF BIRTH: 22-Feb-1957
PLACE OF BIRTH: Famagusta,
Cyprus.
MARITAL STATUS: Married to
Renee Antoniou, USA, French
teacher.
CHILDREN: Nicholas
Antoniou.
SCHOOLS/COLLEGE:
Hampstead Secondary School,
London, England. University of
Nebraska in Lincoln, USA, University of Illinois.
QUALIFICATIONS: Masters Degree in Exercise Science
Ph. D in Kinesiology.
HOBBIES AND INTERESTS: Volunteer for the Shark
Research Institute in the US.
PERSONAL PROFILE: Director of Educational
Programs for the National Swimming Pool Foundation.
Responsible for developing and maintaining all
educational programs and online training programmes.

EFI ANTONIOU
University Lecturer

PLACE OF BIRTH: Cyprus
SCHOOLS/COLLEGE:
Pensylvania State University.
QUALIFICATIONS: Ph. D.
PERSONAL PROFILE: Efi
Antoniou After spending time
in the USA became a Lecturer
of Statistics in the Business
Department of frederick
Institute of Technology in
Cyprus.

KLITSA ANTONIOU
Artist

PLACE OF BIRTH: Cyprus
SCHOOLS/COLLEGE: The
English School, Nicosia. Central
St Martins School of Art and
Design, Pratt Institute New
York and New York University.
QUALIFICATIONS: BA.
MEMBERSHIPS: Cyprus Artists
League.
HONOURS/AWARDS: Path of
Peace Award St Ulrich, Austria.
PERSONAL PROFILE: Klitsa Antoniou is an artist who
has had eight solo exhibitions in both Cyprus and abroad
and participated internationally in Sweden, China, Italy
and New York Just to name a few she now resides in
Cyprus.

GEORGE APOSTOLIDES
Head of the Division of Colon and Rectal
Surgery at Greater Baltimore Medical
Center

PLACE OF BIRTH: Beirut, Parents from Cyprus.
SCHOOLS/COLLEGE: St Josephs University Beirut.
QUALIFICATIONS: MD.
PERSONAL PROFILE: George Apostolides is the Head
of the Division of Colon and Rectal Surgery at Greater
Baltimore Medical Center.

GEORGE APOSTOLOU
Physician practices in Internal Medicine
at Temple University Hospital in
Minnesota

PLACE OF BIRTH: Cyprus.
SCHOOLS/COLLEGE: University of Med and Dentistry
of New Jersey.
PERSONAL PROFILE: George Apostolou is a Physician
practices in Internal Medicine at Temple University
Hospital in Minnesota.

NICHOLAS APOSTOLOU
University lecturer in Accounting

PLACE OF BIRTH: Cyprus.
PERSONAL PROFILE: Dr Nicholas Apostolou is a
lecturer in the Department of Accounting in the College
of Business Administration at the Louisiana State
University.

USA

PAUL CHARLES APOSTOLOU
President of Cornerstones of Carnegie Mellon University

DATE OF BIRTH: 25-Apr-1942
PLACE OF BIRTH: Pittsburgh USA, Grandparents from Pyrga.
MARITAL STATUS: Married to Marilyn.
CHILDREN: Christian, Sales Executive. Alexandra, Architect. Stephanie, Attorney.
SCHOOLS/COLLEGE: University of Notre Dame.
QUALIFICATIONS: Bachelor of Architecture.
MEMBERSHIPS: AHEPA, American Institute of Architects.
HOBBIES AND INTERESTS: Classical guitar, Golf, working on and driving old Porsches.
PERSONAL PROFILE: Former Board Member and President of St. Francis Medical Center. President of Cornerstones of Carnegie Mellon University.

SINOULA APOSTOLOU
Medical

PLACE OF BIRTH: Cyprus.
SCHOOLS/COLLEGE: University of Adelaide.
QUALIFICATIONS: PhD.
PERSONAL PROFILE: Dr Sinoula Apostolou extensive laboratory research experience contributes a valuable perspective as she provides bioinformatics support to Fox Chase research personnel.

ARISTOS ARISTIDOU
Research and Development Manager, Cargill Inc, Minneapolis, Minnesota, USA

DATE OF BIRTH: 12-Jul-1964
PLACE OF BIRTH: Limassol, Cyprus.
MARITAL STATUS: Married to Pirjo, Finnish, Chemical Engineer.
CHILDREN: Andreas, Alexandros.
SCHOOLS/COLLEGE: The English School, Nicosia. Rice University, Houston, Texas.
QUALIFICATIONS: BS Chemical Engineering PhD Biochemical Engineering.
MEMBERSHIPS: American Institute for Chemical Engineers and American Chemical Society.
HONOURS/AWARDS: Fullbright Scholar.
PERSONAL PROFILE: Research and Development Manager, Cargill Inc, Minneapolis, Minnesota, USA.

DR KYRIACOS ARISTOTELOUS
Professor of Economics, Ohio

DATE OF BIRTH: 21-Oct-1961
PLACE OF BIRTH: Orounda.
MARITAL STATUS: Married.
SCHOOLS/COLLEGE: Iowa State University, University of Delaware, The Ohio State University.
QUALIFICATIONS: BS Hotel Management, MA Economics, PhD Economics.
HONOURS/AWARDS: Nominated for Master Teacher Award Otterbain College Westerville Ohio, 2002.
HOBBIES AND INTERESTS: Travelling, History and Hiking.
PERSONAL PROFILE: Professor of Economics, Dept of Business Accounting and Economics, Otterbain College, Westerville, Ohio.

ANDREAS ARTEMIOU
Instructor for Mathematical Statistics at the Pennsylvania State University

PLACE OF BIRTH: Cyprus
MARITAL STATUS: Married.
SCHOOLS/COLLEGE: University of Cyprus and Pennsylvania State University.
QUALIFICATIONS: BSc.
MEMBERSHIPS: Member of the Student Advisory Commitee(2005, 2006) Department of Statistics Pennsylvania State University. Elected for three years (2002, 2003, 2004) as a member of the University Student Unions Council, University of Cyprus.
PERSONAL PROFILE: Andreas Artemiou is an Instructor for Mathematical Statistics at the Pennsylvania State University.

MICHAEL ARTEMIOU
Computer Engineer in the Department of Electrical and Computer Engineering Old Dominion University Virginia, USA

PLACE OF BIRTH: Cyprus.
PERSONAL PROFILE: Michael Artemiou is a Computer Engineer in the Department of Electrical and Computer Engineering Old Dominion University Virginia, USA.

USA

KYRIACOS ATHANASIOU
Bio Engineering

PLACE OF BIRTH: Larnaca
SCHOOLS/COLLEGE: New York Institute of Technology and Columbia University.
QUALIFICATIONS: B. S. M. S. Ph. M and Ph. D.
MEMBERSHIPS: Licensed Professional Engineer Texas State Board of Registration for Professional Engineers.
PERSONAL PROFILE: Kyriacos is based in The Department of Bioengineering at the Rice University in Houston, areas of research are Tissue engineering of cartilage cytomechanics and biomechanics.

IRENE AXENTIOU
Performing Arts coordinator for St Clouds State University

PLACE OF BIRTH: Cyprus.
PERSONAL PROFILE: Irene Afxentiou is the performing arts coordinator for St Clouds State University.

DESPINA AXIOTAKIS
General Secretary of the Cyprus Federation of America

DATE OF BIRTH: 25-Jun-1948
PLACE OF BIRTH: Asgata, Limassol.
MARITAL STATUS: Married to John, Manhattan, parents born in Chios. Retired.
CHILDREN: Irene, Landscaper. Lucas, Event Planner.
SCHOOLS/COLLEGE: Edison Grammar School, Emerson and North Bergen High Schools, Traphagen School of Fashion.
HONOURS/AWARDS: Cyprus Federation of America Recognition Award, the Panpaphian Distinguished Fellow Cyprian Award.
HOBBIES AND INTERESTS: Dancing, ski, oil paint, spend time with grandchildren teaching them Greek language, dance, customs.
PERSONAL PROFILE: Executive Director of the Cyprus USA Chamber of Commerce, General Secretary of the Cyprus Federation of America, Board Member of the Church of the Assumption, Beautification program of Ridgewood, NJ, Asgata Association Cyprus past President and dance instructor.

HELEN BARBAS
Professor at Boston University

PLACE OF BIRTH: Kyrenia
SCHOOLS/COLLEGE: Kean College and Mcgill University.
QUALIFICATIONS: BA and PhD.
MEMBERSHIPS: Society for Neuroscience, The International Brain Research Organisation and the American Association for the advancement of Science.
PERSONAL PROFILE: Helen Barbas is a Professor of the Dept of Health Sciences and Director of the Neutral Systems Laboratory at Boston University.

ANGIE BOWIE
Singer and Author

PLACE OF BIRTH: Cyprus born 1940
SCHOOLS/COLLEGE: St. Georges School in Switzerland. Conneticut College for Women, Kingston Polytechnic.
PERSONAL PROFILE: Angie is the ex-wife of singer David Bowie. She now writes two titles are "Free Spirit" and "Life on the Wild Side" with David Bowie. She is currently living in Tucson, Arizona, USA and has released her first album.

ANDREAS BOYADJIS
Law (retired)

DATE OF BIRTH: 20-Mar-1922.
PLACE OF BIRTH: Mia Milia.
MARITAL STATUS: Married to Lilian Boydajis, American (Greek descent), Retired.
CHILDREN: Chrystalla Daly, Doctor. Terence Boyadjis, Doctor. Anthony Boyadjis, Lawyer. Eleni Boyadjis, Lawyer.
SCHOOLS/COLLEGE: Mia Milia Gymnasium. Rutgers Law School.
QUALIFICATIONS: Juris Doctor, 1964, Rutgers Law School, Undergraduate coursework at Drew University.
MEMBERSHIPS: American Hellenic Education Progressive Association, Cyprus Federation.
HOBBIES AND INTERESTS: Violin, reading, politics.
PERSONAL PROFILE: From a poor village in Cyprus, he achieved tremendous success through sheer force of will, working all night to support a family of 6 while attending law school by day, graduating at age 42.

USA

ANTHONY BOYADJIS
Attorney Mediator for Morris County Superior Court

DATE OF BIRTH: 05-Nov-1958
PLACE OF BIRTH: Morristown, New Jersey Father from Mia Milia.
MARITAL STATUS: Married to Lauren Boyadjis, American, Legal Assistant.
CHILDREN: Hannah, Rachel.
SCHOOLS/COLLEGE: Morristown High School. Cornell University.
QUALIFICATIONS: Bachelor of Arts, Juris Doctor (cum laude).
MEMBERSHIPS: Morris County Bar Association, New Jerset Bar Association, Member of Massachusetts and New York Bar.
HOBBIES AND INTERESTS: Long distance running.
PERSONAL PROFILE: Mediator for Morris County Superior Court.

TERRENCE BOYADJIS
Doctor Psychiatrist

PLACE OF BIRTH: USA Father from Nicosia.
QUALIFICATIONS: MD.
PERSONAL PROFILE: Doctor Psychiatrist based in a Specialty Outpatient Clinic in West Chester.

MELISSA PANAGIDES BUSCH
Research Scientist

PLACE OF BIRTH: USA Father from Limassol
PERSONAL PROFILE: Melissa Busch was a principal Research Scientist at the American Institute of Research currently Vice President Education Studies at JDG Associates a recruitment company.

VANGELIS CALOTYCHOS
Acting Director of the Program in Hellenic Studies at Columbia University

DATE OF BIRTH: 07-Mar-1962
PLACE OF BIRTH: UK Father from Limassol.
SCHOOLS/COLLEGE: University of Birmingham UK Ohio State University and Harvard University.
QUALIFICATIONS: BA MA Ph. D.
PERSONAL PROFILE: Vangelis Calotychos is the Acting Director of the Program in Hellenic Studies at Columbia University. He is also on the Executive Board of the Modern Greek Studies Association.

LINDA CHACHOLIADES
Music Lecturer

PLACE OF BIRTH: USA Father from Omodhos
SCHOOLS/COLLEGE: University of Georgia, Morzarteum Conservatory, Salzburg, Austria and Cleveland Institute of Music.
QUALIFICATIONS: Master of Music Degree and BM.
PERSONAL PROFILE: Linda Chacholiades is a Lecturer at the Best Piano and Keyboard School, Minneapolis, she has performed in several piano competitions.

MILTIADES CHACHOLIADES
Professor of Economics at Georgia State University

DATE OF BIRTH: 22-Jun-1937.
PLACE OF BIRTH: Omodhos.
MARITAL STATUS: Married to Mary.
CHILDREN: Lia, Marina, and Linda.
SCHOOLS/COLLEGE: Athens School of Economics and Masachusetts Institute of Technology.
QUALIFICATIONS: PhD.
PERSONAL PROFILE: He has taught at New York University and the University of California in Los Angeles, and was Professor of Economics at Georgia State University. His articles have been published in a number of international professional economic journals. He also served as the Rector of Cyprus University.

USA

ELENA CHAMBOUS
On the Board of Directors Cyprus
Childrens Fund

DATE OF BIRTH: 28-Mar-1967
PLACE OF BIRTH: USA, Father
from Kalavasos, Mother from
Alona.
CHILDREN: Stefanos.
SCHOOLS/COLLEGE: NYU
Stern school of business.
QUALIFICATIONS: Bachelor of
Science degree in Finance and
International Business.
PERSONAL PROFILE: Certified
financial planner and on the Board of Directors Cyprus
Children's Fund.

PROFESSOR PANOS CHARALAMBIDES
Professor University of Maryland

DATE OF BIRTH: 7-Sept-1955
PLACE OF BIRTH: Ikos
Marathassa
MARITAL STATUS: Married to Dr
Jean Svacina, College Professor.
CHILDREN: Alexi, Student.
Gabe, Student.
SCHOOLS/COLLEGE:
University Of Illinois.
QUALIFICATIONS: BS MSc
and PhD.
HONOURS/AWARDS: won a prestigious five year
Presidential Young Investigator Award from the National
Science Foundation in 1991.
HOBBIES AND INTERESTS: Arts, Poetry, Sports and
World Politics.
PERSONAL PROFILE: Panos Charalambides is a
Professor and Chairman, Department of Mechanical
Engineering, University of Maryland Baltimore County.

ANDREAS CHARALAMBOUS
Award winning Architect

DATE OF BIRTH: 30-Aug-1960
PLACE OF BIRTH: London,
England, parents from
Famagusta.
MARITAL STATUS: Single.
SCHOOLS/COLLEGE: Cornell
University, Ithaca, NY, USA.
QUALIFICATIONS: Bachelor of
Architecture, 1984.
MEMBERSHIPS: American
Institute of Architects.
International Interior Design Association.
HONOURS/AWARDS: Numerous Awards from the

American Institute of Architects in DC, Maryland and
Virginia Magazines _The Washington Post, INTERIOR
Design Magazine, TRENDS magazine.
PERSONAL PROFILE: Accomplished artist, with
personal shows in New York City, Washington DC,
Mexico City, Acapulco, Nicosia.

HARRIS CHARALAMBOUS
Two Cinematography Awards for his
work on the short films

DATE OF BIRTH: 23-Mar-1977.
PLACE OF BIRTH: Paphos.
SCHOOLS/COLLEGE: American Film Institute.
QUALIFICATIONS: MFA in Cinematography.
HONOURS/AWARDS: Two Cinematography Awards
for his work on the short films "Chasing Delight" and
"Apothrasi tis Vasillisas".
PERSONAL PROFILE: Haris Charalambous is a
Photographer/Cinematographer work includes feature
films, short films and commercials.

NELIA CHARALAMBOUS
Visiting Assistant Professor in the
Faculty of Mathematics, University of
California, Irvine

PLACE OF BIRTH: Cyprus
SCHOOLS/COLLEGE:
University of North Carolina
and Cornell University.
QUALIFICATIONS: BS MS
PhD.
MEMBERSHIPS: American
Mathematical association.
PERSONAL PROFILE: Nelia
Charalambous is a Visiting
Assistant Professor in the
Faculty of Mathematics, University of California, Irvine.

CONSTANTINOS CHILIMINDRIS
Doctor

DATE OF BIRTH: 23-Jun-1935.
PLACE OF BIRTH: Famagusta.
MARITAL STATUS: Married.
CHILDREN: Four Children.
PERSONAL PROFILE: Dr Chilimindris runs a general
and family practice in N Charles St Towson, Maryland.

GEORGE CHIMONAS
Professor at the School of Earth and Atmospheric Sciences, Georgia Institute of Technology, USA

PLACE OF BIRTH: Cyprus
SCHOOLS/COLLEGE: Sussex University.
QUALIFICATIONS: PhD.
PERSONAL PROFILE: George Chimonas is a Professor at the School of Earth and Atmospheric Sciences, Georgia Institute of Technology, USA.

CHRIS CHRISAFIS
Executive Film producer of The film's Sea Wolves, Who Dares Wins

PLACE OF BIRTH: From Eptakomi and Komi Kebir.
PERSONAL PROFILE: Chris Chrisafis is a film producer was based at Pinewood Studios now in Hollywood. he was Executive producer of The Sea Wolves, Who Dares Wins, Wild Geese 11 and many others he is currently producing Carry on London.

DEMETRIOS CHRISTODOULIDES
Professor of Optics at the University of Florida

DATE OF BIRTH: 21-Jan-1958
PLACE OF BIRTH: Agglaia Nicosia.
CHILDREN: Nicholas, Alexander, both students.
SCHOOLS/COLLEGE: John Hopkins University.
QUALIFICATIONS: PhD.
MEMBERSHIPS: Fellow of the Optical Society of America.
HOBBIES AND INTERESTS: Swimming.
PERSONAL PROFILE: Demetrios Christodoulides is Professor of Optics at the University of Central Florida.

IOANNIS CHRISTODOULIDES
Physician and Surgeon

DATE OF BIRTH: 28-May-1943.
PLACE OF BIRTH: Kythrea.
MARITAL STATUS: Married to Nancy.
CHILDREN: Alexia, and Chris.
SCHOOLS/COLLEGE: National and Kapodistrian University of Athens.
QUALIFICATIONS: Medical Doctor.

MEMBERSHIPS: Various professional organisations in the USA.
PERSONAL PROFILE: Physician and Surgeon.

DR FLORENTINA CHRISTODOULIDOU
Medical. Has a private practice in Internal Medicine

DATE OF BIRTH: 18-Feb-1951
PLACE OF BIRTH: Paphos, Cyprus.
MARITAL STATUS: Single.
SCHOOLS/COLLEGE: Paphos High School. Aristotelian University School of Medicine, Salonika, Greece.
QUALIFICATIONS: Medical School Graduate.
MEMBERSHIPS: Hellenic Medical Society, New York, Pancyprian Association of America, Cyprus Federation of America.
HONOURS/AWARDS: Pancyprian Association of America Award, (Dance division) Member of the Year Award, the Romanian Medical of New York, Elpides Award in recognition of outstanding service to those in need.
HOBBIES AND INTERESTS: Community work and travel.
PERSONAL PROFILE: Has a private practice in Internal Medicine. Helps students from Cyprus and Greece who have no insurance, gratis. Has written for the Greek newspaper, Proini, a weekly medical article for several years and had a weekly TV Medical program with the National Greek TV for about 2 years. Both were very successful with the Hellenic community.

CHRISTOPHER CHRISTODOULOU
Assistant Professor at the State University of New York

PLACE OF BIRTH: Yialoussa.
QUALIFICATIONS: Ph. D.
PERSONAL PROFILE: Christopher Christodoulou is Assistant Professor, Department of Neurology, State University of New York at Stony Brook.

USA

CHRISTOPHER CHRISTODOULOU
Former Supreme President of the Cyprus Federation of America

PLACE OF BIRTH: Cairo in 1920. Father from Cyprus
MARITAL STATUS: Married to Helen.
CHILDREN: James, Zenon.
SCHOOLS/COLLEGE: Greek High School in Suez, Egypt. University of Munich.
QUALIFICATIONS: PhD in Philosophy.
HONOURS/AWARDS: Ellis Island Medal of Honor Award.
PERSONAL PROFILE: Served as a Priest, Pastor and Archimandrite then taught in the Manhattan School of Printing he later formed his own commercial printing companies. In 1975 he was elected Supreme President of the Cyprus Federation of America.

GEORGE CHRISTODOULOU
Board Member for the Calaveras Office of Education for over 11 years. He served on the Grand Jury for 2 years

DATE OF BIRTH: 04-Apr-1934.
PLACE OF BIRTH: Larnaca, Cyprus.
MARITAL STATUS: Married to Jean, English, Homemaker.
CHILDREN: Nina Kim, Police Officer. Philip Adam, Project Manager. Tracey Sue, Police Officer.
SCHOOLS/COLLEGE: American Acadamy, Larnaca. California Maritime Academy.
QUALIFICATIONS: Bsc Msc in Maritime Engineering.
HONOURS/AWARDS: Professor Emeritus.
HOBBIES AND INTERESTS: Writing books.
PERSONAL PROFILE: Prior to teaching he was a director of Diesel Technology at the American President Lines. He was part of the team that constructed the first flow speed container ships for the American merchant fleet. Since his retirement he has been actively involved in Education. He was Board Member for the Calaveras Office of Education for over 11 years. He served on the Grand Jury for 2 years.

LEO CHRISTODOULOU
Visiting Professor at Virginia Polytechnic Institute and State University

PLACE OF BIRTH: Cyprus.
SCHOOLS/COLLEGE: Imperial College of Science, Technology and Medicine, London. And Carnegie Mellon University in the USA.
QUALIFICATIONS: BSc. and PhD.

HONOURS/AWARDS: Grunfeld Metal and Prize, Institute of Materials 1996.
PERSONAL PROFILE: In 1998 Dr Christodoulou was appointed visiting Professor at Virginia Polytechnic Institute and State University and in 1999 he joined DARPA Defense Sciences Office as a program manager in the Structural Materials R&D area. He has authored or co authored more than 60 technical papers and is a named co inventor on more than 20 US Patents and their Foreign equivalents.

ANDREAS CHRISTOFI
Professor At Monmouth University

PLACE OF BIRTH: Agios Fotios, Pafos born 1949
MARITAL STATUS: Married.
CHILDREN: Two children.
SCHOOLS/COLLEGE: University of New Orleans, Penn State.
QUALIFICATIONS: MBA, PhD.
MEMBERSHIPS: American Finance Association.
HONOURS/AWARDS: Scholarship, Bodosaki Foundation.
HOBBIES AND INTERESTS: Fishing, travelling.
PERSONAL PROFILE: Professor served as Chair of the Economics and Finance Dept at Monmouth University.

PANAGIOTIS CHRISTOFIDES
Professor in Engineering at the University of California

PLACE OF BIRTH: Greece, Grandfather from Cyprus
SCHOOLS/COLLEGE: University of Patras and University of Minnesota.
QUALIFICATIONS: Dipl. Eng MS. and PhD.
PERSONAL PROFILE: Panagiotis Christofides is a Professor in the Department of Electrical Engineering, University of California, Los Angeles.

CLEOPATRA CHRISTOFOROU
Assistant Professor in Mathematics at the University of Houston

PLACE OF BIRTH: Cyprus
MARITAL STATUS: Married to Demetri.
SCHOOLS/COLLEGE: University of Cyprus and Brown University.
QUALIFICATIONS: BS MSc PhD Mathematics.
MEMBERSHIPS: American Mathematical Society, Rose Whelan Society, NSF research grant.
PERSONAL PROFILE: Was BOAS assistant professor Department of Mathematics North Western University USA. Now at University of Houston, Dept of Mathematics Assistant Professor.

PHILIP CHRISTOPHER
President International Coordinating Committee Justice for Cyprus

DATE OF BIRTH: 22-Oct-1948
PLACE OF BIRTH: Kyrenia.
MARITAL STATUS: Married to Christina, School teacher.
CHILDREN: Nick, Attorney at Law.
SCHOOLS/COLLEGE: New York University.
QUALIFICATIONS: BA.
MEMBERSHIPS: Member of the White House Economic Council, Clinton Administration.
HOBBIES AND INTERESTS: Soccer.
PERSONAL PROFILE: Philip is the President of the International Coordinating Committee Justice for Cyprus. He is also President Chief Executive UTStarcom Personal Communications. Mr. Christopher also serves on the Executive Committee of the Cellular Telephone Industry Association.

LOUCAS CHRISTOPHOROU
Ford Foundation Professor of Physics at the University of Tennessee

DATE OF BIRTH: 21-Jan-1937
PLACE OF BIRTH: Pendakomo.
MARITAL STATUS: Married to Eratoula, Senior Clinical Social Worker.
CHILDREN: Penelope, and Yianna.
SCHOOLS/COLLEGE: University of Athens and University of Manchester.
QUALIFICATIONS: BS PhD.
PERSONAL PROFILE: Loucas Christophorou was Ford Foundation Professor of Physics at the University of Tennessee and headed the atomic, molecular and high-voltage physics program at the Oak Ridge National Laboratory.

PENELOPE CHRISTOPHOROU
Lawyer with Cleary Gottlieb in New York also vice-chair of the Uniform Commercial Code Committee of the American Bar Association

PLACE OF BIRTH: USA father from Pentakomo
SCHOOLS/COLLEGE: Georgetown University, Harvard Law School.
QUALIFICATIONS: BS FS JD.
MEMBERSHIPS: member of the Bar in New York. She is presently vice-chair of the Uniform Commercial Code Committee of the American Bar Association and also serves as chair of its Investment Securities Sub committee.
PERSONAL PROFILE: Penelope Christophorou is a Lawyer with Cleary Gottlieb in New York.

USA

DR DEMETRA CHRISTOU
Assistant Professor at Texas A&M University

PLACE OF BIRTH: 1972 in Larnaca
MARITAL STATUS: Married to Evangelos Christou, Assistant Professor at Texas A&M University.
CHILDREN: Andreas.
SCHOOLS/COLLEGE: University of Illinois.
QUALIFICATIONS: BS MS PhD.
PERSONAL PROFILE: Demetra Christou is a Assistant Professor at Texas A&M University in Cardiovascular research. Was a Research Associate at the Department of Integrative Physiology University of Colorado.

EVANGELOS A. CHRISTOU
Assistant Professor at Dept of Health Texas University

DATE OF BIRTH: 26-Mar-1970
PLACE OF BIRTH: Nicosia, Cyprus.
MARITAL STATUS: Married to Demetra Christou, Cypriot, Assistant Professor.
CHILDREN: Andreas Christou.
SCHOOLS/COLLEGE: Truman State University, University of Illinois, University of Colorado.
QUALIFICATIONS: BS MS PhD, Postdoc.
MEMBERSHIPS: International Society of Motor Control, Society for Neuroscience.
HOBBIES AND INTERESTS: Soccer, cycling, cars, weightlifting.
PERSONAL PROFILE: 2004-2006: Senior Research Associate, Dept. of Integrative Physiology, University of Colorado, Boulder. 2006-date: Assistant Professor, Director of Neuromuscular Physiology Laboratory, Dept. of Health and Kinesiology, Texas A&M University.

GEORGE CHRISTOU
Professor of Chemistry at the University of Florida

DATE OF BIRTH: 23-Jun-1969
PLACE OF BIRTH: Limassol.
SCHOOLS/COLLEGE: Exeter University.
QUALIFICATIONS: PhD.
MEMBERSHIPS: On the Scientific Advisory Panel on nanoscience of the Supreme Court of Canada.
HONOURS/AWARDS: Recepient of the 2008 Florida Award in Chemistry.
PERSONAL PROFILE: George Christou is the Drago Professor of Chemistry at the University of Florida been there since year 2001.

NICOLAS CHRISTOU
Lecturer University of California Los Angeles Department of Statistics

PLACE OF BIRTH: Cyprus
SCHOOLS/COLLEGE: National Technical University of Athens, Stern School of Business NYU.
QUALIFICATIONS: Diploma in Mining and Metallurgical Engineering. MS. MPhil. PhD in Statistics and Operations Research.
MEMBERSHIPS: American Statistical Association.
HONOURS/AWARDS: NYU outstanding teaching award 1995-96, 1996 -97.
PERSONAL PROFILE: Lecturer University of California Los Angeles Department of Statistics. Reviewer of several text books in Statistics and Probability Theory. Marathon runner.

USA

There is estimated to be 50,000 Greek Cypriots born in Cyprus or of Cypriot ancestry. Living in the USA.

CHRISTOS G. CHRISTOUDIAS
President of Digital Bungalow Inc providers of interactive services to clients such as Wall St Journal

DATE OF BIRTH: 22-Mar-1977
PLACE OF BIRTH: New York, NY. Father is from Karavas.
MARITAL STATUS: Single.
SCHOOLS/COLLEGE: Tufts University, BA Computer Engineering 1999.
HOBBIES AND INTERESTS: Sports, Snowboarding, Football, Soccer, Boating, Computers and Technology.
PERSONAL PROFILE: Founder of Digital Bungalow Inc. in 1999. Digital Bungalow (www. digitalbungalow. com) is an interactive agency providing outsourced interactive services to B2B companies. Clients include the Wall Street Journal, the New England Patriots and National Amusements.

GEORGE CHRISTOUDIAS
Surgical Oncology

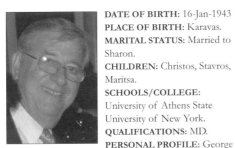

DATE OF BIRTH: 16-Jan-1943
PLACE OF BIRTH: Karavas.
MARITAL STATUS: Married to Sharon.
CHILDREN: Christos, Stavros, Maritsa.
SCHOOLS/COLLEGE: University of Athens State University of New York.
QUALIFICATIONS: MD.
PERSONAL PROFILE: George Christoudias is a Surgeon specializing in Surgical Oncology near Teaneck, New Jersey.

STAVROS CHRISTOUDIAS
Cardiovascular Researcher

PLACE OF BIRTH: USA Father from Karavas.
PERSONAL PROFILE: Stavros Christoudias is involved in Cardiovascular research.

PANOS KYPROS CHRYSANTHIS
Professor of Computer Science and a Founder and Director of the Advanced Data Management Technologies Laboratory at the University of Pittsburgh

DATE OF BIRTH: 01-Feb-1958
PLACE OF BIRTH: Nicosia, Cyprus.
MARITAL STATUS: Married to Areti Papanastasiou, Cypriot, Art Historian- Byzantinology.
CHILDREN: Thalia Maria.
SCHOOLS/COLLEGE: Eleneio Elementary School, Nicosia, Cyprus, Pancyprian Gymnasium, Cyprus. University of Athens, Greece, University of Massachusetts, Amherst.
QUALIFICATIONS: BS MS and PhD.
MEMBERSHIPS: The Scientific Research Society, USA. Hellenic Scientist Association of Boston and various others.
PERSONAL PROFILE: Dr Chrysanthis is a Professor of Computer Science and a founder and director of the Advanced Data Management Technologies Laboratory at the University of Pittsburgh. also an associate editor of the Encyclopedia of Database Systems (Springer-Verlag).

HARRY CHRYSANTHOU
Partner, broker and manager of the Russell group

PLACE OF BIRTH: South Africa parents from Cyprus
MARITAL STATUS: Married to Juanita.
PERSONAL PROFILE: Harry Chrysanthou is a Partner, broker and manager of the Russell group, Nevada a Real Estate Company.

MARIA CHRYSANTHOU
Films

PLACE OF BIRTH: Parents from Cyprus.
SCHOOLS/COLLEGE: University of North Carolina.
PERSONAL PROFILE: Maria began her career in Montevideo in Uruguay where she performed and taught Drama in English to Students at the Alianza Uruguay –Estados Unidos. Maria currently lives in Los Angeles where she continues to work in both theatre and film credits are "Blue Heart", "Crash Diet" are two she done for Wordshed Productions.

USA

CONSTANTINOS CHRYSOSTOMOU
Clinical Instructor, Critical Care Medicine and Pediatrics joint appointment, University of Pittsburgh School of Medicine

PLACE OF BIRTH: Cyprus
MARITAL STATUS: Married.
SCHOOLS/COLLEGE: University Medical school of Debrecen, Hungary, University of Minnesota and University of Pittsburgh.
QUALIFICATIONS: MD.
MEMBERSHIPS: Society of Critical Care Medicine and American College of Cardiology.
PERSONAL PROFILE: Constantinos Chrysostomou is a Clinical Instructor, Critical Care Medicine and Pediatrics joint appointment, University of Pittsburgh School of Medicine.

ANDREAS COMMODROMOS
Treasurer of the World Federation for Overseas Cypriots(POMAK

PLACE OF BIRTH: Vatili
MARITAL STATUS: Married to Anna.
CHILDREN: Eliza, and Demetrios.
SCHOOLS/COLLEGE: St Peters College.
QUALIFICATIONS: BS CPA.
HONOURS/AWARDS: Recipient of the 1996 Ellis Island Medal of Honour and the Newcomen Society of America 1978 Award.
PERSONAL PROFILE: Andreas Comodromos co founded the accounting firm of Comodromos Associates PA with his brother Michael based in New Jersey. Andreas has served as General Secretary of the Cyprus Federation and Chairman of the Justice for Cyprus Commitee from 1989 to 1991. Andreas is Currently Chairman of the Cyprus -US Chamber of Commerce he is the treasurer of the World Federation for Overseas Cypriots(POMAK)and served as a member of the Council of Hellenes Abroad and a member of the Board of the Cyprus Childrens Fund.

DIMITRI CONSTANT
Philosopher

PLACE OF BIRTH: USA father from Nicosia
SCHOOLS/COLLEGE: Yale University Boston University.
QUALIFICATIONS: BA MA.
PERSONAL PROFILE: Dimitri Constant is based in the Department of Philosophy at Boston University USA.

ERRIKOS CONSTANT
Plastic surgeon based in Michigan

DATE OF BIRTH: 15-Apr-1931.
PLACE OF BIRTH: Nicosia.
MARITAL STATUS: Married to Maria.
CHILDREN: Nadina, Dimitri, and Marianna.
SCHOOLS/COLLEGE: Michigan State University.
QUALIFICATIONS: MD.
MEMBERSHIPS: American Society for plastic and Reconstruction Surgery.
PERSONAL PROFILE: Errikos Constant is a plastic Surgeon based at Lansing, in Michigan. His work is confined to Skin Cancer and other skin lesions.

GEORGE CONSTANTINE
Professor of Chemistry, Oregon State University

PLACE OF BIRTH: Cyprus.
SCHOOLS/COLLEGE: University of Utah and Oregon State University.
QUALIFICATIONS: BS MS Ph. D.
PERSONAL PROFILE: George Constantine is a Professor Emeritus, Natural Products Chemistry, Department of Pharmaceutical Sciences Oregon State University.

PROFESSOR ALKIS CONSTANTINIDES
Professor of Chemistry, Rutgers University

DATE OF BIRTH: 29-Jan-1941
PLACE OF BIRTH: Limassol, Cyprus.
MARITAL STATUS: Single.
CHILDREN: Paul, Computer Engineer.
SCHOOLS/COLLEGE: American Acadamy, Larnaca. Columbia University, New York.
QUALIFICATIONS: PhD Chemical Engineering, MS Chemical Engineering, BChE, Chemical Engineering.
MEMBERSHIPS: American Institute of Engineering, American Chemical Society.
HONOURS/AWARDS: Warren l Susman Award for excellence in teaching.
HOBBIES AND INTERESTS: Photography, tennis and skiing.
PERSONAL PROFILE: Teacher of Graduate and Undergraduate courses in Chemical and Biochemical Engineering and Professor at Rutgers University, Consultant to Industry in these areas too. He is also Director of the Microcomputer Laboratory.

CHRISTOS CONSTANTINIDES
Lecturer at University of Wyoming

DATE OF BIRTH: 22-Mar-1931
PLACE OF BIRTH: Nicosia.
MARITAL STATUS: Married.
CHILDREN: Two Sons.
SCHOOLS/COLLEGE: University of Manchester, University of Kansas, Stanford University.
HOBBIES AND INTERESTS: Soccer, was a Referee and a Referee Instructor.
PERSONAL PROFILE: Dr. Constantinides taught in the Department of Electrical and Computer Engineering at the University of Wyoming.

PROFESSOR GEORGE CONSTANTINIDES
Professor of Finance University of Chicago

DATE OF BIRTH: 22-Sep-1947
PLACE OF BIRTH: Nicosia.
MARITAL STATUS: Single.
CHILDREN: Michael, stylianous, Both Students.
SCHOOLS/COLLEGE: Oxford University, Indiana University.
QUALIFICATIONS: Doctor in Business Administration.
HONOURS/AWARDS: Honorary Degree, University of Piraeus, Greece 1999, Academy of Alumni Fellows Award, Indiana University 1994.
PERSONAL PROFILE: Professor of Finance, Graduate School of Business, University of Chicago. Professor Constantinides has written numerous articles in the area he specialises.

MONIKA HELEN CONSTANTINIDES
Constant help to Cypriot Students trying to settle in New York

DATE OF BIRTH: 01-Dec-1965
PLACE OF BIRTH: London, father from Pachna, mother from Munich.
MARITAL STATUS: Single.
SCHOOLS/COLLEGE: St Mary's in Limassol, Dominican Commercial High School in Queens, New York.
HOBBIES AND INTERESTS: Visiting hot water springs, playing scrabble.
PERSONAL PROFILE: She has been in the U. S. for 16 years former owner of Thiasos Nightclub, now owner of a cafe bar in Long Island, Queens. She also owns a property company. She is a constant help to Cypriot students that come over to the States.

USA

The international coordinating committee Justice for Cyprus also known as PSEKA was founded in 1975 by the late president of Cyprus Archbishop Makarios. The organisations headquarters are in Nicosia and has chapters all over the world. The current president is Philip Christopher who is based in New York.

ANDREAS CONSTANTINOU
Professor of Pharmacy at University of Illinois

SCHOOLS/COLLEGE: University of Athens, University of Toledo and MedicalCollege of Ohio.
QUALIFICATIONS: BSc MSc and PhD.
PERSONAL PROFILE: Andreas Constantinou is Associate Professor College of Pharmacy, University of Illinois at Chicago and Professor, Department of Biological Sciences, University of Cyprus.

CHRISTOS CONSTANTINOU
Associate Professor of Urology Stanford University

DATE OF BIRTH: 21-Jul-1939
PLACE OF BIRTH: Limassol.
MARITAL STATUS: Married to Janet, UK.
CHILDREN: Sophia, Philip.
SCHOOLS/COLLEGE: Borough Polytechnic London and Stanford University.
QUALIFICATIONS: HNC MSc PhD.
MEMBERSHIPS: Founding Member, International Society for Dynamics of Upper Urinary TractAmerican Urological Association.
HONOURS/AWARDS: International Prize for Outstanding Contribution to Urology, 1977 (CE Alken). Pharmacology Prize in Experimental Urological Research, 2000.
PERSONAL PROFILE: Associate Professor of Urology at Stanford University.

CLAY CONSTANTINOU
United States Ambassador to Luxembourg

PLACE OF BIRTH: Karavas 1951
MARITAL STATUS: Married.
CHILDREN: Two Children.
SCHOOLS/COLLEGE: New Jersey City University, a JD from Seton Hall University School of Law and New York University School Of Law.
QUALIFICATIONS: BA JD.
HONOURS/AWARDS: Clay Constantinou was awarded the Medal for Exceptional Services, the Republic of Cyprus's highest distinction by president Glafcos Clerides. In addition Archbishop of

Cyprus Chrysostomos bestowed upon him the Medal of Saint Barnabas the Apostle.
PERSONAL PROFILE: Clay Constantinou served as the United States Ambassador to Luxembourg from 1994 to 1999. Following this appointment he was the founding Dean of the John C Whitehead School of Diplomacy and International Relations at Seton Hall University. Prior to his Diplomatic service he was a partner at Wilentz, Goldman & Spitzer a New York Law Firm.

FIVOS CONSTANTINOU
Winner of the u16 3k cross country Nationals in Cyprus

DATE OF BIRTH: 27-May-1981
PLACE OF BIRTH: Aradippou.
SCHOOLS/COLLEGE: American Academy. Massachusetts Institute of Technology.
PERSONAL PROFILE: Fivos Constantinou is studying at the Massachussetts Institute of Technology he is an Athlete in 1997 he won the u16 3k cross country Nationals in Cyprus.

MICHAEL C. CONSTANTINOU
Professor of Civil Engineering Buffalo University

DATE OF BIRTH: 16-Jul-1955
PLACE OF BIRTH: Kyrenia.
MARITAL STATUS: Married to Danai Kontoidi, Athens, Greece, Civil Engineer.
CHILDREN: Alexander, Philip, Nicholas.
SCHOOLS/COLLEGE: Rensselaer Polytechnic Institute, New York. University of Patras, Greece. Rensselaer Polytechnic Institute, New York.
QUALIFICATIONS: BS. MS and PhD in Civil Engineering.
HONOURS/AWARDS: Grand Award, American Council of Engineering Companies(For design of Ataturk International Airport Terminal Turkey)2002. Design Award for Engineering, Technology and Innovation General Services Administration(for design of US Court of Appeals Building San Francisco.
PERSONAL PROFILE: Professor, Dept. of Civil, Structural and Environmental Engineering, University at Buffalo.

USA

SOPHIE CONSTANTINOU
Filmmaker. Produced directed and photographed several documentaries

DATE OF BIRTH: 20-Aug-1967
PLACE OF BIRTH: Stanford California.
MARITAL STATUS: Married to Anthony Tredwell, USA, Artist.
CHILDREN: Milo.
SCHOOLS/COLLEGE: Castilleja School. University College Berkeley.
QUALIFICATIONS: BA Film Studies MA Humanities.
HONOURS/AWARDS: Golden Gate Award 1998 for the Film Between the Lines about women and self injury. Golden Gate Award 1999 for the Film Divided Loyalties.
PERSONAL PROFILE: Sophie Constantinou is a director /Director of Photography She has produced directed and photographed several documentaries including the film" dividing loyalties"a feature length film of the exploration of the conflict in Cyprus. Her Cinematography credits include "Unchained Memories"and "Presumed Guilty".

STAVROS T. CONSTANTINOU
Associate Professor of Geography, Ohio University

DATE OF BIRTH: 28-Apr-1951
PLACE OF BIRTH: Tsada, Paphos, Cyprus.
MARITAL STATUS: Married to Georgette Marie Psarras, Born in US both parents Greek born, Psychologist.
CHILDREN: Theophilos, Alexandra.
SCHOOLS/COLLEGE: Kent State University, Western Kentucky University, Cyprus College, Nicosia, Cyprus, Pedagogical College, Nicosia Cyprus.
QUALIFICATIONS: PhD MS BA.
MEMBERSHIPS: Association of American Geographers, Modern Greek Studies Association, Population Reference Bureau.
HONOURS/AWARDS: He obtained several grants from a variety of academic and other sources to help research efforts in the areas of Greek American ethnicity, migration from Greece and Cyprus, and population geography of Cyprus.
HOBBIES AND INTERESTS: Travel, gardening.
PERSONAL PROFILE: Associate Professor of Geography at the University of Ohio. He has authored numerous articles in professional journals and published collections dealing with the areas of Greek American ethnicity.

TASSOS CONSTANTINOU
Lecturer in Mathematics at the University of Miami

PLACE OF BIRTH: Nicosia
SCHOOLS/COLLEGE: Old Dominion University, University of Miami.
QUALIFICATIONS: BS MA.
PERSONAL PROFILE: Lecturer in Mathematics at the University of Miami.

PETER COSTA
Winner of the sixth series of the popular Late Night Poker television series in the United Kingdom he is based in Las Vegas

DATE OF BIRTH: 17-Jan-1956
PLACE OF BIRTH: Cyprus.
HOBBIES AND INTERESTS: Watching movies.
PERSONAL PROFILE: Professional Poker player based in Las Vegas. He is most well known as the winner of the sixth series of the popular Late Night Poker television series in the United Kingdom. Costas has made four final tables at the World series of Poker. He was nominated for both the 2002 and 2003 European Poker player of the year awards. As of 2007 his total live tournament winnings exceed $1, 700, 000.

ELENI STAVROU COSTEA
Assistant Professor

DATE OF BIRTH: 03-Jan-1968
PLACE OF BIRTH: Nicosia, Cyprus.
MARITAL STATUS: Married to Paul Costeas, Geneticist.
SCHOOLS/COLLEGE: SUNY at Albany, George Washington University.
QUALIFICATIONS: Ph. D, BSc and MBA.
PERSONAL PROFILE: Assistant Professor at University of Cyprus also taught in the USA.

USA

DENNIS COSTIS
Dental surgeon

PLACE OF BIRTH: USA Father from Nicosia.
QUALIFICATIONS: DDS.
PERSONAL PROFILE: Dennis Costis is a General Dentist based in Arlington Heights, Illinois.

CHARLIE CRIST
Governor of Florida USA

DATE OF BIRTH: 24-Jul-1956
PLACE OF BIRTH: Altoona, Pennsylvania Grandfather from Gastria.
MARITAL STATUS: Married.
SCHOOLS/COLLEGE: St Petersburg High School. Florida State University, Samford University and Cumberland School of Law.
QUALIFICATIONS: Law degree.
MEMBERSHIPS: Lifetime Member of the St Petersburg Chapter of NAACP.
HONOURS/AWARDS: Honorary Sheriff by the Florida Sheriffs Association. Only the third person to receive the honor in the organisation's long history.
HOBBIES AND INTERESTS: Fishing, swimming played football for his High School and University.
PERSONAL PROFILE: Charlie Crist was general counsel for the minor league decision of the Baseball Commissioners Office. Governor Crist began his government service as state director for former US Senator Connie Mack. In 1992, he won a seat in the Florida Senate. In 2000, he was elected as Floridas last elected Commissioner of Education. In 2002 he became Floridas first elected Republican Attorney General. On November 7 2006 Governor Charlie Crist was elected to serve as Florida's Governor.

TAKEY CRIST
Obstetrician-Gynecologist

DATE OF BIRTH: 01-Aug-1937
PLACE OF BIRTH: New York Parents from Bellapais.
MARITAL STATUS: Married to Kay, American, Nurse.
CHILDREN: Gloria, Jason, Christopher, David and Stefanos.
SCHOOLS/COLLEGE: University of North Carolina.
QUALIFICATIONS: Clinical Professor of Obstetrics and Gynecology.
MEMBERSHIPS: Director of the Cyprus Museum in Jacksonville.

HONOURS/AWARDS: George Marion Cooper Medical Society Award, Onslow County Jaycees Award.
HOBBIES AND INTERESTS: Stamps, coins, electric trains, collector of maps of Cyprus.
PERSONAL PROFILE: Obstetrician-Gynecologist with his own clinic. In 1973 he founded the Crist Clinic for women in Jacksonville, the first outpatient surgical center and birthing center in North Carolina. The clinic has since expanded to include primary health care services for both men and women family planning and abortion services and counselling. He has written over 40 publications, has been awarded grants for evaluation of IUDS, Birth Control Pills, has done over 140 presentations on areas of womens health. Wrote one of the first papers on the morning after pill.

CHRISTINA CTORIDES FOLEY
Attorney

PLACE OF BIRTH: Cyprus 1968.
MARITAL STATUS: Married to James Foley.
CHILDREN: Two Daughters.
SCHOOLS/COLLEGE: New York University and Brooklyn Law School.
QUALIFICATIONS: BA JD.
MEMBERSHIPS: American Association for Justice.
PERSONAL PROFILE: Christina Ctorides is an Attorney based in New York specialising in medical malpractice and personal injury.

THEOHARIS DAVID
Professor of Architecture at the Pratt Institute

DATE OF BIRTH: 09-Jun-1938
PLACE OF BIRTH: Farmingdale New York USA, Parents from Morphou.
MARITAL STATUS: Single.
CHILDREN: Melissa, Summa Cum Laude BA. Amherst College. Alexis, Student, New School University, Musician, Composer.
SCHOOLS/COLLEGE: Pratt Institute, Yale University.
QUALIFICATIONS: BArch, MArch, Professor of Architecture Pratt Institute, Visiting Professor and Advisor, University of Cyprus.
MEMBERSHIPS: Institute for Urban Design, CIMA (Congress of International Architects), American Planning Association.
HONOURS/AWARDS: Cyprus State Award for Architecture, NYC Board Honor Award, Fellow American Institute of Architects amongst others.

PERSONAL PROFILE: Theo David is a Professor of Architecture at the Pratt Institute his work as an architect and educator has been exhibited and published internationally.

DEMETRIOS DEMETRIADES

Professor of Surgery and Emergency Medicine at the University of California, Los Angeles

PLACE OF BIRTH: Cyprus
SCHOOLS/COLLEGE: University of Witwatersrand and University of Athens.
QUALIFICATIONS: PhD.
MEMBERSHIPS: American Surgical Association and American Association for the Surgery of Trauma.
PERSONAL PROFILE: Demetrios Demetriades is the Professor of Surgery and Emergency Medicine at the University of California, Los Angeles. He is also a Director of the Trauma and Surgical Intensive Care Unit at the same University.

ANDY DEMETRIO

Actor Lead role in the feature film 'Papas'that has been accepted into the prestigious Sundance Film Festival

DATE OF BIRTH: 19-Nov-1979
PLACE OF BIRTH: London Father from Morphou, Cyprus.
MARITAL STATUS: Single.
SCHOOLS/COLLEGE: Italia Academy of Performing Arts. Lee Strasberg Actors Studio.
QUALIFICATIONS: Diploma in Performing Arts.
MEMBERSHIPS: British Actors Equity/London, Screen Actors Guild/USA.
HONOURS/AWARDS: Lead role in the feature film 'Papas' that has been accepted into the prestigious Sundance Film Festival.
HOBBIES AND INTERESTS: Writing screen plays, Theatre, Cinema, Greek Orthodox Religion, Spirituality, Fitness training.
PERSONAL PROFILE: He has performed as an actor all over the UK, Europe and Internationally including London's West End. his film credits include "The Dusty Cold" (2007) "Castell De Ferro" (2007) "The Domestic" (2006) "The Rooms" (2006) and most recently playing the lead role in "Papas" (2007). Andy is now based in Hollywood.

ACHILLES DEMETRIOU

Vice Dean for Clinical Affairs at the Case Western Reserve University School of Medicine

PLACE OF BIRTH: Cyprus
SCHOOLS/COLLEGE: Hebrew University, Jerusalem, Israel and George Washington University, Washington.
QUALIFICATIONS: MD PhD and FACS.
PERSONAL PROFILE: Dr Achilles Demetriou is chief operating Officer and Executive Vice President of University Hospitals and Vice Dean for Clinical Affairs at the Case Western Reserve University School of Medicine in Cleveland Ohio.

ANGELOS DEMETRIOU

Architect designer of the Phinikoudes of today

DATE OF BIRTH: 24-Jul-1929.
PLACE OF BIRTH: Larnaca.
MARITAL STATUS: Married to Eleni.
CHILDREN: Two Children.
SCHOOLS/COLLEGE: Polytechnic in Athens.
PERSONAL PROFILE: The Phinikoudes promenade of today was designed by world-famous architect and town planner, Angelos Demetriou. He has been based in Washington and Athens. Demetriou has worked on many major global projects, from the design of Atlantic City, to the master plan for Islamabad.

USA

Governor of Florida Charlie Crist made a point of saying at his inauguration speech that his grandfather came from the village of Gastria in Cyprus.

ARISTIDES DEMETRIOU
Former President and Founding Member of the Lampousa Organisation

DATE OF BIRTH: 08-Nov-1910
PLACE OF BIRTH: Karavas.
MARITAL STATUS: Married to Maroulla, Karavas, Housewife.
CHILDREN: James, and Dorothy.
MEMBERSHIPS: Lampousa Organisation 1937 to present. Cyprus Federation of America 1951 one of the founding members. St John The Theologian Greek Orthodox Cathedral Tenafly, New Jersey 1968 to present one of the founders.
HONOURS/AWARDS: Lampousa Organization Honorary member 1997. Cyprus Federation of America 2001 for 50 years of outstanding contribution to the Cyprus Community.
PERSONAL PROFILE: Aristides Demetriou at the age of 10 was working in his Father's barber shop in Karavas giving hair cuts to his teachers at 15 he was given the shop by his Father. This was to start a barber career that would take him from Karavas to New York and span over 85 years. He immigrated to the United States in 1930 where he opened up a barbers in Manhattan and then to the Columbia University neighbourhood. He retired in March 2006. He is still active in Community events.

MICHAEL DEMETRIOU
President of the Demetriou Group which are involved in the Insurance market

PLACE OF BIRTH: USA Grandfather from Cyprus.
PERSONAL PROFILE: Michael Demetriou is the President of the Demetriou Group which are involved in the Insurance market. The Company was founded by Peter Demetriou in 1925 since then the company aquired Agency contracts with many of the finest Regional Insurance Companies.

MICHAEL DEMETRIOU
Associate Professor in Mechanical Engineering at Worcester Polytechnic Institute

PLACE OF BIRTH: Cyprus.
SCHOOLS/COLLEGE: University of Southern California.
QUALIFICATIONS: BS MS PhD.
HONOURS/AWARDS: Golden Key National Honor Society.
PERSONAL PROFILE: Michael Demetriou is Associate Professor in Mechanical Engineering at Worcester Polytechnic Institute.

SOPHIA DEMETRIOU
Director of The Career Centre of the City College of New York

PLACE OF BIRTH: Eptakomi
MARITAL STATUS: Single.
SCHOOLS/COLLEGE: City University of New York.
QUALIFICATIONS: PhD, BA, MA.
MEMBERSHIPS: World Association for co-operative Education, American Association for Training and Development, Hellenic American Educators Assoc.
PERSONAL PROFILE: Dr Demetriou has over 20 years experience in teaching and administration at University level. She has taught Spanish language and literature as well as English to non-native speakers and presently Director of The Career Centre of the City College of New York.

STEVEN DEMETRIOU
Pediatric Dentist

PLACE OF BIRTH: Parents from Cyprus
MARITAL STATUS: Married.
CHILDREN: Three Children.
SCHOOLS/COLLEGE: Tufts University.
QUALIFICATIONS: Magna Cum Laude and DMD Degree.
MEMBERSHIPS: American Dental Association.
PERSONAL PROFILE: Dr Steven Demetriou is a Pediatric Dentist has also served as President of the Greater Lowell Dental Society and a Chairman of the Special Fluoridation Committee of the Merrimack Valley Dental Society.

VASSOS DEMETRIOU
Honorary Consul of the Republic of Cyprus at Washington State, USA

DATE OF BIRTH: 10-Feb-1946.
PLACE OF BIRTH: Famagusta, Cyprus.
MARITAL STATUS: Married.
SCHOOLS/COLLEGE: Famagusta Greek Gymnasium. University of Oregan, USA.
QUALIFICATIONS: Bachelor of Architecture.
MEMBERSHIPS: American Institute of Architects, ETEK/Cyprus, AHEPA, American Hellenic Institute.
HONOURS/AWARDS: Numerous awards for Architectural projects. Work featured in several books and other publications.

HOBBIES AND INTERESTS: The Arts.
PERSONAL PROFILE: Honorary Consul of the Republic of Cyprus at Washington State, USA. Past Chair/Board of Advisors, School of Architecture and Allied Arts, University of Oregon. Founding member of Hellenes of the Northwest, which initiated the establishment of the Hellenic Studies Program at the University of Washington, USA.

PHILIP DEMOKRITOU
Adjunct Professor in Physics at Harvard University

PLACE OF BIRTH: Cyprus
PERSONAL PROFILE: Philip Demokritou is the Adjunct Professor of Aerosol Physics Department of Enviromental Health Harvard University.

VICKY HADJIYANIS DIGIOVANNI
Senior Human Resource Systems Consultant

DATE OF BIRTH: 15-Sep-1962.
PLACE OF BIRTH: USA Father from Syngrassi.
MARITAL STATUS: Married to Joseph Di Giovanni, Sicilian, Meteorologist.
CHILDREN: Nico, Marina, Both at School.
SCHOOLS/COLLEGE: St Thomas College, Minnesota and University of Minnesota.
QUALIFICATIONS: BA in Personnel Management. MA in Industrial Relations.
PERSONAL PROFILE: Vicky is a Senior Human Resource Systems Consultant and the Head Teacher for the Greek School in Minneapolis.

ANDREAS DIONYSIOU
President of Rudy's Hot Dog Chain of Restaurants

DATE OF BIRTH: 26-Nov-1928.
PLACE OF BIRTH: Sysklipos.
MARITAL STATUS: Married.
CHILDREN: Two Children.
PERSONAL PROFILE: Andreas is President of Rudy's Hot Dog Chain of Restaurants and is partners with his brother Harry. The company was originally founded by their Uncle Rudy Poturedes the brothers bought the business in 1960.

HARRY DIONYSIOU
Vice president of Rudy's Hot Dog Chain of Restaurants

DATE OF BIRTH: 09-Feb-1939
PLACE OF BIRTH: Sysklipos.
PERSONAL PROFILE: Harry Dionyssiou is the Vice president of Rudy's Hot Dog Chain of Restaurants.

CHRIS DROUSSIOTIS
Vice President Sumitomo Mitsui Banking Corporation

DATE OF BIRTH: 13-Sep-1961
PLACE OF BIRTH: Glasgow, Scotland, brought up in Cyprus now living in New York USA. Father from Limassol.
MARITAL STATUS: Single.
CHILDREN: Amanda, All Students. Christopher, Alec, Troy.
SCHOOLS/COLLEGE: Fairleigh Dickenson University, New Jersey, USA.
QUALIFICATIONS: MBA, Bachelor's, currently teaching as an Adjunct Professor at Fairleigh Dickenson University.
MEMBERSHIPS: Hellenic American Bankers Association, Greek American Chamber of Commerce.
HOBBIES AND INTERESTS: Biking, camping, rock climbing, dancing a mean Zebekiko.
PERSONAL PROFILE: Currently working at Sumitomo Mitsui Banking Corporation, as a Vice President managing the firm's USA. investments in the Leveraged Loan Market. Has previously worked for Bank of America, Canadian Imperial Bank of Commerce and Mizuho Financial, Bank of Tokyo-Mitsubishi.

USA

JOHN ECONOMIDES
Neuroscientist

DATE OF BIRTH: 08-Oct-1971.
PLACE OF BIRTH: Famagusta.
MARITAL STATUS: Single.
SCHOOLS/COLLEGE: Olathe North High School. University of Kansas.
QUALIFICATIONS: BS. PhD.
MEMBERSHIPS: Society of Neuro Science, American Association for the advancement of Science.
HONOURS/AWARDS: National Merit Scholar Ruth L Kirschtein Fellow.
PERSONAL PROFILE: John Economides is a Neuroscientist based in California.

MICHAEL J. ECONOMIDES
Professor in Science at the Cullen College of Engineering, University of Houston

DATE OF BIRTH: 06-Sep-1949
PLACE OF BIRTH: Famagusta, Cyprus.
MARITAL STATUS: Married to Christine Ehlig-Economides, Professor of Engineering, Texas A&M University.
CHILDREN: John, Researcher at University of California. Alexander, Publisher, Energy Tribune Magazine, Houston.
SCHOOLS/COLLEGE: University of Kansas, Stanford University.
QUALIFICATIONS: MS. BS. PhD.
HONOURS/AWARDS: Recipient of the Kapitsa Gold Medal of Honor and the Albert Einstein medal of Honor fron the Russian Academy of Natural Sciences for 'contributions to the field of petroleum engineering', 2004. University of Kansas Hall of Fame, 2004.
PERSONAL PROFILE: Prof. Economides has conducted consulting and advising activities for over 30 countries and major corporations as Managing Partner of Dr. Michael J. Economides Consultants, Inc.

NICHOLAS ECONOMOU
Chief Executive Officer of Confluent Phonotics Corporation

PLACE OF BIRTH: Cyprus
SCHOOLS/COLLEGE: Dartmouth College and Harvard University.
QUALIFICATIONS: BA MA and PhD.
PERSONAL PROFILE: Dr Economou is the Chief Executive Officer of Confluent Phonotics Corporation, a developer and manufacturer of photonic subsystems for the telecommunications and cable TV industries.

SAM ECONOMOU
Plastic Surgeon

PLACE OF BIRTH: Cyprus
CHILDREN: Three Children.
SCHOOLS/COLLEGE: University of Minnesota.
QUALIFICATIONS: MD.
MEMBERSHIPS: American Society of Plastic Surgeons.
PERSONAL PROFILE: Sam Economou is a Plastic Surgeon based in Minnesota, USA.

PETER EFTYCHIOU
Principal of Cresskill High School, New Jersey

PLACE OF BIRTH: USA parents from Karavas
SCHOOLS/COLLEGE: Montclair State University.
QUALIFICATIONS: MA.
PERSONAL PROFILE: Peter Eftychiou is the Principal of Cresskill High School in New Jersey.

MICHAEL ELEFTHERIOU
President and CEO of Catalyst International Inc

PERSONAL PROFILE: Michael Eleftheriou was the President and CEO of Catalyst International Inc. a software products and services company.

CHRISTOPHER ELIA
Thoracic Surgeon

DATE OF BIRTH: 24-Mar-1941.
PLACE OF BIRTH: Ora.
MARITAL STATUS: Married to Patricia.
SCHOOLS/COLLEGE: University of Rochester and Adelphi University.
PERSONAL PROFILE: Christopher Elia is a retired Thoracic Surgeon.

PANAYIOTIS ELLINAS
Primary Care Physician in South Arizona

DATE OF BIRTH: 25-Aug-1962
PLACE OF BIRTH: Famagusta.
MARITAL STATUS: Married to Desdemona from Albania.
CHILDREN: One son and one daughter.
SCHOOLS/COLLEGE: Swarthmore College, Albert Einstein college, University of Albuquerque.
HOBBIES AND INTERESTS: Travel.
PERSONAL PROFILE: Head of non governmental organisation the American Refugee Organisation. Through this position he spent seven months in the jungles of Cambodia serving as a Doctor. He then moved to Kosovo and stayed in the region where he served as the acting head of the World Health Organisation's mission to Albania. He is now a primary care Physician in Douglas in South Arizona.

MICHAEL ERACLEOUS
Associate Professor in Astronomy and Astrophysics

PLACE OF BIRTH: Cyprus.
SCHOOLS/COLLEGE: University of London and Columbia University.
QUALIFICATIONS: BSc. M. A M. Phil Ph. D. B.
MEMBERSHIPS: American Astronomical Society.
PERSONAL PROFILE: Michael Eracleous is an Associate Professor, Department of Astronomy and Astrophysics at the Pennsylvania State University.

EURIPIDES L EVRIVIADES
Former Ambassador of Cyprus to the United States of America

DATE OF BIRTH: 06-Aug-1954
PLACE OF BIRTH: Larnaca.
MARITAL STATUS: Married to Anastasia, Attorney at Law.
SCHOOLS/COLLEGE: University of New Hampshire, John F Kennedy School of Government at Harvard University.
QUALIFICATIONS: Masters degree in Public Administration and a bachelor of science degree in Business administration.
HONOURS/AWARDS: Received a Doctor of Laws, Honoris Causa from his alma mater, the University of New Hampshire.
HOBBIES AND INTERESTS: The arts, music, antiquities, cartography, and motorcycling.
PERSONAL PROFILE: Mr Evriviades started his diplomatic career in 1976 serving initially at the Cyprus Consulate General in New York as Vice Consul(1976-1978) and later as consul(1978-1982). He was also accredited as first secretary at the permanent mission of Cyprus to the United Nations(1980-1982). served as the Ambassador of Cyprus to the United States of America and non resident High Commissioner to Canada(2003-2006). Mr Evriviades is now the Political Director of the Ministry of Foreign Affairs of the Republic of Cyprus.

STEVEN FLORIDES
Artist

PLACE OF BIRTH: London parents from Cyprus born in 1955
MARITAL STATUS: Married to Claudia.
SCHOOLS/COLLEGE: Hunter University.
QUALIFICATIONS: Majored in Astronomy and Mechanical Engineering.
PERSONAL PROFILE: Steven Florides moved to the United States in 1966 His love for Astronomical art has been from a young age his work has been exhibited at many conventions.

USA

MICHAEL PATSALOS FOX

On Mckinseys shareholder committee, the senior governance body of the firm

PLACE OF BIRTH: Cyprus 1953
SCHOOLS/COLLEGE: Sydney University and IMEDE in Switzerland.
QUALIFICATIONS: BSc in Computer Sciences and Pure Mathematics and an MBA. with distinction.
PERSONAL PROFILE: Michael Patsalos Fox is a Director of Mckinsey, Americas, in charge of overseeing the firm's North and South American offices. Patsalos- Fox sits on Mckinseys shareholder committee, the senior governance body of the firm.

DR ELAINE Z. FRANCIS (nee ZAMPAS)

National Program Director for the U.S. Environmental Protection Agency's Pesticides and Toxics Research Program

DATE OF BIRTH: 02-May-1951
PLACE OF BIRTH: USA Father from Karavas, Mother, Greek-American.
MARITAL STATUS: Married to Dr. James Francis, American, Dermatologist.
CHILDREN: Christopher, Sports Management. Jonathan, Attorney.
SCHOOLS/COLLEGE: American University in Washington Thomas Jefferson University in Philadelphia.
QUALIFICATIONS: BS PhD.
MEMBERSHIPS: The Teratology Society, Vice Chair.
HONOURS/AWARDS: Six Bronze One Silver and One Gold medal from the EPA.
HOBBIES AND INTERESTS: Cooking, reading and sport.
PERSONAL PROFILE: Dr. Elaine Francis is the National Program Director for the U. S. Environmental Protection Agency's Pesticides and Toxics Research Program. Before joining EPA she taught anatomy, neuroanatomy, and embryology to medical and graduate students at then Hahnemann Medical College (now Drexel University College of Medicine) in Philadelphia.

JOHN FRANGOS

Founder, Principal Scientist, President and CEO of La Jolla Bioengineering Institute, La Jolla, California

PLACE OF BIRTH: Cyprus
SCHOOLS/COLLEGE: John Hopkins University Baltimore, Stanford University California. And Rice University Houston.
QUALIFICATIONS: BES. MS and PhD.
MEMBERSHIPS: Fellow American Institute for Medical and Biological Engineering and Editorial Board, General Pharmacology.
HONOURS/AWARDS: NSF Presidential Young Investigator Award 1990-1995.
PERSONAL PROFILE: John Frangos is the Founder, Principal Scientist, President and CEO of La Jolla Bioengineering Institute, La Jolla, California.

ANDREAS GEORGE

Radiation Physicist

DATE OF BIRTH: 23-Apr-1931
PLACE OF BIRTH: USA both parents from Neon Chorion.
MARITAL STATUS: Married to Katherine, USA (Greek American), Housewife.
CHILDREN: Stella, Sales. Dian, Teacher. Chris, Construction worker.
SCHOOLS/COLLEGE: Pancyprian Gymnasium, Cyprus. Brooklyn College, Hunter College and City College.
QUALIFICATIONS: BS, MS, MS, Radiation Physicist.
MEMBERSHIPS: Member of the American Associaton of Radon Scientists, Member and Officer in the Order of AHEPA.
HONOURS/AWARDS: Medal and Award from the US Department of Energy for Outstanding and Meritorious Service for his work on radon research and risk assessment.
HOBBIES AND INTERESTS: Volunteered in the 2004 Athens Olympics. He likes farming, reading books on men and women of Science, saints and philosophy.
PERSONAL PROFILE: Radiation Physicist. Has wrote and published a book 'In the Footsteps of Saint Nicholas. Has written more than 100 scientific papers on radon and other radioactive contaminants in the Nuclear Fuel Cycle.

CHRISTOPHER GEORGE
Director of a Network Television company

PLACE OF BIRTH: New York Mother from Cyprus
CHILDREN: Demetra.
SCHOOLS/COLLEGE: St Johns University.
PERSONAL PROFILE: Christopher George is a Director of a Network Television company.

HARRIET PAVLES GEORGE
Retired Civil Court Judge

PLACE OF BIRTH: USA, father born in Droushia.
MARITAL STATUS: Married to Norman George, American, Judge, N. Y. State Supreme Court.
CHILDREN: Six Children.
SCHOOLS/COLLEGE: Hofstra University. Fordham University. Law School.
QUALIFICATIONS: Bachelor of Arts Degree, Doctor of Law Degree, Member of the Bar, State of New York, Member of the Judiciary of the City of New York 1977-1997.
MEMBERSHIPS: Hellenic Womens Club of the North Shore. Hellenic American Lawyers Association.
HONOURS/AWARDS: Honored by the Greek American Lawyers Association, the Hellenic Lawyers Assoc. Selected as one of 6 women of Cypriot descent to receive an award from the Consul General Cyprus.
HOBBIES AND INTERESTS: Art, Music, Opera, Writing, Travel, History, Archaeology.
PERSONAL PROFILE: Retired Civil Court Judge and before that was an attorney in private practice. In 1974 at the time of the Invasion of Cyprus she was appointed to chair the Relief Effort of St. Demetrios Church, Jamaica N. Y. to help Cypriot children affected by the war. $20,000 was raised and donated.

HARRY GEORGE
Law

PLACE OF BIRTH: USA Grandfather from Droushia
MARITAL STATUS: Married to Lisa.
CHILDREN: Michael, Student Grammar School. Andrew, Kindergarten.
SCHOOLS/COLLEGE: Queens College and South Western Law School California.
PERSONAL PROFILE: Harry George is in private practise in a Law firm in Bellmore, Long Island.

KENNETH GEORGE
Patent Attorney

PLACE OF BIRTH: New York Grandfather from Droushia
MARITAL STATUS: Married to Nancy Shenker.
CHILDREN: Austin, College Student. Lowell, High School Student.
SCHOOLS/COLLEGE: New York University and Brooklyn Law School.
PERSONAL PROFILE: Kenneth George is a Patent Attorney and a partner in a New York City Patent Firm.

RALLIS GEORGHAKIS
Vice President of the Long Island Art League

DATE OF BIRTH: 06-Mar-1933
PLACE OF BIRTH: Famagusta.
MARITAL STATUS: Married to Connie.
CHILDREN: Stephen, Executive at the Computer Sciences Corp. Christine, works at Hoffstra University.
SCHOOLS/COLLEGE: American Academy Larnaca. State University of New York, Washington School of Art.
MEMBERSHIPS: Honorary member of the International Society of Artists.
PERSONAL PROFILE: Artist exhibited in USA, UK Greece, Cyprus and is Vice President of the Long Island Art League.

USA

COSTAS GEORGHIADES
Delbert A Whitaker Chair Professor and Department Head with the Electrical and Computer Engineering Department at Texas A&M University

PLACE OF BIRTH: Cyprus
SCHOOLS/COLLEGE: American University of Beirut and Washington University.
QUALIFICATIONS: BE MS and DSc.
MEMBERSHIPS: Fellow of the IEEE.
PERSONAL PROFILE: Costas Georgiades is a Delbert A Whitaker Chair Professor and Department Head with the Electrical and Computer Engineering Department at Texas A&M University.

ANDREAS MICHAEL GEORGHIOU
Chief Executive Officer Spacenet Inc

DATE OF BIRTH: 26-Aug-1949
PLACE OF BIRTH: Steni, Pafos, Cyprus.
MARITAL STATUS: Married to Diane, USA, Educator.
CHILDREN: Angella, Married with children. Lenia, Buyer. Dinos, Studying.
SCHOOLS/COLLEGE: American Acadamy, Larnaca, Cyprus. University of Pennsylvania, Wharton.
QUALIFICATIONS: BSc, Economics and Mathematics, MS Operations Research.
MEMBERSHIPS: Board member, Society of Satellite Professionals (SSPI), Advisory Council member, US Chamber of Commerce.
HOBBIES AND INTERESTS: Travel, books, history.
PERSONAL PROFILE: Chief Executive Officer, Spacenet Inc. which is a $100 million satellite communications company with 250 Employees. Andreas is also Chief Commercial Officer, SES Americom, responsible for the Marketing and Sales operations of this company generating over $500 million of revenue. Senior VP, Asset Management, SES Americom, responsible for Earth station operations and spacecraft engineering.

CHRISTOS GEORGIADES
Assistant Professor of Radiology and Surgery

DATE OF BIRTH: 12-Jul-1965
PLACE OF BIRTH: Morphou.
SCHOOLS/COLLEGE: University of Texas, University of California, Boston University, Harvard Medical School, John Hopkins School of Medicine.
QUALIFICATIONS: PhD MD.
MEMBERSHIPS: Society of Interventional Radiology, Cardiovascular & Interventional Radiology Society of Europe, American Board of Radiology.
PERSONAL PROFILE: Assistant Professor of Radiology and Surgery, Fellowship Program Director, Vascular & Interventional Radiology, John Hopkins Hospital.

DR SAVVAS GEORGIADES
Elected to the Quad City Abuse Council Board Of Directors for 2005-2008

PLACE OF BIRTH: Cyprus
SCHOOLS/COLLEGE: University of Georgia and Florida International University.
QUALIFICATIONS: MSW PhD.
PERSONAL PROFILE: Savvas Georgiades teaches at St Ambrose University School of Social Work. He has also been elected to the Quad City abuse Council Board Of Directors for 2005-2008.

BYRON STEPHEN GEORGIOU
Ran successfully for United States Congress, the Only Greek Cypriot -American ever to do so

DATE OF BIRTH: 22-Jun-1948
PLACE OF BIRTH: Detroit, Michigan, USA, Father from Paphos, Cyprus.
MARITAL STATUS: Married to Theresa Nora Collins, Ireland, Educational Psychologist.
SCHOOLS/COLLEGE: Stanford University, Harvard Law School.
QUALIFICATIONS: JD. Magna Cum Laude 1974.
MEMBERSHIPS: AHEPA and PSEKA.
HONOURS/AWARDS: California Public Official of the Year, from the American Trial Lawyers Association 1982.

USA

HOBBIES AND INTERESTS: Politics, hiking, choral and instrumental music.

PERSONAL PROFILE: Byron is an attorney and investor, of counsel to the law firm of Lerach Coughlin, which exclusively represents investors defrauded in the securities markets. They are a counsel for the class of the defrauded investors in Enron, the most visible of all securities frauds, among others. In 1990 and 1992, Byron ran successfully for United States Congress, the Only Greek Cypriot American ever to do so.

CLEOPATRA GEORGIOU
Creative Director Tommy Hilfinger Europe and USA

PLACE OF BIRTH: Born 1968 in UK Parents from Karavas and Ayios Tychonas
MARITAL STATUS: Single.
SCHOOLS/COLLEGE: St Martins School of Art.
QUALIFICATIONS: BA in Fashion & Textiles.
MEMBERSHIPS: Council of British Fashion Designers, Fashion Global International Network.

HOBBIES AND INTERESTS: Yoga, Health and Fitness, discovering unusual places and markets for inspiration and curiousity.

PERSONAL PROFILE: Cleopatra Georgiou is the creative Director of Tommy Hilfinger Europe and USA, Esprit Europe and Haggar USA. As a Creative Director of Corporate Fashion Houses, unlike UK High Street Labels (M&S, Next.) she is responsible for moving large Global Fashion Brands creatively forward.
research & set the Visionary Trends 2-5 years ahead of time using social political & creative (youth & music) influences, whatever source is relative based on the now & past influences.
Having compiled all this information she then directs the Fashion Designers & Advertising & Marketing chiefs on where they are heading bearing in mind the Brand Identity. taking what is relevant for that particular market. Sees the Fashion Design through to manufacturing steering the ship of these Brands.

ELENA GEORGIOU
Lecturer in creative writing at Hunter College in New York and Goddard College in Vermont

PLACE OF BIRTH: Parents from Cyprus
HONOURS/AWARDS: Recipient of a New York Foundation for the Arts Poetry fellowship and the Astraea Foundation Emerging Writers Award in Poetry.
PERSONAL PROFILE: Elena Georgiou is a Poet her work has been published in numerous literary journals and anthologies. She teaches poetry and creative writing at Hunter College in New York and Goddard College in Vermont.

GEORGE GEORGIOU
Professor and Chairman of the Department of Economics at Towson University

DATE OF BIRTH: 07-Mar-1951
PLACE OF BIRTH: Larnaca.
SCHOOLS/COLLEGE: Drew University, George Washington University.
QUALIFICATIONS: MPh and PhD both in Economics.
MEMBERSHIPS: American Economic Association, American Association of University Professors.
PERSONAL PROFILE: George Georgiou a Fulbright Scholar, and is Professor and Chairman of the Department of Economics at Towson University.

GEORGE GEORGIOU
Playboy Magazine Photographer

PLACE OF BIRTH: USA Parents from Cyprus
PERSONAL PROFILE: George Georgiou is a Photographer for the Playboy Magazine He is also a photo instructor at Columbia College.

GEORGE GEORGIOU
Professor Computer Science Department
California State University

PLACE OF BIRTH: Erimi
SCHOOLS/COLLEGE:
Louisianna State University and
Tulane University.
QUALIFICATIONS: BS MS PhD.
PERSONAL PROFILE: George
Georgiou is an Assistant Dean,
College of Natural Sciences and
Professor Computer Science
Department California State
University.

PETER GEORGIOU
Serves on the Boards of Chicago
Academy for the Performing Arts and
the Bishops Aid Task Force

DATE OF BIRTH: 15-Jun-1961
PLACE OF BIRTH: New York,
father from Larnaca and mother
from Aradippou.
MARITAL STATUS: Single.
SCHOOLS/COLLEGE: Pace
University, National College of
Chiropractic.
QUALIFICATIONS: BA in Human
Services, BSc in Human Biology,
PhD in Chiropractic Medicine.
MEMBERSHIPS: Serves on Chicago Academy for the
Performing Arts and the Bishops Aid Task Force.
HOBBIES AND INTERESTS: Travel, gardening and skiing.
PERSONAL PROFILE: Peter worked as a Flight
Attendant for 11 years while he put himself through
Chiropractic school. He also flew for 5 years while in
private practice and he has currently been in practice for
15 years.

RENOS GEORGIOU
Director of the Cyprus Chamber of
Commerce USA

PLACE OF BIRTH: Neon
Chorion, Kythrea
MARITAL STATUS: Married to
Mary Ann.
CHILDREN: Six Children.
PERSONAL PROFILE:
President of the Reno
Construction Company also
a Director of the Cyprus
Chamber of Commerce USA.

GEORGE GREGORIOU
Political Science Professor at the William
Paterson University

DATE OF BIRTH: 13-Dec-1954.
PLACE OF BIRTH: Cyprus.
QUALIFICATIONS: BA PhD.
PERSONAL PROFILE: George Gregoriou worked as
a Political Science Professor at the William Paterson
University of New jersey has written numerous books
on the Western Geopolitical strategies in the Eastern
Mediteranean particularly the Political forces of British
Coloniasation, the Greek and Cyprus events leading to
the partition in 1974 and the Anglo American policies
outside and inside the United Nations to legitimize the
facts on the ground created by the Turkish occupation of
Northern Cyprus.

GEORGE GREGORIOU
Associate Professor

PLACE OF BIRTH: Cyprus
SCHOOLS/COLLEGE: Drexel
University in Philadelphia.
QUALIFICATIONS: PhD in
Electrical Engineering.
HONOURS/AWARDS: He is a
member of the IEE.
PERSONAL PROFILE: George
worked as a Research Assistant
Professor at Drexel University for
one year and at the University of
North Carolina at Chapel Hill for three years. He is currently
an Associate Professor and Head of the Department of
Engineering at Intercollege. He has presented papers in
numerous conferences and has published more than twenty
papers in conference proceedings and refereed journals
such as the Journal of Nuclear Medicine and the IEEE
Transactions on Nuclear Science.

WILLIAM GROUTAS
Professor in Chemistry at Winchita
University

DATE OF BIRTH: 11-Oct-1945
PLACE OF BIRTH: Dhali.
MARITAL STATUS: Married.
CHILDREN: One son.
SCHOOLS/COLLEGE:
University of Kentucky.
QUALIFICATIONS: PhD.
PERSONAL PROFILE: William
is a Distinguished Professor
Biorganic and Medicinal
Chemistry and Endowment
associations Distinguished Professor to Winchita State
University in Kansas.

USA

MICHAEL HADJIARGYROU
Associate Professor, Dept. of Biomedical Engineering, State University of New York

DATE OF BIRTH: 09-Feb-1964
PLACE OF BIRTH: Larnaca, Cyprus.
MARITAL STATUS: Married to Barbara Monti, American, Artist.
CHILDREN: Sky Liang.
SCHOOLS/COLLEGE: City University of New York.
QUALIFICATIONS: BA, MA, PhD.
MEMBERSHIPS: American Society for Bone and Mineral Research, Federation of American Societies for Experimental Biology.
HONOURS/AWARDS: Who's Who in Medicine and Healthcare, Who's Who in America, Who's Who in Science and Engineering.
HOBBIES AND INTERESTS: Reading The New York Times, Political and Philosophical discussions, playing soccer.
PERSONAL PROFILE: Associate Professor, Dept. of Biomedical Engineering, State University of New York at Stony Brook. Associate Vice President for Research, State University of New York.

PROFESSOR DEMOS P HADJIYANIS
Professor of Economics at the University of St Thomas in Minnesota

DATE OF BIRTH: 01-Dec-1923
PLACE OF BIRTH: Syngrassis.
MARITAL STATUS: Married to Evgenia, Samos, Retired Clerk.
CHILDREN: Katherine Boosalis, Economics BA MBA. Vicky Digiovanni, Human Resources BA MBA. George Hadjiyanis, Engineering BSc MBA.
SCHOOLS/COLLEGE: English School, Tricomo and American Academy Larnaca. Oklahoma State University, Ohio university and University of Minnesota.
QUALIFICATIONS: BSc. MSc. and PhD.
MEMBERSHIPS: American Econ Association and AHEPA(American Hellenic Progressive Association).
PERSONAL PROFILE: Demos Hadjiyanis, Professor Emeritus of Economics, University of St Thomas in Minnesotta has written numerous articles and presentations in Economics. Treasurer of AHEPA Educational Foundation District 14.

GEORGE HADJIYANIS
Vice President Sales and Marketing at Valtira provider of the online marketing platform

PLACE OF BIRTH: Father from Syngrassi
SCHOOLS/COLLEGE: University of minnesota.
QUALIFICATIONS: BSc MBA.
PERSONAL PROFILE: George Hadjiyanis is Vice President Sales and marketing at Valtira provider of the online marketing platform.

CHRISSI HART
Author of the book Under the Grapevine and other Publications

DATE OF BIRTH: 21-Mar-1955
PLACE OF BIRTH: Achna.
MARITAL STATUS: Married to Barry Hart, American, Psychologist.
CHILDREN: Adam, Sophia.
SCHOOLS/COLLEGE: Finchley Manor Hill School. Barnet College, Universities of Hull, Leicester and Lancaster.
QUALIFICATIONS: BA PhD Psychology and Diploma in Clinical Psychology.
MEMBERSHIPS: Society of Childrens Book Writers, Associate Fellow of the British Psychological Society.
HOBBIES AND INTERESTS: Writing, going to Church, gardening, film and travel.
PERSONAL PROFILE: Chrissie Hart is an Author, Psychologist and childrens radio host.
Author of the book Under the Grapevine and other publications.

USA

DEMETRIS HAVADJIAS

President and co founder with his brothers of the Fast Food Restaurant Chain in Southern California called Farmers Boys

PLACE OF BIRTH: Cyprus
HONOURS/AWARDS: KCBS-TV(CBS 2) has named Farmers Boys as the best Burger in Southern California as well as Inland Empire magazines best burger. Farmers Boys have also won Awards for their deep fried Zucchini and monster sized onion rings.
PERSONAL PROFILE: Demetris Havadjias is the President and co founder with his brothers of the Fast Food Restaurant Chain in Southern California called Farmers Boys it has 59 locations with several more currently or soon to be under construction.

MAKIS HAVADJIAS

President of the Monument of Immortals a non profit organisation in California USA and Cyprus dedicated to establishing a monument in Olympia Greece

PLACE OF BIRTH: Cyprus
PERSONAL PROFILE: Makis Havadjias is one of the co founders with his brothers of the Farmers Boys Restaurant Chain. Makis is also the co founder and President of the Monument of Immortals a non profit organisation in California USA and Cyprus dedicated to establishing a monument in Olympia Greece to honour the history and sportsmanship of Olympic competitions and revive the Ancient Tradition of inscribing the names of Olympic Victors.

DIANA SOPHOCLES HEMMENWAY

Executive Director and founder of the Darlington Arts Center

PLACE OF BIRTH: USA Father from Larnaca.
PERSONAL PROFILE: Diana Sophocles Hemmenway is the Executive Director and founder of the Darlington Arts Center which is a non profit school of the Arts located in Garnet Valley, Delaware County. The Center currently serves 4000 people. Darlington has a Faculty of 67 and offers a wide selection of classes in music, visual arts, drama and dance.

ELISABETH HERSCHBACH

Philosopher at Providence College, Rhode Island, USA

PLACE OF BIRTH: USA Great Grandfather from Dhali.
SCHOOLS/COLLEGE: University of Pennsylvania.
QUALIFICATIONS: PhD.
PERSONAL PROFILE: Elisabeth Herschbach is a Philosopher Adjunct Faculty, Department of Philosophy, Providence, College, Rhode, Island, USA.

CHRYSTOM HORATTAS

President of Cyprus Relief Committee

DATE OF BIRTH: 09-Feb-1928
PLACE OF BIRTH: Pano Arodhes.
MARITAL STATUS: Married to Fotine, Greek/American.
CHILDREN: Mark, Medical Doctor. Denise, Pharmacist. Christine, Physical Therapist. Ann Marie, Chemical Engineer.
SCHOOLS/COLLEGE: Paphos Greek Gymnasium. Wayne State University.
QUALIFICATIONS: BSEE, MSEE.
MEMBERSHIPS: AHEPA, GOC, Cyprus Relief, Toastmasters, USAF.
HONOURS/AWARDS: Several Inventions and Patents.
HOBBIES AND INTERESTS: Writing, woodworking, gardening and fishing.
PERSONAL PROFILE: President of Afron GOC, President of Cyprus Relief Committee, President Summit toastmasters, Author of The Love of the Infidel.

MARK HORATTAS

Professor of Surgery at Northeastern Ohio Universities

PLACE OF BIRTH: USA Father from Paphos
SCHOOLS/COLLEGE: NorthEastern Ohio Universities College of Medicine.
QUALIFICATIONS: MD.
PERSONAL PROFILE: Mark Horattas is Professor of Surgery at Northeastern Ohio Universities College of Medicine. He is also Associate Chairman of Medical Education and Research at Akron General Medical Center.

USA

DR CHRISTOS IOANNIDES
Director of the Centre for Byzantine and Modern Greek studies, Queens College City University of New York

PLACE OF BIRTH: Cyprus
PERSONAL PROFILE: Director of the Centre for Byzantine and Modern Greek studies, Queens College City University of New York.

DIMITRIS IOANNIDES
Professor at Missouri University

DATE OF BIRTH: 21-Dec-1961
PLACE OF BIRTH: Nicosia Cyprus (Cypriot father, English mother).
MARITAL STATUS: Single.
CHILDREN: Sasha, Elementary School.
SCHOOLS/COLLEGE: University of Nottingham and Rutgers University.
QUALIFICATIONS: BSc and MA, PhD.
MEMBERSHIPS: Association for American Geographers and the Institute of British Geographers.
HOBBIES AND INTERESTS: Long distance running, road cycling, hiking, supporter for over 30 years of Liverpool Football Club.
PERSONAL PROFILE: Professor of Tourism and Planning and Development, Missouri State University. Was recently offered the Chair Of Human Geography at Mid-Sweden University in Ostersund, Sweden (to begin August 1st, 2008).

SARAH ELIZABETH IOANNIDES
Music director for both El Paso Symphony Orchestra and South Carolina's Philharmonic Orchestra

DATE OF BIRTH: 02-Apr-1972
PLACE OF BIRTH: Canberra, Australia, Father born in Nicosia.
MARITAL STATUS: Married to Scott Hartman, American, Trombonist.
SCHOOLS/COLLEGE: Julliard School of Music, New York. Curtis Institute of Music, Philadelphia, Guildhall School of Music, London, Oxford University, Somerville College.
QUALIFICATIONS: MA, MM.
MEMBERSHIPS: American Symphony Orcheastra League.
HOBBIES AND INTERESTS: Outdoor activities, reading, cooking, languages, travelling, family time and friendship.
PERSONAL PROFILE: Sarah Ioannides has served as a music director for both El Paso Symphony Orchestra and South Carolina's Philharmonic Orchestra since the beginning of 2005-06 season. She is very active in the community life of these cities, providing a network of numerous education and mini-festival events in conjunction with the season performances.

CHRISTOS IOANNOU
Distinguished Instructor in Economics University of Minnesota

PLACE OF BIRTH: Nicosia
MARITAL STATUS: Single.
SCHOOLS/COLLEGE: University of Arizona and University of Minnesota.
QUALIFICATIONS: BS. BA, Business Economics Finance and MA in Economics.
PERSONAL PROFILE: Distinguished Instructor, Dept of Economics, University of Minnesota 2004 and 2007.

CONSTANTINE IOANNOU
Psychiatrist

PERSONAL PROFILE: Dr Constantine Ioannou is a board certified Psychiatrist.

DR GEORGE IOANNOU
Chosen as one of the recipients of the Jan Albrecht Clinical Research Awards in Liver Disease for 2006

PLACE OF BIRTH: Cyprus
MARITAL STATUS: Married to Jannicke.
CHILDREN: Nikolas, Isabelle.
SCHOOLS/COLLEGE: Oxford University in the UK and Duke University in North Carolina.
HONOURS/AWARDS: Dr George Ioannou has been chosen as one of the recipients of the Jan Albrecht Clinical Research Awards in Liver Disease for 2006. The award which consists of $150, 000 in salary support over two years will fund his project in Liver Transplantation.
PERSONAL PROFILE: Dr George Ioannou is acting Professor of medicine at the University of Washington and staff physician at the veterans affairs pugent sound health care system.

GEORGE IOANNOU
Pediatrician based in Astoria, New York

DATE OF BIRTH: 01-May-1932.
PLACE OF BIRTH: Cyprus.
QUALIFICATIONS: MD.
PERSONAL PROFILE: Dr George Ioannou is a Pediatrician based in Astoria, New York.

JOHN MICHAEL IOANNOU
Attorney/Federal Mediator

DATE OF BIRTH: 13-Jan-1955.
PLACE OF BIRTH: New York, parents from Ktima, Paphos, Lakatamia, Nicosia.
CHILDREN: Alexis, Michael, Matthew, Andrew.
SCHOOLS/COLLEGE: New York University, Franklin Pierce Law School.
QUALIFICATIONS: BA, JD.
PERSONAL PROFILE: Attorney/Partner Ioannou and Associates. Federal Mediator, Federal District Court, Eastern District New York.

PETER IOANNOU
Attorney

DATE OF BIRTH: 23-Mar-1958.
PLACE OF BIRTH: Kyrenia.
SCHOOLS/COLLEGE: University of Athens, University of New York and Rutgers University.
QUALIFICATIONS: LLM JD.
MEMBERSHIPS: American Trial Lawyers Association.

PERSONAL PROFILE: Peter Ioannou is an Attorney practising in New Jersey.

PETROS IOANNOU
Professor of Electrical Engineering University of Southern California

DATE OF BIRTH: 03-Feb-1953
PLACE OF BIRTH: Tripimeni.
MARITAL STATUS: Married to Natallia.
CHILDREN: Kira, Student at University of Southern California. Andreas, High School.
SCHOOLS/COLLEGE: University College, London, University of Illinois.
QUALIFICATIONS: BSc. MS and PhD.
MEMBERSHIPS: Control System Society on IEEITS Council Committee.
HONOURS/AWARDS: Recipient of 1985 Presidential Young Investigator Award for his Research in Adaptive Control.
PERSONAL PROFILE: Petros Ioannou is a Professor at the Department of Electrical Engineering, University of Southern California. He is also the Director of the Centre of Adavanced Transportation Technologies, he is also Co-author of five books and over 150 research papers.

PHOTIOS IOANNOU
Professor of Civil & enviromental Engineering at the University of Michigan

PLACE OF BIRTH: Nicosia
SCHOOLS/COLLEGE: University of Michigan.
QUALIFICATIONS: PhD PE.
HONOURS/AWARDS: Recipient of the ASCE John O Bickel Award for his pioneering research contributions in tunnel design and underground construction.
PERSONAL PROFILE: Photios Ioannou is a Professor of Civil & enviromental Engineering at the University of Michigan.

CHRISTODOULOS IORDANOU
Pediatrician in Astoria, New York

PLACE OF BIRTH: Cyprus.
QUALIFICATIONS: M. D.
PERSONAL PROFILE: Dr Christodoulos Iordanou is a Pediatrician in Astoria, New York.

USA

CONSTANTINE IORDANOU
Recipient of the Ellis Island Medal of Honor

PLACE OF BIRTH: Cyprus
SCHOOLS/COLLEGE: University of New York.
QUALIFICATIONS: B. S. in Aerospace Engineering.
HONOURS/AWARDS: Recipient of the Ellis Island Medal of Honor.
PERSONAL PROFILE: Constantine Iordanou is the chief executive Officer, President and Director of Arch Capital Group Ltd.

MICHAEL IORDANOU
Pediatrician Managing Partner of Astoria Pediatric Associates PC

DATE OF BIRTH: 28-Aug-1959.
PLACE OF BIRTH: Nicosia.
MARITAL STATUS: Married to Theana, USA Father from Lefkoniko, Mother from Kyrenia, AVP marketing for AIG.
CHILDREN: Jordan, Christian, Angelika, Jennia.
SCHOOLS/COLLEGE: Davidson College and St Georges School of Medicine.
QUALIFICATIONS: BS MD.
MEMBERSHIPS: Pancyprian Association of America, American Academy of Pediatrics, Former President of Manhasset soccer club.
PERSONAL PROFILE: Dr Michael Iordanou is a Pediatrician practising in Astoria and Bayside New York Managing Partner of Astoria Pediatric Associates PC.

ONISIFOROS IORDANOU
Assistant Professor of Economics at New york University

PLACE OF BIRTH: Cyprus
MARITAL STATUS: Married.
SCHOOLS/COLLEGE: National University of Athens, Long Island Universityand City University of New York.
QUALIFICATIONS: BS MA MPhil and a PhD.
PERSONAL PROFILE: Onisiforos Iordanou served as an Assistant Professor of Economics at New york University and Hunter City College of the City University of New York. He has a special scientist appointment at the University of Cyprus.

THEANA LAZARIDES IORDANOU
Vice President Marketing AIG

PLACE OF BIRTH: Parents from Lefkoniko and Kyrenia.
MARITAL STATUS: Married to Michael, Nicosia, Pediatrician.
CHILDREN: Jordan, Christian, Angelika, Jennia.
SCHOOLS/COLLEGE: Georgetown University.
QUALIFICATIONS: BA.
PERSONAL PROFILE: Theana Lazarides Iordanou is Vice President Marketing AIG.

KAY GEORGE JAIN
Lecturer at Queens College

PLACE OF BIRTH: New York Mother from Cyprus.
MARITAL STATUS: Married to Arvin Jain.
CHILDREN: Kim, Student. Kristen, Student. Lauren, Student.
SCHOOLS/COLLEGE: Smith College.
QUALIFICATIONS: Masters Degree in Linguistics.
PERSONAL PROFILE: Kay George Jain was a lecturer at Queens College.

GUS J. JAMES II
Chairman of the Board, President and Managing Partner of Kaufman & Canoles Supreme President Order of AHEPA

PLACE OF BIRTH: Koma Tou Yialou
MARITAL STATUS: Married to Helen Alexion James, Housewife.
CHILDREN: Dr Mary-Margaret James, Paediatrician. Mrs. Nicole Phillips, Teacher/Housewife.
SCHOOLS/COLLEGE: University of Richmond, College of William and Mary.
QUALIFICATIONS: BS in Business: JD Master of Law and Taxation.
MEMBERSHIPS: Supreme Counselor Order of AHEPA, American Bar Association, Cyprus and Hellenic Affairs Committee and various others.
HONOURS/AWARDS: The National Conference for Community Justice Humanitarian Award, Fellow of the Virginia Law Foundation, Who's Who in American Law and many more.
PERSONAL PROFILE: Chairman of the Board, President and Managing Partner of Kaufman & Canoles, 1994 to present. Supreme President, order of AHEPA 2005-2006, 2006-.

USA

JOHN JOANNOU
Medical Doctor

PLACE OF BIRTH: Born in Cyprus 1961
SCHOOLS/COLLEGE: New York University, School of Medicine.
MEMBERSHIPS: Hellenic Medical Society of New York.
PERSONAL PROFILE: John Joannou is a Medical Doctor specialising in Gerontology works in Astoria, Queens.

ANDREAS S. KACOURIS
Ambassador for the Republic of Cyprus to the United States of America

DATE OF BIRTH: 21-Jul-1960
PLACE OF BIRTH: London. Parents from Famagusta.
MARITAL STATUS: Married to Kareen.
CHILDREN: Stephen, Matthew, Andreana.
SCHOOLS/COLLEGE: Buckingham College for Boys, Lancaster University. Carlton University, Ottawa in Canada.
QUALIFICATIONS: BA (Honours) in Politics; MA (International Affairs).
HOBBIES AND INTERESTS: Current affairs.
PERSONAL PROFILE: Ministry of Foreign Affairs for the Republic of Cyprus since 1984; currently Ambassador for the Republic of Cyprus to the United States of America.

JOHN KAIMAKLIOTIS
Medical

PLACE OF BIRTH: Cyprus.
QUALIFICATIONS: MD.
PERSONAL PROFILE: Dr John Kaimakliotis use to practice Gastroenterology and internal medicine in Astoria, New York. He now resides in Cyprus.

PETER KAKOYIANNIS
President of the Cyprus-US Chamber of Commerce

DATE OF BIRTH: 6-Aug-1947
PLACE OF BIRTH: Brooklyn, New York parents from Cyprus
MARITAL STATUS: Married to Joanne.
CHILDREN: Three Children.
SCHOOLS/COLLEGE: Brooklyn Technical High School.
MEMBERSHIPS: Board member of St Basil Academymember of Hellenic Bankers AssociationCyprus Childrens Fund.
PERSONAL PROFILE: Peter Kakoyiannis is a Lawyer and Partner member of the Law firm of Eiseman Levine Lehrhaupt & Kakoyiannis PC. He is the President of the Cyprus-US Chamber of Commerce and Second Vice President of Cyprus Federation of America. He also serves on the Boards of of the Metropolis of New Jersey and St George Greek Orthodox Church, Trenton, New Jersey and is a former member of the Archdiocese Cousel and legal committee of the Archdiocese.

ANASTASIA KALLI
Researcher in the Chemistry Department with Professor Hakansson at the University of Michigan

PLACE OF BIRTH: Limassol
SCHOOLS/COLLEGE: University of Athens.
QUALIFICATIONS: Studied Chemistry.
PERSONAL PROFILE: Anastasia conducted her undergraduate thesis at the molecular biology department of the Pasteur Institute, Athens, Greece. She is now working in the chemistry department with Professor Hakansson at the University of Michigan.

USA

The first Cypriot arrival to the USA was in the 1920's but the first major wave of Greek Cypriots moving to the USA was in the 1930's.

MARIANNA KALLI
Community partnerships and service coordinator at the University of Indianapolis

DATE OF BIRTH: 05-Jun-1979
PLACE OF BIRTH: Nicosia.
SCHOOLS/COLLEGE: University of Indianapolis.
QUALIFICATIONS: MA in Applied Sociology, BA Major; English and French.
HONOURS/AWARDS: Praxis Award 2004.
HOBBIES AND INTERESTS: Music, technology, poetry, wild life and art.
PERSONAL PROFILE: Marianna was the assistant director IRCIL which is the Indianapolis Resource Centre For Independent Living. She is now the Community partnerships and service co ordinator at the University of Indianapolis.

STAVROS KAMILARIS
President of the Lampousa Cypriot American Association

PLACE OF BIRTH: Karavas.
MARITAL STATUS: Married to Maria.
CHILDREN: Three Children.
SCHOOLS/COLLEGE: Nicosia Technical School and New Jersey Institute of Technology.
QUALIFICATIONS: AS and BSCE degrees.
MEMBERSHIPS: American Concrete Institute.
HONOURS/AWARDS: Recipient of the Engineer of the year Award 2003 from the North Jersey Branch of the American Society of Civil Engineers.
PERSONAL PROFILE: Stavros Kamilaris is the President of the Lampousa Cypriot American Association. and is a Senior Associate and Department Director, managing the Structural Rehabilitation group, the Municipal Engineering Services Group and the Land Surveying Services group based in the company Dewberrys Rutherford office.

JOHN KAMINARIDES
Emeritus Professor of Economics and International Business

DATE OF BIRTH: 07-Apr-1933.
PLACE OF BIRTH: Nicosia.
MARITAL STATUS: Married.
CHILDREN: Two Children.
SCHOOLS/COLLEGE: University of Houston.
QUALIFICATIONS: BA MA.
PERSONAL PROFILE: John Kaminarides is Emeritus Professor of Economics and International Business of Arkansas State University.

EVI PAPALOIZOU KAPLANIS
Lecturer in Modern Greek at the University of North Carolina

DATE OF BIRTH: 30-Dec-1958.
PLACE OF BIRTH: Nicosia.
MARITAL STATUS: Married to Dr. Costas Kaplanis from Nicosia, ex-Investment Banker.
CHILDREN: One son, one daughter.
SCHOOLS/COLLEGE: London School of Economics, London Business School.
QUALIFICATIONS: B. Sc (Econ), M. Sc, Ph. D (Lon).
HOBBIES AND INTERESTS: History of Art.
PERSONAL PROFILE: Former Associate Professor of Finance, London Business School, University of London. Now teaching modern greek at the University of North Carolina, USA.

STALO KARAGEORGI
Scientist

PLACE OF BIRTH: Paphos
SCHOOLS/COLLEGE: Agios Neophytos Lyceum. University of Texas and Imperial College London.
QUALIFICATIONS: BSc. and MSc.
HONOURS/AWARDS: Selected for the National Deans List.
PERSONAL PROFILE: Stalo Karageorgi is enrolled in the five year doctoral program in the USA within the Department of Environmental Health of Cyprus. Stalo is a keen swimmer and participated in the 1997 Cyprus National Competitions.

STAVROS KARAGEORGIS
Instructor California State University

PLACE OF BIRTH: Cyprus.
SCHOOLS/COLLEGE: University of California.
QUALIFICATIONS: BA and MA.
PERSONAL PROFILE: Stavros Karageorgis is an Instructor California State University.

USA

DR DAVID KARAOLIS
Assistant Professor at the University of Maryland

QUALIFICATIONS: PhD.
PERSONAL PROFILE: David Karaolis is an Assistant Professor at the Department of Epidemiology and Preventive Medicine, School of Medicine, University of Maryland.

THEMISTOCLIS KARAOLIS
Medical Researcher

DATE OF BIRTH: 06-Feb-1964
PLACE OF BIRTH: Marathovounos.
MARITAL STATUS: Married to Denise Freilich Karaoli, American, Business Consultant.
CHILDREN: Lia Marie, Nicole Bea.
SCHOOLS/COLLEGE: Pancyprian Gymnasium. Northeastern University.
QUALIFICATIONS: MA, BS in Biotechnology, Summa Cum Laude.
MEMBERSHIPS: Open Water Scuba Instructor, PADI, USA.
HONOURS/AWARDS: Faculty Society Memorial Scholarship for Academic Achievement, 1993, 1994 and 1995, Golden Key National Honor Society, Alpha Sigma Lambda National Honor Society.
HOBBIES AND INTERESTS: Scuba diving, cycling.
PERSONAL PROFILE: Medical Researcher.

MARKOS KASHIOURIS
Doctor based in Baltimore

DATE OF BIRTH: 20-Feb-1980
PLACE OF BIRTH: Limassol.
MARITAL STATUS: Single.
SCHOOLS/COLLEGE: National and Kapodistrian University of Athens. Medical School, Imperial College, London.
QUALIFICATIONS: Graduate Doctor, Honorary Research Officer, Imperial College London.
MEMBERSHIPS: Educational Committee for foreign medical graduates USA.
HOBBIES AND INTERESTS: Water-skiing, Snowboard, Philosophy, Computers.
PERSONAL PROFILE: Markos Kashiouris is a Doctor at Johns Hopkins University/Sinai Hospital Program in Internal Medicine, Baltimore.

TAKIS KASPARIS
Associate Professor in Electrical and Computer Engineering at the University of Central Florida

PLACE OF BIRTH: Limassol born January 1956
MARITAL STATUS: Married to Evridiki, Educator.
CHILDREN: Elena, Both Students. Andrea.
SCHOOLS/COLLEGE: Lanition High School. University of athens, City College of New York and University of New York.
QUALIFICATIONS: Diploma in Electrical Engineering, MS and PhD.
MEMBERSHIPS: Senior member of Institute of Electrical and Electronic Engineers.
HONOURS/AWARDS: Joseph M Biedenbach Outstanding Engineering Educator Award.
HOBBIES AND INTERESTS: Music, vintage amplifier collector.
PERSONAL PROFILE: Takis Kasparis is an Assistant and Associate Professor, Department of Electrical and Computer Engineering University of Central Florida.

YIOTIS KATSAMBAS
Senior Technical Animator at Sony Pictures

DATE OF BIRTH: 10-Jul-1973
PLACE OF BIRTH: Nicosia.
MARITAL STATUS: Married to Aneta Karagiannidou, Greek, Story Development Executive at NewKat Studios.
CHILDREN: Mihalis.
SCHOOLS/COLLEGE: Ringling School of Art, Sarasota, Florida, US.
QUALIFICATIONS: Bachelor of Arts in Computer Animation.
HOBBIES AND INTERESTS: Extreme Sports.
PERSONAL PROFILE: Yiotis has been heavily involved in Hollywood movie productions for the past ten years, producing work for Dreamworks, SKG, Disney and Sony pictures. He did work for the movie Beowulf directed by academy award winner Robert Zemeckis, starring Angelina Jolie, and Sir Anthony Hopkins. He has been fortunate in working on Steven Speilberg's Minority Report, Prince of Egypt, Road to Eldorado, and Spirit Stallion of the Cimmarron. He is currently contracted to Sony Pictures as a Senior Technical Animator, where over the next few years he will be working on breakthrough technical innovations in animation.

PANOS KELALIS
Professor of Urology (Deceased)

DATE OF BIRTH: 17-Jan-1932.
PLACE OF BIRTH: Nicosia.
MARITAL STATUS: Married to Barbara.
SCHOOLS/COLLEGE: University of Dublin.
QUALIFICATIONS: BA MS.
PERSONAL PROFILE: Professor of Urology at Mayo Clinic in Jacksonville. He was also the honorary consul for the Republic of Cyprus. He was a prolific author and lecturer.

COSTAS KELLAS
Develops mission critical client server applications for Industry

PLACE OF BIRTH: Cyprus
PERSONAL PROFILE: Costas Kellas with an education in operations research and statistics moved to South Africa and joined a leading banking group as operations research analyst, specialising in developing computer models for many commercial applications. Now Costas has moved to New Jersey and has a software company that Develops mission critical client server applications for Industry.

COSTA KENSINGTON
Lawyer Lead Counsel in Cyprus Halloumi Trademark Litigation

DATE OF BIRTH: 07-Feb-1948
PLACE OF BIRTH: Bristol, Father from Nicosia.
MARITAL STATUS: Married to Cheryl Lee, American, Teacher.
CHILDREN: C. Ragan Kensington, Student. Costa Nicholas, Student.
SCHOOLS/COLLEGE: Redland View Prep. Rutgers College/Law School.
QUALIFICATIONS: Bachelor Degree in Economics and Juris Doctorate in Law.
MEMBERSHIPS: University Club, New York, Association of the Bar NYC, New York State Bar and American Bar Association.
HONOURS/AWARDS: Henry Rutger Scholar.
HOBBIES AND INTERESTS: Golf, tennis and architecture.
PERSONAL PROFILE: Founding Member of Cyprus U. S. Chamber of Commerce, Lead Counsel in Cyprus Halloumi Trademark Litigation.

NICOLAS K. KENSINGTON
Managing Director Law Firm

DATE OF BIRTH: 07-Feb-1948
PLACE OF BIRTH: Bristol, England, Father from Nicosia.
MARITAL STATUS: Married to Laura Jane Murphy, Irish, Real Estate, Insurance.
SCHOOLS/COLLEGE: Rutgers College, New Brunswick, N. J. Rutgers Law School, Rutgers Business School, New York University.
QUALIFICATIONS: Bachelor Degree, Juris Doctor of Law.
HOBBIES AND INTERESTS: Tennis, Real Estate Development, Develop Investment and Tax Strategies.
PERSONAL PROFILE: Managing Director of Law Firm: Member of many Boards of Directors of various Companies: Trustee of many Trusts: He has taught courses of given lectures at college level. Played in AHEPA Good Will Basket Ball Team (sent to Greece) where the team also played many of the Olympic Basket Ball Teams, including the Russian Team at the time.

SPIROS KITROMILIS
Gynaecologist/Obstetrician

DATE OF BIRTH: 16-Oct-1934.
PLACE OF BIRTH: Karavas.
MARITAL STATUS: Married to Joan.
CHILDREN: Two children.
SCHOOLS/COLLEGE: Syracuse University.
QUALIFICATIONS: MD.
PERSONAL PROFILE: Spyros Kitromilis is a Gynaecologist/Obstetrician based in Liverpool, New York.

STEVEN KODROS
Orthopaedic Surgeon

DATE OF BIRTH: 02-Mar-1920
PLACE OF BIRTH: Nicosia.
MARITAL STATUS: Married to Vivian.
CHILDREN: Steven, Debbie, Paul.
SCHOOLS/COLLEGE: University of Illinois and University of Athens.
QUALIFICATIONS: MD.
MEMBERSHIPS: Former President of the Hellenic Medical society of Chicago.
PERSONAL PROFILE: Andreas Kodros Orthopaedic Surgeon based in Illinois.

GEORGE KOKKINOS
Senior Vice President at Mizuho Alternatives Investments

DATE OF BIRTH: 07-Nov-1960
PLACE OF BIRTH: Katokopia, Cyprus.
MARITAL STATUS: Married to Cathy, American, Accounting.
CHILDREN: Alexandra, Monmouth University. Jon, Randolph High School.
SCHOOLS/COLLEGE: Fairleigh Dickenson University, USA.
QUALIFICATIONS: MBA with Honors.
MEMBERSHIPS: International Association of Credit Portfolio Managers(IACPM).
HONOURS/AWARDS: Graduated college with Honours, Soccer Coach of the Year (Volunteer in Town).
HOBBIES AND INTERESTS: Play and coach Soccer, Travel, History books (especially about Greece and Cyprus).
PERSONAL PROFILE: Works at Mizuho Alternatives Investments, a subsidiary of Mizuho Financial Group, as a Senior Vice President and the Head of Credit Research & Analysis. He has volunteered to coach soccer in his town for the last 10 years. He was also a member of the Greek Educational Committee.

EVRIS KONTOS
Owner of Kontos Flatbread and Fillo Company Kontos Foods is called by many as the Premier Baker of Hand Stretched Flatbread, producing over 22 varieties of flatbread, and the majority are hand-stretched

DATE OF BIRTH: 13-Jul-1930
PLACE OF BIRTH: Karavas, Cyprus.
MARITAL STATUS: Married to Evangelia, Greek, Housewife.
CHILDREN: Steven, College. Kathryn, College. Constantino, High School.
SCHOOLS/COLLEGE: Three years high schol.
MEMBERSHIPS: AHEPA, Leadership 100, Lampousa Cypriot Association.
HONOURS/AWARDS: Archon of Ecumenica Patriarchate, Ellis Island Medal Award of Honor.
HOBBIES AND INTERESTS: Gardening, Fishing, Baseball.
PERSONAL PROFILE: Owner of Flatbread and Fillo Company, Kontos Foods is called by many as the Premier Baker of Hand Stretched Flatbread, producing over 22 varieties of flatbread, and the majority are hand-stretched Past President of Lampousa Cypriot Association, USA.

GEORGE KORNIOTIS
On the Board of Governors of the Federal Reserve System

PLACE OF BIRTH: Cyprus
SCHOOLS/COLLEGE: University of Cyprus and Yale University.
QUALIFICATIONS: BSc and PhD.
PERSONAL PROFILE: George Korniotis is on the Board of Governors of the Federal Reserve System and was an assistant Professor at the University of Notre Dame in Indiana in The USA.

IACOVOS KOUMAS
Robotics and Software Senior Staff Engineer

PLACE OF BIRTH: Nicosia born 1971.
MARITAL STATUS: Single.
SCHOOLS/COLLEGE: Stanford University.
QUALIFICATIONS: MS Computer Science, MS Mechanical Engineering.
HOBBIES AND INTERESTS: Sports, football.
PERSONAL PROFILE: Robotics and Soft Ware Engineer. Senior Staff Engineer at Process Metrix responsible for developing software that controls laser scanning instruments using Microsoft visual.

CHRISTOS KOUTENTIS
Physician, Cardiothracic Anesthesiologist

DATE OF BIRTH: 15-Aug-1968
PLACE OF BIRTH: Born Bristol Parents from Lefkoniko and Trikomo
MARITAL STATUS: Single.
SCHOOLS/COLLEGE: Aberdeen,Boston University and Cornell Johns Hopkins
QUALIFICATIONS: MB ChB
MEMBERSHIPS: Society of Anesthesiology, New York Explorers Club.
HOBBIES AND INTERESTS: Cave diving and exploration.
PERSONAL PROFILE: Physician,Cardiothoracic Anesthesiologist based in New Jersey,USA.

USA

PETROS KOUTRAKIS
Professor of Enviromental Science at Harvard University

PLACE OF BIRTH: Cyprus
SCHOOLS/COLLEGE: Universities of patras and Paris.
QUALIFICATIONS: BS MS PhD.
PERSONAL PROFILE: Petros Koutrakis is a Professor of Enviromental Sciences, Department of Enviromental Health at Harvard University.

DEMETRIOUS KOUTSOFTAS
Associate principal and geo technical group leader Ove Arup & Partners, San Francisco

PLACE OF BIRTH: Mandres
MARITAL STATUS: Married.
CHILDREN: Andrew.
SCHOOLS/COLLEGE: Famagusta Greek Gymnasium. Israel Institute of Technology and Massachusetts Institute of Technology.
QUALIFICATIONS: BSc MSc.
HONOURS/AWARDS: Three prestigious awards from the American Society of Civil Engineers (ASCE): the Ralph B. Peck Award, the Martin S. Kapp Foundation Engineering Award, and the Thomas Middlebrooks Award.
PERSONAL PROFILE: Demetrius is currently a principal in the San Francisco office of Arup, an international multidisciplinary firm headquartered in London. He joined Arup in 2003 to start the Geotechnics group, and since then he has grown the group to 8 professional engineers and two support personnel. He is a registered Civil and Geotechnical Engineer in California. He has more than 36 years of practical experience, during which time he successfully completed scores of projects in California, and in many other states and overseas. He is a nationally-recognized expert in geotechnical engineering, and was recently elected to the National Academy of Engineering.

IOANNIS KYMISSIS
Assistant Professor Electrical Engineering at Columbia University

PLACE OF BIRTH: USA Father from Larnaca
SCHOOLS/COLLEGE: Massachusetts Institute of Technology.
QUALIFICATIONS: SB. M. Eng and Ph. D.
PERSONAL PROFILE: Ioannis Kymissis is an Assistant Professor Electrical Engineering at Columbia University, New York.

PAVLOS KYMISSIS
Professor of Psychiatry

DATE OF BIRTH: 28-Jun-1944.
PLACE OF BIRTH: Larnaca.
MARITAL STATUS: Married to Effie.
CHILDREN: Ann, Ioannis, Charalambos.
SCHOOLS/COLLEGE: University of Athens.
QUALIFICATIONS: MD.
PERSONAL PROFILE: Pavlos Kymissis was a Professor of Psychiatry and Pediatrics at the New York Medical College.

DR JAKOVOS A. KYPRI
Senior Associate at Eurasia Group focusing on Middle East and North Africa

DATE OF BIRTH: 08-Jun-1971
PLACE OF BIRTH: London. Parents from Famagusta.
MARITAL STATUS: Single.
SCHOOLS/COLLEGE: Cambridge University, University Libre De Bruxelles, LSE, and University of Kingston Upon Hull.
QUALIFICATIONS: bachelors, Masters and doctorate.
MEMBERSHIPS: International Institute for Strategic Studies.
PERSONAL PROFILE: Senior Associate at Eurasia Group focusing on Middle East and North Africa. His research interests include Mediterranean Politics Europe's Security Defense Initiative (ESDI), NATO-EU relations, defence and force structures, CBM's and human rights issues.

USA

ANDREAS KYPRIANIDES
Honorary Consul General of Cyprus to Los Angeles

PLACE OF BIRTH: Khoulou. Paphos
MARITAL STATUS: Married to Mika, Cyprus.
CHILDREN: Alexia.
SCHOOLS/COLLEGE: Teachers Training College, Nicosia. Claremont Mckenna College and Claremont Graduate School.
QUALIFICATIONS: BA MA.
MEMBERSHIPS: Founding member and Officer of the save Cyprus Council (now American Hellenic Council of Southern California.
HONOURS/AWARDS: Recipient of the Ellis Island Medal of Honour. The Patriarch Athenagoras Humanitarian Award of the Greek Diocese of San Francisco. During the Olympic Torch Relay for the 2004 Olympic Games in Athens, he was selected to run and carry the Olympic flame at the Los Angeles stage.
PERSONAL PROFILE: Andreas Kyprianides when in Cyprus taught at the Elementary School in Paphos later he worked as a reporter for the daily newspaper AGON in Nicosia. In the USA Andreas taught political philosophy and classics at Pomona College subsequently he started his own business in the field of fine arts and numismatics. He is the Honorary Consul General of Cyprus to Los Angeles.

MIKA KYPRIANIDES
Creative Director Manager

PLACE OF BIRTH: Cyprus
MARITAL STATUS: Married to Andreas, Paphos, Honorary Consul General of Cyprus to Los Angeles.
CHILDREN: Alexia.
SCHOOLS/COLLEGE: California State University.
QUALIFICATIONS: BA in design.
HONOURS/AWARDS: Winner of several Maggie and Publishers awards.
PERSONAL PROFILE: Mika is a Creative Director worked with the lifestyle magazine ALO and Teleflora.

ANNETTE KYPRIANOU
Assistant Professor at the Metro Medical Health Center

PLACE OF BIRTH: USA
Parents from Voni
SCHOOLS/COLLEGE: NorthWestern Ohio Universities, College of Medicine, Rootstown, Ohio.
PERSONAL PROFILE: Annette Kyprianou is an Assistant Professor at the School of Medicine, Metro Health Medical Center and Senior Clinical Instructor at Case Western Reserve University, Cleveland.

NATASHA KYPRIANOU
Lecturer in Cancer Biology at the University of Kentucky

PLACE OF BIRTH: Paphos
SCHOOLS/COLLEGE: University of London, University of Leeds and. University of Wales.
QUALIFICATIONS: BSc. MB. and PhD.
MEMBERSHIPS: British Pharmacological Society and Society of Woman in Urology.
HONOURS/AWARDS: Honorary Kentucky Colonel and SWIU/SBUR Inaugural Award for Outstanding Contributions to Urology Research.
PERSONAL PROFILE: Lecturer, Cancer Biology Course University of Kentucky College of Medicine, Lexington.

Majority of Greek Cypriots are settled in New York, New Jersey and Chicago. They can be found elsewhere in numbers in California, Maryland and Florida.

USA

CHRISTOPHER KYPROS
Musician performed a solo piano concert at The National Gallery of Art in Washington DC in November 2004

PLACE OF BIRTH: Cyprus
SCHOOLS/COLLEGE: Juilliard School in New York and Old Dominion University.
QUALIFICATIONS: Masters Degree.
PERSONAL PROFILE: Christopher Kypros is the Director of Music at the Saint Patrick Catholic School in Norfolk, Virginia. Pianist Christopher has been guest soloist with the Virginia Symphony and various regional College Orchestras. As a chamber musician he has performed with the Feldman String Quartet. Chris performed a solo piano concert at The National Gallery of Art in Washington DC in November 2004.

ANASTASIA KYRIACOU
Control Director at the American Cancer Society

PLACE OF BIRTH: Kyrenia.
PERSONAL PROFILE: Anastasia Kyriacou is a Control Director at the American Cancer Society.

DEMETRIOS KYRIACOU
Associate Professor North Western University

PLACE OF BIRTH: USA Parents from Nicosia
SCHOOLS/COLLEGE: University of California, University of Michigan and London School of Hygiene and Tropical Medicine.
QUALIFICATIONS: MD. PhD, MPH, DTM&H.
PERSONAL PROFILE: Demetrios Kyriacou is an Associate Professor in the Department of Emergency Medicine and Department of Preventive Medicine, North Western University, Feinberg school of Medicine.

KYRIACOS GIG KYRIACOU
Recipient of the year 2000 Volunteer of the Year Award from Los Angeles Superior Court

DATE OF BIRTH: 23-Jul-1959
PLACE OF BIRTH: USA parents from Nicosia.
MARITAL STATUS: Married to Kathleen, Greek, Office manager.
CHILDREN: Christianna, Student. Michael, Student.
SCHOOLS/COLLEGE: University of Southern California and Boalt.
QUALIFICATIONS: BA. JD.
MEMBERSHIPS: International Academy of Mediators, State Bar of California and Southern California Mediation association.
HONOURS/AWARDS: Recipient of the year 2000 Volunteer of the Year Award from Los Angeles Superior Court and the Outstanding volunteer Award from Los Angeles County's Dispute Resolution Program. In 2001 Gig received the case of the year Award from Los Angeles Countys Dispute.
HOBBIES AND INTERESTS: Basketball and Basketball Coaching.
PERSONAL PROFILE: Gig Kyriacou is an Attorney Mediator based in California.

LEE KYRIACOU
Elected Beacon City Councilman

DATE OF BIRTH: 21-Feb-1956
PLACE OF BIRTH: Detroit, Michigan, USA, Father from Droushia, mother from Pedhoulas.
MARITAL STATUS: Married to Elizabeth Ann Barrett, American, Marketing Consultant.
CHILDREN: Anastasia Hope, Sophia Grace.
SCHOOLS/COLLEGE: Woodrow Wilson High School, Long Beach, California. Yale Law School, Yale University, University of California Davis.
QUALIFICATIONS: JD Law, MPhil & MA. Economics, BA. History & Economics.
HONOURS/AWARDS: National Science foundation Graduate Fellow (economics): founding editor, Yale Journal on Regulation.
HOBBIES AND INTERESTS: Politics, crosswords, travel.
PERSONAL PROFILE: Vocation in banking, consulting, managing companies, including Boston Consulting Group, Chase Manhattan Bank, Fleet Bank and Novantas. A vocation in Politics including New York State Democratic Committee, Beacon City Councilman (elected since 1993).

USA

STANLEY KYRIAKIDES
Lecturer in Political Science at the College of Humanities and Social Sciences William Paterson University, USA

DATE OF BIRTH: 01-Nov-1932
PLACE OF BIRTH: Kaimakli.
MARITAL STATUS: Married to Julia.
CHILDREN: Athos, Andria.
SCHOOLS/COLLEGE: Brooklyn College and New York University.
PERSONAL PROFILE: Wrote The Constitution of Cyprus in Constitutions of the Countries of the World, Oceana Publications, 1972. Cyprus: Constitutionalism and Crisis Government, University of Pennsylvania Press, 1968. Stanley is a retired lecturer he taught Political Science at the College of Humanities and Social Sciences William Paterson University, USA.

DR STELIOS KYRIAKIDES
Professor of Aerospace at University of Texas

PLACE OF BIRTH: Cyprus
SCHOOLS/COLLEGE: University of Bristol, UK, California Institute of Technology.
QUALIFICATIONS: BSc First class Honours, MS. and PhD in Aeronautics.
MEMBERSHIPS: Chair Executive Committee, Applied Mechanics Division, ASME.
HONOURS/AWARDS: Fellow of the American Acadamy of Mechanics.
PERSONAL PROFILE: Stelios Kyriakides is a Professor of Aerospace Engineering and Engineering Mechanics. Director, Research Centre for Mechanics of Solids, Structures & Materials at the University of Texas, Austin.

TASSOS KYRIAKIDES
Biostatician/Epidemiologist

DATE OF BIRTH: 02-Mar-1969
PLACE OF BIRTH: Nicosia, Cyprus.
MARITAL STATUS: Married to Kristen Rachele Aversa, American, Obstetrician/Gynecologist.
CHILDREN: Tassos Andreas, Siena Christina, Eleni Katerina.
SCHOOLS/COLLEGE: the English School, Nicosia. UCLA and Yale University.
QUALIFICATIONS: BSC Biochemistry, MPhil Epidemiology, Phd Infectious Diseases Epidemiology.
MEMBERSHIPS: Scientific Expert, European Centres for Disease Prevention and Control, Member Clinical Trials Committee.
HONOURS/AWARDS: John F. Enders Research Grant Recipient, Yale Uni 1997, Honorary Mention, Lantzounis Research Grant.
HOBBIES AND INTERESTS: Soccer, Photography, Wine collection.
PERSONAL PROFILE: Biostatician/Epidemiologist Department of Veterans Affairs Cooperative Studies Program USA. Associate Research Scientist Internal Medicine, Yale University School of Medicine.

THEMIS R KYRIAKIDES
Assistant Professor at Yale University

DATE OF BIRTH: 20-Feb-1965
PLACE OF BIRTH: Nicosia, Cyprus.
MARITAL STATUS: Married to Stacey Fulton, American, International Business.
CHILDREN: Cleo, Elementary School. Maya, Elementary School.
SCHOOLS/COLLEGE: Kykkos Gymnasium, Nicosia. Washington State University.
QUALIFICATIONS: BSc in Microbiology, PhD in Microbiology.
MEMBERSHIPS: American Society for Matrix Biology, American Society of Investigative Pathology, North American Vascular Biology Society.
HONOURS/AWARDS: member of Editorial Board of Biomedical Materials Journal.
HOBBIES AND INTERESTS: Sports (tennis and soccer) collector of antique fountain pens, watches.
PERSONAL PROFILE: Assistant Professor Pathology and Biomedical Engineering, Yale University.

USA

THOMAS (Efthymios) KYRUS (Kyriakides)
Honorary Consul of the Republic of Cyprus in Virginia Beach

DATE OF BIRTH: 20-Jan-1929
PLACE OF BIRTH: Morphou.
MARITAL STATUS: Married to Elaine, Greek American, Housewife.
CHILDREN: Christopher, Architect. Nicholas, Business.
SCHOOLS/COLLEGE: NBorfolk Business College.
QUALIFICATIONS: Business Administration, Accounting.
MEMBERSHIPS: Hellenic American Institute, Hellenic American Congress.
HONOURS/AWARDS: Recipient of the Ellis Island Medal of Honor. Archon of the Patriarchate of Constantinople.
PERSONAL PROFILE: Thomas is Director of the Virginia Beach Foundation, and Director of the Bank of Tidewater, and Honorary Consul of the Republic of Cyprus in Virginia Beach, VA. He is also President and founder of St. Nicholas Greek Orthodox Church, Va. Beach. He entered real estate and development in 1956 and remained until his retirement in 1988. He specialized in commercial and industrial properties, building and development.

ANDREAS LAMBROU
Author

PLACE OF BIRTH: Cyprus.
SCHOOLS/COLLEGE: London University.
PERSONAL PROFILE: Andreas Lambrou is a collector and author on the topic of Fountain pens.

ANGELIKI LAMBROU
Enviromental Health

PLACE OF BIRTH: Cyprus
SCHOOLS/COLLEGE: University of Athens.
QUALIFICATIONS: Nursing Degree and masters of public health.
PERSONAL PROFILE: Angeliki Lambrou is at Harvard University is involved in the doctoral program within the Department of Enviromental Health in Cyprus. She also participated in the Public Health surveillance activities organised for the 2004 Olympic Games.

ANGELO LAMBROU
Fashion Designer

DATE OF BIRTH: 01-Apr-1960
PLACE OF BIRTH: Zimbabwe.
MARITAL STATUS: Single.
SCHOOLS/COLLEGE: Grammar School Limassol. Central St Martins.
QUALIFICATIONS: Degree in Fashion Desgin.
PERSONAL PROFILE: Fashion Designer prominent in South Africa moved to USA. The Fashion business goes under the name Angelos Lambrou.

NICOLE LAMBROU
On the Board of Directors of Oasis For Girls, a non profit organisation in San Francisco that provides art, education for young women aged 10-20

PLACE OF BIRTH: USA parents from Cyprus
SCHOOLS/COLLEGE: Hofstra University in New York.
QUALIFICATIONS: PhD.
PERSONAL PROFILE: Nicole Lambrou works as a Consultant with Jackson Hole Group she works with organizations, teams and individuals to help them realize their potential, maximise effectiveness and drive growth. Nicole is also on the Board of Directors of Oasis For Girls, a non profit organisation in San Francisco that provides art, education for young women aged 10-20.

USA

ANGELIKI CHRISTOFORIDES LAZARIDES
Award from the City of New York for dedicated service to the NYC School System

DATE OF BIRTH: 04-Jan-1936
PLACE OF BIRTH: Kyrenia.
MARITAL STATUS: Married to Chris, Cypriot, Banking.
CHILDREN: Theana, Vice President Marketing AIG. George, Pharmacist.
SCHOOLS/COLLEGE: Kyrenia Gymnasium. Hunter College, St Johns University and Columbia University.
QUALIFICATIONS: BA MA MSc.
HONOURS/AWARDS: Award from the City of New York for dedicated service to the NYC School System.
PERSONAL PROFILE: Angeliki has been a teacher for 15 years at the parochial school of St Demetrios of Astoria and 30 years at a NYC Junior High School.

CHRIS LAZARIDES
Senior Executive Vice President -Atlantic Bank of New York

DATE OF BIRTH: 15-Jun-1935
PLACE OF BIRTH: Lefkoniko.
MARITAL STATUS: Married to Angeliki, Cypriot, Teacher.
CHILDREN: George, Vice President Marketing AIG. Theana, Pharmacist.
SCHOOLS/COLLEGE: Pancyprian commercial Lyceum of Larnaca. Columbia University and Stonier Graduate School of Banking.
QUALIFICATIONS: BA. MA. MSc.
MEMBERSHIPS: American Management Association and Pancyprian Association of America.
PERSONAL PROFILE: Chris Lazarides is the Senior Executive Vice President -Atlantic Bank of New York and President and Chief Executive Officer-Olympian Bank, New York.

GEORGE LAZARIDES
Vice President Marketing AIG

PLACE OF BIRTH: Parents from Lefkoniko and kyrenia.
SCHOOLS/COLLEGE: Georgetown University.
QUALIFICATIONS: BA.
PERSONAL PROFILE: George Lazarides is Vice President Marketing AIG.

GEORGE LAZARIDES
Pharmacist

DATE OF BIRTH: 01-Oct-1964.
PLACE OF BIRTH: USA parents from Lefkoniko and Kyrenia.
SCHOOLS/COLLEGE: St John University.
PERSONAL PROFILE: George Lazarides is the President Double G Pharmaceuticals.

MARKOS LAZARIDES
Sir William Siemens Medal Winner, 2004

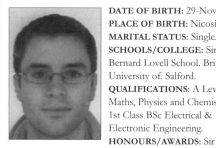

DATE OF BIRTH: 29-Nov-1980
PLACE OF BIRTH: Nicosia.
MARITAL STATUS: Single.
SCHOOLS/COLLEGE: Sir Bernard Lovell School. Bristol, University of. Salford.
QUALIFICATIONS: A Levels Maths, Physics and Chemistry, 1st Class BSc Electrical & Electronic Engineering.
HONOURS/AWARDS: Sir William Siemens Medal Winner, 2004.
HOBBIES AND INTERESTS: Football, keen interest in technology & Environment.
PERSONAL PROFILE: Projects Engineer for Stage Engineering Company, worked on projects in Las Vegas also all over Europe and Asia.

DR CHRISTINE LEMESIANOU
Assistant Professor Mont Clair State University, New Jersey

PLACE OF BIRTH: Nicosia
SCHOOLS/COLLEGE: Rutgers the State University and Adelphi University.
QUALIFICATIONS: BA, MA and Ph. D.
HONOURS/AWARDS: 2006. Outstanding Service Award, New Jersey Communication Association Annual conference.
PERSONAL PROFILE: Christine Lemesianou is an Assistant Professor, Department of Communication Studies, Mont Clair State University, New Jersey.

PROFESSOR CHARIKLIA SOTIRIOU LEVENTIS
Professor of Organic Chemistry at Missouri University of Science and Technology

DATE OF BIRTH: 20-Jan-1960
PLACE OF BIRTH: Nicosia, Cyprus.
MARITAL STATUS: Married to Nicholas, Greece, University Lecturer.
CHILDREN: Theodora, School. Helen, School. Julia, School.
SCHOOLS/COLLEGE: Harvard University, Massachusetts, Northeastern University, Boston, Michigan State University, University of Athens, Greece.
QUALIFICATIONS: PhD-Organic Chemistry, BS Chemistry (Summa Cum Laude).
MEMBERSHIPS: American Chemical Society, American Association for the Advancement of Science.
HOBBIES AND INTERESTS: Art, Theatre and singing.
PERSONAL PROFILE: Professor of Organic Chemistry at Missouri University of Science and Technology with research interests in the areas of organic materials, physical organic and supramolecular chemistry, published 70 journal articles including 2 patents.

PETER LOISIDES
Urologist based in Santa Monica

PLACE OF BIRTH: Cyprus.
SCHOOLS/COLLEGE: University of California and University of Pittsburgh.
QUALIFICATIONS: MD.
MEMBERSHIPS: American Urological Association.
PERSONAL PROFILE: Peter Loisides is a Board Certified Urologist based at the Department of Urology. Loma Linda University Medical Center Santa Monica.

ANTHONY M LOIZIDES
Assistant Professor of Pediatrics

DATE OF BIRTH: 23-Jun-1969
PLACE OF BIRTH: Patchogue, NY, USA, father from Kyrenia, Cyprus.
MARITAL STATUS: Married to Eleni, Speech Language Pathologist.
CHILDREN: Ella, Alexa.
SCHOOLS/COLLEGE: Cornell University, Columbia University, State University of New York at Stony Brook School of Medicine, Harvard University.
MEMBERSHIPS: American Academy of Paediatrics, American Medical Association, International Society for Stem Cell Research and various others.
HONOURS/AWARDS: Rick Brooks Memorial Award, Stony Brook School of Medicine.
HOBBIES AND INTERESTS: Gardening, music, travel.
PERSONAL PROFILE: Assistant Professor of Pediatrics, Albert Einstein College of Medicine, Bronx, NY.

MARIA LOIZOU
Lyric Soprano

PLACE OF BIRTH: USA Father from Paphos
SCHOOLS/COLLEGE: New England Conservatory.
QUALIFICATIONS: Master of Music Degree.
PERSONAL PROFILE: Maria Loizou is a Lyric Soprano she specializes in presenting creative programs of art songs from different epochs. She also works as a Collection Management Librarian at the New England Conservatory of Music.

PHILIPOS C. LOIZOU
Professor of Electrical Engineering

DATE OF BIRTH: 10-Nov-1965
PLACE OF BIRTH: Patriki.
MARITAL STATUS: Married.
SCHOOLS/COLLEGE: Arizona State University.
PERSONAL PROFILE: Professor of Electrical Engineering at the University of Texas.

DESPINA LOUCA
Associate Professor in Physics at the University of Virginia

PLACE OF BIRTH: Larnaca
SCHOOLS/COLLEGE: Pennsylvania University.
QUALIFICATIONS: PhD.
PERSONAL PROFILE: Despina Louca is a Associate Professor in Physics at the University of Virginia.

USA

LOUCAS LOUCA
Research Scientist at the University of Michigan

PLACE OF BIRTH: Cyprus
SCHOOLS/COLLEGE: University of Athens and University of Michigan.
QUALIFICATIONS: MS. PhD.
PERSONAL PROFILE: Loucas Louca worked at the Automotive Research Center as a Research Fellow and assistant Research Scientist at the University of Michigan now based at the University of Cyprus.

ANDREW MAKRIDES
President and Chief Executive Officer of Bovie Medical Corporation

PLACE OF BIRTH: Parents from Cyprus.
SCHOOLS/COLLEGE: Hofstra University and Brooklyn Law School.
QUALIFICATIONS: BA in psychology and Doctor of Jurisprudence.
MEMBERSHIPS: Andrew Makrides is the President and Chief Executive Officer of Bovie Medical Corporation which produces and markets medical products.

DR ANDREW MAKRIDES
Anesthesiologist based in Smithtown New York

DATE OF BIRTH: 07-Jan-1961
PLACE OF BIRTH: USA parents from Agastina and Kaimakli.
PERSONAL PROFILE: Andrew Makrides is an Anesthesiologist based in Smithtown New York.

DR MICHAEL MAKRIDES
Internal Medicine Physician, East Stauket, New York

DATE OF BIRTH: 15-Jul-1959
PLACE OF BIRTH: USA Parents from Angastina and kaimakli.
PERSONAL PROFILE: Michael Makrides is an Internal Medicine Physician, East Stauket, New York.

PROFESSOR NICHOLAS MAKRIS
Professor and Director of the Laboratory for Undersea Remote Sensing at the Massachusetts Institute of Technology

DATE OF BIRTH: 13-Sep-1961
PLACE OF BIRTH: New York Grandparents from Lefkara.
MARITAL STATUS: Married to Margaret.
SCHOOLS/COLLEGE: Massachusetts Institute of Technology.
QUALIFICATIONS: SB in Physics. PhD in Ocean Engineering.
HONOURS/AWARDS: NASA Group Achievement Award to Jupiter Icy Moons Orbiter Science Definition Team 2005. Doherty Professor of Ocean Utilisation july 2000.
HOBBIES AND INTERESTS: Music.
PERSONAL PROFILE: Professor Nicholas Makris is the Director of the Laboratory for Undersea Remote Sensing at the Massachusetts Institute of Technology this involves ocean exploration, undersea remote sensing of marine life and geophysical phenomena, census of marine life, ocean acoustic hurricane classification.

USA

Entrants in Greek Cypriots Worldwide have been nominated for their achievements and contributions.
It is free to nominate someone, or yourself, who deserves to be in the book, just send in the name, contact address, telephone number and email to:
Greek Cypriots Worldwide
111 St Thomas's Road London N4 2QJ
Telephone 0044 207503 3498
cypriotwhoswho@aol.com
www.greekcypriotsworldwide.com

GEORGE A MARCOULIDES
Professor in Science at California State University

PLACE OF BIRTH: Cyprus
SCHOOLS/COLLEGE: California State University and University of California.
QUALIFICATIONS: BA MA and PhD.
MEMBERSHIPS: Royal Statistical Society and Society of Multivariate Experimental Psychology.
HONOURS/AWARDS: Outstanding Professor Award California State University, Fullerton 2000.
PERSONAL PROFILE: George is currently a Professor in the Department of Information and Systems and Decision Sciences at California State University, Fullerton.

PANOS MARCOULLIS
Computers

PLACE OF BIRTH: USA Parents from Cyprus
MARITAL STATUS: Married to Martha.
SCHOOLS/COLLEGE: University of Michigan, George Washington University.
QUALIFICATIONS: BA MS.
PERSONAL PROFILE: Panos Marcoullis is an information systems project manager he is the the creator of the Pseka website.

CONSTANTINE MARKIDES
Short Story Finalist in Another Chicago Magazine Literary awards (2004)

DATE OF BIRTH: 27-Oct-1976
PLACE OF BIRTH: Bangor, Maine, USA Father From Nicosia, Mother from Famagusta.
MARITAL STATUS: Single.
SCHOOLS/COLLEGE: Columbia University and University College London.
QUALIFICATIONS: BA MA.
HONOURS/AWARDS: Short Story Finalist in Another Chicago Magazine Literary awards(2004).
HOBBIES AND INTERESTS: Brazilian Jiu-Jitsu, Blues harmonica, songwriting, tennis, swimming and Lobsterfishing.

PERSONAL PROFILE: Constantine Markides has worked as human rights researcher for former UN member Dr William Corey. Constantine has also worked as a Journalist/reporter for the Cyprus Mail.

DR EMILY JOANNIDES MARKIDES
Lecturer at the University of Maine

DATE OF BIRTH: 28-Jul-1949
PLACE OF BIRTH: Famagusta.
MARITAL STATUS: Married to Dr. Kyriacos Markides, Greek Cypriot, Sociology Professor, University of Maine, USA.
CHILDREN: Constantine, Doing his Masters in Literature at the University College London, UCL. Vasia, Doing her masters in Fine Arts at the School of the Museum of Fine Arts (Tufts) Boston.
SCHOOLS/COLLEGE: Famagusta High School and Highbury Hill High School in London. Munich, Germany, La Neuvville, Switzerland, and Barcelona and Alicante, Spain, University of Maine.
QUALIFICATIONS: BA in German Literature, MA in German Literature, MA in French Literature, Ed. D in Counselor Education, LCPC.
HOBBIES AND INTERESTS: Swimming, reading, hiking, music.
PERSONAL PROFILE: Founding Member of KEGYS, Kentro Gynaikion Spoudon that later became the Peace Centre in Cyprus with Costas Shammas as its current Director. Founder and board member of The International Eco-Peace Village in Cyprus. Also started the Peace Studies Program at the University of Maine where she currently lectures.

KYRIACOS C MARKIDES
Professor in Sociology at the University of Maine

DATE OF BIRTH: 19-Nov-1942
PLACE OF BIRTH: Nicosia.
MARITAL STATUS: Married to Emily, From Famagusta, Adjunct Associate Professor at the University of Maine.
CHILDREN: Constantine, Student. Vasia, Student.
SCHOOLS/COLLEGE: Youngstown University, Bowling Green State and Wayne State University.
QUALIFICATIONS: BS MA PhD.
MEMBERSHIPS: American Sociological Association and Founding member of the Cyprus Sociological Association.
HONOURS/AWARDS: Best Professor Award College of Arts and Sciences.
HOBBIES AND INTERESTS: Swimming, Walking and Chanting.
PERSONAL PROFILE: Kyriacos Markides is a Professor of Sociology at the University of Maine in the USA and Author of eight books.

KYRIAKOS MARKIDES
Professor of Ageing, University of Texas

DATE OF BIRTH: 21-Mar-1948
PLACE OF BIRTH: Nicosia.
SCHOOLS/COLLEGE: Bowling Green State University, Louisiana State University.
QUALIFICATIONS: BA MA PhD.
PERSONAL PROFILE: Kyriacos is currently the Annie and John Gnitzinger Professor of ageing and director of the division of sociomedical sciences at the University of Texas medical branch in Galveston in the department of preventive medicine and community health. He is also the founding and current editor of the journal of ageing and health and the author or co author of over 210 publications. The institute for scientific information has recently selected Dr Markides to be listed among the most cited social scientists in the world.

ELENA MAROULETTI
Founder of AKTINA FM Radio Station in New York

PLACE OF BIRTH: Cyprus
HONOURS/AWARDS: Awarded the "Women of Achievement Pacesetter Award 2000" by former Council Speaker Vallone during a special ceremony on March 28, 2000 at City Hall in Manhattan, New York.
PERSONAL PROFILE: Elena is the founder of AKTINA FM a radio station focusing on English language Greek-American news and on local, national and international news stories of particular interest to its wide New York based audience, as well as hard news stories that examine the national issues of Cyprus and Greece. As an extension of AKTINA FM, in April 2002, Ms. Maroulleti also introduced and established AKTINA TV, the first English language Greek-American TV series in America. Also Elena is President of the first Greek-Cypriot Cultural Organization in America, CYPRECO of America. CYPRECO, founded in 1979.

LUCY MAROULLETI
Community (Deceased)

PLACE OF BIRTH: Egypt Parents from Cyprus
MARITAL STATUS: Married to Kyriacos.
CHILDREN: Angela, Elena, Christiana.
HONOURS/AWARDS: Life time Achievement Award from the World Council of Hellenes Abroad in 2004.
PERSONAL PROFILE: Lucy Maroulleti was the co founder of Cypreco of America a non profit cultural organisation. She also found with her Daughter the Radio program Aktina FM and the English Language Television Program Aktina TV. Lucy was the Author of numerous works of Fiction, plays and Poetry.

USA

ELIZABETH GEORGE MARZULLI
features Editor of Weight Watchers Magazine

PLACE OF BIRTH: New York Grandfather from Cyprus
MARITAL STATUS: Married to Robert Marzulli.
CHILDREN: Zachary, Grammar school. Ava, Kindergaten.
SCHOOLS/COLLEGE: New York University.
PERSONAL PROFILE: Elizabeth George Marzulli is a freelance writer and written several books has also worked as a features Editor of Weight Watchers Magazine and is presently the head of a Department at the Daily News in New York City.

ARCHILLES MAVROMATIS
Deputy Director and the Director of Operations for the New York City Department of Housing Preservation and Development (Deceased)

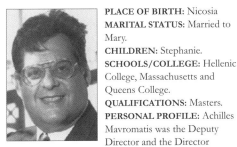

PLACE OF BIRTH: Nicosia
MARITAL STATUS: Married to Mary.
CHILDREN: Stephanie.
SCHOOLS/COLLEGE: Hellenic College, Massachusetts and Queens College.
QUALIFICATIONS: Masters.
PERSONAL PROFILE: Achilles Mavromatis was the Deputy Director and the Director of Operations for the New York City Department of Housing Preservation and Development. He was also Board Chairman of the Patti Fund, Care for Childhood Cancer. He was also an Executive Director of the Hellenic American Political Action committee.

EMILIOS MAVROUDHIS
Chief Engineer Valley Communications Systems

DATE OF BIRTH: 28-Nov-1928.
PLACE OF BIRTH: Nicosia.
MARITAL STATUS: Married to Athena.
PERSONAL PROFILE: Emilios Mavroudhis was the chief engineer and purchasing agent for Valley Communications Systems.

MICHAEL MAVROVOUNIOTIS
Associate Professor Chemical Engineering, North Western University

DATE OF BIRTH: 25-Dec-1961.
PLACE OF BIRTH: Lefkara.
MARITAL STATUS: Married.
SCHOOLS/COLLEGE: University of Athens and Massachusetts Institute of Technology.
QUALIFICATIONS: PhD.
PERSONAL PROFILE: Associate Professor Chemical Engineering Department, North Western University.

CHARALAMBOS MENELAOU
Chairman of Obstetrician/Gynecology Department of Provena Mercy Medical Center

DATE OF BIRTH: 16-Sep-1962
PLACE OF BIRTH: Limassol.
MARITAL STATUS: Single.
SCHOOLS/COLLEGE: University of Wisconsin, George Washington University and Chicago Medical School.
QUALIFICATIONS: MDSC.
MEMBERSHIPS: American College of Obstetrics and Gynecology.
PERSONAL PROFILE: Charalambos Menelaou is an Obstetrician/Gynecologist. He is the chairman of Obstetrician/Gynecology Department of Provena Mercy Medical Center.

NIKOS MENICOU
Dentist with own surgery in California

DATE OF BIRTH: 04-Jun-1970.
PLACE OF BIRTH: San Francisco, parents from Cyprus.
MARITAL STATUS: Married to Danielle, Italian.
CHILDREN: Niko, Stefano, Massimo.
SCHOOLS/COLLEGE: University of Southern California.
HOBBIES AND INTERESTS: Family, Heritage and Hunting.
PERSONAL PROFILE: Nikos Menicou is a Dentist with a Surgery in Davis in Californi.

USA

CONSTANTINOS MICHAEL
Computer Scientist

PLACE OF BIRTH: Cyprus.
SCHOOLS/COLLEGE: English School, Nicosia, Cyprus. The John Hopkins University.
QUALIFICATIONS: BSc, MSc in Computer Science.
HONOURS/AWARDS: Awarded the 2005 computer science outstanding undergraduate award. Honoured with the prestigious CASP undergraduate Scholarship from the Cyprus Fulbright Commission.
PERSONAL PROFILE: Constantinos is involved in Computer Science Research and Development.

DOROS MICHAELIDES
Allergist and Immunologist

DATE OF BIRTH: 07-Jan-1936.
PLACE OF BIRTH: Nicosia.
MARITAL STATUS: Married to Eutychia.
SCHOOLS/COLLEGE: University of Athens, Universities of both London and Liverpool.
QUALIFICATIONS: MSc MD.
PERSONAL PROFILE: Doros Michaelides is an Allergist and Immunologist based in Pennsylvania.

GEORGE MICHAELIDES
one of the leading providers of discount dental plans

PLACE OF BIRTH: USA Father from Pedhoulas.
PERSONAL PROFILE: George Michaelides is the President and co founder of Dentalplans. com one of the leading providers of discount dental plans.

KYRIAKOS MICHAELIDES
Honorary Consul of the Republic of Cyprus for the State of Georgia, USA

DATE OF BIRTH: 19-Dec-1943
PLACE OF BIRTH: Yerolakkos, Cyprus.
MARITAL STATUS: Married to Margaret, American, Homemaker.
CHILDREN: Michael, Works for a retail software development company. Mark, Degree from Atlanta Arts Institute with an Associate Degree in Culinary Arts. Matthew, Senior at Kennesaw University.
SCHOOLS/COLLEGE: English School, Nicosia, Cyprus. Hadassah Medical School, Jerusalem, Israel.
QUALIFICATIONS: Board Certified in Internal Medicine and Gastroenterology.

MEMBERSHIPS: Medical Association of Georgia, (MAG), American Gastroenterological Association, (AGA) amongst others.
HOBBIES AND INTERESTS: Tennis, travel, stamp collecting.
PERSONAL PROFILE: Kyriacos is a Physician Started Digestive Care Associates in 1977. This is a group of 11 Gastroenterologists working together in the North East part of the metro Atlanta Area. In 1985 appointed as the Honorary Consul of the Republic of Cyprus for the State of Georgia, USA, he is still serving in this position today.

MICHAEL MICHAELIDES
Golf Professional/Golf Coach/Received an award from Arthritis Foundation for playing over 100 holes in one day

DATE OF BIRTH: 17-Jan-1976
PLACE OF BIRTH: United States. Parents from Cyprus.
MARITAL STATUS: Married to Pilar C. Michaelides, Hispanic, Vice President and Senior Lending Officer at First Central Savings Bank.
SCHOOLS/COLLEGE: Long Island University.
QUALIFICATIONS: Graduated Long Island University with a Business Degree in Management and Marketing, and a Minor in Finance in 1999.
MEMBERSHIPS: Golf Coaches Association of America, National Golf Coaches Association, United States Golf Association.
HONOURS/AWARDS: Received an award from Arthritis Foundation for playing over 100 holes in one day, Recipient of 2 MPV awards while playing golf at Long Island University, Led mens/team to an NEC Championship and spot in the NCAA regional tournament in 2004.
HOBBIES AND INTERESTS: Music, motorcycles, cars, Art, Sport.
PERSONAL PROFILE: In his fourth full season as head of men's and women's golf coach, Michael returns to help his alma mater return to the top of the Northeast Conference. A former two-time MVP for the LIU men's golf team, he has built a perennial conference title contender to his tenure. He has competed since 2000 in tournaments on the Canadian and Nationwide Tours as well as several regional events.

NICOS MIDDLETON
Enviromental Health

PLACE OF BIRTH: Cyprus
SCHOOLS/COLLEGE: University of Bristol.
PERSONAL PROFILE: Nicos Middleton is conducting research at the Harvard School of Public Health.

PAVLOS MIKELLIDES
Professor of Aerospace Engineering at Arizona State University

PLACE OF BIRTH: Larnaca
SCHOOLS/COLLEGE: Aeronautical and Astronautical Engineering, Ohio.
QUALIFICATIONS: BS MS PhD.
MEMBERSHIPS: American Nuclear Society, American Institute of Aeronautics and Astronautics.
PERSONAL PROFILE: Pavlos Mikellides is a Professor of Aerospace Engineering at Arizona State University.

DR KYRIACOS MOUSKOS
Assistant Professor of Civil and Enviromental Engineering at the New Jersey Institute of Technology

SCHOOLS/COLLEGE: Engineering. University of Texas.
QUALIFICATIONS: BS MS PhD.
PERSONAL PROFILE: Kyriacos Mouskos is the Assistant Professor of Civil and Enviromental Engineering at the New Jersey Institute of Technology.

JOHN NICHOLAS MOUSTOUKAS
Medicine

DATE OF BIRTH: 05-Mar-1984
PLACE OF BIRTH: New Orleans, USA Grandfather from Lefkara, Cyprus.
MARITAL STATUS: Single.
SCHOOLS/COLLEGE: Vanderbilt University, Nashville, Tennessee, Tulane University Medical School, New Orleans, Louisiana.
QUALIFICATIONS: Bachelors of Engineering in Biomedical Engineering.
MEMBERSHIPS: National Hellenic Student Association, American Medical Association.
HONOURS/AWARDS: Tau Beta Pi Engineering Honor Society.
HOBBIES AND INTERESTS: Medicine, Playing Bouzouki and bass, Fly-fishing.
PERSONAL PROFILE: John is a medical student who enjoys organising music events to raise funds for health related charities. Greek Orthodox Young Adult League (YAL).

NICK MOUSTOUKAS
Cardiothoracic and Vascular Surgeon

DATE OF BIRTH: 03-Oct-1952
PLACE OF BIRTH: New Orleans, Louisiana Parents from Cyprus.
MARITAL STATUS: Married to Viki, Greek American, Retired Personnel Manager.
CHILDREN: Diana, Physician. Johnny, Physician.
SCHOOLS/COLLEGE: Tulane University School of Medicine.
QUALIFICATIONS: American Board of Thoracic Surgery.
MEMBERSHIPS: Society of Thoracic Surgeons; Fellow of American College of Surgeons.
HONOURS/AWARDS: Archon of the Ecumenical Patriachate; AOA; Ambassodor Metropolis of Atlanta; Named outstanding Physician by New Orleans Magazine.
HOBBIES AND INTERESTS: Fishing and Photography.
PERSONAL PROFILE: Clinical Associate Professor of Surgery, both Tulane and Louisiana University School of Medicine. Active member, past President and Board member of Holy Trinity Greek Orthodox Cathedral, New Orleans. Participated in the reconstruction of Holy Trinity following Hurricane Katrina. Raised money for the Greek community affected by this devastating storm. Member and president of AHEPA. While president the New Orleans AHEPA received funding from the US government to construct a 44 unit building for low income senior citizens.

USA

379

NICOS MOUYIARIS
Vice President of the Pan Cyprian Association Of America/founder and President of Mana products

PLACE OF BIRTH: Athienou
MEMBERSHIPS: HBA Global Export and Cyprus-US Chamber of Commerce.
PERSONAL PROFILE: Nicos Mouyiaris is the founder and President of Mana products a company producing Beauty Products. He is also the Vice President of the Pan Cyprian Association Of America.

ANDREANE NEOFITOU
Costume Designer her highly acclaimed work for the Royal Shakespeare Company over many years led to her outstanding success with Les Miserables in the West End and on Broadway

PLACE OF BIRTH: Avgorou
HONOURS/AWARDS: Nominated for a Tony Award.
PERSONAL PROFILE: Andreane Neofitou is a Costume designer her highly acclaimed work for the Royal Shakespeare Company over many years led to her outstanding success with Les Miserables in the West End and on Broadway and in many other countries. She endorsed her achievement with Miss Saigon and her designs have been reproduced for the many productions playing Worldwide. Now based in the USA.

ALEXIS NEOPHYTIDES
Actress and Film-Maker has appeared in 'The Education of Max Bickford', Law and Order,

DATE OF BIRTH: 13-Sep-1976
PLACE OF BIRTH: New York, Father from Limassol, Cyprus.
MARITAL STATUS: Single.
SCHOOLS/COLLEGE: Brown University.
QUALIFICATIONS: BA's in Biology and French.
PERSONAL PROFILE: Actress and Filmaker she has appeared in 'The Education of

Max Bickford', Law and Order, 'A Killing on Brighton Beach. She has just returned from Tanzania where she was working on her first Documentary project, 'In the Shadow of Kilimanjaro'.

ANDREAS NEOPHYTIDES
Neurologist at NYU Medical Center

DATE OF BIRTH: 18-Dec-1946
PLACE OF BIRTH: Limassol.
MARITAL STATUS: Married to Andrea.
CHILDREN: Alexia.
SCHOOLS/COLLEGE: University of Athens School of Medicine.
QUALIFICATIONS: MD.
PERSONAL PROFILE: Neurologist at NYU Medical Center specialising back and spine problems, stroke/ cerebrovascular disease, nerve and muscle diseases. General adult Neurology.

NEOPHYTOS NEOPHYTOU
Senior Scientist Leads the research and development on Geospatial Visualisation at Intelepix LLC

DATE OF BIRTH: 23-Jul-1975
PLACE OF BIRTH: Larnaca, Cyprus.
MARITAL STATUS: Married to Mrs. Odaly Cruz-Neophytou, Dominican Republic, Pastry and Culinary Chef.
SCHOOLS/COLLEGE: University of Cyprus, Stony Brook University.
QUALIFICATIONS: BSc and Phd.
MEMBERSHIPS: IEEE, ACM SIGGRAPH.
HONOURS/AWARDS: Renaissance Fellowship, at Stony Brook University, 1998-2001. Recipient outstanding student award, University of Cyprus June 1997
HOBBIES AND INTERESTS: Music, playing keyboard.
PERSONAL PROFILE: Senior Scientist currently leading the research and development on Geospatial Visualisation at Intelepix LLC. Also an active member of the Scientific Visualisation and Geospatial Intelligence communities, and a regular reviewer for ACM/IEEE Journals and conferences.

USA

PANICKOS NEOPHYTOU
Computer Science

DATE OF BIRTH: 20-Dec-1979
PLACE OF BIRTH: Larnaca, Cyprus.
MARITAL STATUS: Single.
SCHOOLS/COLLEGE: University of Cyprus, University of Pittsburgh.
QUALIFICATIONS: BSc in Computer Science from the University of Cyprus. Currently pursuing a PhD in Computer Science at the University of Pittsburgh.
MEMBERSHIPS: IEEE Member for 7 years.
HOBBIES AND INTERESTS: Music, photography, travelling and spending time with friends.
PERSONAL PROFILE: Panickos received his BSc. in Computer Science in 2003, from the University of Cyprus. During those years he served as a student representative in the Board of the Computer Science Dept. After his graduation he worked as a Research Assistant for a year at the Pervasive Computing Lab of the CS Department of the University of Cyprus. Currently he is a graduate student in the Dept of Computer Science at the University of Pittsburgh and a graduate student researcher in the Advanced Data Management Technologies Laboratory. His research interests include Grid, Pervasive, and Distributed Computing and Data Management.

DEMETRIS NICOLAIDES
Science

PLACE OF BIRTH: Cyprus.
PERSONAL PROFILE: Demetris Nicolaides is the co ordinator of Physics in the Department of the Natural Science and Mathematics at Bloomfield College, Jersey USA.

HARRY NICOLAIDES
Mayor of the Village of Munsey Park in the Nassau County of New York

PLACE OF BIRTH: Cyprus.
PERSONAL PROFILE: Harry Nicolaides is the Mayor of the Village of Munsey Park in the Nassau County of New York.

MARIA NICOLAIDES
Assistant professor of Medicine at Cornell University Medical college

PLACE OF BIRTH: Famagusta in 1958
SCHOOLS/COLLEGE: Columbia University.
QUALIFICATIONS: MD.
MEMBERSHIPS: New York academy of Sciences, American College of physicians and the Hellenic Medical Society of New York.
HONOURS/AWARDS: AILF 2004 New York Immigrant Achievement Award.
PERSONAL PROFILE: Maria Nicolaides serves as the Associate Clinical Member at the Memorial Sloan Kettering Cancer Center and as the Assistant professor of Medicine at Cornell University Medical college.

MELINA NICOLAIDES
Recipient of Awards from US National Endowment For The Arts

PLACE OF BIRTH: USA Father from Larnaca.
SCHOOLS/COLLEGE: Princeton University and Maryland Institute College of Art.
QUALIFICATIONS: BA. Masters of fine arts.
HONOURS/AWARDS: Recipient of Awards from US National Endowment For The Arts.
PERSONAL PROFILE: Melina Nicolaides is an artist making abstract paintings has participated in over 30 group exhibitions including the 8th Cairo Biennale, as well as seven solos in the US, Athens, Cyprus and London. Her work can be found in public and private collections in the United States and Europe.

ANDREAS NICOLAOU
Associate Professor in Accounting

DATE OF BIRTH: 25-Jul-1970
PLACE OF BIRTH: Famagusta.
SCHOOLS/COLLEGE: Athens University, Southern Illinois University at Carbondale.
QUALIFICATIONS: CPA, BSc, M Acc, PhD.
MEMBERSHIPS: American Accounting Association.
PERSONAL PROFILE: Associate Professor Lecturer in Accounting Information systems at Bowling Green State University in Ohio, United States of America.

USA

CHRISTOS NICOLAOU
Senior Scientist with Bioreason

PLACE OF BIRTH: Cyprus.
SCHOOLS/COLLEGE: Pedagogical Academy of Cyprus and Florida State University.
QUALIFICATIONS: MSc and BSc in Computer Science.
HOBBIES AND INTERESTS: Enjoys brewing beer.
PERSONAL PROFILE: Was a Senior Scientist with Bioreason a US Chemoinformatics start up company. Christos is now based in Cyprus and is a part time lecturer at the Schools of Computer Science and Education of Intercollege and a consultant to software start up companies.

DR CONSTANTINOS NICOLAOU
Senior scientist and Lab Director at the Sun Chemical Corporation in Cincinatti, Ohio

PLACE OF BIRTH: Akaki.
MARITAL STATUS: Married to Christine, USA.
CHILDREN: Julia, Anna.
SCHOOLS/COLLEGE: University of North London and New York University.
QUALIFICATIONS: BSc. PhD.
HONOURS/AWARDS: Recipient The National Association of Printing Ink Manufacturers Technical Associate Member Service Award for playing a major role in the progress of printing ink technology.
HOBBIES AND INTERESTS: Soccer, Tennis and Travel.
PERSONAL PROFILE: Constantinos Nicolaou is a Senior scientist and Lab Director at the Sun Chemical Corporation, Colors Technology Cincinatti, Ohio.

PROFESSOR KYRIACOS COSTA NICOLAOU
Professor of Chemistry University of California

DATE OF BIRTH: 05-Jul-1946
PLACE OF BIRTH: Karavas, Cyprus.
MARITAL STATUS: Married to Georgette, Born in Cairo Egypt of Greek Parents, Homemaker.
CHILDREN: Colette, Alexis, Christopher, Paul.
SCHOOLS/COLLEGE: University of London, University College.
QUALIFICATIONS: BSc Ph. D.
MEMBERSHIPS: American Chemical Society, European Chemical Society and many others.
HONOURS/AWARDS: Aspirin prize Spain, Schering Prize Germany, Centenary Medal (Royal Society UK) ACS Nobel Laureate Signature Award for Graduate

Education in Chemistry 2003 various others too.
HOBBIES AND INTERESTS: Walking, gardening, cooking, reading, history and geopolitics.
PERSONAL PROFILE: He moved and studied in the UK in 1964 then moved to the United States in 1972 and after post doctoral appointments at Columbia University and Harvard University he joined the faculty at the University of Pensylvania where he rose through the ranks to become the Rhodes-Thompson Professor of Chemistry. In 1989 he accepted joint appointments at the University of California San Diego where he is Professor of Chemistry and the Scripps Research Institute where he is the Chairman of the Department of Chemistry and holds the Skaggs Professorship of chemical Biology and the Darlene Shiley Chair in Chemistry.

DR NICOS NICOLAOU
Dr Nicolaou is a Physicist based at the Fox Chase Center in Philadelphia

DATE OF BIRTH: 14-Apr-1974
PLACE OF BIRTH: Nicosia.
SCHOOLS/COLLEGE: University Of Cape Town.
MEMBERSHIPS: American Board of Radiology.
PERSONAL PROFILE: Dr Nicolaou is a Physicist based at the Fox Chase Center in Philadelphia specializes in treatment of Lymphomas, Head and Neck Cancer, Lung Cancer, Breast Cancer and Nonmelamona Skin Cancers.

CHRYSOSTOMOS L MAX NIKIAS
Provost and Senior Vice President for Scientific Affairs at the University of Southern California

PLACE OF BIRTH: Famagusta.
SCHOOLS/COLLEGE: Famagusta Gymnasium. National Technical University of Athens, State University of New York.
QUALIFICATIONS: MS and PhD.
HONOURS/AWARDS: Honorary Doctorate from the University of Cyprus and Presidential Medallion in the Sciences in 2005 from the Government of Cyprus.
PERSONAL PROFILE: Provost and Senior Vice President for Scientific Affairs at the University of Southern California.

ATHANASIOS ORPHANIDES
Senior Advisor, Board of Governors of the Federal Reserve System

PLACE OF BIRTH: Cyprus
SCHOOLS/COLLEGE: Pancyprian Gymnasium. Massachusetts Institute of Technology.
QUALIFICATIONS: BS. PhD.
PERSONAL PROFILE: Athanasios Orphanides was an Adjunct Professor for Georgetown University and Visiting /Adjunct Professor John Hopkins University and Associate Editor Journal of Economic Dynamics and Control. Athanasios was Senior Advisor, Board of Governors of the Federal Reserve System Now he is the Governor of the Central Bank of Cyprus.

ALEX PAGONIS
Adjunct Professor in the department of restorative dentistry at the University of Pacific

MARITAL STATUS: Married
SCHOOLS/COLLEGE: University of Arizona.
QUALIFICATIONS: BSc.
MEMBERSHIPS: American Dental Association.
HOBBIES AND INTERESTS: Hiking, fishing and travelling.
PERSONAL PROFILE: Alex Pagonis is Adjunct Professor in the department of restorative dentistry at the University of Pacific. He also practices general dentistry at Cupertino Dental Group.

SOPHIA PANAGIS
Clinical Neurophysiologist

PLACE OF BIRTH: USA, Father from Angastina, Cyprus
SCHOOLS/COLLEGE: Ohio State University.
PERSONAL PROFILE: Clinical Neurophysiologist at surgical neuromonitoring associates in Pittsburgh.

ANDREAS PANAYI
Engineering researcher at Michigan State University

PLACE OF BIRTH: Cyprus.
SCHOOLS/COLLEGE: University of Vermont and Michigan State University.
QUALIFICATIONS: BSc MSc.
MEMBERSHIPS: Vice President, Cypriot Greek Association.
HONOURS/AWARDS: 2004 Outstanding Senior Award in Energy engineering, University of Vermont.
PERSONAL PROFILE: Andreas Panayi has worked as a Research Assistant Michigan State University in the development and implementation of a piston dynamics simulation code.

ALEXANDROS PANAYIDES
Professor of Economics at William Patterson University New Jersey

PLACE OF BIRTH: Trachonas
SCHOOLS/COLLEGE: University of Frankfurt and State University of New York.
QUALIFICATIONS: MS MA PhD.
PERSONAL PROFILE: Alexandros Panayides is a Professor of Economics at William Patterson University New Jersey.

MARIOS PANAYIDES
Assistant Professor University of Utah

PLACE OF BIRTH: Nicosia, Cyprus
SCHOOLS/COLLEGE: Oxford University, Yale University.
QUALIFICATIONS: BA (Hons) and MA. (Oxon) MA and PhD in Statistics.
HONOURS/AWARDS: Fulbright Scholar 1998, John Perry Miller Fund Award, Yale University, 2002.
PERSONAL PROFILE: Assistant Professor of Finance, David Eccles School of Business, University of Utah.

USA

ALEXIA PANAYIOTOU
Lecturer in Management

PLACE OF BIRTH: Cyprus
SCHOOLS/COLLEGE: Stanford University and Harvard University.
QUALIFICATIONS: BA MS EdD MPP.
PERSONAL PROFILE: Alexia is a Visiting lecturer at the University of Cyprus and a Teaching Fellow at Harvard University. Her research interests are social constructionism; critical management studies; emotionality of work; feminist analysis of organizations; feminist theory; organizational space and symbolism.

ANDREW PANAYIOTOU
Vice President of innovation and strategy for snacks for Hersheys the famous American chocolate

PLACE OF BIRTH: Cyprus.
PERSONAL PROFILE: Andrew was former vice president of innovation and strategy for snacks for Hersheys the famous American chocolate makers. Prior to this Panayiotou built an independent marketing consulting practice focused on helping companies strengthen marketing strategies and programs. His clients included Mizuno Global Sports, Sears Roebuck and Nike.

DR CHRYS PANAYIOTOU
Professor Electronics Engineering

PLACE OF BIRTH: Limassol
PERSONAL PROFILE: Chrys Panayiotou is a Professor and Departmental Head of Electronics Engineering Technology at Indian River Community College in Fort Pierce, Florida.

DR HERCULES PANAYIOTOU
Associate Professor University of South Alabama

PLACE OF BIRTH: Cyprus
SCHOOLS/COLLEGE: University of Witwatersrand Johannesburg.
QUALIFICATIONS: MD.
PERSONAL PROFILE: Although born in Cyprus Dr Panayiotou grew up in South Africa After University he completed his internship and residency at the Johannesburg Hospital. He joined Vanderbilt University in 1987 where he did a Fellowship in peer reviewed journals. Dr Panayiotou joined the faculty of the University of South Alabama in Mobile in 1990 and rose to the rank of Associate Professor. Dr Panayiotou joined Diagnostic and Medical Clinic in January 1998 in Alabama. He is board certified in internal medicine, cardiovascular medicine and interventional cardiology.

DR THEODORE PANAYOTOU
Professor of Enviromental Management at Harvard University

PLACE OF BIRTH: Cyprus
SCHOOLS/COLLEGE: University of Athens, York University and University of British Columbia.
QUALIFICATIONS: BA MA and PhD.
PERSONAL PROFILE: Theodore Panayotou served as director of the Enviroment and Sustainable Development Programme at the Center for International Development at Harvard University teaching Enviromental Economics. Dr Panayiotou is Director of CIIM and Professor of Enviromental Management.

Entrants in Greek Cypriots Worldwide have been nominated for their achievements and contributions.
It is free to nominate someone, or yourself, who deserves to be in the book, just send in the name, contact address, telephone number and email to:
Greek Cypriots Worldwide
111 St Thomas's Road London N4 2QJ
Telephone 0044 207503 3498
cypriotwhoswho@aol.com
www.greekcypriotsworldwide.com

DR CHRIS PANTELIDES
Professor in Civil and Enviromental Engineering at the University of Utah

PLACE OF BIRTH: Limassol
SCHOOLS/COLLEGE: American University of Beirut and University of Missouri-Rolla.
QUALIFICATIONS: BE MSc PhD.
PERSONAL PROFILE: Chris Pantelides is a Professor and Associate Chair in the Department of Civil and Enviromental Engineering, University of Utah, USA.

KATE PANTELIDES
Assistant Director of the Writing Center at the University of Louisville

DATE OF BIRTH: 25-Feb-1981
PLACE OF BIRTH: New York Parents from Ayia Fyla.
SCHOOLS/COLLEGE: Bowdoin College, University of Nashville and University of Louisville, Opera Academy in Rome.
QUALIFICATIONS: BA.
HONOURS/AWARDS: Disabilities Awareness Award 2007.
HOBBIES AND INTERESTS: Singing.
PERSONAL PROFILE: Kate Pantelides is the Assistant Director of the Writing Center at the University of Louisville and composition instructor. Previously was the Director of the Writing Center and an English teacher at Berkeley Prepatory School in Tampa, Florida.

NATASHA PANTELIDES
Surface Pattern designer

PLACE OF BIRTH: USA Father from Limassol
SCHOOLS/COLLEGE: Syracuse University.
QUALIFICATIONS: Bachelor of Fine Arts.
PERSONAL PROFILE: Natasha Pantelides is a Surface Pattern Designer.

PROFESSOR SOKRATES PANTELIDES
Professor of Physics at Vanderbilt University

DATE OF BIRTH: 20-Nov-1948
PLACE OF BIRTH: Limassol.
MARITAL STATUS: Married to Mimi, American, Equestrian Instructor.
CHILDREN: Kate, Graduate Student. Natasha, Designer (Fabrics).
SCHOOLS/COLLEGE: Laniton High School, Limassol. University of Illinois, Urbana.
QUALIFICATIONS: PhD Physics, University of Illinois, 1973.
MEMBERSHIPS: American Physics Society, Materials Research Society, Institute of Electrical and Electronic Engineers, Fulbright Society.
HONOURS/AWARDS: Fellow, American Physics Society, 1981, Fellow, American Association for the Advancement of Science, 2003.
HOBBIES AND INTERESTS: Literature, gardening.
PERSONAL PROFILE: Researcher and research manager at IBM Research Division in New York (1975-1994). McMinn Professor of Physics at Vanderbilt University, Nashville, TN since 1994. Editor of 8 technical books and author or co-author of over 300 technical articles.

ANNA PANTELIDOU
Assistant researcher in the Department of Electrical and Computer Engineering at the University of Maryland

PLACE OF BIRTH: Nicosia
SCHOOLS/COLLEGE: University of Athens and University of Maryland.
QUALIFICATIONS: BS MS PhD.
PERSONAL PROFILE: Anna Pantelidou is an assistant researcher in the Department of Electrical and Computer Engineering at the University of Maryland.

USA

MARIA PAPADAKIS
Professor Coordinator of the Urban and Regional studies Minor, James Madison University

SCHOOLS/COLLEGE: Indiana University.
QUALIFICATIONS: Ph. D.
PERSONAL PROFILE: Maria Papadakis is Professor Coordinator of the Urban and Regional studies Minor, James Madison University.

PROFESSOR DEMETRIOS PAPAGEORGIOU
Professor in Mathematics

DATE OF BIRTH: 23-Mar-1960
PLACE OF BIRTH: Nicosia, Cyprus.
MARITAL STATUS: Married to Iva-Maria Varda, Greek.
CHILDREN: Chloe-Theodora.
SCHOOLS/COLLEGE: University College, London, Imperial College London.
QUALIFICATIONS: BSc Mathematics (Hons), PhD Mathematics.
MEMBERSHIPS: American Physical Society, American Association of University Professors, Hellenic Society of Rheology.
HONOURS/AWARDS: National Aeronautics and Space Administration Group Achievement Award, ICASE Fluid Mechanics Group (1993).
HOBBIES AND INTERESTS: Reading and writing, History, Archeology, Architecture.
PERSONAL PROFILE: Demetrios is a Professor of Mathematical Sciences at the New Jersey Institute of Technology, USA. He has held various administrative posts including Associate Chair and Director of Graduate Studies. Work funded by several federal agencies including the National Science Foundation, NASA, NATO and the Air Force Office for Scientific Research.

STELIOS PAPAGEORGIOU
Owner of Zenon Taverna renowned Chef. Best Chef in Hotel and Catering Institute for 2 years, 1977-1978 and 1978-1979

DATE OF BIRTH: 25-Sep-1959
PLACE OF BIRTH: Nicosia.
MARITAL STATUS: Married to Theodora, Greek-Cypriot, Chef.
CHILDREN: Constantina, Elena, Angela, all students.
MEMBERSHIPS: Hotel and Catering Institute.
HONOURS/AWARDS: Best Chef in Hotel and Catering Institute for 2 years, 1977-1978 and 1978-1979.
HOBBIES AND INTERESTS: Cooking, hunting.
PERSONAL PROFILE: Stelios is the owner of Zenon Taverna worked very hard to help the Greek-Cypriot community flourish in Astoria, by donating food and services to those around him.

CHRISTOS PAPALOIZOU
Alexandria City, Washington Award

DATE OF BIRTH: 22-Jun-1954
PLACE OF BIRTH: Nicosia.
MARITAL STATUS: Married to Dionysia, Partner in Business.
CHILDREN: Maria, Family business. Nicos, Family business. Stavros, University.
SCHOOLS/COLLEGE: Southbank College.
HONOURS/AWARDS: Alexandria City, Washington Award "Make Alexandria beautiful" for his Restaurant Garden.
PERSONAL PROFILE: Christos Papaloizou with his wife Dionysiou own the Restaurant Taverna Cretekou in Alexandria, Washington it is one of the regions top Greek restaurants.

Cyprus Federation of America was formed in 1950 its purpose to bring all the Cypriots and Cypriot organisations in the USA under one umbrella.

USA

PETER PAPANICOLAOU
President of the Cyprus Federation of America

PLACE OF BIRTH: Nicosia
SCHOOLS/COLLEGE: New Jersey Institute of Technology.
QUALIFICATIONS: BSc in civil engineering, MSc in construction, engineering and management.
MEMBERSHIPS: Cyprus Chamber of Commerce.
HONOURS/AWARDS: Awarded the Ellis Island Medal of Honour.
PERSONAL PROFILE: Principal of J. F. contracting a Brooklyn based construction and engineering company. President of the Cyprus Federation of America. Member of the advisory board of Queens College.

GUS PAPAPETROU
Psychologist in Forest Hills New York

PLACE OF BIRTH: USA Parents from Karavas.
MARITAL STATUS: Married to Helen.
CHILDREN: One son and one daughter.
PERSONAL PROFILE: Gus Papapetrou is a Psychologist has his own practice in Forest Hills New York.

ANDREAS PAPAS
Founder and President of Yasoo Health Inc

DATE OF BIRTH: 29-Oct-1942
PLACE OF BIRTH: Kato Moni.
SCHOOLS/COLLEGE: University of Illinois.
QUALIFICATIONS: PhD.
HONOURS/AWARDS: Fullbright Scholarship.
PERSONAL PROFILE: Andreas Papas is the adjunct Professor at the College of Medicine at East Tennessee State University and a senior scientific advisor of the cancer prevention Institute at Harvard's School of Epidemiology. Founder and President of Yasoo Health Inc.

PETER J PAPPAS
Former Chairman and President of the Cyprus Childrens Fund

DATE OF BIRTH: 08-Dec-1939
PLACE OF BIRTH: New York, One of his parents from Cyprus.
MARITAL STATUS: Married to Catherine.
CHILDREN: Peter, James, Tara.
HONOURS/AWARDS: An Archon of the Greek Orthodox Church. Awarded by the President of the Republic of Cyprus the gold medal of the Republic of Cyprus.
PERSONAL PROFILE: Businessman, President of P. J. Mechanical Corp. a major air conditioning installation contractor, service and maintenance organisation in New York. Former Chairman and President of the Cyprus Children's Fund.

DEMOS PARNEROS
Staples President of US stores

PLACE OF BIRTH: Born in Cyprus
SCHOOLS/COLLEGE: New York University.
PERSONAL PROFILE: Demos Parneros is Staples President of US Stores responsable for retail operations throughout the United States. Staples operates more than 2000 Office Superstores.

USA

ANDREAS PARPERIDES

Founder of the New York Salamina Soccer Club The team has successfully competed in Men's Semi-Pro soccer in the USA

DATE OF BIRTH: 02-Sep-1962
PLACE OF BIRTH: Famagusta.
MARITAL STATUS: Married to Theodora Theodosiadou, Greek Cypriot, Educational Director for St. Margaret Mary's School in Astoria.
SCHOOLS/COLLEGE: Long Island City High School. Queens College, City University New York.
QUALIFICATIONS: Bachelor of Liberal Arts in Philosophy, 1985.
MEMBERSHIPS: Member of the New York State Board of Realtors, Astoria Democratic Club, Olympiakos Pireaus Fan Club of New York, New York Salamina Soccer Club.
HONOURS/AWARDS: Manager of the Year, 2004-05, Northeastern Super Soccer League, President's Club, RE/MAX Realtors 1996.
HOBBIES AND INTERESTS: Football, Soccer, Literature, History, Philosophy, World Politics, Rock Music.
PERSONAL PROFILE: Founder of the New York Salamina Soccer Club on August 14, 1999. The team has successfully competed in Men's Semi-Pro soccer for the last eight seasons in the United States.

CHRIS PARTRIDGE

Director of a Real Estate Development Company in New York

DATE OF BIRTH: 22-Mar-1943
PLACE OF BIRTH: Kato Drys, Cyprus.
MARITAL STATUS: Married to Carmen, Puerto Rico.
CHILDREN: Christopher, Derek.
SCHOOLS/COLLEGE: Long Island City High School. Law Course at The New School NYC.
HOBBIES AND INTERESTS: Body-building, swimming, jogging, cooking.
PERSONAL PROFILE: Director of a Real Estate Development Company. Father was in the USA from the 1920's.

DEMETRIUS PARTRIDGE

Director of Partridge Realty Real Estate Company in New York

DATE OF BIRTH: 13-Mar-1955
PLACE OF BIRTH: Parents from Kato Drys.
MARITAL STATUS: Married to Victoria.
CHILDREN: Roxanne, Adam.
SCHOOLS/COLLEGE: Long Island High School. Queens College.
HOBBIES AND INTERESTS: Collector of Wrist watches.
PERSONAL PROFILE: Director of Partridge Realty Real Estate company in New York. Restaurants in Manhattan, his father Harry started the Business in 1954.

DEREK PARTRIDGE

Directed and co produced winner of the 1997 Best Feature Film at the New York Independant Film Festival and World Film Festival Bronze Award

PLACE OF BIRTH: New York Father From Kato Drys
MARITAL STATUS: Single.
HONOURS/AWARDS: Feature Film "No Deposit No Return"which he directed and co produced Winner of the 1997 Best Feature Film at the New York Independant Film Festival and World Film Festival Bronze Award.
PERSONAL PROFILE: Derek Partridge is a Film writer/ Director. He runs an independant production company Vista Clara Productions for music videos, commercials and feature films.

ANDRE PATSALIDES

Member of the teaching and supervising faculty at the University of California

PLACE OF BIRTH: Cyprus.
PERSONAL PROFILE: Andre Patsalides is a practising psychoanalyst in Berkeley, founder and faculty member of the Lacanian School of Psychoanalysis. member of the teaching and supervising faculty at the University of California. Professor at the University of Louvain Belgium. He is the author of numerous articles on psychoanalysis.

EUGENIOS PATSALIDES
Professor of Information Technology

DATE OF BIRTH: 08-Jun-1963.
PLACE OF BIRTH: Nicosia.
MARITAL STATUS: Married to Terry, Kentucky.
CHILDREN: Andrea, student. Jordan, School.
SCHOOLS/COLLEGE: Brescia University
(Undergraduate work) Owensboro Kentucky, Western
Kentucky University (Graduate work) Bowling Green,
Kentucky presently attending the University of Kentucky.
QUALIFICATIONS: Masters Degree, Computer Science
and Education.
HOBBIES AND INTERESTS: Travelling, gardening,
soccer.
PERSONAL PROFILE: Professor of Information
Technology, Henderson Community College, Henderson,
Kentucky.

PAULA PAVLIDES
Trial Attorney

PLACE OF BIRTH: USA Parents from Cyprus.
SCHOOLS/COLLEGE: Molloy College School of
Nursing. Loyola College and St Johns University.
QUALIFICATIONS: BA Juris Doctor.
MEMBERSHIPS: Queens County Bar Association.
PERSONAL PROFILE: Paula Pavlides is a Trial Attorney
specialising in municipal insurance defence.

CONSTANTIA PAVLOU
Treasurer of the Cyprus Childrens Fund

DATE OF BIRTH: 25-Aug-1931.
PLACE OF BIRTH: Marathovounos.
MARITAL STATUS: Married to Andreas Pavlou, Cyprus,
Business.
CHILDREN: George, Doctor Gastroenterologist.
Theophanis, Doctor Pulmonary.
SCHOOLS/COLLEGE: Teachers College, Nicosia,
Hunter College. St Johns University.
QUALIFICATIONS: Bachelors Degree in Mathematics,
Master of Arts in Education.
PERSONAL PROFILE: Works in Education, has
developed Greek bilingual curriculum and authored
books. Treasurer of the Cyprus Childrens Fund. Board
Member of the Pan Cyprian Association of America.

DR GEORGE PAVLOU
Gastroenterologist based in West
Paterson, New Jersey

PLACE OF BIRTH: USA Mother from Marathovouno.
QUALIFICATIONS: MD.
PERSONAL PROFILE: Dr George Pavlou is a
Gastroenterologist based in West Paterson, New Jersey.

PAUL A. PAVLOU
Assistant Professor of Information
Systems at the University of California

DATE OF BIRTH: 04-Jul-1975
PLACE OF BIRTH: Nicosia,
Cyprus.
MARITAL STATUS: Married to
Angelika Dimoka, Professor.
SCHOOLS/COLLEGE:
Rice University, Houston,
TX, University of Southern
California, Los Angeles, CA.
QUALIFICATIONS: BSc
Electrical Engineering, MSc
Electrical Engineering, PhD Business Administration.
HONOURS/AWARDS: I.
PERSONAL PROFILE: Paul Pavlou is an Assistant
Professor of Information Systems at the University of
California at Riverside. His research focuses on online
auction marketplaces, electronic commerce.

DR THEOPHANIS PAVLOU
Chief of Pulmonary Medicine at Holy
Name Hospital

PLACE OF BIRTH: USA Parents from Marathovouno.
QUALIFICATIONS: MD. FCCP.
PERSONAL PROFILE: Dr Theophanis Pavlou is board
certified in Internal Medicine, Pulmonary Disease,
Critical Care Medicine and Sleep Medicine. He is chief
of Pulmonary Medicine at Holy Name Hospital. Dr
Pavlou is also the Director of the Sleep Center at Pascack
Valley Hospital.

GEORGE PERDIKIS
Neurosurgeon

PLACE OF BIRTH: Cyprus.
SCHOOLS/COLLEGE: Irvine Medical Center University
of California.
QUALIFICATIONS: MD.
PERSONAL PROFILE: Dr George Perdikis practices
Neurosurgery in Lancaster in California.

USA

ANDREAS PERICLI
Chairman, CEO and Chief Strategist of
Euclid Financial Group

DATE OF BIRTH: 30-Jun-1960
PLACE OF BIRTH: Paphos.
MARITAL STATUS: Married
to Penka Trentcheva, Sophia,
Bulgarian, Statistician.
CHILDREN: Christina.
SCHOOLS/COLLEGE:
Graduate School, CUNY.
QUALIFICATIONS: BSc MA
PhD.
MEMBERSHIPS: Several
Economic and Financial Management Associations.
HOBBIES AND INTERESTS: Community Activities,
Reading, Hiking, Other Sports.
PERSONAL PROFILE: Dr. Pericli is the Chairman,
CEO and Chief Strategist of Euclid Financial Group.
Community Activities: Member of the parish council of
Saint Katherine's Greek Orthodox Church President of
the Greek Cypriots in the Metro Washington Area, 1998
to 2004. President of the Finance & Economics Society,
CUNY, New York, 1989-1990.

NICOS A PETASIS
Professor of Chemistry

PLACE OF BIRTH: Cyprus
SCHOOLS/COLLEGE:
Aristotelian University of
Thessaloniki, Greece and
University of. Pennsylvania.
QUALIFICATIONS: BS and
PhD.
PERSONAL PROFILE: Nicos
is a Professor of Chemistry
at the University of Southern
California.

MICHAEL PETROU
Associate Professor in Civil and
enviromental engineering

PLACE OF BIRTH: Cyprus
SCHOOLS/COLLEGE:
University of Athens and Case
Western Reserve University
Cleveland, Ohio.
QUALIFICATIONS: MS PhD.
MEMBERSHIPS: American
Society for Engineering
Education.
PERSONAL PROFILE: Michael
Petrou was an Associate
Professor in the Department of Civil and environmental

Engineering at the Universitie's of South Carolina, Volos
and Cyprus. Now based in Cyprus.

TASSOS PETROU
Assistant Professor In the Library and
Information Science Program at Denver
University

PLACE OF BIRTH: Cyprus
SCHOOLS/COLLEGE:
University of California and
Mankato University.
QUALIFICATIONS: BS MA
MBA PhD.
PERSONAL PROFILE: Tassos
Petrou is a Assistant Professor
In the Library and Information
Science Program at Denver
University.

CHARLES PISTIS
State Coordinator for Michigan Sea
Grant Extension

PLACE OF BIRTH: New York
Mother from Karavas, Father
from Kyrenia.
MARITAL STATUS: Married.
CHILDREN: One son, one
daughter.
SCHOOLS/COLLEGE: City
College of New York and Texas
A&M University.
QUALIFICATIONS: Bs Ms.
HONOURS/AWARDS: Michigan
State University's Distinguished Academic Staff Award 2002.
PERSONAL PROFILE: Chuck Pistis is State Coordinator
for Michigan Sea Grant Extension he is also an advisor to
the Great Lakes Fishery Commission and is a member of
the Michigan Department of Natural Resources Citizen
Advisory Committees for Lakes Michigan and Erie.

MARY PITTAS
Professor of Modern Greek Language

DATE OF BIRTH: 23-May-1942
PLACE OF BIRTH: Alexandria,
Egypt. Paternal Grandfather was
from Dhali.
MARITAL STATUS: Married
to Dennis R. Herschbach,
California, California. Professor
at University of Maryland.
CHILDREN: Robert, Alissa,
Elizabeth.

USA

SCHOOLS/COLLEGE: St. Joseph's School (Nicosia), University of Illinois, University of Maryland.
QUALIFICATIONS: PhD.
MEMBERSHIPS: Modern Greek Studies Association; American Philological Association.
HOBBIES AND INTERESTS: Theatre, travel, archaeology.
PERSONAL PROFILE: Coordinator of Modern Greek Program University of Maryland Department of Classics; Professor of Modern Greek Language and Literature and Classical Literature Book and articles on classical drama and modern Greek theatre. Member of St. Sophia Greek Orthodox Cathedral, Washington D. C.

ANDREAS A. POLYCARPOU
Professor at the Department of Mechanical Science and Engineering at the University of Illinois

PLACE OF BIRTH: Nicosia
MARITAL STATUS: Married to Mary, Famagusta.
CHILDREN: Aryeris (Aris), Andrea.
SCHOOLS/COLLEGE: State University of New York.
QUALIFICATIONS: BS MS PhD.
MEMBERSHIPS: Member, Executive Committee, Tribology Division, 2001-2006.
HONOURS/AWARDS: 2007 Edmond E. Bisson Award.
HOBBIES AND INTERESTS: Outdoor activities (involved with Boy Scouts of America), travelling and archeology.
PERSONAL PROFILE: Andreas A Polycarpou is a Professor and Kritzer Faculty Scholar at the Department of Mechanical Science and Engineering at the University of Illinois Urbana-Champaign and the author and co-author of over 100 archival journal papers.

MARIOS POLYCARPOU
Professor in Electrical and Computer Engineering

DATE OF BIRTH: 27-Aug-1962
PLACE OF BIRTH: Nicosia.
MARITAL STATUS: Married to Maria, Cyprus, Artist.
SCHOOLS/COLLEGE: Rice University in Houston and University of Southern California.
QUALIFICATIONS: BA BSc MS and PhD in Electrical Engineering.

HONOURS/AWARDS: Recipient of the William H Middendorf Research Excellence Award at the University of Cincinnati.
HOBBIES AND INTERESTS: Hiking, Swimming and Literature.
PERSONAL PROFILE: Previously Marios Panayiotou was an Associate Professor at the Department of Electrical and Computer Engineering at the University of Southern California. Now hes in the Department of Electrical and Computer Engineering at the University of Cyprus where he is a Professor.

PAUL POLYCARPOU
1999 Best Director Award winner for his work on the groundbreaking documentary Faces in the Forest

PLACE OF BIRTH: Larnaca.
HONOURS/AWARDS: 1999 Best Director Award winner for his work on the groundbreaking documentary Faces in the Forest currently airing on The Learning Channel and National Geographic Worldwide.
PERSONAL PROFILE: Paul Polycarpou is the founder and creative vision behind Envision after moving to America from Great Britain where he started his career in video production producing healthcare specific educational programs. Hundreds of programs later Paul has become an acomplished director in this field.

POLYXENI POTTER
Medical/Science writer

PLACE OF BIRTH: Limassol
MARITAL STATUS: Married to Morris, USA, Veterinarian.
CHILDREN: Alexia, Writer. Elliott, Electrical Engineer.
SCHOOLS/COLLEGE: First Gymnasium for Girls, Limassol, Cyprus. Baldwin-Wallace College, Berea, Ohio, Purdue University, Lafayette, Indiana.
QUALIFICATIONS: BA in English Literature, MA in American Studies.
MEMBERSHIPS: Council of Science Editors, American Medical Writers Association.
HONOURS/AWARDS: Received Young Scholar's Essay Award from the city of Limassol.
HOBBIES AND INTERESTS: Drawing, Art, History.
PERSONAL PROFILE: Taught English Language and American Culture classes at Georgia State University, Atlanta for 10 years. Transferred her interest in Language to a science writer-editor position at the centres for Disease Control and Prevention. Has published over 70 articles between art and science.

USA

DR ELIZABETH PRODROMOU
Assistant Professor University of Boston

PLACE OF BIRTH: Born in 1959 Father from Aradippou **SCHOOLS/COLLEGE:** Tufts University, The Fletcher School of Law and Diplomacy and Massachusetts Institute of Technology. **QUALIFICATIONS:** BA MA PhD. **PERSONAL PROFILE:** Elizabeth Prodromou is an Assistant Professor, Dept of International Relations;Associate Director. Institute on Culture, Religion and World Affairs at Boston University.

CHRISTOS RIALAS
Program administrator for New York State Academic Dental Centers and Associated Medical Schools of New York

PLACE OF BIRTH: Cyprus **MARITAL STATUS:** Married to Olivera Jakovljevic, Concert Violinist. **CHILDREN:** Philip. **SCHOOLS/COLLEGE:** State University of New York, Adelphi University and New School University. **QUALIFICATIONS:** BS MS MA. **PERSONAL PROFILE:** Christos Rialas is Program administrator for New York State Academic Dental Centers and Associated Medical Schools of New York.

DEBBIE (DESPINA) RIGA
Sales Director of the Year Hyatt Hotels

DATE OF BIRTH: 03-Dec-1958.
PLACE OF BIRTH: Detroit, Michigan. Parents from Limassol and Paphos.
MARITAL STATUS: Married to Doros Evangelides, Larnaca, Director of Animation.
MEMBERSHIPS: Cyprus Federation of America, Panpaphian Association Cyprus Childrens Fund.
HONOURS/AWARDS: Sales Director of the Year Hyatt Hotels.
Member of the Year award Panpaphian Association.
HOBBIES AND INTERESTS: Writing Poetry, writing plays in the Greek Cypriot dialect.

PERSONAL PROFILE: Debbie Riga is the General Manager of Morgans Hotel in New York. A career in the travel industry spanning 36 years. She has written two Greek Cypriot Plays which have been produced locally. Writes articles for local papers and an active member of the community.

ALEXANDER ROSSIDES
President and Co Founder of Growth Philanthropy Network

PLACE OF BIRTH: Washington, Grandparents from Cyprus **SCHOOLS/COLLEGE:** Dartmouth College and Columbia Business School. **QUALIFICATIONS:** BA MBA. **PERSONAL PROFILE:** Alexander Rossides is the President and Co Founder of Growth Philanthropy Network(GPN)its initial program focus is on youth education and development, health, and family economic success.

ELENI ROSSIDES
Executive Director of the Washington Tennis and Education Foundation

PLACE OF BIRTH: Washington, Grandparents from Cyprus **MARITAL STATUS:** Married to Nikolas. **CHILDREN:** Two sons. **SCHOOLS/COLLEGE:** Stanford University and North Western University. **QUALIFICATIONS:** MBA. **PERSONAL PROFILE:** Eleni Rossides is the Executive Director of the Washington Tennis and Education Foundation. As a Tennis player she spent eight years on the womens professional tennis tour. She was ranked in the top 50 US womens Tennis Professionals.

GALE ROSSIDES
Territorial Security Administration (TSA) Permanent Deputy Administrator

PLACE OF BIRTH: Washington, Grandparent from Cyprus
SCHOOLS/COLLEGE: Wheaton College and George Washington University.
QUALIFICATIONS: BA MA.
PERSONAL PROFILE: Gale Rossides became The Territorial Security Administration (TSA) permanent deputy administrator. Rossides led a team of Government and private sector personnel that successfully trained and certified more than 50, 000 screeners in less than six months. She also led the team that successfully federalized the first domestic airport, Baltimore/ Washington International Thurgood Marshall Airport. From September 2004 through August 2005, Rossides served at the Department of Homeland Security as the Senior Advisor to the Deputy Secretary and Director of Business Transformation in the Office of the Under Secretary for Management.

GENE ROSSIDES
Founder, American Hellenic Institute and American Hellenic Institute Foundation

DATE OF BIRTH: 23-Oct-1927
PLACE OF BIRTH: Brooklyn, NY USA, Parents from Cyprus.
MARITAL STATUS: Married to Aphrodite Macotsin.
CHILDREN: Five children two from previous marriage.
SCHOOLS/COLLEGE: Columbia College, New York City, AB 1949. Law School Attended Columbia University Law School NYC JD 1952.
MEMBERSHIPS: American Bar Association.
PERSONAL PROFILE: Retired senior Partner of Rogers & Wells, now Clifford Chance, US LLP. Founder, American Hellenic Institute and American Hellenic Institute Foundation. Served as Assistant Secretary US Treasury Department.

ANDREAS S SAVVA
He is the producer and host of a local weekly Cypriot Radio show airing in the New York City Tri State area

PLACE OF BIRTH: Limassol, Cyprus in 1960
SCHOOLS/COLLEGE: Queens college of the city university of New York, New York Institute of Technology, and University of Wexford.
QUALIFICATIONS: BA and PhD.
HOBBIES AND INTERESTS: Community work.
PERSONAL PROFILE: Began as a Lecturer at Technical Colleges Business Schools in New York City. Andreas is the founder of and CEO of ARC Technologies an information Technology Partnership. He serves on the Board of Directors of several community, political and charitable organisation's. Andreas has also served as a volunteer Police Officer. He is the producer and host of a local weekly Cypriot Radio show airing in the New York City Tri State area.

DR CHRISTOS SAVVA
Assistant Research Scientist at the Texas A&M University

PLACE OF BIRTH: Larnaca
SCHOOLS/COLLEGE: University of Leeds and Texas A&M University.
QUALIFICATIONS: BSc PhD.
PERSONAL PROFILE: Christos Savva is an Assistant Research Scientist at the Microscopy and imaging Center at the Texas A&M University.

DR GEORGE SAVVAS
Family Doctor in Illinois

PLACE OF BIRTH: Cyprus.
QUALIFICATIONS: MD.
PERSONAL PROFILE: Dr George Savva is a Family Doctor in Champaign, Illinois.

USA

THEODORE SAVVAS
Chiropractor

PLACE OF BIRTH: Cyprus
PERSONAL PROFILE:
Theodore Savva has family
Chiropractic practise in Virginia
Beach, Virginia.

ANDREAS SAVVIDES
Assistant Associate, Full Professor
Department of Economics, Oklahoma
State University

PLACE OF BIRTH: Cyprus.
SCHOOLS/COLLEGE: Birmingham University UK and
University of Florida.
QUALIFICATIONS: BSc BCom MA PhD.
PERSONAL PROFILE: Andreas Savvides is an Assistant
Associate, Full Professor Department of Economics,
Oklahoma State University.

ANDREAS SAVVIDES
Assistant Professor of Electrical
Engineering and of Computer Science at
Yale University

PLACE OF BIRTH: Cyprus
SCHOOLS/COLLEGE:
University of California.
QUALIFICATIONS: PhD.
PERSONAL PROFILE:
Andreas Savvides is an Assistant
Professor of Electrical
Engineering and of Computer
Science at Yale University.

CHRISTOPHER SAVVIDES
Business

PLACE OF BIRTH: USA Father from Lapithos.
PERSONAL PROFILE: Christopher Savvides is the
Owner of the Black Angus Restaurant in Virginia Beach
actively involved with the Cypriot Community in the
USA.

JOANNA SAVVIDES
President of the World Trade Center of
Greater Philadelphia

PLACE OF BIRTH: Cyprus
CHILDREN: Two Children.
PERSONAL PROFILE: Joanna
Savvides is the President of the
World Trade Center of Greater
Philadelphia which is a non
profit organisation which has
assisted over 500 companies
to expand their International
business. Joanna is an adjunct
Professor of Global Business
Strategy and International Marketing at Saint Josephs
University in Philadelphia.

MARIOS SAVVIDES
Research Assistant Professor with
an appointment in Carnegie Mellons
CY Lab and Electrical & Computer
Engineering Department

PLACE OF BIRTH: Cyprus
SCHOOLS/COLLEGE:
University of Manchester and
Carnegie Mellon University.
MEMBERSHIPS: BEng MS
PhD.
PERSONAL PROFILE: Marios
Savvides is currently a Research
Assistant Professor with an
appointment in Carnegie
Mellons CY Lab and Electrical
& Computer Engineering Department. His Research
interest is in biometric recognition of face. Iris and
Fingerprint and Palm print modalities.

PHOTIS SAVVIDES
Accountant

PLACE OF BIRTH: Limassol.
PERSONAL PROFILE: Photis Savvides is an Accountant
with his own practice located in the Bronx area of
New York. Active member of the New York Cypriot
Community.

USA

MICHAEL SELEARIS
World Champion Arm Wrestler 1998

PLACE OF BIRTH: USA Parents from Cyprus
SCHOOLS/COLLEGE: New Town High School.
PERSONAL PROFILE: Michael Selearis won the Arm Wrestling World Championships in 1998 he has also been the USA National Champion several times.

SOPHIA SERGHI
Distinguished Associate professor of Music at the College of William and Mary in Virginia, USA

DATE OF BIRTH: 05-Oct-1972
PLACE OF BIRTH: Nicosia.
MARITAL STATUS: Married to Aris Aristides, UK, Senior Business Analyst.
CHILDREN: Ariadne.
SCHOOLS/COLLEGE: Makarios C' Lyceum. Columbia University.
QUALIFICATIONS: DMA. Doctor of Music Arts, MA Master of Music Arts, BA Honors, Music.
MEMBERSHIPS: American Association of University Women.
HONOURS/AWARDS: 2005-2008 Robert F and Sarah M Boyd Distinguished Associate Professor of Music.
HOBBIES AND INTERESTS: Sailing, tennis, hiking.
PERSONAL PROFILE: Sophia is a Cypriot Composer, now resident in the USA, of stage, orchestral, chamber, vocal and multi-media works that have been performed in Europe and the USA. She is the Robert F and Sarah M Distinguished Associate professor of Music at the College of William and Mary in Virginia, USA.

LAURA SERGIS
Pediatrician in Carson, California

PLACE OF BIRTH: Father from Cyprus.
PERSONAL PROFILE: Dr Laura Sergis is a Pediatrician in Carson, California.

MARINA SIRTIS
Actress played Deanna Troi on the Television and Film Series Star Trek

DATE OF BIRTH: 22-Mar-1955
PLACE OF BIRTH: London Parents from Cyprus.
MARITAL STATUS: Married to Michael Lamper.
SCHOOLS/COLLEGE: Guildhall School of Music and Drama.
PERSONAL PROFILE: Marina Sirtis is an Actress who is most noted for playing Deanna Troi on the Television and Film Series Star Trek. Has also appeared in films one where she was the wicked lady with Faye Dunaway also had a major role in the Charles Bronson film Death Wish 111.

KONSTANTIA SOFOKLEOUS
Artist Her work includes short animated movies and drawings

DATE OF BIRTH: 15-Apr-1974.
PLACE OF BIRTH: Limassol.
MARITAL STATUS: Married to Savvas Houvartas, Greek, Musician.
SCHOOLS/COLLEGE: University of Westminster, London, UK, New York University (NYU), USA.
QUALIFICATIONS: Master of Science in Computer Animation with Distinction.
HOBBIES AND INTERESTS: Reading and researching.
PERSONAL PROFILE: Artist. Her work includes short animated movies and drawings. Shown work in international Art Exhibitions and Film Festivals. She represented Cyprus at the 51. Venice Biennale International Art Festival.

USA

STAVROULLA (VOULLA) SOLONOS (nee Epiphanou)

Served as Vice President Tommy Hilfinger USA inc

DATE OF BIRTH: 23-Jan-1964
PLACE OF BIRTH: Teaneck New Jersey, Parents from Karavas.
MARITAL STATUS: Married to George Solonos, Mia Milia, Self Employed.
CHILDREN: Marissa, Both in School. Katerina.
SCHOOLS/COLLEGE: Moore College of Art Philadelphia.
QUALIFICATIONS: BFA.
HOBBIES AND INTERESTS: Travelling, Painting, Gardening, Cooking, Reading and Swimming.
PERSONAL PROFILE: Served as Vice President Tommy Hilfinger USA inc. Designed two menswear signature pieces. prep crew with crest 1990 and Tommy Flag Sweater 1992 both are still used today. Designed Hip Hop Logo Sweater first worn by Michael Jackson in early 90's and flag centenial sweater worn by Ronald Reagan in 1993.

MARIOS SOPHOCLEOUS

Senior Scientist, Geohydrology Section, Kansas Geological Survey, The University of Kansas

PLACE OF BIRTH: Cyprus
SCHOOLS/COLLEGE: University of Athens, University of Kansas and University of Alberta.
QUALIFICATIONS: BSc MSc PhD.
PERSONAL PROFILE: Marios Sophocleous is Senior Scientist, Geohydrology Section, Kansas Geological Survey, The University of Kansas.

DEAN SOPHOCLES

Clinical Assistant Professor in the Department of Preventative and Restorative Sciences at the University of Pennsylvania School of Dental Medicine

PLACE OF BIRTH: USA Father from Larnaca
MARITAL STATUS: Married.
CHILDREN: Two children.
SCHOOLS/COLLEGE: Trinity College Harford, University of Pennsylvania School of Dental Medicine.
HONOURS/AWARDS: Dr. Sophocles has twice been selected by his peers as one of the top cosmetic dentists in the Western Philadelphia suburbs, as reported in Main Line Today in August 2006 and June 2008.
PERSONAL PROFILE: Dean is Clinical Assistant Professor in the Department of Preventative and Restorative Sciences at the University of Pennsylvania School of Dental Medicine. By night, Dean has established himself as a session player, a solo jazz pianist, and an ensemble keyboardist in both the rock and jazz genres. He began studying both piano and violin at the age of five; by the age of twelve, he was traveling throughout the U. S. with a young chamber group, the Young Concerto Soloists, led by veteran Philadelphia Orchestra member Jerome Wigler. Dean studied classical and jazz piano with various well known Philadelphia-based teachers, as well as in a master class with Bruce Hornsby. Dean is a former member of the Doug Markley Band and is currently performing with Three the Hard Way.

VASSOS SOTERIOU

Assistant Instructor at Princeton University

PLACE OF BIRTH: Born in Limassol 1976
SCHOOLS/COLLEGE: Rice University and Princeton University.
QUALIFICATIONS: BSEE MA. PhD.
HOBBIES AND INTERESTS: Travel, Weight Training, reading and photography.
PERSONAL PROFILE: Vassos Soteriou was an assistant instructor at Princeton University also a visiting Lecturer in the Department of Electrical and Computer engineering at the University of Cyprus.

USA

ZOE STAVRI
Assistant Professor at Oregon Health Sciences University

PLACE OF BIRTH: USA Parents from Cyprus
PERSONAL PROFILE: Zoe Stavri is the Assistant Professor at Oregon Health Sciences University.

MARIO STAVROU
Owner of a chain of Celebrity hair and beauty salons in Bergen County with over 70 employees

PLACE OF BIRTH: Cyprus.
PERSONAL PROFILE: Marios Stavrou is the owner of a chain of Celebrity hair and beauty salons in Bergen County, New Jersey with over 70 employees.

THEOFANIS G. STAVROU
Lecturer at the University of Minnesota

DATE OF BIRTH: 12-Jul-1934
PLACE OF BIRTH: Dhorios Kyrenia.
MARITAL STATUS: Married to Freda.
CHILDREN: Gregory, Lyn, Michael.
SCHOOLS/COLLEGE: Indiana University.
QUALIFICATIONS: PhD.
HONOURS/AWARDS: College of Liberal Arts Teaching Award, University of Minnesota 1976, Hellenic Society of Translators of Literature Award, Morse Amoco/Alumni Teaching Award, University of Minnesota, 2000.
PERSONAL PROFILE: Lecturer in Modern Russia and Cultural History of Modern Greece in the Dept. of History at the University of Minnesota. Co-edited books on Greece, Russia and South Eastern Europe.

MARIOS STEPHANIDES
Lecturer in Sociology

DATE OF BIRTH: 26-Apr-1945.
PLACE OF BIRTH: Polis Chrysochous.
MARITAL STATUS: Married to Ourania.
CHILDREN: Three children.
SCHOOLS/COLLEGE: Wayne State University.
QUALIFICATIONS: BA MA PhD.
PERSONAL PROFILE: Marios Stephanides has taught sociology at Universities, Wayne State, Louisville and Spalding. Has also writen books on the Greeks in Detroit, St Louis and Louisville, Kentucky.

DR MICHAEL STEPHANIDES
Plastic Surgeon

PLACE OF BIRTH: Parents from Cyprus
SCHOOLS/COLLEGE: Stanford University School of Medicine, California.
QUALIFICATIONS: MD.
HOBBIES AND INTERESTS: Water Sports and Hiking.
PERSONAL PROFILE: Dr Stephanides is a Plastic Surgeon based in Nashville, Tennessee.

STEPHANOS STEPHANIDES
Poet and Literary Scholar

DATE OF BIRTH: 22-Oct-1949
PLACE OF BIRTH: Trikomo.
MARITAL STATUS: Married to Kathleen, Washington DC, Editor.
CHILDREN: Katerina, Student.
SCHOOLS/COLLEGE: Cardiff University.
QUALIFICATIONS: BA (Hons) PhD Modern Languages and Literatures.
MEMBERSHIPS: ACLALS (Association for Commonwealth Literature and Language Studies) ESSE (European Society for the Study of English).
HONOURS/AWARDS: Cavaliere (Knight) of the Republic of Italy (OSSI Order of the Star for Italian Solidarity).
HOBBIES AND INTERESTS: All the arts especially literature and film.
PERSONAL PROFILE: Poet, literary scholar and critic, translator, ethnographer. He has lived in many countries was mainly based in the USA after leaving Cyprus at the age of eight and returned 35 years later as a founding member of the University of Cyprus where he is currently Dean of Humanities.

USA

GABRIEL STYLIANIDES
Assistant Professor of Mathematics at the University of Pittsburgh

PLACE OF BIRTH: Cyprus
SCHOOLS/COLLEGE: University of Cyprus and University of Michigan.
QUALIFICATIONS: BA MSc and PhD.
PERSONAL PROFILE: Gabriel Stylianides is an Assistant Professor of Mathematics at the University of Pittsburgh.

ANTONIS STYLIANOU
Professor of Management Information Systems

PLACE OF BIRTH: Nicosia
SCHOOLS/COLLEGE: Kent State University.
QUALIFICATIONS: BS MBA PhD.
PERSONAL PROFILE: Antonis Stylianou is a Professor of Management Information Systems at North Carolina University.

DESPINA A. STYLIANOU
Associate Professor of Mathematics at the City University of New York

DATE OF BIRTH: 02-Sep-1970
PLACE OF BIRTH: Nicosia, Cyprus.
MARITAL STATUS: Married to Juan M. Huerta, Mexican, Research Scientist.
CHILDREN: Juan Manuel Huerta-Stylianou, Christina Isabel Herta-Stylianou.
SCHOOLS/COLLEGE: Pedagogical Academy of Cyprus, Boston University, University of Pittsburgh.
QUALIFICATIONS: EdD MA MEd BS.
MEMBERSHIPS: American Education Research Association, National Council of Teachers of mathematics, amongst others.
HONOURS/AWARDS: National Science Foundation, USA, Early Career Award.

PERSONAL PROFILE: Despina is an Associate Professor of Mathematics Education at The City College of the City University of New York. Her work has been published in several Journals one of being Journal of Mathematical Behaviour.

HARRY STYLIANOU
Councilman in Dumont New Jersey/ Attorney

PLACE OF BIRTH: Parents from Cyprus
MARITAL STATUS: Married.
SCHOOLS/COLLEGE: Rutgers University and California Western School of Law.
QUALIFICATIONS: BS JD.
MEMBERSHIPS: New Jersey State Bar Association.
HONOURS/AWARDS: Award for Outstanding Trial Performance from Citi Bank.
HOBBIES AND INTERESTS: Mr Stylianou serves as Councilman in Dumont New Jersey. He successfully ran for re-election in November 2006. He is an Attorney and is a partner in the Firm of Eichenbaum & Stylianou LLC.

STEVE STYLIANOU
Honorary Consul of Cyprus in Michigan

DATE OF BIRTH: 15-Jun-1944.
PLACE OF BIRTH: Larnaca.
CHILDREN: Three children.
SCHOOLS/COLLEGE: Wayne State University and Detroit College of Law.
PERSONAL PROFILE: Steve Stylianou is the Honorary Consul of Cyprus in Michigan. He is a Lawyer with his own practice in Michigan.

SYMEON SYMEONIDES
Judge Albert Tate Professor of Law at Louisiana State University

PLACE OF BIRTH: Lythrodontas 1949
MARITAL STATUS: Married to Haroulla.
SCHOOLS/COLLEGE: Aristotelian University of Thessaloniki, Greece and Harvard.
QUALIFICATIONS: LLm DJS.
PERSONAL PROFILE: In 1989 Symeon became the Judge Albert Tate Professor of Law at Louisiana State University. (LSU), teaching there until 1999. While a professor he served as U. S. National

Reporter to the International Congress of Comparative Law in 1994, and as Rapporteur Général in 1998. During his time at LSU he also served as a vice chancellor. In March 1999, Symeon C. Symeonides was hired as the Dean at Willamette University's law school located in Salem, Oregon.

GEORGE SYRIMIS
Associate Program Chair of Hellenic Studies Program Yale University

PLACE OF BIRTH: Skylloura born 1966
SCHOOLS/COLLEGE: Nicosia Grammar School. Cornell University and Harvard University.
QUALIFICATIONS: PhD in Comparative Literature.
MEMBERSHIPS: Modern Greek Studies Association of North America.
HOBBIES AND INTERESTS: Greek Music and cooking.
PERSONAL PROFILE: Associate Program Chair of Hellenic Studies Program Yale University and Lecturer in Comparative Literature.

MICHAEL G. SYRIMIS
Assistant Professor in Italian Tulane University

DATE OF BIRTH: 23-Jul-1962
PLACE OF BIRTH: Nicosia, Cyprus.
MARITAL STATUS: Single.
SCHOOLS/COLLEGE: Gymnasio Kykko. Rutgers University, New Brunswick, New Jersey, The University of Chicago, Chicago Illinois.
QUALIFICATIONS: BS Ba PhD. Phi Beta Kappa.
MEMBERSHIPS: Modern Language AssociationAmerican Association for Italian Studies.
HOBBIES AND INTERESTS: Film, Music, Reading, Exercising.
PERSONAL PROFILE: Since July 2005: Assistant Professor (Italian), Department of French and Italian, Tulane University, New Orleans, Louisianna, USA.

CHRISTINE TALARIDES
Senior Counsel at Lucas Film Limited

PLACE OF BIRTH: USA Father from Cyprus.
SCHOOLS/COLLEGE: Harvard Law school. University of California.
QUALIFICATIONS: BA Psychology.

PERSONAL PROFILE: Corporate General Counsel/Senior Counsel with substantial in house legal experience at Technology companies. Currently Senior Counsel at Lucas Film Limited.

DIANA GEORGE TELEMACHOU
Accountant

PLACE OF BIRTH: New York Mother from Cyprus
MARITAL STATUS: Married to Demetris Telemachou, Cyprus, Assistant Principal in a High School and former Basketball player.
CHILDREN: Tatiana, Grammar School. Harry, Kindergarten.
SCHOOLS/COLLEGE: Queens College.
PERSONAL PROFILE: Diana George Telemachou is an Accountant born and lived most of her life in the USA now living in Cyprus.

GEORGIOS THEOCHAROUS
Professor in Computer Science

DATE OF BIRTH: 18-Feb-1971
PLACE OF BIRTH: Cyprus.
MARITAL STATUS: Single.
SCHOOLS/COLLEGE: University of South Florida, Michigan State University and Masachussets Institute of Technology.
QUALIFICATIONS: PhD in computer Science, Research area is artificial intelligence, machine learning and robotics.
PERSONAL PROFILE: Professor in Computer Science at the University of Florida.

USA

DR ANDREAS THEODOROU
Professor of Clinical Pediatrics
University of Arizona

DATE OF BIRTH: 15-Nov-1955
PLACE OF BIRTH: Cyprus.
MARITAL STATUS: Married to maria.
SCHOOLS/COLLEGE: Wayne State University.
QUALIFICATIONS: MD.
MEMBERSHIPS: Member of the Arizona Health and Hospital Associations Patient Safety Steering Committee.
HOBBIES AND INTERESTS: Honoured with Care Award from The Brain Injury Association of Arizona.
PERSONAL PROFILE: Andreas Theodorou is a Professor of Clinical Pediatrics and Section Chief of Pediatric Critical Care with the University of Arizona Department of Pediatrics.

ANDREW THEODOROU
Elected as Chairman of Tourism Board, Newport Beach

DATE OF BIRTH: 18-Feb-1951
PLACE OF BIRTH: Reading, England parents from Cyprus.
MARITAL STATUS: Married to Susan, American, Optometric Assistant.
CHILDREN: Kristina, Student. Joseph, Navy Officer.
SCHOOLS/COLLEGE: American Acadamy, Larnaca.
QUALIFICATIONS: BA (diploma) Hotel Management, (diploma) Sales and Marketing.
MEMBERSHIPS: Member of Commodores Group, (leading business members in Newport Beach, Member of Chamber of Commerce of both Newport Beach and Santa Ana, Board of Directors.
HONOURS/AWARDS: Elected as Chairman of tourism board, Newport Beach, two terms, 2006-2008, 100 year (centennial), awarded by John Wayne Family for his contributions towards the celebration of the life of John Wayne (movie star). amongst other honors.
HOBBIES AND INTERESTS: Travel, sports, Politics, Cyprus problem and reading.
PERSONAL PROFILE: Chairman, Newport Beach, Conference and Visitors Bureau, (Tourism) Newport Beach, CA, USA. 2006-2008. Board member of many charities.

ANTONIS THEODOROU
Business

PLACE OF BIRTH: Cyprus
SCHOOLS/COLLEGE: Technical University of Berlin and University of Chicago.
QUALIFICATIONS: MS MBA.
PERSONAL PROFILE: Antonis Theodorou is the President and Founder of a Machine Tool Operation.

SUSIE THEODOROU
Food writer and stylist

DATE OF BIRTH: 09-Oct-1965
PLACE OF BIRTH: Father from Livadhia Mother from Morphou.
MARITAL STATUS: Single.
SCHOOLS/COLLEGE: Enfield Chase School. Polytechnic of North London.
QUALIFICATIONS: HND in Home Economics.
HOBBIES AND INTERESTS: Food and Travel.
PERSONAL PROFILE: Susie Theodorou is a freelance food writer and stylist, and the author of "Coffee and Bites" and "Can i freeze it books". She has worked for numerous publications in both the United States and the United Kingdom, including Food editor for She and Bella. Also worked for Gourmet, Martha Stewart Everyday Food, Real Simple, Waitrose Food Illustrated, Conran's Live It, and She magazine. She is a regular contributor to Australian Vogue Entertaining & Travel.

STELLA Z. THEODOULOU
Holds the the position of Dean College of Social & Behavioural Sciences, California State University

DATE OF BIRTH: 16-Jun-1955
PLACE OF BIRTH: UK, parents from Rizokarpasso.
SCHOOLS/COLLEGE: City of London Polytechnic, Essex University, Tulane University.
QUALIFICATIONS: BA (Hons}, MA; Ph. D.
HONOURS/AWARDS: Harvard University Institute of Leadership and Management in Higher Education Fellowship.

PERSONAL PROFILE: Since 2001 Dr. Stella Theodoulou has held the position of Dean College of Social & Behavioural Sciences, California State University. She was formerly Professor and Chair, Dept. of Political Science CSU, Northridge. She was also Vice President and Producer of AMER PRODUCTIONS 1990-2005. Produced movie 'Riders of Purple Sage, starring Amy Madigan and Ed Harris. She is author of six books.

STEVE THEOFANOUS
President of the Cyprus Brotherhood of Greater Chicago

DATE OF BIRTH: 15-Nov-1957
PLACE OF BIRTH: Nicosia.
MARITAL STATUS: Married to Maria, Greek Cypriot.
CHILDREN: Katerina, Television Journalist. Andrea, Fashion Broker/Distributor. Anna, Student.
QUALIFICATIONS: Food Service Management.
HONOURS/AWARDS: Board member of the Greek American Restaurant Association, past President of the McHenry County Restaurant Association, Cyprus Federation of America-Illinois Governor, past President of the Cyprus Brotherhood of Greater Chicago.
HOBBIES AND INTERESTS: Time with family, Golf, dining out, travelling.
PERSONAL PROFILE: Owner and Operator with his brother Fano: Around the Clock Restaurant and Bakery in Crystal Lake, Illinois.

MICHAEL TOUMAZOU
Professor of Classics at Davidson College in North Carolina

DATE OF BIRTH: 11-Dec-1952
PLACE OF BIRTH: Famagusta.
MARITAL STATUS: Married.
SCHOOLS/COLLEGE: Franklin & Marshall College, Loyola University of Chicago and Bryn Mawr College.
QUALIFICATIONS: BA MA PhD.
MEMBERSHIPS: Archaelogical Institute of America.
HONOURS/AWARDS: Recipient of the Hunter-Hamilton Teaching Award 2003.
PERSONAL PROFILE: Michael Toumazou is a Professor of Classics at Davidson College in North Carolina he specializes in art and archaeology and offers courses in Greek Language and Literature as well as in Classical and Cypriot Art And Archaeology. He has directed the Athienou Archaeological Project on Cyprus since 1990.

ANDREAS TSANGARIS
Active member of the Astoria community New York

PLACE OF BIRTH: Cyprus.
PERSONAL PROFILE: Andreas Tsangarides is an active member of the Astoria community New York he is an Accountant with his own practice in New York.

SAVAS TSIVICOS
President of the Cyprus Childrens Fund, former President of the Cyprus Federation of America

DATE OF BIRTH: 14-Jan-1963
PLACE OF BIRTH: Innia.
MARITAL STATUS: Married to Maria.
CHILDREN: Haralambos, Elpetha, Evangelos.
SCHOOLS/COLLEGE: Fairleigh Dickinson University, George Washington University.
QUALIFICATIONS: Bachelors degree and an MBA.
HONOURS/AWARDS: Awarded the Ellis Island medal of honour.
PERSONAL PROFILE: President of the Cyprus Childrens Fund, Former President of the Cyprus federation of America. Has served for several years as Vice President of the International Coordinating Committee Justice for Cyprus. He is President of Paphian Enterprises Inc a New Jersey based general contracting company specialising in government contracts.

IAKOVOS VASILIOU
Executive Officer PhD. MA program in Philosophy at the City University of New York

PLACE OF BIRTH: USA Grandfather from Chirokitia.
SCHOOLS/COLLEGE: Cornell University and University of Pittsburgh.
QUALIFICATIONS: BA. and PhD.
PERSONAL PROFILE: Iakovos Vasiliou Executive Officer PhD. MA program in Philosophy at the City University of New York.

USA

PROFESSOR ANDREAS VASSILIOU
Professor Emeritus in the Department for Earth and Environmental Services at Rutgers University USA

DATE OF BIRTH: 30-Nov-1936
PLACE OF BIRTH: Ora, Larnaca.
MARITAL STATUS: Married to Marika.
CHILDREN: Alexia, Katia.
SCHOOLS/COLLEGE: Columbia University USA.
QUALIFICATIONS: MA PhD.
MEMBERSHIPS: President of the American Cyprus Congress and the American Acadamy Alumni Association.
HONOURS/AWARDS: Rutgers University Award for Excellence in Teaching (The Warren I Susman Award).
PERSONAL PROFILE: Professor Emeritus in the Department for Earth and Environmental Services at Rutgers University USA.

DEMETRIOS VASSILIOU
Education

DATE OF BIRTH: 22-Dec-1939
PLACE OF BIRTH: Troulli.
MARITAL STATUS: Married to Panayiota, Greek Cypriot, Teacher.
CHILDREN: Pantelis Vassilou, Reliability Engineer. Vassilia Demitri Young, Physician/Dermatologist.
SCHOOLS/COLLEGE: Pancyprian Commercial Lyceum, Larnaca, Cyprus. University of Northern Colorado.
QUALIFICATIONS: Master of Arts, Special Education, Master of Science in Statistics & Research, Doctor of Education.
HONOURS/AWARDS: The Rotary Foundation of Rotary International Award, Whos Who in American Education 1989-90, National Aging Leadership Award, USA 1997, amongst others.
HOBBIES AND INTERESTS: Travel, Sports, Politics.
PERSONAL PROFILE: Now retired from North Dakota Centre for Persons with Developmental Disabilities at Minot State University where he served for the past 15 years as a teacher, trainer and mentor.

MARIOS VASSILOU
Executive Director at Rockwell International Science Center

DATE OF BIRTH: 07-Jun-1953
PLACE OF BIRTH: Nicosia, Cyprus.
MARITAL STATUS: Married to Cynthia Vassilou, USA, Engineer.
CHILDREN: Simos.
SCHOOLS/COLLEGE: UN International School, New York. Harvard University, Cambridge MA, University Of Southern California, California Institute of Technology.
QUALIFICATIONS: MS MBA, PhD.
MEMBERSHIPS: Institute of Electrical and Electronics Engineers, Society of Exploration Geophysics.
HONOURS/AWARDS: Vice President Al Gore's Hammer Award for Reinventing Government (in connection with leadership of the Advanced and Interactive Displays Federated Laboratory).
HOBBIES AND INTERESTS: Language and Dialectology, History, Photography.
PERSONAL PROFILE: Currently Analyst at the Institute for Defence Analyses, advising the United States Government in the areas of energy security, research planning and management technology readiness assessment, risk management, and acoustic and electromagnetic propagation issues. Executive Director at Rockwell International Science Center.

HARIS VIKIS
Research Assistant Professor of Surgery

PLACE OF BIRTH: Father from Moni, Mother from Limassol
SCHOOLS/COLLEGE: University of Michigan.
QUALIFICATIONS: PhD in Bio Chemistry.
PERSONAL PROFILE: Haris Vikis is a Research Assistant Professor of Surgery, Division of General Surgery, Washington University.

KIMON VIOLARIS
Doctor, Co Director of Neonatology, The Brooklyn Hospital

PLACE OF BIRTH: Kyrenia.
QUALIFICATIONS: MD.
PERSONAL PROFILE: Kimon Violaris is a Doctor, Co Director of Neonatology, The Brooklyn Hospital Center, Apnea Center, Brooklyn, New York.

USA

HERCULES VLADIMIROU
Research Associate at Princeton
University

PLACE OF BIRTH: Limassol
MARITAL STATUS: Married.
SCHOOLS/COLLEGE: Duke
University and Princeton
University.
QUALIFICATIONS: BSE MA
PhD.
MEMBERSHIPS: Institute for
operations research and the
management sciences.
PERSONAL PROFILE: Hercules
served as a Research Associate at Princeton University
and as research staff member at the IBM Thomas J
Watson Research Center in New York. At present he is
an Associate Professor of management science at the
University of Cyprus.

CHRISTOS XENOPHONTOS
Assistant Professor Loyola College
Baltimore

PLACE OF BIRTH: Cyprus
SCHOOLS/COLLEGE: College
of William and Mary and
the University of. maryland,
Baltimore County.
QUALIFICATIONS: BS. MS.
and PhD.
PERSONAL PROFILE: Dr
Christos Xenophontos is an
Assistant Professor in the
Department of Mathematical
Science, Loyola College, Baltimore.

DEMITRIS XYDAS
Chiropractor

PLACE OF BIRTH: Cyprus.
PERSONAL PROFILE: Demetris Xydas practises as a
Chiropractor in Houston Texas.

GARO YEPREMIAN
former National Football League
Placekicker he played for the Detroit
Lions, Miami Dolphins, New Orleans
Saints and Tampa Bay Buccaneers

PLACE OF BIRTH: Larnaca
HONOURS/AWARDS: Garo
was voted Kicker of the Decade
by the Pro Football hall of Fame
between 1970 and 1980 and in
1981 was elected to the Florida
Sports Hall of Fame.
PERSONAL PROFILE: Garo
Yepremian is a former National
Football League Placekicker. He
played for the Detroit Lions,
Miami Dolphins, New Orleans Saints and Tampa Bay
Buccaneers during a career that spanned from 1966 to
1981. He is currently a motivational speaker and the
Author of several books including an autobiography
titled I Kick a Touchdown.

DR SOTIRA YIACOUMI
Researcher at the School of Civil and
Enviromental Engineering at the
Georgia Institute of Technology

PLACE OF BIRTH:
Peristeronopyi
SCHOOLS/COLLEGE: Aristotle
University(Greece) and Syracuse
University.
QUALIFICATIONS: Dipl. Engr.
MS and PhD.
HONOURS/AWARDS: 1997
National Science Foundation
Career Award. Project Title.
PERSONAL PROFILE:
Researcher in interfacial and Colloidal Phenomena
in Environment Systems at the School of Civil and
Enviromental Engineering at the Georgia Institute of
Technology.

USA

Entrants in Greek Cypriots Worldwide have been nominated for their
achievements and contributions.
It is free to nominate someone, or yourself, who deserves to be in the book, just
send in the name, contact address, telephone number and email to:
Greek Cypriots Worldwide
111 St Thomas's Road London N4 2QJ
Telephone 0044 207503 3498
cypriotwhoswho@aol.com
www.greekcypriotsworldwide.com

ANDREW YIANGOU
Founding partner in the Law firm Bergman & Yiangou in Ohio

DATE OF BIRTH: 03-Sep-1961
PLACE OF BIRTH: Nicosia.
MARITAL STATUS: Single.
SCHOOLS/COLLEGE: Wittenburg University and Ohio State University.
QUALIFICATIONS: BA. JD.
HOBBIES AND INTERESTS: Motor Sports, Reading and Rembetika.
PERSONAL PROFILE: Andrew Yiangou was admitted to the bar 1991 Ohio;1993 US District Court, Southern District of Ohio. He is a Founding partner in the Law firm Bergman & Yiangou in Ohio.

PROFESSOR ANDREW YIANNAKIS
Professor and Director, Clemson International Institute

DATE OF BIRTH: 24-May-1944
PLACE OF BIRTH: Famagusta.
MARITAL STATUS: Married to Linda Yiannakis, USA, Speech Pathologist.
SCHOOLS/COLLEGE: Madeley College (University of Keele) UK, University of North Carolina, University of New Mexico, UCLA, Los Angeles (post doc).
QUALIFICATIONS: PhD, MA, CertEd.
MEMBERSHIPS: North American Society for the Sociology of Sport.
HOBBIES AND INTERESTS: Travel and exploration reading historical novels, playing the violin, the martial arts, Native American cultural practices and traditions.
PERSONAL PROFILE: Professor and Director, Clemson International Institute for Tourism Research and Development PRTM Dept. Professor Yiannakis has also had a book published-'The Complete Guide to Successful Fund Raising'.

JOHN KIMON YIASEMIDES
Managing Consultant in the Disputes Resolution Group within the Company, Warner

PLACE OF BIRTH: Father from Morphou
SCHOOLS/COLLEGE: University of Florida and University of Maryland.
PERSONAL PROFILE: He is Managing Consultant in the Disputes Resolution Group within the Company, Warner. He has also worked in Florida with Centex where he managed a variety of commercial and educational construction projects.

VASSILIA DIMITRI YOUNG
Physician/Dermatologist

DATE OF BIRTH: 08-Oct-1966
PLACE OF BIRTH: USA Parents from Troulli.
MARITAL STATUS: Married.
PERSONAL PROFILE: Vassilia Dimitri Young is a physician/ dermatologist at University of WI Hospital.

IACOVOS ZACHARIADES
President and Chief Executive of Global Reach Internet Productions

PLACE OF BIRTH: Cyprus
SCHOOLS/COLLEGE: Iowa State University.
HONOURS/AWARDS: Technology company of the year award in the small company category by Software and Information Technology of Iowa.
HOBBIES AND INTERESTS: Soccer.
PERSONAL PROFILE: Iacovos Zachariades is the president and chief executive of Global Reach Internet productions in Ames, Iowa in the United States. They also have offices in Cyprus and Korea. and have over 250 clients and 21 staff.

IOANNIS ZACHARIOU
Lecturer in The Department of Mathematics of the University of Kansas

PLACE OF BIRTH: Cyprus
SCHOOLS/COLLEGE: University of Kansas.
QUALIFICATIONS: BSc. MA. and PhD in Mathematics.
MEMBERSHIPS: American Statistician and American Mathematical Society.
HONOURS/AWARDS: Florence Black Teaching Award 2004, International Mathematical Olympiad 1992 and 1995.
PERSONAL PROFILE: Yiannis Zachariou is a lecturer in the Department of Mathematics of the University of Kansas.

TASOS ZAMBAS
Alternate President of PSEKA and Chairman Justice for Cyprus committee for Cyprus Federation of America

DATE OF BIRTH: 08-Sep-1960
PLACE OF BIRTH: Prastio, Morphou.
MARITAL STATUS: Married to Sharon, American, Banker.
CHILDREN: Demetrios.
SCHOOLS/COLLEGE: Syracuse University.
QUALIFICATIONS: BS in Finance.
PERSONAL PROFILE: Tasos Zambas is the Alternate President of PSEKA and Chairman Justice for Cyprus committee for Cyprus Federation of America.

JOANNA ZAMPAS
Research and Editorial Assistant to USA Greek Cypriot's Who's Who Worldwide edition/Project Coordinator National Academy for Excellent Teaching, Teachers College Columbia University

DATE OF BIRTH: 29-Feb-1964
PLACE OF BIRTH: New York Parents from Karavas.
CHILDREN: One son.
SCHOOLS/COLLEGE: Glassboro State College (Rowan University), New York University.
QUALIFICATIONS: BA MA.
MEMBERSHIPS: Sahaja Yoga International Society St.

Anthony's Eastern Orthodox Church.
HONOURS/AWARDS: Had poems published.
HOBBIES AND INTERESTS: Reading Fiction, Fitness, Creative Writing.
PERSONAL PROFILE: Joanna is an administrator for the National Academy for Excellent Teaching whose mission is to establish a new national model of effective professional development for high school teachers that significantly and measurably improves the achievement of under-performing and under-served students, first in New York City and then across the country. Joanna is also Research and Editorial Assistant to USA section of Greek Cypriot's Who's Who Worldwide edition.

MIKE ZAPITI
Editor and publisher of the Hellenic voice newspaper, Producer of TV program and journalist

DATE OF BIRTH: 17-Dec-1926
PLACE OF BIRTH: Khirokitia.
MARITAL STATUS: Married to Olympia (deceased).
CHILDREN: Harry, Clara.
SCHOOLS/COLLEGE: High school.
PERSONAL PROFILE: Editor and publisher of the Hellenic voice newspaper, Producer of TV program and Journalist. In 1966 he was instrumental in convincing the department of motor vehicles to give the written exams for licensing in several languages such as Italian, greek etc in order to help the new immigrants get their driving privileges as soon as possible. this offered opportunities to our new immigrants to make a decent living in this country.

USA

PANAYIOTIS ZAVOS
Reproductive Specialist

PLACE OF BIRTH: Tricomo
SCHOOLS/COLLEGE: Emporia State University in Kansas, University of Minnesota.
QUALIFICATIONS: BS in Biology, MS in Biology-Physiology, Biochemistry and Statistics. Professor of Emeritus of Reproductive Physiology and Andrology at the University of Kentucky.
MEMBERSHIPS: American Society of Andrology, The European Society of Andrology, The European Society for Human Reproduction and Embryology.
PERSONAL PROFILE: Dr. Zavos has a long career as a reproductive specialist and he has devoted more than 25 years to academia and research. He is one of the chief scientists in the development of several new innovative technologies in the animal and human reproductive areas with worldwide implications. He has authored and co-authored more than 400 publications. He has made many television and radio appearances all over the world.

ENDY ZEMENIDES
On the Editorial Board and Board of Advisors of the National Strategy Forum a Chicago Based Foreign Policy Organisation

PLACE OF BIRTH: Komi Kebir
MARITAL STATUS: Married.
CHILDREN: Two Children.
SCHOOLS/COLLEGE: Georgetown University Law Centre and De Paul university in the USA and Essex University.
QUALIFICATIONS: BA. MA.
PERSONAL PROFILE: Endy Zemenides is a partner in the Law firm of Acosta, Kruse & Zemenides LLC. Endy is also a registered Lobbyist. He serves on the Editorial Board and Board of Advisors of the National Strategy Forum a Chicago Based Foreign Policy Organisation. He is the President of the Hellenic American Leadership has been a lecturer in De Pauls University Political Science Department. He is the Executive Director of the Greeks for Obama Organisation.

DR STAVROS ZENIOS
Known internationally for his work in computational finance and financial services

PLACE OF BIRTH: Born 1959 Nicosia
MARITAL STATUS: Married.
CHILDREN: Three Children.
SCHOOLS/COLLEGE: London University, Princeton University and University of Pennsylvania.
QUALIFICATIONS: BSc BEng MA PhD.
HONOURS/AWARDS: Marie Curie Fellow of the European Commission.
PERSONAL PROFILE: Stavros Zenios was a Tenured Faculty member of the Wharton School of University of Pennsylvania. He is now based at the University of Cyprus as the Dean of the School of Economics And Management.

STEFANOS ZENIOS
Professor of Operations Information and Technology at Stanford University USA

PLACE OF BIRTH: Cyprus
SCHOOLS/COLLEGE: University of Cambridge and Massachusetts Institute of Technology.
QUALIFICATIONS: BA. MA. PhD.
HONOURS/AWARDS: Recipient of the National Science Foundation Award 2000.
PERSONAL PROFILE: Stefanos Zenios is a Professor of Operations Information and Technology at Stanford University USA.

ANDREW ZENIOU
Physician /Doctor

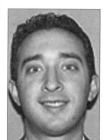

PLACE OF BIRTH: Cyprus
PERSONAL PROFILE: Andrew Zeniou is a doctor practising from a general surgery in East Setauket in New Jersey.

GEORGE ZENIOU
Medical

PLACE OF BIRTH: Born USA father from Famagusta
PERSONAL PROFILE: George Zeniou provides home based Pediatric services for occupational, Physical and Speech Therapies serving Orange, Durham and Person counties, North Carolina.

NICOS ZITTIS
Vice president of the Cyprus Childrens Fund

PLACE OF BIRTH: Nicosia.
SCHOOLS/COLLEGE: Rutgers University.
QUALIFICATIONS: BSc MBA.
PERSONAL PROFILE: Hes a Business analyst with Lynx network services. Former president of the New Jersey Cypriot Association. Vice president of the Cyprus Childrens Fund.

Entrants in Greek Cypriots Worldwide have been nominated for their achievements and contributions.

It is free to nominate someone, or yourself, who deserves to be in the book, just send in the name, contact address, telephone number and email to:

Greek Cypriots Worldwide
111 St Thomas's Road,
London, N4 2QJ
Telephone 0044 207503 3498
cypriotwhoswho@aol.com
www.greekcypriotsworldwide.com

USA

Argentina

NEOPHITOS MICHAELIDES
Cypriot Champion in Swimming and the holder of several records

DATE OF BIRTH: 10-Dec-1958
PLACE OF BIRTH: Nicosia.
MARITAL STATUS: Married to Ursula, Argentinian, Housewife.
CHILDREN: Manolis, Diogenes.
SCHOOLS/COLLEGE: Polytechnic of Zurich.
QUALIFICATIONS: Bachelor in Business & Administration.
HONOURS/AWARDS: Cypriot Champion in Swimming and the holder of several records.
PERSONAL PROFILE: Neophitos was the Vice Director of a Private Bank in Vaduz Liechenstein, He is now the Independant Portfolio Manager of Michaelides Vermogensverwaltung GmbH. He is now based in Argentina.

Bahrain

PETER PANAYIOTOU
Deputy Chief Executive Officer and Chief Investment Officer Gulf Finance House

PLACE OF BIRTH: Parents from Cyprus
SCHOOLS/COLLEGE: Oxford University.
QUALIFICATIONS: Degree in Jurisprudence.
MEMBERSHIPS: Fellow of the Institute of Chartered Accountants.
PERSONAL PROFILE: Peter Panayiotou is Deputy Chief Executive Officer and Chief Investment Officer for Gulf Finance. He holds numerous directorships including Chairman of Injazat Capital Bank, Vice Chairman of Bahrein Alluminium Extrusion Company, Director of Bahrain Financial Harbour.

Belgium

PANAYIOTIS DEMETRIOU
Member of the European Parliament

DATE OF BIRTH: 06-May-1939
PLACE OF BIRTH: Cyprus.
MARITAL STATUS: Married to Maria.
CHILDREN: Two Children.
SCHOOLS/COLLEGE: Cyprus Teacher Training College.
QUALIFICATIONS: Barrister.
HONOURS/AWARDS: Knight in the Order of Merit of the French Republic.
PERSONAL PROFILE: Panayiotis Demetriou is a member of the European Parliament, was Deputy Chairman of DHSY.

CONSTANTINOS ELIADES
Ambassador to the Kingdom of Belgium and to the Grand Duchy of Luxembourg

DATE OF BIRTH: 18-Nov-1955
PLACE OF BIRTH: Free Town Sierra Leone Parents from Cyprus.
MARITAL STATUS: Married to Constantia, Professor of the French Language.
CHILDREN: Chara, Fashion Designer.
SCHOOLS/COLLEGE: Second Gymnasium For Boys Limassol. Universite Aix Marseille Aix En Provence France.
QUALIFICATIONS: Bachelors and Masters Degree.
HONOURS/AWARDS: Medal of St Marc from the Patriachate of Alexandria and all Africa.
HOBBIES AND INTERESTS: Reading, tennis, painting and model making.
PERSONAL PROFILE: Constantinos Eliades is the Ambassador to the Kingdom of Belgium and to the Grand Duchy of Luxembourg.

LOU SPYROU
Musician

PLACE OF BIRTH: UK parents from Cyprus
PERSONAL PROFILE: Leo Spyrou resides in Belgium and performs and writes music was the road manager for the Argonauts originally, and has played in various bands since notably the Nozes played in the UK, Netherlands and Belgium.

Brazil

MILTON JERONOMIDES
Art

PLACE OF BIRTH: Nicosia
SCHOOLS/COLLEGE: Pacific Union College and Manhattan College of Art.
QUALIFICATIONS: MSc.
HONOURS/AWARDS: In 2002 he received the III Art Supply Award.
PERSONAL PROFILE: Milton Jeronomides paintings are in Oil and Acrylic revealing a colorful tropical richness, where Insistent Geometric Forms stand out among Abstract and Figurative Images. He has participated in several exhibitions of contemporary art.

ALEXIS PANAGIDES
Chief Technical Officer of Innova

PLACE OF BIRTH: USA father from Limassol.
PERSONAL PROFILE: Alexis Panagides is a Co founder and Chief Technical Officer of Innova based in Brazil. Has also held technical positions at the World Bank in Washington DC and was the World Bank's Technology Consultant to the Brazilian Government.

COSTAS TAKKAS
Cayman Island Football Hall of Fame Order of Merit-Ex General Secretary

DATE OF BIRTH: 15-Feb-1957
PLACE OF BIRTH: Mia Milia.
MARITAL STATUS: Single.
SCHOOLS/COLLEGE: Holloway. Imperial College London.
QUALIFICATIONS: B. Sc. (hons), ARCS in Physics A. C. A.
MEMBERSHIPS: Institute of Chartered Accountants in England & Wales.
HONOURS/AWARDS: Cayman Island Football Hall of Fame Order of Merit-Ex General Secretary.
HOBBIES AND INTERESTS: Football, Theatre, Film and Golf.
PERSONAL PROFILE: Costas Takkas is a Accountant semi -retired concentrating on personal projects. Involved in development and construction of low income housing in Brazil.

Bulgaria

CHRISTOPHER VIOLARIS
Owner of Eurolink finance a major Land Bank in the Balkan Peninsula

DATE OF BIRTH: 14-Jan-1956
PLACE OF BIRTH: Lapithos.
MARITAL STATUS: Married to Anastasia, Bulgaria, Architect.
CHILDREN: Stelios, Accountant. Yolanda, Journalist. Stephanie, Student.
SCHOOLS/COLLEGE: Pancyprian Gymnasium. London School of Economics.
QUALIFICATIONS: BSc MSc PhD.
HOBBIES AND INTERESTS: Music, hunting, nature, archaeology and architecture.
PERSONAL PROFILE: Christopher Violaris is the owner of Eurolink finance a major Land Bank in the Balkan Peninsula.

More Places

409

GREEK CYPRIOTS WORLDWIDE

Cape Verde

STAHIS PANAYIDES
Resident Country Director in Cape Verde, Millenium Challenge Corporation

DATE OF BIRTH: 27-Oct-1937
PLACE OF BIRTH: Limassol.
MARITAL STATUS: Married to Joy, USA.
CHILDREN: Melissa, Vice President ICF International. Alexis, IT Director. Lela, HR Microsoft Corporation.
SCHOOLS/COLLEGE: Kansas State University and Iowa State University.
QUALIFICATIONS: BS PhD.
HONOURS/AWARDS: Blue Key National Honor Society USA. Brotherhood Award, Kansas State University, USA.
HOBBIES AND INTERESTS: Rembetika and opera.
PERSONAL PROFILE: Dr Stahis Panayides is Resident Country Director in Cape Verde, Millenium Challenge Corporation worked in senior positions with the World Bank, The Ford Foundation and the University of California.

Cayman Islands

PHILIP PASCHALIDES
Attorney at Law/Founder member of an experimental drama group on the Cayman Islands

DATE OF BIRTH: 01-Jul-1970.
PLACE OF BIRTH: Kaimakli.
MARITAL STATUS: Married to Emerentienne, French.
CHILDREN: Hector.
SCHOOLS/COLLEGE: Bloxham School. University of St Andrews.
QUALIFICATIONS: MA(Hons) English and Theology First Class. CPE/Diploma in Law-Commendation.
MEMBERSHIPS: Honourable Society of the Inner Temple, London.
HOBBIES AND INTERESTS: Wine, Literature, opera, antiques, travel and shooting.
PERSONAL PROFILE: Philip Paschalides is an Attorney at Law currently a partner in the finance department of an offshore law firm in the Cayman Islands. Founder member of an experimental drama group on the Island.

Cuba

JOSEF KOUMBAS
Artist

DATE OF BIRTH: 08-Nov-1944
PLACE OF BIRTH: London. Father from Rizokarpasso.
SCHOOLS/COLLEGE: Gifford St Secondary School, Central St. Martins.
QUALIFICATIONS: BA Honours in Critical Fine Art.
HONOURS/AWARDS: Received a Reconocimiento Award from UNEAC for his support and contribution to the Cuban Culture.
HOBBIES AND INTERESTS: Travel.
PERSONAL PROFILE: Living in Cuba started Cuba Arts fund on his initiative to raise funds for Cuban artists. Had his own band in the 1970s, played and recorded in those days with Dave Stewart before Eurythmics. Appeared in films Merlin, Shakespeare in Love and Gladiator. As an artist he produced stone slabs based on a panel cast from one of the original Parthenon frieze slabs, displayed at Wood Green shopping centre and St. Martins Art College.

Denmark

ANDREAS STEPHANOU
Computers

DATE OF BIRTH: 30-Aug-1954
PLACE OF BIRTH: Lefka.
MARITAL STATUS: Single.
CHILDREN: Alexander, Stephanie.
SCHOOLS/COLLEGE: English School Nicosia. Polytechnic of Central London.
QUALIFICATIONS: Bachelor of Science.
MEMBERSHIPS: Institute of Electrical Engineers and Danish society of Engineers.
HOBBIES AND INTERESTS: Philosophy, arts, film, theatre and music.
PERSONAL PROFILE: Andreas Stephanou is the IT Systems Administrator/Engineer for the Computer Systems department of the University of Southern Denmark.

More Places

France

MARCOS BAGHDATIS

World Ranking Tennis Player, Finalist at the Australian Open

DATE OF BIRTH: 17-Jun-1985
PLACE OF BIRTH: Paramytha.
MARITAL STATUS: Single.
SCHOOLS/COLLEGE: He trained at the Mouratoglou Tennis Academy in Paris on an Olympic Solidarity Youth Development Programme Scholarship since the age of 13 and learned to speak French.
HONOURS/AWARDS: 2005 Cyprus Male Athlete of the Year.
ITF WORLD JUNIOR TENNIS CHAMPION IN 2003.
HOBBIES AND INTERESTS: Playing and watching football.
PERSONAL PROFILE: Marcos Baghdatis is a World Ranking Tennis Player was the runner-up at the 2006 Australian Open and a semifinalist at the 2006 Wimbledon Championships.

SAVVAS CHRISTODOULIDES

Artist

PLACE OF BIRTH: Paphos in 1961
SCHOOLS/COLLEGE: School of Fine Arts, Toulouse, National School of fine arts, Paris, National school of decorative arts Paris. University of Provence.
PERSONAL PROFILE: Artist given exhibitions in London, Athens, Paris, Berlin and several other places around the world.

MELANIE GEORGIADES DIAMS

Singer/Songwriter won the Award for the best French act at the 2006 MTV Europe Music Awards

DATE OF BIRTH: 25-Jul-1980
PLACE OF BIRTH: Cyprus.
HONOURS/AWARDS: Won the Award for Best French Act at the 2006 MTV Europe Music Awards.
PERSONAL PROFILE: Diams now living in France is a top French Rap Singer. Her album Dans Ma Bulle went on to be the biggest selling French Album in France in 2006.

CYPRIEN KATSARIS

Pianist and Composer has collaborated with Conductors such as Leonard Bernstein

DATE OF BIRTH: 05-May-1951
PLACE OF BIRTH: Marseilles France. Father from Lapithos, Mother from Nicosia.
MARITAL STATUS: Single.
SCHOOLS/COLLEGE: Paris Conservatoire.
QUALIFICATIONS: Piano First Prize 1969. First Prize in Chamber Music 1970.
HONOURS/AWARDS: Knight of Merit of Cameroon(1977). Artist of Unesco for Peace(1997). Knight of the Order of Arts and Letters (France 2000). Record of the year 1984 Germany for the 9th Symphony of Beethoven /Liszt).
HOBBIES AND INTERESTS: Backgammon, Ping Pong, French and Belgium comics and remote control aeroplanes.
PERSONAL PROFILE: Cyprien Katsaris has performed with the World's greatest orchestras most notably the Berlin Philarmonic, Cleveland Orchestra, National Symphony Orchestra Washington, DC and Moscow Philarmonic Orchestra. He has collaborated with Conductors such as Leonard Bernstein. Has recorded solo works by some of the great masters.

More Places

ANDREAS D. LIVERAS
Founded Liveras Yachts, a company that owns and charters luxury super yachts (Deceased)

DATE OF BIRTH: 01-Apr-1935
PLACE OF BIRTH: Anayia.
CHILDREN: Mary, Sophia, Dion, Krita.
MEMBERSHIPS: Monaco Yacht Club; Mediterranean Yacht Brokers Association.
HONOURS/AWARDS: Awarded the Medaille de la Paix et de la Reconciliation (1999) by HM King Kigeli V, for assisting the cause of Rwandan refugees who were victims of genocide. Awarded the Adwa Centenary Medal (1999) by HRH Prince Haile-Selasse, for supporting the Crown Pri.
HOBBIES AND INTERESTS: Tennis, and water- and snow-skiing. Keen pilot.
PERSONAL PROFILE: Andreas arrived in England in 1963, and started work as a salesman for a patisserie in London. Within five years, he had bought the company, and 15 years later it was the leading manufacturer of quality frozen gateaux in the UK. He sold the business to Grand Met in a multi-million pound deal, then, in 1986, he founded Liveras Yachts, a company that owns and charters luxury super yachts. Andreas Died in November 2008 shot in tragic circumstances in a terrorist attack at the Taj Mahal Hotel in India.

EVAGORAS MAVROMMATIS
President of the International Coordinating Committee Justice for Cyprus for Europe

PLACE OF BIRTH: Cyprus
QUALIFICATIONS: Masters degree in Social and economic administration.
PERSONAL PROFILE:
Evagoras Mavrommatis is the President of the International Coordinating Committee Justice for Cyprus for Europe. He has served as the President of the Cypriot Community in France for several years. Also a Director of the Daedalos Institute of Geopolitics. He owns restaurants with his brother in Paris and has one in the Four Seasons Hotel in Limassol too.

EFSTATHIOS ALONEFTIS
First Cypriot Footballer to compete in the Bundesliga

DATE OF BIRTH: 29-Mar-1983
PLACE OF BIRTH: Nicosia.
PERSONAL PROFILE: An attacking midfielder he started his career with Omonia Nicosia making his first appearance for the senior squad during the 2000-01 season. He moved to the Greek side AEL Larissa in 2005 for a transfer fee CYP £136, 000. On May 31st 2007 German side Energie Cottbus announced the signing of Aloneftis(Bosman ruling free transfer) making him the first Cypriot Footballer to compete in the Bundesliga. He is a regular in the Cyprus national Football team. Now back in Cyprus playing for Omonia.

GRIGORIS ANTONIOU
Scientist

PLACE OF BIRTH: Cyprus
PERSONAL PROFILE: Grigoris Antoniou is a scientist based in the Department of Computer Science, University of Bremen in Germany. He has also written several publications in non monitoring reasoning.

ARIS ARISTIDOU
Head of Investment at Hypove Reinsurance Bank In Germany

PLACE OF BIRTH: Cyprus.
PERSONAL PROFILE: Dr Aris Aristidou is the Head of Investment at Hypove Reinsurance Bank In Germany.

MARC CHRYSANTHOU
Senior Lecturer in Sociology, University of Salford, born in Germany

DATE OF BIRTH: 25-Jul-1959
PLACE OF BIRTH: Wgberg, Germany Father from Kontea.
MARITAL STATUS: Married to Judi, Social Worker.
CHILDREN: One step son and one step daughter.
SCHOOLS/COLLEGE: Wolverhampton University and Pembroke College, Oxford University.
QUALIFICATIONS: BA(Hons) M. Litt Politics and Ph. D Public Health.
HOBBIES AND INTERESTS: Climbing, song writing. Writing Poetry, films and keeping fit.
PERSONAL PROFILE: Senior lecturer in Sociology, University of Salford. Editor of the Owl and the Cragrat an anthology of climbing poetry.

MARIOS ELIA
Theodor-Koerner Fonds Composition Prize awarded by the Austrian Federal President, Vienna (2007)

DATE OF BIRTH: 19-Jun-1978
PLACE OF BIRTH: Paphos.
MARITAL STATUS: Single.
SCHOOLS/COLLEGE: University of Music and Dramatic Arts Salzburg and Vienna University of Music.
QUALIFICATIONS: Magister Artium (Mozarteum).
HONOURS/AWARDS: 1st Prize at the Edison Denisov International Composition Competition, Moscow 2007. Theodor-Koerner Fonds Composition Prize awarded by the Austrian Federal President, Vienna (2007).
PERSONAL PROFILE: Elias Compositions have recieved performances from Hanover State Opera, Stuttgart State Opera, Rubinstien Quartet and many others. Has performed in many concert halls worldwide to name a few the Berlin Philarmonic, Warsaw Philarmonic and Expo Athens.

LUKAS BENO IOANNIDES
Lecturer at the Leipzig academy of Music and drama

PLACE OF BIRTH: Born in 1980 London. Father from Cyprus
HONOURS/AWARDS: 1997 & 1998 won first prizes in the federal competition Jugend Musiziert Germany.
PERSONAL PROFILE: Musician Trumpeter 1st solo Trumpeter in the Gewandhaus orchestra Leipzig. Lecturer at the Leipzig Academy of Music and drama.

YIANNIS KYRIAKOU
Scientist at the University of Erlangen in Nuremburg

PLACE OF BIRTH: Germany Father from Paphos Mother from Germany
PERSONAL PROFILE: Yiannis Kyriakou is a scientist specializing in CT imaging at the Institute of Medical Physics at the University of Erlagen in Nuremburg.

ANGELOS MICHAELIDES
Scientist

PLACE OF BIRTH: Ireland
SCHOOLS/COLLEGE: Queens University of Belfast.
QUALIFICATIONS: BSc PhD.
HONOURS/AWARDS: Royal Irish Academy Prize for Young Chemists in 2000.
PERSONAL PROFILE: Dr Angelos Michaelides is a Staff Scientist at the Fitz Haber Institute in Berlin. He will soon be moving to the London Centre for Nanotechnology.

More Places

413

Dr STATHIS PHILIPPOU
Chairman Dept of Pathology Ruhr University

PLACE OF BIRTH: Cyprus.
PERSONAL PROFILE: Dr Stathis Philippou is the Chairman Department of Pathology Ruhr University Bochum, Germany.

RIKO VANEZIS
Lawyer and partner in Clifford Chance, Frankfurt

PLACE OF BIRTH: Born in London Parents born in Egypt Grand parents from Paphos
SCHOOLS/COLLEGE: University of Sussex and University of Konstanz.
QUALIFICATIONS: BA in Law and German.
PERSONAL PROFILE: Riko Vanezis is a Lawyer and partner in the Law Company Clifford Chance, Frankfurt. He is also the Head of Banking and Capital Markets Germany.

IOANNIS VOTSIS
Post Doctoral Fellow University of Dusseldorf

DATE OF BIRTH: 20-Jun-1973
PLACE OF BIRTH: Nicosia.
SCHOOLS/COLLEGE: Archbishop Makarios. University of California, London School of Economics and University of Dusseldorf.
QUALIFICATIONS: BA PhD.
MEMBERSHIPS: European Philosophy of Science Association.
PERSONAL PROFILE: Post Doctoral Fellow University of Dusseldorf was a teaching fellow in philosophy at the University of Bristol and researcher in philosophy at the London School of Economics.

Ireland

PETROS SERGHIO FLORIDES
Associate Professor in Applied Mathematics, Trinity College, Dublin

DATE OF BIRTH: 16-Feb-1937
PLACE OF BIRTH: Lapithos (Kyrenia) Cyprus.
MARITAL STATUS: Married to Despina, Athens, Housewife.
CHILDREN: Serghios, IT. Andros, Economist. Constandinos, IT.
SCHOOLS/COLLEGE: Commercial Lyceum (Famagusta). Northern Polytechnic (now University of North London) & Royal Holloway College (University of London).
QUALIFICATIONS: BSc MA PhD.
MEMBERSHIPS: Fellow of the Royal Astronomical Society, Member of the Society of General Relativity & Gravitation, Senior Fellow of Trinity College, Dublin.
HOBBIES AND INTERESTS: music and reading.
PERSONAL PROFILE: Associate Professor in Applied Mathematics, Trinity College, Dublin. Professor in Applied Mathematics (Grade A) at the University of Crete (1984-88), Member of the Preparatory Committee for the Establishment of the University of Cyprus.

STEFANOS JACQUES
Executive Director of Fostering First Ireland

DATE OF BIRTH: 04-Jul-1972
PLACE OF BIRTH: Kornos.
SCHOOLS/COLLEGE: American Academy Larnaca and Woodhatch School Reigate. Sheffield University.
QUALIFICATIONS: BA.
MEMBERSHIPS: General Social Care Council UK/Ireland.
HOBBIES AND INTERESTS: Travel, reading, cooking and theatre.
PERSONAL PROFILE: Stefanos Jacques is an Executive Director of Fostering First Ireland Ltd a non statutory foster care agency in the Republic of Ireland in association with the FCA Group of Companies who provide foster care to over 2500 children and young people throughout the UK and Ireland. Stefanos is also an operations manager with the FCA.

More Places

NICHOLAS LESTAS
Honorary Commissioner for Cyprus in Northern Ireland

DATE OF BIRTH: 19-Jul-1962
PLACE OF BIRTH: Reading Father from Zodhia Mother from Paphos.
MARITAL STATUS: Married to Michelle.
CHILDREN: Finn, Aron.
SCHOOLS/COLLEGE: University of East London and University of Ulster.
QUALIFICATIONS: MBA and Psychology Degree.
MEMBERSHIPS: Member of Institute of Marketing.
HOBBIES AND INTERESTS: Karate and property development.
PERSONAL PROFILE: Nicholas Lestas is the Honorary Commissioner for Cyprus in Northern Ireland. He is a management consultant with Lestas Consulting in partner with his wife. Previous to this he was the Director of Development for a local authority in Northern Ireland specialising in EU funding and economic and Tourism development.

Israel

PANAYIOTIS ARTEMIOU
Heart Surgeon based in Tel Hashomer, Israel

PLACE OF BIRTH: Cyprus.
PERSONAL PROFILE: Panayiotis Artemiou is a Heart Surgeon based at the Chaim Sheba Medical Center at Tel Hashomer in Israel.

To nominate someone, or yourself, just send in the name, contact address, telephone number and email to:

Greek Cypriots Worldwide
111 St Thomas's Road,
London, N4 2QJ
Telephone 0044 207503 3498

cypriotwhoswho@aol.com
www.greekcypriotsworldwide.com

Italy

TESSA KIROS
Acclaimed Food Writer wrote the books Apples for Jam, Falling Cloudberries, Twelve and Piri Piri Starfish Portugal Found

DATE OF BIRTH: 09-Jul-1945
PLACE OF BIRTH: London. Father from Cyprus, Mother from Finland.
MARITAL STATUS: Married to Giovanni from Italy.
PERSONAL PROFILE: Acclaimed Food Writer wrote the books Apples for Jam, Falling Cloudberries, Twelve and Piri Piri Starfish Portugal Found.
She was born in London. The family moved to South Africa when she was four and at the age of 18, Tessa set off to travel and learn all she could about the world's cultures and traditions and new ways of living and eating. She has cooked at Londons Groucho club and in Sydney, Athens and Mexico. Tessa now resides in Tuscany, Italy.

Japan

DANIELLE DEMETRIOU
News Reporter at the Daily Telegraph Formerly worked at the Evening Standard. Now working freelance from Tokyo

DATE OF BIRTH: 22-Dec-1974
PLACE OF BIRTH: Sevenoaks, Kent. Father from Nicosia, Cyprus.
MARITAL STATUS: Single.
SCHOOLS/COLLEGE: King's School, Canterbury, Trinity College, Dublin.
QUALIFICATIONS: BA Honours French & Italian. Postgrad Journalism Diploma.
PERSONAL PROFILE: Currently based in Tokyo and working freelance for a number of UK, US and Canadian newspapers and magazines. Was a News Reporter at the Daily Telegraph. Formerly worked at the Evening Standard.

More Places

ANDREAS A. IOANNIDES
Heads the laboratory for Human Brain Dynamics at the Brain Science Institute, RIKEN near Tokyo, Japan

DATE OF BIRTH: 20-Mar-1952
PLACE OF BIRTH: Morphou.
MARITAL STATUS: Married to Dr. Lichan Liu, Neuroscientist.
CHILDREN: from first marriage 3 children, second marriage twin daughters.
SCHOOLS/COLLEGE: Greek Gymnasium of Morphou 1963-69. Surrey University B. Sc. Physics (1st Class Hers). Surrey University PhD Nuclear Physics.
QUALIFICATIONS: PhD.
MEMBERSHIPS: Institute of Physics (UK), New York Academy of Science (USA), Society for Neuroscience (USA).
HOBBIES AND INTERESTS: Basketball, Reading Literature.
PERSONAL PROFILE: Andreas Ioannides has worked in nuclear Physics from 1976 to 1986, at Surrey University, Daresbury Laboratory and the Open University, all in the UK. Heads the laboratory for Human Brain Dynamics at the Brain Science Institute, RIKEN near Tokyo, Japan.

Kuwait

ANDREAS CHRISTOFOROU
Professor of Engineering Kuwait University

PLACE OF BIRTH: Limassol
SCHOOLS/COLLEGE: University of Utah, Salt Lake City, USA.
QUALIFICATIONS: BS MS and PhD.
PERSONAL PROFILE: Andreas Christoforou is a Professor in the Department of Mechanical Engineering College of Engineering and Petroleum, Kuwait University.

Lebanon

CHRISTOS ANASTASIOU
Assistant Professor of Environmental Engineering at the America University of Beirut in Lebanon

DATE OF BIRTH: 13-Jun-1972
PLACE OF BIRTH: Zodhia, Cyprus.
MARITAL STATUS: Married to Eleni Louka, Cypriot, Secondary School Teacher.
CHILDREN: Georgia.
SCHOOLS/COLLEGE: University of Florida, North Carolina State University.
QUALIFICATIONS: PhD ME BS.
MEMBERSHIPS: American Society of Civil Engineers.
HOBBIES AND INTERESTS: Philosophy and Politics, Martial Arts, Home brewing and Scuba.
PERSONAL PROFILE: Before joining the faculty of CLL Harvard Dr. Anastasiou worked as a consultant in the US, Cyprus and Lebanon, as an officer at the Research Promotion foundation in Cyprus, and more recently as an Assistant Professor of Environmental Engineering at the America University of Beirut in Lebanon.

Malawi

STEPHEN CONSTANTINE
First team coach of the Malawi National Team

DATE OF BIRTH: 16-Oct-1962
PLACE OF BIRTH: London. Father from Paphos.
MARITAL STATUS: Married to Lucy, English Cypriot, Housewife.
CHILDREN: Paula, Christiana.
SCHOOLS/COLLEGE: Southgate, the Grammar School, Limassol.
QUALIFICATIONS: FA Advanced License, UEFA License FIFA Instructor.
MEMBERSHIPS: FA Coaches (FACA) FIFA.
HONOURS/AWARDS: Nepalese OBE received medal from King of Nepal.
HOBBIES AND INTERESTS: Military Modeling.
PERSONAL PROFILE: Football manager, Nepal National Team, APEP, and Achilleas in Cyprus. Assistant Manager at Apollon in Cyprus. Bournemouth FC Youth Team Manager. Played for AEL in Cyprus, Enfield Town in UK. Former India National Team Manager. Was first team coach at Millwall 2005/6. At present Stephen is the first team coach of the Malawi National Team.

Netherlands

MICHAEL EFTHYMIOU

Named as Offshore Pioneer in Hall of Fame of Offshore Energy Centre for Reliability based Design of Marine Structures, 2002, Houston, Texas USA based in Netherlands

DATE OF BIRTH: 23-Apr-1953
PLACE OF BIRTH: Dhali.
MARITAL STATUS: Married to Maria, Manchester Father from Famagusta and Mother from Nicosia, School Administrator.
CHILDREN: Margarita, Sophia, Both University students.
SCHOOLS/COLLEGE: English School Nicosia. Manchester University.
QUALIFICATIONS: Bsc Msc and PhD.
MEMBERSHIPS: Royal Institute of Naval Architects.
HONOURS/AWARDS: Named as Offshore Pioneer in Hall of Fame of Offshore Energy Centre for Reliability based Design of Marine Structures, 2002, Houston, Texas USA.
HOBBIES AND INTERESTS: Travelling, swimming.
PERSONAL PROFILE: Michael Efthymiou joined Shell in 1981 as a Research Scientist in the Netherlands, he has been with them for 25 years. He is currently Head of Offshore structures in a global shell unit responsible for execution of major oil and gas projects worldwide.

TASSOULLA HADJITOFI

Nominated by the Cyprus section of the International Association for the Promotion of women of Europe for the 2007 Women of Europe Award

DATE OF BIRTH: 23-Feb-1959
PLACE OF BIRTH: Famagusta.
MARITAL STATUS: Married to Dr Michael Hadjitofi.
HONOURS/AWARDS: Nominee of the Cyprus Association of the International Association for the promotion of Women in Europe for her twenty-one years of activism and volunteering work in recovering stolen cultural and religious objects from the occupied territories of Cyprus. Her work has led to the location of some 5, 000 objects and the repatriation of 60, including 6th century Kanakaria mosaics, 12th century frescoes and 15th century icons.

For her endeavours and achievements in 1999 she was awarded the highest honour in Cyprus the order of St Barnabas.
PERSONAL PROFILE: Mrs Hadjitofi served as the Honorary Consul of Cyprus in the Netherlands from 1986 until 1999. In 1987 she established in The Hague her own company Octagon to specialise in the provision and coaching of international professional manpower. Since 2008 she has been appointed as the Ambassador to the Board of medical checks for children, a volunteer organisation that aims to provide medical checks for children in developing countries. Mrs Hadjitofi is often asked to be a public speaker at academic and political forums for issues related to diversity, integration, immigration and identities in the broader sense.

NICHOLAS KOUNIS

Macro Economist with Fortis Investment Bank in Amsterdam

DATE OF BIRTH: 28-Jun-1976
PLACE OF BIRTH: London. Parents from Paphos.
MARITAL STATUS: Married to Dorien Buckers who is a 'New Economy' policy analyst with a Government Ministry in Netherlands.
SCHOOLS/COLLEGE: London Guildhall University, Durham University.
QUALIFICATIONS: BA (Honours) in Economics, MSc in Corporate and International Finance.
HOBBIES AND INTERESTS: Football, cycling and politics.
PERSONAL PROFILE: Macro-Economist with Fortis Investment Bank in Amsterdam advising on UK and Swedish economic performance as relating to financial markets and securities. Previously with H. M. Treasury on UK Macroeconomic and Fiscal Policy and on UK economic policy towards Russia & Ukraine.

More Places

Tassoulla Hadjitofi was nominated for the 2007 Women of Europe Award

YANNIS KYRIAKIDES
Musician Composes work for esembles such as ASKO NL Icebreaker UK

DATE OF BIRTH: 01-Aug-1969
PLACE OF BIRTH: Limassol.
MARITAL STATUS: Married to Ayelet Harpaz, Singer.
SCHOOLS/COLLEGE: Eton College, York University and Royal Conservatoire.
QUALIFICATIONS: BMus. MA.
HONOURS/AWARDS: Gaudeamus International Composition Prize 2000. Honorary Mention Prix Ars Electronica 2006.
PERSONAL PROFILE: Yannis Kyriakides currently lives in Amsterdam where he has collaborated as composer on three projects with Dick Raaijmaakers and Paul Koek. He works on combining traditional performance practices with digital media. Composes work for ensembles such as ASKO NL Icebreaker UK.

SOCRATES LOUCAIDES
Researcher in Geochemistry at Utrecht University

PLACE OF BIRTH: Limassol
SCHOOLS/COLLEGE: University of North Carolina.
QUALIFICATIONS: MS BS.
PERSONAL PROFILE: Socratis Loucaides is a researcher in Geochemistry in the Department of Earth Sciences Faculty of Geosciences, Utrecht University, Netherlands.

PHEDON NICOLAIDES
Professor at the European Institute of Public Administration, Maastricht

PLACE OF BIRTH: Cyprus
QUALIFICATIONS: BA Political Philosophy and Art History. MA Economics. PhD Economics.
PERSONAL PROFILE: Dr Phedon Nicolaides is a Professor at the European Institute of public administration, Maastricht Served as a Minister Plenipotentiary in the Ministry of Foreign Affairs of Cyprus. Author of books and numerous academic papers.

New Zealand

RITA CHRISTINA DAVID
News Reporter

DATE OF BIRTH: 12-Jan-1974
PLACE OF BIRTH: London. Parents from Deftera, Cyprus.
MARITAL STATUS: Single.
SCHOOLS/COLLEGE: Christ Church CE School, North Finchley, Southgate College, University of Sussex, Harlow College (For Post Graduate).
QUALIFICATIONS: BA Honours History, University of Sussex. NCTS Post Graduate Journalism Diploma Assoc Board Royal Schools of Music (ABRSM).
HONOURS/AWARDS: Ted Bottomly Award, Newspaper Journalism, 1998. Grade 8 Piano.
HOBBIES AND INTERESTS: Watersports and literature, (fiction & non).
PERSONAL PROFILE: She is now working in New Zealand on mainstream magazines. Was News Reporter, Retail Week Magazine, previously Reporter on the Enfield Gazette + Advertiser. Contributor to Parikiaki. Also taught Piano & hosted a local Radio News Programme. (Radio North NID).

KYRIAKOS ECONOMOU
Former President of the Greek Association in Wellington, New Zealand

DATE OF BIRTH: 25-Oct-1915
PLACE OF BIRTH: Marathovounos.
CHILDREN: George, Pharmacist. Chrystalla, Restauranteur. Anthoulla, Accountant. Andronikos and Merobe And Christoforos, Restauranteur and Restauranteur and motelier.
HOBBIES AND INTERESTS: Gardening and reading.
PERSONAL PROFILE: Kyriakos Economou was President of the Greek association in Wellington, New Zealand. While he was in Cyprus in 1974 he was held prisoner by the Turkish Army for three weeks despite having a New Zealand Passport he was moved from location to location within the Northern part of the Island. He is now back living in New Zealand.

More Places

ANDRONICOS ECONOMOUS
President of the Cyprus Community in New Zealand

DATE OF BIRTH: 25-May-1956.
PLACE OF BIRTH: New Zealand Parents from Cyprus.
MARITAL STATUS: Married to Tina, Greece.
MEMBERSHIPS: Porsche Club New Zealand.
HOBBIES AND INTERESTS: Music.
PERSONAL PROFILE: Andronicos Economous is the President of the Cyprus Community in New Zealand.

GIANNIS MICHAELIDES
Major pita bread makers in New Zealand

PLACE OF BIRTH: Cyprus.
MARITAL STATUS: Married to Despo.
CHILDREN: Andreas, All in Business. Kyriacos, Stelios.
PERSONAL PROFILE: Giannis arrived in New Zealand when he was 19 years old and he hooked up with his uncles in the fishing industry. In 1991 he and his wife opened a bakers shop, he specialised in lahmajoun a small middle eastern Pizza. They have now diversified into producing pita bread and they are the biggest pita bread makers in New Zealand. They also have started producing Giannis pita bread chips.

Norway

ANDREAS HATJOULLIS
Established Dolly Dimple's one of Norway's largest restaurant chains, comprising a total of 84 restaurants all over the country

DATE OF BIRTH: 20-Apr-1944
PLACE OF BIRTH: Perachorion, Nisou.
MARITAL STATUS: Married to Gunhild Lima, Norwegian, Interior Decorator.
CHILDREN: Alexia, Product Director Graduate University of Bath MBA. Pierre, Finance Director Economics Graduate University of Bergen. Marie, Logistic manager in Shipping Garduate in Travel.
SCHOOLS/COLLEGE: Tollington Park.
MEMBERSHIPS: Rotary Sandnes Sør.
HONOURS/AWARDS: Entrepreneur of the year Norway.
BEST COMPANY OF THE YEAR ROGALAND, NORWAY.
HOBBIES AND INTERESTS: Sports, photography, reading, music.

PERSONAL PROFILE: Andreas Hatjoullis created one of the largest pizza chains in Norway. "Dolly Dimples. Dolly Dimple's is one of Norway's largest restaurant chains, comprising a total of 84 restaurants all over the country. The chain was established by the Cypriot Andreas Hatjoullis in Sandnes in 1986, which is the location of the company headquarters. The chain employs a total of 1, 600 people. Hes also a"building a childrens home in Kenya, Nairobi.

Russia

JOHN MYLONAS
Managing Director of General Motors Russia

DATE OF BIRTH: 22-Dec-1945
PLACE OF BIRTH: Kato Platres.
MARITAL STATUS: Married to Magdalena, Tyrol, Austria.
CHILDREN: James, Fireman. Tara, Tourism.
SCHOOLS/COLLEGE: Mitsis Commercial College, Tottenham Tech, Kingston University.
QUALIFICATIONS: HND in Mechanical Engineering, BSc in Production Engineering, MSc in Air Transport Engineering IE (Industrial Engineering) Practitioner.
HONOURS/AWARDS: GM President Honours Award.
HOBBIES AND INTERESTS: Flying, theatre, football and backgammon.
PERSONAL PROFILE: On completion of Masters Degree worked with BEA for a short period. Joined Vauxhall Motors Luton Plant as Production Operator on assembly line (nobody knew of his qualifications), then progressed through a number of senior appointments. In 1989 he took an international assignment for General Motors (GM) as the Implementation Director setting up two factories in Hungary for Astra Cars and to manufacture Opel engines. Then he was Operations Director for GM Poland. In 1998 John moved to Moscow, where he is now the Managing Director of GM Russia for the joint venture between General Motors and the Russian Autovaz that produces the Lada vehicles.

More Places

419

STAVROS PANAYI
Solicitor

DATE OF BIRTH: 05-Jul-1977
PLACE OF BIRTH: London. Father born in Kato Drys, Mother's parents from Yialoussa.
SCHOOLS/COLLEGE: University College School, Hampstead 1990-1995, Cambridge University 1995-98, Law School 1998-1999.
QUALIFICATIONS: Law BA Honours, MA. Solicitor of England & Wales.
MEMBERSHIPS: Law Society.
HOBBIES AND INTERESTS: Reading philosophy and history, Bolshoi theatre, good food, wine and cigars.
PERSONAL PROFILE: Lawyer with City Law firm Denton Wilde Sapte, 19 International Offices & around 700 Lawyers worldwide. Specialises in Capital Markets. Works in the Moscow office.

Spain

MARIA ELEFTHERIOU
Assistant Professor in Economics at University Carlos in Madrid

PLACE OF BIRTH: Cyprus.
PERSONAL PROFILE: Maria Eleftheriou is Assistant Professor in the Department of Economics at University Carlos III in Madrid.

IOANNIS OKKAS
Cyprus International Footballer Played for Celta Vigo in Spain

DATE OF BIRTH: 11-Feb-1977
PLACE OF BIRTH: Larnaca.
HONOURS/AWARDS: At the age of 19, he was called into the Cypriot National team and has been a regular ever since, passing the 50 cap mark in 2003. He has captained his national squad since the 2006 FIFA World cup.
PERSONAL PROFILE: Ioannis is a striker renowned as one of the most talented players to emerge from Cyprus. He started his career at the age of 16 with New Salamis then joined Anorthosis four years later. Okkas helped Anorthosis win the Championship four times in a row. In year 2000 Okkas signed for Paok Fc and scored seven times during a first year which brought success in the Greek cup and the Cypriot player of the year award. In the final against Olympiakos, Okkas scored two goals and Paok won 4-2. In year 2003 Okkas joined AEK but following FIFA intervention over unpaid wages he secured a fresh start with Olympiakos in Greece where he helped them complete the double twice. For two consecutive seasons Okkas scored the first league goal of the season in Greece with Aek in 2003-4 and Olympiakos the next season. In august 2007 he signed a one year deal with Celta Vigo The Spanish League club. Now playing for Omonia in Cyprus.

Sweden

STAVROS LOUCA
Mathematics Prize of The Royal Swedish Academy of Sciences 2006

DATE OF BIRTH: 20-Dec-1953
PLACE OF BIRTH: Famagusta.
HONOURS/AWARDS: Mathematics Prize of The Royal Swedish Academy of Sciences 2006. Also awarded by the Royal Society Pro Patria.
PERSONAL PROFILE: Stavros Louca is the Vice Chairman of the Swedish Cypriots Association in Stockholm. He is a Mathematics teacher at the School of Rinkeby in Stockholm.

CHRISTINA ZAMPAS
Senior Regional Manager and Legal Adviser, Europe for the Center for Reproductive Rights

DATE OF BIRTH: 07-Sep-1967
PLACE OF BIRTH: New York Parents from Karavas.
MARITAL STATUS: Married to Magnus Lanje, Sweden, Photographer.
SCHOOLS/COLLEGE: Rutgers University and Syracuse University.
QUALIFICATIONS: BA in Political Science and Juris Doctorate with a certificate in International Law. Lawyer licensed to practice law in New York State and International Law.
MEMBERSHIPS: Democrats Abroad Sweden;ABA.
HONOURS/AWARDS: Deans List.
HOBBIES AND INTERESTS: Yoga, Reading and Gardening.
PERSONAL PROFILE: Christina is Senior Regional Manager and Legal Adviser, Europe for the Center for Reproductive Rights. She has taken cases to the European Court of Human rights. Started the first ever training of lawyers in Europe focusing on protecting

More Places

and promoting womens human rights. She has published several articles in journals and written reports documenting human rights violations. Sat on boards of womens rights organizations and on the board of the US Democratic party organization in Sweden and expert committees of the Council of Europe and the World Health Organization.

Switzerland

ANDREAS ANDREADES
Chief Executive Officer of Temenos one of the world's leading suppliers of packaged banking software

PLACE OF BIRTH: Cyprus
SCHOOLS/COLLEGE: Cambridge University.
QUALIFICATIONS: Engineering Degree he is a Chartered Accountant.
PERSONAL PROFILE: Andreas Andreades is the Chief Executive Officer of Temenos one of the world's leading suppliers of packaged banking software.

DEMETRIOS CHRISTODOULOU
Professor of Mathematics and Physics

DATE OF BIRTH: 19-Oct-1951
PLACE OF BIRTH: Athens, Grandfather from Ayios Theodoros Paphos and Grandmother from Khirokitia.
SCHOOLS/COLLEGE: Princeton University.
QUALIFICATIONS: MA PhD in Physics.
HONOURS/AWARDS: Elected to the American Academy of Arts and sciences. Honorary Doctorate in the Sciences Brown University.
HOBBIES AND INTERESTS: Professor Demetrios Christodoulou is a Professor of Mathematics and Physics at the Swiss Federal Institute of Technology Zurich. Has also lectured at Universities in Greece and the USA.

MICHAEL EVANGELOU
Lecturer at the Swiss Federal Institute of Technology Zurich

PLACE OF BIRTH: Parents from Cyprus
SCHOOLS/COLLEGE: RWTH Aachen University.
QUALIFICATIONS: PhD.
MEMBERSHIPS: Soil Protection Group of the Institute of Terrestrial Ecosystems(ITES).
PERSONAL PROFILE: Dr Michael Evangelou is a Lecturer at the Swiss Federal Institute of Technology Zurich in Biology.

THEODOROS MICHAELIDES
Air Pilot/Project Manager for the Development of a Scooter

DATE OF BIRTH: 29-Oct-1968
PLACE OF BIRTH: Larnaca.
MARITAL STATUS: Single.
SCHOOLS/COLLEGE: Swissair Pilots School.
HOBBIES AND INTERESTS: Flying, motor sport, water sports, wheelchair basketball, reading and music.
PERSONAL PROFILE: Theodoros Michaelides is a former Airline Pilot (Swissair, Luftansa) he is the CEO of www. doros. ch owner of a restaurant, project manager for the development of a scooter and an ambassador of an organisation for disabled people.

ALIKI PANAYIDES
General Secretary of the Swiss Peoples Party in Berne

DATE OF BIRTH: 13-May-1964
PLACE OF BIRTH: Doros, Switzerland Father from Limassol mother Swiss.
MARITAL STATUS: Single.
SCHOOLS/COLLEGE: University of Berne and Barcelona.
QUALIFICATIONS: Dr. Phil. hist.
HOBBIES AND INTERESTS: Arts and crafts, sci fi, swimming.
PERSONAL PROFILE: General Secretary of the Swiss Peoples Party in Berne. Member of the local government of Ostermundigen.

More Places

ZACHARIAS ZACHARIOU
Professor of Paediatric Surgery

DATE OF BIRTH: 25-Nov-1957
PLACE OF BIRTH: Limassol.
MARITAL STATUS: Married to Ulrika, German, Physician.
CHILDREN: Ioannis.
SCHOOLS/COLLEGE: Lanition Gymnasium. University of Heidelburg Germany.
QUALIFICATIONS: Professor of Paediatric Surgery.
MEMBERSHIPS: Swiss Association of Paediatric Surgery.
HOBBIES AND INTERESTS: Stained glass windows, Byzantine medicine and culinary arts.
PERSONAL PROFILE: Director of the Department of Surgical Paediatrics, University of Berne.

Thailand

HARRY NICOLAIDES
Author/Lecturer in Tourism and Hospitality at Mae Fah Luang University

PLACE OF BIRTH: Melbourne Parents from Cyprus
SCHOOLS/COLLEGE: La Trobe University.
QUALIFICATIONS: BA.
PERSONAL PROFILE: Harry Nicolaides is an Australian author. His first book Concierge Confidential published in 2002 generated national publicity. In 2003 he relocated to live in Thailand. He is a Lecturer in Tourism and Hospitality at Mae Fah Luang University.

Syria

THEODOSIS KONTOU
Oil and Gas Project Manager with Shell

DATE OF BIRTH: 27-Feb-1949
PLACE OF BIRTH: Achna.
MARITAL STATUS: Married to Jennifer, Dutch, Hr Manager.
CHILDREN: Yiannis, Investment Banking. Pavlos, Business Science. Eleni, Police Officer.
SCHOOLS/COLLEGE: 1st Gymnasium Famagusta. Salford University.
QUALIFICATIONS: MSc in Underwater Science and Technology.
MEMBERSHIPS: Chartered Engineer. Dive Marshall British Sub Aqua Club.
HOBBIES AND INTERESTS: World affairs, reading and diving.
PERSONAL PROFILE: Theodosis Kontou is a senior member of staff with the Shell group specializing in underwater engineering and has lived in diverse locations such as Borneo East Malaysia, Houston USA and Lagos Nigeria, where he helped to develop oil and gas sub sea projects. He is currently attached to Al Furat Petroleum, a joint venture between Shell and Syrian government interests. He has always been involved in community affairs and was elected Chairman of the Greek communities of Great Yarmouth UK and Lagos in Nigeria.

United Arab Emirates

MARIO PISHIRI
Area Director of Hyder Consulting in Dubai

PLACE OF BIRTH: UK Father from Komi Kebir
PERSONAL PROFILE: Mario Pishiri is the Area Director of Hyder Consulting in Dubai.

Zimbabwe

NESTORAS NESTOROS
Honorary Consul of the Republic of Cyprus to Zimbabwe

DATE OF BIRTH: 06-May-1958.
PLACE OF BIRTH: Philia.
MARITAL STATUS: Single.
CHILDREN: Panayiotis, Anthoulla, Maria, Eleni, all four are students.
QUALIFICATIONS: Diploma of a Marine Officer in Engineering.
HONOURS/AWARDS: Member of the World Council of Hellenes.
PERSONAL PROFILE: Nestoras Nestoros is the Honorary Consul of the Republic of Cyprus to Zimbabwe he served as Chairman of the Hellenic Cypriot Brotherhood of Zimbabwe. Nestoras has his own Company Pylos Investments we are project managers for Building projects.

PROFILES INDEX: BY OCCUPATION

GREEK CYPRIOTS WORLDWIDE

GREEK CYPRIOTS WORLDWIDE

PROFILES INDEX: BY OCCUPATION

PROFILES INDEX: BY OCCUPATION

GREEK CYPRIOTS WORLDWIDE

Index

GREEK CYPRIOTS WORLDWIDE

Index

xii

Index

INDEX OF LOCATIONS IN CYPRUS

Index

Index

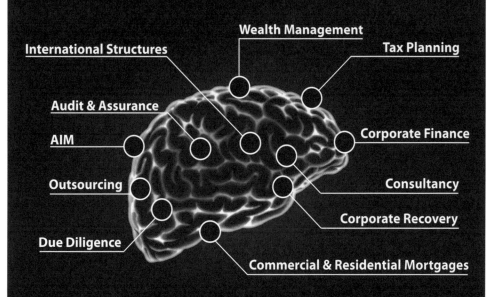

Wealth Management

International Structures

Tax Planning

Audit & Assurance

AIM

Corporate Finance

Outsourcing

Consultancy

Corporate Recovery

Due Diligence

Commercial & Residential Mortgages

TURNING KNOWLEDGE
INTO GOOD ADVICE
www.bondpartners.co.uk

KEY CONTACTS:
Corporate Recovery - Pat Papanicola (Head Office)
Tax Planning & Audit - Michael Michaelides (Head Office)
AIM / Corporate Finance/ Due Diligence - Mike Marcus (Head Office)
Audit & Assurance - Costas Morfakis (Head Office)
Commercial & Residential Mortgages - Nick Kounis (City Office)
Consultancy / Outsourcing - George Ioannides (Head Office)
Financial Services - Nick Kounis (City Office)

Bond Partners is one of the UK's fastest growing independent accountancy practice. Multi-cultural in constitution and philosophy Bond Partners is ideally positioned to understand and service the diverse business communities within the UK economy.

Bond Partners strength is in creating and sustaining long-term supportive partnerships with our clients. This enables us to develop sophisticated finance and accounting strategies, aligning perfectly with your business objectives.

Our aim at Bond Partners is to earn the status of trusted business advisor from our clients, and our efforts are focused on helping them to build the inherent value of their business. Bond Partners are committed to maintain a comprehensive knowledge of your business strategy and financial circumstances in order to continue to provide the guidance and support both you and your business require.

Many of our Partners managed their own practice prior to joining Bond Partners and this makes them all the more able to advise the owner-managed business and SME's with whom we predominantly work.

Bond Partners is a fully integrated and connected business. Our individual specialists work within multi-disciplinary teams to ensure our ability to deliver the right combination of support and advice for your specific needs.

The principle areas of our practice comprise: audit and assurance, taxation, corporate/business recovery/rescue and insolvency, bookkeeping services, through our Bond Financial Controller unit, and financial services through our FSA authorised subsidiary, Bond Financial Network.

Within each of these practice areas we provide an enormous range of services to both individual and corporate clients. Bond Partners goal is to provide all clients with pro-active, circumspect business and financial advice, capable of protecting and advancing their interests.

t: +44(0)870 850 6007

Head Office:
The Grange
100 High Street
London N14 6TB
T: 0870 850 6007
F: 0870 850 6008

City Office:
111 Charterhouse Street
London
EC1M 6AW
T: 0870 240 3007
F: 0870 240 3008

www.bondpartners.co.uk

CuroCare

CuroCare - THE 'NEW KID' ON THE HEALTH CARE BLOCK

Introduction to the *'new kid'*

This article introduces a 'new kid' on the block in the learning disability/mental health field. Behind this 'new kid' is over 20 years experience of providing services in this sector, but recent changes mean the 'kid' has a different shape, a new name and a lot of 'chutzpah'! The experience and expertise of the old company has been retained; delivering individualised care services in high quality surroundings is at the heart. *Watch out – CuroCare are about!*

CuroCare's roots

CuroCare provide continuing care and day services to clients with learning disabilities and other complex needs or challenging behaviours. This small, innovative, company has a successful track record, and wide range of planned service developments are occurring.

   Services include Day Service and Constance House, a seven bed in-patient unit for females with learning disabilities and complex needs; we have recently open two new services in North London.

CuroCare's mission and service philosophy

'We seek to provide excellence in all areas: high quality functional environments; positive clinical risk taking for clients and their families; evidenced based clinical activities, and close partnership working. We believe small, bespoke, local services are key, and we aim to be at the heart of local communities providing specialist services for people with complex physical needs, learning disabilities or mental health issues.'

For more information

www.curocare.co.uk

CuroCare

"passionate about care"

At CuroCare we work as one, providing specialist services for adults with a learning disability, associated mental illness, personality disorder and challenging behaviour.

As an independent healthcare provider, we can offer a range of community based services to include:

- High ratio skilled experienced professionals
- Safe, therapeutic environment
- Comfortable homely surroundings
- Person centred approach
- Outcome focused
- Care pathways
- Lifestyle opportunities

Our inspirationally designed bespoke service in **North London** is now open and taking referrals!

- **Eden Court** - a 9 bedded continuing care service
- **Olive Grove** - a 5 bedded rehabilitation service

To arrange a visit or to discuss your requirements in detail, please contact **Ruth Georgiou**.

t. 0844 887 8700   e. ruth@curocare.co.uk

www.curocare.co.uk

Haji-Ioannou Dynasty

Loucas Haji-Ioannou was born in 1927 in the Troodos Mountains village of Pedhoulas the eldest of 12 children. He went out to work to help the family at the age of 16. His early career was a salesman with his uncle in Saudi Arabia. When his uncle died unexpectedly Loucas started his own import-export business in Saudi Arabia becoming one of the few businesses allowed to trade within the kingdom without a local partner. During the Saudi construction boom of the late 1950's he became the sole importer of Heraklis and Titan cement, this is where he built the foundations of his commercial empire.

In 1959 Loucas Haji-Ioannou relocated to London where at the age of 32 he purchased his first ship a 10,500-tonne cargo ship named Nedi after his wife. He lived in London until 1965 while he built up a fleet of more than 20 general cargo vessels, becoming a major client of British Shipbrokers in particular Clarksons. His first vessels carried dry cargoes such as food and building materials.

After moving to Athens in the mid 60's he realised the future of shipping lay in the booming international oil trade. He bought his first tanker in 1969 and for most of the second half of the 20th century he dominated the global shipping industry. Niarchos and Onassis may have led more glamourous lives, but Haji-Ioannou owned more tonnage.

By 1990 Haji-Ioannou was the world's largest independent shipowner with Troodos Shipping controlling a fleet of more than 50 vessels. He employed about 2,000 people.

During the Iran-Iraq war of the 1980's oil tankers loading from Iran's Kharg Island oil export terminal were easy targets for Iraqi missile carrying aircrafts, shipping insurance rates went sky high deterring many owners from entering the war zone,after taking advice from British security specialists Haji-Ioannou equipped his ships with extra safety systems that enabled him to obtain insurance at cheaper rates as one of the few owners prepared to lift from the Kharg his charter rates were so high that the purchase price of a tanker could be recouped within two round trip voyages from Kharg to the safety of the Strait of Hormuz.

He endowed a Haji-Ioannou Foundation with more than $10 million dollars his daughter Clelia is President of the Haji-Ioannou Foundation she is also a noted art collector. Among other things the foundation founded a school in the village of Pedhoulas where he was born. The charity also supports the Greek Institute of Cardiology.

He has two sons **Polys** who runs a shipping fleet of his own under the name of Polyar Tankers AS and is also a major shareholder in Tottenham football Club.

And **Sir Stelios** the founder of Easy Jet the leading low cost airline which he started with £5 million capital provided from his father Easy Jet Stelios is often credited as the pioneer who changed the European aviation scene for the benefit of millions of consumers. Easy Jet is Europe's leading low-fares airline, and in June 08 it is operating 157 aircraft on 392 routes between 101 airports in  26 countries. Easy Jet carried over 40 million passengers in the past 12 months. The airline was partially floated on the London Stock Exchange in 2000 but Stelios remains the largest single shareholder and a member of its board of directors.

In November 2006, at the age of 39, Stelios received a knighthood from Queen Elisabeth II for services to entrepreneurship. On the giving back side, Stelios is active in supporting education, encouraging entrepreneurship and promoting environmentally sustainable development strategies. First amongst various philanthropic projects he has started is the environmental charity **www.cymepa.org** in Cyprus in 1992. On education he has pledged 200 scholarships over 10 years at his alma mater (the LSE and the City University). In 2007 he created the "disabled entrepreneur of the year award" in the UK in partnership with the disability charity "Leonard Cheshire" (see **www.lcdisability.org/stelios**).

Katsouris Fresh Foods

In June 1992 the office of the UK's Prime Minister, the Rt. Hon John Mayor, phoned Tony Yerolemou at Katsouris Fresh Foods to invite him to a charity reception , the 50th Anniversary of the Animal Health Trust", being held at No. 10 Downing Street. With the invitation came the the shy request "You couldn't provide some taramasalata for the canapés, could you? We are all addicted to it here."

Tony, as any generous Cypriot would, offered to provide more than just taramasalata; he would provide a whole range of canapés based on dishes produced by Katsouris Fresh Foods (KFF). KFF supplied all the British major supermarkets. At that time 33% of KFF's production went to Marks & Spencer both in the UK and through them to France, Spain and Belgium; 30% went to Sainsbury, 20% to Tesco, 18% to Waitrose and the rest to Safeways, Morrison and even Boots' health foods.

KFF operating from Wembley, West London, was the single biggest producer of ethnic ready- made meals making not only Greek dips, such as taramasalata, houmous and tzatziki but other dishes like dolmades, moussaka, keftedes and samosas. KFF's flexibility, its insistence on quality and consistency ensured that the major retailers relied on KFF's expertise and flair. "All the major supermarkets helped us to develop," Tony acknowledges. "Without M&S's pledge of business back in 1983 we would never have moved from the tiny kitchen in Holloway to a factory in Wembley. Sainsbury was our first customer for samosas. Waitrose, the first customer for Moussaka and it was with Safeway that we delivered our very first order for Greek dips."

From left to right:
Theodosis, Yiannis and Loizos Katsouris

Yet in 1974 Katsouris Brothers (KB), which was to enable the establishment of KFF, was on the verge of collapsing. The import export business built up painstakingly by the brothers John, Theodosis and Louis Katsouris in 1952 was faced with the loss of its suppliers in Cyprus because of the War. It was John Katsouris who first came to England to sell the produce from Cyprus and the family agricultural lands – olives, vine leaves, trahana and vegetables. John couldn't adjust to the English climate and returned to Cyprus. Theodosis who came in his place stayed and learnt the import trade. He stopped bringing vegetables by air as they often spoilt and concentrated on dry goods which Cypriots in London wanted, such as Evrika washing powder, wine vinegar, pure lemon juice. Theodosis was a businessman but it wasn't till his energetic, dashing nephew, the first born of all the family, son of Katina and Prodromos Yerolemou arrived that Katsouris Bros. received a boost to its development. Tony was full of ideas and had the energy to implement them. He was a leader who trusted people to make day to day decisions giving them fully responsibility and in that way earned the loyalty of employees.

The first innovation was the gift tins where families in Cyprus were able to fill a tin of their own home-grown produce and send them to the UK through KB. Their relatives would collect them from KB offices in London. This together with the "Cypressa" brand name made Katsouris Bros. known throughout the Cypriot and Greek Community. At one stage there was almost an Agent for KB in every main village in Cyprus sending on tins to Famagusta from where they were shipped to the UK. "I had the beginnings of a Cypriot DVHL" laughed Tony, " but I failed to see the potential. However, although that was one idea that got away, there were plenty of others. " In the 1970s KB developed the "Cypressa" label denoting high quality products and also became a large supplier to the newly emerging organic and health food stores and restaurants. Katsouris pre- packed pulses, vine leaves and other products themselves, at one stage even bottling wine, and went on to supply Selfridges, Harrods, even Biba in the flagship Kensington High Street store. From a shop in Mornington Crescent in 1962 KB moved on to a warehouse in Holloway. It was there that the popular "That's Life" prime TV programme hosted by Ester Rantzen commended "Cypressa" on its cooking instructions for red kidney beans which could be toxic if not cooked long enough.

However, the 1974 war in Cyprus put a halt to KB's ambitions. As the eldest, Tony felt responsible for the fortunes of the family. The supplies of halloumi, feta, olives, trahana etc stopped completely with the war and Tony had to source goods from all over the world. He was joined by his cousins, Panicos Katsouris, Demos Hapeshis and Costa Constantinou and slowly the company recovered and grew in strength.

The war taught Tony not to keep all his eggs in one basket. To diversify, he opened a restaurant the Wine & Moussaka in 1976 with his wife, Barbara and his cousins. It was from the Wine and Moussaka in 1978 that Tony first made taramasalata for sale to Safeways Supermarket for their deli counter. By 1981 there were three restaurants but more importantly for the future development of the company, a central kitchen was established to supply the restaurants at the Holloway base in Islington. With the encouragement of Safeways, Tony called this new venture "Katsouris Fresh Foods" and it was

Barbara Yerolemou Ealing Councillor diplaying products of Cypressa and Katsouris food products.

formally inaugurated in 1982. KFF began operating from ex-United Biscuits factories in Wembley. The major boost to the company came in 1998 when Tesco asked them to take on production of its "Finest "range, the first products being mashed potato and chicken breasts in sauce. By 2000 there were five huge factories plus a separate company Fillo Pastry Ltd.

Many companies had bid to buy KFF over the years and eventually the family sold the Katsouris Fresh Foods and Fillo business in 2001 for £100m. In the meantime the Katsouris Bros. arm of the family business had also been steadily developing and expanding: with the energies of the third generation of family members who have joined the business, *who knows what innovations will occur?*

Inside one of the Katsouris Fresh Foods Factories with Tony Yerolemou showing dignitaries around

Tony Yerolemou with the Chairman of Tescos at the time, Tony Gardner, at the opening of a Katsouris Fresh Foods Factory in Wembley, London

Outside one of the factories Archbishop Gregorios and the Katsouris Fresh Foods Management

Laiki Bank

Marfin Popular Bank, in its present form, was created by the recent merger of three Groups: *Marfin Financial Group, Laiki Group and Egnatia Bank.*

Marfin Popular Bank offers a wide range of financial services through its subsidiary companies and its branch network of 415 branches in Cyprus, Greece, Australia, UK, Ukraine, Russia, Romania, Estonia, Serbia, Malta and Guernsey and a labor force of more than 8,000 employees.

2007 has been a year of great success and robust expansion for Marfin Popular Bank. Group Net Profit after tax and minorities reached a record of € 563.4m recording an increase of 130% compared of the proforma results of 2006 and total assets of the Group amounted to €30.3bn an increase of 34% compared to the proforma figures at the end of 2006.

Mayfair
12 Hay Hill,
W1J 8NR
United Kingdom, London
ukenquiries@laiki.com
Tel: +44-20-7307-8400, Fax: +44-20-7307-8444

Finchley
995 High Road, North Finchley,
N12 8PW
United Kingdom, London
ukenquiries@laiki.com
Tel: +44-20-8492-2000, Fax: +44-20-8492-2020

Holloway
95 Seven Sisters Road,
N7 6BZ
United Kingdom, London
ukenquiries@laiki.com
Tel: +44-20-7561-7000, Fax: +44-20-7561-7007

Palmers Green
246 Greens Lanes,
N13 5XT
United Kingdom, London
ukenquiries@laiki.com
Tel: +44-20-8920-1000, Fax: +44-20-8920-1011

Erdington
154 Gravelly Hill North, Erdington,
B23 6BE
United Kingdom, Birmingham
ukenquiries@laiki.com
Tel: +44-121-377-3200, Fax: +44-121-377-3210

Taking the lead

�# **MARFIN LAIKI BANK**

**9 top distinctions
open up new roads**

By joining forces we have won the
greatest distinctions in the banking sector,
awarded by prestigious international economic magazines.

We have achieved this leading position through
effort, dynamism, passion, vision and your own cooperation.

We thank you for your trust.

- **Bank of the Year 2007**
  The Banker (Financial Times Magazine)
- **Best Domestic Bank in Cyprus**
- **Best Private Banking Services Overall**
- **Best Private Bank for Entrepreneurs in Cyprus**
- **Best Private Bank for Corporate Executives in Greece**
  Euromoney Magazine
- **Best in Class for Custody Services**
- **Innovation Award**
  Money Markets Magazine
- **Bronze Award for Cheapest Home Loan in Australia**
- **Bronze Award for Best Term Deposit in Australia**
  Money Magazine

Tel: +44 (20) 7307 8400   www.laiki.com

Lorrells Georgiou Nicholas

Georgiou Nicholas was formed on 18th July 1988 with two partners, *George Georgiou* who was born in London, his parents from Ayios Andronicos and Vothylakas and *Steve Nicholas* born in London, parents from Ayios Amvrosios who both went to the same schools and colleges. Their first office was in John Street, London EC1 and it was just the two partners and a secretary.

They were predominantly involved in property law and as they grew in size they then moved to new offices in 2005 to Goswell Road EC1. The company is well known in the Cypriot community not only in providing legal services also for their philanthropic help.

On 1st September 2008 the company decided to merge with another Law firm Lorrells and are now practising under the name **Lorrells Georgiou Nicholas LLP Solicitors.** They are now able to offer more services Litigation, Personal Injury, Debt Collection, Commercial Law as well as Residential and Commercial Property Law.

They are now located in Temple Bar House in Fleet Street EC4 and in Ely Place London EC1. The four senior partners are now Mark Lorrell, George Georgiou, David Richards and Chris Theo and the practise has 45 employees.

They have a client base built largely on reputation through referrals and recommendations. They have worked hard to maintain its vision of being the firm with a difference, providing a variety of benefits for clients. Their specialists are experts in their particular fields and offer an exceedingly high level of intelligent and appropriate advice that is clear, honest and always jargon-free. Blinding clients with technical terms and waffle is not their style. At Lorrells Georgiou Nicholas they have invested considerably in up-to-the-minute technology. They are dedicated to making the best possible use of their investment, and unlike many of their competitors, they pass the resulting time saving benefits of their advanced systems onto their clients, thus keeping their bills to a minimum.

They use e-mail as much as possible, preferring to scan and send rather than copy and post. This means return correspondence that could take more than a week only takes a few days.

Lorrells Georgiou Nicholas has a vision of being the firm with a difference; and because of that vision keeps them on track to provide clients with the ultimate in quality of service, they will continuously work towards it.

LORRELLS
GEORGIOU
NICHOLAS | LLP

Temple Bar House, 23-28 Fleet Street, London EC4Y 1AA
Tel: 020 7822 7430
Fax: 020 7353 7454
DX: 309 LONDON CHANCERY LANE

25 Ely Place, London EC1N 6TD
Tel: 020 7681 8888
Fax: 020 7539 4599

Email: enquiries@lorrells.com

Task Systems

task systems™ clients include

10 Downing Street • Adecco • Anglo Irish Bank
Ashley Associates • Axola • Baker Tilly • Bank of Cyprus
Bartle Bogle Hegarty • Beresford Blake Thomas • Bank of Ireland
Blackmore Borley • Blue Jelly • Blue Arrow • Bray Leino • BSM
Cabinet Office • Cable & Wireless • Charles Russell Solicitors
Clear Channel • Coalition • Computer People • Deutsche Bank
Dron and Wright • Elliott Ross Associates • European Interior Contracting
Exeter Crown Court • Fair Isaac • Fortis Bank • Fortis Investments
Four Capital • GBB • Hamptons International • Harris McMillan
Hermes Pension Management • Hiscox Plc • HMKM Holmes Place
HSBC Assets Management • Independent Newspaper • Insolvency Service
Interior Design Management • International Cricket Council • ISG Interior Exterior
Leo Burnett Advertising • Lloyds TSB Development • London Bridge Software
London Clinic • McDonalds • McCann Erickson Advertising
McGregor Boyall Associates • Mellon Bank • Metropolis Planning and Design
Michelmores Solicitors • Ministry of Defence • Mitsubishi • Models One
MOT Models • Motley Fool MTT Consulting • National Bank of Pakistan
Nesta / CBS Interiors • Nestor Health Care Group Plc • NICEIC • Nomura
Office Angels • Pargon Consulting Group • Phoenix Adminstration Service
Prudential Portfolio • Re: Source • Real Media • Red Lorry Yellow Lorry
Romeike International • RW Baird • Saatchi & Saatchi Advertising
Schroders Investment Management • Select Appointments • Societe Generale
Superdrug • The Football Association • The Mill • Tyler Capital • UBS
Unisys • Vantis • Victoria & Albert Museum • Visit London • Volkswagen Group
Westminster Abbey • Wilmington Publishing Ltd • Winkworth
Wolf Rock Capital LLP • WPA • Xansa UK

task systems™ company of ideas

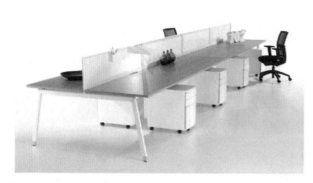

T: (0)20 7729 5088
www.tasksystems.co.uk
marketing@tasksystems.co.uk

The Ability Group

Andreas Panayiotou

The Ability Group was founded in 1996 by Andreas Panayiotou, who has led the Group as Chairman ever since. The son of Cypriot immigrants, Andreas was born in East London. His life took a dramatic turn when he decided to abandon a career in professional boxing, to help run his parents' Launderettes. Soon after joining the business, Andreas put in place a strategy to move the company into Property Development and 'The Ability Group' was born.

Andreas saw the growth potential of the East London residential market. So using his existing knowledge of the area, focused on acquiring unwanted or dilapidated buildings. This often allowed the company to buy-and-build properties at between £100 and £200 per square foot. Today, finding properties in the same areas at under £900 per square foot, is a huge challenge. As the markets have grown so much over the years, mirrored by the growth of The Ability Group.

What started out as the conversion of small apartments in un-fashionable areas of London such as Islington, Hackney and Clerkenwell. Became a property empire that now owns in access of 6,000 residential units and is valued at over £1bn. Today, the group remains active in the residential property market where its development arm, 'Ability Developments', has a workforce of over 900 people, currently building projects of over 1 million square feet in Central London. However, it has also expanded into the leisure arena through its acquisition and development of Hotels, Commercial, Retail and Office properties.

Unlike the majority of developers, Andreas adopted a long-term strategy of retaining ownership of the properties he built. Rather than simply, selling them at attractive prices. He thereby pioneered the concept of 'Build to Let' in the London residential market and built a strong and stable business that has gone from strength to strength.

Driven by the energy of its management, The Ability Group grew at a phenomenal rate and in 2000 entered a new phase. By initiating its first New Build projects on the Kingsland Road in East London. By 2002, the group was developing new apartment complexes in Dalston Lane and Central Street in Islington, and had built over 1,000 new apartments and 50 B1 Retail units.

Currently, the group is nearing the completion of Ability Place in Millharbour, Ability Central in Limeharbour and Ability Parkview on Baker Street. These properties will add a further 900 apartments to the group's portfolio. The group has also acquired a unique 40,000 square foot development property. Situated on The Bishop's Avenue in Hampstead, that sits on two acres of land. Under the group's ambitious re-development plans this property will set new standards of luxury for a single house in the capital. It is expected that once completed, the house may command the highest price ever paid for a UK residential property.

Hilton, Liverpool

More recently the group has begun to diversify its portfolio, to include Commercial property, such as Hotels, Offices and Retail properties. Whilst also widening its geographic scope, by acquiring seven Retail Centres throughout Europe. Thereby quickly establishing itself as a major player, within the Hospitality business.

This latest venture has been entirely financed by The

East Weald, The Bishops Avenue   Dunblane Hydro Hotel

Ability Group, after the sale of 5,000 apartments in Central London. One portfolio of properties, of which was sold to Grainger for £205 million in 2006.

Ability has developed close relationships with Hotel Operators. So therefore is looking to acquire both vacant Hotels, to operate under newly installed management, and existing Hotels, that would complement its current portfolio. It is particularly interested in opportunities that enable it to employ its Development and Hotel expertise simultaneously.

The group plans to acquire other Commercial properties, particularly Hotels, in International markets including France, Italy, Spain, Portugal, Eastern Europe and the United States. It intends to increase the value of its portfolio to over £3 billion by 2010.

The Commercial portfolio began with the acquisition of 7 Shopping Centres in Germany, financed by a €100 million credit line from Hypo Real Estate Bank. Ability then acquired its first Hotel, the Hilton Liverpool, from Grosvenor. This is the first five star Hotel in Liverpool, part of the £1 billion re-generation scheme run by Grosvenor, one of the largest property Companies in the UK.

During 2007 the group acquired the Cambridge Garden House Hotel in the heart of Cambridge, from Goldman Sachs. The Hotel features 122 rooms and Ability are planning to develop an extra 58 rooms. This would increase the market share to 32% of the 4 Star Hotels market in Cambridge.

The Group has acquired the Dunblane Hydro Hotel from Starwood Capital and is planning a £10 million facelift for the 206 bedroomed Hotel. As well as re-positioning and re-branding the Hotel, within the luxury Hoteliers market.

Over the years, The Ability Group has also become involved in the acquisition, management and charter of luxury Aircraft and Yachts. The next addition to Ability's fleet will be a $40 million Gulfstream 450. Which, with its transatlantic range, advanced avionics and sumptuous interior, represents the pinnacle of excellence in business Aviation. When delivered in the summer of 2009, the Aircraft will be the first Gulfstream G450 on the UK charter market.

Ability also own a 56 metre, five deck luxury Motor Yacht, which is available for summer charter in the Mediterranean and winter charter in the Caribbean. The most recent addition to the Ability family is the Mangusta 130, a 40 metre Sports Yacht, acquired in 2007.

The Ability Group
Head Office
No 7, Portland Place, London W1 B1PP

T: 020 7580 1234 F: 020 7580 7271
E: info@theabilitygroup.com www.theabilitygroup.com

Anastasia Lodge & Autumn Gardens Care Homes

Anastasia Lodge

The above family business owes its origins to Melis Ourris who came to England in the mid 60's from the Village of Ayios Sergios in Cyprus at the age of 17. He trained and became an Electrician and eventually had his own electrical contracting company. While he was doing this he started a property development company. The next venture was the purchase of Elena Hotel in Islington.

The next stepping stone was in 1990 when he opened a care home in Winchmore Hill, London N21 which he named Anastasia Lodge. It was originally 20 beds in 2005 and extended to 29 beds in 2006. It became a family business where all his family are involved in some way.

In 2006 they purchased Autumn Gardens in Southgate N14. This was an empty rundown Care Home, it now has 40 beds and they are hoping to double the size in the next two years.

Autumn Gardens

The Official Grand opening took place on Sunday October the 5th it was opened by the First Lady of the Republic of Cyprus the President's Wife Elsie Christofias.

The homes are Care Homes for the community mainly the Cypriot community offering them care within a Cypriot environment through food, activities and outings within their culture.

Although the family are involved in the Care Home business they still find time to help the community in many ways. Melis is an active supporter of many community causes, he was previously Chairman of Ayios Sergios Village Association. His wife Anastasia is on the Committee of St Demetrius Church in Edmonton. His son Tony is the owner of Anthony Webb Estate Agents in Palmers Green which was opened by Stephen Twigg in Year 2000 and is a member of the committee of the Green Lanes Business Association. His son Tom owns Essex Lettings supporting housing for vulnerable young people. His daughter Elena is a Solicitor working for Mischon Reyes.

Autumn Gardens
opened by the
First Lady of the
Republic of Cyprus,
Elsie Christofias
in 2008.
Present in the photo
are Teresa Villiers MP,
Melis Ourris, family
and guests

Anastasia Lodge
10-14 Arundel Gardens
London N21 3AE

Tel: 020 8886 1034
Fax: 020 8886 1034
Email: info@anastasialodge.com
Web: www.anastasialodge.com

Autumn Gardens
73 Trent Gardens
London N14 4QB

Tel: 020 8344 2600
Fax: 020 8344 2610
Email: info@autumn-gardens.com
Web: www.autumn-gardens.com

DALSA Corporation

DALSA Corporation is an international high performance semiconductor and electronics company that designs, develops, manufactures and markets digital imaging products and solutions, in addition to providing specialized water foundry services.Products include image sensor components; electronic digital cameras; vision processing hardware components. Their products are vital components in equipment for manufacturing machines for semiconductor foundries, automated machines for manufacturing electronic components and boards, digital x-ray equipment, DNA based laboratory test equipment, industrial automated manufacturing systems, professional photography, HDTV cameras, and many other industrial applications.

DALSA was founded in Waterloo, Ontario, Canada in 1980 by imaging pioneer Dr. Savvas Chamberlain, Born in Dhikomo, Cyprus, Dr. Chamberlain pursued his university studies in England he obtained his first degree from North London Polytechnic in London, and M.Sc. and Ph.D. degrees from Southampton University, U.K.

He is highly regarded as a pioneer in the field of digital imaging. He has published more than 150 papers in scientific journals in the area of CCDs, MOSFET's and silicon semiconductor devices and has authored and co-authored more than 20 patents. In 1999, he was awarded the position of Distinguished Professor Emeritus for his 25-year contribution to the University of Waterloo. He received the Ernst & Young 2003 Ontario Entrepreneur of the Year award for the Technology and Communications industry segment, and in 2004 was awarded the Automated Imaging Association Life Time Achievement Award for World Industry Leadership in imaging. In 2007 Dr. Chamberlain accepted the Premier's Catalyst Award for Lifetime Achievement in Innovation from Ontario Premier and Minister of Research and Innovation Dalton McGuinty at the inaugural Premier's Innovation Awards.

Dr. Chamberlain capitalized DALSA in November 1984 and went public on the Toronto Stock Exchange (TSX: DSA) in May 1996. The company has grown into a world industry leader in digital imaging and semiconductor technology, employing approximately 1000 people world-wide with sales revenue running at approximately $200 million per annum. Sales offices across North America as well as in Germany, Japan and China support an international distribution network serving more than 40 countries.

DALSA Digital Imaging offers the widest range of machine vision components in the world. From industry-leading image sensors through powerful and sophisticated cameras, frame grabbers, vision processors and software to easy-to-use vision appliances and custom vision modules, our innovative technology helps give you competitive advantage in your imaging application, whatever it may be.

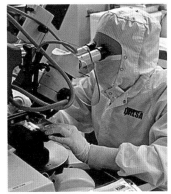

In 2005, DALSA acquired Coreco Imaging. DALSA began offering innovative vision processing hardware and software and smart cameras, elegantly complementing its traditional sensors and cameras.

Mission
To grow profitably the revenue of their company to $500 Million dollars by end of 2010.

DALSA in the Community
At DALSA they believe that their associates and technology are their strengths. In tune with these strengths, their corporate donations focus on **improving the community** as well as **promoting technological advancement.** DALSA supports a variety of worthy causes in the Waterloo Region, where their head office and the majority of their associates are located, helping to make it a better place to live. To promote technological advancement DALSA sponsors a research chair at the University of Waterloo.

Arts and community
DALSA is an active supporter of the cultural arts in the Waterloo Region, including the Kitchener-Waterloo Symphony and Opera. DALSA has sponsored a number of concerts including Madame Butterfly. DALSA also recognizes and participates in helping the underprivileged in the community.

Contact DALSA
DALSA is headquartered in Waterloo, Ontario, Canada, with US operations in Colorado.
We have sales offices in Europe and Asia, plus a worldwide network of representatives and agents to serve you efficiently. Links to maps and directions are listed below.

CORPORATE OFFICES

DALSA Waterloo
605 McMurray Road, Waterloo,
Ontario, Canada
N2V 2E9
Tel: 519 886 6000
Fax: 519 886 8023

DALSA Montreal
7075 Place Robert-Joncas
Suite #142
St. Laurent, Quebec
Canada, H4M 2Z2
Tel: 514 333 1301
Fax: 514 333 1388

DALSA Billerica
700 Technology Park Drive
Billerica, MA
USA, 01821
Tel: 978-670-2000
Fax: 978-670-2010
Email: Sales.Americas@dalsa.com

DALSA Europe
Breslauer Str. 34
D-82194 Gröbenzell (Munich)
Germany
Tel: +49 - 8142 - 46770
Fax: +49 - 8142 - 467746
Email: Sales.Europe@dalsa.com

DALSA Asia Pacific
Ikebukuro East 13F
3-4-3 Higashi Ikebukuro, Toshima-
ku, Tokyo, Japan
Tel: +81 3 5960 6353
Fax: +81 3 5960 6354
Email: Sales.Asia@dalsa.com

DALSA Eindhoven
High Tech Campus 27 (M/S 14)
5656 AE Eindhoven
The Netherlands
Tel: +31 40 2599000
Fax: +31 40 2599005

DALSA Semiconductor
18, boul. de l'Aéroport
Bromont, Québec
Canada , J2L 1S7
Tel: 450-534-2321
 or 1-800-718-9701
Fax: 450-534-3201
Email: sales@dalsasemi.com

Erotica Limited

Savvas Christodoulou arrived in the UK with his mother, father, sister and brother from their native Cyprus at the tender age of just 9 years old – not being able to speak a word of the English language. Savvas had to adapt to the UK fast and it is this inherent ability to acclimatize to different environments that has assisted Savvas in adjusting to a range of different business challenges and succeeding in such a variety of entrepreneurial opportunities over the past 30 years or so.

Savvas gained his first taste of the English education system by way of attending Holloway Boys School and thereafter further chance to express his ability at Stratford Grammar School. By 1970 Savvas had been admitted to the London School of Economics where he succeeded in gaining an honours degree in Economics specialising in Accounting & Finance. TOUGH-TALKING businessman Savvas Christodoulou has come a long way since graduating from the London School of Economics back in 1974.

From there a successful career with one of the top firms of City Accountants following culminating by 1978 in Savvas being admitted to the Institute of Chartered Accountants in England and Wales.

However auditing simply did not provide the breadth of challenges that Savvas was seeking and soon after qualifying Savvas quickly found a role as Chief Accountant with the renowned Rock Band Pink Floyd. There were 33 companies under the umbrella of Pink Floyd Music Limited; the Group operated a diverse range of activities and not all aligned to music. Touring with the Band on their US Tour as well as witnessing the coming together of The Wall Album were just a couple of a wide range of experiences Savvas gained whilst working with the Floyd.

However, having gained first hand knowledge at being at the sharp end of industry, the lure of being in business for himself was too strong and Savvas' next major business move was to own and run a Greek Tour Operator "Twelve Islands" which specialised in providing inclusive holidays to the Dodecanese group of islands in the Aegean. In 1980 at the inception of Twelve Islands the business contracted a modest 30 seats a week to Rhodes and Kos from London Gatwick – providing holiday makers that personal touch of service together with a specialised knowledge of the area, something Savvas had gained personally whilst working as a Tour Guide in his holidays whilst at University.

Twelve Islands quickly expanded, by 1987 whole planes were being chartered and Twelve Islands was one of just a few leading tour operators to this idyllic area of Greece.

Not content with having one success story behind him, almost simultaneously with the exciting growth of Twelve Islands, he is also now pioneering overseas property development, headed by his 57 year old brother Giannis, in the Greek Dodecanese Islands, his 27 year old son Pavlos successfully launched a multi million pound property development business this year in Dubai, as well as continuing with major UK projects. Savvas turned his eye to property originally by starting to develop residential care homes culminating in him being the largest operator of Residential Care Homes for the elderly in the London Borough of Havering. The same period also witnessed an aggressive building plan of holiday homes in Rhodes, Kos, Symi and Leros – all adding to the maestro's worth!

Still concurrently Savvas expressed his full entrepreneurial flare by Operating a bar and night-clubs in Havering, ultimately expanding into North London with the Operation of Club UN, which was voted in 1996 as the Best Club of the Year by Kiss FM. His portfolio boasted a bar and five night clubs. The nightclub is something that Savvas has continued to be involved in despite selling off the majority of his ownerships to make way for major Town developments. By this time Savvas had sold the Twelve Islands Tour Operation to Owners Abroad – now the First Choice Holiday Group – partly in order that he could dedicate his time and energy into what was going to be his biggest challenge yet – EROTICA!!

The creation of Erotica Limited, the first company in the UK ever to be granted a Sex Establishment Licence for the purpose of holding a public exhibition of erotic material has developed into an extraordinary success story with the brand gaining recognition across all genres in the UK. Between 1997, when it was conceived and 2007 there have been 14 Erotica Shows in the UK, eleven at London Olympia and three at the G-Mex, Manchester. Erotica 2007 at  Olympia London attracted 80,000 visitors. Today Erotica is the largest attended adult lifestyle exhibition in the UK with over 250 exhibitors and such star attractions as Dita Von Teese appearing regularly as part of the amazing stage show that supports the event.

The Brand doesn't stop there! There is an Erotica Membership scheme, Erotica Events and parties, a Winter Ball and an Erotica Website that attracts over 20 million hits in the month of November. The Erotica Brand continues to develop from strength to strength; a number of TV opportunities are currently under negotiation and the 2008 Erotica promises to break even more records.

If all that wasn't enough Savvas still found time in 2001 to change the use to "residential" of one of his business properties with a development value of £30m it was sold to a major property developer.

Back to Erotica and in 2002 Savvas successfully launched the Adult Industry's very first trade association the "Association of Adult Trades and Services". Somewhat inevitably Savvas was also appointed Chairman of the Association and remained so for three years.

Still not content to rest on his Laurels, in 2004 Savvas purchased a freehold site adjacent to one of his properties in Romford High Street with a 25 year lease forming a two-acre site in Romford Town Centre. More property deals followed most notable of which was when Savvas negotiated a joint venture with the Mayor for a two-acre residential development with a sales value in excess of £200m. Even more property deals followed, success followed success – just the numbers got bigger and bigger.

Today Savvas still is actively involved in the property market, he travels extensively having homes in many countries across the world.

Savvas dedicates some of his free time to assisting Charities especially those from his home area in the London Borough of Havering.

Savvas is not seeking to retire just yet, rather emulate his first industry employers Pink Floyd and carry on building "another brick in the wall"

Mr Christodoulou has worked hard to get where he is today. From bars and nightclubs to property development and exhibitions, he has learned the trade from the bottom upwards. From a humble Cypriot lad born in Strovolos who arrived at a young age from the Cypriot shores, he has put his stamp on the UK by becoming an entrepreneur in the truest sense.

Erotica UK
Secrets House, 26-44 North Street, Romford, Essex RM1 1BH

T: 01708 768000   F: 01708 768918
E: info@erotica-uk.com
www.erotica-uk.com

Global Foods (NSW) Ltd

Global foods Ltd is a family owned and operated business which began its operations in 1978 in Sydney, Australia.

The Company began operations out of one single warehouse open for retail and wholesale trade with two employees delivering goods to smaller retail outlets after hours to keep up with demand. Today Global Foods operates from premises in excess of 12,000 sq metres to ensure prompt delivery of goods to Australia's leading supermarket chains, independent supermarket chains, independent supermarkets and other retail outlets.

Global foods deals with many Australian and internationally renowned brands across a broad range of products. Global Foods imports some of the largest and most well known Greek brands, including Dodonis Greek Feta, the world's best Misko pasta and Loumidis Coffee both market leaders in Greece, as well as Yiotis desserts and many other grocery lines. Global foods is one of the largest importers of Greek olives and olive oils in Australia and its range covers all sizes and varieties.

In addition to the highest quality Greek olives, Global foods also imports a range of Spanish olives, including black sliced and green stuffed.

In July 2007 the Global foods family expanded its operations by taking over the already successful business of Galaxy imports, thus broadening its product range into the beans and nuts industry.

Today the Global Foods/Galaxy Imports family have over 30 employees who help to provide quality service and products to customers throughout New South Wales, Australia as well as interstate.

Global Foods(NSW) Pty Ltd
Galaxy Imports(NSW) Pty Ltd
114 Christina Road
Villawood
NSW 2163 Australia

Tel: 02 9723 5066
Fax: 02 9723 5044
Email: sales@galaxyglobalfoods.com.au

www.cyprusairways.com

Hornsey Agencies

Hornsey Agencies has been established since 1958, and has become as synonymous to Crouch End as the clock tower. They are an independent firm of estate agents with over 40 years experience of selling and letting residential and commercial properties in the North London area.

Hornsey Agencies provide to the following service:
- They prepare full particulars of your property for circulation to all prospective tenants.
- Advertise your property on two nationwide web sites, local newspapers and other publications.
- Obtain and carefully scrutinise essential references.
- Collect an advance rental payment and further deposit against possible dilapidations.
- Prepare a professionally drafted Tenancy Agreement with relevant notices to include any particular requirements regarding your property.
- Draw up an inventory if required.

Hornsey Agencies historically have had a large commercial base. They are now able to give more specialist advice on the sales, lettings and acquisitions of all types of property; including freehold, retail, office, industrial, investment and development sites and premises.

With a mixed management portfolio of commercial and residential properties, every client is important and we ensure our professional advice is coupled with a friendly and attentive service.

They offer a full range of services to their clients including;
- Acquisitions and disposals.
- Rent reviews and lease renewals.
- Management; rent collection and maintenance.
- General property consultancy.

Much of their work is concentrated within North London. However their specialist expertise extends over a wider geographical area and we undertake work outside these boundaries when needed.

Hornsey Agencies is one of the main providers of the private sector leasing to a number of Local Authorities and Housing Associations. They can arrange leases for terms of 3, 5 and 10 years. They provide a service second to none and ensure that we actively manage all our residential properties.

They are well aware of the difficulties faced by Housing Associations and Local Authorities alike and we have therefore devised a bespoke management process specifically for short term housing management. They have a dedicated in house team including property managers, caretakers, maintenance operatives and a finance controller ensuring the best possible service both to landlords and tenants.

The company has historically had a reputation of being one of North London's first estate agents. Building on experience they have adopted new computerised systems to aid us in our management of an extensive portfolio with the majority of our landlords having been with us in excess of 10 years.

They have the professionalism to manage both commercial and residential properties and with an in house surveying department we can provide expert advice on all matters relating to the property.

Comprehensive property management service includes:
Collecting rents and directing them to you or your bank on a monthly or quarterly basis.
- Remit on your behalf various bills, rates, insurance etc.
- Undertake quarterly inspections on your behalf to ensure the property is being adequately maintained.
- Check tenants into the property and arrange vacation at the end of the agreement.
- Supervise inventory check on vacation by tenants.
- Undertake repairs/maintenance on your behalf.
- Their commission rate is based on the term of the contract.

They pride ourselves on meeting our clients' needs and providing a high quality service. Having been in North London for over 40 years we have extensive knowledge in the residential market, specifically in Crouch End and surrounding areas. They have clients, investors and first time buyers who are constantly looking for properties. With their extended relationship with councils and Private Sector Leasing can guarantee our investors good yields on their investment.

Hornsey Agencies strive to employ professional and friendly staff. They advise on all aspects of the property cycle. Starting with site/property acquisition, planning and development advice through to sales and lettings and finally to property management. This all encompassing service relates to both residential and commercial sectors of the property market including one off flats, houses, shops, offices, warehouse space and moreover the management of large blocks of flats and commercial properties.

Their substantial client list and the prominent location of our office provide a constant source of new enquiries. Therefore they are in need of new properties in your area to meet current demand. As part of our professional package, we offer free market appraisals to give you an accurate and unbiased value of your property.

Hornsey Agencies
7 Topsfield Parade, Crouch End Broadway, London N8 8PR

Telephone: 0208 348 1111 or 0208 348 2545   Fax: 0208 348 5902
Email: enquiries@hornseyagencies.com

Joannou & Paraskevaides Group

Stelios Joannou

George Paraskevaides

When in World War II Britain needed a swift extension to the runway at Nicosia airport to cater for allied bombers charged with destroying Hitler's fuel depots in Romania, the colonial authorities in Cyprus turned to a local construction company. Given the deadline, it had seemed a mission impossible. But the British military were confident that J&P, named after its co-founders, Stelios Joannou and George Paraskevaides, could do the job. The Company was already involved in upgrading the facilities and infrastructure of British military bases on the island as part of the war effort and its efficiency and reliability had impressed. The vital runway was completed on time. J&P, established in 1941, went on to play a key role in developing the island's early infrastructure but by the time Cyprus won independence in 1960, the company's size, ambition and dynamism inevitably meant it would seek new challenges abroad. The company cut its teeth overseas in Libya in the early 1960s, first with projects at the British Base of El Adem, followed by housing projects for the Government and civil works projects for international oil companies. Having proved its mettle in these difficult desert conditions, J&P was ready in 1969 to expand operations to the Arab states of the Arabian Gulf. It was a timely move. The exploitation of the region's oil spawned a 15 year construction boom in which J&P played a leading role. It built mountain roads and desert highways, bridges and flyovers, airports, luxury hotels, hospitals, palaces and whole townships, with contacts in **Saudi Arabia, Oman, the United Arab Emirates, Iraq, Algeria, Ethiopia, Egypt, Qatar and Jordan.** J&P is still heavily involved in Libya, specialising in oil-gas separation plants. It is currently working in 10 different oil fields there, spanning a distance of 2,000 kilometres. Today, J&P has a global reach as one of the biggest companies of its kind in the world, employing 16,000 people and with regional offices in London, Athens, Nicosia and Dubai. Through the years, the company gained rightfully a reputation for top quality work – completing projects on time and on budget. J&P International is ranked today among the top 30 building contractors in the world according to the ENR (Engineering News Record) magazine. *"Human resources are our major asset," says Mr Paraskevaides. "Cypriot technicians are tough workers and they are the backbone of the company. They can endure odd and difficult environments and they have a drive for good quality work."* Oil and gas projects account for around 30 per cent of J&P's turnover, but it is active in all areas of construction including airports, hotels, hospitals, roads and highways, residential homes sports facilities, dams & irrigation projects To name but a few from a long list of completed projects are the Al Bustan Palace Hotel in Oman, Doha Intercontinental Hotel in Qatar, the Al Safa Interchange, Dubai Ring Road and the Emirates Engineering Centre in Dubai Airport, in the United Arab Emirates, the Lahore International Airport in Pakistan, built in a record two-and-a-half years, The King Fahd International Airport in Dammam, Saudi Arabia. The Queen Alia International Airport in Amman Jordan is one of the most recent projects awarded to J&P.

In recent years J&P has had sizeable contracts in Greece, its springboard into Europe where the company is relishing the fresh opportunities that came with Cyprus's accession to the EU. Major projects for the Athens 2004 Olympics were completed ahead of time. The Company had also a leading part in the consortiums that built the Rion-Antirion Road Bridge over the Gulf of Corinth, and the Attiki Odos, two of the most significant infrastructure projects in Greece. J&P AVAX S.A a member company of the Group is now building highways in Poland and infrastructure projects in Albania. The Company is also active in the Hospitality Sector, with holdings in the Athens Intercontinental Hotel, and through YES chain of hotels, whose flagship is the Semiramis hotel in Kifissia, Athens.

In Cyprus J&P is also well known for its generous charity work in the local community. The George and Thelma Paraskevaides Foundation, for instance, paid for more than 1200 children to receive medical care in the US in the past decade. J&P has also established a state-of-the art kidney transplant centre in Nicosia, the only one of its kind in the world that offers

Al Bustan Palace Hotel, Muscat

Allama Iqbal International Airport, Lahore, Pakistan

Doha InterContinental Hotel, Qatar

a free service to those with limited means. Some 800 operations have so far been performed. The Christos Steliou Ioannou Foundation meanwhile is a model center offering high standard specialised programs and services to adults, with moderate and mild mental handicap from all over Cyprus, while the late Mr. Joannou was also one of the founders of a rehabilitation centre for young people with drug problems.

J&P UK Representative Office
16 Hanover Street, London W1S 1YL

Tel: +44(020)7462 5000   Fax:+ 44 (020)7493 0059
Email:london@jandp.org

Leventis Group

Anastasios Leventis with Archbishop Makarios

Anastasios G Leventis was born in December 1902 in the Cypriot mountain village of Lemythou. The earliest records of his family dates back to the 18th century when a young ancestor traveled to the Peloponnese to join in the abortive 1770 uprising against Ottoman rule.

At the end of the First World War the young Anastasios, determined to improve his education and prospects, travelled to visit his elder brother, George, who was already in Egypt and from there took ship to Marseilles, where he first found work and then completed his commercial education at the Ecole Superieure de Commerce in Bordeaux. Through a Marseilles contact he found employment with an Anglo-Greek Manchester-based company in a rural part of south-eastern Nigeria in 1920 and, two years later, with a British company, also based in Manchester, as the manager of their branch in Abeokuta in the south-west of Nigeria.

Anastasios Leventis was, above all, a dynamic and inspired man of business; his employers, G.B. Ollivants, recognized this at an early stage; by 1928 he was Deputy General Manager in Nigeria and, in 1929, at the age of 26, he was transferred to Accra, capital of the Gold Coast (now Ghana), to take over as General Manager of the company's business in that country and in Ivory Coast and Togo. The Gold Coast was the most advanced of the British colonies in West Africa and already had an embryonic system of local self-administration, with a Legislative Council at its apex. Anastasios Leventis was chosen by the commercial community as a member of the Legislative Council to represent its interests. He also served as Chairman of the Accra Chamber of Commerce.

In the 1930's Anastasios Leventis left to form his own company, A.G. Leventis & Company Limited, joined by George Keralakis and, a little later, by Christodoulos Leventis, Anastasios' younger brother.

The new company, although established at the height of the depression, made rapid progress and soon had branches in all parts of the Gold Coast; in 1942 Christodoulos moved to Nigeria to set up branches.

By the time of his death in October 1978, it was one of the largest enterprises and one of the two largest employers in Nigeria and was on the point of expanding into other parts of the world. They now own Nigerian bottling Company (NBC) has 15 Factories and 90 Depots located throughout Nigeria. In the early 80s, Leventis took up the Franchise of Coca Cola in Europe (Greece) and they expanded into Eastern Europe. Now the Leventis Coca Cola business under the umbrella of CCHBC is operating in 28 countries and is the 3rd biggest bottler of Coca Cola in the world. They also own Frigoglass Group: Due to the difficulty in some essential materials for its operation, NBC embarked on vertical integration whereby they created manufacturing facilities for Glass bottles, Plastic containers, Crowns, PET and Coolers. In 1996 it was decided to separate the manufacturing of packaging materials by the creation of the Frigoglass

Group. AG Leventis Group also owns Leventis Motors who represent Mercedes Benz and Volkswagen in Nigeria the division also provides on site fleet maintenance for big field operators. The Division has Showrooms, spare part stores and workshops throughout Nigeria.

They have formed a partnership with the world leader in diesel engines and power generation, it changes the business landscape. Together, Leventis and Cummins are developing a power generator set manufacturing facility in Lagos, strengthening our engine parts and service capabilities, and bringing an unprecedented commitment to providing world-class products and support in this region. It's a partnership built on a foundation of strength that promises to be part of a brighter tomorrow for Nigeria

Leventis Foods is 51% owned by A. G. Leventis (Nig.) Plc and 49% owned by foreign Technical Partners consisting of Katselis S.A and Alatini S.A. Both of which are members of the Leventis group.

The Company has the largest Bakery in Nigeria, which is a fully automated plant.

In addition to bread, the Company has expanded the product range in 2007, by introducing successfully the new snacks named Meaty-sausage rolls and Hotty-savory pies into the Nigerian market. Before Anastasios Leventis died he provided for the establishment of a foundation to support educational, cultural, artistic and philanthropic causes in Cyprus, Greece and elsewhere. The Foundation formally came into being in May 1979 and was operating on a small scale by the end of the year. The Main areas of the foundations activities in Cyprus, Greece and the rest of the World are to focus to a large extent on culture and education with a special emphasis on the cultural heritage of Cyprus. There has also been an interest in the Cypriot and Greek Community in Britain. As to West Africa where Anastasios Leventis spent his early and middle working years for technical reasons not been able to set up the Leventis Foundation (Nigeria) till 1988 its main activity has been the establishment of agricultural schools in Nigeria specialising in the training of small farmers to improve both productivity, efficiency and environmental sensitivity. This has since been extended to Ghana. The Scholarship programme has consistently been the largest item in the foundations expenditure, the University of Cyprus has been supported in many ways. The Foundation also supports medical research, Grants have been made in support of hospitals and an old peoples home in Cyprus as well as medical care for people in need.

Louisianna Investments

Pantelis Savva

The Family business **Louisianna Investments** foundations go back to the Village of Alethrico in Cyprus where Pantelis Savva was born 8th of April 1936.

At nine years old he left the village to go and live with another family in Larnaca where he found employment in the indoor market in Larnaca. At 15 years old he took the big step of going by boat to London like many fellow Cypriots to seek a better life.

Panteli's first job was as a waiter in Stafford Hotel and continued to do so with various other catering institutions, he met and married Louiza in 1955, who was originally from Famagusta and they had a family of five children, daughter Bobbie and four sons Savva, Mario, Andrew and Philip.

In 1961, he opened a Shoe repair shop in Tufnell Park where the weekly rent was £6.00, over the years he expanded into six shops, as well as repairs they were also selling Shoes and Luggage.

Pantelis Savva started buying Commercial and Residential properties for letting and renting and in 1976, he went into the Hotel business under the name of Louisianna Properties, where at one time he had eight hotel's providing accommodation for the homeless. While these businesses

Andrew, Mario, Savva (seated) and Philip

were expanding, Pantelis was also active within the Cypriot Community as the Chairman of Alethrico Association UK and Anorthosis FC UK and he was well known for his charitable work, he received the Freedom to the city of London in 1985.

Sadly, Pantelis Savva passed away at the age of 53 in 1989.

He left his family in good stead, the companies are now a family affair run by his son's Savva, Mario, Andrew and Philip. The sons have carried on their father's legacy and have diversified into other fields of business. They have invested in Banking, Luxury Car retailers, Commercial properties and development. They have followed in their father's beliefs by continuing to support charities, Schools, Churches and local sports. Since 1994 providing outreach support for 15-18 year olds for independent living. Bobbie is also involved in charitable work and is the main driving force behind the Eleni Pericleous Trust Fund which raises monies for leukaemia research.

Head Office
67 Arlington Road, London N14 5BB

Tel: 020 8211 3663
Fax: 020 8211 3662
Email: louisianaprop@btconnect.com

Congratulations on
producing the first-ever
Greek Cypriot Who's Who
Worldwide

Oak Insurance Services

Oak Insurance Services was formed in 1995 by the two partners Andrew Gavas and Kiran Meisuria. Andrew was born in Sydney, Australia of Cypriot origin and Kiran was born in Kenya of Indian origin. They started in the Florentia Village and within a year moved on to new offices in Haringey. In 2005 operations continued from their own premises in Enfield where they remain today.

They have grown to become a multi line Insurance Consultancy offering, Business, Commercial Policies, Let Properties, Property Portfolios, Tenant Reference, Liabilities and Professional Indemnity Covers, Home and Motor Insurance.

The customer service provided is as one would expect and appreciate. Oak Insurance are particularly proud of the relationships that they maintain with their Clients. They provide a large variety of cover within their customer base which ranges from Sole Proprietor to Multi National Companies. Clients are guided through the maze of Insurance wordings and help is always at hand particularly when potential 'Claim' incidents may arise.

Customer priorities include:
✔ Identifying Risk Exposures
✔ Negotiating Risk Management Solutions with clients
✔ Arranging Insurance Protection where appropriate.
✔ Will accompany Insurer Surveyors to customer premises to ensure a fair solution
✔ Liaise with Loss Adjusters, Surveyors, Architects and Solicitors on your behalf
✔ Arranging Local Papers for overseas projects

O A K
INSURANCE
SERVICES

OAK HOUSE
268 Willow Road, Enfield EN1 3AR

Tel: 020 8367 5000
Fax: 020 8367 5600
Email:ois@oakinsurance.co.uk

Introducing...

When you place your business with The Press, as distinguished printers we guarantee a level of service and quality that is second to none. Established in 1991, we offer economy, integrity, trust and ethical work practices, attributes that we pride ourselves on and constantly strive to maintain.

Your Partner In Print

Our *IN–HOUSE* services include a fully automated CTP Reprographics Department, multi-press Print Room, finishing and delivery.

When a job comes into our care, we constantly monitor the quality and speed of production throughout the process ensuring the smooth running of every project undertaken. We are well equipped to be your ideal partner in print and our sound financial structure ensures the most competitive quotes in the market.

Plant List

Pre Press

Fully Automated B1 CTP (Computer to plate)

B1 Digital Proofing

Sheet Fed Presses

6 Colour Speedmaster 102 CD (B1)

10 Colour Speedmaster 102
(B1, Perfecting 5/5 or as straight 10 colour)

Finishing

Polar 115 Guillotine
(with fully automated lift, jogger and stacker)

MBO folders x 2

Muller Martini Presto saddle sticher

Heidelberg Cylinder (cutting and creasing up to B2)

Bench work, drilling, shrink wrapping, ram bundling
and delivery

Bambos Charalambous started the print company 17 years ago in 1991. From modest beginnings Bambos has grown The Press to its present day form through hard work, sound financial control and vision. The Press now serves an array of customers ranging from multi nationals such as Syngenta, T-Mobile, and HSBC to local businesses and designers. Located in North London it is ideally placed to serve customers both within the heart of London and nationwide due to the proximity of the M25.

Thomas Anthony Group of Companies

Thomas Anthony Mortgage and Financial Services Ltd was formed in 1997 and quickly found a niche market that is still served today and skilfully expanded on. They are independent financial advisors and provide financial advice in general for their clients. This includes commercial/business finance and personal loans. They are also in a position to recommend products that protect the debt in the event of death, critical illness, accident, sickness and unemployment.

Thomas Anthony services do not just centre on raising finance, independent advice on investments and savings including bonds, unit trusts and ISA's is also available. The business growth in this area has seen the establishment of Thomas Anthony Wealth Management Ltd in October 2004. The Company has taken the issue of investment advice to the next level and incorporated the issues of pensions, inheritance tax planning, will writing and corporate financial planning. In an effort to expand their services to cover a wider geographical client base Thomas Anthony Financial Services Ltd was formed in April 2004 and operates from its base in the West Midlands.

Over the years the Directors of Thomas Anthony Group of Companies have built a great personal and professional relationship with the professional people that attend their regular seminars and with many others in the future.

Director Profiles

Nicholas Antoniou MLIA. Aff. SWW

Nick commenced his career in the financial services sector with Prudential in 1982 subsequently being promoted to senior financial manager and then area manager. He then joined Halifax as a financial advisor dealing in all areas of financial planning and following a successful spell there he moved to Barclays Private Clients Premier sector. Nick has also advised small businesses and director/shareholders on a personal and corporate basis at Barclays. He joined Thomas Anthony Wealth Management in 2004 as a director from St James Place. He now specialises in Inheritance Tax planning and savings & investments he holds the requisite financial planning Mortgage advice and regulated Equity release certificates and is also an affiliate member of the society of will writers.

Tony Antoniou FPC CeMAP CF Dip

Tony has over 30 years experience in financial services starting as a trainee with Prudential where he worked for 8 years before setting up as a financial adviser independently in 1985 until 1997 when he co founded Thomas Anthony Mortgage and Financial Services also Director of Thomas Anthony Wealth Management Ltd and Thomas Anthony Financial Services Ltd which is based in Birmingham.

Tony is well known within the Cypriot Community through his involvement in Football he is the President of Omonia Youth in the UK.

Vassos Koni MBA ACIB CeFA CeMAP CeRER Aff SWW

Vassos has been involved in financial services for 25 years. He worked with the Bank of Cyprus for 20 years moving to the positions of Branch Manager and then Area Manager. He is also an Associate member of the Chartered Institute of Bankers and has an MBA from Henley Management College.Vassos joined the Thomas Anthony Group in 2004 as the main director of Thomas Anthony Financial Services Ltd based in Birmingham and also holds the requisite equity release certificates. He is also a member of the society of will writers .

Tom Theodorou FPC CeMAP

Tom has been involved in the financial services industry for over 20 years focusing predominantly in the mortgage market and has built up a wealth of experience from over 15 years as a legal & General Appointed Representative.

Tom co founded Thomas Anthony Mortgage & Financial Services in 1997 and is also a director of their associated companies Thomas Anthony Wealth Management and Thomas Anthony Financial Services and Thomas Anthony Financial Solutions.

For more information regarding Thomas Anthony Group of Companies and their range of services visit

London Office		**Birmingham Office**
Lonburry House		417a Birmingham Road
495 Green Lanes		Sutton Coldfield
Palmers Green		West Midlands
London N13 4BS		B72 1AU

Tel: 020 8886 5500	Tel: 0121 382 4870
Fax:020 8886 8004	Fax:0121 382 4919
Email:enquiries@thomasanthony.com	Email:info@thomasanthony.com

or Visit the website www.thomasanthony.com

Travelmania

THE COMPANY THAT TOOK THE COMPILER OF THE BOOK MICHAEL YIAKOUMI ROUND THE WORLD IN ONE YEAR.

John Neophytou, Anna Papaphoti and Andrew Neophytou

The idea of Travelmania came from the mind of Andrew Neophytou, whose passion in life revolved around airplanes flying and holidaying in the island of Cyprus where his parents where from. Andrew was at the time employed at Cyprus Airways and had also worked previous to that at one of the first Greek travel agents, "Homatas".

Andrew's younger brother, John, was at the time at college and was indecisive as to what career to pursue, so it was Andrews idea to get John to take the same diploma in Travel and Tourism and to eventually have some sort of career in travel.

John passed his exams with flying colours and got a job straight away at Apollo Travel based in Camberwell, South London. He then went on to Cyprair Holidays which was the tour operating arm of Cyprus Airways.

At the same time, John and Andrews younger first cousin, Anna Papaphotis, had also become interested in the same diploma. With Andrew and Johns help she became one of the youngest people in the UK to graduate at the age of 16. Anna than went on to work at the established Hercules Travel in Wood Green, North London.

Now, with three people in the same family all with the same qualification, it wasn't long before the cousins united and had the idea to start up a travel agency for themselves. After an extensive search, the name Travelmania was agreed upon. The reasoning for this was the enthusiasm of the founders and the fact that the name did not limit the destinations that the office would offer. Making it a worldwide travel agents. Another family member, our cousin Andrew Anastasiou, was called upon to design our company logo.

Fortunately, Anna's father, Nicos Papaphotis, was in a good position to help. Nicos was successfully trading as a clothing manufacturer. His factory was located in Holloway Road, Islington, and was then producing garments for the likes of Chelsea Girl now known as River Island. All three approached him and it was agreed that part of the clothes factory would be converted in to a small shop front.

In January 1988 the Company was incorporated with all four members of the family being equal shareholders, and on March 24th, 1988 Travelmania opened its doors to the public. Within the first year, the company obtained its ABTA and IATA licences. Initially only John and Anna were working full time and at minimal wages. Nicos had let them have the office on a rent free basis to allow the business to grow. All investments in the company came from Nicos who was now the main guarantor, Johns parents, Anna and Nicos Neophytou and Andrew Neophytou's own personal savings.

In 1991, Andrew left his job at the airlines to come and help at the office as it was now at the point where all hands were needed. The company now employed at least 5 full time members of staff. Travelmania grew from strength to strength, and in 1992, it obtained its own ATOL license to allow the company to operate as a tour operator this subsequently lead to the launched of "Cyprus Elite". This was a high end of the market product, selling only 5 star accommodation in Cyprus as package holidays.

In 1998, Nicos Papaphotis decided to retire and sell his factory. Travelmania bought one of the properties from Nicos and relocated the offices 2 doors away. John was made Managing Director and has steered the company from strength to strength. In 2007, the Company was nominated and was a finalist in the category of small offline agency of the year at the Agent Achievement Awards.

In 2008, the Company celebrated its 20th Anniversary with a fabulous party at the Kensington Roof Gardens along with its co-hosts, The Four Seasons Hotel Limassol, and the Cyprus Tourist Organization. Travelmania was honoured with an award from Cyprus Airways in recognition for the long standing good relationship that the two companies had formed over the years and also an award from the Four Seasons Hotel to commemorate their 15 year relationship.

The Company's success can be put down to a number of factors, the hard work and dedication of the staff and directors of the company, the guidance from the company's accountant, Chris Pieri from Kallis & Partners, a regular loyal customer clientele. Travelmania overall outlook on business is to try and offer the best service it can offer and a wealth of knowledge of destinations, climates and advice plus an unbiased view. The interest of the client is at the heart of every sale. If they feel that a holiday is inappropriate, they would rather forgo the sale than have a dissatisfied customer. With so many forms of sale in the market, including internet, teletext, teleshopping etc, they feel that it is a great achievement to keep the Company growing. They thank all their clientele for all their help and all their staff for they're continued dedication and hard work. Michael Yiakoumi the compiler of the book Greek Cypriots World Wide would also like to thank Travelmania for arranging and organising his trips Worldwide to Australia, Canada, The Arab States, Europe, The Far East, Africa and USA so that this book could be completed.

Travelmania

Travelmania is based at
125 Holloway Road, Islington, London N7 8LT

Tel 020 7700 4844 Fax 020 7609 7179
Email: Enquiries@travelmania.ltd.uk
Web: www.travelmania.ltd.uk

Yianis Group

Four Seasons Hotel, Canary Wharf

The Founder John Christodoulou, the man who fled his homeland of Cyprus in 1974 after the Turkish invasion has done himself proud since then. Leaving school at 16, he trained as a diamond mounter, and at 18 started his own business, taking advantage of a government-sponsored scheme. He saved up to buy his first property, a North London studio flat, and by 1994 he was investing and developing in the property market full-time. He is a premier property developer in urban regeneration. A company that has the expertise and perception to develop passe, defunct buildings into vogue, trendy accommodation for today's lifestyle.

The Yianis Group is now one of the largest private investment and property development companies in the UK. With a dynamic infrastructure and drive for success through sustained growth, they are a name for the present and future... Yianis Christodoulou is the second largest freeholder at London's Canary Wharf with 2m sq. feet of assets there. He was in the news in mid-2006 when he bought the Marriott Hotel in Canary Wharf to include to his Four Seasons hotel collection. Recently he purchased a further two hotels one at Heathrow Airport 11.5 acres with 881 bedroom suites, plus the Manchester Marriot Hotel. Future plans the company is expected to develop 2.2 million square feet of properties consisting of leisure, retail and hotels and should be completed in year 2012 and increase the income of their existing portfolio substantially. Last two years also John has focused his intentions on Europe where he spends most of his time to expand his global ambitions.

Here at Yianis, a team of professionals led by Mr John Christodoulou ensure that the company remains focused on the main philosophy of providing quality, exciting, live and work spaces, which in turn attracts young professionals and blue chip companies to their ever expanding portfolio.

Yianis Air and Yianis shipping his other interests focuses on luxury yachts and planes and will take delivery of a further yacht in the first quarter of 2009 which will be the fastest luxury open yacht ever made and the twelve passengers will be able to have breakfast in Portofino, lunch in Sardinia and dinner in St Tropez same day.

Freehold plot of Yianis group in Canary Riverside

www.yianisgroup.com

Zela Shipping Company Limited

Kyriacos Mouskas

Zela Shipping Company Ltd is a privately owned independent company established in the City of London over 45 years ago with its roots in the international maritime industry. Over the years, the Company has consistently delivered the highest standards of shipping services within its industry.

The Company was formed by Mr. Kyriacos Mouskas senior in 1963. His integrity, strength and natural leadership transformed his vision of Zela Shipping as a thriving family firm into reality. He retired in 1977 leaving the Company in the capable hands of his two sons Zenon and George Mouskas. The family's third generation is also involved in the business with Kyriacos Z. Mouskas having joined the company in 1993 and Antonis Mikellides (son of Zenon's and George's sister) having joined the company in 2002 and most recently Kyriacos G. Mouskas having joined in 2007.

Mr Kyriacos Mouskas senior, founder and architect of Zela Shipping, was born in Cyprus in 1917. He was a man of renowned integrity and strength and a natural leader. At the age of 19, he came to England filled with ambition and dreams. But those early years in a foreign country soon to be at war were testing ones; he learned about hardship, deprivation and endurance. It was not until the end of WWII that the course of his life was set. He joined the Greek Mercantile Marine Service and then the Greek Shipping Co-operation Committee. He simultaneously attended the

Kyriacos Mouskas, Antonis Mikellides, Zenon Mouskas and George Mouskas

City of London College for shipping studies where his remarkable memory and mathematical abilities, for which he was noted and admired, soon distinguished him from his fellow students and made it clear that a prosperous future lay ahead. In 1951 he joined a London shipowning company and broadened his experience until it encompassed all aspects of shipping such as operations, chartering, accounts, insurance and sale and purchase. Four years later in 1955 he was elected a member of the Baltic Exchange. In 1963 he founded Zela Shipping as a shipowning company by purchasing an American Liberty replacement vessel, whilst also being appointed as agent for several other Liberty ships. He dedicated himself entirely to building Zela Shipping, to become one of the leading Greek Shipping Companies in London and Athens, together with his eldest son Zenon and they were later joined by his other son George. Staff, associates and crew have not only profitably participated with the company, but have also been absorbed into the extended Zela family. The respect that Zela Shipping Company enjoys today for its honesty and financial astuteness is directly attributable to Mr Kyriacos Mouskas senior.

Head Office Kenville House

London Office:
Kenville House
Spring Villa Business Park
Edgware, Middlesex, London HA8 7EB

Tel: **020 8099 8099**   Fax: **020 8099 9000**
Email: mail@zelashipping.com

Athens Office:
Seascope Shipping Agency Ltd
70 Vouliagmenis Avenue
16777 - Elliniko, Athens – Greece

Tel: **+30 210 428 3218**   Fax: **+30 210 428 3252**
E-mail: mail@seascopesa.com

Launch of Greek Cypriots in the UK
A Directory of Who's Who –
a star studded event

The Launch of **Greek Cypriots in the UK – A Directory of Who's Who** took place Thursday 2nd February 2006 at the Hellenic Centre in Paddington street London.

The event proved a huge success with over 600 people attending. Guests were greeted with complimentary glasses of wine and food provided by One Stop Co-ordinations and were able to view photos by the late Andy Nicola as well as the logos of the sponsors projected on a large screen.

The evening began with the host actor **Peter Polycarpou** welcoming the guests and congratulating Cypriot tennis player **Marcos Baghdatis** on his success of reaching the final of the Australian Open Tournament throughout the evening he made the crowd laugh with his witty humour.

Peter introduced the first speaker **Joanne Anthony** of Pen Press the publishers of the directory who congratulated the author of the book, Michael Yiakoumi.

Archbishop Gregorios of Thyateira & Great Britain also praised the book and wished the compilers all the best for a future edition.

The Cyprus Consul General **Mr Nicos Christodoulides** gave a special mention to the authors for their hard work and dedication. *"One feels proud when one identifies with a certain community. The directory features at least three generations of Greek Cypriots; the oldest being Mr Sergios Florides who recently celebrated his 103rd birthday."*

From left to right:
Kyriacos Tsioupras
Tony Yerolemou
Janet Paraskeva
Nicos Adonis
Archbishop Gregorios
Lord Adonis
Michael Yiakoumi

Next to speak was special guest **Peter Andre.** The host introduced the singer by saying *"this man was offered a recording contract live on television, went on to have seven top 5 hits, a platinum and gold album in the UK and he was the first Australian artist to debut at No 1 in the UK."*

Followed by a very loud applause from the audience Peter addressed the guests *"good evening yia sas, sas agapo poli. First of all thank you for featuring me in this fantastic book, there's one disappointment though you didn't put me on the front cover,"* he joked.

"I'm proud to be Cypriot, everyone knows that and I'm actually building a home in Cyprus right now so that me, my wife and my children can go and stay there a few months every year. My wife is back there by the way," everyone turned to the upstairs balcony where Jordan seemed to be shying away from the cameras.

He concluded *"thank you very much, sas sevoume ke sas agapo efcharistoume."*

As the press snapped away the host introduced the next speaker former editor of Hello Magazine **Maggie Koumi.**

In her moving speech Maggie spoke about growing up in the UK she advised everyone to talk to their parents and grandparents because *"their experience is so interesting it's unbelievable what you can learn".*

Psychologist **Linda Papadopoulos** followed *"I feel overwhelmed to be here tonight"*, she said. *"As Cypriots I think we know not only about surviving but about adapting and that's precisely why we've gone from everywhere from the Australian Open to revolutionising the airline industry to redeveloping the world of medicine. We have accomplished this because we take pride in our identity. The Directory has bought together not only what we can do as individuals but what we mean as a society. For me a Greek Cypriot is someone who can adapt, someone who is willing to learn, who has pride to themselves and their culture. Thank you so much everybody."*

Peter Andre

Linda Papadopoulos and Peter Polycarpou

Peter Polycarpou then introduced *"someone we all know very well indeed. A Cypriot who has made our lives a bit easier, he's the founder of easy jet, easy internet café, easy rent a car, easy cruise* **Stelios Haji-ioannou** *via video link up."* Stelios sent the following message:

"I was pleasantly surprised when I first saw the book at how many successful Greek Cypriots we have in the UK. I'm someone who was born outside the UK but built my business here. I'm a great believer of people who have the courage to leave their own country and live and work somewhere else. The directory is one of a kind publication and I'm proud to be part of it."

Chief Executive of the Law Society **Janet Paraskeva** highly praised the publication saying *"We have achieved something great together"*.

Lord Andrew Adonis spoke at his amazement of seeing so many Cypriots *"I have never seen such a large congregation of Cypriots since I was about 11 standing outside the Greek Church in Camden Town when Archbishop Makarios came in 1975. I am extremely happy to have my father here with me tonight can I give my congratulations to Michael Yiakoumi: I have never met anybody so dedicated than him putting together a collection of a thousand and a bit profiles is a massive undertaking."*

He joked *"I made the biggest mistake of giving Michael my mobile number, I remember my phone going off while I was in the House of Lords."* *"All of us here tonight are a great example of just how many successful Cypriots we have in the UK"* he concluded.

Mr Kyriacos Tsioupras former editor of Parikiaki and managing director of LGR and co-author of the directory said in his brief speech *"going through this book it is like looking in a mirror showing the Greek Cypriot Community with respect to all those who are mentioned, the real achievers of the Greek Cypriot Community story are mostly the ones that are not in these pages: the fathers, mothers and in many cases the grandparents, who have gone through so many difficulties and so many problems to realise their dream."*

From left to right:
Kyriacos Tsioupras
Janet Paraskeva
Maggie Koumi
Linda Papadopoulos
Michael Yiakoumi

Lord Adonis

The final speaker **Michael Yiakoumi** was introduced as a dedicated searcher of Cypriots, he's co-author of the book and the reason why we are all here this evening. In his speech Michael thanked everybody for attending especially those who had travelled from all over the UK and as far as Cyprus. He presented a bouquet and said a special thank you to Sophie Toumazis who turned this directory from an ordinary book into something great.

He also thanked Koulla Anastasi for all her help at the earlier stages of compiling the directory and the family of the late Andy Nicola for allowing them to use his photographs.

He concluded *"I just want to point out that although I have been given a lot of credit for the book it's the people in the book that have made this publication possible and hopefully we can go on from here and publish a new edition. Thank you very much for all your support and attendance"*.

Peter Polycarpou thanked all the speakers and turned to the audience and said *"Im sure in one way and another we have all learnt something more about ourselves. The book is not only about where we come from. Michael you're responsible for giving us a glimpse of ourselves, a kind of incredible look into our own past and in some ways of our future. Thank you"*.

From left to right:
Michael Yiakoumi
Tony Vourou
Stelios Haji-Ioannou
Sophie Toumazis
Maggie Koumi

Scene from the launch at the Hellenic Centre

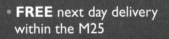
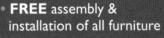

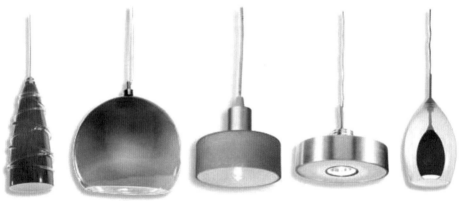

@

ANTONIOU
HAIR & BEAUTY

The Ultimate in Hair and Beauty

Antoniou Salons

16 Orange Street, Canterbury T: +44 (0)1227 456956

21 High St. Ashford T: +44 (0)1233 633171

2 West St. Faversham T: +44 (0)1795 533471

79A Preston St. Faversham T: +44 (0)1795 591867

21 The Borough, Canterbury T: +44 (0)1227 784746

PH Academy

T: +44 (0)1227 784746
T: 44 (0)1795 531867

PH Academy are providers of:

- NVQ Level 2 and 3
- Key Skills
- A1 & A2 Assessors Awards
- V1 Internal Verifyer
- Private courses in hair dressing

www.ahbgroup.co.uk

APOLLONIA
Restaurant & Taverna

376-378 Cranbrook Road, Gants Hill, Ilford, IG2 6HW
Tel: 020 8554 1121   Website: www.theapollonia.co.uk

Importers and Distributors of
Finest Quality Continental Foods

Bevelynn House,
Unit 33 Riverwalk Industrial Park,
Riverwalk Road EN3 7QN
Tel: 020 8805 8558   Fax: 020 8804 5569
Email: main@bevelynn.co.uk

chelepis watson

Chartered Accountants
Registered Auditors

67 Westow Street

Upper Norwood

London SE19 3RW

Telephone: +44 (0)20 8768 6277

Fax: +44 (0)20 8771 4623

office@chelepiswatson.co.uk

www.chelepiswatson.co.uk

A clear view of your world.

Choice

Home

Flavour

Flair

+ 4 magazines

THE CYPRUS
WEEKLY

One weekly newspaper in Cyprus has been your window to the world for almost 30 years. Now that same newspaper is opening a window to an even bigger world. Yours. Get a complete view of fashion, cooking, shopping and home living with our four new weekly magazines. Every Friday with the Cyprus Weekly.

web
theoria

web design | digital media

- web design & development
- flash development
- full hosting - personal support
- 3d animation and after effects
- motion graphics
- interactive presentations
- branding
- search engine optimization
- database development

info@webtheoria.com | www.webtheoria.com

GEORGE THEODOULOU
CONSTRUCTION LTD

91 TRENT GARDENS, SOUTHGATE, LONDON N14 4QB
TEL: 020 8449 9049   MOBILE: 07885 107 571

You owe it to yourself...
Take the best financial advice.

Our History ...
Credible and successful for over 65 years…

Our Knowledge...
Over 85% Qualified Professionals…
Registered to Carry out Audit work…
Registered Training Office…

Our Services...
Offered in a friendly and professional manner, drawing upon our extensive experience and knowledge...

Our Commitment...
Excellence and value for money…

Our Clients...
From all sizes, nationalities, professions, commerce and industry…

Loyalty…
Over 80% of our clients have been with us for more than 20 years…

GOODMAN LAWRENCE & CO.
FOUNDED 1942

CHARTERED
CERTIFIED
ACCOUNTANTS

56A HAVERSTOCK HILL
LONDON NW3 2BH

TEL: +44 (0) 20-7428 1000
FAX: +44 (0) 20-7428 1005

E-MAIL:
info@goodmanlawrence.com
www.goodmanlawrence.com

PRINCIPAL:
DEMETRIOS ZEMENIDES
FCCA, MCIM, MSc, DHP, MCH

OUR REASON FOR BEING IS
TO OFFER THE BEST
SOLUTIONS, AND GIVE OUR
CLIENTS THE FINANCIAL
FLEXIBILITY TO BE MORE
PROFITABLE, THROUGH
THE PROVISION OF SOUND
FINACIAL ADVICE AND
HIGH QUALITY OF SERVICE

Member of the
HAT GROUP OF ACCOUNTANTS

REGISTERED AS AUDITORS
AND REGULATED FOR A RANGE OF
INVESTMENT BUSINESS ACTIVITIES
BY THE ASSOCIATION OF
CHARTERED CERTIFIED
ACCOUNTANTS
ACCA No: 8005588

VAT No: 365 5621 41

honeystone
DESIGN

Unique Graphic Design
Visual Solutions
Branding & Communciation Consultants
Digital Media
Inspirational Promotional Ideas

Honeystone Design uses a blend of creative skills and commercial awareness to create, evolve and revitalise brands to achieve your companies objectives.

Call +357 9909 9185
or email sawas@honeystonedesign.com
to discuss your requirements

Magic Concepts
AMAZING MEDIA

Honeystone Design is the sole authorised agent of Magic Concept & Rubiks promotional products in Cyprus

Magic Concepts
AMAZING MEDIA

Magic Concepts: The first commercial break your customers will thank you for!

Once in hand, always in mind: Inspiring an irresistible urge to play, Magic Concepts objects rise above the flood of information and relieve advertising fatigue with a refreshing sense of wonder. New studies show that multisensory messages with tactile appeal are more engaging and memorable, achieving up to triple the brand recall effect.

The amazing folding action of Magic Concept® makes your message fun, fascinating, and highly memorable.

PROMOTIONAL GIFT AWARD 2007

To arrange a meeting or to find out more please call:
+357 9909 9185 or visit: **www.honeystonedesign.com**

honeystone DESIGN

Mirror Mirror
Bridal Boutiques
LONDON

LINEA RAFFAELLI

INSPIRATIONAL BRIDAL COLLECTIONS AND BESPOKE DESIGN

Mirror Mirror Couture
37 Park Road
Crouch End
N8 8TE
020 8348 2113

By appointment

www. mirrormirror.uk.com

Mirror Mirror Angel
56 Penton Street
Islington
N1 9QA
020 7713 9022

Put a little
Sparkle
in your Event

Onestop Coordinations organises bespoke events for an intimate gathering of friends through to an elaborate production for thousands. Onestop continuously support their clients in the desire to achieve the unexpected through their ability to reinvent a space and understand the important intricacies that create a truly successful event. Their mission is to give a personal and professional service to all, from conception to completion regardless of the project size.

We strive to deliver a quality, creative, tailor-made solution within the required budget and ensure complete satisfaction.

For more information please contact Tony Vourou on **+44 (0)20 8445 6720** or email **info@onestopcoordinations.com**

PARIKIAKI

THE NEWSPAPER OF THE CYPRIOT COMMUNITY IN BRITAIN

Parikiaki 140 Falklands Road, London N8 ONP
Tel: +44 (0) 20 8341 5853 or +44 (0) 20 8341 0751   Fax: +44 (0) 20 8341 6642

natural ingredients   **modern** manufacturing   **traditional** goodness

Tims Dairy Limited • Mopes Farm • Denham Lane • Chalfont St Peter • Buckinghamshire • SL9 0QH
T - +44 (0) 1753 888 380 • F - +44 (0) 1753 893 538 • E - info@timsdairy.co.uk

www.timsdairy.co.uk

A Bridge Opens Up...
...New Opportunities

Visit **www.tiutaplc.com** today or speak to one of our Business Development Managers on **0870 777 7205** to find out how short-term finance could benefit your long-term plans.

The Straight-Talking Bridging Loan Company

VIVENDI ARCHITECTS LLP

FULL RIBA SERVICES PLANNING APPLICATIONS BUILDING REGULATIONS INTERIOR DESIGN MASTER PLANNING

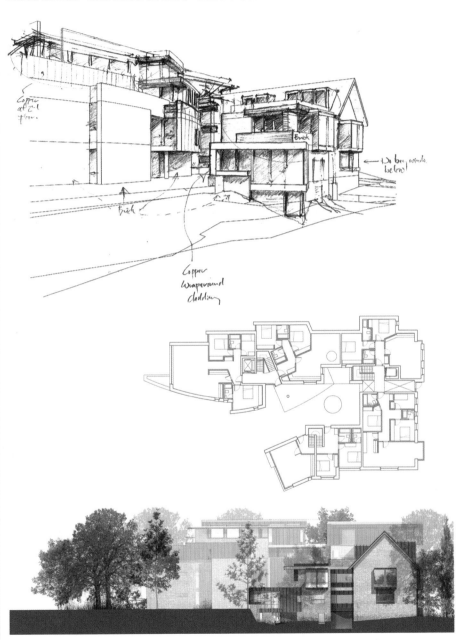

Vivendi Architects LLP, Unit E3U, Bounds Green Industrial Estate, Ringway, London N11 2UD
t/f: +44(0)20 3232 4000 e: info@vivendiarchitects.com w: www.vivendiarchitects.com

BETTER SERVICE : BETTER SPACE : BETTER SECURITY : BETTER VALUE

PERMANENTLY LOW PRICES

Safe and Secure

- 24 hour manned security
- Individually alarmed units with PIN access
- You are the only key holder
- 24 hour CCTV security
- Full insurance cover available

Personal Space

- Are you running out of space at home?
- Are you thinking of moving?
- Why not store your overflow with us - we'll look after anything from a bicycle to a Brontosaurus
- From 10sq ft to as much as you like

Business Space & Office Rentals

- No long-term leases or contracts
- Releases expensive floor or office space when storing such items as stock, stationery or files, office furniture and display equipment
- Manage the space and cost by transferring into the size you need - big or small
- Whatever the nature of your business we have the space

Flexible Short or Long-term Contracts

We have a wide range of units 10 sq ft to 10,000 sq ft. Hire space you need for as long as you need

WE ALSO PROVIDE VAN RENTALS

Restaurant   Office Rental   WE ALSO SELL BOXES, BUBBLE WRAP, TAPE

NO VAT

555 White Hart Lane

HOW TO FIND US:		OPENING HOURS:	
Bus:	W3	Monday - Friday	8 am - 7 pm
Tube:	Wood Green	Saturday	8 am - 6 pm
Rail:	White Hart Lane	Sunday	10 am - 4 pm

ssa
self storage association
United Kingdom

555 WHITE HART LANE
(Near the New River Sports Centre)
0800 597 5000
www.sssuk.com

ARIELLA COUTURE

Cocktail, Evening & Special Occasion wear

sales@ariella.co.uk   www.ariella.co.uk   tel: +44 (0) 20 8800 5777

Ariella Fashions Ltd, Zenith House, 69 Lawrence Road, London, N15 4EY

Greek Business (London) A to Z 2009

Κυκλοφορεί σύντομα το καινούργιο ανανεωμένο τεύχος του 2009

BEST WISHES

FROM

THE LINCOLN GROUP

Dolly Dimple's

Dolly Dimple's is a leading Norwegian pizza restaurant chain founded by Andreas Hatjoullis in 1986.

Dolly Dimples is a chain of restaurants all across Norway known for their tasty pizzas. The restaurants have a young and modern profile and uses only first class ingrediens. The chain is constantly growing and new restaurants opens every year. Some of the restaurants are owned and run by the Head Office, others by independent franchisees.

Company facts (2008):
- 90 restaurants throughout Norway
- Turnover app. € 90 mill
- 1500 employees

Company vision:
"To be perceived as the most professional restaurant chain in Norway with best pizza and best service"

Web: dolly.no
E-mail: dolly@dolly.no
Telephone: +47 51 96 99 00
Address: Dolly Dimple's Head Office/PAM AS,
Luramyrveien 75, N-4313 Sandnes, Norway

WITH YOUR
SundayMail

Lifestyle, events, entertainment
Everything you need to know,
every Sunday

SEVEN

Lefkosia: 24 Vassiliou Voulgaroctonou Street, P.O. Box 21144, 1502,
Tel: 22818585, Fax: 22676385, E mail: mail@cyprus-mail.com

thecypriot.com

Connecting Greek Cypriots around the world

Sport
Sports news from
Cyprus & Greece

News
Daily news from
Cyprus

Entertainment
music, film, literature,
arts, video

Lifestyle
religion, travel,
cooking, property

Business Directory
Greek & Cypriot
businesses around the
world

Online Community
Connect with Greek
Cypriots worldwide

Visit www.thecypriot.com

Aroma Patisseries

424 GREEN LANES,
PALMERS GREEN,
LONDON N13 5PB

TELEPHONE:
020 8886 8083

34 GREEN LANES,
PALMERS GREEN,
LONDON N13 6HJ

TELEPHONE:
020 8889 4324

Δεχόμαστε παραγγελίες
για Γάμους, Ονομαστικές Εορτές, Βαπτίσεις,
Γενέθλια και για οποιεσδήποτε δεξιώσεις.

Andreas & Maria

Philip Christopher

President & CEO, Personal Communications Devices, LLC.

President, Pan Cyprian Association of America

and the International Coordinating Committee Justice for Cyprus

Congratulations

on producing the book

Greek Cypriot Who's Who

Worldwide

Lewis
Charles
Securities

Services include:

Brokerage – UK and International stockbroking service for equities, cfds, spread betting, telephone and online trading

Fund Management – Discretionary fund management in a suite of financial products, including derivatives, FX and Options

Equity Research – Fundamental analysis of small-cap and growth companies

Corporate Finance – Advisory, Pre-IPO fund raising, AIM admissions, primary and secondary fund raising

Foreign Exchange – Money Transfers, Currency Hedging, Travel Currency

Clearing – We provide an outsourced, highly-customised solution to small and medium sized financial institutions in the areas of clearing, settlement and custody

www.lewischarles.com

Tel: +44 (0) 20 7456 9100 Lewis Charles Securities, LCS House, 44 Worship Street, London EC2A 2EA

THE HELLENIC CENTRE

CELEBRATING 15 YEARS—1994-2009

EXHIBITIONS . LECTURES . PARTIES . WEDDINGS .
DINNERS . CHRISTENINGS . PRODUCT LAUNCHES .
CONFERENCES . PRESS EVENTS . CONCERTS

Situated in the heart of fashionable Marylebone, the Hellenic
Centre has a number of versatile spaces to accommodate all
cultural, corporate and private events.
Visit our website to enjoy a full virtual tour of our spaces.

16-18 PADDINGTON STREET . MARYLEBONE . LONDON . W1U 5AS
Main line: 020 7487 5060 . Venue Hire: 020 7463 9834
www.helleniccentre.org . bookings@helleniccentre.org

A Private Company Working in Partnership with the Public Sector

Putting People and Property Together

Dedicated to Lettings and Property Management

A Modern, Stream-lined, Pro-active Company

WE OFFER LANDLORDS:

Comprehensive Professional Service

Free Rent Appraisals

Guaranteed Rents with No Agency Fees and No Void Periods

Prompt Rental Payments

Guaranteed Vacant Possession

Fixed Term Contracts (of between 1-5 years)

Competitive Rates (ex-'Right to Buys' especially welcome)

In-house Maintenance

Regular Property Inspections

More than 22 Years Experience

CALL 020 8482 5511

137 Tottenham Lane · Crouch End · London N8 9BJ
Tel: 020 8482 5511 · Fax: 020 8348 8711
www.smarthousinggroup.com

ΖΟΥΜΕΡΟΣ

ΔΗΜΙΟΥΡΓΙΚΟΣ

ΑΙΧΜΗΡΟΣ

Ανοίξτε τον ΠΟΛΙΤΗ!...

Αν θέλετε η εφημερίδα σας
να έχει "άποψη",
να έχει πάντα "ζουμί",
να είναι "διαφορετική"
και πάνω απ' όλα έγκυρη,
ανοίξτε τον ΠΟΛΙΤΗ.
Η μόνη εφημερίδα στην Κύπρο
που τα έχει όλα και...
Τα λέει όλα!

ΠΟΛΙΤΗΣ *Τα λέει όλα*

VRISAKI RESTAURANT

COME TO "VRISAKI" FOR GOOD FOOD & SERVICE

AUTHENTIC CYPRIOT CUISINE

73 MYDDLETON ROAD, LONDON N22 8LZ
TELEPHONE: 020 8889 8760

(open Monday-Saturday 12 noon to midnight)
Sunday 12 noon to 9.00pm

Evening Standard Award and London Tonight Award 2003

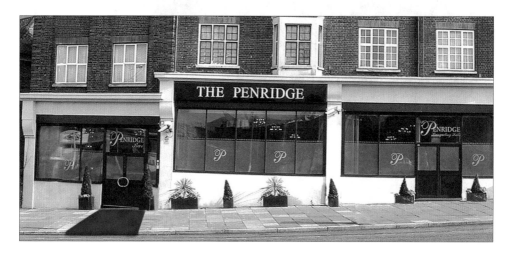

JonChristopher
Chartered Surveyors

T: 020 8444 0055
F: 020 8444 0222
info@jonchristopher.com
www.jonchristopher.com

84 High Road
East Finchley
London N2 9PN

TRIOS
BANQUETING

The Elegant Choice

Available for:
Weddings - Engagements - Christenings - Birthdays - Barmitzvahs
Conferences - Club Functions - Office Parties
Christmas Parties - Anniversaries

248 Green Lanes, Palmers Green, London N13 5TU
Tel: 020 8886 2985 Fax: 020 8886 5453
Email: enquiries@trios.fsnet.co.uk

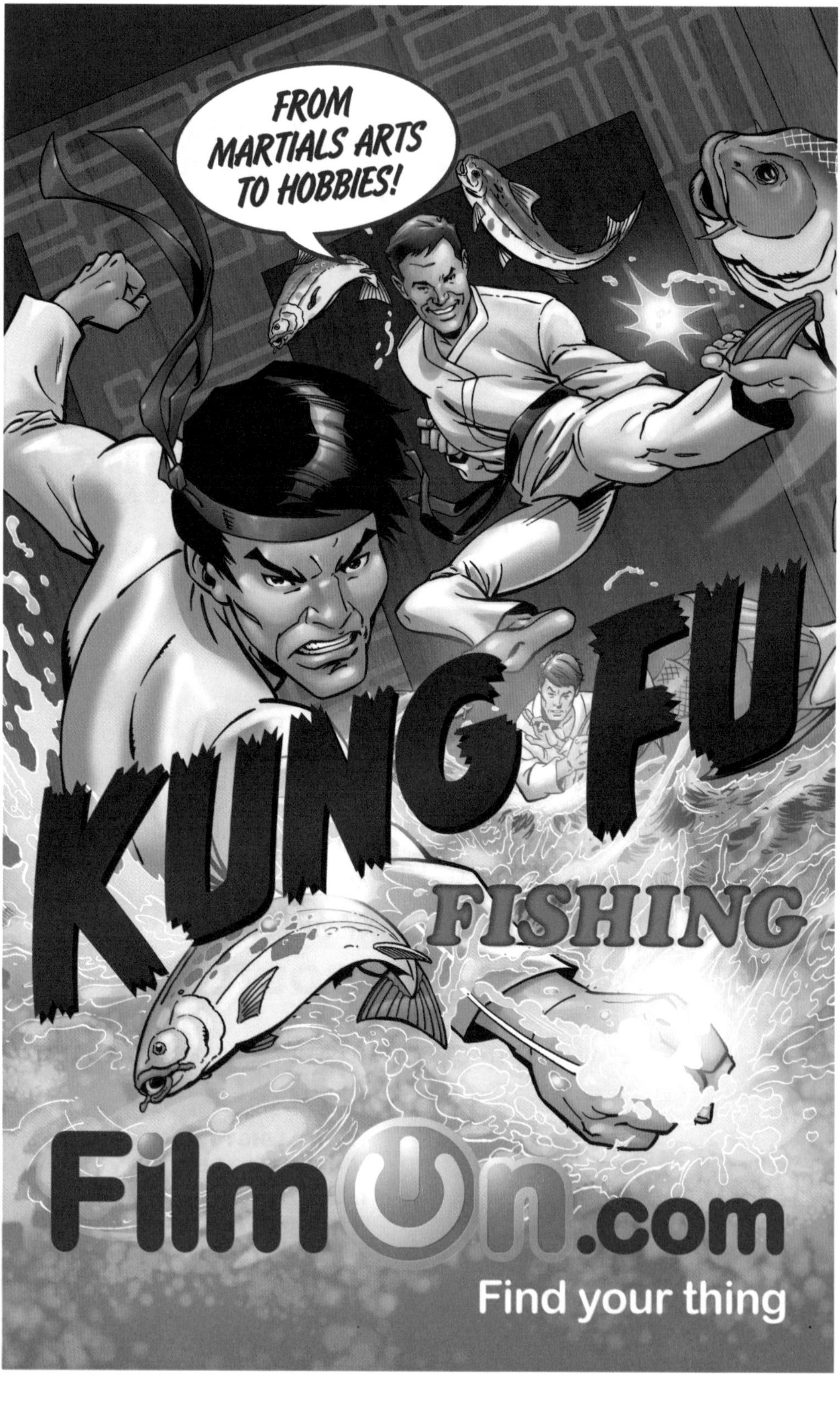
FROM MARTIALS ARTS TO HOBBIES!
KUNG FU
FISHING
FilmOn.com
Find your thing

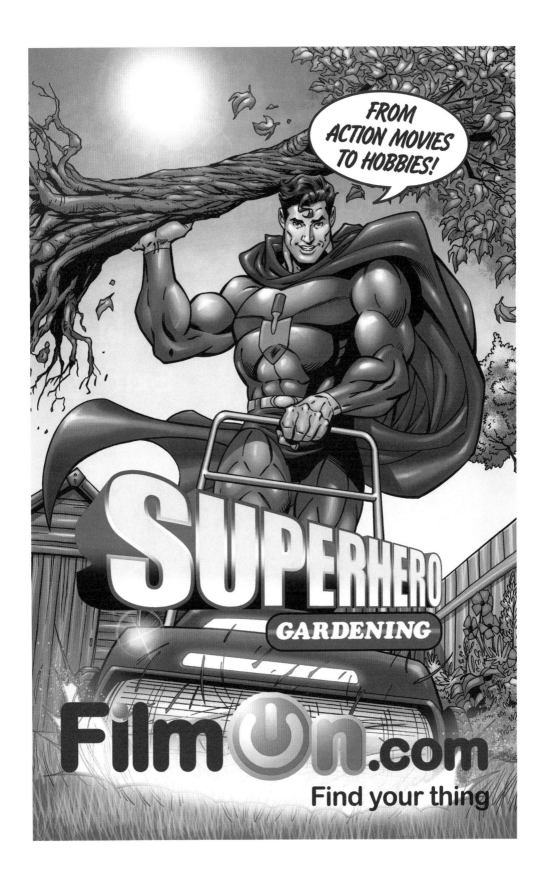

St Raphael's
Integrity Care Home

Mr & Mrs P. Joannides RGN, OND, Cert Ed, BSc Hons.
93/95 Stanhope Gardens, Haringey, London N4 1HZ
Tel. 081 800 6393/0429

DESPINA'S FOOD STORE

Butchers, Supermarket, Fruit & Veg, Off Licence

Despina's Food Store is a family-run business

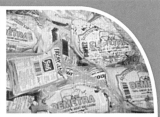

EVERYTHING YOU NEED FOR YOUR WEEKLY SHOPPING & MORE!

Koubes, Daktila, Bourekia, Anari, Sheftalia, Ravioli, Olives, Spinach & Halloumi Pittas, Flaounes, Fresh Fruit & Vegetables from Cyprus. A vast selection of Olives & Olive Oil. A wide variety of dips (taramas, houmous etc.) WE ALSO CATER FOR SMALL PARTIES!

7 Days a Week 7.30am – 8.30pm

Tel: 020 8368 8855

456-458 Bowes Road, New Southgate, London N11 1NL

CHARTERED ACCOUNTANTS

BANK HOUSE
36-38 Bristol Street, Birmingham B5 7AA
Tel: 0121 622 3633 Fax: 0121 622 5845
Email: dmd@markou.com

OPENGATE
Mortgage Solutions Ltd

JMH House, 481 Green Lanes, London N13 4BS
Tel: 0208 886 4999

Opengate Mortgage Solutions Ltd was founded with the good intention to operate on a high professional level that would ensure that all our clients constantly receive the best service possible.

Choosing a mortgage or any other loan is a skilled job that should not be underestimated because you will effectively be entering into a contract that in most cases will result in your property being used as security.

It is therefore in our opinion, always better to speak to an independent mortgage advisor who will then be able to recommend the best deal that fits in with your past present and future circumstances which are based on a highly detailed questionnaire.

We are proud to be able to offer our services to advise and arrange any *Residential or Buy to Let Mortgage with No Broker Fee* because we want to give you the confidence to approach us first before you make any decisions.

Other services we offer are Commercial Loans, Income Protection, Life Cover and General Insurance.

We are committed to Treating Customers Fairly.

George Pornaris
Managing Director

In memory of my father Takis Koutalianos (Asha)

Greek & Mediterranean Cuisine

212-216 High Road, East Finchley, London N2 9AY

Tel: 020 88 83 83 83
Email info@genzorestaurant.co.uk
www.genzorestaurant.co.uk

In Association With:

S.C. TRIMS DIRECT S.R.L
ROMANIA
OLTENITA, CALARASI 8350
Tel: 0040-242-515833
Fax: 0040-242-515782
E-MAIL: samleva@ARtelecom.net

ANGEL TRIMMINGS LTD

38 Crown Road, Enfield, Middx EN1 1TH
Tel: 020 8805 8007 Fax: 020 8805 8006

Email: sales@angeltrimmings.co.uk

www.angeltrimmings.co.uk

Simon Fisher

LOSS ASSESSOR

ΞΕΡΕΙ ΤΗ ΔΟΥΛΕΙΑ ΤΟΥ

P.O. BOX No. 1970
LONDON NW2 2PF

TEL: 020 7794 4261

AlexanderLawsonJacobs

Chartered Accountants
Corporate Recovery & Insolvency Specialists

1 KINGS AVENUE
WINCHMORE HILL
LONDON N21 3NA

Telephone: +44 (0) 20 8370 7250
Fax: +44 (0) 20 8370 7251
DX 36953 Winchmore Hill

Email: enquiries@alexanderlawsonjacobs.com
www.alexanderlawsonjacobs.com

ALEX JOHNSON LIMITED

Chartered Certified Accountants and Registered Auditors

97 JUDD STREET
LONDON
WC1H 9JF

Tel: 020 7387 6504
Fax: 020 7388 7935
Email: admin@alex-johnson.co.uk

Vasos Georgiou FCCA
Managing Director

LAWSON LIMITED

SAGE SOLUTION CENTRE

97 JUDD STREET
LONDON
WC1H 9JF

Tel: 020 7121 6390
Fax: 020 7388 7935
Email: office@lawson.ltd.uk

Kyriacoulla Georgiou
Director

Business Partner

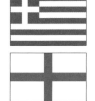

John Alexander Limited
Accountants and Registered Auditors

John Alexander & Co., originally a sole tradership was established in 1974, servicing businesses, families and individuals. In 2001 the growing family practice was incorporated into the status of a limited company.

John Alexander Limited is registered with the Chartered Institute of Certified Accountants and is entitled to practise as a firm of Registered Auditors.

We pride ourselves on our professional abilities and providing clients with a personal and individual service.

In cases where specialist or technical knowledge is required, we have at hand a team of specialist advisors - able to provide our clients with a high quality service and up to date information. We work closely with the specialist advisors to ensure our clients are accommodated.

At all times we work alongside our client to provide a level of service appropriate to individual needs and to meet the requirements of any associated third parties. It is our aim to advise and assist in the successful management of our clients' businesses.

A close association enables us to take a more proactive involvement with our clients' business development and fund raising thereby extending our services to areas other than the traditional accounting and taxation.

Our approach to clients is to hold consultations and interviews whereby we can best determine their needs and aspirations and establish how we can best assist their businesses in achieving their objectives.

We believe that close liaison and personal "tailoring" of services is crucial to providing best service and that it provides a better solution for the client.

115 Chase Side, Southgate
London N14 5HD
Tel: 020 8882 5133

THE HELLENIC CYPRUS BROTHERHOOD OF SOUTH AFRICA
ΕΛΛΗΝΙΚΗ ΚΥΠΡΙΑΚΗ ΑΔΕΛΦΟΤΗΣ ΝΟΤΙΟΥ ΑΦΡΙΚΗΣ

Congratulations on

producing the first-ever

Greek Cypriot Who's Who Worldwide

from

The Executive Committee of the

Hellenic Cyprus Brotherhood

PANCYPRIOT ASSOCIATION OF REPATRIATED CYPRIOTS FROM ENGLAND

PATMOY, 1 ZAKAKI, 3046
LIMASSOL, CYPRUS

Andreas Chialoufas
Tel and Fax: 00357 25711746 Mob: 00357 99687228

Paphos
Takis Mantis
Mob: 00357 99666400

Nicosia
P. Paschalis
Mob: 00357 99680410

Ant Trimikliniotis
Mob: 00357 99686348

Larnaca
Nicos Georgiou
Tel: 00357 24667953

Lefkara
Evdokia Stavri
Mob: 00357 99125341

Ammochostos
V. Christoforou
Mob: 00357 99429899

The Association was formed in 1995 to assist in solving the problems that Cypriots faced when returning to Cyprus from all countries of the diaspora. Returning Cypriots can join the association no matter where they are coming from whether UK, Australia, the USA, Africa, Canada or Greece.

There are more than 10,000 members and we have Cypriots from all over the world ringing for advice and information before they take the decision for repatriation.

The Association continuously helps on a variety of issues and work closely with the Cyprus Government, Ministers and MP's.

We have offices in all main towns of Cyprus and very active within the community in general and advise our members to mix with the rest of our compatriots and to participate in every aspect of life.

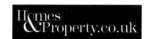

NATIONAL FEDERATION OF CYPRIOTS
IN THE UNITED KINGDOM

Britannia Road, London, N12 9RU.
Tel: 020 8445 9999 Fax: 020 8445 9977 **www.cypriotfederation.org.uk**

National Federation of Cypriots in the UK
Working for a Free, United Cyprus

AIMS

The main aims of the National Federation of Cypriots in the United Kingdom are:

✔ To lead and coordinate the UK Cypriot community's efforts which are aimed at bringing about an equitable and lasting resolution of the Cyprus problem for the benefit of all Cypriots.

✔ To help the Republic of Cyprus in its struggle to reunite the island, its people, economy and institutions on the basis of United Nations resolutions and the principles of international and European Union law so that the human rights of all Cypriots can be safeguarded.

✔ To initiate and coordinate actions designed to facilitate the progress and enhance the contribution of the UK Cypriot community in all fields of British society and in British institutions.

✔ To contribute actively to the development of friendly relations between Cyprus and the United Kingdom and to the enhancement of cultural, economic, trade and other links between the two countries.

✔ To cultivate the idea of rapprochement and harmonious co-existence among all Cypriots irrespective of ethnic origin or religion.

✔ To maintain close links and a regular dialogue with representatives of the British Government and British political parties and UK parliamentarians.

✔ To communicate actively with the British mass media in order to promote the cause of a reunited Cyprus and the contribution of the Cypriot community to the social, economic and political development of British society.

**The Secretariat of the Federation
wish your publication every success!**

Omega Lettings Ltd
Omega House
495 Lea Bridge Road
Leyton, London E10 7EB

T 020 8988 2838
F 020 8988 2839

omega@omegalettings.com
www.omegalettings.com

The Olive Tree
Greek Restaurant

George, Vasoulla, Solos

and the Staff

are pleased to be associated with

The Cypriots of the World Who's Who

Headingley
74-76 Otley Road
Headingly
Leeds
LS6 4BA
Tel: 0113 274 8282

Chapel Allerton
88-190 Harrogate Road,
Chapel Allerton
Leeds
LS7 4NZ
Tel: 0113 269 8488
Fax: 0113 256 1116

Rodley
'Oaklands'
55 Rodley Lane
Rodley
Leeds
LS13 1NG
Tel: 0113 256 9283

Website – www.olivetreegreekrestaurant.co.uk
Email – contact@olivetreegreekrestaurant.co.uk

CYPRUS FEDERATION OF AMERICA INC.

email: **cyprusfederation@aol.com**

tel: **201 444 8237**

Congratulations on

producing the first-ever

Greek Cypriot Who's Who Worldwide

CYPRIOT FEDERATION OF CANADA

6 Thorncliffe Park Drive
Toronto, Ontario M4H 1H1

Phone: (416) 696-7400
Fax: (416) 696-9465
Email: cypriotfederation@rogers.com

On behalf of the

Cypriot Federation of Canada

we would like to congratulate you on

producing the first-ever

Greek Cypriot Who's Who Worldwide

FEDERATION OF CYPRUS COMMUNITIES OF AUSTRALIA AND NZ

President
Michael Christodoulou D.O
58-76 Stanmore Road, Stanmore,
Sydney, NSW 2048
Ph: 02 9557 1256 Fax: 02 9516 1679
Mob: 0412 622 467
E-mail: cyprusclub@optusnet.com.au

Secretary
Charles Kapnoulla
23 Ham Road, Mansfield,
Brisbane, QLD 4122
Ph. & Fax: 07 3216 8567
Mob: 0411 533 529
E-mail: charleskapnoulla@hotmail.com

Congratulations on

producing the first-ever

Greek Cypriot Who's Who Worldwide

These Emigrants are proud of their Greek Cypriot Heritage

Who are these Greek Cypriot Emigrants who are so successful world wide as Professors, Scientists, Medical Doctors, Business men, innovators and great citizens?

The majority of them left Cyprus from their villages in the 1950's when Cyprus was still a British Colony.

These villages were closely knit communities. In the 1950's the unwritten purpose of these villages was to serve the big cities of Cyprus. Life in these villages was very poor. There were no doctors, no medical clinics, no garbage collection, no high schools, and the clean running water was at a premium. Babies were delivered by a self taught 'mammou".

Every morning, six days a week, the workers got up early, go into the packed busses, reached the cities by 7 am, served the citizens of the big Cypriot cities and returned at around 7 pm. The opportunities for self advancement were almost none existent.

There was no other way to escape the "village trap" except to emigrate. They emigrated as young men, to Europe, Britain, The United States, Canada, Australia and other countries. They suffered all the ills of been an immigrant, been a foreigner in a new country, it was not easy. They had to learn the new language, they suffered loneliness, they learned as to how it feels not to have enough to eat and to be cold. But they worked hard, educated themselves at their own expense, went to colleges and Universities, created families, educated their children, and with hard work they became successful.

They kept their unique property which characterizes the Greek Cypriots of the 1950's. They give unconditional compassion to their family, friends, and strangers. They propagate their Greek Cypriot culture in their new adopted country, they regularly visit Cyprus, they help economically their relatives in Cyprus, they help the underprivileged where ever there may be.

I would like to congratulate Mike Yiakoumi on producing the first-ever Greek Cypriot Who's Who Worldwide. It gives an identity to the Greek Cypriot Emigrants.

**Dr. Savvas Chamberlain – Founder and Chairman
of DALSA Corporation**

GEORGE'S
FISH & SOUVLAKI BAR

YOUR LOCAL AWARD WINNING FISH & CHIPS / GREEK RESTAURANT.
HOLDER OF THE SEA FISH FRYERS QUALITY AWARD 2008
LONDONS PERFECT PORTION AWARD 2009

Caroß Tree

Greek Mediterranean Kitchen

15 Highgate Road
London NW5 1QX (Corner of Swains Lane)
Tel: 020 7267 9880

Proprietors: **Louis Loizou, Steven Webster**

Toff's
of Muswell Hill

Licensed Fish Restaurant – Est. 1968

Established in 1968, Toff's is an award winning fish and chip shop. A fully licensed restaurant and take away in Muswell Hill. It prides itself on serving fresh food at reasonable prices in a family friendly atmosphere.

FIRST FLOOR SEATING NOW AVAILABLE

Open Mon-Sat 11.30am – 11pm

38 Muswell Hill Broadway, London N10 3RT

T: 020 8883 8656

ToffsFish@gmail.com

www.toffsfish.co.uk

We at Toffs wish the Publishers all the success in seeking all our fellow patriots around the world

Thomas Properties

Tasos Papaloizou, Kypros Koufou and John Papaloizou

Established in 1999 **Thomas Properties** was set up to provide a number of different types of accommodation. Thomas Properties procure and manage housing stock on behalf of Local Authorities, Government and other housing providers that are used to house people in need of temporary accommodation and emergency accommodation. The company also has a rapidly growing portfolio of properties that are offered to the private sector by way of short term rentals; these properties cover all sections and range from the very modest of flats right up to the luxury end of the market. The homes and properties offered to both market sectors have to comply with extremely high standards and levels of repair decoration and furnishing in order for the staff at Thomas Properties to include the property in its portfolio. One of the fundamental principles held by Thomas Properties is a belief that no matter what a clients financial situation may look like they deserve to live in good clean and aesthetically pleasing accommodation. Thomas Properties has a number of professional service people in its employ including plumbers, electricians, builders and carpenters dedicated to keeping the standard of their housing stock in excellent condition. This means that when a repair is carried out the workmanship is first class, the repair sturdy and the problem fixed. Thomas Properties takes great pride its dealings with all its tenants, landlords, suppliers and customers and believes in treating each person it deals with as an individual upon whom the company relies on for its very existence, ensuring that each person or organisation involved with them in what ever capacity gets the very best attention possible. The Aim: To match properties to people in a way that ensures both tenants and landlords are happy, that the quality of the properties are good and each property is maintained to an extremely high standard giving the tenant a great place to live and the landlord an good income coupled with the piece of mind that comes from knowing his investment is secure.

The Directors are John Papaloizou a Chartered Quantity Surveyor, Kypros Koufou a Mortgage and Life Insurance Broker and Tasos Papaloizou a Chartered Accountant.

The Company has 15 members of Staff office and maintenance staff that have a wide range of experience in the property business that can also advise on property investments.

The Company is situated at **Thomas Properties**
167 Stroud Green Road, London N4 3PZ
Tel: 020 7281 2000 Fax: 020 7281 2001   Web: www.thomas-properties.com

Summer Product Range

Big K Charcoal Merchants Ltd, Unit 20 Millmead Industrial Centre,
Millmead Road,
Tottenham Hale, London N17 9QU

Tel: (01366) 501485 Fax: (01366) 500395 E-Mail: sales@bigk.co.uk www.bigk.co.uk

VICKEAL LTD. T/A

MARCOS TRIMMINGS

Zips ● Cottons ● Buttons ● Canvas ● Elastics etc.

TAVISTOCK ROAD
LONDON N4 1TD

TEL: 020-8800 9918/9903
FAX: 020-8809 6776

E-mail: eptakomi@aol.com
Website: www.marcostrimmings.com

ZIPS, COTTONS, BUTTONS, CANVAS, ELASTICS ETC.

J&P

Joannou & Paraskevaides Group

International
Building & Civil Engineering Contractors

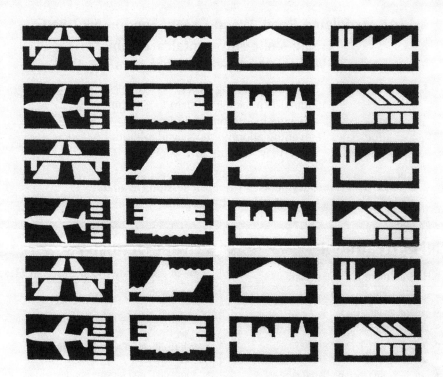

UK Representative Office
16 Hanover Street London W1S 1YL
Tel: +44 (020) 7462 5000 Fax: +44 (020) 7493 0059
Email: London@jandp.org

my dental care

www.my-dentalcare.com

New Patients Welcome
Tel: 020 8889 3773

Dentists
Mr Mark Marcou BDS (Lond.)

Dental therapist/hygienist:
Irene Kaimakamis MJDF, BDS
Funmi Sijuwade BDS

141 Myddleton Road, Wood Green, London N22 8NG
Email: smile@my-dentalcare.com
Web: www.my-dentalcare.com

Opening Times:
Monday to Thursday: 9.00am to 6.00pm
Lunch: 1.00pm to 2.00pm
Tuesday late evening appointments available until 8.00pm
Friday: 8.00am to 2.00pm

Private Hygienist / therapist sessions available
Enquire at Reception

NHS Treatment

NHS treatment is FREE if you:-

- are under 18 years of age
- are pregnant
- are a mother and your baby is under 1 year
- are receiving income support
- are receiving pension credit
- are receiving income based job seekers allowance
- are a student who is 18 years and in full time education
- have an exemption certificate i.e. HC2
- receive families tax credit or disability tax credit
- If you are on a low income and none of the above apply please ask the receptionist for a HC2 form for help with NHS charges

Private Dentistry

Some of the private treatments available:-

- Tooth whitening
- Tooth Cleaning – Power Clean treatment
- White fillings / Porcelain fillings
- Tooth coloured crowns / bridges
- Gold crowns and inlays
- Dentures

The

Kelmanson

Partnership

CHARTERED CERTIFIED ACCOUNTANTS

REGISTERED AUDITORS

INSOLVENCY PRACTITIONERS

AVCO HOUSE, 6 ALBERT ROAD
BARNET, HERTFORDSHIRE EN4 9SH
TELEPHONE: 020 8441 2000
FACSIMILE: 020 8441 3000

EMAIL: moss@kelpart.co.uk
WEBSITE: www.kelpart.co.uk

Broxbourne Dental Care

– Mr S. Efstratiou BDS (RAND) –

Unit 1, The Precinct

High Road

Broxbourne

Herts EN10 7HY

Tel: 01992 478578

Η ΕΛΛΗΝΙΚΗ ΕΦΗΜΕΡΙΔΑ ΤΟΥ ΛΟΝΔΙΝΟΥ

ΕΛΕΥΘΕΡΙΑ

ΚΑΘΕ ΠΕΜΠΤΗ
ΜΕ ΝΕΑ ΤΗΣ ΠΑΡΟΙΚΙΑΣ
ΚΑΙ ΤΟΥ ΕΛΛΗΝΙΣΜΟΥ
ΑΠ' ΟΛΟ ΤΟΝ ΚΟΣΜΟ

«ΕΛΕΥΘΕΡΙΑ»
ΑΝΕΞΑΡΤΗΤΗ ΕΒΔΟΜΑΔΙΑΙΑ ΕΛΛΗΝΙΚΗ ΕΦΗΜΕΡΙΔΑ ΤΟΥ ΛΟΝΔΙΝΟΥ
757 HIGH ROAD, FINCHLEY, LONDON N12 8LD
ΤΗΛ: **020 8343 7522** • ΦΑΞ: **020 8343 7524**
email: **michael@eleftheria.biz**

Cutwater Construction Limited

12 Corri Avenue
Southgate
London N14 7HL

Telephone:	0208 882 4534
Facsimile:	0208 882 4534
Mobile:	07836 752123

PROPERTY DEVELOPMENT
ARCHITECTURAL PLANNING
DESIGN CONSULTANTS

- *We carry out all Design & Building requirements*
- *Consultation with Client Pre-Design*
- *Consultation on Draft Designs*
- *Submission of plans for approval*
- *Production of detailed quotation*
- *Management and/or completion of development*
- *NHBC guarantee – 10 years (new buildings)*
- *Extensions, Conversions & New Builds*
- *Architectural Landscaping*
- *Complete follow-up service available*

Director: T Efstathiou B.A. Arch   Secretary: G.A. Efstathiou   Registered in England No. 5165369
V.A.T. Registration No. 858 7080 85